Monastic Life in Anglo-Saxon England, *c.* 600–900

This major new history of monasticism in early Anglo-Saxon England explores the history of the church between the conversion to Christianity in the sixth century and a monastic revival in the tenth. It represents the first comprehensive revision of accepted views about monastic life in England before the Benedictine reform. Sarah Foot shows how early Anglo-Saxon religious houses were simultaneously active and contemplative, their members withdrawing from the preoccupations of contemporary aristocratic society while in a very real sense remaining part of that world. Focusing on the institution of the 'minster' (the communal religious household) and rejecting a simplistic binary division between active 'minsters' and enclosed 'monasteries', Foot argues that historians have been wrong to see minsters in the light of ideals of Benedictine monasticism. Instead, she demonstrates that Anglo-Saxon minsters reflected more of contemporary social attitudes; despite their aim for solitude, they retained close links to aristocratic secular society.

SARAH FOOT is Professor of Early Medieval History in the Department of History at the University of Sheffield.

Monastic Life in Anglo-Saxon England, *c.* 600–900

SARAH FOOT

University of Sheffield

For Dominic
who has taught me much
about observant Benedictinism

with warmest wishes
from Sarah

CAMBRIDGE
UNIVERSITY PRESS

CAMBRIDGE UNIVERSITY PRESS
Cambridge, New York, Melbourne, Madrid, Cape Town, Singapore, São Paulo, Delhi

Cambridge University Press
The Edinburgh Building, Cambridge CB2 8RU, UK

Published in the United States of America by Cambridge University Press, New York

www.cambridge.org
Information on this title: www.cambridge.org/9780521859462

© Cambridge University Press 2006

First published 2006
Reprinted 2008

Printed in the United Kingdom at the University Press, Cambridge

A catalogue record for this publication is available from the British Library

Library of Congress Cataloging in Publication data
Foot, Sarah.
Monastic life in Anglo-Saxon England, c. 600–900 / Sarah Foot.
        p.   cm.
Includes bibliographical references and index.
ISBN-13: 978-0-521-85946-2 (hardback)
ISBN-10: 0-521-85946-8 (hardback)
1. Monastic and religious life – England – History – Middle Ages, 600–1500.
2. England – Church history – 449–1066.   I. Title.
BX2592.F66 2006
271.00942'09021 – dc22
2006013834

ISBN 978-0-521-85946-2 hardback

Contents

Plates

Figures

Preface

Readers who have also undergone the academic rite of passage that is the successful defence of a doctoral thesis will recall how their euphoria was tempered by the conflicting advice they were given about publishing their research. Few will have proved so unwise as to reject all of it and sit on a wholly-unrevised manuscript for many years. This book now takes a form quite distinct both from the original thesis from which it derives and from the various versions that I might have written earlier. I do not, however, regret the delay. Various projects that have filled the intervening period – particularly my work on female monasticism – have led me to a different understanding both of the nature of the religious life in early Anglo-Saxon England and of the factors that have clouded historical understanding of the early English church. The revisionist interpretation offered here modifies some of my own earlier statements as well as questioning conventional readings of the contemporary literature.

Over the years on which I have worked on this project I have incurred debts to so many individuals that it would be invidious to attempt to list them all here, but some deserve particular thanks. Rosamond McKitterick supervised the original thesis and has continued to offer support and assistance ever since. No less significant in shaping my thinking and understanding of the pre-Conquest period has been Simon Keynes. Nicholas Brooks has been unfailingly supportive. He and Thomas Charles-Edwards read the entire manuscript in draft and offered a number of suggestions for its significant improvement: they bear no responsibility for the errors that remain. I have also learnt a great deal from Lesley Abrams, Julia Crick, David Dumville and

Susan Kelly. It is a great sadness that Patrick Wormald, to whom I owe so much, did not live to see this finished text. My early thinking about Anglo-Saxon minsters is heavily indebted to John Blair, with whom I have had numerous stimulating exchanges. This manuscript was completed before the appearance of his book, *The Church in Anglo-Saxon Society* (Oxford University Press, 2005), which offers a different reading of early English religion, but I have not thought it right to revise my book to take account of his. All the staff of Cambridge University Library have been unfailingly helpful and I owe particular thanks to Godfrey Waller and his colleagues in the Manuscripts Room. My own colleagues at Sheffield have shown great patience in tolerating the long delay in producing this text. Meanwhile my doctoral students – James Palmer, Morn Capper, Geoff Little and Martha Riddiford – have not only taught me a great deal but also patiently endured many conversations about minsters of only tangential relevance to their own work. In the production of this book Debby Banham's assistance has been invaluable.

On a personal note, I must acknowledge the significant encouragement given over many years by Geoff Schrecker: without his continuing faith in this project I would have abandoned it many times. My gratitude to Michael and Matthew for their loving support during my immersion in minsters goes beyond words.

Abbreviations

Alcuin, *Ep.*	*Epistolae*, ed. Ernst Dümmler, *MGH*, *Epistolae Karolini Aevi* II
Alcuin, *Versus*:	'Versus de patribus regibus et sanctis euboricensis ecclesiae', in Peter Godman (ed.), *Alcuin: The Bishops, Kings and Saints of York* (Oxford: Clarendon Press, 1982)
Alfred, Preface	Alfred, prose preface to his translation of Gregory the Great, *Cura pastoralis*, ed. Henry Sweet, *King Alfred's West Saxon Version of Gregory's Pastoral Care*, 2 vols., EETS, o.s. 45 and 50 (London: N. Trübner, 1871–2)
AntJ	*Antiquaries Journal*
ArchJ	*Archaeological Journal*
ASC	Anglo-Saxon Chronicle
ASE	*Anglo-Saxon England*
BAR	British Archaeological Reports
BCS	Walter de Gray Birch, *Cartularium Saxonicum: A Collection of Charters relating to Anglo-Saxon History*, 3 vols. (London: Whiting & Co, 1883–99)
Bede, *Homelia*	*Bedae venerabilis opera, pars III: Opera homiletica*, ed. David Hurst, CCSL 122 (Turnhout: Brepols, 1955)
Boniface, *Ep.*	*Epistolae*, ed. Michael Tangl, *Die Briefe des Heiligen Bonifatius und Lullus*, *MGH*, *Epistolae selectae* I (Berlin, 1916)
C&S	*Councils & Synods, I: AD 871–1204, with other Documents relating to the English Church*, ed. Dorothy Whitelock, Martin Brett and C. N. L. Brooke (Oxford: Clarendon, 1981)
CCSL	Corpus Christianorum, Series Latina (Turnhout: Brepols)

DACL	*Dictionnaire d'archéologie chrétienne et de liturgie*
EETS	Early English Text Society
EHD	*English Historical Documents, I: c. 500–1042*, ed. Dorothy Whitelock (2nd edn, London: Eyre Methuen; New York: Oxford University Press, 1979)
EpEcg	Bede, *Epistola ad Ecgberhtum episcopum*, ed. Charles Plummer, *Venerabilis Bedae, opera historica*, 2 vols. (Oxford: Clarendon Press, 1896), I, 405–23
HA	Bede, *Historia abbatum*, ed. Charles Plummer, *Venerabilis Bedae, opera historica*, 2 vols. (Oxford: Clarendon Press, 1896), I, 364–87
HBC	*Handbook of British Chronology*, 3rd edn, E. B. Fryde, S. Porter and I. Roy, Royal Historical Society Guides and Handbooks 2 (London: Royal Historical Society, 1986)
HE	Bede, *Historia ecclesiastica*, ed. and trans. Bertram Colgrave and R. A. B. Mynors, *Bede's Ecclesiastical History of the English People* (Oxford: Clarendon Press, 1969)
H&S	Arthur West Haddan and William Stubbs (eds.), *Councils and Ecclesiastical Documents relating to Great Britain and Ireland*, 3 vols. (Oxford: Clarendon Press, 1869–78)
JEH	*Journal of Ecclesiastical History*
LBG	*Liber beatae Gregorii papae*, ed. Bertram Colgrave, *The Earliest Life of Gregory the Great* (Lawrence, KS: University of Kansas Press, 1968; paperback edition Cambridge: Cambridge University Press, 1985)
Liebermann, *Die Gesetze*	*Die Gesetze der Angelsachsen*, ed. Felix Liebermann, 3 vols. (Halle: Max Niemeyer, 1903–16)
MA	*Medieval Archaeology*
MGH	*Monumenta Germaniae Historica* (Hanover)
PL	*Patrologia Latina*, ed. J. P. Migne (Paris, 1844–64)
RCHM	Royal Commission on Historical Monuments (England)
Resting-places	*Die Heiligen Englands*, ed. Felix Liebermann (Hanover: Hahn, 1889)
RM	*Regula Magistri*, ed. Adalbert de Vogüé, *La Règle du Maître*, Sources chrétiennes 105–7 (Paris: Editions du Cerf, 1964–5)
RSB	*Regula S. Benedicti*, ed. and trans. Timothy Fry, *The Rule of St Benedict in Latin and English with Notes* (Collegeville, MN: Liturgical Press, 1981)

S	P. H. Sawyer, ed., *Anglo-Saxon Charters: An Annotated List and Bibliography*, Royal Historical Society guides and handbooks 8 (London: Royal Historical Society, 1968). Now superseded by the Electronic Sawyer: http://www.trin.cam.ac.uk/sdk13/chartwww/eSawyer. 99/eSawyer2.html
SC	*Sources chrétiennes* (Paris)
SEHD	*Select English Historical Documents of the Ninth and Tenth Centuries*, ed. Florence E. Harmer (Cambridge: Cambridge University Press, 1914)
Settimane	*Settimane di studio del Centro italiano di studi sull'alto Medioevo* (Spoleto)
SSRM	*Scriptores rerum Merovingicarum*
TRHS	*Transactions of the Royal Historical Society* (London)
VSB	*Vita S. Bonifatii*, ed. Reinhold Rau, *Briefe des Bonifatius: Willibalds Leben des Bonifatius. Nebst einigen zeitgenössischen Dokumenten* (Darmstadt: Wissenschaftliche Buchgesellschaft, 1968)
VSCeol.	*Vita S. Ceolfridi*, ed. Charles Plummer, *Venerabilis Bedae, opera historica*, 2 vols. (Oxford: Clarendon Press, 1896), I, 388–404
VSCuth.	*Vita S. Cuthberti*, ed. and trans. B. Colgrave, *Two Lives of Saint Cuthbert: A Life by an Anonymous Monk of Lindisfarne and Bede's Prose Life* (Cambridge: Cambridge University Press, 1940)
VSG	*Vita S. Guthlaci*, ed. and trans. Bertram Colgrave, *Felix's Life of Saint Guthlac* (Cambridge: Cambridge University Press, 1956; paperback edition, 1985)
VSL	Rudolf, *Vita Leobae abbatissae Biscofesheimensis*, ed. G. Waitz, *MGH, Scriptores*, XVI (Hanover: Hahn, 1887), 118–31
VSW	*Vita S. Wilfridi*, ed. and trans. Bertram Colgrave, *The Life of Bishop Wilfrid by Eddius Stephanus* (Cambridge: Cambridge University Press, 1927)
Wallace-Hadrill, *Commentary*	J. M. Wallace-Hadrill, *Bede's Ecclesiastical History of the English People: A Historical Commentary* (Oxford: Clarendon Press, 1988)

CHAPTER 1

Introduction: situating the problem

At the heart of the monastic life lies the quest for spiritual perfection, the individual journey of the soul towards the love of God and the promise of eternal life. First of all things, the seventh-century Irish monk Columbanus reminded the members of his own communities in Gaul at the opening of his Rule for monks, 'we are taught to love God with the whole heart and the whole mind and all our strength, and our neighbour as ourselves, next our works'.[1] Only by renouncing the will and arming the soul with the 'strong and noble weapons of obedience', could the monk 'do battle for the true King, Christ the Lord' argued St Benedict of Nursia.[2] He wrote his 'little rule for beginners' in sixth-century Italy for the monks of his abbey at Monte Cassino, south of Rome, but copies circulated in northern Frankia and in England in the seventh century.[3] 'Nothing must be refused in their obedience by Christ's true disciples, however hard and difficult it

---

[1] Columbanus, *Regula monachorum*, prologue (ed. Walker, *Sancti Columbani Opera*, pp. 122–3); the quotation of Christ's injunction is from Matthew 22: 37 and 39. Columbanus wrote his two rules, the *Regula monachorum* and the *Regula coenobialis*, for the guidance of the members of the communities he had established at Annegray, Luxeuil and Fontaine in Frankia and Bobbio in northern Italy: see Donald Bullough, 'The career of Columbanus', in Michael Lapidge (ed.), *Columbanus: Studies on the Latin Writings* (Woodbridge: Boydell Press, 1997), pp. 1–28, at pp. 11–13; and Jane Barbara Stevenson, 'The monastic rules of Columbanus', *ibid.*, pp. 203–16, at p. 206.

[2] *RSB*, prologue, 3; ch. 73, 8 (pp. 156–7 and 296–7).

[3] See plate I: Oxford, Bodleian Library, MS, Hatton 48, fo. 93. This eighth-century manuscript is the earliest surviving copy of Benedict's Rule and has a south-western provenance; it may have been copied in a minster in the south-west with which Bishop Wilfrid had connections: Patrick Sims-Williams, *Religion and Literature in Western England, 600–800* (Cambridge: Cambridge University Press, 1990), pp. 117–18; for the early circulation of the Rule see Marilyn Dunn, *The Emergence of Monasticism: From the Desert Fathers to the Early Middle Ages* (Oxford: Blackwell, 2000), pp. 192–4.

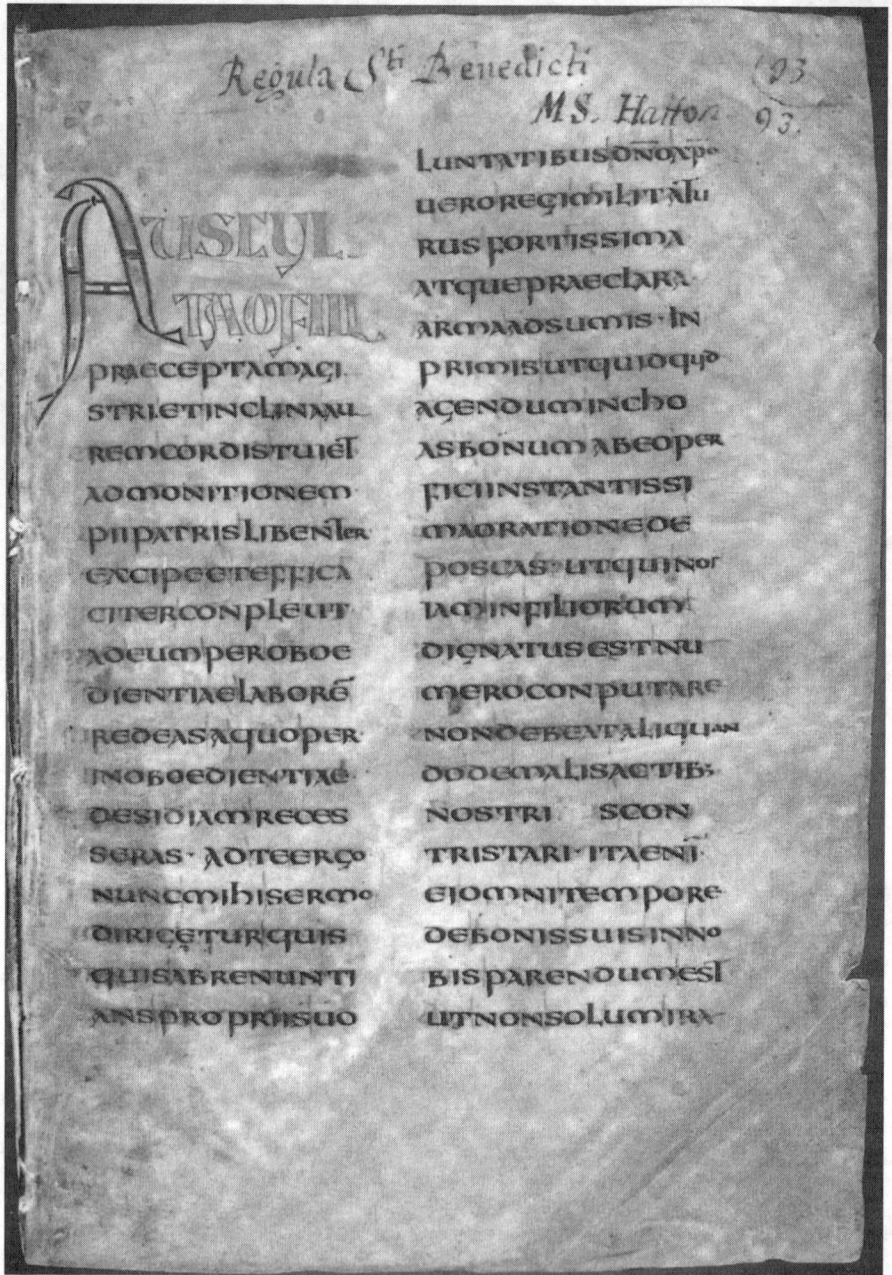

PLATE I: The Rule of St Benedict: Oxford, Bodleian Library, MS Hatton 48, fo. 93.

be, but it must be seized with zeal, with gladness, since if obedience is not of this nature, it will not be pleasing to the Lord.'[4] Benedict acknowledged that the path to salvation was bound to be narrow at the outset, but 'as we progress in this way of life and in faith, we shall run on the path of God's commandments, our hearts overflowing with the inexpressible delight of love. Never swerving from his instructions, then, but faithfully observing his teaching in the monastery until death we shall through patience share in the sufferings of Christ that we may deserve also to share in his kingdom.'[5]

Monastic rules reveal with particular clarity the ideals that shaped the evolution of the communal religious life in the Christian Latin West and would outwardly seem to offer a valuable route into a study of the nature of the conventual monastic life in the same period. The words of St Benedict's rule were so familiar to the eighth-century Northumbrian Bede that his writings, particularly his homilies, were frequently coloured with allusions to a text that he must have known well by heart.[6] In the autobiographical statement with which he concluded his *Ecclesiastical History*, Bede defined himself as a servant of Christ, *famulus Christi*. He explained how he had spent his entire life from the age of seven at the *monasterium* of Saints Peter and Paul at Wearmouth and Jarrow 'amid the observance of the discipline of the rule and the daily task of singing in the church', devoting himself with joy to learning, teaching or writing.[7] Ceolfrith, Bede's abbot, had similarly 'for many years carried out the discipline of observance of the rule, a discipline which its father and provider had handed down on authority of traditional practice for the benefit both of his followers and himself' before he elected in old age to visit once more the shrines of the holy apostles in Rome.[8] Adherence to a rule, or to a clearly articulated set of organising principles, was one of the defining characteristics of monasticism and the key to its differentiation from secular life-styles. Caesarius of Arles admonished the nuns in sixth-century Arles for whom he wrote his rule, 'with your whole heart and with your whole soul you should strive earnestly to fulfil the

---

[4] Columbanus, *Regula monachorum*, ch. 1 (pp. 124–5).   [5] *RSB*, prologue, 49–50 (pp. 164–7).
[6] A. G. P. van der Walt, 'Reflections of the Benedictine Rule in Bede's homiliary', *JEH* 37 (1986), 367–86. See also Patrick Wormald, 'Bede and Benedict Biscop', in Gerald Bonner (ed.), *Famulus Christi: Essays in Commemoration of the Thirteenth Centenary of the Birth of the Venerable Bede* (London: SPCK, 1976), pp. 141–69, at pp. 142–4; and Henry M. R. E. Mayr-Harting, *The Venerable Bede, the Rule of St Benedict and Social Class*, Jarrow Lecture 1976 (Jarrow, 1977), pp. 8–9.
[7] *HE* V. 24 (pp. 566–7).   [8] *HA*, ch. 16 (p. 380).

precepts included above, through which you may happily attain your eternal reward'.[9]

Monasticism was the predominant form of religious expression in England in the period between the conversion of the Anglo-Saxons to Christianity in the late sixth and seventh centuries and the end of the First Viking Age *c*. 900. Most of the religious men and women whose pious and charitable deeds we find reported in contemporary narratives were, for at least a part of their careers, associated with a communal religious establishment. Even those whose ascetic fervour found fulfilment in the eremitic life often had formal connections with a conventual house and had frequently spent some time sharing in a life of communal devotion before they adopted a solitary existence.[10] The *monasterium* was the focus of all Anglo-Saxon piety: it satisfied the devotional aspirations of pious men and women, served the spiritual and often the charitable needs of its lay neighbours and fulfilled a valuable social function as a focal point in its own locality. Although the words might refer to diverse sorts of establishment, the Latin noun *monasterium* and its Old English derivative, *mynster*, were used synonymously in early English sources to denote communal religious establishments. Contemporaries made no distinction between different sorts of congregation on the basis of the identity (or gender) of their occupants, or the types of task in which they were most regularly engaged.[11] It is thus important to clarify at the start of this study the terms that will be used to describe both

---

[9] Caesarius, *Regula ad uirgines*, ch. 63 (ed. de Vogüé and Courreau, pp. 248–9). Caesarius, who had trained at the monastery of Lérins, was archbishop of Arles from 502 until 542; taking a particular interest in the Christian community in Arles, he reorganised the life of his own cathedral congregation and established a female community, headed by his sister and after her his niece, writing a rule specifically for the women's use: Dunn, *The Emergence of Monasticism*, pp. 98–107.

[10] Not all of those known to have lived as solitaries (for example the anchorites named in Durham's *Liber vitae*) can be associated with specific minsters and it is not possible to comment on any preparation or training they might have received before entering a hermitage. In his poem about the church of York, Alcuin described the spiritual prowess of two anchorites, Balthere and Echa (*Versus*, lines 1319–87 and 1388–1407), neither of whom appears to have lived at York; that Alcuin was seemingly so well-informed about their deeds and that both their deaths were recorded in the York Annals (*s.a.* 756 and 767) implies that neither man was totally cut off from the organised Church of his own day. See Donald Bullough, 'Hagiography as patriotism: Alcuin's "York poem" and the early Northumbrian "vitae sanctorum"', in Pierre Riché and Evelyne Patlagean (eds.), *Hagiographie, Cultures et Sociétés ive–xiie siècles: Actes du Colloque organisé à Nanterre et à Paris (2–5 mai, 1979)* (Paris: Etudes augustiniennes, 1981), pp. 339–59, at pp. 349–52.

[11] Compare Christopher Brooke, 'Rural ecclesiastical institutions in England: the search for their origins', *Settimane* 28 (1982), 685–711, at 697–8: 'there is no kind of religious community, or church bereft of a religious community, that was not at one time or another called a *monasterium*. The confusion is compounded by our ignorance of the nature of the communities or groups of clergy who served the majority of the minster churches for most of the period 600–1100.'

communal religious establishments in early Anglo-Saxon England and those who dwelt within them.

Definition of terms

As I have argued elsewhere, the Latin noun employed most consistently in early medieval England (and indeed the rest of western Europe) to denote a congregation of people living together, apart from the world under religious vows, was *monasterium*.[12] Cathedral communities, groups of religious mostly in clerical orders, who lived in a household led by a bishop were generally described either as *sedes episcopales* (the seats of bishops) or sometimes simply as *ecclesiae*.[13] We shall look further at the relationship between episcopal and monastic communities in the next chapter,[14] yet apart from bishops' households, all other religious congregations were consistently called *monasteria*. This blanket term could conceal a variety of types of institution ranging from a small community of a handful of men, living at a distance from secular settlement on a small portion of land with perhaps a wooden oratory or church, to a large, well-endowed congregation of men and women, living in a planned enclosure organised around one or more stone-built churches. The household of a widow living in quiet seclusion with her unmarried daughters might be thought of as a *monasterium*, just as was a new community created by the royal grant of a portion of land to an aspiring abbot and a group of like-minded men. What differentiated a *monasterium* from a secular household was that its inmates had determined to devote their collective lives to religion, yet beyond this it is difficult to define the word.[15]

The modern noun 'monastery' is not an ideal choice as a translation either for the Latin *monasterium* or its old English equivalent, the Latin loan word, *mynster*. In current usage 'monastery' carries with it connotations of contemplative regularity, particularly perhaps Benedictine or Cistercian regular observance, which do not apply to English circumstances before the tenth

---

[12] This argument is articulated at length in my 'Anglo-Saxon minsters: a review of terminology', in John Blair and Richard Sharpe (eds.), *Pastoral Care before the Parish* (Leicester, London and New York: Leicester University Press, 1992), pp. 212–25.

[13] James Campbell, 'The church in Anglo-Saxon towns', in his *Essays in Anglo-Saxon History* (London: Hambledon Press, 1986), pp. 139–54, at p. 140.

[14] Below, pp. 61–9.

[15] Richard Morris has argued that the word 'is not susceptible to exact or exclusive definition': 'Alcuin, York and the *alma sophia*', in L. A. S. Butler and R. K. Morris (eds.), *The Anglo-Saxon Church* (London: Council for British Archaeology, 1986), pp. 80–9, at p. 80.

century. At a period in which, as we shall see, distinctions were not drawn between contemplative 'monks' and secular clergy engaged actively in pastoral ministry, it is not wise to use a noun for their households that is generally taken to imply regularity of observance or strict enclosure.[16] My own preference here has been to use the noun 'minster'. Some scholars have in recent years chosen to use this word in a specialised sense to refer to those Anglo-Saxon institutions that lay behind the mother churches of Domesday Book, collegiate churches that were distinguishable from other religious houses because of the primarily pastoral function they exercised in serving the spiritual needs of the villages and other settlements within their *parochiae*.[17] Yet to restrict the use of 'minster' to represent only those houses which in the later Anglo-Saxon period took pastoral responsibility for wide geographical areas is to lose much of the diversity of meaning which the nouns *mynster* and *monasterium* conveyed in the earlier period. There were wide differences in the composition, status and function of religious houses active in England between 600 and 900, yet that diversity was encompassed within the remarkably consistent vocabulary used by contemporaries to define households that stood out from their secular counterparts because of their communal dedication to religion. We, too, should adopt a single term that can embrace this variety and I have thus chosen to use 'minster' consistently in this study.[18]

Distinctions made by later generations of monks between institutions on the basis of adherence to the precepts of the Rule of St Benedict are not appropriate in our period when the monastic life was characterised in England, as elsewhere in Europe, by the observance of no single rule of life. Study of the variety of monastic rules, together with the range of other sorts of advisory or prescriptive literature that sought to regulate the internal organisation of religious communities or define the limits of their inmates' congress with their lay neighbours, would patently answer many questions about how the monastic life was practised in the first Christian centuries in England. In the next chapter we shall explore the available rules in some detail and consider the ways in which they helped to shape English attitudes

---

[16] Much of the debate around this issue in recent years has focused on the question of the exercise of pastoral care; this is discussed in detail in chapter 7.

[17] Compare, for example, M. J. Franklin, 'The identification of minsters in the Midlands', in R. Allen Brown (ed), *Anglo-Norman Studies VII*, pp. 69–88, at p. 69; Patrick Hase, 'The development of the parish in Hampshire, particularly in the eleventh and twelfth centuries' (unpublished PhD thesis, University of Cambridge, 1975), p. 13.

[18] Patrick Sims-Williams took the opposite decision when addressing the same problem: *Religion and Literature*, p. 117.

towards the conventual life. Yet there are dangers in over-reliance on such texts. The monastic legislator, whether writing a rule for the guidance of a particular group of avowed men or women, or trying to couch general pre-scriptions for the organisation of religious institutions and the behaviour of their members within an ecclesiastical province, constructed an idealised picture of a perfect and harmonious institution. As we shall see, the diver-sity of custom to which non-prescriptive texts bear witness was consider-able. Narrative sources from seventh- and eighth-century England describe the behaviour and habits of many holy Englishmen and women in ways that frequently fail to correspond neatly to the templates which the normative rules or canons of church councils provide. Reading these accounts of indi-viduals' actions in the expectation that they could – or should – be made to adhere to the principles that governed an ideal monastery is to deny much of the distinctiveness that characterised the early English minster and thus to misrepresent its nature.

If we are to come closer to understanding the nature of the monastic life in early Anglo-Saxon England, we need to read the non-prescriptive literature in a different way, neither measuring descriptions of the behaviour of reli-gious men and women against contemporary regulatory norms, nor seeing their actions through the retrospective lens of later generations of monas-tic reformers. In many instances, it will prove necessary to read between the lines of the narrative sources or to focus on incidental remarks made by hagiographers and historians. It is often in the scene-setting prelude to an account of a saint's performance of a miracle or his uttering of impor-tant spiritual truths that a hagiographer will, perhaps unwittingly, shed useful light on the day-to-day routine within a minster. Extremes of a saint's ascetic devotion (whether in fasting, prayer, bodily mortification or sleep-deprivation) were frequently accentuated by being set in the context of the more mundane habits pursued by the rest of the community to which the holy man or woman belonged. Thus for us the most valuable information is to be found not, paradoxically, in a hagiographer's demonstration of the distinctiveness of his subject but in his depiction of what was commonplace about the monastic backdrop against which the saint's holiness was painted.

Questioning the assumptions that underlie the sources may lead us fur-ther to think critically about another linguistic problem. If we describe the men and women who lived in early English minsters by the conventional labels monk and nun, do we thereby prejudice our view of the life-styles they led? Was a monk inevitably a brown-cowled figure, to be found bent over the herbs in his garden, reading in the cloister, or standing chanting 7 in the candle-lit choir? Must a nun have worn a veil and lived in total exclusion from the secular, especially the male, world around her? These, as will rapidly become apparent, are images that fit uncomfortably with the narratives found in our sources, although they may resonate more readily with some of the recommendations of the admonitory or prescriptive literature. Language relating to male religious in the pre-Viking Age church does appear to offer some insight into the different roles and functions performed by different groups of religious, and suggests that we should not bracket them all together unthinkingly. While male monastics might often be described by the general term brothers (*fratres*), as tonsured men, that mark being the symbol that most obviously marked them out from their lay counterparts, or simply as *clerici*, there was a sharp linguistic distinction drawn in narrative and prescriptive sources between religious generally and those who were ordained to clerical rank. Priests and deacons stood apart from all men, their ecclesiastical rank conferring upon them particular obligations but also a special status, and hence protection under the law. While this readily answers questions about how best to refer to early English clergy it does not tell us whether other men who lived a religious life in minsters but were not ordained to the ranks of the clergy were all called 'monks'. This is a question to which we shall return in the next chapter.[19] Certainly the canons of English church councils drew sharp contrast between *monachi* and *clerici*, between *ecclesiastici* and *monasteriales* and applied higher penalties to the transgressions of both groups than to the sins of other religious.[20] It is difficult to find the same linguistic clarity in the narrative sources and thus hard to make firm decisions about the extent to which one described as a brother in a minster was a professed monk or one who had made a lesser commitment to life under a rule. Where I have quoted from monastic rules, or from other sorts of prescriptive literature, I have retained the language of the texts and referred to the obligations placed upon monks, but in general I have chosen to avoid that noun and to talk more loosely about brethren and religious, without further clarification.

In a previous study of religious women in Anglo-Saxon England, I argued in similar vein that it could be positively misleading to talk about nuns

[19] Below, pp. 66–9.
[20] Council of Hertford, AD 672/3, chs. 4 and 5 (*HE* IV. 5, pp. 348–53); Ecgberht's *Dialogi, responsiones* 3, 7, 12 and 14 (H&S III. 405–6, 408–9); Council of *Clofesho*, AD 747, chs. 4–5, 7–8, 8–12, 28–9 (H&S, III. 364–7 and 374); Legatine synods, AD 786, ch. 4 (ed. Dümmler, p. 22). See further my 'Language and method: the *Dictionary of Old English* and the historian', in M. J. Toswell (ed.), *The Dictionary of Old English: Retrospects and Prospects*, Old English Newsletter, Subsidia 26 (1998), 73–87, at pp. 76–7, and *Veiled Women*, I: *The Disappearance of Nuns from Anglo-Saxon England* (Aldershot: Ashgate Publishing, 2000), p. 28.

in either the pre- or the post-Viking-Age church. In the period between the seventh and ninth centuries, contemporaries described religious women by a variety of nouns (for example *ancilla Dei, Deo deuota, famula Christi, femina consecrata, monacha, nonna, nunnona, sanctimonialis, soror*) which appear, so far as one can tell, to have been thought more or less synonymous. Certainly the various terms reveal nothing of the nature or organisation of the congregation in which a religious woman might have lived; the same nouns refer to young girls in the double houses at Whitby and Barking and widows living in seclusion within their own homes. A sharper contrast was drawn between women who entered the cloister as virgins and those who came either with a living husband's consent or in widowhood, suggesting that the extent of a woman's previous sexual experience was a more significant issue to writers about the early English church than was the outward forms by which religious chose to express their devotion.[21] While some of the women whose activities we shall explore might have lived lives that would conform to later medieval (and indeed modern) views of a nun's behaviour, others were far less withdrawn from secular society than later generations might think customary and lived not so much at as across the margins of the temporal and spiritual worlds. As far as is possible, I have avoided the word 'nun' to describe women in the pre-Viking Age church, except in translation of monastic rules and the canons of church councils, where legislators wrote specifically about their expectations of the behaviour of *sanctimoniales*.

In English texts written during and after the monastic revolution of the tenth century, the language used of both female and male religious changed sharply; then institutional arrangements did, at least in vernacular writing, determine the words used to differentiate the cloistered from those who lived in the world. Women dwelling within the walls of institutions ordered by the precepts of Benedict's Rule were called *mynecenas*; their male equivalents were monks, *munecas*. Women who lived a religious life under vows while remaining in the world were, however, called *nunnan*, equivalent to the male *preostas*, secular clergy.[22] As I have argued previously, it is clearer

---

[21] This is argued at length in my *Veiled Women*, I, 26–30.

[22] This distinction may be seen most clearly in Archbishop Wulfstan's Institutes of Polity: *I Polity*, 84–5, ed. Karl Jost, *Die 'Institutes of Polity, Civil and Ecclesiastical'* (Bern: Francke, 1959), p. 129, trans. Michael Swanton, *Anglo-Saxon Prose* (2nd edn, London: Dent, 1993), pp. 187–201, at p. 199. For full discussion see my *Veiled Women*, I, 96–104; the issue has also been explored by Mary Clayton, 'Ælfric's *Judith*: manipulative or manipulated?', *ASE* 23 (1994), 215–27, at pp. 225–7; and Pauline Stafford, 'Queens, nunneries and reforming churchmen: gender, religious status and reform in tenth- and eleventh-century England', *Past and Present* 163 (1999), 3–35, at p. 10.

in modern English to translate *mynecenas* as 'cloistered' women and to call *nunnan* 'vowesses', than it is to translate either Old English noun as 'nun'. The differentiation of vowesses from their religious sisters who were cloistered paralleled the marking of a similar distinction between clerics active among the secular community and monks who dwelt in enclosed contemplation and reflects the significant changes made to the organisation of the religious life in tenth-century England. The imposition of Benedict's Rule as a single standard for the governance of the conventual life marked a substantial shift, even revolution, in English ecclesiastical life. This study is preoccupied, however, with circumstances before that reform and with a period when boundaries between action and contemplation were much more blurred.

Approach and method

Throughout the rest of this book I shall seek to build a picture of the nature of monasticism before the tenth-century monastic revolution, and to do so cumulatively, by collecting references and allusions from a range of sources in order to illustrate particular elements of religious behaviour or to cast light on specific aspects of the monastic day. There are dangers in such an approach. At one level, one could argue that this technique misses nuances in the evidence and creates a slightly bland picture of the early English church, from which the peaks of spiritual fervour (and troughs of unduly-secular irregularity) have been ironed out. This method may further be over-descriptive and so tend to accentuate similarities between institutions, whereas it is a central thesis of the study that early English minsters were in fact characterised by their dissimilarity. Much of the book's purpose is to refocus scholarly attention away from an unduly polarised view of the pre-reform church that contrasts a Benedictine monastic ideal (as presented by Bede and the reformers of Edgar's reign) with a pastorally-active, but ideologically-imperfect, reality, and to point attention towards a more integrated view of early English monasticism that gives equal weight to all shades in the contemporary spectrum of religious observance. Each of the numerous examples adduced serves to support this central argument about the diversity of early Anglo-Saxon monasticism in a way that local surveys and individual case studies cannot. I have indeed deliberately chosen not to provide any narrative descriptions of particular minsters and their congregations, nor to construct the sort of catalogue of institutions that constitutes the second part of my *Veiled Women*. This is a study of monasticism as a social and spiritual phenomenon, not a survey of the evidence about separate institutions.

I shall argue that much historical understanding of the early English church has depended on a number of misconceptions about the essential nature of Anglo-Saxon monasticism in the period before the tenth century. Historians, influenced by the writings of Bede (particularly but not exclusively his *Ecclesiastical History*) and by the rhetoric of the monks who reformed the monasteries in the 960s and 970s, have tended to see the monasticism of earlier centuries as conforming to a certain uniform type. Any departure from the standards to which Bede and the draughtsmen of conciliar canons aspired has often been represented in terms of a 'decline' from monastic standards attained when the English religious life reached its peak in the late seventh and early eighth centuries. Contemporary criticisms of ecclesiastical behaviour in general and monasticism particularly do shed useful light on eighth-century attitudes, but again tend to emphasise consistency over individuality or diversity. An alternative but equally influential mode of studying the church in this period has been via the question of the provision of pastoral care for the laity. In much of that debate, active 'minsters' and enclosed 'monasteries' have been understood as binary opposites and historians have sought to shape malleable evidence to fit one or other institutional model. Here I shall argue that early English monasteries were neither enclosed houses constructed on the Benedictine model (communities organised exclusively for prayerful, inward-looking contemplation) nor primarily mission-stations perched precariously in the wilds and struggling to cope with the pastoral needs of a barely Christianised population, while displaying only the vestiges of a conventional monastic ideal. Rather, I shall suggest that Anglo-Saxon minsters were houses created to follow mixed rules in which action and contemplation were treated as complementary routes towards the fulfilment of both individual and collective spiritual quests. Their founders and early inmates interpreted the ideologies of earlier generations of monastic legislators in diverse and imaginative ways and thereby invented a novel, but distinctively Anglo-Saxon, version of monasticism.[23] In order to explain why prevailing orthodoxies might need to be challenged, it is necessary to consider the perspectives from which the English church

---

[23] Anglo-Saxon monasticism did not, of course, emerge in isolation and owed much to contemporary forms of communal religious observance, particularly but not exclusively those of Ireland and Merovingian Gaul (which were themselves interconnected). The monastic institutions founded in England in the seventh and eighth centuries were thus similar to their Irish and Frankish counterparts, although they reflected certain uniquely English characteristics.

has previously been studied and to explore the contexts within which an alternative reading could be located.

Retrospective readings

A substantial impediment to the study of early English monasticism is the apparent impermanence of many of the religious houses that were founded in the seventh and eighth centuries. Some royal and noble institutions served the familial needs of their founders' kin for only one or two generations; no longer proving useful to family strategies their valuable landed estates were seemingly reabsorbed within secular patrimonies. Others, perhaps never adequately endowed, fade from view not being economically viable as separate units.[24] More significant for the church as a whole was the impact of the Scandinavian wars and ensuing settlements in the ninth and tenth centuries. One can argue about the extent to which religion really suffered during the First Viking Age and question both contemporary and later accounts of the destruction of monastic houses, but it is impossible either in the medieval or the later historiography entirely to escape the vikings' shadow. Dom David Knowles, whose magisterial survey of the monastic order in England begins in 940 with the major religious reform that sought to restore the church after the decline of the previous century, summarises – and indeed to an extent was subsequently to dictate – conventional wisdom. 'Historians of the last century were commonly agreed that at the epoch of Dunstan's boyhood and the reign of Æthelstan [924–39] monasticism was wholly extinct in England and that the renaissance under King Edgar [957/9–75] was modelled wholly on lines borrowed from abroad.' Although Knowles qualified the second of these observations, noting that by the time he was writing it was accepted that the origins of the renaissance were to be found in England before Edgar's reign, he was not minded to adjust the first: 'all available evidence from the reign of Alfred points to a complete collapse of monasticism by the end of the ninth century'.[25] Whether that collapse should rightly be blamed on the vikings is a matter that cannot detain us here. Tenth-century reformers tended not to dwell on

---

[24] The foundation and endowment of minsters is examined in chapter 3.

[25] Dom David Knowles, *The Monastic Order in England: A History of its Development from the Times of St Dunstan to the Fourth Lateran Council, 940–1216* (2nd edn, Cambridge: Cambridge University Press, 1963), pp. 32–3.

this as a cause,[26] but the generation preceding them had, in looking at a range of causes for the inadequacies of the church in their own day, drawn direct connections between the activities of the Danes as the tools of God's anger on the one hand, and the irreligious English and the lack of interest among the Anglo-Saxon nobility in monastic observance on the other.[27]

Whatever had caused the decay, that English monasticism had declined almost to the point of extinction was certainly the view taken by the ecclesiastics who promoted the tenth-century monastic revival. Bishop Æthelwold (abbot of Abingdon before he became bishop of Winchester and responsible for much of the ideological literature relating to the Benedictine revolution) argued that before the reform of the male community at Abingdon in the 960s 'there were only a few monks in a few places in so large a kingdom who lived by the right rule. This was in no more places than one, which is called Glastonbury, where [Edgar's] father, King Edmund, first established monks.'[28] In similar vein, he explained in the preface to the *Regularis concordia* the necessity for the reforms being instituted through the ensuing text, the report of the 'monastic agreement' reached at a council held in Winchester in the king's presence in the 970s. Æthelwold's preface placed responsibility for this revolution in monastic organisation firmly on the king's shoulders, suggesting that it was his perception of the decay of monastic institutions that was driving the reform agenda:[29]

When therefore he learned that the holy monasteries in all quarters of his kingdom, brought low and almost wholly lacking in the service of our Lord Jesus Christ, were wasting away and neglected, moved by the grace of the Lord, he most gladly set himself to restore them everywhere to their former good estate. Wherefore he drove out the negligent clerks with their abominations, placing in their stead for the

---

[26] Eric John, *Orbis Britanniae and Other Studies* (Leicester: Leicester University Press, 1966), p. 155; but see Antonia Gransden, 'Traditionalism and continuity during the last century of Anglo-Saxon monasticism', *JEH* 40 (1989), 159–207, at p. 169.

[27] We shall return to this issue in the final chapter. I have explored the question of the impact of the Danes on women's religious houses in particular in my *Veiled Women*, I, pp. 71–84, and looked at contemporary perceptions of viking violence in 'Violence against Christians? The vikings and the church in ninth-century England', *Medieval History* 1.3 (1991), 3–16.

[28] Æthelwold, 'An account of King Edgar's establishment of monasteries' (*C&S* I, 148–9, no. 33).

[29] *Regularis concordia*, proem §2 (ed. Hallinger, pp. 69–70; trans. Symons, pp. 1–2). The king's role in this process has been much discussed, see particularly, John, *Orbis Britanniae*, pp. 154–80; N. Banton, 'Monastic reform and the unification of tenth-century England', in Stuart Mews (ed.), *Religion and National Identity* (Oxford: Basil Blackwell for the Ecclesiastical History Society, 1982), pp. 71–85. Antonia Gransden's suggestion that Edgar might have been following the example of the Carolingian emperor Louis the Pious, who summoned a council at Aachen in 816 to discuss the reform of Frankish religious communities, is a good one: 'Traditionalism', pp. 164–5.

service of God, throughout the length and breadth of his dominions, not only monks but also cloistered women,[30] under abbots and abbesses; and these, out of gratitude to God, he enriched with all good things.

Central to the reformers' ideology was the claim that their efforts would restore the English church to its former, more perfect state. Historical example was used to justify a (wholly unwarranted) assertion that nothing novel was being effected by the reforms, that these were no more than a royally-sponsored and protected means of returning the religious houses of England to orthodox life under a single rule.[31] The monks' collective 'memory' (perhaps better conceived as a collective act of construction rather than recollection) manufactured a sense of the Anglo-Saxon ecclesiastical past which was, to quote Alan Thacker, 'all of a piece and all monastic'.[32] Political realities of the mid-tenth century placed a further constraint upon their acts of restoration: the reform was, necessarily, an exclusively southern and midland enterprise. None of the former Northumbrian houses was revivified in Edgar's reign.[33]

Æthelwold's narrative of King Edgar's establishment of monasteries, written as a prologue to his own translation of the Rule of St Benedict into Old English, set the efforts of the king and his bishops in a wide chronological context. His text begins with an account of the conversion of the English (a grievously deluded race, practising devil worship) effected through the good offices of St Gregory (the Great) and his emissary Augustine. Following papal instruction, Augustine acquired the English for the Lord, and founded minsters to the praise and honour of Christ, establishing for the servants of God the same mode of life which the apostles maintained with their society

---

[30] For reasons explained at length in my *Veiled Women*, I, 104–10, I prefer to use this term to the more conventional 'nun' to describe religious women living in cloistered communities in England after the tenth-century reform.

[31] *Ibid.*, pp. 162–3.

[32] Alan Thacker, 'Æthelwold and Abingdon', in Barbara Yorke (ed.), *Bishop Æthelwold, his Career and Influence* (Woodbridge: Boydell Press, 1988), pp. 43–64, at p. 63. This idea has been further developed by Simon Coates, 'Perceptions of the Anglo-Saxon past in the tenth-century monastic reform movement', in R. N. Swanson (ed.), *The Church Retrospective* (Woodbridge: Boydell Press for the Ecclesiastical History Society, 1997), pp. 61–74.

[33] See figure 2. Stenton commented on the fact that the strength of the monastic reform movement lay almost entirely in the southern half of England and that it had only a limited impact on western Mercia: *Anglo-Saxon England* (Oxford: Clarendon Press, 1943; 3rd edn 1971, pp. 455–6). It is perhaps surprising that Oswald did not do more to promote reform in the north in his capacity as archbishop of York: H. R. Loyn, *The English Church 940–1154* (London: Longman, 2000), p. 19. An ambiguous passage in Byrhtferth's *Vita Oswaldi* (ed. Raine, p. 462) has been thought to describe Oswald's reintroduction of monks to Ripon, but the allusion is probably to Worcester: A. Hamilton Thompson, 'Northumbrian monasticism', in A. Hamilton Thompson (ed.), *Bede: His Life, Times, and Writings* (Oxford: Clarendon Press, 1935), pp. 60–101, at p. 98.

FIGURE 1: Map of houses connected with the tenth-century monastic revolution.

at the beginning of Christianity.[34] They lived, as had the first Christian community in Jerusalem, having no possessions of their own but holding all things in common (Acts 4: 32).[35] 'This same mode of life, therefore, through the admonition of the holy man, was for a long time progressing and prospering well in the minsters of the English nation. But . . .': here the text breaks off. The manuscript is damaged and at least one, perhaps as many as three folios are missing.[36] When the text resumes much time has elapsed, for the young Edgar is being praised for his early commitment to the church and he is soon installed on the throne following his brother Eadwig's death (in 959) and made responsible for bringing back to unity the division of the kingdom. It is not difficult to supply the missing narrative. If Æthelwold continued to follow Bede as closely as he had done in discussing the conversion, he would have shown the expansion of faith across the separate English kingdoms, the foundation of bishoprics and minsters in each realm, the institution of a single, central authority over the whole church by Archbishop Theodore (669–90) and then – presumably – the gradual decay from that high point during the later eighth and ninth centuries, if not the devastation wrought by pagan, Scandinavian invaders.[37] Certainly such a narrative would contextualise and help to explain the statement about the unique position of Glastonbury as the sole preserver of the 'right rule' at the start of Edgar's reign quoted above, and would further account for the young king's energy in setting monasteries in order, 'cleansing holy places from all men's foulnesses' (in Mercia as well as in Wessex) and 'driving out canons who abounded beyond measure' in sin.[38] Invective of this sort

[34] Æthelwold, 'An account', pp. 143–5; his narrative is based on Bede's account of the background to the mission to the English, Augustine's arrival in Kent in 597 and the creation of the first churches there: *HE* I. 23–6, 33; II. 1. Dorothy Whitelock demonstrated that this anonymous work was written by Æthelwold: 'The authorship of the account of King Edgar's establishment of monasteries', reprinted in her *History, Law and Literature in 10th–11th Century England* (London: Variorum, 1981), no. VII.

[35] Here, Æthelwold followed *HE* I. 27, where Bede reports Gregory's answer to Augustine's question as to how he should live with his clergy in England, although he quotes more of the passage from Acts than Gregory had done in the *Liber responsionum*. The implication that this apostolic life-style was that followed by all English minsters in the succeeding generation is Æthelwold's own, however.

[36] The text survives only in a damaged twelfth-century manuscript: London, British Library, MS Cotton Faustina A. x, fos. 148–51r; see *C&S* I, 142 and 145n.

[37] Patrick Wormald, 'Æthelwold and his continental counterparts: contact, comparison, contrast', in Barbara Yorke (ed.), *Bishop Æthelwold: His Career and Influence* (Woodbridge: Boydell Press, 1988), pp. 13–42, at p. 40.

[38] Æthelwold, 'An account' (*C&S* I, 150). Some responsibility for the poor state of affairs he also placed on Edgar's brother, Eadwig 'who had through the ignorance of childhood dispersed this kingdom and divided its unity and also distributed the lands of holy churches to rapacious strangers': *ibid.*, p. 146.

against the unreformed clerical communities is found in other texts from the reform era and may also have had historical roots. The language of these texts (the *Regularis concordia*, Wulfstan of Winchester's Life of St Æthelwold, Byrhtferth's Life of St Oswald and Edgar's foundation charter for the New Minster at Winchester) is reminiscent of both Bede's *Ecclesiastical History* and of the letter that Bede wrote to Bishop Ecgberht of York in 734, in which he complained about declining religious standards in his own day.[39]

One additional area that particularly concerned the reformers was that of the involvement of seculars in the control of monastic houses. The *Regularis concordia* was particularly outspoken on the subject: 'The assembly wisely, and under severe censure and anathema, forbade the holy monasteries to acknowledge the overlordship of secular persons (*secularium prioratus*), a thing which might lead to utter loss and ruin as it did in past times.'[40] Towards the end of his account of the reform Æthelwold articulated his prayerful hopes for the future of the reformed monasteries, urging his fellow abbots that neither they or anyone else should seek to diminish God's patrimony (either the church's estates or its other possessions) lest 'the fire of holy religion should become lukewarm and grow cold'. He was sure that 'the observance of this holy rule was impaired in former times through the robbery of evil men and through the consent of the kings who had little fear of God'.[41] The reformers' response to the problem of lay control was to place the reformed monasteries directly in royal hands; as John argued, 'the *Concordia* replaced *saecularium prioratus* by royal *dominium*'.[42] This was perhaps a slightly risky strategy since it relied upon the continuing presence of a king benevolently disposed towards the reform and its ideals. There certainly was secular opposition to the ways in which new and re-established institutions acquired landed possessions, especially in contexts where those had formerly been in lay hands, as is shown by the reaction of some of

---

[39] Wulfstan of Winchester, *Vita S. Æthelwoldi*, chs. 16, 18, 20 (ed. Lapidge and Winterbottom, pp. 30–1, 32–3, 36–7); Byrhtferth, *Vita S. Oswaldi*, II (ed. Raine, I, 411); S 745 (New Minster foundation charter) and compare also S 782, a charter issued for Bishop Æthelwold. The parallels were noted and discussed by Dorothy Whitelock, 'The authorship', pp. 130–3. The connection with Bede's language has been explored in detail by Gransden, 'Traditionalism', pp. 166–8; also Coates, 'Perceptions of the Anglo-Saxon past', pp. 62–4. It is interesting, as I observed in *Veiled Women*, I, 93–5, that the same criticisms were not levelled at unreformed communities of religious women. Equally noteworthy is the failure of 'B', the earliest of Dunstan's biographers, to indulge in the abuse of non-monastic congregations. That he may have been himself a member of a clerical community may be relevant here: Michael Lapidge, 'B. and the *Vita sancti Dunstani*', in Nigel Ramsay, Margaret Sparks and Tim Tatton-Brown (eds.), *St Dunstan: His Life, Times and Cult* (Woodbridge: Boydell Press, 1992), pp. 247–59.

[40] *Regularis concordia*, proem §10 (ed. Hallinger, p. 75; trans. Symons, p. 7).

[41] Æthelwold, 'An account' (*C&S* I, 152–3).   [42] John, *Orbis Britanniae*, p. 178.

the dispossessed nobles after the death of King Edgar.[43] Yet here again the reformers were following Bede's guidance in his condemnation of the secularisation of minsters in his own day when lay nobles had appropriated monastic lands to their own uses.[44]

Such vilification of an old order that reformers seek to supplant is, unsurprisingly, often found in the literature of reform movements. Patrick Wormald has commented on the fact that the sources from the Lotharingian house at Gorze may give 'too desolate and/or dissolute an impression of pre-reform conditions'.[45] Similarly, after the Conquest, the new Norman ecclesiastical hierarchy, in particular Archbishop Lanfranc, expressed forcibly the distaste with which they viewed the English monasteries and their saints.[46] What is significant about the English literature produced in support of the tenth-century reform is not the nature of these denigrating comments but the historical character of these texts, most markedly those associated with Æthelwold.[47] The reformers believed that the poverty they witnessed in the expression of monasticism in their own day was result of a decline from a former glorious state; their stated aim was 'to *restore* the church to its former good estate' by implication to the condition of the church of Bede's youth.[48]

Æthelwold's rhetorical and propagandist writings enshrined as historical truth the notion that there had been Benedictine houses and monastic cathedrals in the eighth century. He and the other reformers created a uniform image of the earlier church, where the Rule of St Benedict had been the dominant model of monastic organisation, and they did so by appealing to the authority of Bede.[49] Not only did Æthelwold's writings include quotations from and significant verbal similarities with Bede's, the bishop had also absorbed some of the broader themes of Bede's *Ecclesiastical History*, particularly the concept of unity which was central to Bede's purpose in writing. Æthelwold conferred as much praise on Edgar for having 'brought back to unity the division and the kingdom and ruled everything so prosperously',

---

[43] D. J. V. Fisher, 'The anti-monastic reaction in the reign of Edward the Martyr', *Cambridge Historical Journal* 10 (1950–2), 254–70; Gransden, 'Traditionalism', pp. 169–70.

[44] *EpEcg.*, §11 (ed. Plummer, pp. 415–16).   [45] Wormald, 'Æthelwold', pp. 27–8.

[46] S. J. Ridyard, '*Condigna veneratio*: post-Conquest attitudes to the saints of the Anglo-Saxons', *Anglo-Norman Studies* 9 (1986), 179–206, at p. 206; Frank Barlow, *The English Church 1066–1154* (London: Longman, 1979), pp. 185–6; H. R. Loyn, *The English Church 940–1154* (London: Longman, 2000), pp. 82–3.

[47] Wormald, 'Æthelwold', pp. 38–41. He also drew attention (p. 40) to two 'more or less authentic' texts for Ely and Peterborough (S 779 and 782) which made specific reference to Bede's testimony.

[48] *Regularis concordia*, prologue §2 (ed. Hallinger, pp. 69–70).

[49] Coates, 'Perceptions of the Anglo-Saxon past', p. 64.

as he did for his restoration of the minsters, reinforcing his approval in typically Bedan fashion by reference to the eternal reward that would await the king in heaven.[50] The second generation of reformed monastics such as Ælfric perpetuated Æthelwold's reinterpretation of England's ecclesiastical past; a homily on the prayer of Moses encapsulates Ælfric's viewpoint:[51]

We can well reflect on how well it went with us when this island was dwelling in peace, and monasteries were held in reverence, and laymen were ready against their enemies, so that our reputation spread widely throughout the earth. How was it then afterwards, when men overthrew monasteries and held God's services in scorn, but that pestilence and famine came to us and afterwards a heathen army held us to scorn?

William of Malmesbury, the twelfth-century monastic historian and a Benedictine himself, also reinforced the images created by the reformers of a golden age in the time of Bede, followed by a period in which the monastic life was almost extinguished before it was wonderfully restored *in statum pristinum* by Edgar.[52] Further, William accepted the view that the early Anglo-Saxon cathedral at Canterbury was staffed by monks, not secular priests; he described Oda as the first archbishop of Canterbury not to have been in monastic orders, and stressed that since the time of Archbishop Lawrence there had always been monks at Canterbury.[53]

Historians have long dismissed the monks' criticisms of the clerks who occupied the unreformed minsters as hyperbole and have also rejected the reformers' assertion that early English houses followed the Rule of St Benedict exclusively. As I have already suggested, early Anglo-Saxon monasticism was characterised by a diversity and individuality that encompassed multiple expressions of spiritual ideals within a single institutional model, that of the *monasterium* or minster.[54] Yet it is worth pausing and considering further the textual underpinning of the reformers' representation of the Anglo-Saxon past. The far-reaching influence of the tenth-century literature on historical perceptions of the reform itself and the condition of the minsters in the

[50] Æthelwold, 'An account' (*C&S* I, 147).
[51] Ælfric, 'On the prayer of Moses', ed. Walter W. Skeat, *Ælfric's Lives of Saints*, EETS, reprinted in 2 vols. (London: Oxford University Press for the Early English Text Society, 1966), I, 294; trans. Whitelock, *EHD*, no. 239f.
[52] Compare William of Malmesbury, *Vita S. Dunstani*, II. 2 (ed. Stubbs, *Memorials of St Dunstan*, p. 290); *idem, Gesta pontificum Anglorum*, I. 18 on Edgar's ejection of the clerks (ed. Hamilton, p. 27); II. 75 and 80: Æthelwold's reform (pp. 166–7, 178); III. 116: the Danish destruction of Northumbrian minsters (pp. 253–4), V. 198: Aldhelm's minsters of Frome and Bradford (p. 346).
[53] William of Malmesbury, *Gesta pontificum Anglorum*, I. 14 and 20 (pp. 21 and 32).
[54] Sims-Williams, *Religion and Literature*, pp. 115–17.

century that preceded this revolution have until recently been less readily appreciated.[55]

A contemporary perspective

In his preface, Bede described what was to be his last major work as a 'history of the English church and people' (*historia gentis Anglorum ecclesiastica*).[56] A central theme that runs through the entire narrative is the growth of the Christian religion in England from the first mission of Augustine to Canterbury in 597 until the 'favourable times of peace and prosperity' in which Bede was writing.[57] The *Ecclesiastical History* is with some justification regarded as one of the outstanding works of medieval historiography; indeed so great was Bede's skill, especially in his adroit manipulation of diverse kinds of evidence, that it has been difficult to resist the temptation to judge his work with modern standards of historical criticism. Many others have analysed Bede's qualities as an historian and I shall not retrace their steps here.[58] Instead, I shall look at the ways in which his *History* can help in understanding the nature of early Anglo-Saxon monasticism.

An obvious but nonetheless important difficulty is that Bede was not a contemporary witness to most of the events he described. Indeed, he made few references in his *History* to the events of his own lifetime, and the bulk of his text concentrates on the period before 716.[59] According to his own account, Bede completed his *History* 'about 285 years after the coming of the English to Britain, in the year of our Lord 731'; this interval may have struck him as computistically significant and perhaps led him to feel that one cycle of English history had been completed and another era was about to begin.[60] As a brother in the community at Jarrow, Bede was often

---

[55] Wormald, 'Æthelwold', pp. 40–1; Coates, 'Perceptions of the Anglo-Saxon past', p. 64.

[56] *HE* preface (pp. 2–3). In the list of his writings that he appended to the work's final chapter, Bede called it 'historia ecclesiastica nostrae insulae ac gentis in libris v': V. 24 (p. 570). See plate II, a page from a mid-eighth-century manuscript of the *History* made at Monkwearmouth–Jarrow from the copy of the text now known as the St Petersburg Bede: London, British Library, Cotton MS Tiberius A. xiv, fo. 84.

[57] *HE* V. 23 (pp. 560–1).

[58] Wilhelm Levison, 'Bede as historian', in A. Hamilton Thompson (ed.), *Bede: His Life, Times and Writings* (Oxford: Clarendon Press, 1935), pp. 111–51; James Campbell, 'Bede', in T. A. Dorey (ed.), *Latin Historians* (London: Routledge and Kegan Paul, 1966), pp. 159–90, reprinted as 'Bede I', in his *Essays in Anglo-Saxon History* (London and Ronceverte: Hambledon Press, 1986), pp. 1–27; *idem*, 'Bede II', *ibid.*, pp. 28–48; Walter Goffart, *The Narrators of Barbarian History (AD 550–800): Jordanes, Gregory of Tours, Bede, and Paul the Deacon* (Princeton, NJ: Princeton University Press, 1988), ch. 4.

[59] Goffart, *The Narrators*, p. 246.

[60] *HE* V. 23 (p. 560). The year 285 years before AD 731 was 446, one of the dates Bede had previously assigned to the *aduentus Anglorum*.

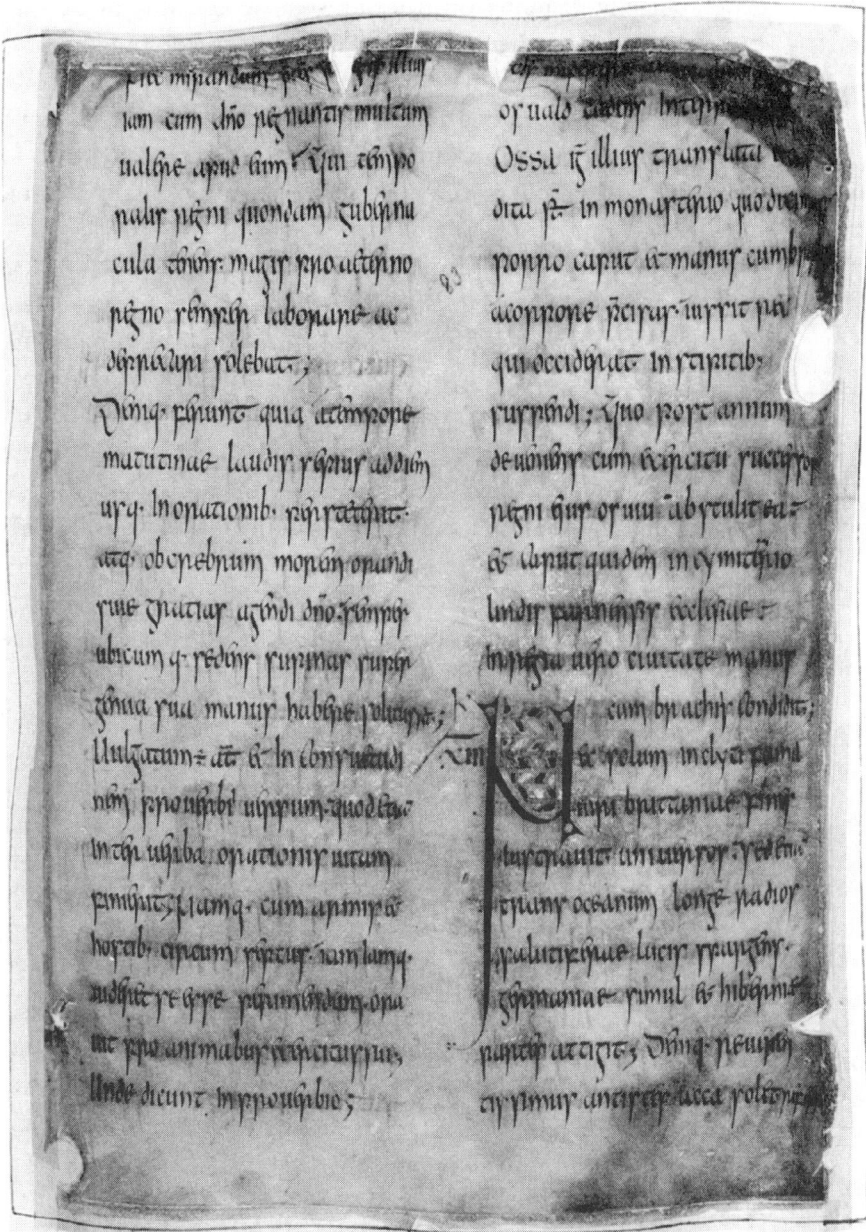

PLATE II: Bede, *Historia ecclesiastica*: London, British Library, Cotton MS Tiberius A. xiv, fo. 84.

geographically distant from the minsters whose way of life he described; his own spiritual milieu – a crucial element in forming and developing his ideas – was arguably equally far from the life-style found in other contemporary institutions. It is difficult not to anticipate that Bede would, albeit subconsciously, have compared the habits of other monastic houses with the standards of Benedict Biscop's two institutions where he had dwelt all his life.

Bede's primary purpose in writing was didactic. 'Should history tell of good men and their good estate', he wrote in the prefatory letter dedicating the work to King Ceolwulf of Northumbria, 'the thoughtful listener is spurred on to imitate the good'; equally, should it record the fate of evil men, the devout listener might be inspired to reject 'what is harmful and perverse'.[61] Explaining how he had collected information from a wide variety of sources, Bede asserted 'in accordance with the principles of true history, I have simply sought to commit to writing what I have collected from common report for the instruction of posterity'.[62] Many of the episodes related in the *Ecclesiastical History* leave the reader in no doubt as to the ultimate fate of those who turned from the right path (a message reinforced through Bede's use of other-worldly visions, for example that of Dryhthelm),[63] yet the work is in fact, as many commentators have noted, predominantly a 'gallery of good examples'.[64] The crimes of the evil were seldom catalogued in any detail. Bede dwelt at some length on the qualities of his chosen exemplary characters, notably the monastic bishops such as Aidan and Cuthbert, describing their simple lives of devotion and poverty and their attention to pastoral obligations, virtues that he hoped his monastic contemporaries would imitate.[65] He did not need to define explicitly the contrast between their restraint and the laxity and opulence he observed among some episcopal households in his own generation. Bede's reticence in this respect has been attributed to unwillingness on his part, lest he should undermine its authority, to denounce the church overtly in a work which was intended for a general audience.[66] However, as James Campbell has argued, one could

---

[61] *HE* preface (pp. 2–3). See Calvin B. Kendall, 'Imitation and the Venerable Bede's *Historia ecclesiastica*', in Margot King and Wesley Stevens (eds.), *Saints, Scholars and Heroes* (Collegeville, MN: Hill Monastic Manuscript Library, Saint John's Abbey and University, 1979), I, 161–90.

[62] *HE* preface (pp. 6–7).   [63] *HE* V. 12 (pp. 488–99).

[64] Campbell, 'Bede I', p. 25; Patrick Wormald, 'Bede, "Beowulf" and the conversion of the Anglo-Saxon aristocracy', in R. T. Farrell (ed.), *Bede and Anglo-Saxon England*, BAR, Brit. ser. 46 (Oxford: BAR, 1978), 32–95, at p. 61.

[65] Campbell, 'Bede II', pp. 37–9. Kendall, 'Imitation', pp. 169–71.

[66] The vices he explored in his letter to Ecgberht, bishop of York, in 734. Campbell, 'Bede I', pp. 19–20; H. E. J. Cowdrey, 'Bede and the English people', *Journal of Religious History* 11 (1981), 501–21, at p. 516.

read Bede's analysis of secular affairs as intended to show the working of God's providence on earth.[67] While the pattern of God's judgement had yet to emerge, he could make only implicit criticisms of his contemporaries, ecclesiastical or lay.

Bede did not therefore devote much space to irregular monastic houses from which we might have been able to learn more about the monastic qualities of which he would have approved, although he did describe the sins of the double house at Coldingham, burnt down because of the wickedness of those who dwelt there and especially of those who were supposed to be its leaders.[68] There are, additionally, some useful comments in his history on the habits of various model houses such as Whitby, Melrose or Barking, which are also included for edification. But it is not sufficient merely to understand the didactic intent underlying Bede's writings: we need to recognise the clarity of his ideas about monasticism and thus understand the nature of the monastic system he recommended. He did not, any more than any of his contemporaries, assume that there was only one rule on which the monastic life was modelled, but he did hold that the religious life should be regular. At Barrow in his day he felt that only traces of the regular life remained (*regularis uitae uestigia*); in his letter to Bishop Ecgberht he defined quite sharply what the consequences of a slide into irregularity would be.[69]

Part of Bede's educational purpose in the *Ecclesiastical History* is visible in his attempt to instil in his contemporaries an awareness of their common heritage as the *gens Anglorum*, united by their Christian faith and use of the Latin language.[70] Irish and British particularism he saw as an especial threat to the integration of the nation.[71] In promoting the ideal of a unified church in England, Bede had a habit of playing down the importance not just of dispute but of diversity. For one whose thought was clearly so

Compare, however, L. W. Barnard, who suggested that because Bede lived at a time of comparative political stability, he projected the same peacefulness into the contemporary Church and tried to minimise its internal quarrels: 'Bede and Eusebius as church historians', in Bonner (ed.), *Famulus Christi*, pp. 106–24, at pp. 119–20.

[67] Campbell, 'Bede I', p. 15.   [68] *HE* IV. 25 (pp. 420–7).

[69] *HE* IV. 3 (pp. 336–7); Ian Wood, 'Anglo-Saxon Otley: an archiepiscopal estate and its crosses in a Northumbrian context', *Northern History* 23 (1987), 20–38, at p. 25.

[70] Patrick Wormald, 'The venerable Bede and the "church of the English"', in Geoffrey Rowell (ed.), *The English Religious Tradition and the Genius of Anglicanism* (Wantage: Ikon, 1992), pp. 13–32; I have discussed this also in 'The making of *Angelcynn*: English identity before the Norman Conquest', *Transactions of the Royal Historical Society*, 6th series, 6 (1996), 25–49, at p. 39. Now see also Nicholas Brooks, *Bede and the English*, Jarrow Lecture 1999 (Jarrow: [St Paul's Church], 2000), particularly pp. 12–14 and 20–2.

[71] Cowdrey, 'Bede and the English people'.

indebted to Gregory the Great, it is perhaps surprising that he did not display greater sympathy with that pope's tolerance of 'diversity within unity'.[72] While Gregory was content, so long as all churches were bound by unity of faith, to allow them to use diverse customs,[73] Bede was more concerned with conformity of practice and clearly shared the views he put into the mouth of King Oswiu at the start of the synod of Whitby in 664. He had the king declare that 'it was fitting that those who served one God should observe one rule of life and not differ in the celebration of the holy sacraments, seeing that they all hoped for one kingdom in heaven'.[74] When he described the nature of the monastic life followed within minsters in different parts of England, Bede preferenced similitude over distinctiveness. On some of the occasions when he made direct comparison between the habits of different houses, he remarked on points of contact between minsters that were dependent one on another or were governed at different times by a single abbot or abbess: Cuthbert, for example, introduced to Lindisfarne the same rule of life that he had known at Melrose, and Hild took to Whitby a system of government already established at Hartlepool.[75] But other parallels may seem less obvious. In both the *Ecclesiastical History* and his prose Life of Cuthbert, Bede compared the manner of life followed at Lindisfarne with that of Augustine's community at Canterbury, quoting in relation to both houses Pope Gregory's injunction that episcopal clergy should live as had the earliest Christians in Jerusalem, holding all things in common.[76] Perhaps Bede used the example of Lindisfarne which he knew well to explain the less familiar customs at Canterbury. Alternatively, he may have been trying to demonstrate that a fundamental uniformity of practice linked discrete institutions across kingdoms. It is striking how similar the minsters described in Bede's *History* seem to be: they all appear to be governed by like principles and to follow remarkably similar sorts of rule. If Bede had written to some extent as if their habits were standard, it would have reinforced

---

[72] Paul Meyvaert, 'Diversity within unity, a Gregorian theme', reprinted in his *Benedict, Gregory, Bede and Others* (London: Variorum, 1977), no. VI; *idem, Bede and Gregory the Great,* Jarrow lecture 1963 (Jarrow: [St Paul's Church], 1964).

[73] As was demonstrated, for example, by his response to Augustine's question about the customs in different churches: *HE* I, 27 (pp. 80–3).

[74] *HE* III. 25 (pp. 298–9); quoted by Meyvaert, *Bede and Gregory the Great,* p. 17. It was at Whitby in 664 that the dispute over the different means of calculating the date of Easter was settled, the synod deciding in favour of the Roman system.

[75] *HE* IV. 27 (pp. 434–5); Bede, *VSCuth.,* ch. 16 (pp. 206–7); *HE* IV. 23 (pp. 408–9). A further, yet more obvious example would be that of Jarrow, where Ceolfrith instituted observance of the same rule that had pertained at Wearmouth: *VSCeol.,* ch. 11 (pp. 391–2).

[76] Compare *HE* IV. 27 (pp. 434–5) with Bede, *VSCuth.,* ch. 16 (p. 208); on both occasions he quoted *HE* I. 27 and Acts 4: 32.

his ambition to reveal the underlying unity that characterised England's common ecclesiastical heritage.

Recognising that Bede's representation of the nature of monasticism in the sixth and seventh centuries may not have been entirely the objective and disinterested narrative it outwardly appears is important not so much for what that perception would reveal about Bede, but because of the enormous influence his account had on later generations of monastic historians. For this narrative has shaped historical perceptions of the nature of the early Anglo-Saxon church. His history was widely read on the continent from the late eighth century onwards; King Alfred considered it one of those books most necessary for all men to know and included it among those texts translated into Old English in the latter part of his reign. It was also still being read, as we have seen, in the mid-tenth century, when religious leaders used Bede's *History* and his letter to Ecgberht selectively to good effect to provide an historical justification for their attempts to reform the monastic way of life according to the precepts of the Benedictine Rule. If Bede's account over-emphasised the uniformity and lack of diversity within the early Anglo-Saxon church to serve particular needs he perceived within ecclesiastical structures of his own day, this throws into yet sharper relief the equally present-minded accounts of early monastic history offered by later reformers, especially Æthelwold.

Considering the diversity and range of other materials for the study of the early English church, it is remarkable both how few general studies there have been of Anglo-Saxon monasticism before the tenth century and how much Bede's image of his own church, viewed through the lens of Æthelwold and other tenth-century reformers, has dominated the historiography until recently.

Historiographical contexts

There has, in fact, never been a major study of monastic life in England before the Benedictine revolution of the tenth century, although there have been some studies of female monasticism in this period.[77] Cuthbert Butler's *Benedictine Monachism*, published in 1919, offered an historical survey of the Benedictine life and rule and drew on various early medieval examples, but

---

[77] Stephanie Hollis, *Anglo-Saxon Women and the Church: Sharing a Common Fate* (Woodbridge: Boydell Press, 1992); Barbara Yorke, *Nunneries and the Anglo-Saxon Royal Houses* (London and New York: Continuum, 2003) and my own *Veiled Women*.

it is as much a study of Benedictine spirituality as it is any kind of history of the order.[78] David Knowles is perhaps still the most significant historian of pre-Conquest monasticism, even though as we have already observed, his study of the monastic order in England began with Æthelwold's church, not with Bede's. It is also important to remember that Knowles was, as much as Butler, a Benedictine historian. He sought to argue that English minsters in the time of Bede were Benedictine in spirit if not in fact, as part of a wider argument both about the historicity of English monastic institutions but also about the non-involvement of early English monastic houses in the obligations of pastoral care.[79] In his study of the conversion of Anglo-Saxon England, Henry Mayr-Harting devoted considerable attention to early English monasticism and particularly the prayerful life of the minster, scholarship and learning, and the influence of monastic culture on wider lay society; this remains the single most valuable account of the nature of early English monastic spirituality.[80] Yet no other study, beyond an unpublished MA dissertation, has attempted to explore the nature of monasticism in this period; Thomas Allison's examination of English religious life in the eighth century does examine, albeit rather perfunctorily, most aspects of monastic life at the time, but it does so from the specific perspective of contemporary correspondence.[81] The collection of essays commemorating the thirteenth centenary of the birth of the Venerable Bede similarly contributes much to our understanding of Bede's place in shaping the way we understand the early English church.[82]

Among histories of the Anglo-Saxon church in general, where monasticism is considered as one element within a larger picture, the general studies by Margaret Deanesly and John Godfrey are of especial value. Both, however, convey a similar picture of a seventh- and eighth-century golden age, followed by a dramatic decline in the Viking Age that reaches its nadir in Alfred's reign, before there is a glorious revival under Edgar.[83] Frank Barlow

---

[78] Cuthbert Butler, *Benedictine Monachism: Studies in Benedictine Life and Rule* (London and New York: Longmans, Green, 1919).

[79] For discussion of the influences on the development of Knowles's thought see Giles Constable, 'Monasteries, rural churches and the *cura animarum* in the early Middle Ages', *Settimane* 28 (1982), 349–89, at p. 351.

[80] Henry Mayr-Harting, *The Coming of Christianity to Anglo-Saxon England* (London: Batsford, 1972; 3rd edn, 1991).

[81] R. A. Timson, 'English monasticism before 735' (unpublished MA dissertation, University of London, 1956); I owe this reference to Patrick McGurk. Thomas Allison, *English Religious Life in the Eighth Century as Illustrated by Contemporary Letters* (London: SPCK and New York: Macmillan, 1929).

[82] Bonner (ed.), *Famulus Christi*.

[83] Margaret Deanesly, *The Pre-Conquest Church in England* (2nd edn, London: Adam & C. Black, 1963); John Godfrey, *The Church in Anglo-Saxon England* (Cambridge: Cambridge University Press, 1962).

and, more recently, Henry Loyn, in their studies of the later English church began essentially where Knowles had done, with the reform of the tenth century, and touched on the earlier church only in general terms.[84] A different perspective may be found in Richard Morris's work, which has taken the material record (architectural and archaeological) as it starting point. His survey of the church in British archaeology explored (and tabulated) all the evidence for seventh-century church building in England, considered where churches were built and the relationship between politics and church patronage.[85] In his study of English parish churches, Morris made an important contribution to the so-called 'minster debate' looking at the nature of early English monasticism, its relationship with royal and noble kin groups and the connections between early minsters and later parish churches.[86]

A critical contribution to modern views of the Anglo-Saxon church and the relationship between early minsters and later parish churches has been made by John Blair. Landscape and the evidence of extant fabric and excavated archaeological remains have lain at the heart of his work, perhaps rather more than early textual evidence, and this has inevitably led Blair to conclusions that are sometimes at variance from my own when he has argued for a greater degree of continuity across time in the organisation of pastoral provision.[87] He edited a valuable collection of local studies of the church between the tenth and twelfth centuries, a critical period for the development of the parish, and co-edited a volume on pastoral care before the parish, which set Anglo-Saxon churches in a wider, insular context.[88] His own local studies of early medieval Surrey, in which the church took a central role, and on the churches of the Thames valley, have been followed more recently by a magisterial survey of saints' cults in Britain.[89] Blair's

---

[84] Frank Barlow, *The English Church 1000–1066: A History of the Later Anglo-Saxon Church* (1963, 2nd edn, London: Longman, 1979); H. R. Loyn, *The English Church 940–1154* (London: Longman, 2000).

[85] Richard Morris, *The Church in British Archaeology*, Council for British Archaeology, Research Report 47 (London: Council for British Archaeology, 1983), ch. 3; table III lies at pp. 35–8 and records the evidence for 99 seventh-century churches.

[86] Richard Morris, *Churches in the Landscape* (London: Dent, 1989), chs. 3 and 4.

[87] For Blair's work on landscape see particularly his 'Minster churches in the landscape', in Della Hooke (ed.), *Anglo-Saxon Settlements* (Oxford: Basil Blackwell, 1988), pp. 35–58; and 'Anglo-Saxon minsters: a topographical review', in John Blair and Richard Sharpe (eds.), *Pastoral Care before the Parish* (Leicester, London and New York: Leicester University Press, 1992), pp. 226–66.

[88] John Blair (ed.), *Minsters and Parish Churches: The Local Church in Transition 950–1200* (Oxford: Oxford University Committee for Archaeology, 1988); with Richard Sharpe (eds.), *Pastoral Care Before the Parish* (Leicester, London and New York: Leicester University Press, 1992).

[89] John Blair, *Early Medieval Surrey: Landholding, Church and Settlement before 1300* (Stroud: Alan Sutton and Surrey Archaeological Society, 1991); 'The minsters of the Thames', in John Blair and Brian Golding (eds.), *The Cloister and the World: Essays in Medieval History in Honour of Barbara Harvey* (Oxford: Oxford

forthcoming monograph on *The Church in Anglo-Saxon Society* will in many ways complement this volume, laying greater stress on archaeological and topographical approaches than does this.[90]

There are other important studies which have concentrated on the early pre-Conquest period generally, rather than on its ecclesiastical history specifically, and have much to say about the monastic life and its impact on early Anglo-Saxon society and culture. One might single out particularly Peter Hunter Blair's *The World of Bede* and *Northumbria in the Days of Bede* or two important *Festschriften*, for Dorothy Whitelock and for J. M. Wallace-Hadrill.[91] David Dumville's essays on Wessex and England in the tenth century make a valuable contribution to our understanding of the background to the tenth-century monastic revolution.[92] The question of the provision of pastoral and spiritual care for the laity in the early medieval period has attracted growing attention in recent years; interpreting such studies remains, however, difficult in the absence of any agreed understanding of just what made an Anglo-Saxon minster.[93]

Local studies have perhaps been of the greatest significance in focusing historians' minds on the distinctiveness of English expressions of monastic culture. Much the most important of these is Patrick Sims-Williams' investigation of religion and literature in the western counties, which asks many of the same questions as does this, wider-ranging study but concentrates particularly – as this does not – on the intellectual Latin culture of monastic houses in western Mercia.[94] Nicholas Brooks' study of a single cathedral community, Christ Church Canterbury, also frequently employs the specific

University Press, 1996), pp. 5–28; and 'A saint for every minster? Local cults in Anglo-Saxon England', in Alan Thacker and Richard Sharpe (eds.), *Local Saints and Local Churches in the Early Medieval West* (Oxford: Oxford University Press, 2002), pp. 455–94.

[90] John Blair, *The Church in Anglo-Saxon Society* (Oxford: Oxford University Press, 2005); this volume had not yet appeared when I completed this manuscript.

[91] Peter Hunter Blair, *The World of Bede* (London: Secker and Warburg, 1970); *idem*, *Northumbria in the Days of Bede* (London: Book Club Associates, 1976); Peter Clemoes and Kathleen Hughes (eds.), *England before the Conquest* (Cambridge: Cambridge University Press, 1971); Patrick Wormald, *et al.* (eds.), *Ideal and Reality in Frankish and Anglo-Saxon Society* (Oxford: Basil Blackwell, 1983).

[92] David N. Dumville, *Wessex and England from Alfred to Edgar: Six Essays on Political, Cultural, and Ecclesiastical Revival* (Woodbridge: Boydell Press, 1992); equally important are his *Liturgy and the Ecclesiastical History of Late Anglo-Saxon England: Four Studies* (Woodbridge: Boydell Press, 1992) and *English Caroline Script and Monastic History: Studies in Benedictinism, AD 950–1030* (Woodbridge: Boydell Press, 1993).

[93] In addition to Richard Morris's work already cited, of most significance here are the essays in Blair and Sharpe (eds.), *Pastoral Care*. The so-called 'minster debate' is explored in ch. 7.

[94] Patrick Sims-Williams, *Religion and Literature* (1990). See also Michael J. Franklin, 'Minsters and parishes: Northamptonshire studies' (unpublished PhD thesis, University of Cambridge, 1982); and the essays in Blair (ed.), *Minsters and Parish Churches*.

as a means of illustrating the general.[95] It can, however, be difficult to know how widely the experiences of individual communities or of regions can be extrapolated into arguments that apply to the whole of one kingdom, let alone to the whole of the country. This volume aims to offer a broad framework against which more detailed local studies might be measured.

Reflecting a wider historiographical interest in the cult of saints, there has been a profusion of recent volumes of collected papers considering the lives and work of individual saints from Anglo-Saxon England. Each of the major tenth-century reformers now has his own commemorative volume (issued following a conference to mark the millennium of his death).[96] Many aspects of early Northumbrian monasticism are considered in volumes of essays about St Wilfrid and St Cuthbert; studies of St Augustine and the conversion, Columbanus' Latin writings and Archbishop Theodore and his school have also illuminated a number of significant aspects of ecclesiastical thinking in the period.[97] Susan Ridyard has explored the cults of royal saints in pre-Conquest England and a recent volume has looked at local cults.[98] While each such investigation sheds much light on local understanding and expression of spiritual ideals, and illuminates much about the function of an audience for hagiography, they do not collectively entirely succeed in explaining the nature of the minsters in which each saint dwelt for at least a part of his or her life.

Monastic life in England *c.* 600–900

Despite this profusion of literature about various aspects of English ecclesiastical culture, it is remarkable that there is still no study of the institution at the heart of expression of the religious ideal in the era before the reform,

[95] Nicholas Brooks, *The Early History of the Church of Canterbury: Christ Church 597–1066*, Studies in the Early History of Britain (Leicester: Leicester University Press, 1984).

[96] Barbara Yorke (ed.), *Bishop Æthelwold: His Career and Influence* (Woodbridge: Boydell Press, 1988); Nigel Ramsey *et al.* (eds.), *St Dunstan: His Life, Times and Cult* (Woodbridge: Boydell Press, 1992); Nicholas Brooks and Catherine Cubitt (eds.), *St Oswald of Worcester: Life and Influence* (London: Leicester University Press, 1996).

[97] D. P. Kirby, *St Wilfrid at Hexham* (Newcastle upon Tyne: Oriel Press, 1974); Gerald Bonner *et al.* (eds.), *St Cuthbert, his Cult and his Community to AD 1200* (Woodbridge: Boydell, 1989); see also Clare Stancliffe and Eric Cambridge (eds.), *Oswald: Northumbrian King to European Saint* (Stamford: Paul Watkins, 1995). Richard Gameson (ed.), *St Augustine and the Conversion of England* (Stroud: Sutton, 1999); Michael Lapidge (ed.), *Columbanus: Studies on the Latin Writings* (Woodbridge: Boydell Press, 1997); idem (ed.), *Archbishop Theodore: Commemorative Studies on his Life and Influence* (Woodbridge: Boydell Press, 1995).

[98] Susan Ridyard, *The Royal Saints of Anglo-Saxon England: A Study of West Saxon and East Anglian Cults* (Cambridge: Cambridge University Press, 1988); Alan Thacker and Richard Sharpe (eds.), *Local Saints and Local Churches in the Early Medieval West* (Oxford: Oxford University Press, 2002).

the minster. This study thus breaks new ground in attempting to define the nature of monasticism between the conversion of the English to Christianity in the seventh century and the monastic revolution of the tenth. As will rapidly become clear, its primary focus will be on the seventh and eighth centuries, the period in which the monastic expression of religious fervour was at its height. The book offers a broad perspective, standing back from the close focus of local studies to look more generally at the nature of the monastic institution. It does not concentrate in any detail on the theology or Latin culture of the early English church, but asks a more fundamental question: what was an Anglo-Saxon minster like?[99] That question is answered under two broad headings which serve to structure the volume: what were the characteristics of the institution itself and how did the minster and its inmates relate to the secular world outside the cloister?

As I have already suggested, much of the secondary discussion of the religious life in our period tends – with varying degrees of self-consciousness – to locate examples of holy or less edifying behaviour to which the contemporary sources bear witness in the context of the prescriptions of normative literature such as monastic rules, penitential canons or reports of the deliberations of church councils. In chapter 2 we shall explore various different models against which the behaviour within early English monastic houses might be compared and assess their usefulness for explaining conditions in our own period. The first section of the book then investigates life within the cloister walls. How and why minsters were created and provided with a landed endowment is the subject of chapter 3. In the fourth chapter, we explore the monastic community: who joined minsters and why, what ceremonies marked a postulant's transition from lay to religious status, how were children admitted to the cloister and how was the congregation ordered and controlled? The final chapter in the first part looks at daily life within the cloister, attempting if not to depict a 'typical' monastic day (for the diversity of minsters was such that this is an impossible task), but to show which activities were distinctive of the religious way of life, the structure of the monastic day and how religious of both sexes may have relaxed in such leisure time as they had available.

At the end of that fifth chapter, we shall find ourselves investigating spheres of activity in which the cloister's wall proved permeable, contexts where lay and religious life-styles seem to have mingled. In the second part

---

[99] Several of the questions explored here I first rehearsed in my 'What was an Anglo-Saxon monastery?', in Judith Loades (ed.), *Monastic Studies* (Bangor: Headstart History, 1990), pp. 48–57.

of the study we look outside the walls to consider the place of the minster within contemporary Anglo-Saxon society. Chapter 6 focuses on institutions once more by investigating the nature of the relationships that could exist between separate minsters. Although some houses were entirely independent establishments, associated only with other minsters by virtue of sharing with them a place in the national and universal church, others had much closer ties with other communal religious houses, sometimes as part of a cluster in their own vicinity, sometimes much farther afield. We shall here look at colonies and confederations of minsters and ask what benefits an individual community might have gained from associating itself with other houses within an affinity. In the final substantive chapter, we turn from the institution of the minster back to its community and explore the relationship between professed religious and their lay neighbours. Here we will address the 'minster debate' and consider sorts of services, pastoral and other, which minsters may have provided for their lay neighbours in the early Anglo-Saxon period, and the corresponding obligations the laity had to the maintenance of churches in their vicinity. A brief final chapter looks forward to the events of the tenth-century reform sketched above and shows how a novel understanding of the nature of early Anglo-Saxon monasticism subtly alters our reading of the rhetoric of Æthelwold and his contemporaries.

Before we can explore in closer detail the ways in which early English monastics worked out their communal aspiration to devotion, we need to pause to reflect a little on the sorts of the ideals to which they were urged to aspire. In the next chapter we will explore three possible models that might serve as interpretative tools through which to gain a deeper understanding of the frameworks within which English minsters operated.

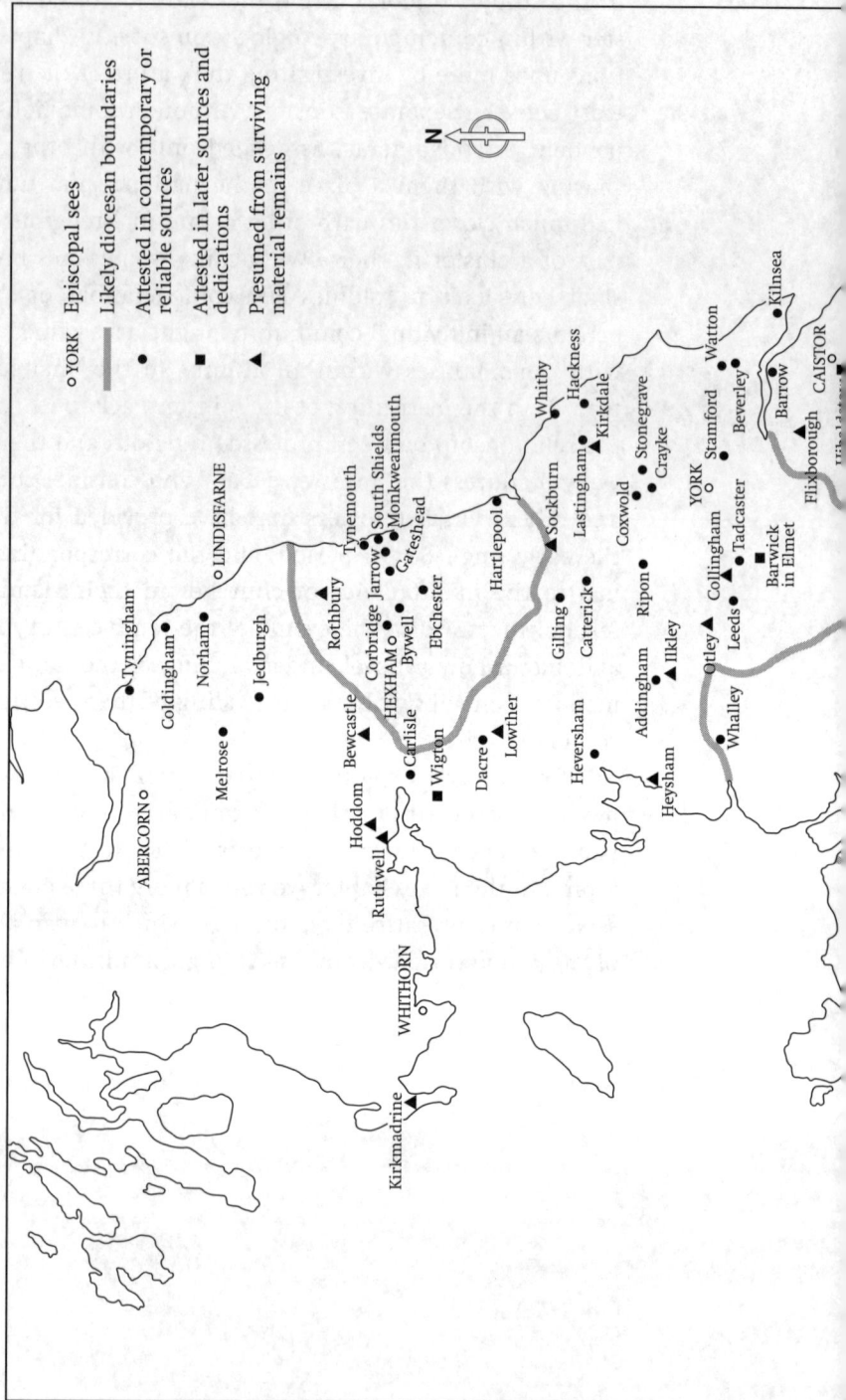

Episcopal sees

Likely diocesan boundaries

Attested in contemporary or reliable sources

Attested in later sources and dedications

Presumed from surviving material remains

N

Tyningham
Coldingham
Norham
Jedburgh
ABERCORN
Melrose
Bewcastle
Hoddom
Ruthwell
Carlisle
Wigton
WHITHORN
Kirkmadrine
Dacre
Lowther
Heversham
Heysham
Whalley
Addingham
Ilkley
Otley
Leeds
Collingham
Barwick in Elmet
Tadcaster
YORK
Ripon
Coxwold
Catterick
Gilling
Lastingham
Sockburn
Hartlepool
Ebchester
Bywell
HEXHAM
Corbridge Jarrow
Rothbury
Monkwearmouth
Gateshead
South Shields
Tynemouth
LINDISFARNE
Whitby
Hackness
Kirkdale
Stonegrave
Crayke
Stamford
Beverley
Watton
Barrow
Kilnsea
Flixborough
CAISTOR

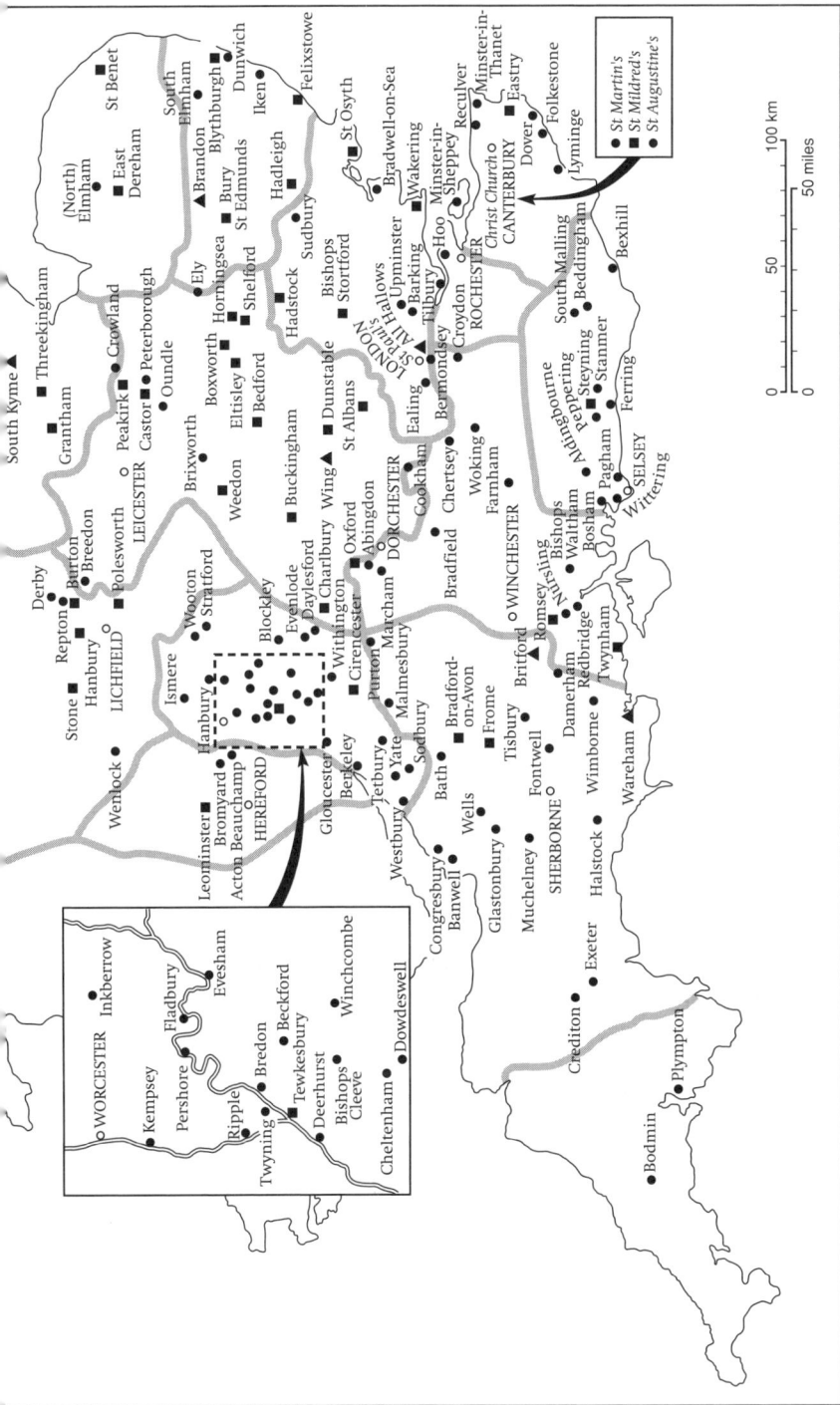

FIGURE 2: Map of bishoprics and minsters to c. 850 (after Campbell (ed.), *The Anglo-Saxons*, fig. 72).

CHAPTER 2

The ideal minster

A minster was both a physical space and a social institution. Walls or other symbolic barriers created physical boundaries around the sacred and domestic space, separating a minster's inhabitants from the secular world outside. But religious men and women were equally restrained and confined by the distinctively-religious social framework which ordered their shared existence. Monastic rules and the written and oral customs devised by congregations defined structures designed to minimise the tensions between individual spiritual aspirations and the collective needs and obligations of the community as a whole. The insistence in many rules on the necessity for obedience affords one of the clearest signs of the potential for discord within such an artificially-created society, one that could encompass a wide range of social backgrounds and behavioural expectations. 'Up to what measure is obedience laid down?' inquired the Irishman Columbanus in his Rule for Monks; 'up to death it is assuredly enjoined', he responded, echoing the words of Cassian, 'since Christ obeyed the Father up to death for us'.[1] By their very nature, monastic rules present archetypical pictures of perfect institutions, places where all action is ordered within the structured framework of the liturgical *cursus*, every task is performed in God's service and each member of the community journeys under his superior's guidance towards perfection and the heavenly city. Yet the physical environment had to be ordered, too, if the idealised society that monastic legislators aspired

---

[1] Columbanus, *Regula monachorum*, ch. 1 (ed. and trans. G. S. M. Walker, *Sancti Columbani opera*, Dublin: Dublin Institute for Advanced Studies, 1970), pp. 124–5. Compare Philippians, 2: 8 and Cassian, *Institutes*, 12, 28 (ed. Guy, SC 109, 494–5).

to create was successfully to achieve its collective goals while simultaneously satisfying the ambitions of its individual members.

At some time in the early ninth century a Frankish monk drew a diagrammatic plan of a Benedictine monastery on a large piece of parchment apparently created for the purpose by the expedient of sewing five smaller sheets together. At the heart of the drawing (although not in the precise centre of the space) was a large church, 200 feet in length from east to west, with semi-circular eastern and western apses.[2] The rest of the plan depicts forty separate buildings, some for domestic use, others with agricultural or light-industrial functions, many drawn with internal divisions, plus open areas for gardens and a cemetery. Precise and technical inscriptions explain the purpose of most of the buildings and rooms within them, showing clearly where buildings had upper storeys, sometimes even indicating to what use the furniture within should be put. A dedicatory inscription at the top of the drawing explains that this sketch illustrating the 'layout of monastic buildings' had been sent by an anonymous person (customarily identified with Haito, abbot of Reichenau, 806–23), to a certain Gozbert, abbot of the Swiss monastery of St Gall from 816 until 836 or 837, in whose monastery it remained.[3]

Known as 'the plan of St Gall', this schematic representation of the layout of all the buildings needed for the running of a Benedictine abbey has attracted substantial scholarly attention. This plan may have been intended to represent a paradigmatic statement of the shape and layout of an idealised monastery, as Horn and Born argued in their three-volume study of the plan.[4] If it were, the St Gall plan would not only shed light on the implementation of the monastic reforms instituted by the Frankish emperor Louis the Pious in councils held at Aachen in 816–17, but it would also – more significantly for our purposes – provide a model or template against which the evidence from other early medieval monasteries might be measured.

---

[2] See plate III. The length of the nave and its width (40 feet, with nave aisles 20 feet wide), are specified in three prose inscriptions on the drawing: Walter Horn and Ernest Born, *The Plan of Saint Gall: A Study of the Architecture and Economy of, and Life in a Paradigmatic Carolingian Monastery* (3 vols., Berkeley, Los Angeles and London: University of California Press, 1979), III, 23–5. For a discussion of these measurements and the possibility that the Plan is a copy based on an earlier prototype depicting a 320-foot church with 10 nave bays see Calvin B. Kendall, 'The plan of St Gall: an argument for a 320-foot church prototype', *Mediaeval Studies* 56 (1994), 279–97.

[3] In the late twelfth century, the Life of St Martin was copied onto the blank side of the sheet, which had been folded for the purpose. In that folded form it was preserved in St Gall's library, where it is now Stiftsbibliothek MS 1092. Warren Sanderson, 'The plan of St Gall reconsidered', *Speculum* 60 (1985), 615–32, at p. 615.

[4] Horn and Born, *The Plan of Saint Gall*.

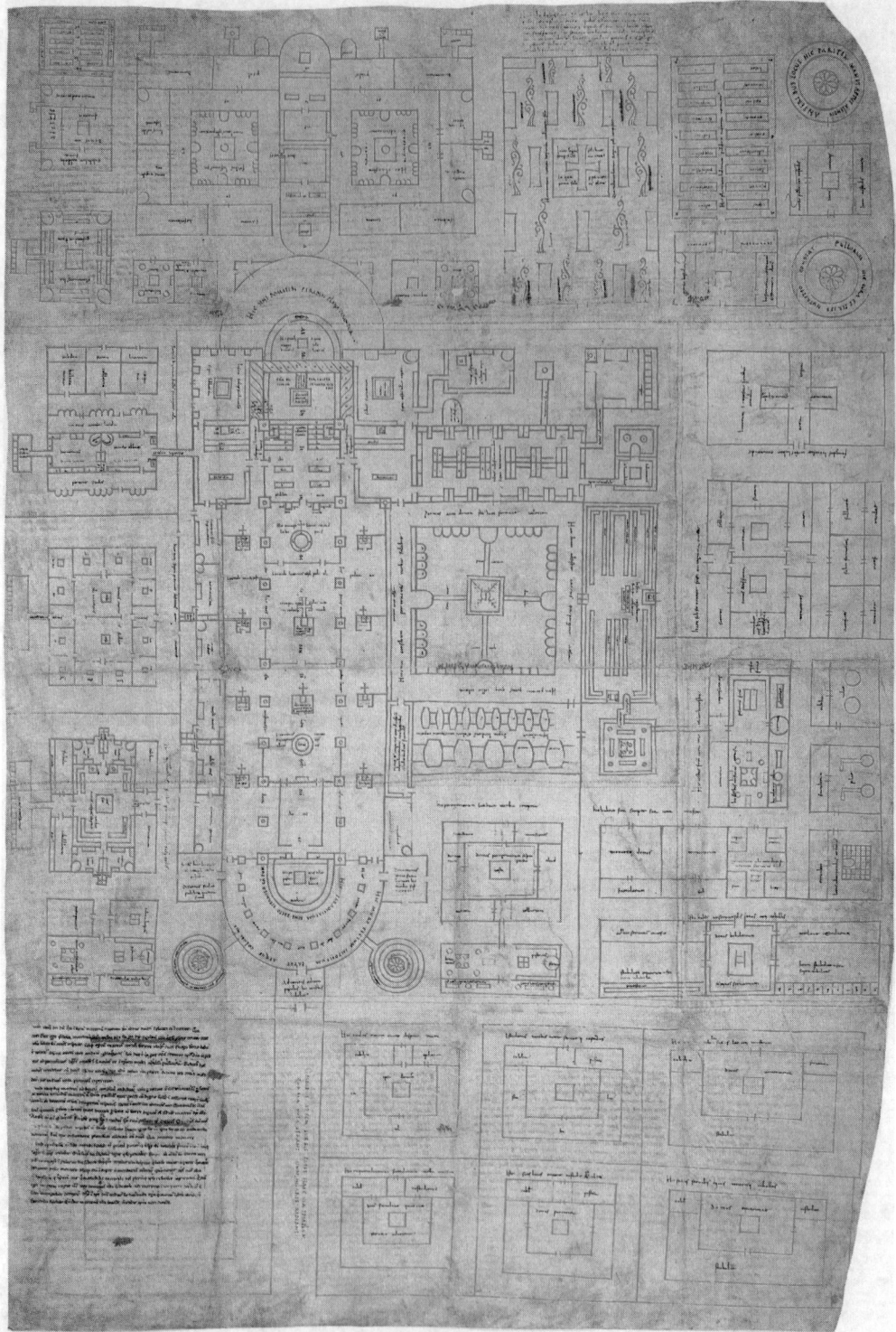

PLATE III: The St Gall plan: St Gall, Stiftsbibliothek, MS 1092.

One might compare the evidence afforded by the plan as to the different buildings a monastery ought to contain, and the various functions to be performed within them, with accounts in narrative sources about the physical settings in which cloistered religious carried out their daily tasks. Similarly, excavated monastic remains could be interpreted according to whether or not they appeared to reflect the structures and organisational layout prescribed as ideal by the draughtsman of the plan.[5] Further, if monastic rules are considered to represent alternative idealised models against which the practice of separate early medieval religious communities should be measured, one would want to compare the details of the St Gall plan with the wording of Benedict's Rule and verify not only how effectively the Aachen councils' stipulations about the implementation of the revised version of the *RSB* were being followed, but also the extent to which this ideal diverged from those identified by other monastic legislators of the early medieval period.[6]

This chapter articulates three discrete models of paradigmatic or artificially-constructed societies against which the minster communities of early Anglo-Saxon England might be measured. It will reflect a little on the nature of the minster as an institution, comparing it with other social institutions from different times and places. This will lead us further to consider the organisation of sacred and domestic space within a quintessential monastic environment, before we turn to the systems of regulation known and followed (to varying degrees) within minsters in England between the seventh and ninth centuries, and ask what other sorts of texts might usefully have offered images of idealised monasticism to which the devout English man or woman might aspire. Model-building presents its own problems and is often avoided by medieval scholars, who usually feel more comfortable confining their enquiries to the evidence provided by contemporary texts, allowing them to speak for themselves. One obvious danger is that the search for a paradigmatic ideal might lead to the confection of a chimera, an ideal so divorced from reality that it could never have been imagined in practice. Yet, in their detailed exploration of separate aspects of early English monastic life as it was observed within and without cloistered walls,

---

[5] Compare Richard Hodges 'San Vincenzo al Volturno and the plan of St Gall', in Richard Hodges (ed.), *San Vincenzo al Volturno, 2: The 1980–86 Excavations, Part II* (London: British School at Rome, 1995), pp. 153–75.

[6] For a general discussion of the organised use of space within early medieval Benedictine monasteries and the way in which early monastic rules constructed the geography of cenobitism see Patrice Noisette, 'Usages et représentations de l'espace dans la Regula Benedicti: une nouvelle approche des significations historiques de la règle', *Regula Benedicti Studia, Annuarium Internationale* 14/15 (1985), 69–93.

historians frequently return to images of ideal monasteries and compare the representations they have found and the aspirations of the early medieval authorities with these semi-artificial prescriptions and notional models. If we were clearer at the outset about how and in what contexts these ideals found expression, it might prove easier to measure their distance from (or the proximity to) ideal typologies and imbue those contemporary narratives with more subtle meanings.

Minsters as total institutions

All social institutions necessarily exercise some degree of power over the individual at least to the extent of defining the limits of individual freedoms and the requirements for co-operation and compromise between members; without these, no social group can function effectively. Each type of social institution (the family, the school, the army, the religious community) articulates its own tools for social control distinctively. Yet there are some social institutions that exercise a greater, arguably a total, control over their populations in such a way that they appear to constitute a particular type of society, even though separate establishments within this group are created to fulfil widely different functions. Prisons, hospitals, asylums, boarding schools, army camps and monasteries have all been described as 'total institutions'.[7]

The encompassing total character of such organisations is symbolised by the physical barrier to social intercourse with outsiders around their perimeter (whether man-made walls or fences or natural topographical features: cliffs, watercourses, forests, moors and hillsides) and frequently by further internal obstacles: walls, locked doors, bars or grilles. Total institutions do not constitute a separate category of social establishment; rather they are specific foundations which exhibit certain of the characteristics common to all institutions to a notably intense degree.[8] They constitute a sort of social hybrid, being part residential communities and part formal organisations, characterised by their tendency to alter the nature of the personalities of those who reside within them.[9] Above all, total institutions break down the

---

[7] Erving Goffman, 'On the characteristics of total institutions: the inmate world', in Donald R. Cressey (ed.), *The Prison: Studies in Institutional Organization and Change* (New York: Holt, Rinehart and Winston, 1961), pp. 15–67, at p. 16. See also Erving Goffman, *Asylums: Essays on the Social Situation of Mental Patients and other Inmates* (Chicago: Aldine Publishing Co., 1961). I am extremely grateful to Jane Sayers for first suggesting that I explore the idea of total institutions further.

[8] Samuel E. Wallace, 'Introduction' in his *Total Institutions* (Chicago: Aldine Publishing Co., 1971), p. 2.

[9] Goffman, 'The inmate world', p. 22.

barriers between sleep, work and play which most societies tend to perform in separate spaces. Inside a total institution all activities take place within the same space, under a single authority and in the company of all the others who belong to the same group. All activity is tightly scheduled into a rigidly demarcated timetable, and all is governed by a single rational plan articulating the aims of the institution.[10] The space within the institution is sub-divided and functionally-ordered to maximise both communal identity and efficiency, but the sense of confinement and loss of the self is common to the prison, the barracks or even the early-industrial factory, as well as to the monastery.[11]

Outwardly, the similarities between monastic communities and other 'total' institutions are appealing; these can, however, be over-stated and it is as important to look for the characteristics distinctive to cloistered establishments. Many total institutions such as prisons, hospitals and to a lesser extent boarding schools are organised around a fundamental dichotomy between the large managed group of inmates (prisoners, patients or pupils) and a small supervisory staff with minimal social mobility or overlap between the two groups. While the staff may have contact with the outside world – returning to their own homes at the end of a working shift – the inmates are permanently confined for the duration of their sentence, period of treatment or school term.[12] Although there are of necessity certain office holders within a monastic community – the abbot or abbess and their deputies charged with organisation of specific aspects of the corporate life – those titular officers have little or nothing in common with the staff of other total institutions. All members of a monastery share some of the basic deprivations that characterise the ascetic lifestyle; monastic communities function as a single collegial group, one that in a Benedictine congregation is stratified internally according to the date of each member's profession, but not otherwise formally divided.[13] A convent is further distinctive in that all its inmates (or at least the vast majority within a community)[14] entered

---

[10] *Ibid.*, p. 17.

[11] Michel Foucault, *Discipline and Punish: The Birth of the Prison* (London: Allen Lane, 1977), pp. 142–3.

[12] Goffman, 'The inmate world', pp. 18–19.

[13] *RSB*, ch. 63, 1 (pp. 178–9): 'The monks keep their rank in the monastery according to the date of their entry, the virtue of their lives, and the decision of the abbot.' See Erving Goffman, 'On the characteristics of total institutions: staff–inmate relations', in Cressey (ed.), *The Prison*, pp. 68–106, at p. 101.

[14] Confinement to the cloister could be imposed penitentially by a priest in expiation for sin or punitively as part of a legal process; some of those confined to the cloister in childhood may have become similarly reluctant adult monks; see further below, ch. 4. However, such reluctant adult postulants were always in the minority. To the category of unwilling (or unwitting) entrants

its walls voluntarily, deliberately choosing to abandon the world and its fleshly pleasures for a life of ascetic austerity and spiritual devotion.[15] Like prisoners, the compulsorily detained patients in mental hospitals or army conscripts, however, monastics go through initiation ceremonies on their entry to the cloister, ceremonies which serve in part to mark the permanence of an entrant's break with his past life. Admission procedures in all such institutions are designed to strip the individual of their autonomy, to deprive them of their clothes and personal possessions, to reclothe them within the garb distinctive to their new state and often to rename them.[16] Denied many of the attributes that had defined their identity outside in the world, including their social status, new entrants to any sort of total institution are in a sense reborn into a new role, one that is articulated within the community's distinctive terms of reference. Entry to the monastic life was explicitly compared to the new birth of baptism by St Jerome in the fourth century; writing to Paula about her daughter, Jerome reminded her that it was only four months since Blesilla 'by the grace of God was washed by a kind of second baptism, that of profession'. Many later medieval monastic writers echoed the same theme.[17]

Every aspect of life within a total institution is directed towards the fulfilment of the central purpose for which the establishment was founded; each activity is organised according to a rigid timetable that breaks up the hours of daylight (and, in a monastery, darkness) into periods specified for the completion of tasks directed towards the achievement of that goal. The institution disciplines the mind, body and emotions of each individual

---

we might, perhaps, add children, some of whom were consigned to the cloister long before the age of reason. That they grew up knowing no other life-style cannot be thought to imply that they never yearned for the earthly life. The entry of children to the cloister is discussed below, ch. 4.

[15] Otto Gerhard Oexle, 'Les moines d'occident et la vie politique et sociale dans le haut Moyen Age', *Revue bénédictine* 103 (1993), 255–72, at p. 257: 'Car le monastère n'est pas seulement une institution dirigée par un abbé, c'est aussi, comme on sait, un groupe, une communauté d'hommes ou de femmes, dans laquelle – c'est au moins le cas normal – l'individu s'engage volontairement.'

[16] Caesarius forbad postulants immediately to assume the religious garb but directed that they should wait an entire year in their lay clothes until their will to adopt the monastic life had been proved by trials: *Regula ad uirgines*, ch. 4 (ed. de Vogüé, SC 345, 182); compare Cassian, *Institutes*, 4, 5 (ed. Guy, SC 109, 126–7). Benedict similarly described the process of re-clothing a new monk at the end of his initiatory period: *RSB*, ch. 58, 27 (pp. 270–1). See Goffman, 'The inmate world', pp. 23–8 and further below, pp. 152–6.

[17] Jerome, *Epistola* 39, 3 (ed. Hilberg, I, 299). For parallels between monastic profession and baptism see Timothy Fry, *The Rule of St Benedict in Latin and English with Notes* (Collegeville, MN: Liturgical Press 1981), pp. 15 and 441; Giles Constable, 'The ceremonies and symbolism of entering the religious life and taking the monastic habit, from the fourth to the twelfth century', *Settimane* 33 (1987), 771–834, at pp. 799–802.

inmate according to its distinctive hierarchy of internal relations.[18] As Max Weber observed, 'the monk is the first human who lives rationally, who works methodically and by rational means toward a goal, namely the future life. Only for him did the clock strike, only for him were the hours of the day divided – for prayer.'[19] Many have noted the monastic influence in this respect on the partitioning of time in the nineteenth-century school or factory as well as the prison; 'for centuries the religious orders had been masters of discipline: they were the specialists of time, the great technicians of rhythm and regular activities'.[20] The careful structuring of the rhythm of the monastic day was, however, made for an explicitly spiritual purpose, not simply for reasons of order or discipline or to improve individual productivity, let alone to facilitate crowd-control. Cassian explained this most succinctly in his *Monastic Institutes*, in a passage clarifying why the canonical hour of Morning Prayer (*matutina*) had been instituted in his monastery during his own lifetime. 'This office literally fulfils the number which the holy David foretold . . . "seven times daily have I spoken praise to you for the rightness of your judgements". For by adding this Office, we make seven meetings for prayer in the course of the day and are shown to be "speaking praise to the Lord seven times in the day".'[21] In each of these seven offices on each day of the week prescribed psalms were recited so that, according to Benedict's Rule, 'the full complement of one hundred and fifty psalms is by all means carefully maintained every week and that the series begins anew each Sunday at Vigils'.[22]

Superficially a minster displays many of the characteristics of a total institution, but at a more profound level the parallel is unconvincing. It is not merely that its inhabitants have, predominantly, chosen willingly to enter the confines of the cloister, nor that egalitarian principles govern much of the ordering of the activities of the membership, extending even to their shared poverty: monks, 'leaving all things and daily following the Lord Christ with the cross of fear, have treasures in heaven' (Matthew 19: 21).[23] The monastic life involves the renunciation of the self, the struggle for mastery

---

[18] Roberta Gilchrist, *Gender and Material Culture: The Archaeology of Religious Women* (London and New York: Routledge, 1994), p. 18.

[19] Max Weber, *General Economic History*, trans. Frank H. Knight (London: Allen and Unwin, 1927), p. 365.

[20] Foucault, *Discipline and Punish*, p. 167.

[21] Cassian, *Institutes*, 3, 4 (ed. Guy, SC 109, 103–5), quoting Psalm 118: v 164: 'septies in die laudem dixi tibi super iudicia iustitiae tuae'. Compare *RSB*, 16, 1–4 (pp. 210–11).

[22] *RSB*, 18, 23 (pp. 214–15).

[23] Columbanus, *Regula monachorum*, ch. 4 (ed. Walker, pp. 126–7). Compare *RSB*, chs. 33, 6 (pp. 230–1); 34, 1 (*ibid.*); 55, 20, quoting Acts 4: 32, and 35 (pp. 264–5). *RM*, ch. 82, 12–14, quoting Matthew 6: 25–33, and ch. 82, 18, quoting 2 Timothy, 2: 4 (pp. 338–9).

over the body and the temptations of the world in obedience to God, in search of spiritual perfection and the heavenly home. That journey is made within the nurturing, self-sufficient environment of the cloister and within the framework of repeated corporate psalmody and communal as well as private prayer. Yet ultimately, each is engaged in a private struggle for his own soul. As Benedict wrote, he who could keep 'this little rule for beginners' might then set out 'for the loftier summits of the teaching and virtues' mentioned by other monastic legislators and catholic Fathers.[24] Those who could not conform and amend their ways were to be banished 'lest one diseased sheep infect the whole flock'.[25] The total institution that is the modern prison or mental hospital may be well equipped for the treatment of the non-conformist, but it has no place for the discovery of the individual soul: it rather seeks to change the personalities within that artificial society towards an abstract, non-spiritual but highly disciplined goal.[26]

Organising space

In his monastic rule, Benedict of Nursia recommended that 'the *monasterium* should, if possible, be so constructed that within it all necessities, such as water, mill and garden are contained, and the various crafts are practised. Then there will be no need for the monks to roam outside, because this is not at all good for their souls.'[27] So closely does the draughtsman of the ninth-century plan of St Gall appear to have adhered to the Benedictine ideal, and to the principles enunciated at the reforming councils of Aachen in 816–17, that Horn and Born argued that this was not a plan for a specific site, 'but rather an ideal scheme that demonstrates what buildings an exemplary Carolingian monastery should be composed of and in what manner they should be arranged'.[28] In the organisation of the space the designer appears to have had Benedict's desiderata in the forefront of his mind. The plan's scheme encompasses mill and granary, garden and orchard, barns for animals and their keepers and workshops for shoe-makers, wood- and leather-workers as well as the domestic buildings necessary to house and feed the professed brothers, novices, abbot and distinguished visitors

---

[24] *RSB*, ch. 73, 8–9 (pp. 296–7). Compare the *Regula ad uirgines* of Caesarius of Arles, which also presented the enclosed life of a dedicated virgin as an individual spiritual journey towards eternal blessedness with the choir of holy and wise virgins in heaven: *Regula ad uirgines*, chs. 1 and 63 (pp. 170–1 and 246–9). See Mother Maria Caritas McCarthy, *The Rule for Nuns of St Caesarius of Arles: A Translation with a Critical Introduction* (Washington, DC: Catholic University of America Press, 1960), p. 52.

[25] *RSB*, ch. 28, 8 (pp. 224–5). [26] Goffman, 'The inmate world', p. 22.

[27] *RSB*, ch. 66, 6 (pp. 288–9). [28] Horn and Born, *The Plan of Saint Gall*, I, 20. See plate III.

together with pilgrims and paupers. Here are sufficient resources to keep the community within its enclosure. The brothers' own needs take priority in the organisation of the space: an area to the south of the church is ordered around an open courtyard so that they may pray, eat, sleep, read and study and deal with all their bodily needs without having to leave this inner area. Although close scrutiny reveals that this inner complex is not wholly secluded from the rest of the enclosure and hence from the outside world, this was still obviously intended, as Richard E. Sullivan has argued, to be a reserved space within which to constitute Benedict's 'school for the Lord's service'.[29]

Complete segregation from the noise, commercial bustle, animal husbandry and potentially dangerous human distractions of the secular world was not, however, attempted by the St Gall planner. It cannot be coincidental that he offered so many windows out from the safe, prayerful environment of the monastic cloister onto the alarmingly seductive exterior world. The abbot's house provided a formal setting in which outsiders might be interviewed, but in fact lay people and lay preoccupations were visible (and audible) to the cloistered brothers in many parts of their enclosure; from the external school, the hospice for pilgrims and paupers and the guest-house for noble visitors to the wide range of workshops for artisanal craftsmen and agricultural workers.[30] Sullivan has offered an attractive explanation for this apparent relaxation in the maintenance of a strict ascetic ideal:

It is easy to dismiss this matter by saying that the worldly presence involved nothing more than providing the material needs of the holy men, but that is not the point. The Plan reflects a concern with giving structure, order, and proportion to that dimension of monastic life. It says that to be a monk involves coping with worldly people and activity; being holy is defined by how this involvement was managed. This is another way of saying that the Plan was designed by someone thinking about those relationships in terms of redefining monasticism.[31]

For Sullivan, the plan offers an answer to questions about the nature of Carolingian monasticism; it appears to him to offer a contemporary solution to the central problem that had compromised the pursuit of the ascetic ideal

---

[29] *RSB*, prologue, 45 (pp. 164–5); Richard E. Sullivan, 'What was Carolingian monasticism?' in Alexander Callander Murray (ed.), *After Rome's Fall: Narrators and Sources of Early Medieval History* (Toronto, Buffalo and London: University of Toronto Press, 1998), pp. 251–87, at p. 271. Horn and Born (*The Plan of Saint Gall*, II, 356), were less struck by the potential routes out of this space but saw it rather as 'an inner fortress, in which the monks could perform their spiritual offices without being exposed to contamination by the outside world'.

[30] Sullivan, 'What was Carolingian monasticism?', pp. 273–6.   [31] *Ibid*, p. 278.

in earlier centuries by creating space for the professed religious to fulfil their spiritual needs while at the same time enabling them to engage in fruitful encounter and intercourse with the outside world.[32]

Appealing as this argument is, it depends on two premises that are both open to challenge. It may readily be demonstrated from the literature describing such endeavours that the earliest experiments made in the medieval West for the creation of communities of the holy, designed for the collective pursuit of spiritual perfection, were driven by an idealistic desire for self-sufficient isolation and total separation from the distractions and temptations of the world. The same literature makes it abundantly clear, however, just how far reality fell short of those ideals. Successive generations of aspiring monastics from St Anthony onwards struggled with the apparent inevitability of the world's incursion into their holy fastnesses, regardless of the remoteness of the location chosen, or the strength of their initial determination to keep the world out.[33] Although in the sixth and seventh centuries the perfect monastery was perceived as an isolated enclave or island outside the Christian community, as Sullivan has suggested,[34] none ever achieved total separation from relationships with the corrupting, mainland world. It is thus difficult to sustain Sullivan's argument that the Carolingian period represents the 'decisive period in the revolutionary transition from autarchic to collectivized, socialized monasticism', of the type apparent from about 1000.[35] The plan of St Gall may indeed have offered a practical and workable solution to the problem of integrating necessary (inevitable) temporal elements into the margins of the monastic world without unduly compromising the integrity of the brothers' spiritual experience that lay at its heart, but this was by no means the first occasion on which western monks had sought to negotiate their interaction with the world.[36] This leads to the second premise on which Sullivan's argument in part depends: that the plan of St Gall, in offering in visual form a pioneering statement about the

---

[32] *Ibid.*, p. 283.

[33] For a general discussion of this problem see L. J. R. Milis, *Angelic Monks and Earthly Men: Monasticism and its Meaning to Medieval Society* (Woodbridge: Boydell Press, 1992); and for some specific early medieval Frankish and English examples see my 'The role of the minster in earlier Anglo-Saxon society', in Benjamin Thompson (ed.), *Monasteries and Society in Medieval England* (Stamford: Paul Watkins, 1998), pp. 35–58, at pp. 35–7. Oexle has considered the integration of ninth-century Carolingian monasteries in contemporary political, ecclesiastical and social cultures: 'Les moines d'occident', pp. 263–6.

[34] Sullivan, 'What was Carolingian monasticism?' p. 283.   [35] *Ibid.*, p. 284.

[36] These questions about the extent of the separation of the monastic life-style from the secular world will recur throughout this study; they are perhaps explored in closest detail in chapter 4, which deals with the endowment of monastic houses with temporal possessions, and chapters 6 and 7 which explore minsters' relationships with their lay neighbours.

relationship between the spiritual and the worldly, was creating a model for others to implement.

In their monumental study of the St Gall plan, Walter Horn and Ernest Born argued that the drawing was a copy of an official architectural statement, a visual equivalent to the written statutes of the Aachen synods, demonstrating, in an ideal scheme, of what buildings an exemplary Carolingian monastery should be composed and in what manner they should be arranged.[37] It thus constituted 'a statement of policy drawn up on the highest levels of political and ecclesiastical administration and conceived within the framework of a monastic reform movement whose overriding preoccupation was to establish unity (*unitas*) where life had been controlled by disparate traditions (*diuersitas*), to put a "single rule" (*una regula, una consuetudo*) in place of the mixed tradition (*regula mixta*)'.[38] Although one cannot deny that the plan appears to conform closely to the ideals of Louis the Pious' reform, doubts have been cast on many elements on this interpretation. Several aspects of the plan – from the meaning of the dedicatory (or transmittal) note at the top right-hand corner of the parchment sheet, through the question of whether the drawing was copied or traced from a pre-existing original, to the issue of the monumental size of the abbey's church – have been used to support the view that this was not a paradigmatic plan for an ideal monastery drawn up after 817.[39] Richard Sullivan has wondered whether the plan might have been paradigmatic not in the sense of specifying the template for an official building programme to be applied everywhere in the Frankish realm, but rather as offering a 'menu of options from which abbots and their patrons might select' when deciding to build or rebuild a monastery, a visual analogue to the numerous *florilegia* of literary texts compiled in the Carolingian era.[40] Although he rejected this supposition in favour of the suggestion that the plan was designed as a guide to an actual construction programme (drawn at Reichenau to provide a model for Abbot Gozbert's new building at St Gall), Sullivan's overall conclusion still depends on the assumption that the plan had an admonitory function: 'the central message of the Plan is a call to all concerned [with defining the nature of the monastic life] to seek ways to give order and structure to a space within which the sacred and the profane *must* intersect

[37] Horn and Born, *Plan of Saint Gall*, I, 20.   [38] *Ibid.*, I, 52.
[39] Sanderson, 'The plan of St Gall', pp. 617–21; Lawrence Nees, 'The plan of St. Gall and the theory of the program of Carolingian art', *Gesta* 25 (1986), 1–8 and Sullivan, 'What was Carolingian monasticism?' p. 266, all provide references to the various reviews and articles critical of Horn and Born's edition.
[40] Sullivan, 'What was a Carolingian monastery?' pp. 267–8.

so that each might sustain the other'.[41] Not, then, a paradigmatic proto-type but a visual response to the dilemma at the heart of early medieval monasticism.

Other communal residential institutions such as those we discussed previously had a similar need to order, control and confine spaces for the better segregation of the inmates from the corrupting influences of the exterior world, but also for their more effective manipulation. In his work on the history of prisons, Michel Foucault explored the ways in which total institutions such as prisons, army-camps, schools and hospitals used the ordering of space as a means of controlling and disciplining their inmates, creating a 'discipline of power'. He drew heavily in this argument on another visual representation of an idealised conception of the effective use of space: Jeremy Bentham's penitentiary Panopticon of 1791, an architectural scheme for an annular building with individual prison cells, all facing inwards towards a central 'control tower', which surveyed their every movement.[42] To Foucault, the building itself here became an instrument of power 'reduced to its ideal form', 'a figure of political technology'.[43] The Panopticon can however also be viewed, as Megan Cassidy-Welch has argued, as 'an example of how the articulation of space can successfully maintain and express institutional interests'. She has drawn direct comparison between penitential organisations and other discursive regimes at work in the production of physical space and the monastery, which uses principles of enclosure to express its institutional need for segregation from the world.[44] In many ways the medieval monastery provides one of the best examples of the organised use of space; as Valerie Flint suggested, the space within a monastery, 'in framing a monk's activities, seems to sculpture and direct them, too'.[45]

When one turns from these abstractions to look at the organisation and layout of English monastic enclosures, it is frequently difficult to determine the relative weight a founding abbot would place on the prescriptions of monastic legislators or the extent to which he might have preferred to allow the natural topography of his chosen site to dictate the layout of

---

[41] *Ibid.*, p. 283.

[42] Foucault, *Discipline and Punish*, pp. 200–4; illustrated on plate 3 (between pp. 130 and 131).

[43] *Ibid.*, p. 205.

[44] Megan Cassidy-Welch, *Monastic Spaces and their Meanings: Thirteenth-Century English Cistercian Monasteries* (Turnhout: Brepols, 2001), p. 8.

[45] Valerie I. J. Flint, 'Space and discipline in early medieval Europe', in Barbara A. Hanawalt and Michal Kobialka (eds.), *Medieval Practices of Space* (Minneapolis and London: University of Minnesota Press, 2000), pp. 149–66, at p. 149.

buildings and their inter-relationships.[46] Early Anglo-Saxon minsters were commonly located at earlier settlement sites, within prehistoric hillforts or inside Roman enclosures; other more isolated sites sought solitude within the natural landscape, seeking the seclusion of islands, river or coastal locations. In both such environments the internal layout of the minster was inevitably determined as much by the natural topography of the site and the location of any pre-existing buildings as by any idealised notions of the founders as to the proper organisation of its space.[47] Those who strove for spiritual perfection in solitary isolation, such as Hereberct who lived as a hermit on an island in Derwentwater, or Guthlac who struggled with devils in the misty gloom of his island hermitage at Crowland, could use the topography of the natural landscape to secure their spatial confinement (relying on the services of an unconfined assistant to provide for their bodily needs).[48] But for those who laboured within the confines of a larger community, the organisation of space was subject to a wider range of conflicting pressures, and determined as much by the nature of the original land donated for the minster's establishment, its proximity to lay settlement, and the location and suitability of the agricultural terrain from which the congregation was sustained.

Prescriptive literature from the early Anglo-Saxon period was considerably more preoccupied with St Benedict's injunctions against wandering monks and clergy than in ensuring that his recommendation that the economic necessities for sustaining the communal life be provided.[49] Prohibitions on wandering religious and clerics were announced so frequently in the canons of church councils in early medieval England that the principle was seemingly understood (if not necessarily welcomed) by those who dwelt in minsters. Abbess Eangyth and her daughter Bugga, writing to Boniface in the hope that he would permit them to travel on pilgrimage to Rome, acknowledged that there were many in the church in their day who

[46] For conceptions of monastic layouts in different early monastic rules see W. Horn, 'On the origins of the medieval cloister', *Gesta* 12 (1973), 13–52, at pp. 19–21.

[47] David Parsons, 'The Mercian church: archaeology and topography', in Michelle P. Brown and Carol A. Farr (eds.), *Mercia: An Anglo-Saxon Kingdom in Europe* (London: Leicester University Press, 2001), pp. 50–68, at pp. 55–7; John Blair, 'Anglo-Saxon minsters: a topographical review', in John Blair and Richard Sharpe (eds.), *Pastoral Care before the Parish* (Leicester, London and New York: Leicester University Press, 1992), pp. 226–66, at pp. 227–31.

[48] For Hereberct – *uitam ducens solitariam* – see *HE* IV, 29 (pp. 440–1). Guthlac's choice of solitude was described by Felix, *VSG* chs. 27–8 (pp. 90–5). Guthlac had a servant, a *clericus* called Beccel: ch. 35 (pp. 110–13).

[49] The council of *Clofesho* held in 747 demanded that the seniors of houses ensure they had sufficient economic resources to support their communities: chs. 4 and 28 (H&S III, 364, 374); discussed further in ch. 3.

disapproved of this form of devotion, who 'support their opinion by the argument that the canons of councils prescribe that everyone shall remain where he has been placed, and where he has taken his vows, there he shall fulfil them before God.'[50] Yet only were Benedict's other recommendation – that the physical needs of a monastic community be provided from resources within its confines – also satisfied, could any requirement for stability be enforced. We will investigate the provision of land and other temporal necessities for the foundation of minsters, and explore the practical solutions adopted by individual founders to the conflicting pressures of physical space, economic hardship and the ideologies articulated in monastic legislation, in the next chapter. Meanwhile, it is to monastic rules that we must turn.

Regulating communal life

All social groups require some degree of regulation, or at least the tacit acceptance of a set of norms to govern both individual and collective behaviour, if they are to function effectively. Families establish spoken and unspoken rules to reduce friction between relations and smooth the daily running of the household; tribes and peoples necessarily agree on conventions to control social interaction and laws to prevent (or when required, to punish) anti-social and criminal behaviour.[51] Institutionalised social groups require more formal regulatory mechanisms than do families; inevitably they must formulate rules and guidelines for the effective governance of the communal life, boundaries that frame (circumscribe) the individual's freedoms within the group. Anything less would bring not just the anarchy to be anticipated within any genuinely rule-less society, but the rapid and complete collapse of the corporate ethos. In total institutions of the types we have been discussing, the regulatory system can be punitive and oppressive, perhaps no less for the 'staff' than for the 'inmates'. By contrast, the rules of a West End London club (frequently not recorded in writing) may seem occasionally irritating, or bafflingly antiquated, but they scarcely limit a man's – even, in these enlightened times, a woman's – personal freedom, let alone his sense of himself. A monastery is here, as elsewhere, distinguishable both from other total institutions and from different sorts of voluntary social and

---

[50] Boniface, *Ep.* 14 (p. 25).

[51] Henry Sumner Maine, *Ancient Law: Its Connection with the Early History of Society and its Relation to Modern Ideas* (1861; with introduction and notes by Frederick Pollock, London: John Murray, 1906), pp. 123–85.

charitable association in that the 'rule' of a monastery is far more than the system by which the lives of those who obey it are regulated.[52] The rule is the very essence of the monastic life itself: 'The reason we have written this monastic rule', reported Benedict in the last chapter of his Rule, 'is that, by observing it in monasteries, we can show that we have some degree of virtue and the beginnings of monastic life.'[53]

A superficial study of the language used to describe the communal religious life in early Anglo-Saxon England demonstrates rapidly that it was regulation that distinguished the religious way of life from that followed in secular households. Phrases such as *uita regularis*,[54] *regularis conseruatio*,[55] and *regularis uitae disciplina*[56] suggest that for contemporaries a defining characteristic of the religious life was that it was subject to some form of externally imposed discipline and authority. Even though, according to Cuthbert's anonymous biographer, the saint's early adult life had been distinguished by remarkable ascetic feats, it was in order to bind himself by the more rigid law of life in a minster (*disponens duriori se uite lege in monasterio constringere*) that Cuthbert chose to leave his secular life. Bede described the same decision in his life of the saint in similar terms: having forsaken the things of the world, Cuthbert hastened to submit to monastic discipline (*relictis seculi rebus monasterialem properat subire disciplinam*).[57] Adopting a life of religion, for women as well as for men, involved an agreement to live under a rule. Benedict decreed that his rule should be read straight through to a postulant seeking to join a monastic community, who should then be told, 'This is the law (*lex*) under which you are choosing to serve. If you can keep it, come in. If not, feel free to leave.'[58] That the lives of the inhabitants of early English minsters were rule-governed is easily established; determining which rule (or rules) they might have followed is much more difficult. Yet it is necessary to explore this question in some detail if we are to have a

---

[52] *RSB*, rubric to ch. 1 (pp. 168–9): 'Incipit textus regulae: regula appellatur ab hoc quod oboedientum dirigat mores;' 'Here begins the text of the rule: it is called a rule because it regulates the lives of those who obey it.' See the discussion of this phrase (which is not found in all manuscripts of the Rule), in Fry, *The Rule*, p. 168n.

[53] *RSB*, ch. 73, 1 (pp. 294–5).

[54] Thus Stephen described the way of life adopted by Wilfrid at Lindisfarne: *VSW* ch. 2 (pp. 6–7); Bede used the same language on many occasions, for example of Hild's Whitby: *HE* III. 24 (pp. 292–3).

[55] *VSCeol.* ch. 3 (p. 389).   [56] Alcuin, *Ep.* 42 (p. 86).

[57] Anon., *VSCuth.* II, 1 (pp. 74–5); Bede, *VSCuth.* ch. 6 (pp. 172–4).

[58] *RSB*, ch. 58, 9–10 (pp. 266–9). Caesarius of Arles, also, envisaged that the rule he wrote for his sister's community in Arles would provide them with a system by which all aspects of their life might be ordered. Having written one version at the time of the nunnery's foundation, he later produced a revised text in which he 'so moderated the rule under God's inspiration that with the help of God you can keep it in entirety': *Regula ad uirgines*, ch. 48 (pp. 232–5).

clear understanding of the ideals that may have shaped the expression of monastic fervour in the early English church.

St Benedict's Rule was certainly well-known in seventh-century England. Indeed, the earliest surviving manuscript copy of the rule was made in England in the eighth century and is generally accepted as having a south-western provenance.[59] Such was the strength of Bede's own devotion to St Benedict's Rule and so convincing are the references to its observance in his own lifetime[60] that it was commonplace until the middle years of the twentieth century for historians to argue that early English monasticism was Benedictine in its organisation, and had indeed been so since its first inception. Cuthbert Butler saw the Venerable Bede as the first Benedictine student and scholar, 'the type for all time . . . In range of subjects and in manner and temper of treatment, as in character and outlook on life, St Bede was the forerunner, the archetype of the succession of Benedictine scholars.'[61]

Bede was not, however, the first Benedictine in England, or even in Northumbria. Stephen, biographer of Bishop Wilfrid, gave that honour to his subject, asserting that Wilfrid had brought the Rule to Ripon in the 660s.[62] He suggested that this was a claim the bishop had made for himself in the impassioned speech he put into the bishop's mouth on the occasion when Wilfrid conducted his own defence at the council of Austerfield in 702–3.[63] Editing Stephen's Life for publication in 1927, Bertram Colgrave

---

[59] Oxford, Bodleian Library, MS Hatton 48, illustrated in plate I. N. R. Ker, 'The provenance of the oldest manuscript of the Rule of St Benedict', *Bodleian Library Record* 2 (1941), 28–9. Patrick Sims-Williams has suggested that this copy of the rule might have been written for one of the minsters associated with St Wilfrid in the Worcester diocese, perhaps Bath, which was dedicated to St Peter and St Benedict: *Religion and Literature in Western England, 600–800* (Cambridge: Cambridge University Press, 1990), p. 118.

[60] For example, the much-repeated story from Bede's childhood about the occasion when plague had so reduced the community at Jarrow that Ceolfrith abandoned the chanting of antiphons in the office except at matins and in the evening, as would have been permitted by Benedict's Rule: *VSCeol.* ch. 14 (p. 393; compare *RSB*, ch. 17, 6, pp. 212–13). See Patrick Wormald, 'Bede and Benedict Biscop' in Gerald Bonner (ed.), *Famulus Christi* (London, SPCK, 1976), pp. 141–69, at p. 145. Bede's own intimate knowledge of the Rule has already been mentioned: above, n. 6, and see van der Walt, 'Reflections', p. 376. For a contrary view see Walter Goffart, *The Narrators of Barbarian History (AD 550–800): Jordanes, Gregory of Tours, Bede and Paul the Deacon* (Princeton, NJ: Princeton University Press, 1988), pp. 314–15.

[61] Cuthbert Butler, *Benedictine Monachism: Studies in Benedictine Life and Rule* (London and New York: Longmans, Green, 1919), p. 326.

[62] Extraordinarily, this claim finds no mention in Bede: Goffart, *The Narrators*, pp. 314–15.

[63] *VSW* chs. 46–7 (pp. 93–9). For the date of this council see Catherine Cubitt, *Anglo-Saxon Church Councils c. 650–c. 850* (London and New York: Leicester University Press, 1995), p. 259. The debate at the synod was discussed by Eric John, 'The social and political problems of the early English church', in Joan Thirsk (ed.), *Land, Church, and People: Essays presented to Professor H. P. R. Finberg* (Reading: British Agricultural History Society, 1970), pp. 39–63, at p. 51. Goffart has suggested that it was precisely because the Rule was held to be synonymous with Wilfrid that Bede's writings 'maintain a resolute distance from it': *The Narrators*, p. 315.

reacted energetically to these statements about the origins of the rule in England: 'The rule of St Benedict was of course introduced to England by St Augustine and his fellow-monks in 597. The monastery he established was probably the first Benedictine house outside Italy.'[64] This was conventional wisdom in this period. Also writing about Wilfrid's promotion of the Rule, Stenton argued in 1943 that 'religion had been introduced into England by monks trained in the Benedictine tradition and a church which owed its foundation to Gregory the Great was bound to revere the monastic saint whom Gregory regarded as his master'.[65] Gregory's own monastery of St Andrew on the Caelian hill in Rome was assumed to have followed Benedict's Rule; the reluctant brothers who accompanied Augustine through Gaul towards the pagan shores of Britain were thus thought to have been brought up in that tradition. Further, on the Benedictine model, they were taken to be bound in obedience to Augustine as to Christ himself once their former prior had been promoted to be their abbot by Gregory.[66] That Benedict's own recommendations precluded the use of monks in pastoral activity beyond the cloister was not considered an insuperable problem. It was incongruous to use monks for missionary work, Margaret Deanesly observed, but she argued that a bishop could remove a monk 'from the monastic to the clerical servitude at need'; she considered it unlikely that any secular clergy would have wanted to accompany the monks on so precarious a mission.[67]

Two important studies by Guy Ferrari and Kassius Hallinger, both published in 1957, challenged the conventional view that early Roman monasteries had followed Benedict's precepts and that Pope Gregory had been a major figure in the promotion of the Rule of St Benedict for the organisation of

---

[64] Bertram Colgrave, *The Life of Bishop Wilfrid by Eddius Stephanus* (Cambridge: Cambridge University Press, 1927), p. 161, commenting on *VSW* ch. 14. Compare David Knowles, *The Monastic Order in England: A History of its Development from the Times of St. Dunstan to the Fourth Lateran Council, 940–1216* (2nd edn, Cambridge: Cambridge University Press, 1963), p. 18.

[65] F. M. Stenton, *Anglo-Saxon England* (Oxford: Clarendon Press, 1943), p. 158.

[66] Gregory's letter to the missionaries in July 596 instructing them to continue with their journey to Britain under Augustine's abbatial leadership was reproduced by Bede, *HE* I. 23 (pp. 70–1).

[67] Margaret Deanesly, *The Pre-Conquest Church in England* (2nd edn, London: Adam & C. Black, 1963), p. 46; compare also p. 54. Although on neither occasion did Deanesly mention Benedict's Rule by name, she appears to have intended readers to understand that this was the rule she had in mind, for it is to these pages that the reference in the index to St Benedict's Rule refers the reader. She had been much more cautious in her early essay about the composition of the Christ Church community published in T. F. Tout's *Festschrift* in 1925, where she argued that although a monk, Augustine had not been trained in a Benedictine tradition: 'The *familia* at Christ Church, Canterbury, 597–832', in A. G. Little and F. M. Powicke (eds.), *Essays in Medieval History* (Manchester: Manchester University Press, 1925), pp. 1–13; at p. 4.

monastic life in the early medieval West.[68] Although Hallinger's suggestion that Gregory had never read the Rule can be challenged from a close study of the pope's own writings,[69] his central argument that Gregory did not seek to impose any single rule of life upon western monasteries has important consequences for our understanding of the origins of monasticism in England.[70] For if Augustine and his companions were not Benedictines, what sort of monks were they? Were they even really monks at all?[71] If it is accepted, as scholars now generally agree, that no sixth- or seventh-century monastery could be called 'Benedictine' in the sense in which a modern audience would understand the term,[72] then it becomes rather less necessary to distinguish between the exponents of different ideals of conventual, monastic living. In this age of *regula mixta* (mixed rules) in which the leaders of monastic houses drew together precepts from a range of earlier authorities in order to create a synthetic model of holy living for the guidance of their own communities, there was no single regulatory norm against which any individual community of religious could be measured and found wanting. Benedict himself certainly embodied one ideal of monastic perfection and served as an important personal example of religious living for Gregory, Bede and others. But his was not the only available model and his rule was only one of several at the disposal of seventh-century abbots, albeit, at least for the English, a remarkably ubiquitous one.[73]

If Rome's direct role in the transmission of the Rule of St Benedict to England is now diminished, then that played by Gallic monasteries, notably those associated with the Irishman Columbanus, has proportionately

---

[68] Guy Ferrari demonstrated that there are hardly any indications of the use of the *RSB* in Rome before the tenth century; each abbot tended to create a rule for his own house, compiling a composite customary on the basis of the various pre-existing rules with which he was familiar: *Early Roman Monasteries: Notes for the History of the Monasteries and Convents at Rome from the V through the X Century* (Città del Vaticano: Pontifico Istituto di archeologia cristiana, 1957), pp. 379–407. Kassius Hallinger, 'Papst Gregor der Grosse und der heilige Benedikt', *Studia Anselmiana* 42 (1957), pp. 231–319.

[69] Adalbert de Vogüé and Jean Neufville (eds.), *La règle de Saint Benoît*, SC 181–6 (6 vols., Paris: Editions du Cerf, 1971–2), I, 150–7; Henry Mayr-Harting, *The Venerable Bede, the Rule of St Benedict and Social Class*, Jarrow Lecture, 1976 (Jarrow: St Paul's Church, 1977), p. 6; Conrad Leyser, 'St Benedict and Gregory the Great: another dialogue', in Salvatore Pricoco *et al.* (eds.), *Sicilia e Italia suburbicaria tra IV e VIII seculo* (Rubbettino: Soveria Mannelli, 1991), pp. 21–43, at p. 25.

[70] Eric John, '"Secularium prioratus" and the Rule of St Benedict', *Revue bénédictine* 75 (1965), 212–39, at pp. 213–14. For a nuanced reading of Gregory's views about the proper conduct of the monastic life see Conrad Leyser, *Authority and Asceticism from Augustine to Gregory the Great* (Oxford: Clarendon Press, 2000), pp. 151–7.

[71] See further below, pp. 62–6.   [72] Wormald, 'Bede and Benedict Biscop', p. 142.

[73] Mayr-Harting, *The Venerable Bede*, p. 7: 'whatever other rules may have been known amongst the Anglo-Saxons, however, RB seems to crop up almost everywhere and occupies a commanding place in the evidence'.

increased.[74] Columbanus wrote his two complementary rules (the *Regula monachorum*, written for the guidance of an individual monk, and the *Regula coenobialis*, which explores how monks should live together) for the inhabitants of the houses he founded in Gaul and Italy.[75] Like Benedict, Columbanus promoted the coenobitic ideal over the eremitic, although whether it was he or other Frankish monastics who introduced Benedict's Rule to Frankia is disputed.[76] By his own account, when he came to compile his own rules, Columbanus drew on the practices of the *seniores* of his own monastery at Bangor. He would seem also to have been influenced by contemporary monasticism in Gaul, particularly Cassian's *Conferences* and *Institutes* (which reflected many of the ideas of the first monks of the Egyptian desert), and possibly by St Martin of Tours.[77] Further, it seems likely that he did know the Rule of Benedict.[78] As Thomas Charles-Edwards has argued, the 'rule of Columbanus' that his followers disseminated was probably an oral rule of monastic life, one that had textual sources including Benedict, Cassian and Basil as well as Columbanus' own writings, but incorporated also the Irishman's spoken teachings.[79]

[74] John, '"Secularium prioratus"', pp. 215–9.

[75] Jane Barbara Stevenson, 'The monastic rules of Columbanus', in Michael Lapidge (ed.), *Columbanus: Studies on the Latin Writings* (Woodbridge: Boydell Press, 1997), pp. 203–16, at pp. 206–7. For discussion of Columbanus' influence on Frankish monasticism see Pierre Riché, 'Columbanus, his followers and the Merovingian church', in H. B. Clarke and Mary Brennan (eds.), *Columbanus and Merovingian Monasticism*, BAR, International series 113 (Oxford: BAR, 1981), 59–72; Friedrich Prinz, 'Columbanus, the Frankish nobility and the territories east of the Rhine', *ibid.*, pp. 73–87; Ian Wood, *The Merovingian Kingdoms 450–751* (London and New York: Longman, 1994), pp. 184–9; and Marilyn Dunn, *The Emergence of Monasticism: From the Desert Fathers to the Early Middle Ages* (Oxford: Blackwell, 2000), pp. 158–90.

[76] T. M. Charles-Edwards, *Early Christian Ireland* (Cambridge: Cambridge University Press, 2000), pp. 384–8, John, '"Secularium prioratus"', pp. 216–18. For Columbanus' views on the advantages of communal living see his *Regula*, ch. 10 (ed. Walker, pp. 140–3).

[77] Friedrich Prinz, *Frühes Mönchtum im Frankenreich: Kultur und Gesellschaft in Gallien, den Rheinlanden und Bayern am Beispiel der monastischen Entwickeln (4. bis 8. Jahrhundert)* (Munich and Vienna: R. Oldenbourg, 1965), pp. 645–6. Although we know little about monasticism in the British church in this period, the British writer, Gildas had a substantial influence upon Columbanus' Latin prose style: Michael Winterbottom, 'Columbanus and Gildas', *Vigiliae Christianae* 30 (1976), 310–17. Jane Stevenson has argued plausibly that Gildas is thus likely to have had some impact on the Irishman's views about monasticism: 'The monastic rules', pp. 207–9.

[78] De Vogüé and Neufville (eds.), *La règle de Saint Benoît* I, 163–9; Charles-Edwards, *Early Christian Ireland*, pp. 386–8.

[79] Charles-Edwards, *Early Christian Ireland*, p. 388. Columbanus's followers promoted mixed rules drawing on a range of sources: Waldpert of Luxeuil composed a rule combining the precepts of Benedict and Columbanus for the nuns of Faremoutiers, and Donatus of Besançon drew in addition on the *Regula uirginum* of Caesarius of Arles in writing his own nuns' rule: Adalbert de Vogüé, *Les règles monastiques anciennes (400–700)*, Typologies des sources, 46 (Turnhout: Brepols, 1985), pp. 59–60 (on the *Regula Waldeberti*, preserved by Benedict of Aniane under the anonymous title *Regula cuiusdam ad uirgines*) and *ibid.*, p. 56 (on the *Regula Donati*). See also de Vogüé, 'La règle de Donat pour l'abbesse Gauthstrude', *Benedictina* 25 (1978), 219–313, and Prinz, *Frühes Mönchtum*, pp. 286–7 and 149–51.

Knowledge of the Rule of St Benedict probably came to the English church not from Rome but via the monasteries of the Columbanian connection in northern Gaul.[80] Bede noted the close connections between English and Gallic churches in the seventh century – particularly the Franks who were appointed to English bishoprics, the English clerics consecrated to episcopal office in Gaul, and the popularity in the 630s of northern Gallic monasteries among devout royal women, unable to fulfil their vocations to the monastic life in England, where no religious houses for women had yet been built.[81] His account can, as James Campbell has shown, be supplemented from other sources, which serve further to emphasise the direct relationship between English churches and the monasteries connected with St Columbanus and his disciples. Wilfrid spent three years with Archbishop Annemundus of Lyons between 655 and 658 and could have encountered Benedict's Rule then or, Patrick Wormald has suggested, in the two years after 664 when he spent time with his patron Agilbert, himself a member of the Columbanian connection.[82] It may well have been from Wilfrid that the brothers of Bede's abbey at Wearmouth and Jarrow learnt to admire Benedict of Nursia.[83] Wilfrid had been Ceolfrith's abbot at Ripon before the latter joined the community at Jarrow and he was a vigorous bishop in Northumbria, seeing the control of monastic discipline within his diocese as a proper part of his function.[84]

Benedict Biscop, Wearmouth's first abbot, was himself a frequent visitor to Francia and Rome; he made several journeys during the period when he was attempting to set his new minster onto a secure footing in order to collect books, sacred vessels and vestments, indeed 'everything necessary for the service of church and altar'.[85] On these journeys (and presumably

[80] Wormald, 'Bede and Benedict Biscop', pp. 145–6; Mayr-Harting, *The Venerable Bede*, p. 6; Dunn, *The Emergence of Monasticism*, pp. 191–3.

[81] James Campbell, 'The first century of Christianity in England', in his *Essays in Anglo-Saxon History* (London: Hambledon Press, 1986), pp. 49–67, at p. 55; discussed further in my *Veiled Women*, I, 36–7.

[82] *VSW*, chs. 6, 12 and 28 (pp. 12–15, 24–7, 54–7); Wormald, 'Bede and Benedict Biscop', p. 145.

[83] Wormald, 'Bede and Benedict Biscop', pp. 144–5; see also John, '"Secularium prioratus"', pp. 218–20; Goffart, *The Narrators*, pp. 314–15.

[84] *VSCeol.* chs. 3, 5, 8 (pp. 389–91); for Ceolfrith's links with Wilfrid see Henry Mayr-Harting, *The Coming of Christianity to Anglo-Saxon England* (London: Batsford, 1972; 3rd edn, 1991), p. 166. Wormald, 'Bede and Benedict Biscop', p. 159, n. 27.

[85] *HA* ch. 5 (p. 368), cf. chs. 4 and 6 (pp. 367 and 368–9). Ceolfrith travelled with Benedict to Rome and played a significant role in the founding and expansion of the Wearmouth–Jarrow library: *VSCeol.* chs. 9–10 and 20 (pp. 391 and 394–5); Simon Coates, 'Ceolfrid: history, hagiography and memory in seventh- and eighth-century Wearmouth–Jarrow', *Journal of Medieval History* 25 (1999), 69–86, at p. 73.

also during his travels as a young man, when he spent some months at the island monastery of Lérins in southern Gaul),[86] Biscop took a lively interest in contemporary customs for the organisation and regulation of the religious life, storing away 'in the coffer of his breast' whatever valuable customs he had observed anywhere, and bringing these back to Britain for his brethren to follow.[87] Even at the last, Biscop dwelt on the necessity for his community to persist in the observance of the rule he had given them. On his deathbed, Bede had him say, 'You must not think that the ordinances (*decreta*) I laid down for you were the result of my own untutored invention. No, all I found best in the life of the seventeen monasteries I visited during my long and frequent pilgrimages, I stored up in my mind and have handed on to you, to be steadfastly adhered to for your own good.' When it came to the election of a new abbot in his stead, Benedict's advice was clear: the brothers were to consult both the rule of 'the great St Benedict our founder', and the decretals of the papal privileges for this house, before meeting together to agree on the candidate who best would serve their needs.[88]

Wearmouth–Jarrow was in many ways far from typical among seventh-century minsters. As the home of the Venerable Bede, it has always attracted particular attention from historians, whose interest is stimulated by the abundant anecdotal evidence in Bede's own Lives of the abbots and the anonymous Life of Abbot Ceolfrith (possibly also written by Bede).[89] A modern government would clearly hail this institution as a centre of excellence and probably, dwelling on its educational role in rearing and training young religious, make it a 'specialist college'. Yet it is striking that, for all Bede's personal commitment to uniformity of observance, even at his own abbey no

---

[86] *HA* ch. 2 (pp. 365–6). It is not clear precisely when Benedict was at Lérins, where he was tonsured, and thus whether he was there before or after Aigulf of Fleury had arrived at that monastery and tried to impose the reformed monasticism practised in the Columbanian houses: Wormald, 'Bede and Benedict Biscop', p. 144. Equally, Biscop's adoption of the cognomen Benedict provides further evidence for his devotion to the Italian saint, but we do not know when he took the name. He can more confidently be thought to have encountered the joint rules of Benedict and Columbanus in practice during the winter of 668–9, when he travelled back from Rome in the company of the newly consecrated Archbishop Theodore, staying with Agilbert, bishop of Paris, or with Emmo of Sens and Burgundofaro of Meaux, both with close Columbanian connections: *HE*, IV, 1 (330–1); *HA*, ch. 3 (p. 366); Wormald, 'Bede and Benedict Biscop', pp. 144–5.

[87] *VSCeol*. ch. 6 (p. 390).

[88] *HA* ch. 11 (pp. 374–5); compare *VSCeol*. ch. 16 (p. 390). Wormald, 'Bede and Benedict Biscop', pp. 141–2. For discussion of the, now lost, privilege of Pope Agatho for Wearmouth see Wilhelm Levison, *England and the Continent in the Eighth Century* (Oxford: Oxford University Press, 1946), pp. 247. See also Peter Hunter Blair, *The World of Bede* (London: Secker and Warburg, 1970), pp. 197–9.

[89] Judith McClure, 'Bede and the Life of Ceolfrid', *Peritia* 3 (1984), 71–84.

one rule of life legislated for all eventualities.[90] Beside the Rule of St Benedict and the papal privilege already mentioned, Benedict Biscop seemingly drew up a composite set of guidelines for the minsters' future guidance.[91] Zelzer argued that these might better be thought of as an early customary ('usus cotidianus'), prescriptions covering aspects of the organisation of daily monastic life that could be used as a supplement to the fundamental guidelines provided by a written rule.[92] These need not have been preserved in writing; Catherine Cubitt has suggested that they may have been handed down (together with the precepts later passed on by Benedict's successor Ceolfrith) within the community's collective memory, preserved as oral traditions about the example and teaching of the minster's early abbots.[93] When Alcuin wrote to the brothers of these same minsters in 793 and recommended them to keep the observance of the regular life that their former abbots Benedict and Ceolfrith had laid down for them, he further advised that the Rule of St Benedict be read frequently among the assembled brethren and explained in their own language, so that all might understand it.[94] If that rule had already been the sole system for regulating the minster, one might think such a suggestion otiose.

Similarly composite systems of regulation were apparently used in other early English minsters. When Cuthbert arrived at Lindisfarne from Melrose, his anonymous biographer reported that the saint 'arranged our rule of life which we composed then for the first time and which we observe even to this day along with the Rule of St Benedict'.[95] It is hard to believe that this was the first occasion on which any sort of system of regulation had been imposed on the congregation at Lindisfarne; perhaps the author meant to imply that the rule being followed in his own day was first recorded in Cuthbert's time. What his account does show clearly, however, is that Benedict's rule was here, as at Wearmouth and Jarrow, being used alongside another set of written instructions. St Benedict's Rule was apparently also

---

[90] Goffart has stressed Bede's reluctance to mention the *RSB* directly; there is no reference to the Rule at all in his *Ecclesiastical History* and it is only in relation to Benedict Biscop's death-bed instructions that Bede referred to the Rule in his History of the Abbots: *The Narrators*, pp. 314–15.

[91] Others within the same community did leave written records for the minster's future organisation, for example John, the arch-chantor from Rome who taught the brothers how to recite psalms in the Roman fashion, writing down his instructions for posterity: *HE* IV. 18 (388–9); *HA* ch. 6 (p. 369).

[92] Klaus Zelzer, 'Zur Frage der Observanz des Benedict Biscop', in Elizabeth A. Livingstone (ed.), *Studia Patristica 20: Papers Presented to the Tenth International Conference on Patristic Studies held in Oxford 1987* (Leuven: Peeters Press, 1989), 323–9, at pp. 325–6.

[93] Catherine Cubitt, 'Monastic memory and identity in early Anglo-Saxon England', in William O. Frazer and Andrew Tyrell (eds.), *Social Identity in Early Medieval Britain* (London and New York: Leicester University Press, 2000), pp. 252–76, at pp. 273–4.

[94] Alcuin, *Ep.* 19 (p. 54).   [95] Anon., *VSCuth.* III. 1 (pp. 94–7).

known and followed, at least to some degree, in southern England in the seventh century. Wynfrith-Boniface had some experience of its teachings during the period he spent as a boy and young man in the West Saxon minsters at Exeter and Nursling, although both places appear to have followed a mixed rule that probably also incorporated the teachings of Columbanus.[96] Aldhelm of Malmesbury certainly knew of the merits of Benedict of Nursia, and proclaimed his own participation (with mediocre talent) in celebrating the saint's blessedness 'ringing out with harmonious voice in the holy celebration of the Psalms with its two divisions, and reverberating "Osanna" among the twin melodies'.[97] Although his account of the saint provides insufficient ground from which to argue that Aldhelm claimed to live by Benedict's Rule,[98] it is not unlikely that Malmesbury's daily life drew on the combined precepts of Benedict and Columbanus. If there is any truth in William of Malmesbury's assertion that Aldhelm was trained at Malmesbury by an Irishman Máeldub, 'a monk by profession', who had left Ireland in search of the solitary life,[99] one need not assume that he had come to England direct from Ireland. If the putative Irish founder of Malmesbury had spent time in Francia *en route*, he could, like the West Saxon bishops Agilbert and Leutherius, have brought knowledge of the mixed rules from the Columbanian connection to Wessex.[100]

That early English minsters drew on various pre-existing monastic rules to order their internal affairs, and above all to set the pattern for their collective worship, the *opus Dei*, seems certain. In the process of creating a mixed rule for their own use, many communities may have turned for guidance to separate rules – the Rule of St Benedict, the writings of Columbanus, one or other of the rules of Caesarius of Arles, perhaps also the rules of St Augustine

---

[96] Willibald, *VSB* ch. 1 (Exeter, ed. Rau, pp. 462–4); ch. 2 (Nursling, pp. 466–8). Christopher Holdsworth, 'St Boniface the monk', in *The Greatest Englishman: Essays on St Boniface and the Church at Crediton*, ed. Timothy Reuter (Exeter: Paternoster Press, 1980), pp. 49–67, at pp. 54–6. Boniface was certainly sufficiently interested in St Benedict's teachings to encourage the monks of Fulda to follow his precepts and to send Sturm to Tuscany to explore how the rule worked in practice there: Eigil, *Vita Sancti Sturmi*, ch. 14 (*MGH* Scriptores, II, 371). Mayr-Harting, *The Venerable Bede*, p. 7.

[97] Aldhelm, *De uirginitate*, xxx (ed. Gwara, pp. 381–2; trans. Lapidge and Herren, *Aldhelm*, pp. 89–90).

[98] Holdsworth, 'St Boniface', p. 66, n. 46; *contra* Wormald, 'Bede and Benedict', p. 146.

[99] William of Malmesbury, *Gesta pontificum*, §189 (ed. Hamilton, pp. 333–4). Not only was William writing long after these events in the twelfth century, but he may, in identifying an Irish teacher for Aldhelm, merely have been extrapolating from Bede's description of Malmesbury as *urbs Maildubi*, that is the town of a man called Maildub (Máeldub): *HE* V, 18 (pp. 514–15); Lapidge and Herren, *Aldhelm*, pp. 181–2.

[100] Holdsworth, 'St Boniface', p. 57. Agilbert, bishop of Wessex 650–60, had spent time in Ireland before he came to Britain (*HE* III, 7, pp. 234–5) and had family connections with the Columbanian house at Jouarre where he was buried: Campbell, 'The first century', p. 58. His nephew, Leutherius, was bishop of Wessex from 670–676: *HE* III, 7 (236–7).

or of St Basil, both of which were well-known in the Latin West[101] – or they may of course have drawn on an anthology of regulatory material previously created elsewhere in England, or, as we have seen, in Francia. While Benedict Biscop looked for models abroad, other Englishmen travelled around their own country in an attempt to discover how best to organise the religious life. When Ceolfrith had been ordained to the priesthood at Ripon, he visited Kent 'from a desire to learn fully the practices of the monastic life and of the order which he had undertaken', and then went on to visit Abbot Botwulf in East Anglia.[102] It seems not to have been anticipated that all minsters would follow identical rules, but there was, as we have already shown, a widespread notion that the religious life when properly observed was regular and that there were such places as true minsters.[103]

The various ecclesiastical synods that offered guidance on the internal organisation or external supervision of minsters during the eighth and early ninth centuries largely restricted their advice to general admonitions about the regular governance of minsters, and did not attempt to direct what sort of rule was to be followed. At *Clofesho* in 747, for example, bishops were instructed to verify that abbots and abbesses represented exemplary good living and that those subject to such leaders conducted themselves regularly.[104] Similarly, the council convened in 803 by Archbishop Æthelheard, which also met at *Clofesho*, forbade the election of laymen as abbots of minsters and urged monastic communities to 'take care to comply with their monastic obligations by the rule and observance of discipline'.[105]

More precise recommendations about the proper performance of the religious life are found in the canons of the councils held on the occasion of

---

[101] Mayr-Harting, 'The Venerable Bede', p. 7.   [102] *VSCeol.* chs. 3–4 (pp. 388–9).

[103] See, for example, Bede's letter to Bishop Ecgberht of York, §12 (pp. 415–16), in which he criticised those without experience of the *vita regularis*, who set up minsters on land acquired from kings under false pretences. It is important, as Patrick Sims-Williams has shown, to read this letter in a tradition of monastic polemic extending back at least to Cassian and to recognise both the rhetorical conventions on which Bede drew as well as the fact that not all 'family minsters' were necessarily irreligious, nor founded without episcopal licence: *Religion and Literature*, pp. 126–30.

[104] Council of *Clofesho*, AD 747, ch. 4 (H&S III, 364); for a wide-ranging discussion of the reform programme announced at this council see Cubitt, *Anglo-Saxon Church Councils*, pp. 110–22.

[105] Council of *Clofesho*, AD 803 (H&S III, 546): 'ea regula et obseruantia disciplinae sua monastica jura student observare'. Compare by contrast the 742 *Concilium Germanicum*, ch. 7 (ed. Tangl, *Die Briefe*, p. 101, no. 56), which decreed that monks and maidservants of God should live according to the Rule of St Benedict, by whose precepts they should govern their lives. The influence of Boniface on this council was discussed by Levison, *England and the Continent*, pp. 83–6 and Holdsworth, 'St Boniface', pp. 60–1.

a visit of papal legates (Bishop George of Ostia and Theophylact of Todi) to England in 786, and incorporated in the report of their visit.[106] As had the chapters of the Council of *Clofesho* in 747, the legatine canons stressed the necessity for bishops to make annual diocesan visitations and correct errors, particularly in the religious observance of the laity.[107] But the 786 council issued much more specific injunctions about the proper behaviour of religious, urging bishops to 'take great care that canons (*canonici*) live canonically and monks and nuns behave themselves regularly (*regulariter*) both in dress and in diet, so that there may be a distinction (*discretio*) between a canon, a monk and a secular'.[108] No such distinction had previously been made in an English context;[109] this canon is usually taken to reflect contemporary Frankish practice and to have been inspired by the rule for canons of Chrodegang of Metz, which sought to impose elements of monastic discipline and a corporate liturgical practice onto cathedral clergy living communally.[110] Chrodegang's influence might further be apparent in the emphasis placed at the same council on the necessity for conformity with the practice of the church of Rome, but important as these clauses are for the history

---

[106] The legatine report is best printed by Dümmler among Alcuin's correspondence: *Epistolae Karolini Aevi* II, no. 3 (pp. 19–29); a partial translation is in *EHD*, no. 191. Conventionally, the legates' visit has been associated with Mercian affairs, particularly King Offa's decision to raise the status of the bishopric of Lichfield to archiepiscopal status in 787 and his consecration of his son, Ecgfrith, as his heir in the same year: Frank Merry Stenton, *Anglo-Saxon England* (3rd edn, Oxford, 1971), pp. 215–18. More recently, however, attention has focused on the possible Northumbrian context for the mission: P. Wormald, 'In search of Offa's law-code', in I. N. Wood and N. Lund (eds.), *People and Places in Northern Europe 500–1600* (Woodbridge: Boydell Press, 1986), pp. 25–45, at pp. 28–34; Cubitt, *Anglo-Saxon Church Councils*, pp. 153–90.

[107] Cubitt, *Anglo-Saxon Church Councils*, pp. 159–60.

[108] Legatine synod, ch. 4 (ed. Dümmler, p. 22): 'Quartus sermo, ut episcopi diligenti cura preuideant, quo omnes canonici sui canonice uiuant et monachi seu monachae regulariter conuersentur, tam in cibis quam in uestibus seu peculiare, ut discretio sit inter canonicum et monachum uel secularem.' The sixth chapter of the same text (*ibid.*) also echoed Chrodegang's *Regula canonicorum*, ch. 2 (ed. Schmidt, p. 3), in insisting that priests and deacons should persist in the exact rank and title to which they had been ordained (ut nullus episcoporum presbiterum aut diaconum ordinare presumat, nisi probatae uitae fuerint et officium suum rite implere possint, et in illo titulo perseuerent, ad quem consecrati sunt, ita ut nullus de alterius titulo presbiterum aut diaconum suscipere presumat absque causa rationabili et literis commendaticiis.)

[109] Hanna Vollrath, *Die Synoden Englands bis 1066* (Paderborn: Schöningh, 1985), p. 167 and nn. 131–2. Vollrath was cautious in declaring this the first occasion in an English context when monks and canons had been differentiated, and noted that Archbishop Ecgberht had legislated for the *canonica*, that is the canoness as distinct from full nuns in his Penitential: Penitential of Ecgberht, preface and ch. 5.8, ed. H&S, III, 417, 422; see Levison, *England and the Continent*, pp. 105–6.

[110] Chrodegang's Rule was written for his own community at Metz *c.*755–6; its composition is closely associated with the Council of Ver of 755, which was concerned with articulating a clearer distinction between clerical and monastic lives: *Capitularia regum Francorum*, ed. A. Boretius, *MGH Leges* II (Hanover: Hahn, 1883), no. 14, pp. 32–7; see Brigitte Langefeld, '*Regula canonicorum* or *Regula monasterialis uitae*? The Rule of Chrodegang and Archbishop Wulfred's reforms at Canterbury', *Anglo-Saxon England* 25 (1996), 21–36, at p. 27.

of the early English church, they do not prove that Chrodegang's Rule was known in England.[111] Since Alcuin (the English cleric and scholar educated at York who spent much of his adult career at the court of Charlemagne) was not only present at both the Northumbrian and Mercian synods in 786, but may have played some role in the drafting of the 'capitulary' that resulted from them,[112] it is perhaps unsurprising that these reflect many issues of current concern in the Frankish church. Recommendations for the closer scrutiny of the canonical life had been made at various Frankish synods from the time of Boniface onwards,[113] but in the later eighth century such advice became much more specific. Direct reference was made to the *regula* or *instituta* by which canons' lives should be regulated, for example in the *Admonitio generalis* of 789, another text in whose drafting Alcuin may have played some part.[114] In Francia, the canonical life was formally placed under written guidelines at Louis the Pious' reforming synods at Aachen in 816–17, when the *Institutio canonicorum* was recommended as the clerical equivalent to the *Regula monachorum*, a revised and elaborated version of the Rule of St Benedict devised by Benedict of Aniane for all monastic communities.[115] Whether the advice about the organisation of clerical communities offered in England in 786 had much impact on the bishops charged with its implementation is hard to determine. This text does, however, raise wider questions about the way of life followed in English cathedral communities before the tenth century.

---

[111] Legatine synods, chs. 4 and 8 (ed. Dümmler, p. 22); Langefeld, 'The Rule of Chrodegang', 27.

[112] Cubitt, *Anglo-Saxon Church Councils*, p. 164.

[113] For example: Pippin III, Council of Ver 755 (ed. Boretius, *MGH, Capitularia*, I, 32–7, no. 14) Pippin of Italy, Council of 782×786, ch. 2 (ed. Boretius, p. 191); for a general discussion of reforming councils before Charlemagne see Rosamond McKitterick, The *Frankish Church and the Carolingian Reforms, 789–895* (London: Royal Historical Society, 1977), pp. 47–9; J. M. Wallace-Hadrill, *The Frankish Church* (Oxford: Clarendon Press, 1983), pp. 170–3.

[114] *Admonitio generalis*, 789, ch. 73 (ed. Boretius, *MGH, Capitularia*, I, 60, no. 22): 'similarly it is our will that those who enter upon the clerical status we call the canonical life (*canonica uita*) live in all respects as canons in accordance with their rule (*secundum suam regulam*) and the bishop is to rule their life as the abbot does that of monks'. For Alcuin's role in the drafting of the *Admonitio generalis* see Friedrich-Karl Schiebe, 'Alcuin und die *Admonitio generalis*', *Deutsches Archiv* 14 (1958), 221–29; T. F. X. Noble, 'From brigandage to justice: Charlemagne, 785–794', in Celia M. Chazelle (ed.), *Literacy, Politics and Artistic Innovation in the Early Medieval West* (Lanham, MD, and London: University Press of America, 1992), pp. 49–75, at pp. 57–60. Patrick Wormald drew attention to the parallel between the *Admonitio generalis* and the English 786 'capitulary', showing not just that both texts cover much the same ground, but that both use the same biblical quotations to bolster their arguments: 'In search of Offa's law-code', pp. 42–3. Further Cubitt, *Anglo-Saxon Church Councils*, pp. 160–6.

[115] *Institutio canonicorum*, ed. Werminghoff, *MGH, Concilia 2, Concilia Aevi Karolini I* (Hanover and Leipzig: Hahn, 1906), 312–421; Langefeld, 'The Rule of Chrodegang', p. 22; Brooks, *The Early History*, p. 156; Wallace-Hadrill, *The Frankish Church*, pp. 264–5.

Rules for cathedral communities

Clear evidence for the influence of contemporary continental ideas about the proper organisation of communities of canons on arrangements made for English cathedral clergy is found only in the time of Wulfred, archbishop of Canterbury 805–32. Charter subscriptions made by the congregation in the time of his predecessor, Æthelheard (archbishop 793–805), suggest that the Christ Church community then consisted of secular clergy organised under *praepositi* with an archdeacon (*archidiaconus*) to assist the archbishop.[116] It was Archbishop Wulfred, previously archdeacon at Christ Church, who claimed to have 'revived the holy monastery of the church of Canterbury by renewing, restoring and rebuilding it with the aid of the priests, deacons and all the clergy of the said church', urging his congregation diligently to frequent the canonical hours in the church of Christ and to share a common refectory and dormitory 'according to the rule of monastic discipline' (*iuxta regulam monasterialis disciplinæ uitæ*).[117] Chrodegang's *Rule* provides close parallels for the separate elements of Wulfred's reform of his clergy, both the archbishop's insistence on the celebration of the canonical hours and on the sharing of common living arrangements, and also the concession Wulfred made in the same charter for priests to retain their private property on condition that it never be alienated from the community, nor put to improper use.[118] In other grants that Wulfred made to the Christ Church *familia*, the archbishop urged the congregation to almsgiving, the recitation of psalms and the celebration of masses;[119] he further donated a court (*curtis*) that he had acquired within the *monasterium* to the community as a separate dwelling for sick or infirm members of the congregation, an arrangement that conforms with Chrodegang's recommendation about the segregation of the sick.[120] It seems, as Nicholas Brooks has argued, that one of the archbishop's primary motives in reordering his congregation was to inspire them to corporate chanting

---

[116] S 1259, a charter of 805, by which Æthelheard recovered for Christ Church land in Kent previously confiscated by King Offa, was attested by two *praepositi*, eight priests, Wulfred, *archidiaconus*, a deacon, a subdeacon and two others without title: Brooks, *The Early History*, p. 155.

[117] S 1265, attested by a *presbyter abbas*, eight priests, two deacons and a *praepositus*; the charter, which survives only in an antiquarian copy, cannot be dated more closely than to 808 × 813. See Deanesly, 'The familia at Christ Church', p. 10; J. Armitage Robinson, 'The community at Christ Church, Canterbury', *Journal of Theological Studies* 27 (1926), 226–40, at pp. 237–8; Brooks, *The Early History*, p. 156.

[118] Brooks, *The Early History*, p. 156, drawing attention to *Regula Chrodegangi*, chs. 3 and 4–6, and the provisions for canons made at the 816–17 Aachen councils, *Institutio canonicorum*, chs. 118, 123, 126–31. Also John, '"Secularium prioratus"', p. 226.

[119] S 1188, 1268 and 1414.

[120] S 1268, compare *Regula Chrodegangi*, ch. 28; Brooks, *The Early History*, p. 156 and n. 10 (p. 357).

and worship, in the hope perhaps that this would restore Canterbury to its historic pre-eminence in chanting in the Roman manner.[121] Whether he should be thought to have done so on the basis of Chrodegang's Rule or whether this was rather, as Brigitte Langefeld has argued, an attempt to restore the *monastic* life-style at Canterbury, following the more familiar *RSB*, is unclear.[122] In Wulfred's own time there is little evidence for the spread of continental ideas about the organisation of clerical communities beyond Canterbury, nor is there any indication that the recommendations made at the 786 synods had had much impact on either minsters or cathedral churches.[123] Of greater significance for our purposes here is the relationship between Wulfred's domestic and liturgical reorganisation of Christ Church and the arrangements originally suggested by Pope Gregory to Augustine for the ordering of the first episcopal community at Canterbury.

Persuaded by the force of the Roman missionaries' preaching and the excellence of the example of their pure life, King Æthelberht of Kent had accepted baptism in 597 and given his teachers 'a place to settle in, suitable to their rank, in Canterbury his chief city' as well as various possessions appropriate to their needs.[124] This donation enabled Augustine to institute his episcopal see, restoring a church in the city of Canterbury and dedicating it to the Saviour, he established a dwelling (*habitatio*) for himself and all his successors.[125] In his narrative of the progress of the mission, Bede had already drawn attention to the behaviour of Augustine and his companions from their first arrival in Kent. Once they had obtained a temporary *mansio*

---

[121] Brooks, *The Early History*, pp. 156–7. Brooks has set the references in these various charters in the context of a letter Alcuin had written to Wulfred's predecessor, Æthelheard, in 797, recommending that he reform the Canterbury *familia* by inspiring them to zeal in Scripture and service in the choir: *Epistola*, no. 128 (p. 190). Bede had commented on the impact of the chanting of Augustine's companions in Canterbury at the start of the mission to the English (*HE* I. 26, pp. 76–7) and on the role of Canterbury in disseminating skill in liturgical singing among the churches of the English (*HE* IV. 2, pp. 334–5).

[122] Langefeld, 'The Rule of Chrodegang', pp. 30 and 35–6. An important element of Langefeld's argument is the evidence that when the Rule of Chrodegang did become known in Anglo-Saxon England it was in its enlarged version, compiled in western France after the 816–17 Aachen councils, not in Chrodegang's original text.

[123] At Worcester, as J. Armitage Robinson showed, the early ninth-century *familia* consisted of presbyters, deacons and *clerici*; in the middle years of the century the clergy were led by a *praepositus* (S 1272, 1273, 1278): *St Oswald and the Church of Worcester*, British Academy supplemental papers 5 (London: Oxford University Press for the British Academy, 1919), pp. 8–10. In Robinson's view, the Worcester charters show that the bishop and the *familia* were joint holders of the estates of the church. 'There is but one church of Worcester and but one *familia*. And there is no hint anywhere of monasticism' (p. 10). Although, early in the next century, one witness to a charter of 904 was described as *abbas* (S 1280), it is not clear that this Cynelm was a monk, let alone that his congregation was monastic.

[124] *HE* I. 26 (pp. 76–9).   [125] *HE* I. 33 (pp. 114–15).

from the king, 'they began to imitate the way of life of the apostles and of the primitive church. They were constantly engaged in prayers, in vigils and fasts'; they preached energetically, spurning all worldly goods and accepting only basic necessities from their flock.[126] When Augustine tried to formalise the arrangements suitable for a permanent episcopal community he turned to Pope Gregory for advice, asking how bishops should live with their clergy and how the offerings of the faithful should be divided between them.[127] Augustine's uncertainty presumably stemmed from his monastic background; for although he and his companions had clearly established an impressively spiritual mode of communal living characterised by simplicity and poverty, he must have struggled to translate this into the context of an active cathedral set within the city of Canterbury.[128]

Gregory's reply to this question laid stress on his new bishop's familiarity with monastic rules and recommended that Augustine should not live apart from his clergy in the English church; 'you ought to institute that manner of life which our fathers followed in the earliest beginnings of the Church: none of them said that anything he possessed was his own, but they had all things in common'.[129] The image of the apostolic community in Jerusalem had of course stimulated many monastic legislators in the early Christian West, including Benedict of Nursia, who quoted the same passage from Acts in the chapter of his Rule forbidding monks to have any private possessions.[130] Yet, as Conrad Leyser has shown in his important recent

---

[126] *HE* I. 26 (pp. 76–7).

[127] *Ibid.*, I. 27 (pp. 78–81). The celebrated list of Augustine's questions and Gregory's answers known as the *Libellus responsionum* does not survive in the Register of the pope's letters but is now generally accepted as a genuine document, even though Bede made use of a flawed text; see Paul Meyvaert, 'Bede's text of the *Libellus Responsionum* of Gregory the Great', in Peter Clemoes and Kathleen Hughes (eds.), *England Before the Conquest* (Cambridge: Cambridge University Press, 1971), pp. 15–33; Wallace-Hadrill, *Commentary*, pp. 37–8.

[128] That Augustine and his companions were already following some sort of rule seems probable (Wallace-Hadrill, *Commentary*, p. 76); that this was the *RSB* is, as we have already seen, highly unlikely. Margaret Deanesly returned to the question of the rule of life followed by St Augustine in a lengthy appendix on the Rule of the Master and the Rule of St Benedict at the end of her *Augustine of Canterbury* (London: Nelson, 1964), pp. 134–50. She argued (p. 149) that although neither Christ Church nor the monastery of Sts Peter and Paul at Canterbury could have been Benedictine houses and must have followed mixed rules, the *RSB* must have been among the rules studied as part of Augustine's Roman training and thus have represented a significant influence on his own thought.

[129] *HE* I. 27 (pp. 80–1), quoting Acts 4: 32: 'And the multitude of believers had but one heart and one soul. Neither did any one say that aught of the things which he possessed was his own: but all things were common unto them.' See Leyser, *Authority*, p. 152.

[130] *RSB*, ch. 33. 6 (230–1). Compare also Cassian, *Institutes*, 2, 5, (ed. Guy, *SC* 109, 64–5); Caesarius of Arles, *Regula ad uirgines*, ch. 20 (pp. 194–5). But compare also Columbanus, *Regula monachorum*, ch. 4 (ed. Walker, p. 126), which announces the ideal of monastic poverty without reference to the Jerusalem community.

study of Gregory, this pope was less interested than many earlier monastic legislators in the idea of creating the monastery as a separate space whose inmates would set new examples of social organisation to the laity who dwelt outside. For Gregory, the imperative (an urgent one, since he believed that the Last Days were imminent) was to articulate an authoritative model by which the whole church community might co-exist with each other and with the laity.[131] In the pressing conditions of the late sixth century, the spiritual elitism of the true ascetic could no longer be encouraged; the Bible not the convent was the route to spiritual perfection. Scripture would bring spiritual consolation to those able to read it for themselves (and a necessary peaceful rest for those labouring in the heat of the world).[132] More importantly, it could also provide succour for all the faithful according to their need, through the work of teachers and preachers.[133] Gregory's vision, in Leyser's compelling analysis, lay not in his perpetuation of an earlier separation between the faithful within the walls of the cloister and the believers outside, nor the Augustinian three-fold division between the married, the continent and the church's rulers, but in a more fundamental dichotomy between those who preach and those who hear. Augustine of Canterbury's mission was as a preacher, he was to take the word to the heathen in Britain and, once settled there, to establish communities whose function was to teach the faithful and so bring them closer to heaven. The life of such congregations was to be organised under ecclesiastical rule and characterised by morality, psalmody and righteous living.[134] In this context, Gregory's advice to Augustine and indeed his choice of brothers from his own monastery as missionaries seems less contradictory than it has done to some commentators. Although Gregory had written about the incompatibility of the monastic and the priestly life, the imminence of the approach of the End rendered institutional and ascetic competitiveness redundant.[135]

---

[131] Leyser, *Authority*, pp. 155–9. See also Robert Markus, 'Living within sight of the end', in Chris Humphrey and W. S. Ormrod (eds.), *Time in the Medieval World* (York: York Medieval Press, 2001), pp. 23–34, at pp. 31–4.

[132] Gregory pictured himself withdrawing into the shade of sacred text, where he might pick the green shoots of ideas while reading and interpret them meditatively: *Homilies on Ezekiel*, I. 5. 1, quoted by Leyser, *Authority*, p. 177.

[133] *Ibid.*, pp. 176–8, quoting and commenting on Gregory's description of Scripture in the preface to his *Moralia on Job*: 'Scripture is as it were a kind of river, if I may so liken it, which is both shallow and deep, wherein the lamb may find a footing and the elephant float at large.'

[134] *HE* I. 27 (pp. 80–1); for further discussion of Gregory's missionary strategy see also Robert Markus, 'Gregory the Great and a papal missionary strategy', *Studies in Church History* 6 (1970), 29–38, and his 'Augustine and Gregory the Great', in Richard Gameson (ed.), *St Augustine and the Conversion of England* (Stroud: Sutton, 1999), pp. 41–9.

[135] Leyser, *Authority*, pp. 158–9. Gregory's most outspoken statement on priests and monks was made in a letter to John of Ravenna: *Epistola* V.1, ed. Dag Norberg, *S. Gregorii Magni registrum epistularum*,

For understanding the structures of the early English church, it is the reception and interpretation of Gregory's advice to Augustine that should most concern us. Whether Gregory's recommendations were followed precisely it is difficult to determine, although, as Brooks has suggested, the preservation of the *Libellus responsionum* at Canterbury implies some continuing interest in the counsel the text could offer after Augustine's own time. The creation of a second religious community at Canterbury, the minster of Sts Peter and Paul built outside the walls of the city, might have offered a convenient resolution to the problem of housing together religious not all of whom had obligations to the lay population.[136] In that second establishment it would have been unnecessary to qualify the aspiration to corporate poverty for there, unlike Christ Church, no provision was needed to enable married clergy in minor orders to retain their own property and receive separate stipends.[137] If Bede had, as Wallace-Hadrill suggested, intended his detailed account of the formation of the Canterbury community to function in some sense as a practical guide for the churches of his own day as well as an historical statement of conditions that pertained in the first Christian century, it is important to be clear about Bede's own ideas here.[138] Twice Bede made direct comparison between the way of life followed by the first community at Canterbury and that adopted by Aidan's congregation at Lindisfarne. In his prose Life of St Cuthbert he explained why it was that the island minster was at the same time the seat of a bishop and the home of an abbot and monks: for Aidan, the first bishop, was a monk and lived according to monastic rule with his followers, adopting a mode of life of which we know, from Gregory's advice to Augustine, the pope greatly approved.[139] In his *Ecclesiastical History*, Bede recast the same passage more succinctly to explain again that at Lindisfarne there was a bishop living with his clergy and an abbot with his monks, the monks nonetheless belonging to the bishop's household, for this was the arrangement Aidan had adopted

---

CCSL 140A (Turnhout: Brepols, 1982), p. 266. Gregory's views on monasticism were discussed by F. H. Dudden, *Gregory the Great: His Place in History and Thought*, (2 vols., London: Longmans and Co., 1905), II, 189–94, and by Jeffrey Richards, *Consul of God: The Life and Times of Gregory the Great* (London: Routledge and Kegan Paul, 1980), pp. 251–8.

[136] *HE* I. 33. J. Armitage Robinson suggested persuasively that the second *monasterium* might have been established for just this purpose: 'The early community', p. 232. For the suggestion that the arrangement of the site was modelled rather on the arrangement of cathedrals and monasteries in Rome, see Brooks, *The Early History*, p. 89; and Ian Wood, 'The mission of Augustine of Canterbury to the English', *Speculum* 69 (1994), 1–17, at p. 16.

[137] *HE* I. 27, §1 (pp. 78–81); Brooks, *The Early History*, pp. 155–9.

[138] Wallace-Hadrill, *Commentary*, p. 38.

[139] Bede, *VSCuth.* ch. 16 (pp. 208–9). Robinson, 'The community at Christ Church, Canterbury', pp. 232–3.

in the same way as had Augustine previously in Kent, on Pope Gregory's advice.[140]

Outwardly, Bede appears to have suggested that a single model of life, commended by the apostle to the English, should be applied to episcopal and monastic congregations alike, indeed that groups of professed religious who had not ordained and men of clerical rank could (as the Lindisfarne example showed most clearly) live together in harmony. This need not imply, however, that he recognised no distinction between the functions performed by abbots and their congregations of brothers and by bishops and cathedral clergy. Bede's enthusiastic advocacy of the example presented by the lives of monastic bishops such as Aidan, Cuthbert, John of Hexham and Theodore of Canterbury, and his stress on the merits of their continued scholarly, contemplative and ascetic activities, is articulated within a clear understanding of the primacy of their episcopal role as preachers of the Gospel.[141] For Bede it was most important to demonstrate that it was within an active, preaching context that these bishops maintained a contemplative, devotional and monastic life, living within the social framework of corporate poverty after the example of the first apostles.[142] His suggestion, made in the letter he wrote to Bishop Ecgberht of York in 734, that the sites of minsters in Northumbria be adapted into the dwelling places of bishops, here made perfect sense: a bishop's active, pastoral obligations were best fulfilled out of a contemplative context.[143] But the translation of minsters to cathedrals would not by definition turn the brothers living there into the bishop's clergy. Such men might also be preachers – indeed Bede offered many exemplary portraits of monastics who taught – but they were not necessarily ordained to the ranks of the clergy.[144] The primary

---

[140] *HE* IV. 27 (pp. 434–5).

[141] Simon Coates, 'The bishop as pastor and solitary: Bede and the spiritual authority of the monk-bishop', *JEH*, 47 (1996), 601–19, at pp. 617–19.

[142] Archbishop Theodore had argued that any member of a minster community ordained to clerical orders would, regardless of the burden of the new duties he acquired by virtue of his ordination, persist in his performance of his devotional obligations: 'any monk whom a congregation has chosen to be ordained to the rank of presbyter for them ought not to give up his former habit of life'; *Penitential*, II.vi.12 (ed. Finsterwalder, *Die Canones Theodori*, p. 321).

[143] Bede, *EpEcg*, ch. 10 (p. 413). Alan Thacker, 'Bede's ideal of reform', in Patrick Wormald *et al.* (eds.), *Ideal and Reality in Frankish and Anglo-Saxon Society* (Oxford: Basil Blackwell, 1985), pp. 130–53, at pp. 131–3.

[144] If, indeed, they heeded the advice of Benedict's Rule, there would be few ordained to the priesthood among their number. Benedict had some misgivings about ordained monks, preferring the majority of his community to remain in the lay state. Although he provided for abbots to ordain suitable candidates to the priesthood (*RSB*, ch. 62, pp. 276–7) and was willing to permit previously ordained priests to join a monastic congregation (*RSB*, ch. 60, pp. 272–5), in which he differed from the Rule of the Master, Benedict was careful to stress that ordination did not elevate a man's

difference between a monastic and an episcopal *familia* (beyond that of the status of the authoritative figure at the head of the congregation) lay in the proportion of each community in clerical orders. Simon Coates is right to argue that too much attention has been paid in the recent literature to the nature and function of the institutions that housed religious in the early English church, and insufficient consideration given to the status of the personnel who undertook pastoral care within the locality.[145] Distinctions between *monachi* and *clerici*, their life-style, organisation and social status were made explicitly in the prescriptive literature of the period.[146] Since, as Catherine Cubitt has observed, the conciliar literature was concerned predominantly with clerical duties and their proper execution, it did not necessarily explore questions of accommodation in any detail, although that all religious (monks, priests and lesser clergy alike) were expected to live in *monasteria* seems to have been taken for granted.[147] Priests, clerics and other religious may often have dwelt together, but their roles within and without their communities were not identical.

Questions about the provision of pastoral care for the lay population will be addressed in greater detail in a later chapter.[148] Our concern there will be, as elsewhere in this volume, with the activities of those who dwelt in minsters under the authority of abbots, not with the role and function of the members of episcopal communities. Both Cubitt and Coates have drawn attention to the need for a full-scale study of bishops in the English church, and have further stressed the necessity to differentiate between the liturgical and pastoral ministry of ordained clergy and the educational and charitable work frequently performed by enclosed men (and women).[149]

status within the community: all were to remain in the place that corresponded to the date of their entry to the monastery and to submit themselves to discipline. See Fry, *The Rule*, p. 96. The question of priests within minster communities is explored further in chapter 4.

[145] Simon Coates, 'The role of bishops in the early Anglo-Saxon church: a reassessment', *History* 81 (1996), 177–96, at p. 195.

[146] Council of Hertford, chs. 4–5 (*HE* IV. 5, pp. 350–1); Council of *Clofesho*, 747, ch. 6 (H&S III, 364); Dialogues of Ecgbert, §12 (H&S III, 408); Theodore, *Penitential*, I.i.2–3, II.ii and II.vi (ed. Finsterwalder, pp. 289, 313–15, 319–21). One of the most important contributions to this debate is Catherine Cubitt, 'Pastoral care and conciliar canons: the provisions of the 747 council of *Clofesho*', in John Blair and Richard Sharpe (eds.), *Pastoral Care before the Parish* (Leicester, London and New York: Leicester University Press, 1992), pp. 193–211, at pp. 195–7 and 205–6.

[147] Cubitt, 'Pastoral care', p. 205. I have explored this question elsewhere: 'Parochial ministry in early Anglo-Saxon England: the role of monastic communities', *Studies in Church History* 26 (1989), 43–54, and 'Anglo-Saxon minsters: a review of terminology', in Blair and Sharpe (eds.), *Pastoral Care before the Parish*, pp. 212–25. See also Cubitt, 'Pastoral care', p. 205.

[148] See chapter 7.

[149] Catherine Cubitt is currently working on a history of the Anglo-Saxon church to be published by Longmans; John Blair's forthcoming book on the same subject will deal also with the question of the spiritual care of the laity.

Where appropriate, comparison will be made with cathedral churches and their communities, but this will always be a secondary consideration since it is the nature of monasticism which is primarily under investigation.

With a strictly monastic vision in mind, Bede's account of the establishment of the first cathedral community at Canterbury and Archbishop Wulfred's attempt to reorganise that congregation in the early ninth century may seem only tangentially pertinent. This lengthy digression has, however, clarified some important issues against which the prescriptions in the conciliar literature about the organisation of congregations of *clerici* as well as *monachi* come into sharper focus. In addition to the question of the provision of pastoral services by priests and other clergy is the issue of the retention of personal property by clergy in minor orders and the related subject of their right to keep wives. Gregory, as we have seen, suggested that Augustine allow his minor clergy to marry, ensuring that stipends be made available for them while still taking care that they lived under ecclesiastical rule, attending to the chanting of psalms.[150] In his attempts to re-order the Christ Church community, Wulfred, too, made arrangements about the personal property held by some of his clerks. Although one need not argue from this that Wulfred was following the precepts laid down in Chrodegang's Rule, it is difficult to reconcile his acceptance of this right with a desire on his part to institute Benedict's monastic rule at Canterbury.[151] It seems more likely that Wulfred's reform was influenced at some level by late-eighth-century Frankish efforts to regularise the organisation of episcopal communities and that, as at the legatine synods in 786, Alcuin may have played a central role in communicating those ideas to Canterbury. Many aspects of the life of cathedral clergy in England before the tenth-century reform were indeed 'monastic'; professed religious and secular clergy could and did live side-by-side within one institution, sharing common eating and sleeping arrangements as well as the regular chanting of the monastic hours. Yet in terms of their relationships with the wider world there were subtle but significant distinctions separating the professed monastic from the ordained cleric. That some bishops and archbishops found it necessary to clarify the regulatory framework within which their clergy lived and worked should not surprise us. Only, however, once the Rule of Benedict had been prescribed as the sole system by which to organise English monastic communities (when it was imposed by the Council of Winchester held under King

[150] *HE* I. 27 (pp. 80–1).   [151] *Contra* Langefeld, 'The Rule of Chrodegang', pp. 35–6.

Edgar's supervision in the early 970s), would it prove possible to make definitive statements about the regulation of congregations of secular canons.

The monastic family

Although the prescriptive literature read and written by members of the early Anglo-Saxon church may shed a good deal of light on contemporary perceptions of what epitomised an ideal minster, we have already remarked on the potential gulf between those principles and their pursuit in practice. Monastic rules, while providing – like the rules that govern the collective behaviour of other social groups – a framework for controlling and ordering the unpredictability of human nature, sought to do more than to structure every aspect of the individual and collective lives of confessed religious. As we have seen, the rule was the defining characteristic of the monastic life, that which, perhaps above all, distinguished the religious from the secular life. A ninth-century Carolingian commentary on the Rule of St Benedict attributed (erroneously) to Paul the Deacon,[152] brings out the totality of the monastic experience with particular force, demonstrating that the monastic ideal did not consist in the practice of any one virtue, but rather in the more intensive service of God, in becoming a more perfect Christian than was possible for someone who lived in the world.[153] The degree of perfection achieved by a brother would depend on the motives with which his service was performed. A comparative secular analogy brings the point home: 'if [the monk] serves God from fear of punishment, lest he be excommunicated or beaten, he is a slave; if he serves God because of the profession which he has promised, he is, as it were, a vassal; if he serves God in order to receive the inheritance of the heavenly country, he is a mercenary; if he serves God only to possess His good pleasure and not to know His anger, he is a perfect son'.[154]

Recognising the gulf between the idealised statements found in monastic legislation and other advisory or admonitory texts on the one hand and the

---

[152] The commentary is generally agreed to post-date the organisational reforms of Louis the Pious and so to have been wrongly associated with Paul the Deacon, who died in 800; it is more plausibly to be connected with Hildemar (a monk of Corbie in the 820s) or his pupils. For a summary of the arguments and full references see Richard Yeo, *The Structure and Content of Monastic Profession: A Juridical Study, with Particular Regard to the Practice of the English Benedictine Congregation since the French Revolution*, Studia Anselmiana 83 (Rome: Pontificio Ateneo S. Anselmo, 1982), pp. 139–43.

[153] Schroll, *Benedictine Monasticism*, p. 190.

[154] *Pauli Warnefridi, diaconi casinensis, In sanctam regulam commentarium*, ch. 5 ([Monte Cassino]: Abbey of Monte Cassino, 1880), p. 124.

daily customs followed inside separate minsters on the other brings us little further forward in determining what an early English minster was really like. The last example given does, however, suggest one further paradigm worth exploring briefly before we turn to explore the narrative and other accounts of the running of early Anglo-Saxon minsters, that of the family.

It was commonplace in early medieval hagiography to depict an individual's decision to adopt a life of religion as marking a complete separation from the bonds of the family (parents, siblings, spouse and children) as well as the ties of material possession and earthly preferment.[155] After a brief military career, Guthlac decided at the age of twenty-four to devote himself to the service of God; according to his biographer he not only renounced the displays (*pompae*) of this world and disregarded the reverence due to his royal blood, but he also spurned his family (*parentes*).[156] Similarly the boy Sturm, offered to the missionary bishop Boniface by his spiritually ambitious parents along with other sons of the Norican nobility, joyfully set out on a journey with his patron 'leaving behind all his relations' (including his, now grieving, parents).[157] Renunciation of the bonds of kin did not, however, separate professed religious from all the consolations of family life: early English sources consistently described monastic communities in the language of kindred.[158] The Latin noun *familia* denoted both a secular and a religious household, the term referring in a secular context simply to the nuclear family (in religious terms presumably those who had taken vows), not to the wider group including retainers or servants; it could further be used of the nominal unit of peasant land-holding, the hide.[159] Within that overarching familial framework, relationships inside the minster were also defined in terms of kinship, but this was a kindred identified in terms of affinity to Christ and to the saints (particularly a founding patron) not of blood. In his homily for the feast day of Benedict Biscop, founder of his

---

[155] Julia M. H. Smith, 'The problem of female sanctity in Carolingian Europe, c. 750–920', *Past and Present* 146 (1995), 3–37, at p. 25.

[156] *VSG* ch. 19 (pp. 82–3).   [157] Eigil, *Vita S Sturmi*, ch. 2 (ed. Pertz, *MGH*, Scriptores II, 366).

[158] I have discussed this at greater length in 'The role of the minster in earlier Anglo-Saxon society', in Benjamin Thompson (ed.), *Monasteries and Society in Medieval England* (Stamford: Paul Watkins 1998), pp. 35–58, at pp. 39–42.

[159] *Dictionary of Medieval Latin from British Sources* (Oxford: Oxford University Press, 1975–), fasc. IV, *s.v.* *familia*. David Herlihy, *Medieval Households* (Cambridge, MA, and London: Harvard University Press, 1985), pp. 2–3. For a definition of a hide as *terra unius familiae* see Bede, *HE* IV, 23 (pp. 406–7). The Old English *hired* likewise referred to both secular and religious establishments and the nouns for hide, *hid* and *hiwisc*, carried the same dual meaning of family and land. That the familial reference is to the social unit created by the relationship between man and wife is shown by Thomas Charles-Edwards, 'Kingship, status and the origins of the hide', *Past and Present* 56 (1972), 3–33, at pp. 6–7.

own minster at Jarrow, Bede drew attention to the ways in which a religious family could be both inspiration and replacement for earthly relations:

The children which [Benedict] disdained to have in a fleshly way he deserved to receive hundredfold as spiritual children . . . Now we are his children, since as a pious provider he brought us into this monastic house. We are his children, since he has made us to be gathered spiritually into one family of holy profession, although in terms of the flesh we were brought forth of different parents. We are his children if by imitating him we hold to the path of his virtues, if we are not turned aside by sluggishness from the narrow path of the rule which he taught.[160]

For Bede, as Mayr-Harting has argued, 'kinship constituted not the reality, but the analogy by which monastic and priestly society should work'.[161] Cloistered men and women, brothers and sisters in Christ, may have seen themselves in the first instance as children of their father-abbot or mother-abbess ('all who knew Hild, the handmaiden of Christ and abbess, used to call her mother because of her outstanding devotion and grace').[162] Yet in joining a minster they became part of a social brotherhood, a *fraternitas*, of a singular kind, a fraternity (sorority) determined by the group's commitment to a particular life of prayer and collective devotion.[163] The same ninth-century commentary on the Rule of St Benedict already quoted laid great stress on the fraternal attachments which should bind the brothers of a Benedictine monastery together.

It is well that he [St Benedict] ordered them to be called *fratres* because they have been reborn in the same sacred font of Baptism, they have been sanctified by the same Spirit, they have pledged the same profession, they hope to attain to the same reward, and are all sons of Holy Mother Church. It is to be noted that this spiritual brotherhood is greater than that of the flesh.[164]

---

[160] Bede, *Homelia*, I. 13 (ed. Hurst, p. 93; trans. Martin and Hurst, *Homilies on the Gospels*, p. 131). See also Wormald, 'Bede and Benedict Biscop', p. 141.

[161] Mayr-Harting, *The Venerable Bede*, p. 16.

[162] *HE* IV. 23 (pp. 410–11). Compare Aldhelm's letter to Wilfrid's abbots reminding them of how their bishop had nurtured them, his foster-children, like a wet-nurse, rearing and teaching them in his paternal love: Aldhelm, *Ep.* 12 (ed. Ehwald, p. 501; trans. Lapidge and Herren, *Aldhelm*, p. 169). Foley has commented on Wilfrid's fatherly treatment of his monks: *Images of Sanctity in Eddius Stephanus' 'Life of Bishop Wilfrid', an Early English Saint's Life* (Lewiston, NY, Queenston, ON and Lampeter: Edwin Mellen Press, 1992), ch. 3.

[163] Oexle, 'Les moines d'occident', pp. 257–8.

[164] 'Paul the Deacon', *In sanctam regulam commentarium*, ch. 63 (p. 469); *Expositio regulae ab Hildemaro tradita*, ed. Rupert Mittermüller (Regensberg, NY, and Cincinnati, 1880), p. 579. These passages have been discussed by Sister Mary Alfred Schroll, *Benedictine Monasticism as reflected in the Warnefrid–Hildemar Commentaries on the Rule* (New York and London: Columbia University Press and P. S. King & Son, Ltd, 1941), p. 139, and Patricia A. Quinn, *Better than the Sons of Kings: Boys and Monks in the Early Middle Ages*, Studies in History and Culture 2 (New York: P. Lang, 1989), p. 97.

Beyond this immediate familial relationship, their spiritual profession made religious also relations in a much wider family: a holy kindred consisting of the whole community of those who had previously dwelt in their own minster or its dependencies.[165] That sacred family bond not only replaced the ties of blood family but theoretically severed all links and obligations to each member's own kin.[166] As we shall see, however, here as in so much else, the ideal and the reality diverged. Many monastic kindreds retained close links with the blood-families of the members in the world, ties that were sustained in some cases for generations beyond a minster's first foundation.[167] It is time to turn from the abstract to the concrete and look more closely at the process of monastic foundation in early Anglo-Saxon England, the reasons that inspired the devout to dedicate land to the service of God, and the means by which minster communities obtained sufficient earthly possessions to fulfil their spiritual ambitions.

---

[165] Catherine Cubitt has explored the ways in which religious communities forged their identity in commemoration of their early founders, 'Universal and local saints in Anglo-Saxon England', in Alan Thacker and Richard Sharpe (eds.), *Local Saints and Local Churches in the Early Medieval West* (Oxford: Oxford University Press, 2002), pp. 423–53, at pp. 437–8.

[166] For further discussion see my 'The role of the minster', pp. 41–2 and the examples given there.

[167] See below, chapters 3 and 4. Discussed also in relation to women's communities in *Veiled Women*, I, 44–8.

PART I

Within the walls

CHAPTER 3

The making of minsters

During the First Viking Age of the ninth century and its immediate after-math, before the monastic revolution of the 960s and 970s, various English-men enviously compared the material and devotional poverty of religious institutions in their own time with the substantial landed possessions, move-able wealth and spiritual strength of the early Anglo-Saxon church. Lament-ing the lack of learning among his contemporaries, King Alfred looked back regretfully to the time 'before everything was ravaged and burnt' when 'the churches throughout England stood filled with treasures and books'.[1] Some-what later, Æthelwold (abbot of Abingdon from 955 and bishop of Winch-ester 963–84) recalled the prosperity of English religious houses after the con-version and lamented the privations experienced by tenth-century abbeys. His biographer, Wulfstan of Winchester, stressed that before the saint under-took the minster's reform, the house at Abingdon was neglected and empty, its buildings worthless and supported by only forty hides, and that of Ely equally destitute, with all its possessions in the royal treasury.[2] Several expla-nations were proposed by different authors for this state of affairs. Æthel-wold, at least, attributed much of the blame for this material decay to the 'overlordship of secular persons, a thing which . . . led to utter loss and ruin . . . in past times'.[3] There may, however, be grounds for questioning not

---

[1] Alfred, prose preface to the Pastoral Care, ed. Henry Sweet, *King Alfred's West Saxon Version of Gregory's Pastoral Care*, 2 vols., EETS, o.s. 45 and 50 (London: N. Trübner, 1871-2), I, 4–5.

[2] Æthelwold, 'An account of King Edgar's establishment of minsters' (*C&S* I, 145); Wulfstan, *Vita Æthelwoldi*, ed. Michael Lapidge and Michael Winterbottom, *Wulfstan of Winchester, The Life of St Æthelwold* (Oxford: Clarendon Press, 1991) chs. 11, 23, pp. 18–21, 38–9.

[3] *Regularis concordia*, proem, ch. 10 (ed. Hallinger, p. 75).

only the accuracy of the picture of decay presented in the reforming literature, but also the widespread presumption that early Anglo-Saxon religious
houses were generally affluent.

The property and endowments of early English cathedrals and the larger
minsters, notably those still (or once more) active after the Norman Conquest, are better recorded in surviving sources than are the possessions of
the smaller minsters. Although more numerous, the latter may have with-
stood the vicissitudes of changing political circumstances less well than did
the great houses, because of their relative poverty. Most Anglo-Saxon charters (the primary witnesses to pre-Viking-Age land-ownership) are preserved
only in later copies, frequently in the post-Conquest cartularies of large religious houses; these relate for the most part to the estates of large and often
wealthy institutions. Fewer surviving documents provide evidence for the
endowments of the less prestigious establishments, particularly those which
were no longer active in the later Anglo-Saxon period. Narrative sources tend
also to concentrate on the histories of religious houses associated with kings
and prominent nobles and to reveal less about the smallest, poorest minsters.
Overwhelmingly, the sources give the impression of a steady proliferation
of minsters from the middle years of the seventh century until the start of
the Viking Age, each house initially endowed with some lands and wealth
and subsequently enriched by further gifts from kings and other lay people.
While making allowance for the rhetorical or hyperbolic nature of many of
the texts in which such views were expressed, it does seem that writers in
the ninth and tenth centuries had a similar impression of the substantial
material prosperity of the early Anglo-Saxon church to that apparently given
by the earlier materials.[4] It may be, however, that the predominantly ecclesiastical nature of much of the evidence for early Anglo-Saxon history has
tended to exaggerate the economic status of the church in society and to
present a misleading impression of the proportion of the material wealth of
Christian Anglo-Saxons that was devoted to the support of religion. Before
the full extent of the church's wealth and its economic status within contemporary society can be assessed, some account should be given of why the
English chose to invest lands and wealth in the new religion following their
conversion to Christianity.[5]

[4] Æthelwold seems likely to have derived his understanding of the history of the early English church
from an, albeit selective, reading of Bede: Antonia Gransden, 'Traditionalism and continuity during
the last century of Anglo-Saxon monasticism', *JEH* 40 (1989), 159–207, at pp. 165–9. Others may have
read the early sources in the same way.

[5] A general survey of the spread of monasticism in England may be found in Henry Mayr-Harting, *The
Coming of Christianity to Anglo-Saxon England* (London: Batsford, 1972; 3rd edn, 1991); for the growth

The foundation of minsters

The establishment of the first minsters in England was closely connected with the conversion of the Anglo-Saxons.[6] Mission stations, from which groups of religious would go out to preach to the local people, were intentionally positioned at or near centres of population, particularly royal vills, and these first communities deliberately established close and lasting contacts with their lay neighbours. Thus, as we saw in the last chapter, Augustine settled his group of missionary clergy in Kent in the city of Canterbury at King Æthelberht's invitation; similarly Paulinus created a see at York with the assistance of the Northumbrian king, Edwin, and built the first church in Lindsey in the city of Lincoln.[7] Roman settlements and sites with pre-existing fortifications often proved attractive to the founders of minsters. While some minsters lay in more isolated places – islands, promontories or peninsulas – these were often, even so, created to fulfil a missionary role.[8] When Wilfrid arrived in Sussex, he was given eighty-seven hides at Selsey in a place surrounded on all sides by the sea, except on the west where it could be approached by a very narrow piece of land; from this site the saint undertook the conversion of the South Saxons, apparently more successfully than had the first community of religious in the kingdom, that of Dícuill at Bosham, an equally remote place, surrounded by woods and the sea.[9]

Many early minsters as well as *sedes episcopales* were founded in or near places of secular administrative importance, often *villae regales*, and took responsibility for missionary endeavour in areas coterminous with those controlled by the vills.[10] The pre-existing political relationship between royal and ecclesiastical power within a kingdom was obviously often a significant factor in determining the location of such sites. Several seventh-century royal palace-complexes, such as Bamburgh and Yeavering, included churches,

---

of networks of minsters in particular areas see, for example, M. Franklin, 'Minsters and parishes: Northamptonshire studies' (unpubl. PhD dissertation, Cambridge University, 1982), and the essays in John Blair (ed.), *Minsters and Parish Churches: The Local Church in Transition 950–1200* (Oxford: Oxford University Committee for Archaeology, 1988). Less work has, however, been done on the complex motives that may have inspired kings, nobles and others to found new houses.

[6] Mayr-Harting, *The Coming of Christianity*, pp. 67–77 and 94–102.

[7] *HE* I. 25 and II. 14, 16 (pp. 74–5, 186–7, 192–3).   [8] Above, ch. 3.   [9] *HE* IV. 13 (pp. 372–5).

[10] Aidan used royal vills as the basis of his missionary work: *HE* III. 17 (pp. 262–3). See James Campbell, 'The church in Anglo-Saxon towns', in Derek Baker (ed.), *The Church in Town and Countryside*, Studies in Church History 16 (Oxford: Basil Blackwell, 1979), 119–35; reprinted in his *Essays in Anglo-Saxon History*, pp. 139–54, at p. 139; and Peter Sawyer, 'The royal *tun* in pre-Conquest England', in Patrick Wormald *et al.*, *Ideal and Reality in Frankish and Anglo-Saxon Society* (Oxford: Basil Blackwell, 1983), pp. 273–99, at pp. 277–8.

but many royal minsters were in the proximity of royal power-centres rather than absolutely contiguous with them.[11] Twinned with important secular settlements, these minsters were topographically somewhat distant from the lay habitations, set in their own lands and within a distinct enclosure. Lindisfarne for example was connected with but distant from Bamburgh, and Coldingham was linked with a nearby secular fortified site;[12] Gloucester was placed within a former Roman settlement, with the royal vill on open ground outside it.[13] It can be hard to tell which establishment, the secular or the ecclesiastical, pre-dated the other. In East Anglia it is difficult to state with any confidence where the episcopal sees lay, although we know that the first was established by the Christian king Sigeberht in the 630s and that from the 670s (in the time of Archbishop Theodore) there were two East Anglian bishops.[14]

While the creation of mission-stations (especially those attached to episcopal sees), of royal family minsters and to a lesser extent of so-called 'pseudo-minsters' is relatively well catalogued and has been discussed extensively in the secondary literature, rather less is known about why other monastic foundations were created in the seventh and eighth centuries, especially those for which no foundation charters survive and whose creation was attributable to persons of lesser birth. Kings and nobles who chose to involve themselves in the creation of new religious communities, or the endowment of existing houses, were seemingly driven to do so by a range of factors, not all of them religious. Yet contemporary authors had little to say about the motives which persuaded particular individuals to patronize

[11] Brian Hope-Taylor, *Yeavering: An Anglo-British Centre of Early Northumbria* (London: HMSO, 1977), pp. 70–85. Arnold Angenendt, 'The conversion of the Anglo-Saxons considered against the background of early medieval mission', *Settimane* 32 (1986), 747–92, at pp. 767–77; John Blair, 'Anglo-Saxon minsters: a topographical review', in John Blair and Richard Sharpe (eds.), *Pastoral Care before the Parish* (Leicester, London and New York: Leicester University Press, 1992), pp. 226–66, at p. 231.

[12] Rosemary Cramp, 'Anglo-Saxon settlement', in J. C. Chapman and H. C. Mytum (eds.), *Settlement in North Britain 1000 BC–AD 1000*, BAR, British series, 118 (Oxford: BAR, 1983), 263–97, at pp. 278–9; Blair, 'Anglo-Saxon minsters', p. 231.

[13] John Blair, 'Minster churches in the landscape', in Della Hooke (ed.), *Anglo-Saxon Settlements* (Oxford: Basil Blackwell, 1988), pp. 35–58, at pp. 41–4. For the ecclesiastical re-use of Roman structures see Blair, 'Anglo-Saxon minsters', pp. 235–46.

[14] The problems of identifying the location of the southern see at the *ciuitas* called *Dommoc* (sometimes identified with Dunwich or with Felixstowe in Suffolk, or even with Hoxne or Eye, both also in Suffolk) and of determining at which of the Elmhams the northern see lay have been explored – but not resolved – by James Campbell, 'The East Anglian sees before the Conquest', in Ian Atherton *et al.* (eds.), *Norwich Cathedral: Church, City and Diocese, 1096–1996* (London: Hambledon Press, 1996), pp. 3–21; reprinted in his *The Anglo-Saxon State* (London and New York: Hambledon and London, 2000), pp. 107–27. On figure 2 I have therefore elected to mark only the presumed boundary between the two East Anglian sees and not to attempt to decide where the *sedes episcopales* were to be found before the First Viking Age.

churches and alienate their property from their own kin, making it difficult to draw sweeping conclusions about the ways in which minsters were founded and endowed in the pre-Viking period. Precisely how the aristocracy were inspired to devote an apparently sizeable amount of their collective wealth to the church within a century of Augustine's arrival at Canterbury remains unclear. That they did so, however, is certain.[15]

One possible incentive for a lay noble to endow a new church or minster was the opportunity such an act presented for the ostentatious display of wealth. In the Late Antique world, the erection of a new building offered a means by which the urban governing classes could demonstrate their social standing; churches were built in part for this purpose by bishops and laymen. The Emperor Justinian legislated against laymen who built churches without providing them with sufficient endowments to support the maintenance of services within them, suggesting, Peter Brown has argued, that in the sixth century 'prestige continued to be measured in stone'.[16] In post-Roman Gaul, similar motives are visible; as Ian Wood has shown in relation to Burgundy *c*. 500, church building reflected secular aristocratic values, and the public display of wealth in the endowment and adornment of churches had a competitive aspect. A donor's status was enhanced not only among his or her peers, but also with the wider population, by his generosity in providing for a new ecclesiastical structure.[17] In Anglo-Saxon England, the precedent provided by kings, who generously endowed episcopal churches and royal minsters to mark their adoption of the new faith, came gradually to be imitated by the lay nobility who might, among other reasons, hope that such lavish gifts would ensure that their names would be remembered in perpetuity by these new communities. Building in stone (a technique unknown to the Anglo-Saxons before the conversion)[18] provided new media for the expression of wealth in monumental display. Surviving

---

[15] Generosity in endowment was as marked in houses for women as in those established for men only: Patrick Wormald, 'St Hilda, saint and scholar (614–80)', in Jane Mellanby (ed.), *The St Hilda's College Centenary Symposium: A Celebration of the Education of Women* (Oxford: St Hilda's College, 1993), pp. 93–103, at p. 95.

[16] Peter Brown, 'Art and society in late antiquity', in Kurt Weitzmann (ed.), *Age of Spirituality: A Symposium* (New York: Metropolitan Museum of Art, 1980), pp. 17–27, at p. 20.

[17] Ian Wood, 'The audience of architecture in post-Roman Gaul', in L. A. S. Butler and R. K. Morris (eds.), *The Anglo-Saxon Church: Papers on History, Architecture, and Archaeology in honour of Dr H. M. Taylor* (London: Council for British Archaeology, 1986), at pp. 74–9, pp. 76–7. Wood has noted that the former wives of several bishops contributed financially to the building and upkeep of churches, viewing this as an activity appropriate to their new status.

[18] Rosemary Cramp, 'Monkwearmouth and Jarrow in their continental context', in Catherine E. Karkov (ed.), *The Archaeology of Anglo-Saxon England: Basic Readings* (New York and London: Garland Publishing, 1999), pp. 137–53, at p. 140.

church-dedication inscriptions dating from the tenth and eleventh centuries suggest that at least by the later Anglo-Saxon period some patrons were sufficiently conscious of the prestige accruing to such donations to wish to advertise their generosity to the widest possible audience.[19] Changes in burial practice may also illustrate attitudes to church patronage; the correspondence in England in the mid-eighth century between the decline in burial with grave-goods in barrows and the rise in church building may, Philip Rahtz has argued, have been in part because resources that were formerly 'conspicuously wasted or economically sterilised in the ground' were being given to the church instead.[20] The church represented an alternative outlet for visible expenditure in ways, Donald Bullough suggested, 'that even more clearly than the traditional ones perpetuated the reputation of the giver and could make lasting provision for his kinfolk'.[21]

Devotional piety was paramount among the range of motives which may have stimulated laymen to found new minsters or to make donations to pre-existing houses, although self-interest may in some cases have been a further contributory factor. That the pious sentiments which had provoked the granting of lands or wealth to minsters were articulated on behalf of donors by charter scribes in formulaic statements of religious zeal, need not lead us to question the genuineness of the patrons' fervour.[22] Charter formulae recording that grants were made for the remedy (or the redemption) of the soul of the donor and the absolution of his sins were echoed in the contemporary literary sources and may indeed have reflected genuine

---

[19] Dedicatory inscriptions naming church patron(s) survive from several churches and have been catalogued by Elisabeth Okasha, *Handlist of Anglo-Saxon Non-Runic Inscriptions* (Cambridge: Cambridge University Press, 1971): Aldborough, ER Yorks. (no. 1), Deerhurst, Gloucs. (no. 28), Kirkdale, NR Yorks. (no. 64), St Mary-le-Wigford, Lincoln (no. 73), and St Mary Castlegate, York (no. 146). A fuller list of dedicatory inscriptions is given by John Higgitt, 'The dedication inscription at Jarrow and its context', *AJ* 59 (1979), 343–74, at pp. 367–70. For such self-aggrandisement to work, the patrons may have assumed that there would be sufficient literate people at the churches able to interpret their inscriptions or the sentiment behind them to illiterate visitors. Compare, however, Wood's remarks about inscriptions on church vessels and ecclesiastical furnishings that can never have been visible to the wider congregation: Wood, 'The audience', p. 77.

[20] Philip Rahtz, 'Artefacts of Christian death', in S. C. Humphries and H. King (eds.), *Mortality and Immortality: The Anthropology and Archaeology of Death* (London: Academic Press, 1981), pp. 117–36, at p. 118.

[21] Donald Bullough, 'Burial, community and belief in the early medieval West', in Patrick Wormald *et al.* (eds.), *Ideal and Reality in Frankish and Anglo-Saxon Society* (Oxford: Basil Blackwell, 1983), pp. 177–201, at p. 196.

[22] For example S 7, a charter recording a grant made to St Augustine's, Canterbury, by Hlothhere, king of Kent, 'for the remedy of my soul and the absolution of my sins' ('pro remedio anime mee et absolucione peccatorum meorum'); or S 102, granted to Worcester by King Æthelbald of Mercia, 'for the redemption of my soul' ('pro redemptione animæ meæ'). See Richard Abels, *Lordship and Military Obligation in Anglo-Saxon England* (Berkeley and Los Angeles, CA: University of California Press, 1988), pp. 47–9, and p. 224, n. 26.

piety.[23] King Alhfrith was said to have chosen, 'for the redemption of his soul', to give Abbot Eata land at Ripon to build a minster;[24] and King Wulfhere of Mercia 'for the benefit of his soul' gave to Wilfrid several estates in various places, on which Wilfrid forthwith founded minsters for the servants of God.[25]

Many minsters were created to satisfy a perceived local spiritual need or to fulfil the pious hopes of an individual or family, who hoped either to serve God themselves or to provide the means for others to pray for their salvation. So much has been written in the past about the iniquities of 'pseudominsters', established fraudulently in order to obtain the advantages and privileges pertaining to ecclesiastical land, that it is sometimes forgotten to what extent the Christian church was able to tap genuine sentiments of lay piety for its own material support.[26] An individual might elect to found a minster as a means of expressing a personal religious vocation, appropriating a portion of his own landed wealth for him to retire from the world (alone or with companions), and devote himself exclusively to prayer and the service of God. Before he became bishop of London, Eorcenwold founded for himself a minster at Chertsey, at the same time establishing another minster at Barking for his sister as abbess of a company of women devoted to God.[27] Actions of this kind, if regularised by the production of charters specifying that the land was henceforward to be permanently reserved for ecclesiastical use, would theoretically remove the estates in question from the control of the rest of a founder's kin, but in fact many such minsters retained close links with one family over several generations.[28] Wilfrid, for example, appointed his kinsman, Tatberht, as his successor over his minster at Ripon

[23] For a more cautious approach to the language of these documents, especially in a period when the charter started to become a convenient medium for purely secular conveyancing, see Patrick Sims-Williams, *Religion and Literature in Western England, 600–800* (Cambridge: Cambridge University Press, 1990), pp. 147–8.

[24] Bede, *VSCuth.* ch. 7 (pp. 174–5).   [25] *VSW* ch. 14 (pp. 30–1).

[26] Patrick Wormald, 'Bede, "Beowulf" and the conversion of the Anglo-Saxon aristocracy', in R. T. Farrell (ed.), *Bede and Anglo-Saxon England*, BAR, Brit. ser. 46 (Oxford: BAR, 1978), 32–95, at pp. 51–4.

[27] *HE* IV. 6 (pp. 354–7). See also the spurious charter S 1246.

[28] For discussion of early Anglo-Saxon proprietary minsters see Heinrich Böhmer, 'Das Eigenkirchentum in England', in Heinrich Böhmer *et al.* (eds), *Texte und Forschungen zur englischen Kulturgeschichte: Festgabe für Felix Liebermann zum 20. Juli 1921* (Halle: M. Niemeyer, 1921), pp. 301–53, at pp. 338–45; Charles Plummer, *Venerabilis Baedae opera historica*, 2 vols. (Oxford: Clarendon Press, 1896), II, 262–3; Eric John, 'The social and political problems of the early English church', in Joan Thirsk (ed.), *Land, Church, and People* (Reading: British Agricultural History Society, 1970), pp. 39–63, at p. 61. This situation was not unique to English conditions; compare, for example, Iona, where most of Columba's successors until 704 were members of his family, the Cenél Conaill: A. O. Anderson and M. O. Anderson, *Adomnán's Life of Columba* (revised edn, Oxford: Clarendon Press, 1991), p. xxxviii; Máire Herbert, *Iona, Kells, and Derry: The History and Hagiography of the Monastic Familia of Columba* (Oxford: Clarendon Press, 1988), pp. 36–46.

and twice in the succession of abbots at the cell of Lindisfarne described in
Æthelwulf's poem *De abbatibus*, brother succeeded brother.[29] Noble women
in early Anglo-Saxon England found the communal religious life equally
appealing: both the unmarried and the widowed succeeded in obtaining
the landed wealth necessary to establish minsters, although the relationship between these communities and the families of their first founders
was often complex. Withington minster in Gloucestershire was bequeathed
by its first abbess, Dunne, to her grand-daughter Hrothwaru, but the latter
had difficulty in gaining possession of the house from her mother who had
had charge of it during Hrothwaru's minority.[30]

Rather than founding a minster for his or her own use, a prospective
lay benefactor might have been persuaded to relinquish some part of their
landed property to enable another person, not necessarily a relative, to pursue a religious career. Since the grantor would expect to benefit from the
prayers of the community established by means of his or her munificence,
such donations may reflect as much the religious zeal of the benefactor as of
those persons who actually served God on the lands in question. Nothhelm
(or Nunna), king of the South Saxons, made a grant of a total of thirty-eight
hides of land at different places in Sussex to his sister, Nothgyth, to found
a minster and build a church to be 'devoted to the divine praises and hon-
ouring of the saints', for the relief of his soul. He declared that he knew
'that whatever I devote from my own possessions to the members of Christ
will benefit me in the future'.[31] In about 700, the East Saxon king Swæfred
elected for the benefit of his own soul to alienate some land to be used for
religious purposes, with less concern as to who precisely would serve God on
the donated estates.[32] He gave thirty hides at Nazeing in Essex to a certain

[29] *VSW* ch. 63 (pp. 136–9); Æthelwulf, *De abbatibus*, chs. 13 and 15 (pp. 32–4 and 38–9). Richard Fletcher, *The Conversion of Europe: from Paganism to Christianity 371–1386 AD* (London: HarperCollins, 1997), pp. 181–2.

[30] S 1429; S 1255; discussed by Sims-Williams, *Religion and Literature*, pp. 130–4. For a full discussion of female enthusiasm for the conventual forms of the religious life in the pre-Viking Age see my *Veiled Women*, I, ch. 2.

[31] S 45. Compare also S 44, a composite document in the Selsey archive which includes an account of a grant made by the same king of land at Peppering to a certain Beorhtfrith, *famulus Dei*, to found a minster made apparently 'so that day and night in that place the prayers said for me may rise to God' ('ut in eo loco die noctuque ad Deum proueiant [for *prouehant*] oraciones orancium pro me').

[32] S 65a. This is one of the recently discovered Ilford Hospital charters, Ilford Hospital MS 1/6. 15v; the text is printed by Kenneth Bascombe, 'Two charters of King Suebred of Essex', in Kenneth Neale (ed.), *An Essex Tribute: Essays presented to Fredrick G. Emmison* (London: Leopard's Head, 1987), pp. 85–96, at p. 86. I am grateful to Susan Kelly for drawing my attention to this document. Swæfred was son of King Sæbbi of the East Saxons, and ruled jointly in Essex with his brother Sigeheard from *c.* 694. The date of neither brother's death is known; the next king of Essex, Offa, abdicated in 709: *HBC*, p. 10.

Ffymme for the beneficiary either to share in building a minster (*domus dei*) there, or to hand the land over to someone else who would use it for the same purpose.[33]

Parents may have sought to satisfy their own pious aspirations vicariously through their children, who could by their prayers provide for the future spiritual health of the entire family. King Alfred established the minster at Shaftesbury as a residence suitable for nuns with his own daughter Æthelgifu, a virgin consecrated to God, as its first abbess.[34] By this means the king provided for the future spiritual benefit of the West Saxon royal family just as he had protected their present earthly interests by marrying his eldest daughter Æthelflæd to Æthelred, the Mercian ealdorman, and as he was later to do in the marriage of his youngest, Ælfthryth, to Baldwin of Flanders.[35] Oswiu dedicated his baby daughter to God after his victory at the battle of *Winwæd* in 655, consigning the infant Ælfflæd to Hild's minster at Hartlepool; in adulthood, Ælfflæd was to play an important role in the fostering of her family's cult at the minster at Whitby.[36] Karl Leyser suggested that other, rather less spiritually respectable, motives may also have played a part in the creation of houses for women, arguing that in Frankia and Old Saxony as well as in Anglo-Saxon England such institutions may have been founded by members of the nobility in order to dispose of their unmarried daughters.[37] By this means, women would leave the world in part for their

---

[33] Swæfred subsequently added a further ten hides at *Ettunende obre* to the original grant, to be used for the same purpose: S65b; Bascombe, 'Two charters', p. 86. Both charters survive only in sixteenth-century copies and the name *Ffymme* is almost certainly corrupt; although the name could refer to either a man or a woman, Bascombe has assumed ('Two charters', pp. 89, 93–4) that *Ffymme* was female and that these are foundation charters of a nunnery, possibly dependent on Barking.

[34] Asser, Life of King Alfred, ch. 98 (ed. Stevenson, p. 85). The forged Shaftesbury foundation charter, S 357, maintained that Æthelgifu entered the minster because of ill-health. See further Simon Keynes, 'King Alfred the Great and Shaftesbury Abbey', in Laurence Keen (ed.), *Studies in the Early History of Shaftesbury Abbey* (Dorchester: Dorset County Council, 1998), pp. 17–72, at pp. 40–1.

[35] Asser, Life of King Alfred, ch. 75 (ed. Stevenson, pp. 57–8); Æthelweard, *Chronicon*, prologue (ed. Campbell, p. 2). King Æthelstan behaved similarly in marrying some of his numerous sisters into other royal families and placing the rest in the church: Reginald Lane Poole, 'The Alpine son-in-law of Edward the Elder', in Austin Lane Poole (ed.), *Studies in Chronology and History* (Oxford: Clarendon Press, 1934, reprinted 1969), pp. 115–22; Sheila Sharp, 'The West Saxon tradition of dynastic marriage with special reference to the family of Edward the Elder', in N. J. Higham and D. H. Hill (eds.), *Edward the Elder 899–924* (London and New York: Routledge, 2001), pp. 79–88.

[36] *HE* III. 24 (pp. 290–3). Peter Hunter Blair, 'Whitby as a centre of learning in the seventh century', in Michael Lapidge and Helmut Gneuss (eds.), *Learning and Literature in Anglo-Saxon England* (Cambridge: Cambridge University Press, 1985), pp. 3–32, at pp. 8–12.

[37] K. J. Leyser, *Rule and Conflict in an Early Medieval Society: Ottonian Saxony* (London: Edward Arnold, 1979), p. 64. Margaret Clunies Ross has drawn attention to the innovative nature within Germanic societies of this practice of grouping celibate women in communal isolation: 'Concubinage in Anglo-Saxon England', *Past and Present* 108 (1985), 3–34, at pp. 32–3. I have discussed the influence of demographic pressures on recruitment to nunneries in my *Veiled Women*, I, ch. 2.

own personal safety, but also for the wider benefit of the kin group, since nuns within the cloister were less likely to conceive further heirs to threaten their family's inheritance.

The maintenance or promotion of the cult of an individual or an entire family frequently inspired donations to monastic houses. A bequest of land or moveable property in a will could provide for the future benefit of an individual donor's soul; early in the ninth century Æthelric, son of Æthelmund, ealdorman of the Hwicce, left several estates to the minster at Deerhurst 'if it shall befall me that my body shall be buried there', but 'on condition that that community carries out their vows as they have promised me'.[38] Such grants were not made exclusively to the place of burial; Æthelric also made a grant to the church of Gloucester and left his other estates to revert to Worcester. The ninth-century ealdorman of Surrey, Alfred, similarly left instructions that one hundred swine should be given to both Christ Church and Chertsey for himself and his soul, ordering that the surplus was to be divided among the minsters of God's churches in Surrey and Kent, as long as they remained minsters.[39] Alternatively, new minsters could be created specifically to sustain the cults of particular people. Ecgbert, king of Kent, gave the land for the foundation of Minster-in-Thanet to Domne Eafe in compensation for the killing of her brothers Æthelred and Æthelberht, the sons of Eormenred. In the various forms of the Mildrith legend Ecgbert is represented as thus appeasing God by endowing Minster in payment of the princes' wergild.[40] Similarly, Queen Eanflæd requested that a minster be built at Gilling to atone for Oswiu's murder of Oswine; the church was given to a servant of God, Trumhere, so that prayer might continually be offered there for the eternal welfare of both kings.[41] Whitby maintained a close association with both the Bernician and Deiran royal families: not only through Oswiu's daughter Ælfflæd, but also her mother, Eanflæd, who ruled after Hild's death in 680.[42] Edwin (Eanflæd's father), Oswiu, Eanflæd and Ælfflæd were all buried there.[43] The closeness of the link between royalty and nunneries, and especially double houses, is particularly striking, and

[38] S 1187; Sims-Williams, Religion and Litearature, pp. 174–6.   [39] S 1508; trans. Whitelock, EHD, no. 97.

[40] D. R. Rollason, The Mildrith Legend: A Study in Early Medieval Hagiography in England (Leicester: Leicester University Press, 1982), pp. 49–51, 56.

[41] HE III. 14, 24 (pp. 256–7, 292–3); Molly Miller, 'The dates of Deira', Anglo-Saxon England 8 (1979), 35–61, at pp. 37–9.

[42] HE IV. 26 (pp. 428–31).

[43] HE III. 24. See Miller, 'The dates of Deira', p. 39; Hunter Blair, 'Whitby as a centre of learning in the seventh century', pp. 3–32, p. 14; Karl Heinrich Krüger, Königsgrabkirchen der Franken, Angelsachsen, und Langobarden (Munich: Wilhelm Fink Verlag, 1971), pp. 305–15.

such communities were frequently the guardians of the family's memory.[44] Other houses were established so that they might serve as burial places in the future, such as Sts. Peter and Paul (later St Augustine's), Canterbury, which was to serve as the mausoleum for the kings of Kent and bishops of Canterbury.[45] King Œthelwald wanted to establish a minster at Lastingham so that during his lifetime he might go there to pray and hear the Word, and that after his death he might be buried there, 'for he firmly believed that the daily prayers of those who served God there would greatly help him'.[46]

Some minsters were established specifically to meet the wider pastoral needs of the local population, particularly during the conversion period.[47] For example, when Cedd was made bishop of the East Saxons he 'established churches in various places and ordained priests and deacons to assist him in preaching the word of faith and in the administration of baptism, especially in the city called [Bradwell-on-Sea] and also in the place called Tilbury'.[48] The minster at Farnham in Surrey, a place which lies within a concentration of place-names referring to pagan religious practices, may have been founded in the 680s 'with a view to mopping up an obstate enclave of paganism'.[49] The donation by Osric, king of the Hwicce, of land at Bath to Abbess Berta to found a minster in 675 could also have been made to meet pastoral needs, since the gift purported to be part of a wider scheme for the creation of minsters for both men and women 'for the increase of the catholic and orthodox faith', after the reception of baptism by the Hwiccean people.[50] Archbishop Theodore emphasised the importance of providing continuity

[44] See further Dagmar Schneider, 'Anglo-Saxon women in the religious life: a study of the status and position of women in an early mediaeval society' (unpubl. PhD thesis, University of Cambridge, 1985), p. 34; Pauline Stafford, 'Sons and mothers: family politics in the early Middle Ages', in Derek Baker (ed.), *Medieval Women* (Oxford: Blackwell for the Ecclesiastical History Society, 1978), pp. 79–100, at p. 97; my *Veiled Women*, ch. 2 and most recently Barbara Yorke, *Nunneries and the Anglo-Saxon Royal Houses* (London and New York: Continuum, 2003), chs. 1–2.

[45] *HE* I. 33 (pp. 114–15); Krüger, *Königsgrabkirchen*, pp. 264–89.

[46] *HE* III. 23 (pp. 286–7); Krüger, *Königsgrabkirchen*, pp. 300–4.   [47] See further below, chapter 7.

[48] *HE* III. 22 (pp. 282–5). Mayr-Harting, *The Coming of Christianity*, pp. 100–2.

[49] Margaret Gelling, 'Further thoughts on pagan place-names', in Kenneth Cameron (ed.), *Place-name Evidence for the Anglo-Saxon Invasion and Scandinavian Settlements: Eight Studies* (Nottingham: English Place-Name Society, 1975), pp. 99–114, at pp. 104–5. Farnham's foundation charter, S 235, refers to two of these 'pagan' place-names: *Cusanweoh*, meaning 'the sanctuary of Cusa', and *Besingahearh*, 'the sanctuary of the Besings'. It is not, as John Blair noted, specifically stated that this minster should be at Farnham, but there was a well-established church there by 1086, with 'all the marks of an old minster': *Early Medieval Surrey: Landholding, Church and Settlement before 1300* (Stroud: Alan Sutton and Surrey Archaeological Society, 1991), p. 97.

[50] S 51. Patrick Sims-Williams, 'St Wilfrid and two charters dated AD 676 and 680', *JEH* 39 (1988), 163–83, at pp. 167–74, and *Religion and Literature*, pp. 56–7.

in the exercise of pastoral care in his penitential, where he stipulated that if the site of a minster were moved, 'a priest should be released for the ministry of the church in the former place'.[51] We shall look further at the foundation of minsters specifically to provide for the pastoral needs of the laity in chapter 7, when we explore the place of minsters in the early Anglo-Saxon landscape.

In addition to those who were inspired by personal piety or concern for the spiritual needs of the laity in their establishment of minsters there were, according to Bede at least, those who founded houses for fraudulent motives, attempting to acquire the privileges associated with ecclesiastical land for estates which were, in reality, still being used for secular purposes.[52] While Bede's censure may readily be understood, especially when such proprietary churches are viewed in light of the high standards which appear to have pertained at his own minster at Jarrow, the patronage of the nobility was clearly essential for the establishment of sufficient religious institutions in the early Christian period, and many of these family minsters became (if they had not always been) part of a parochial network.[53] Had the desire for personal gain initially been a more powerful motive driving the creation of such establishments than was the religious devotion of the individual founder, or his perception of the spiritual needs of the neighbouring populace, the creation of such family minsters nevertheless played a vital role in the spread of Christianity in the English countryside. However irregular such institutions may have appeared to be in comparison with more strictly regulated houses, their significance in the history of the English church should not be minimised. It seems less important to distinguish between worldly and pious motives than to recognize that a web of interrelated aspirations drove the founders of most early Anglo-Saxon minsters, although this fact may frequently have been deliberately obscured in contemporary sources. Authors of the lives of saints were perhaps particularly unwilling to draw attention to any motives other than those which conformed to their preconceptions of saintly behaviour. For example, Alcuin stated that Wilgils, father of Willibrord, founded his cell on a Northumbrian headland because

[51] Theodore, Penitential, II.vi.7 (ed. Finsterwalder, p. 320): 'Si quis uult monasterium suum in alium locum ponere . . . dimittat in priori loco presbiterum ad ministeria ecclesiae.'
[52] EpEcg, §11 (pp. 414–15). Discussed further below, pp. 128–30.
[53] Blair, 'Minster churches', pp. 39–40. See also Ulrich Stutz, 'The proprietary church as an element of mediaeval Germanic ecclesiastical law', in Geoffrey Barraclough (trans.), Mediaeval Germany 911–1250: Essays by German Historians, 2 vols. (Oxford: Basil Blackwell, 1938), II, 35–70; also for consideration of minsters outside a pastoral network, Sims-Williams, Religion and Literature, pp. 170–6.

of his 'zeal for the spiritual life', but the house remained in the possession of Wilgils's family until coming 'by lawful succession' to Alcuin.[54] As Patrick Wormald convincingly demonstrated, Christianity in Anglo-Saxon England was 'successfully assimilated by a warrior nobility which had no intention of abandoning its culture, or seriously changing its way of life, but which was willing to throw its traditions, customs, tastes and loyalties into the articulation of the new faith'.[55]

The endowment of minsters

All exponents of early medieval monasticism shared a desire to recreate in their own time the apostolic way of life practised by the first disciples and detailed in the early chapters of Acts. Making particular use of the verse 'neither did any one say that aught of the things which he possessed was his own: but all things were common unto them,' monastic rules stressed the virtues of individual poverty and the corporate ownership of all essential property.[56] At the same time they urged adherence to Christ's command, 'If thou wilt be perfect, go sell what thou hast and give to the poor and thou shalt have treasure in heaven. And come follow me.'[57] One of the paradoxes of early medieval monasticism lies in the substantial temporal wealth and landed possessions of many religious houses. These were accumulated originally on the grounds that an essential prerequisite for the foundation of any religious house was the permanent possession of an adequate landed endowment for the collective support of the community.[58] No religious

---

[54] Alcuin, *Vita S. Willibrordi*, ch. 1 (ed. Levison, p. 116).

[55] Patrick Wormald, 'Bede, "Beowulf" and the conversion of the Anglo-Saxon aristocracy', p. 57.

[56] Acts 4. 32. The only early rule with which I am familiar which does not use some portion of this verse when recommending the ideal of monastic poverty is that of Columbanus: *Regula monachorum*, ch. 4 (ed. Walker, p. 126). See Glenn Olsen, 'Bede as historian: the evidence from his observations on the life of the first Christian community at Jerusalem', *JEH* 33 (1982), 519–30; David Ganz, 'The ideology of sharing: apostolic community and ecclesiastical property in the early middle ages', in Wendy Davies and Paul Fouracre (eds.), *Property and Power in the Early Middle Ages* (Cambridge: Cambridge University Press, 1995), pp. 17–30.

[57] Matt. 19: 21. In one of his sermons, Bede explained that this injunction referred only to those who had taken monastic vows; other devout Christians might rightly retain their possessions and use them to give alms to the poor: Bede, *Homelia*, I. 13, lines 41–7 (ed. Hurst, p. 89). Quoted by Gerald Bonner, 'The Christian life in the thought of the Venerable Bede', *Durham University Journal*, 63 (1970), 39–55, at 45.

[58] It was the rejection of the substantial wealth and consequent temporal power of the old monasteries, especially those associated with Cluny, which in part inspired the growth of the new monastic orders and the upsurge of interest in the eremitic life in the eleventh and twelfth centuries: C. H. Lawrence, *Medieval Monasticism: Forms of Religious Life in Western Europe in the Middle Ages* (London: Longman, 1984), pp. 125–45; Henrietta Leyser, *Hermits and the New Monasticism: A Study of Religious Communities in Western Europe 1000–1150* (London: Macmillan, 1984), pp. 18–28. For a broad ranging

community could subsist without any property at all.[59] The ability of a new minster's first inmates to persuade individuals or groups to donate land for their cause was thus a critical factor in determining their ultimate success. If the expectation of receiving a heavenly reward for earthly generosity were indeed a sufficient incentive to persuade noble patrons to contribute to the costs of such enterprises,[60] donors would have been anxious to ensure that their names were gratefully – and prayerfully – remembered by their beneficiaries. For the recipients, the imperative was to safeguard their title to the newly acquired property against future disputes over ownership, especially disputes with the donor's heirs.

Ecclesiastical recipients of royal generosity probably developed the diploma as evidence of the nature of the estates and privileges they had received, as one mechanism for ensuring that donations of land to churches would remain permanent and inalienable. If this presumption is correct, one might expect to find such diplomas recorded from the earliest Christian period when the first such grants were made.[61] Bede's account of the establishment of the earliest religious houses in each kingdom would seem to support this view, since he stressed particularly the acquisition by cathedral communities and other minsters of permanent landed endowments. That there is, before the late seventh century, no documentary proof of such transactions need not cause us to doubt Bede's testimony that that such perpetual grants were made.[62] Since Bede considered that royal and noble wealth should properly be used to support the permanent endowment of the church, he was keen to draw attention to laymen who legitimately granted land into ecclesiastical ownership. Only kings could free estates from secular obligations and from the control of kin groups; their names are thus necessarily prominent in the historical record of early English monasticism.[63]

---

discussion of monastic vows of poverty and the sources of the material wealth of medieval monasteries see Ludo J. R. Milis, *Angelic Monks and Earthly Men: Monasticism and its Meaning to Medieval Society* (Woodbridge: Boydell Press, 1992), pp. 17–40.

[59] Abels, *Lordship*, pp. 43–8.   [60] *Ibid.*, pp. 47–8.

[61] Patrick Wormald, *Bede and the Conversion of England: The Charter Evidence*, Jarrow Lecture 1984 (Jarrow: [St Paul's Church], 1985), pp. 21–3; Eric John, *Land Tenure in Early England: A Discussion of Some Problems* (Leicester: Leicester University Press, 1964), pp. 10–11, 24–5; Abels, *Lordship*, pp. 45–7; Pierre Chaplais, 'The origin and authenticity of the royal Anglo-Saxon diploma', reprinted in Felicity Ranger (ed.), *Prisca munimenta* (London: University of London Press, 1973), pp. 28–42.

[62] Wormald, *Bede and the Conversion*, pp. 13–19.

[63] *Ibid.*, p. 19. Clare Stancliffe has explored the role of kings: 'Kings and conversion: some comparisons between the Roman mission to England and Patrick's to Ireland', *Frühmittelalterliche Studien* 14 (1980), 59–94, at pp. 70–7 and 89–94; see also Arnold Angenendt, 'The conversion of the Anglo-Saxons, considered against the background of early medieval mission', *Settimane* 32 (1986), 747–92, at pp. 747–66. Sims-Williams, *Religion and Literature*, p. 96.

One immediate consequence of a king's reception of missionaries into his kingdom and his acceptance of the Christian faith was the creation of a *sedes episcopalis*, a site where the proselytising bishop and his entourage might settle, and whence they could go out to carry the faith to the rest of the king's people. Bede rightly stressed the paramount role of royal families in the formation of many early sees and thus the central part they played in the institution of Christianity among the English. This, for example, was the pattern of the conversion of Kent, followed by the establishment of Christ Church, Canterbury. According to Bede, Augustine and his followers were provided by Æthelberht of Kent with a place in which to settle suitable to their rank, and with 'possessions of various kinds for their needs'.[64] Similarly, the conversion of the West Saxons led to the foundation of Dorchester, given jointly to the missionary bishop, Birinus, by the newly baptised king, Cynegils, and his godfather, Oswald of Northumbria.[65] On the acceptance of Christianity by the South Saxons their king, Æthelwealh, gave to Wilfrid 'eighty-seven hides of land [on which] to maintain his exiled followers' at Selsey, 'with all the stock on it, together with fields and men' for an episcopal see.[66] The Irish conversion of Northumbria took place in slightly different circumstances since King Oswald was already a Christian, but his first act on welcoming the missionary Aidan was to provide him with an episcopal see at Lindisfarne.[67] Houses other than cathedrals also received permanent landed grants from kings. After his victory over Penda in the battle of *Winwæd* of AD 655, Oswiu, in fulfilment of a vow, dedicated his daughter, Ælfflæd, to perpetual virginity, and gave 'twelve small estates on which, as they were freed from any concern about earthly military service, a site and means might be provided for the monks [*monachi*] to wage heavenly warfare and to pray with unceasing devotion'.[68] For the foundation of St

---

[64] *HE* I. 26 (pp. 74–5). Nicholas Brooks, *The Early History of the Church of Canterbury: Christ Church 597–1066* (Leicester: Leicester University Press, 1984), pp. 8–11.

[65] *HE* III. 7 (pp. 232–3); Barbara Yorke, *Wessex in the Early Middle Ages* (London and New York: Leicester University Press, 1995), pp. 65–6 and 171–2.

[66] *HE* IV. 13 (pp. 374–5). The spurious charter S 232 purports to record Selsey's foundation, being a grant from King Cædwalla of 87 hides of land at Selsey and in other places to Wilfrid 'for the support of the servants of Christ who lead the monastic life and for the construction of a minster'. See S. E. Kelly (ed.), *Charters of Selsey* (Oxford: Oxford University Press for the British Academy, 1998), no. 1.

[67] *HE* III. 3 (pp. 218–21). A cathedral minster was not, however, necessarily the first house to be founded in every kingdom; there were already minsters in western Mercia before the establishment of sees for the peoples of the Hwicce and Magonsætan between *c.* 675 and 680: Sims-Williams, *Religion and Literature*, pp. 87–91.

[68] *HE* III. 24 (pp. 292–3). John, *Land Tenure*, pp. 13–14; Abels, *Lordship*, p. 49.

Peter's minster at Wearmouth, King Ecgfrith gave Benedict Biscop an area comprising seventy hides from his personal property.[69]

In the foundation of the first sees, the role of the king, and possibly of other members of the royal family, was clearly central to the success of the new religion, but the faith could only expand and thrive within a kingdom once it had succeeded in inspiring the interest of the rest of the land-owning class. The progress of the creation of these episcopal houses may fairly readily be determined from Bede's *Historia ecclesiastica*, and can be supplemented for some places from early saints' lives. Establishing a chronology for the growth of religious houses not directly associated in Bede's narrative with the initial nominal conversion of a kingdom is rather more difficult, as is the task of calculating how many such houses there were by *c.* 700. Bishops tended to be the central figures in Bede's conversion narratives, and he was seemingly rather less interested in recounting the missionary endeavours of those who did not attain high ecclesiastical rank. Yet there may, more widely than has sometimes been recognised, have been other missionary endeavours as well as those largely successful enterprises described by Bede. Patrick Sims-Williams has suggested, for example, that the English peoples of the Hwicce and the Magonsætan may have been converted 'in an unobtrusive and ultimately unmemorable way by the Britons among them'.[70] Many of the allusions to minsters in the *Ecclesiastical History* relate to incidents within already established houses and provide no more than a *terminus ante quem* for their foundation. Even where diplomas survive recording the gift of land to religious foundations, it is not always clear when such houses were first set up. Charters, including documents which purported to establish a new minster on a given piece of land, may serve only to regularise the status and landed possessions of a pre-existing community.[71] Thus it is frequently unclear how or why these minsters were founded, or which individuals were initially responsible for ensuring that money and estates would be available for their support.

The first step towards the creation of a minster was, as has already been stressed, the acquisition of a portion of land suitable for the support of its members. While pursuit of the ascetic ideals of the renunciation of property and separation from the world might lead aspiring religious to favour the remotest and most inhospitable sites, practical considerations dictated that the land chosen should not only be of sufficient quantity to support the

[69] *HA* ch. 4 (ed. Plummer, p. 367).   [70] Sims-Williams, *Religion and Literature*, pp. 78–9.
[71] *Ibid.*, p. 92.

community, but also agriculturally suitable.[72] When Sturm was searching for a site for the community eventually established at Fulda, he commented to Boniface on the lie of the land, the fertility of the soil and the availability of running water.[73] Guthlac had only himself to consider when looking for somewhere to live as a hermit; the island in the middle of a marsh on which he ultimately settled was as yet uncultivated (*inculta*), but not apparently because it was uncultivable. Previous potential occupants had been deterred by the phantoms of demons (*fantasiae demonum*) that reputedly dwelt there.[74] While he was still living as a solitary in his small chapel dedicated to St Andrew, Willibrord's father, Wilgils, may have been able to support himself: perhaps it lay on land already in his possession. But once he had gathered a community around him and wanted to build a church there, he needed the small landed properties close to his headland which the king and the nobles of the Northumbrians gave to him in perpetual gift.[75] In this case, the pious gifts of the local nobility were being made to one already known for his choice of a religious life, just as Wilfrid *confessor* acquired ten hides at *Stanforda* from the Northumbrian king Alhfrith in *c.* 660, and Æthelbald of Mercia issued a charter granting land at Daylesford in Gloucestershire to a *seruus Dei* called Bægia.[76] Several laymen, however, received such grants before they had taken the habit and there is no need to presume that all these did so for the bogus reasons detailed in Bede's letter to Ecgberht.[77]

That few records survive of houses other than those established by kings and nobles may serve to create a distorted impression of the total range of monastic institutions created in the early period. Freemen of lesser birth may also have been setting up minsters from their own households, or within their own much more modest estates, without obtaining royal

---

[72] Rosalind Hill, 'Christianity and geography in early Northumbria', *Studies in Church History* 3 (1966), 126–39, at pp. 128 and 132; John Blair, 'Anglo-Saxon minsters: a topographical review', pp. 227–31.

[73] Egil, *Vita Sturmi*, chs. 4–5 (ed. Pertz, *MGH* Scriptores II, 367).

[74] *VSG* ch. 25 (pp. 88–9); here Felix was quoting directly from Bede's Life of Cuthbert, ch. 17 (pp. 214–15).

[75] Alcuin, *Vita S. Willibrordi*, ch. 1 (ed. Levison, p. 116). Although there are no surviving early Anglo-Saxon charters relating to Northumbria, this passage from Alcuin's Life of Willibrord apparently relates to the same process of creating a minster as is witnessed in a number of charters relating to lands in southern England from the 670s onwards.

[76] *VSW* ch. 8 (pp. 16–17). In describing this grant, Stephen seems to have been quoting from a charter-text; see my 'Reading Anglo-Saxon charters: memory, record or story?', in E. M. Tyler and Ross Balzaretti (eds.), *Narrative and History in the Early Medieval West* (Turnhout: Brepols, forthcoming). Æthelbald's grant of Daylesford is S 84, dated 718 for ?727. For discussion of the authenticity of this charter see Anton Scharer, *Die angelsächsische Königsurkunde im 7. und 8. Jahrhundert* (Vienna: Böhlau, 1982), pp. 164–6.

[77] *EpEcg*; Wormald, 'Bede, "Beowulf" and the conversion', pp. 53–4.

charters to do so. Temporary endowments, those tenable only for the life-time of the original donor, were, however, of less benefit to prospective minsters, whose founders would ideally have preferred the security of lands divorced from all secular claims, whether of king or family, in order to concentrate on the service of God. Ultimately, only the king might grant permanent title to landed estates, although some minsters did acquire such freedom via members of the nobility.[78] The earliest surviving charter by which a layman not of royal blood, in this case a thegn called Dunwald, alienated to a religious house land which he had received from a king with the right of free disposition dates only from AD 762, but there is no reason to doubt that minsters frequently received land from nobles in this way before that time.[79] A number of perfectly genuine minsters must have been founded in this fashion during the seventh and eighth centuries and even have retained close contacts with members of the founder's family, for all that Bede's letter to Bishop Ecgberht dwelt on the undesirable consequences of the lay exploitation of land designated for the service of God.[80] Pragma-tism clearly shaped episcopal attitudes to the control of minsters by pow-erful local kindreds rather more than did the idealism of the prescriptive literature.[81]

Wealth and monastic endowment were thus inextricably linked. Without substantial monetary resources, it was apparently impossible to establish a new minster; occasional references are even found to those whose insuffi-ciency of means thwarted their monastic ambitions. The anonymous Whitby Life of Gregory the Great described how the relics of King Edwin were trans-lated from Hatfield Chase to Whitby by a priest Trimma, who then lived for a time at the site of the first burial and was reported to have said that 'if he could have done so, he would have liked to build a minster there'.[82] Why this should have proved impossible is unknown, but lack of sufficient money may well have been a significant issue. In fact, the initial landed possessions of many foundations about which information does survive were often rel-atively modest. Æthelbald's grant of land to found a minster at Stour in Ismere in 736, for instance, was only of ten hides, while in the 670s Cenred gave just thirty hides at Fontmell in Dorset to Abbot Bectun.[83] Abbess Hild's first minster was established on only one hide of land on the north side of the river Wear, although she lived the monastic life there with a small band of companions for a year before she was appointed to Hartlepool in

---

[78] Wormald, *Bede and the Conversion*, p. 22.   [79] S 1182.
[80] Wormald, 'Bede, "Beowulf" and the conversion', pp. 53–4.
[81] Sims-Williams, *Religion and Literature*, p. 130.   [82] *LBG* ch. 19 (pp. 104–5).   [83] S 96 and S 1164.

Heiu's place.[84] Grandiose claims may be one sign of a diploma's doubtful authenticity.[85]

Charter-formulae used to describe a grant offer some insights into the nature of estates given for religious purposes. In 822 King Ceolwulf of Mercia gave five plough-lands at Milton in Otford in Kent to Archbishop Wulfred, 'with all the advantages duly belonging to it, with fields, woods, meadows, pastures, water, mills, fisheries, fowling grounds, hunting-grounds, and whatever is contained in it'.[86] Those already living and working on the land were granted to religious houses together with the estate. Even if the professed members of a house participated in some manual labour, they cannot have farmed the whole of their wider estates with their own hands, but rather organised their cultivation by the peasants and slaves who previously had worked them for a secular landlord.[87] Booked land, that given in perpetuity by means of a charter, was freed from the normal secular burdens of providing labour and food-rents to the king or ealdorman; any revenues and rents together with the profits of justice were thus available for the support of the minster.[88] The three common burdens of military service, building fortresses and constructing bridges were, however, still exacted from all lands, including those in the church's possession. These obligations were not specifically reserved in any charter before AD 749, but they were probably always due from all land.[89]

Grants of land for church endowment were not necessarily made unconditionally. There are various references in charters to land being given to minsters in exchange for monetary payments from the recipients. Archbishop Wulfred obtained an estate of five sulungs at Milton in Otford on

---

[84] *HE* IV. 23.

[85] As, for example, the purported foundation charter for Shaftesbury, mentioned above: S 357. See S. E. Kelly (ed.), *Charters of Shaftesbury Abbey* (Oxford: Oxford University Press for the British Academy, 1996), no. 7. The list of estates in this charter bears suspicious similarity to the statement of Shaftesbury's landholdings in Domesday Book, I, fo. 78vb. Doubt is similarly cast on S 70, Æthelred of Mercia's grant in 679 to his *ministri* Osric and Oswald, by its references to initial endowments of three hundred hides at Gloucester and Pershore, which would appear to allude to the triple hundreds of Gloucester and Pershore of the later Anglo-Saxon period: H. P. R. Finberg, *The Early Charters of the West Midlands* (Leicester: Leicester University Press, 1961), p. 163; Sims-Williams, *Religion and Literature*, p. 95; Scharer, *Die angelsächsische Königsurkunde*, pp. 146–8.

[86] S 186.

[87] The involvement of religious men and women in manual labour will be explored in chapter 5.

[88] Compare the explicit statements of exemption in S 177 and S 1217, and the references made to monastic freedom from secular obligation by Bede (*EpEcg* § 12, p. 415) and Boniface (*Ep.* 73; ed. Tangl, p. 152). Nicholas Brooks, 'The development of military obligations in eighth- and ninth-century England', in Peter Clemoes and Kathleen Hughes (eds.), *England before the Conquest* (Cambridge: Cambridge University Press, 1971), pp. 69–84, at p. 71; Abels, *Lordship*, p. 49.

[89] S 92. Brooks, 'The development', pp. 73–4. But see also Abels, *Lordship*, pp. 50–7, who has argued that the common burdens were newly imposed on booked land by the eighth-century Mercian kings.

payment to King Ceolwulf of *placabilis pecunia*, namely a gold ring containing 75 mancuses.[90] Similarly a certain Cuthswith (probably abbess of Inkberrow in Worcestershire) paid 600 *solidi* to Æthelheard and Æthelweard, sons of Oshere, king of the Hwicce, for five hides at Ingon;[91] and William of Malmesbury recorded that one of Glastonbury's abbots, Tyccea, had paid 100 gold *solidi* to King Sigeberht for two estates in the Polden Hills, although the charter recording this transaction no longer survives.[92] Although the individual members of minsters were supposed to have no personal property, some monastic households obviously held substantial sums in common if their heads were able to find the wherewithal to make such payments. Other grants were made in return for prayer for the donor from the community, or for the provision of certain liturgical services.[93] Early in the ninth century an ealdorman Oswulf and his wife Beornthryth gave an estate at Stanstead to Christ Church, Canterbury, in return for which the community undertook to perform certain religious offices including the saying of masses and singing of psalms for the donors' souls each year on their anniversaries.[94]

Not all the lands owned by religious houses were acquired by direct grant made in perpetuity to the minster or to one of its members. A minster at Bibury in Gloucestershire, for instance, seems to have been founded at least in part on lease-land. Wilfrid, bishop of the Hwicce 718–54, leased five hides of land at Ablington in Bibury beside the river Coln to the *comes* Leppa ('on account of the old friendship between us') and the latter's daughter, Beage, to revert after their lives to the see of Worcester.[95] The place Bibury was seemingly named after Leppa's daughter – *Beagan byrig* – and the leased land apparently formed part of the endowment of a separate minster. When the land did return to Worcester's possession, the right to the ancient dues of church-scot and soul-scot were reserved by Bibury church.[96] In the archives

---

[90] S 186; Brooks, *The Early History*, pp. 135–6.

[91] S 1177; Sims-Williams, *Religion and Literature*, pp. 191–2. Compare also S 70, the foundation charter for Gloucester, which states that the Hwiccean ruler, Osric, obtained the *ciuitas* of Gloucester from King Æthelred of Mercia, and paid him 30,000 unspecified coins for the right to establish a minster there and the right to bequeath it to his heirs, before he gave it to his sister for a minster. The surviving text of this charter is very corrupt, but it seems to be based on older materials; see Sims-Williams, *Religion and Literature*, pp. 35, 94; Finberg, *The Early Charters of the West Midlands*, pp. 158–61.

[92] *De antiquitate Glastonie ecclesie*, ch. 47 (ed. Scott, p. 104); S 1610.

[93] For example S 11, a grant of *c.* 690 from King Swæfheard of Kent to Æbba, abbess of Minster-in-Thanet, of land in Kent, made in order that those serving God there should pour out prayers for the king's life without failing. S. E. Kelly (ed.), *Charters of St Augustine's Abbey, Canterbury and Minster-in-Thanet* (Oxford: Oxford University Press for the British Academy, 1995), no. 41; see also Scharer, *Die angelsächsische Königsurkunde*, pp. 83–4, 92.

[94] S 1188.   [95] S 1254.

[96] S 206, 1279. Sims-Williams, *Religion and Literature*, pp. 152, 170 and 379.

of various larger churches, notably but not exclusively cathedrals, it is not uncommon to find copies of charters in favour of other beneficiaries, only some of which may subsequently have been passed on to the church; that fact need not of course have prevented the holder of the charter from laying claim to the estates concerned.[97] Other lands were legitimately acquired by cathedrals and minsters through reversionary grants, particular estates being earmarked in charters and wills for ultimate reversion to a named religious community although they might in the interim provide other beneficiaries, secular or ecclesiastical, with immediate enjoyment for up to three lives. A ninth-century West Saxon thegn, Dunn, left an estate near Rochester to his wife to enjoy for the rest of her life with the intention that it would ultimately revert to the church of St Andrew at Rochester, unless his children were to lease the land from St Andrew's at a fair rent.[98] Offa, king of Mercia 757–96, gave an estate at Evenlode in Gloucestershire to his thegn Ridda on condition that after the deaths of Ridda, his wife and daughter the land should pass to the minster at Bredon in Worcestershire. That house had been founded by Offa's grandfather Eanwulf, and Offa gave it other properties on condition that they remain within his kindred's control for ever.[99] Worcester cathedral substantially enhanced its own endowment by acquiring control of a number of smaller minsters within its diocese, including the minster at Bredon; the archive of the cathedral church preserves several eighth-century leases relating to small minster churches and other estates that were leased to various people, lay and ecclesiastical, with ultimate reversion to the cathedral. Abbess Æthelburh, daughter of *comes* Ælfred, for example, held minsters at Withington in Gloucestershire and Twyning and Fladbury in Worcestershire, each of which was destined for eventual episcopal ownership.[100] The advantages to both sides of such arrangements are obvious, yet ultimately these smaller minsters, precariously established

---

97 The archive of St Augustine's Canterbury includes some grants to other beneficiaries that appear to have been 'improved' in order to give the abbey a direct title to the land involved; Kelly, *Charters of St Augustine's*, pp. lxii–lxiii and cvii–cviii. Abingdon's archive, on the other hand, contained a number of title deeds for lands in which the abbey had no demonstrable interest: Stenton, *The Early History of the Abbey of Abingdon* (Reading: University College, 1913; reprinted Stamford: Paul Watkins, 1989), pp. 40–3; S. E. Kelly (ed.), *Charters of Abingdon Abbey*, 2 vols. (Oxford: Oxford University Press for the British Academy, 2000–1), I, cxxxi–cxl.

98 S 1514. Dunn had originally received this estate as a grant from King Æthelwulf in 855: S 315.

99 S 109; compare S 116. In fact, the church of Worcester successfully claimed ownership of Bredon at the synod of Brentford in 781 and the minster was among the cathedral's possessions in the 840s: S 1257. Bredon's history has been discussed by Sims-Williams, *Religion and Literature*, pp. 152–5 and 163.

100 S 1255 records Bishop Milred's grant of Withington to Æthelburg, on condition that 'after her death she return it again for the eternal redemption of [Milred's] soul to the church of [Worcester]' and that she 'also return the minster at Twyning, with all the goods that are there, after her day to

on leased lands, frequently fade from the historical record beyond the later eighth century, their estates being absorbed within the territorially coherent holdings of their richer and more powerful monastic and episcopal neighbours.

The physical character of early minster sites

Although the sites of many churches dating from the Anglo-Saxon period can be located, no early medieval domestic or industrial buildings erected for religious purposes remain standing, and relatively few monastic complexes established in England between c. 600 and c. 900 have been excavated.[101] Recent archaeological work has served to emphasise the difficulty of distinguishing on the ground between high-status secular and ecclesiastical sites, particularly when the building material used was wood, as at the excavated sites of Tynemouth and Hartlepool.[102] In England, as in Gaul and Ireland, monastic dwellings were not designed or constructed differently from those found in purely secular contexts. Even so, in all three societies, ecclesiastical sites often reveal a higher proportion of small buildings, placed more densely within what may have been planned complexes, frequently separated from their surroundings by man-made fences or ditches, or by natural topographical features.[103] Among recently excavated sites those

---

the church of Worcester, as was the injunction of her father, Alfred'. Discussed by Sims-Williams, *Religion and Literature*, pp. 37–8 and 157–8.

[101] A convenient summary of sites excavated before 1976 is found in Rosemary Cramp, 'Monastic sites' in David Wilson (ed.), *The Archaeology of Anglo-Saxon England* (Cambridge: Cambridge University Press, 1976), pp. 201–52. Richard Morris has provided a full survey of seventh-century churches in his *The Church in British Archaeology* (London: Council for British Archaeology, 1983), pp. 33–48 with a valuable table (III, pp. 35–8), recording the nature of the evidence for almost one hundred seventh-century churches. More recent surveys of the state of Anglo-Saxon archaeology are provided by Kelley M. Wickham-Crowley, 'Looking forward, looking back: excavating the field of Anglo-Saxon archaeology', in Catherine E. Karkov (ed.), *The Archaeology of Anglo-Saxon England: Basic Readings* (New York and London: Garland Publishing, 1999), pp. 1–23 and Martin O. Carver, 'Exploring, explaining, imagining: Anglo-Saxon archaeology 1998', *ibid.*, pp. 25–52.

[102] Cramp, 'Monastic sites', pp. 219–20, 222–3. Also Cramp, 'Monkwearmouth and Jarrow', pp. 138–9.

[103] For the layout of Gallic monastic sites see Edward James, 'Archaeology and the Merovingian monastery', in H. B. Clarke and Mary Brennan (eds.), *Columbanus and Merovingian Monasticism*, BAR, International series, 113 (Oxford: BAR, 1981), pp. 33–55; for Ireland see A. D. S. MacDonald, 'Aspects of the monastery and monastic life in Adomnan's Life of Columba', *Peritia* 3 (1984), 271–302, and Michael Herity, 'The buildings and layout of early Irish monasteries before the year 1000', *Monastic Studies* 14 (1983), 247–84. For parallels between Northumbria and Ireland see Rosemary Cramp, 'Northumbria and Ireland', in Paul E. Szarmach with the assistance of Virginia Darrow Oggins (eds.), *Sources of Anglo-Saxon Culture* (Kalamazoo, MI: Medieval Institute Publications, Western Michigan University, 1986), pp. 185–201, at pp. 192–9. The layout of English monastic sites is considered by R. J. Cramp and R. Daniels, 'New finds from the Anglo-Saxon monastery at Hartlepool, Cleveland', *Antiquity* 61 (1987), 424–32, at pp. 425–8; and Blair, 'Anglo-Saxon minsters', pp. 258–64.

at Brandon, Suffolk, and Flixborough, South Humberside, are of particular significance; although there is documentary evidence for the existence of a minster at neither site, at each place a case can be made for the presence of a monastic component in the middle Saxon period. At Brandon a church and attendant cemeteries have been excavated, and one of the buildings at Flixborough has burials within its walls, albeit lying underneath subsequent residential layers. Both sites offer some evidence for the use of writing.[104]

If contemporary literary material is used to supplement the archaeological record, it is possible to draw some general conclusions about the preferred locations for new minsters and about the layout of monastic buildings within their enclosures.

All minsters appear to have been in some manner enclosed, deliberately separated from the secular world outside, in order that their occupants might concentrate on their divine labours without undue interruption or distraction, but in reality the sites of many religious communities in Gaul, Ireland and North Britain as well as in England were prominent rather than remote.[105] Some houses were so positioned that the natural topography of the site isolated them from the lay population, while at the same time giving the minster some geographical conspicuousness.[106] Islands obviously provided the greatest seclusion, but those associated with monasticism in Anglo-Saxon England seem to have been occupied not by substantial communities on the model of Iona, but rather by solitary ascetics such as the hermit Hereberct who inhabited an island in Derwentwater, Guthlac, who chose to live in solitude on an island in the middle of a marsh at Crowland, or St Cuthbert who dwelt for a time on Farne.[107] The natural

[104] See fig. 3. See R. D. Carr *et al.*, 'The middle Saxon settlement at Staunch Meadow, Brandon', *Antiquity* 62 (1988), 371–7; Leslie Webster and Janet Backhouse (eds.), *The Making of England: Anglo-Saxon Art and Culture, AD 600–900* (London: British Museum Press, 1981), pp. 81–8 (Brandon), 95–101 (Flixborough); Chris Loveluck, 'A high-status Anglo-Saxon settlement at Flixborough, Lincolnshire', *Antiquity* 72 (1998), 146–61, at pp. 154–5.

[105] Charles Thomas, *The Early Christian Archaeology of North Britain* (London and New York: Oxford University Press for the University of Glasgow, 1971), pp. 27–32; Blair, 'Anglo-Saxon minsters', p. 227. The ideal of enclosure was, for example, expounded by St Benedict: *RSB* chs. 4, 78, and 66, 6–7 (pp. 186–7 and 288–9). Compare Columbanus, *Regula coenobialis*, ch. 8 (ed. Walker, p. 155), which punishes a monk who has 'gone outside the wall [*extra vallum*], that is outside the bounds of the monastery, without asking'. When in the tenth century Æthelwold reorganised the monastic buildings at Winchester, bringing the three communities into a single enclosure defined by walls and fences, his aim was to obtain seclusion for the religious men and women to serve God in tranquillity, *a ciuium tumultu remoti*: S 807; Martin Biddle, *Winchester in the Early Middle Ages: An Edition and Discussion of the Winton Domesday* (Oxford: Clarendon Press, 1976), p. 322.

[106] Morris, *Churches*, pp. 104–12.

[107] For Hereberct see anon., *VSCuth.* IV. 9 (pp. 124–5). For Guthlac's choice of Crowland see Felix, *VSG*, ch. 25 (pp. 88–9); although Orderic Vitalis asserted that a religious community had been

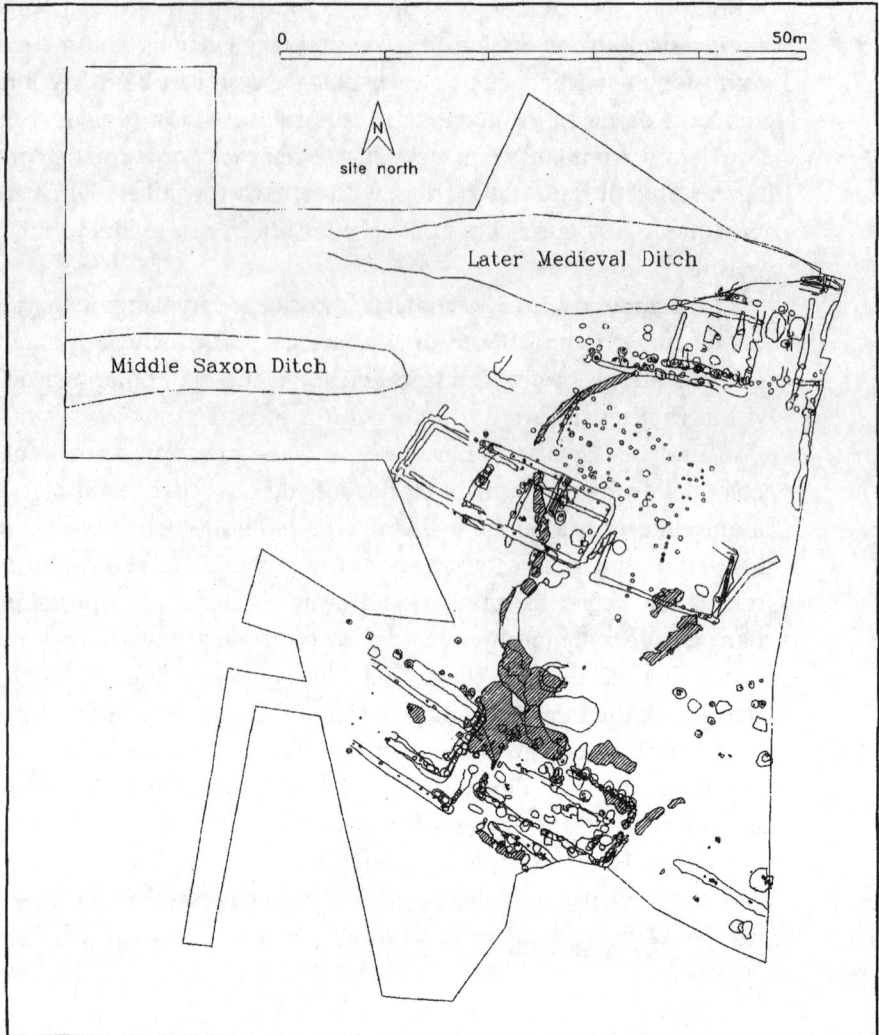

FIGURE 3: Plan of the excavations at Flixborough (after Loveluck, 'A high-status Anglo-Saxon settlement').

seclusion of the island was, however, insufficient for that saint, who constructed around his dwelling a circular enclosing wall 'higher than a man standing upright' and cut away further inside 'so that the pious inhabitant

established on this site after the hermit's death, there is no certain evidence of a minster there before the mid-tenth century: Colgrave, *Felix's Life of Saint Guthlac*, pp. 7–9. St Cuthbert's time on the island of Farne was described *VSCuth.* book III (pp. 94–107). Also *HE* IV. 27–9 (pp. 430–43).

could see nothing except the sky from his dwelling, thus restraining both the lust of the eyes and of the thoughts and lifting the whole bent of his mind to higher things'.[108] Places which were cut off from the mainland at high tide, such as Lindisfarne, were more popular locations for communal establishments;[109] Brandon in Suffolk, where the excavated settlement lies on a sand-ridge surrounded by peat, was similarly prone to isolation since it stands as an island in time of flood, and thus seems appropriate for monastic use.[110] Other sites such as Selsey in Sussex were virtual islands being almost totally surrounded by the sea, and inland islands, formed by loops of rivers or at their confluence, were frequently chosen by monastic founders.[111] Ely was similarly a virtual island, lying on high ground amid the fens.[112] Wareham minster lay between two rivers, the Frome and the Tarrant, and was according to Asser 'in a very secure position except on the west where it is joined to the mainland'; the site was further fortified in the ninth century as a defence against foreign incursions.[113] Headlands and promontories might similarly afford both natural seclusion and some element of defence; several Northumbrian minsters had coastal sites, such as Hartlepool or Wilgils's minster on the Humber estuary.[114] Women's houses lay in equally isolated spots, for example the Kentish minsters for women on the islands of Sheppey and Thanet, or the double house at Whitby which occupied a coastal site. For women, issues of safety must have been paramount in the selection of a suitable site. Bede's Life of Cuthbert offers a cautionary warning as to the vulnerability of such congregations, describing how a group of Northumbrian nuns fled from their minster in the face of a Pictish army and had to be given another place of refuge by the saint.[115]

Hill-top sites such as Aylesbury in Buckinghamshire, Hanbury in Worcestershire and Breedon-on-the-Hill in Leicestershire offered obvious attractions to potential religious founders.[116] Lastingham appealed to Cedd because

---

[108] Bede, *VSCuth.*, ch. 17 (pp. 216–17).

[109] Cuthbert's anonymous hagiographer referred to Lindisfarne as 'this island of ours', '*haec insula nostra*' (III. 1, pp. 94–5), but Holy Island was and is accessible from the mainland at low tide.

[110] Carr *et al.*, 'The middle Saxon settlement', p. 371.   [111] *HE* IV. 13 (pp. 414–5).

[112] *HE* IV. 19 (pp. 394–5): 'the district of Ely [*regio Elge*] is surrounded on all sides by waters and marshes'.

[113] Asser, *Life of King Alfred*, ch. 49 (ed. Stevenson, p. 46). See also *RCHM*, Dorset II, part 2, pp. 322–4.

[114] Hartlepool: *HE* IV. 23 (pp. 406–7); Cramp and Daniels, 'New Finds'; Wilgils' cell: Alcuin, *Vita S. Willibrordi*, ch. 1 (ed. Levison, p. 116). Morris (*Churches*, p. 110), has identified the headland on which Alcuin said this minster was built with Spurn Head, and argues that this headland may in this period have been temporarily partly detached from the mainland, and like Lindisfarne only approachable at low tide.

[115] Bede, *VSCuth.* ch. 30 (pp. 254–5).

[116] Thomas, *The Early Christian Archaeology*, p. 33; Blair, 'Minster churches', pp. 41–5, and 'Anglo-Saxon minsters', pp. 227–30; Morris, *Churches*, pp. 111–12.

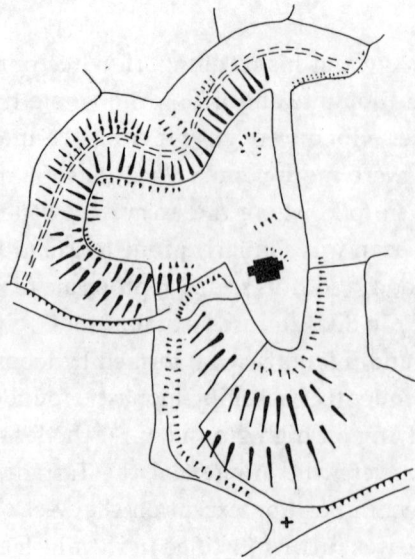

(a) HANBURY

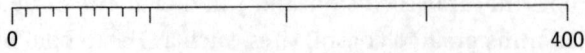

metres

0   400

(b) AYLESBURY

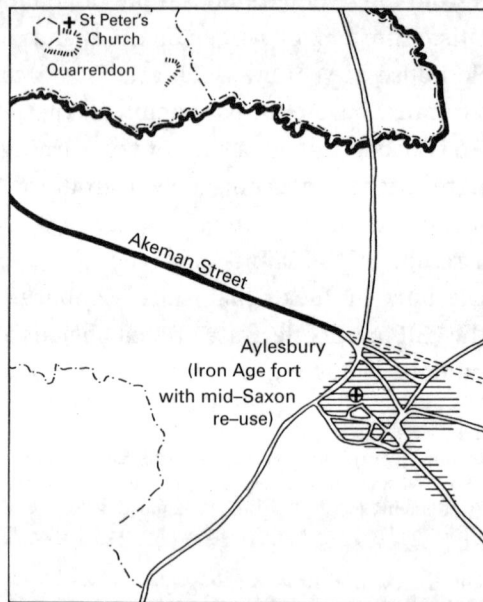

St Peter's
Church

Quarrendon

Akeman Street

Aylesbury
(Iron Age fort
with mid–Saxon
re–use)

⊕ Mother church   Roman road ≡ Medieval built-up area
⬡ Royal vill (inferred)   + Other church or chapel

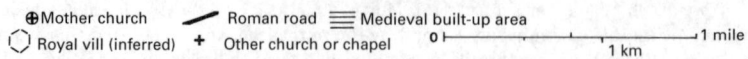

0   1 mile
                         1 km

FIGURE 4: Minsters situated at Iron Age hill-forts: (a) Hanbury (after Hooke, *Anglo-Saxon Landscapes of the West Midlands*, fig. 2.6 (iii)); (b) Aylesbury (after Blair, 'Minster churches in the landscape', fig. 2.1).

of its 'steep and remote hills which seemed better fitted for the haunts of robbers and the dens of wild beasts than for human habitation'; according to Bede he created a minster there in order that 'the fruit of good works might spring up where once beasts dwelt or where men lived after the manner of beasts'.[117] Similarly Ecgberht (the English holy man living in Ireland) told Eanmund, founder of Æthelwulf's minster, to choose a particular small hill, protected by thick thorn bushes and once a den of robbers, on top of which to build his church.[118] Man-made defences could afford equal protection: the minsters at Aylesbury, Hanbury and Breedon all lay within the ramparts of Iron Age hillforts,[119] while others such as Lincoln, Reculver in Kent, Bradwell-on-Sea in Essex, or *Cnobheresburg* (?Burgh Castle in Suffolk) were placed in Roman stone-walled forts.[120] Former Roman sites would provide a ready source of stone for building, and the prior existence of an enclosing wall which could serve as a *vallum monasterii* might have been a further attraction.[121]

Elsewhere, if none already existed, the community would erect some form of boundary to separate themselves physically as well as symbolically from the outside world; such enclosures were frequently curvilinear in form.[122]

---

[117] *HE* III. 23 (pp. 286–7).

[118] Æthelwulf, *De abbatibus*, ch. 6 (ed. Campbell, pp. 12–13). The site of Æthelwulf's minster has not certainly been identified; see Campbell, *Æthelwulf, De abbatibus*, pp. xxv–xxvi. Michael Lapidge has made a persuasive case for this apparent cell of Lindisfarne having been at Crayke, near York: 'Aediluulf and the School of York', in A. Lehner and W. Berschin (eds.), *Lateinische Kultur im VIII. Jahrhundert. Traube Gedenkschrift* (St Ottilien: EOS Verlag, 1990), pp. 161–78, at pp. 174–8.

[119] Blair, 'Anglo-Saxon minsters', pp. 233–4. See fig. 4.

[120] See fig. 5 Cramp, 'Monastic sites', p. 204; Blair, 'Anglo-Saxon minsters', pp. 237–40. Warwick Rodwell, 'Churches in the landscape: aspects of topography and planning', in Margaret Faull (ed.), *Studies in Late Anglo-Saxon Settlement* (Oxford: Oxford University Department for External Studies, 1984), pp. 1–23, at pp. 3–9. *Cnobheresburg* is traditionally equated with Burgh Castle, but the archaeological evidence for such an identification is at best equivocal: Stephen Johnson, *Burgh Castle: Excavations by Charles Green 1958–61*, East Anglian Archaeology, Report 20 (Dereham: Norfolk Archaeological Unit, 1983), pp. 119–21. David Parsons has looked more generally at the location of churches within former Roman forts: 'England and the Low Countries at the time of St Willibrord', in Elisabeth de Bièvre (ed.), *Utrecht: Britain and the Continent, Archaeology, Art and Architecture* ([London?]: British Archaeological Association, 1996), pp. 30–48, at pp. 35–7.

[121] Consider for example the seventh-century church at Escomb, County Durham, below and plate IV. It was built from Roman masonry, and excavations suggest that a curvilinear enclosure surrounded the church: M. Pocock and H. Wheeler, 'Excavations at Escomb church, County Durham, 1968', *Journal of the British Archaeological Association*, 3rd ser. 34 (1971), 11–29; John Blair, 'Escomb', in Michael Lapidge *et al.* (eds.), *The Blackwell Encyclopaedia of Anglo-Saxon England* (Oxford: Blackwell, 1999), p. 174.

[122] Thomas, *The Early Christian Archaeology*, pp. 40–3; Blair, 'Anglo-Saxon minsters', p. 229, fig. 10.2 and pp. 231–2. See fig. 6.

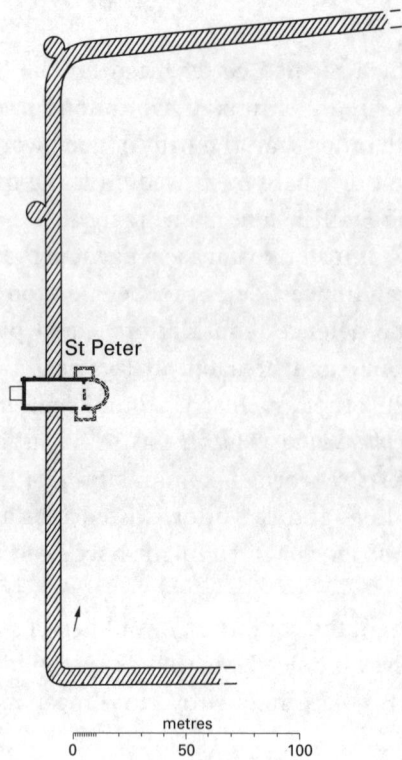

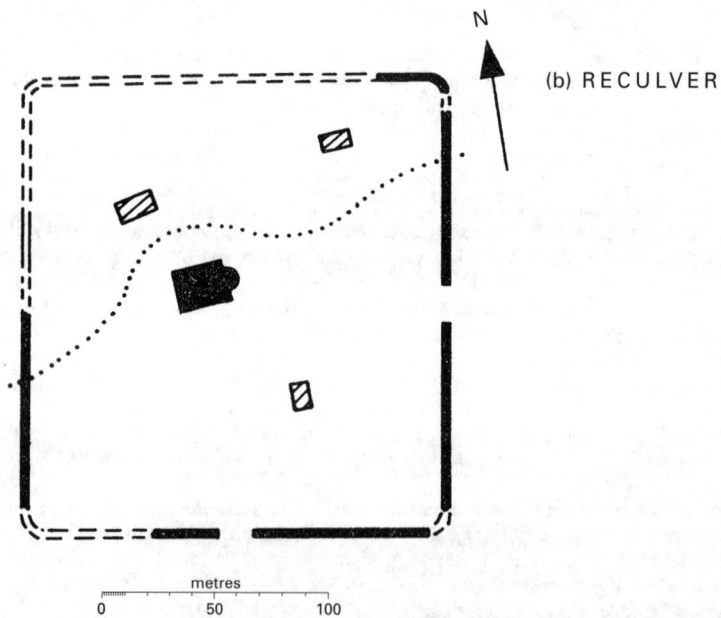

FIGURE 5: Minsters located in former Roman forts: (a) Bradwell-on-Sea and (b) Reculver (after Blair, 'Anglo-Saxon minsters', fig. 10.6); (c) Burgh Castle (after Charles Green); (d) Lincoln (after Rodwell, 'Churches in the landscape', fig. 2).

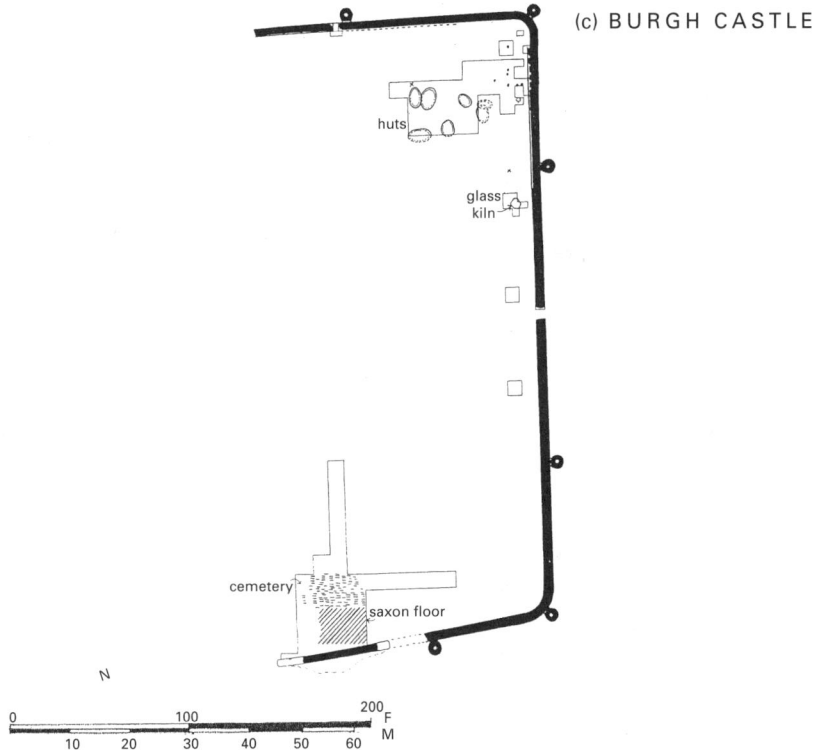

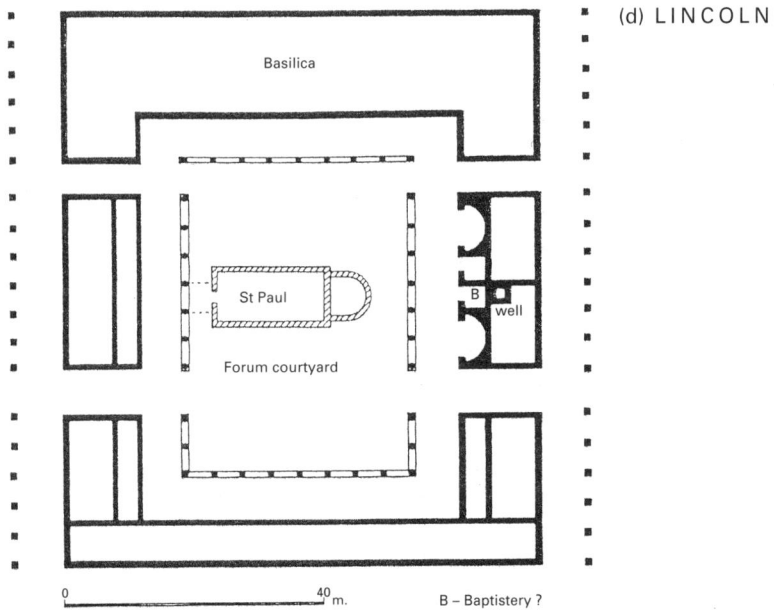

FIGURE 5: (cont.)

PLATE IV: Escomb church, County Durham.

This is not a feature peculiar to Anglo-Saxon monasticism; Irish and Merovingian monasteries were also enclosed within a wall or ditch.[123] Although already removed from the mainland as an island, the brethren who dwelt on Iona, for example, further separated their monastery from its surroundings by constructing a substantial *vallum*, a complex system comprising an earthen rampart and outer ditch.[124]

According to Stephen, a great hedge of thorn surrounded Wilfrid's house at Oundle, and Bede reported that a rampart also enclosed the secluded oratory at Hexham to which John of Beverley retired when he was able.[125] There were also apparently 'strong and lofty walls' around the double minster at Wimborne.[126] The archaeological discovery of an artificial boundary is often

---

[123] James, 'Archaeology', pp. 39–41; Herity, 'The buildings', pp. 248–9.

[124] Anderson and Anderson, *Adomnán's Life of Columba*, p. xlvi; MacDonald, 'Aspects', pp. 280–1.

[125] *VSW* ch. 67 (pp. 144–5). Compare Gregory of Tours' description of the monastery in Clermont, which had a garden within the enclosure, separated from the ouside world by a thick thorny hedge: Gregory of Tours, *Liber vitae patrum*, XIV. 2 (ed. B. Krusch, *MGH, SSRM* I. 2, 719); James, 'Archaeology', p. 40. For Hexham see *HE* V. 2 (pp. 456–7).

[126] *VSL* ch. 2 (p. 123). There were equally high walls at the Gallic nunneries of Faremoutiers and Sainte-Croix in Poitiers: James, 'Archaeology', pp. 40–1.

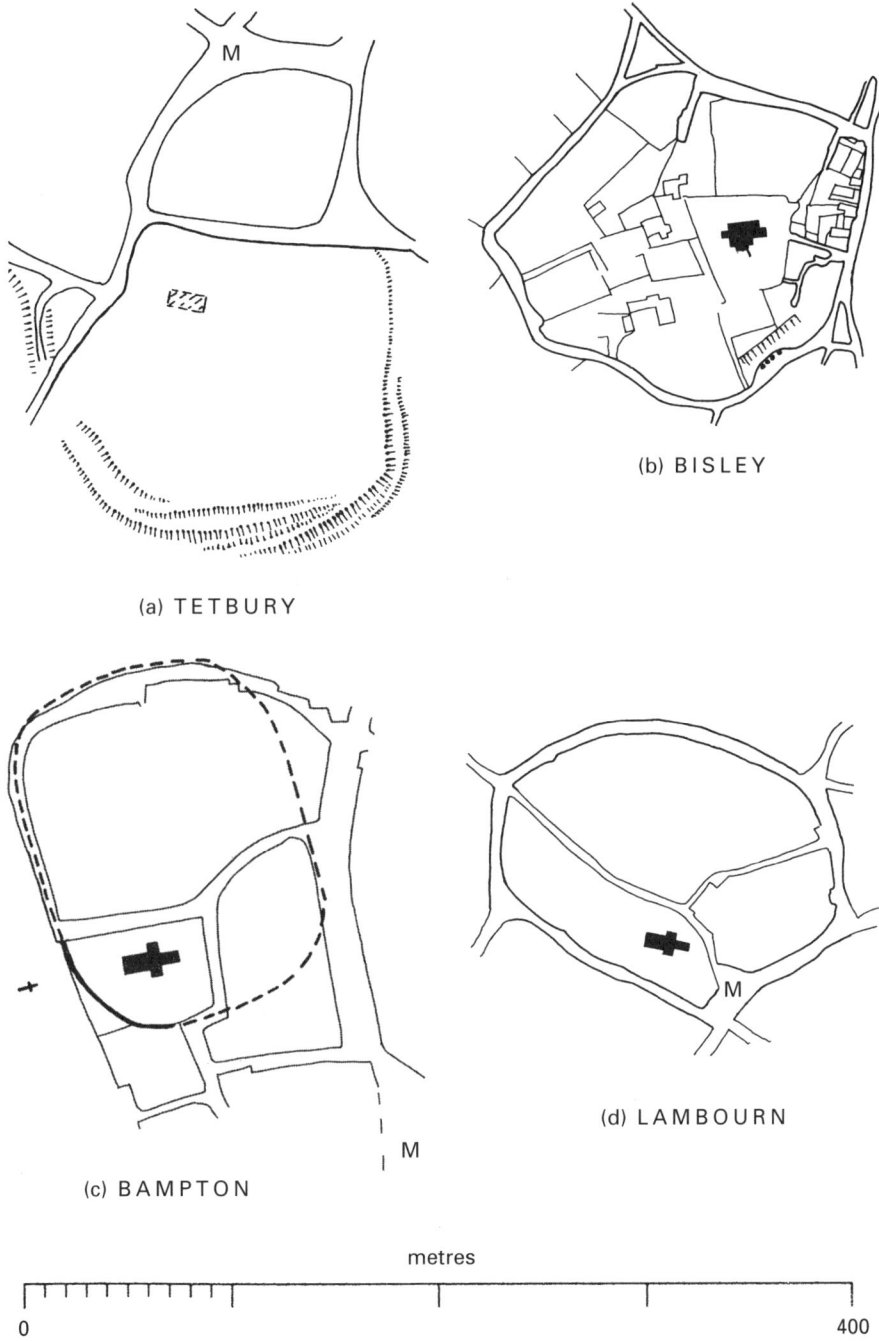

FIGURE 6: Curvilinear monastic enclosures: (a) Tetbury; (b) Bisley; (c) Bampton; and (d) Lambourn (after Blair, 'Anglo-Saxon minsters', fig. 10.2).

taken as one indication of the monastic nature of a site; for example a rectangular earthwork of enclosure ditches has been excavated at Brandon in Suffolk.[127] Excavations in the vicinity of the present twelfth-century church at Hartlepool have revealed evidence of a boundary complex constructed of three separate components of deep post-pits and palisade trench; although some of the buildings discovered lie outside this boundary (as is also the case at Whitby where some features are found beyond the putative *vallum monasterii*). These features have been interpreted as the enclosure of the seventh-century minster of *Heruteu*.[128]

Monastic enclosures were seemingly subdivided internally, both to separate different functions within the minster and to keep the inmates apart from visiting outsiders. In England, the sexes were often physically separated in double houses; at Barking this was done so strictly that men and women were originally even buried apart, although the two burial grounds were later combined because of pressure of space, but at Æthelhild's minster near Partney the *locus virorum* was separated from the women's area only by a gate.[129] According to the description given by Rudolf, Leoba's hagiographer, the high walls at Wimborne served as much to divide the sexes as to protect them all from the outside world. Since Rudolf so abhorred the very concept of a double house that he strove to prove that the men and women at Wimborne had no contact whatsoever, it is, however, unclear to what extent this evidence for their isolation should be taken literally.[130] The topography of the modern town of Wimborne Minster may demonstrate the former existence of two independently enclosed religious establishments, both lying within a larger enclosure, with the church lying at the centre of a concentric precinct. This might, John Blair has argued, indicate an Anglo-Saxon arrangement, although the town plan would also admit of alternative interpretations.[131]

---

[127] Carr *et al.*, 'The middle Saxon settlement', pp. 371, 376.

[128] Cramp and Daniels, 'New finds', p. 428; R. Daniels, 'The Anglo-Saxon monastery at Church Close, Hartlepool, Cleveland', *AJ* 145 (1988), 158–210.

[129] Barking: *HE* IV. 7, 10 (pp. 356–7 and 364–5); Æthelhild's minster: *ibid.*, III. 11 (pp. 246–9).

[130] *VSL* ch. 2 (ed. Waitz, p. 123). The problems of this Life have been explored by Hollis, *Anglo-Saxon Women*, pp. 270–80; Schneider, 'Anglo-Saxon women', pp. 42–3 and n. 38; and more recently by Yitzhak Hen, '*Milites Christi utriusque sexus*: gender and politics of conversion in the circle of Boniface', *Revue bénédictine* 109 (1999), 17–31, at pp. 23–30.

[131] John Blair, 'Wimborne Minster', *Archaeological Journal* 140 (1983), 37–8. That an early monastic enclosure could dictate the shape and street-plan of a modern town is demonstrated by the town-plans of Wimborne and Lambourn. Compare also Manglieu in the Auvergne: James, 'Archaeology', p. 41. See figure 7.

FIGURE 7: Monastic influences on modern town-plans: (a) Wimborne, Dorset, and (b) Lambourn, Berkshire (after Blair, 'Minster churches in the landscape', fig. 2.3).

Other considerations as well as gender governed the internal organisation of many communities: the young, the old and the sick were frequently segregated from the rest of a monastic congregation, for their mutual protection. The small children of both sexes at Barking lived with the women.[132] At Whitby, the novices lived in a place positioned at the remotest part of the minster until they had been fully instructed and entered into the fellowship of the community, perhaps in order to ensure that those who did not advance to full membership could not compromise the vocations of the professed women.[133] The sick seem to have been kept apart in private cells; Benedict Biscop and Sigeberht each lay in individual *cubicula* during their last illnesses, and Eosterwine was prevailed upon to leave the dormitory for a more secluded place two days before he died.[134] Whitby also housed the sick and the infirm (who may have been mostly the very old) away from the rest of the men; at Barking the old and feeble nuns had separate *cubicula*, away from the sisters' common dormitory.[135]

When people from the outside world came into minsters, whether as guests, on business or through sickness, efforts seem to have been made in some establishments to restrict them to the outermost parts of the enclosure, presumably in order to ensure that their presence affected the normal life of the community as little as possible. The guest-house at Ripon, of which Cuthbert was given charge, was at some distance from the other buildings;[136] Wilfrid died in a house set right against the fence at the edge of the enclosure of the minster of Oundle, which he was visiting at the time of his final illness.[137] Excavations at Jarrow suggest that the guest-house there (if correctly identified) was also set at a little distance from the monks' own communal buildings.[138] The guest-house at Æthelhild's minster was separated from both the male and female quarters: when a guest fell ill during the night, a servant called at the abbess's gate to fetch Æthelhild; she went out of the minster's door to the men's dwelling, where she called a priest and together they went from there to the guest-house.[139] Columbanian houses also made separate provision for the reception of guests, hospitality being an important function of these communities

---

[132] *HE* IV. 8 (pp. 358–9).   [133] *HE* IV. 23 (pp. 414–15).

[134] *HA* chs. 8, 13 (ed. Plummer, pp. 372 and 376).   [135] *HE* IV. 24, IV. 9 (pp. 418–9, 360–1).

[136] Anon., *VSCuth.* II. 2 (pp. 76–7); Bede, *VSCuth.* ch. 7 (pp. 176–7).

[137] *VSW* ch. 67 (pp. 144–7). Cramp, 'Monastic sites', p. 204.

[138] Fig. 8; Rosemary Cramp, 'Monastic sites', pp. 240–1.   [139] *HE* III. 11 (pp. 248–9).

JARROW 1975

Saxon

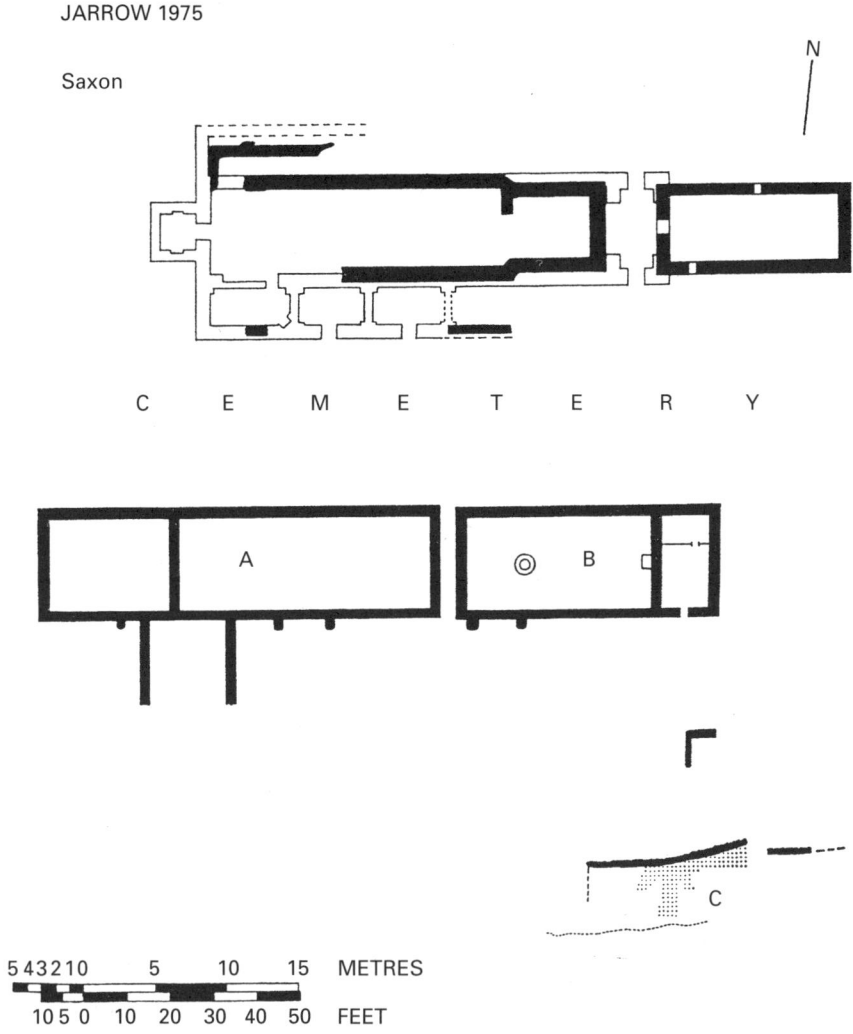

FIGURE 8: Jarrow, layout of church and monastic buildings (after Cramp, 'Jarrow church', fig. 30). A, Refectory; B, East Range (assembly hall and abbot's private room); C, Guest House.

in the seventh century.[140] The way in which the outside world was kept separate from the professed community at Wimborne – where the superior was reputed to talk to outsiders only through a window – may have been unprecedented.[141]

[140] MacDonald, 'Aspects of the monastery', pp. 291–2.
[141] *VSL* ch. 2 (ed. Waitz, p. 123).

Comparison with contemporary Irish and Merovingian evidence can offer useful pointers towards the way in which Anglo-Saxon monastic sites may have been laid out, but traditional perceptions of Celtic monasticism have been challenged in recent years, and a marked difference between regular, planned Gallic houses and more haphazard Irish arrangements is not apparent.[142] Herity has demonstrated considerable consistency in the organisation of Irish Christian sites, with three focal monuments – cross-slab, saint's tomb, and oratory or church with an open space in front – being arranged in a recurring pattern. He has shown that the domestic buildings on such sites were frequently separated from this area by a low wall, and it is striking how often the brothers' dwellings were positioned on the west side of the enclosure, in apposition to the focal monuments and burials on the north, south and east.[143] The eighth-century Life of St Philibert provides a description of an elaborate and tightly planned complex at Jumièges, although other Frankish sites may not have been so well organised: excavations of the monastery at Nivelles give no indication of any planned relationship between the three churches there.[144] In England, as we have already seen, it is hard to draw close parallels between the injunctions of monastic legislators about the best way in which to order a religious enclosure and the evidence for the formal planning of monastic enclosures.[145]

Monastic churches

A main church where the whole community might worship together was the focal point of each enclosure, but this may not always have been positioned centrally. In the Roman forts of Reculver and Chester-le-Street, the principal church lies roughly centrally; in other enclosures, Roman and non-Roman, the church is against the boundary of the defended area as at

[142] Christopher D. Morris, *Church and Monastery in the Far North: An Archaeological Evaluation*, Jarrow Lecture, 1989 (Jarrow: Saint Paul's Church, 1990). For the planning of Merovingian sites see James, 'Archaeology', pp. 38–47.

[143] M. Herity, 'The layout of Irish Early Christian monasteries', in P. Ní Chatháin and M. Richter (eds.) *Irland und Europa: Die Kirche im Frühmittelater* (Stuttgart: Klett-Cotta, 1984), pp. 105–16, Herity, 'The buildings', p. 264.

[144] James, 'Archaeology', pp. 38–41, 43.

[145] See above, chapter 2, and further, Walter Horn, 'On the Origins of the Medieval Cloister', *Gesta* 12 (1973), 13–52, at pp. 19–21. John Blair has suggested that, rather than trying to match the idealistic statements of monastic rules (or the potentially prescriptive function of the St Gall plan) it might be more helpful to envisage a broad tradition of western monastic planning, 'in which formal main buildings co-existed with a high density of informal lesser ones': Blair, 'Anglo-Saxon minsters', p. 260.

Caistor-by-Norwich or Horncastle, and Bampton and Lambourn.[146] At Barking the oratory apparently lay on the west side of the minster.[147] Most religious communities of any significance in England, as in Gaul and possibly in Ireland, had more than one church and there is evidence that groups of churches were laid out consistently according to a linear pattern following Frankish conventions of the sixth and seventh centuries.[148] The English landscape differs from the Gallic and Italian, in that special baptismal churches are not generally found in this country.[149] Among English sites with more than one church are Lindisfarne, where there would seem to have been two, both made of wood, and Glastonbury where in Dunstan's time there were reputedly two churches, one wooden and the other built in stone.[150] John Blair has shown that at most minsters with identifiable groups of churches, the churches are arranged in linear plan from west to east. As well as Lindisfarne, other examples of sites thus arranged include St Augustine's Canterbury, Glastonbury and Wells.[151] On other sites there may have been one central church and a collection of smaller chapels or oratories; Ceolfrith, for example, built several oratories at Wearmouth and Jarrow during his time as abbot.[152] As part of their attempt to find themselves some degree of solitude within their over-busy lives, John of Beverley and Chad also built themselves oratories which lay apart from the other minster buildings, although they were probably still within the minster's wider enclosure.[153]

In common with other Germanic peoples, the Anglo-Saxons had no tradition of building in stone, and many Anglo-Saxon churches were, like Irish

---

[146] Martin Biddle, 'The archaeology of the church: a widening horizon', in Peter Addyman and Richard Morris (eds.), *The Archaeological Study of Churches*, Council for British Archaeology, Research report 13 (London: Council for British Archaeology, 1976), pp. 65–71, at p. 67. Blair, 'Anglo-Saxon minsters', p. 239. Compare figures 5 for Reculver and 6 for Bampton and Lambourn.

[147] *HE* IV. 7 (pp. 356–7).　　[148] Blair, 'Anglo-Saxon minsters', pp. 247–50.

[149] I have discussed this in '"By water in the Spirit": the administration of baptism in Anglo-Saxon England', in John Blair and Richard Sharpe (eds.), *Pastoral Care before the Parish* (Leicester, London and New York: Leicester University Press, 1992), pp. 171–92, at pp. 180–2; see also Blair, 'Anglo-Saxon minsters', p. 150.

[150] Lindisfarne: *HE* III. 17, 25 (pp. 264–5 and 294–5); Deirdre O'Sullivan, 'The plan of the early Christian monastery on Lindisfarne: a fresh look at the evidence', in Gerald Bonner *et al.* (eds.), *St Cuthbert, his Cult and his Community* (Woodbridge: Boydell Press, 1989), pp. 125–42, at p. 129. Glastonbury: William of Malmesbury, *Vita S. Dunstani*, ch. 16 (ed. Stubbs, p. 271). We have already seen that, at least according to Rudolf, Wimborne minster also had two churches: *VSL* ch. 2 (ed. Waitz, p. 123). The same multiplicity of churches characterised monastic sites in Gaul at this period: James, 'Archaeology', pp. 41–3.

[151] See figure 9. For more examples see Blair, 'Anglo-Saxon minsters', figs. 10.8–10.10.

[152] *HA*, ch. 15 (p. 379). Ian Wood, *The Most Holy Abbot Ceolfrid*, Jarrow Lecture 1995 (Jarrow: [St Paul's Church], 1996), p. 15.

[153] *HE* V. 2, IV. 3 (pp. 456–7 and 338–9).

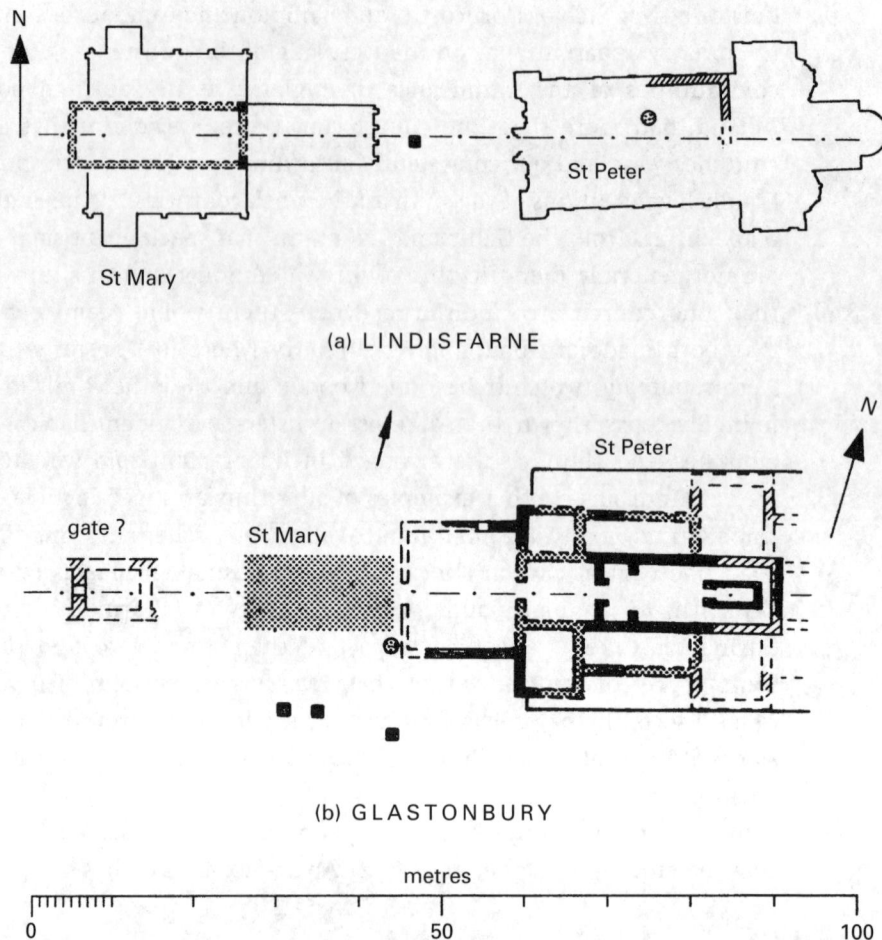

(a) LINDISFARNE

(b) GLASTONBURY

metres

0   50   100

FIGURE 9: Aligned church-groups: (a) Lindisfarne (after Blair, 'Early churches at Lindisfarne'); (b) Glastonbury (after Radford, 'Glastonbury Abbey before 1184' and Blair, 'Anglo-Saxon minsters', fig. 10.10); (c) Wells (after Rodwell, 'Churches in the landscape', fig. 6); (d) St Augustine's, Canterbury (after Taylor and Taylor, *Anglo-Saxon Architecture*, fig. 61).

ones, made of wood.[154] Aidan's first church at Lindisfarne was presumably wooden, as was the church he built on the royal estate near Bamburgh,

[154] For Irish wooden churches see Macdonald, 'Notes', pp. 305–6, 313–14, Herity, 'The buildings', pp. 249–50, and Catherine Karkov, 'The decoration of early wooden architecture', in Catherine Karkov and Robert Farrell (eds.), *Studies in Insular Art and Archaeology* (Oxford, OH: American Early Medieval Studies and the Miami University School of Fine Arts, 1991), pp. 27–48, at pp. 30–4.

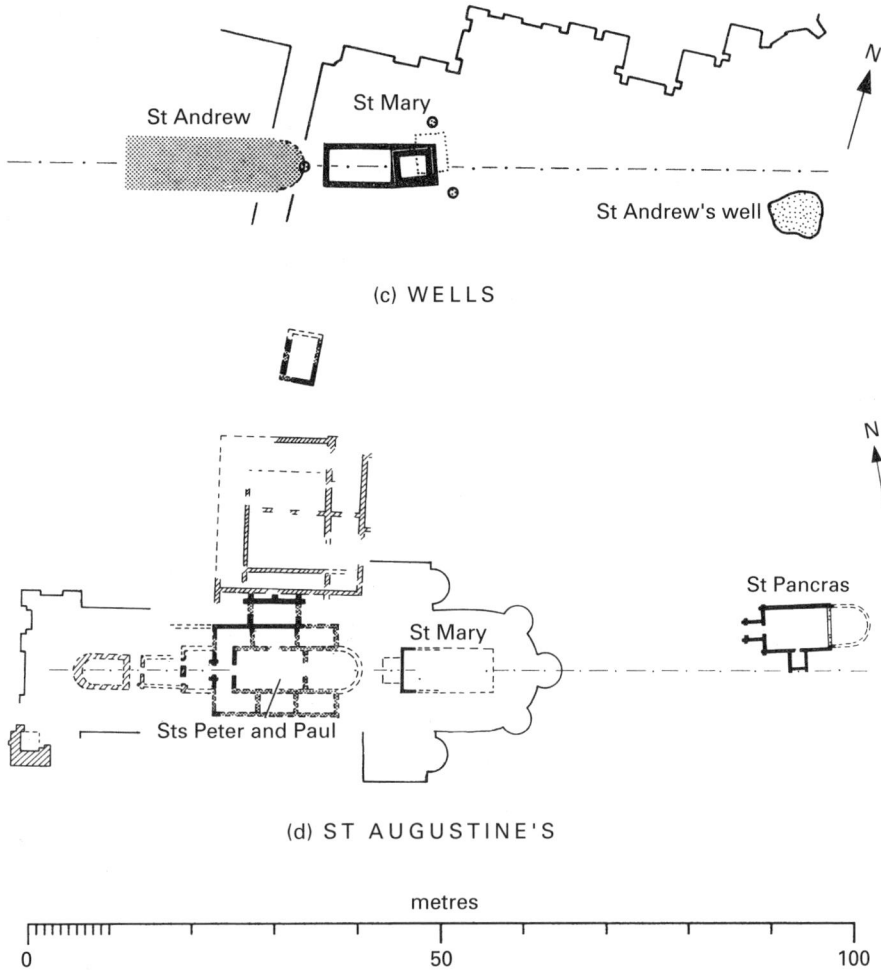

(c) WELLS

(d) ST AUGUSTINE'S

FIGURE 9: *(cont.)*

against the buttress of which he died. This building subsequently burnt
down twice, but on each occasion the buttress was not injured by the flames;
splinters from the fabric were reputed to be efficacious in curing sickness.[155]
Finan had the second church at Lindisfarne built *more Scottorum*, not of stone
but of oak, and thatched with reeds; a subsequent bishop of Lindisfarne,
Eadberht (688–98), removed the reed thatch from Finan's church and had

[155] *HE* III. 17 (pp. 264–5). Rosemary Cramp, 'The artistic influence of Lindisfarne within Northumbria',
in Gerald Bonner *et al.* (eds.), *St Cuthbert, his Cult and his Community* (Woodbridge: Boydell Press,
1989), pp. 213–28, at p. 215 and n. 6, and p. 218. Also O'Sullivan, 'The plan', p. 129.

the whole building, roof and walls, covered with sheets of lead.[156] The first church of St Peter at York, built hastily for the baptism of King Edwin in 627, was made of wood but a stone structure to replace it was soon begun. Paulinus also built a wooden church in the royal dwelling at *Campodonum*, but this was later burnt down apart from its altar, which Bede reports escaped the fire through being made of stone.[157] At Lastingham a stone church was built some time after the minster's foundation, again replacing an earlier wooden structure.[158] When Benedict Biscop founded Wearmouth, he needed to bring masons (*cementarii*, those who could make mortar) from Gaul to construct a stone church,[159] and subsequently also glaziers, 'craftsmen hitherto unknown in Britain, to put windows in the chancel, the *porticus* and in the refectory'.[160] Eanmund built a stone church for his minster (perhaps at Crayke); it had high walls, lead on the roof and glass windows.[161] The church at Escomb in County Durham, which probably dates from the late seventh century, was built from re-used Roman masonry from the nearby fort at Vinovia. Although the best preserved of the early Northumbrian churches, there is no documentary evidence relating to this church or the community that served it.[162] William of Malmesbury thought that the church of St Laurence at Bradford-on-Avon standing in his own day had been built by St Aldhelm; in fact the surviving stone building is a rebuilding of that earlier structure, of the tenth or early eleventh century, but is, as John Blair

---

[156] *HE* III. 25 (pp. 294–5). Karkov, 'The decoration', p. 37. For a general discussion of church building in wood in England and on the continent, and handlists of such churches described in medieval sources see W. Zimmermann, '*Ecclesia lignea* und *ligneis tabulis fabricata*', *Bonner Jahrbücher* 158 (1958), 414–58. For discussion of the enshrining of the whole church building (rather than just the roof) in lead see Cramp, 'The artistic influence', p. 218.

[157] *HE* II. 14 (pp. 186–7); see Plummer, *Baedae opera* II, 101–2. One of the timber structures excavated at the Northumbrian royal site of Yeavering, building B, has been identified as a possible church, associated with the cemetery which surrounds it: Brian Hope-Taylor, *Yeavering: An Anglo-British Centre of Early Northumbria* (London: HMSO, 1977), pp. 73–8, 278–9, but for a contrary view see Cramp, 'The artistic influence', p. 218. Two phases of timber building have been identified from excavations at Hartlepool, although the church has not been found: R. Daniels, 'The Anglo-Saxon monastery at Church Close, Hartlepool, Cleveland', *AJ* 145 (1988), 158–210, at pp. 160–81. The earliest building phase at Whitby may also have been of timber before stone structures were erected: Cramp, 'A reconsideration', pp. 65–6.

[158] *HE* III. 23 (288–9).

[159] *HA*, ch. 5 (p. 368); Peter Hunter Blair, *Northumbria in the Days of Bede* (London: Book Club Associates, 1976), p. 122.

[160] *HA*, ch. 5. Edward James has argued convincingly ('Archaeology', p. 46) that the term *porticus* in this context refers to a covered walk linking the church with the other monastic buildings, and has identified this with the structure found in the excavation of Wearmouth and presumed to serve such a purpose. Compare Cramp, 'Monastic sites', p. 234.

[161] Æthelwulf, *De abbatibus*, chs. 6, 20 (ed. Campbell, pp. 12–15, 48–51). However, compare Aldhelm, *Carmen ecclesiasticum* III (ed. Ehwald, pp. 14–18), discussed by Campbell, *De abbatibus*, p. xlvi.

[162] See plate IV. H. M. and Joan Taylor, *Anglo-Saxon Architecture*, 3 vols. (Cambridge: Cambridge University Press, 1965–78), I, 234–8; Pocock and Wheeler, 'Excavations at Escomb church'.

PLATE V: Church of St Laurence, Bradford-on-Avon, Wiltshire.

has observed, remarkable for the atmosphere of Anglo-Saxon religious space that it conveys.[163]

While from the later seventh century, as a result of continental and Mediterranean influences,[164] stone gradually came to be used more widely for building, the use of wood persisted throughout the Anglo-Saxon period; that wood was the ordinary building material is implied by the fact that the Old English verb to build is *getimbrian*.[165] Archbishop Theodore's Penitential indicates that wooden churches were common in England in his time, for in a section devoted to church buildings and their uses he ordered that the wood of a church ought not to be put to any use other than for another church, unless it were be kept for the benefit of the brethren of a minster and burnt to bake bread for them.[166] Anglo-Saxon missionaries on the

---

[163] See plate V; William of Malmesbury, *De gestis pontificum Anglorum*, ed. N. E. S. A. Hamilton, Rolls Series 52 (London, 1870), pp. 346–7. John Blair, 'Bradford-on-Avon', in Michael Lapidge *et al.* (eds.), *The Blackwell Encyclopaedia of Anglo-Saxon England* (Oxford: Blackwell, 1999), p. 72.

[164] Thomas, *The Early Christian Archaeology*, pp. 74–5.

[165] Bosworth and Toller, *An Anglo-Saxon Dictionary*, *s.v.*; Plummer, *Baedae opera*, II.101.

[166] Theodore, Penitential, II.1.3 (ed. Finsterwalder, p. 312).

continent may also have first erected wooden churches on the sites of their new monastic foundations. Boniface certainly had a wooden oratory built at Geismar, the site of a notable pagan shrine, but on this occasion the saint was making a symbolic statement about the power of the Christian God by reusing for the church the timber from the oak sacred to Jupiter which he had felled.[167] On their final flight from Lindisfarne, the community of St Cuthbert had taken with them not only their most precious relics but also the wooden church erected by Aidan, re-erecting it first at Norham and then at Chester-le-Street, once the congregation settled there between 882 and 884.[168] According to Simeon of Durham, Æthelric, bishop of Durham 1041–56, pulled down the wooden church at Chester-le-Street in order to build a stone one there, seeing this as a more appropriate memorial to St Cuthbert.[169] There is some evidence for the continued erection of wooden churches in England in the tenth century, and also for the continued ecclesiastical use of older wooden structures into the late Anglo-Saxon period and beyond. Abbo of Fleury reported in his *Passio Sancti Eadmundi*, written at the commission of the monks of Ramsey, that at some time after King Edmund's martyrdom, the saint's body was translated to the *villa regia* of *Beodricesworth*, where a wooden church was built to house his relics.[170] Edith, wife of Edward the Confessor, apparently had a stone church built at the minster where she was educated, Wilton, because the church there was still made of wood.[171] At Glastonbury, to the west of the stone church, William of Malmesbury claimed to have seen a 'wattled building with a layer of boards, covered from the top down with lead', which he identified with the old church, *vetusta ecclesia*, on that site.[172] The only standing timber fabric

---

[167] *VSB*, ch. 6 (ed. Rau, p. 494).

[168] *Historia de S. Cuthberto*, ch. 9 (ed. Johnson South, pp. 48–9); Cramp, 'The artistic influence', p. 215. A. P. Smyth has discussed the wanderings of the Cuthbert community: *Scandinavian York and Dublin: The History and Archaeology of Two Related Viking Kingdoms*, 2 vols. (Dublin: Templekieran Press, 1975–9), I, 41–4, 77–8, 96–103, 107–8, 112.

[169] Simeon of Durham, *Historia Dunelmensis ecclesiae*, III. 9 (ed. Arnold, I, 92).

[170] Abbo, *Passio Sancti Eadmundi*, ch. 13 (ed. Michael Winterbottom, *Three Lives of English Saints*, p. 82). The twelfth-century Ramsey chronicler also asserted that a wooden chapel for three monks was first built at that site in the 970s by the abbey's benefactor Ealdorman Æthelwine (*Chronicon abbatiae Rameseiensis*, ch. 18, ed. W. D. Macray, Rolls Series, 1886, p. 36), but this story is not found in Byrthferth's account of the foundation of the abbey by Oswald. He reported rather that the saint hired *caementarii* during his first winter at Ramsey, who laid out the plan of the church in the shape of a cross and then built in stone to that design: *Vita Oswaldi*, ch. 4, ed. James Raine, *Historians of the Church of York*, 3 vols. (London: Rolls Series, 1879–94), I, 434.

[171] *Vita Ædwardi Regis*, ch. 6 (ed. Barlow, pp. 46–7); discussed further by me in *Veiled Women*, II, *s.n.* Wilton.

[172] William of Malmesbury, *De antiquitate Glastonie ecclesiae*, ch. 6 (ed. Scott, pp. 52–3); *Gesta regum Anglorum* I, 20 (ed. Mynors *et al.*, I, 804–5). See further J. A. Robinson, 'The historical evidence as

known to have survived from any pre-Conquest church in England is the late Anglo-Saxon nave of St Andrew's church at Greensted in Essex.[173] Remains of timber churches have, however, been found under later stone structures in excavations at, for example, St Botolph's church at Iken in Suffolk (where the nave of the Norman stone church cuts through the timber foundations of an earlier building),[174] and at Wharram Percy in Yorkshire and Potterne in Wiltshire, both of which timber churches have tentatively been dated to the tenth or eleventh century.[175]

Domestic buildings

The nature of the buildings reserved for the use of the monastic *familia* varied from site to site, and it might be expected that the traditions which influenced the form of the coenobial life adopted at a particular house would also have affected the layout and purpose of buildings erected. Several of the literary sources referred to the presence of communal buildings, such as a refectory at Wearmouth, and dormitories at Hackness, Lindisfarne and Wearmouth.[176] The buildings at Wimborne included one that was sufficiently large to hold all the sisters (of whom there were at that time apparently fifty), who gathered there to celebrate the early morning offices when they were unable to get into the church because its keys had been lost.[177] To a visitor arriving at Coldingham, its lofty buildings (*aedificia . . . sublimiter erecta*) were the most striking; these may have been storeyed, as apparently was a

---

to the Saxon church at Glastonbury', *Proceedings of the Somersetshire Archaeological and Natural History Society* 73 (1928), 40–9, at pp. 44–5; C. R. Radford, 'Glastonbury Abbey before 1184: interim report on the excavations 1908–64', in *Medieval Art and Architecture at Wells and Glastonbury* (London: BAR, 1981), pp. 110–34, at pp. 111–12. Evidence for other examples of tenth- and eleventh-century wooden churches at Colchester, Croyland, Spalding and Whistley, Berkshire, was collected by Zimmermann, 'Ecclesia lignea', nos. II, 27, II, 20, I, 48, I, 57.

[173] Taylor and Taylor, *Anglo-Saxon Architecture*, I, 262–4; see H. Christie *et al.*, 'The wooden church of St. Andrew at Greensted, Essex', *Antiquaries Journal* 59 (1979), 92–112.

[174] S. E. West, N. Scarfe and R. Cramp, 'Iken, St Botolph, and the coming of East Anglian Christianity', *Proceedings of the Suffolk Institute of Archaeology and Natural History* 35 (1984), 279–301, at p. 284.

[175] R. D. Bell and Maurice Beresford (eds.), *Wharram Percy: The Church of St Martin*, J. G. Hurst and P. H. Rahtz (gen. eds.), *Wharram: A Study of Settlement on the Yorkshire Wolds* III (London: Society for Medieval Archaeology, 1987), pp. 55–7, 98–9, 200; N. Davey, 'A pre-Conquest church and baptistery at Potterne', *Wiltshire Archaeological and Natural History Magazine* 59 (1964), 116–23

[176] For the refectory at Wearmouth see *HA* ch. 5 (p. 368); the brothers' dormitory there, outside which there was an oratory to St Lawrence, was described by Bede, *ibid.*, ch. 17 (p. 382). For the buildings at Hackness see *HE* IV. 23 (pp. 414–5); and for Lindisfarne, Bede, *VSCuth.* ch. 16 (pp. 210–1).

[177] *VSL* ch. 5 (ed. Waitz, p. 124).

multi-purpose building at Jumièges in the seventh century.[178] Irish sources mention a *magna domus* (also called simply *monasterium*), a large building of rectilinear or possibly curvilinear ground plan, divided into individual *cubicula* giving onto an open floor space; this had no specialised use, but apparently housed a range of activities: teaching, reading and writing, and – since it often also contained the kitchen and bake-house – was probably also a refectory.[179] Unfortunately excavated sites cannot always add greatly to the picture given in the written sources. If there were communal buildings at Whitby, they were presumably south of the church in the area which has not been excavated. A range of different buildings lay to the north of the church, some of which may have been used for the domestic activities of the women, such as spinning, weaving, or sewing; others may have housed the various manufacturing tasks that the finds indicate were carried out there: working of bronze and silver, and glass-making.[180] More informative are the sites at Wearmouth and Jarrow, which included various stone buildings, some identified as serving communal purposes, such as a refectory with a dormitory over it, and a room for assemblies at Jarrow. These may be compared both with monastic buildings in contemporary Gaul,[181] and with the plans of Anglo-Saxon secular buildings, for example those at Yeavering. Rosemary Cramp has suggested that 'the Wearmouth/Jarrow buildings could therefore be seen as a direct translation into stone of Germanic timber structures'.[182] The difficulties experienced in providing confident explanations of the purpose of the recently-excavated sites at Brandon and Flixborough accentuate again the dependence of monastic architects on domestic models.

In addition to these larger communal areas, there were also much smaller buildings within most monastic enclosures. The heads of houses appear to have slept apart, for Bede remarked that Abbot Eosterwine continued to sleep with the rest of the brethren after his election to the abbacy, clearly implying that it was normal in other houses for the abbot to occupy a single

---

[178] *HE* IV. 25 (pp. 424–5); Blair, 'Anglo-Saxon minsters', p. 261. For Jumièges see anon., *Vita S. Philiberti*, ch. 8 (ed. Levison, *MGH SSRM*, V. 589–90); James, 'Archaeology', p. 40.

[179] MacDonald, 'Aspects', pp. 284–7.

[180] Cramp, 'Monastic sites', p. 229; *eadem*, 'Northumbria and Ireland', p. 194.

[181] See Eric Fletcher, 'The influence of Merovingian Gaul on Northumbria in the seventh century', *Medieval Archaeology* 24 (1980), 69–86, at pp. 82–3, who has shown how Merovingian architecture and building techniques were influential upon Wilfrid as well as Benedict Biscop. Richard Bailey has discussed the possible Frankish and other models that might have inspired Wilfrid's building at Ripon and Hexham: 'St Wilfrid, Ripon and Hexham', in Catherine Karkov and Robert Farrell (eds.), *Studies in Insular Art and Archaeology* (Oxford, OH: American Early Medieval Studies and the Miami University School of Fine Arts, 1991), pp. 3–25, at pp. 17–22.

[182] Cramp, 'Northumbria and Ireland', p. 196. Compare figure 8.

cell.[183] Abbess Tetta of Wimborne apparently had access at least to a place where she might pray in private during the night while the nuns were sleeping, even if she did not also sleep alone.[184] The possession of an individual dwelling may have been a privilege accorded to senior and trustworthy members of the house; one of the older sisters at Barking, Torhtgyth, appears to have lived in her own cell.[185] However, Bede's account of Adomnan's vision of Coldingham reveals that there were a number of *domunculae* within that enclosure, although these were apparently intended for praying and reading, not sleeping. The beds which the angel found empty would appear to have been in a different place from the little cells.[186]

To Bede's mind, a certain minimum number of buildings was essential for the practice of the religious life. When the Irish left Lindisfarne he commented approvingly that 'there were very few buildings there except for the church, in fact only those without which the life of a community was impossible'.[187] Precisely which buildings Bede deemed necessary it is hard to tell; it was the simplicity of the life followed by the Irish of which Bede particularly approved and, in his rejection of ostentation, he may have minimised references to superfluous buildings and laid undue stress on the communal. Another text written in the same milieu, the anonymous Life of Abbot Ceolfrith, appears to convey a similar picture of appropriate monastic buildings. That author reported that Ceolfrith first went to Jarrow with his twenty-two companions only 'when all the buildings especially required by the needs of a minster had first been erected there'.[188] Some other member of the Wearmouth and Jarrow community, most probably Benedict Biscop, would seem to have held strong views on the importance of restricting the dwellings on a monastic site to a specified minimum.[189] While it may be assumed, on the basis of other known early medieval monastic rules, that the result of such a policy would be for religious to engage in almost all their daily activities (praying, reading, eating and sleeping) inside communal dwellings, it remains uncertain just how many separate constructions would be needed for the maintenance of a way of life designed to strengthen the corporate nature of the community.

---

[183] *HA* ch. 8 (p. 372).   [184] *VSL*, ch. 5 (ed. Waitz, p. 124).   [185] *HE* IV. 9 (pp. 360–1).

[186] *HE* IV. 23 (pp. 424–5). This point is made by James, 'Archaeology', p. 45, commenting upon Cramp, 'Monastic sites', pp. 206–7.

[187] *HE* III. 26 (pp. 310–11).

[188] *VSCeol*. ch. 11 (p. 391). This is to presume that the Life of Ceolfrith was not written by Bede; the Life was attributed to Bede's authorship by Judith McClure, 'Bede and the life of Ceolfrid', *Peritia*, 3 (1984), 71–84.

[189] Ian Wood has emphasised the extent to which the initial work at Jarrow was Benedict's: *The Most Holy Abbot*, p. 16.

The economic basis of the religious life

Few religious houses possessed of any sort of material endowment can have existed in genuine obscurity; close relationships developed in the mission and post-conversion periods between the royal and noble families and the ecclesiastical institutions founded within each English kingdom. In a later chapter we will look further at the consequences for professed religious of living in such proximity to their founders and donors as well as to a gradually Christianised wider population.[190] Here, we will concentrate purely on issues relating to the church's economic status within early Anglo-Saxon society.

Earlier we investigated the location of early churches in the landscape and their close association with centres of royal power and other pre-existing settlements, but minsters could themselves become the foci for the growth of towns.[191] Some communities were located on the best agricultural land, namely on precisely such ground as would be most likely to attract further lay settlement, or was most likely to find favour with local royal families. The positions chosen by many monastic founders also gave their churches a visual dominance over the local landscape. This was certainly the case in the West Midlands and in Northumbria.[192] Even if they were originally positioned at a distance from secular dwellings, minsters might act as an impetus for lay settlement in the locality, the populace being motivated by both the spiritual and the economic advantages accruing from their proximity to the church. Markets were frequently established near minsters; communities with large estates were liable to produce a surplus that they might sell at their gates, the more readily since the churches attracted regular gatherings of people.[193] By the early tenth century it would seem to have been common for markets to be held on Sundays, presumably when people from the neighbourhood came to the minster for mass, for King Æthelstan

---

[190] Below, chapter 7.

[191] Campbell, 'The church in Anglo-Saxon towns', pp. 141–2; Blair, 'Minster churches in the landscape', pp. 47–50. For consideration of the same issue in other parts of early medieval Europe see Donald Bullough, 'Social and economic structure and topography in the early medieval city', *Settimane* 21 (1974), 351–99, at pp. 357–62, and for Francia see Rosamond McKitterick, 'Town and monastery in the Carolingian period', in Derek Baker (ed.), *The Church in Town and Countryside*, Studies in Church History 16 (Oxford: Basil Blackwell, 1979), pp. 93–102.

[192] Sims-Williams, *Religion and Literature*, pp. 368–71, 394–5; Hill, 'Christianity and geography', pp. 137–9. Also Blair, 'Anglo-Saxon minsters', pp. 230–1.

[193] P. H. Sawyer, 'Fairs and markets in early medieval England', in Niels Skyum-Nielsen and Niels Lund (eds.), *Danish Medieval History: New Currents* (Copenhagen: Museum Tusculanum Press, 1981), pp. 153–68, at p. 160.

legislated against the practice.[194] Indeed, a marked coincidence between
churches and markets is visible in Domesday Book, despite the incomplete
record of both institutions provided by that survey.[195] Merchants bearing
raw materials, for example precious metals and stones for the making of
liturgical vessels, silk for vestments, or pigments for manuscript decoration,
would congregate at an emporium beside a minster; they might, moreover,
bring those products which a minster could not manufacture for itself, such
as spices, oil, and in some areas probably wine.[196] Many minsters were also
either positioned at harbours, as were Whitby and Wearmouth,[197] or were
closely associated with ports, such as Eling, on the opposite side of the estuary of the river Test from *Hamwic*,[198] or Reculver and Minster-in-Thanet in
Kent, which lay near Fordwich and Sandwich.[199]

Whether a church was established at or near a pre-existing town or village or whether its foundation subsequently served as the stimulus for the
formation of a secular settlement is often unclear; some of the more afflu-
ent and economically active minsters such as Whitby must have themselves
been very like small towns.[200] Not all lay communities welcomed the placing
of a church in their midst. Paulinus had difficulty founding churches in the
kingdom of Deira, and had to baptise the people in the river Swale outside
the town of Catterick, because he could not build an oratory or baptistery
there.[201] Some churches may alternatively have been positioned at recognised meeting-places, crossroads or river junctions, or at pagan shrines or
cemeteries, where there may not previously have been a secular settlement,
but where one might thereafter have developed. The availability of preaching
and of sacraments, particularly of those of baptism and burial, the presence
of a shrine with relics of proven thaumaturgic power, or a potential distribution of largesse all proved further stimulus to the accumulation of lay
populations around minsters. People flocked to Lindisfarne on Sundays to

[194] II Æthelstan, ch. 24 (ed. Liebermann, *Die Gesetze*, I, 164). See also Richard Morris, *Churches in the Landscape* (London: Dent, 1989), pp. 212–13.
[195] Richard Morris, *The Church in British Archaeology* (London: Council for British Archaeology, 1983), p. 76.
[196] Cramp, 'Anglo-Saxon settlement', p. 280.
[197] For the connections between early Northumbrian minsters and ports and harbours see Hill, 'Christianity', p. 132.
[198] Patrick Hase, 'The mother churches of Hampshire', in John Blair (ed.), *Minsters and Parish Churches: The Local Church in Transition, 950–1200* (Oxford: Oxford University Committee for Archaeology, 1988), pp. 45–66, at p. 45.
[199] See Susan Kelly, 'Trading privileges from eighth-century England', *Early Medieval Europe* 1 (1992), 3–28.
[200] Campbell, 'The church in Anglo-Saxon towns', p. 141.   [201] *HE* II. 14 (pp. 188–9).

hear the word of God, and the poor assembled at the gates of Æthelwulf's minster, to be rewarded with Abbot Sigwine's generosity.[202] Minsters' physical character, geographical location and material prosperity all significantly shaped the nature and the extent of their dealings with secular society.

Since the possession of wealth and the ability to endow monastic foundations were inextricably linked, it is unsurprising that the contemporary sources tended to concentrate overwhelmingly on the role of those of royal or noble birth in the establishment of minsters. The preponderance of such figures in accounts of lay generosity to the church may be taken to reflect more than a hagiographical *topos* that nobility of birth was an essential prerequisite for future sanctity. Vocations to the religious life were not restricted to the highest strata of society, nor were only those of noble birth educated to a sufficient understanding of Christianity to voice spiritual ambitions. Even so, it must have been difficult for those of peasant stock to express a pious ambition to renounce the world. Not only did they lack the material resources to create their own religious houses, they were also bound in service to a secular lord. Cædmon's story is patently exceptional, and even he would never have come to the monastic life had he not attracted the attention of Whitby's reeve while he was working on the minster's estates.[203]

Although responsibility for creating new minsters probably did lie with the relatively restricted social group that possessed sufficient means to make such gifts, the establishments created by royal and noble donors were not invariably wealthy. Occasional references may be found to houses which suffered through the inadequacy of their endowments. Bishop Cwichhelm was apparently obliged to abandon his see at Rochester for lack of means (*prae inopia rerum*).[204] An Abbess Eangyth and her daughter Heaburg wrote to Boniface lamenting that they were oppressed by their poverty and lack of temporal goods, by the meagreness of the produce of their fields and by the exactions of the king.[205] Bishop Wilfrid was not typical in the extent and value of his material possessions, yet even he was not immune from financial anxiety; the repeated references in Stephen's Life to his attempts to secure not only his minsters at Ripon and Hexham but more importantly their revenues further illustrate the difficulties experienced in maintaining

---

[202] *HE* III. 25 (pp. 310–11). Æthelwulf, *De abbatibus*, ch. 15 (pp. 38–9). Discussed further in chapter 7.
[203] *HE* IV. 24 (pp. 414–21).   [204] *HE* IV. 12 (pp. 368–9).
[205] Boniface, *Ep.* 14 (ed. Tangl, p. 23); Sims-Williams, *Religion and Literature*, pp. 134–5.

the religious life without sufficient material support.[206] The Irish at Lindisfarne were obviously unusual in supposedly having contrived to exist without money; the generosity of their landed endowment and their sufficient supply of cattle were, however, necessary preconditions for their renunciation of coin.[207] In fact the community must have been able to mobilise relatively substantial quantities of silver (or goods to make payment in kind) for Bishop Eadberht to have been able to afford to have the entire wooden structure of his church covered with sheets of lead.[208] Inadequate resources may have threatened the survival of a number of eighth-century religious establishments, for an attempt was made at the reforming council at *Clofesho* in 747 to limit the size of congregations within under-endowed minsters. Heads of minsters were charged not to admit a greater congregation than the foundation had the means to support, and advised that if anyone had unwarily done this, they should exact less work of the additional persons 'until they can give them food and clothing suitable to their profession'.[209]

There were, however, substantial economic advantages to be gained from holding land designated for the service of God. A minster might normally expect to be exempt from the rendering of food-rents to the king or to another secular landlord who had acquired the right to such revenues. For example, the charter recording the grant made by ealdorman Oswulf and his wife Beorngyth of an estate at Stanstead to Christ Church, Canterbury early in the ninth century includes a confirmation by Archbishop Wulfred, incorporating this land into the church's estate at Lympne and specifying the amount of food-rent to be collected annually at the latter place and sent thence to the community:

One hundred and twenty wheaten loaves, thirty fine loaves, one full-grown bullock, four sheep, two flitches, five geese, ten hens and ten pounds of cheese, if it be a flesh day. If, however, it be a fast day, they are to give a wey of cheese, and of fish, butter

---

[206] *VSW* chs. 44, 60 (pp. 90–1 and 132–3). Wilfrid's relationship with the minsters in his 'affinity' is discussed at length in chapter 6.

[207] *HE* III. 26 (pp. 310–1).   [208] *HE* III. 25 (pp. 294–5), discussed above.

[209] Council of *Clofesho*, AD 747, ch. 28 (H&S III, 374). The notion that a minster community might be considered as a unit of lordship has been discussed by James Campbell, 'Elements in the background to the Life of St Cuthbert and his early cult', in Gerald Bonner *et al.* (eds.), *St Cuthbert, his Cult and his Community to AD 1200* (Woodbridge: Boydell, 1989), pp. 3–19, at p. 13. Compare also canons 7 and 8 of the council held at Chelsea in 816 (H&S III, 582), which stressed that monastic lands were inviolable, their charters were not to be challenged and that once land had been granted to God it should remain sanctified for ever.

and eggs, as much as they can procure, and thirty ambers of good Welsh ale . . . and a *mitta* full of honey, or two of wine.[210]

A certain proportion of the produce was set aside to provide a feast for the community on the anniversary of the benefactors, and at the same time the brethren would give 120 *gesufl* loaves as charity for the good of the souls of Oswulf and his wife.[211] Food-rents were not, however, invariably granted with the lands from which they were paid. Some late eighth- and early ninth-century charters show that churches in the Worcester diocese were required to pay substantial food-rents to the king, from which obligation they were only exempted in the mid-ninth century.[212] The earliest such exemption is found in a charter by which King Coenwulf of Mercia granted to the bishop of Worcester and his *familia* the renders due from Worcester and its dependent minsters in exchange for the minster at Twyning and some other land.[213]

There were further secular obligations from which ecclesiastical land was normally freed, including labour on public works, royal vills and palaces, and legal rights such as the fines imposed by popular courts, but there is no evidence that minsters were ever exempt from the obligation to provide the three essential services.[214] Minsters owed further dues to their diocesan bishops, which could prove burdensome, as Abbess Eangyth complained to Boniface.[215] A synod at *Clofesho* in 803 settled a dispute between the bishops of Hereford and Worcester over their right to the annual food-rent payable from two minsters in the Worcester diocese.[216] Even so, the benefits of holding land freed from many secular concerns were such as to offer sufficient incentives to the fraudulent for it to be worth pretending to establish minsters on their own estates, while in fact continuing to live in a basically secular fashion with their wives and children.[217] Privileges granted with

---

[210] S 1188; for discussion of the values of the Anglo-Saxon measures the wey, amber and *mitta* see Harmer, *SEHD*, pp. 73–4.

[211] The meaning of *gesufl* is not entirely clear; it seems to refer to some kind of bread: Harmer, *SEHD*, p. 74; Bosworth and Toller, s.v. *gesufel*. Also discussed by Ann Hagen, *A Handbook of Anglo-Saxon Food: Processing and Consumption* (Pinner: Anglo-Saxon Books, 1992), p. 12, and Debby Banham, *Food and Drink in Anglo-Saxon England* (Stroud: Tempus, 2004), p. 17.

[212] For example, S 146, discussed by Sims-Williams, *Religion and Literature*, p. 137.

[213] S 172. See Christopher Dyer, *Lords and Peasants in a Changing Society: The Estates of the Bishopric of Worcester, 680–1540* (Cambridge: Cambridge University Press, 1980), pp. 16, 28–9.

[214] Brooks, 'The development', p. 71.

[215] Boniface, *Ep.* 14 (p. 23); Sims-Williams, *Religion and Literature*, p. 109.

[216] S 1431 (H&S III, 544–5); Frank M. Stenton, 'Medeshamstede and its colonies', in J. G. Edwards *et al.* (eds.), *Historical Essays in Honour of James Tait* (Manchester: privately printed, 1933), pp. 313–26; reprinted in Doris M. Stenton (ed.), *Preparatory to Anglo-Saxon England* (Oxford: Clarendon Press, 1970), pp. 178–92, at p. 187; Sims-Williams, *Religion and Literature*, pp. 138–9.

[217] *EpEcg*, § 11–13 (pp. 414–17).

monastic estates were not, however, necessarily inviolable. Boniface may have had some specific cases in mind when he protested to Archbishop Cuthbert that religious were wrongfully being forced to participate in royal building programmes.[218]

Once established, minsters were mostly still considered as their founders' property, to be passed on to the relatives of the first heads of the house. Such a view applied both to proprietary minsters (where the owner of the estates, or one of his female relations, was the first head) and to minsters set up on land donated to, or bought by, a third party. Benedict Biscop was obviously unusual in going to considerable lengths to ensure that his brother might not inherit his minsters at Wearmouth and Jarrow after him, a practice he viewed as an abuse.[219] The material worth of many minsters, however, occasioned in particular by the rights and privileges they enjoyed, led to a number of disputes over their ownership as, for example, the rival claims voiced by the communities of Berkeley and Worcester to possession of the minster of Westbury, which were resolved at a council in 824.[220] An abbot Forthred had to resort to appeal to Rome in order to try to reclaim three minsters at Stonegrave, Coxwold and *Donæmuthe* granted to him by an abbess but subsequently seized by Eadberht, king of Northumbria (between 737 and 757/8) and given to the king's brother, the *patricius* Moll. Pope Paul I duly wrote to the king and to Ecgberht, archbishop of York, another of his brothers, instructing them that permission should never again be granted to any layman or any person whatsoever to invade the possessions of religious places.[221] Yet, as we shall see, the appropriation of monastic lands by laymen was a recurrent problem within the early Anglo-Saxon church, one that may well have been exacerbated by the blurring of questions of ownership through the leasing of ecclesiastical land.

By the late eighth century, it seems to have become common for minsters to lease part of their estates to lay people for up to three lifetimes, in return for an annual render of produce, or a monetary rent, or a single payment, instead of farming them directly.[222] This practice had become so widespread

---

[218] Boniface, *Ep.* 78 (ed. Tangl, p. 171).

[219] *HA* ch. 11 (pp. 374–5); *VSCeol.* ch. 16 (pp. 393–4). See below, chapter 4, for a fuller discussion of the inheritance of minsters within families.

[220] S 1433. Patrick Wormald, 'Charters, law and the settlement of disputes in Anglo-Saxon England', in Wendy Davies and Paul Fouracre (eds.), *The Settlement of Disputes in Early Medieval Europe* (Cambridge: Cambridge University Press, 1986), pp. 149–68, at pp. 152–7; see also *idem*, 'A handlist of Anglo-Saxon lawsuits', *Anglo-Saxon England* 17 (1989), 247–81.

[221] *EHD* no. 184.

[222] The earliest recorded lease was S 1254, Bishop Wilfrid's lease of five hides at Bibury, discussed above. An example of a lease made in exchange for a single monetary payment is S 218; compare S

by the end of the eighth century, and was clearly causing such serious deple-
tion of ecclesiastical estates, that the council of Chelsea in 816 directed that
no portion of a minster's lands might be alienated from the church for
longer than one lifetime.[223] However, even if a minster retained direct control of all its estates, the bulk of the labour of cultivating these must have
fallen to the peasants and slaves who lived on them, acting under the direction of the minsters' representatives. For the cathedrals and larger minsters
this must have been the case regardless of whether the professed members
of their communities actually engaged in manual labour; the sheer size
and wide geographical spread of their endowments would have rendered
any other system impossible. For example, the estates of Whitby in the seventh century were farmed by peasants subject to a *uilicus*, a reeve; the latter
was directly responsible to the abbess, for it was to Hild that the reeve took
Cædmon, having heard of his miraculous powers of song.[224] Although there
is little early documentary evidence for the way in which monastic estates
were managed, it is likely that much of the manual labour on many smaller
minsters also fell to the tenants living on the lands. A charter of King Edward
the Elder includes a record in Old English of the dues and services to be rendered from the peasants living on an estate at Hurstbourne in Hampshire
belonging to the *familia* of Winchester Cathedral:

they must plough three acres in their own time and sow them with their own seed
and bring it to the barn in their own time, and give three pounds of barley as rent,
and mow half an acre of meadow as rent in their own time, and make it into a
rick, and supply four fothers of split wood as rent, made into a stack in their own
time . . . and at Easter they shall give two ewes with two lambs . . . and they must
wash the sheep and shear them in their own time.[225]

Whether similar arrangements applied also to the estates of smaller houses
whose archives do not survive is uncertain.

1285 (*SEHD* no. 17), a lease made by Bishop Denewulf and the Winchester community to Beornwulf
in exchange for an annual rent of forty-five shillings paid at the autumn equinox, and given on the
understanding that he and his children would contribute each year to the repair of the church to
which the estate belonged, pay the church-scot, and perform the military service and construction
of bridges and fortresses.

[223] Council of Chelsea, AD 816, ch. 7 (H&S III, 579–85, at p. 582).

[224] *HE* IV. 24 (pp. 416–17): '[Cædmon] ueniensque mane ad uilicum, qui sibi praeerat, quid doni per-
cepisset indicauit, atque ad abbatissam perductus iussus est'. The Old English Bede translated
this passage: 'to þæm tungerefan þe his ealdormon wæs', that is 'to the estate reeve who was his
superior': Thomas Miller (ed.), *The Old English Version of Bede's Ecclesiastical History of the English People*,
EETS, o.s. 95–6 (Oxford: EETS, 1890; reprinted 1959), p. 344.

[225] S 359; A. J. Robertson, *Anglo-Saxon Charters* (Cambridge: Cambridge University Press, 1956), no. 110.
Rosamond Faith, *The English Peasantry and the Growth of Lordship* (London and Washington: Leicester
University Press, 1997), pp. 56–7 and 77.

A minster's external pursuits were not necessarily exclusively agricultural. Charters show that religious houses played an active part in local trade and in small-scale production. An exchange made between the church of Worcester and the Mercian king, Æthelbald, in 716 or 717 shows that the community at Worcester was involved in salt production in the shire. The king gave to the community a piece of land on the river Salwarp 'on which salt is wont to be made', for the construction of three salthouses and six furnaces in exchange for six other furnaces in two salthouses owned by the minster already.[226] Some minsters also engaged in sea-borne trade. A collection of documents surviving uniquely in one archive relates to the exemption of the community of Minster-in-Thanet from the tolls due on ships, and similar documents are known which remit tolls on behalf of other houses.[227]

The control of monastic lands and endowments

The value of ecclesiastical land, and the privileges it carried with it, rendered the church's estates particularly liable to exploitation by the unscrupulous, and not merely by those who masqueraded as abbots. During the late seventh and eighth centuries the evidence of charters and of church councils suggests that the holders of monastic lands faced a variety of different pressures from within and without the church, as interested parties struggled for control of these valuable assets. Solutions proposed to these problems at church councils may not always have served the best interests of the minsters, although they certainly would, if successful, have strengthened the power of the church as a whole against the encroachments of the laity.[228]

The prospect of acquiring ecclesiastical lands for their own benefit was sometimes irresistible to kings: the valuable minster of Cookham in Berkshire, originally given by King Æthelbald to Christ Church, Canterbury, was first seized by Cynewulf of Wessex and then taken from him by Offa, and only restored to the church after a long dispute.[229] Offa and Coenwulf of Mercia even contrived to have their proprietary rights over minsters confirmed by

---

[226] S 102.   [227] Kelly, 'Trading privileges'; Kelly, *Charters of St Augustine's*, pp. xxv–xxvii.

[228] For general discussions see C. J. Godfrey, *The Church in Anglo-Saxon England* (Cambridge: Cambridge University Press, 1962), pp. 163–6; and Edward James, *Britain in the First Millennium* (London: Arnold, 2001), pp. 184–8.

[229] S 1258. See Brooks, *The Early History*, pp. 103–4. Compare also the example of the three minsters lost by Abbot Forthred quoted above (*EHD* no. 184).

papal privilege.[230] One of the charges laid by Boniface against the Mercian king, Æthelbald, was that he had violated the privileges of churches and minsters and deprived them of their property; warning the king to amend his own ways and prevent his *praefecti* and *comites* from oppressing religious and priests, Boniface reminded Æthelbald of the fates of two earlier kings renowned for their abuse of the church and its privileges, Ceolred of Mercia and Osred of Northumbria.[231] The West Saxon royal house was swift to appropriate the valuable lands of the Kentish minsters, whether soon after Wessex gained control of Kent, or once sustained viking attacks on their coastal sites had rendered the monastic life virtually untenable there.[232] Later historians at Abingdon accused King Alfred of having appropriated their minster and its possessions: 'Like Judas among the twelve, heaping evil upon evil, he violently seized the vill in which the abbey was sited ... with all its appurtenances.'[233]

Not only kings and their families abused monastic lands. Bede's celebrated letter of 734 to Ecgberht, bishop of York, censured laymen who:

not experienced in the usages of the life according to the rule or possessed by love of it, give money to kings, and under the pretext of founding minsters buy lands on which they may more freely devote themselves to lust, and in addition cause them to be ascribed to them in hereditary right by royal edicts and even get those same documents of their privileges confirmed ... by the subscription of bishops, abbots and secular persons.[234]

Bede's objections to this practice were two-fold; firstly on religious grounds he abhorred the presence of laymen within minsters, people who 'call themselves abbots and at the same time reeves or thegns or servants of the

---

[230] Wilhelm Levison, *England and the Continent in the Eighth Century* (Oxford: Clarendon Press, 1946), pp. 29–33, 255–7.

[231] Boniface, *Ep.* 73 (ed. Tangl, pp. 152–3).

[232] Brooks, *The Early History*, pp. 205–6. It is possible that King Alfred referred to these in his will where he bequeathed 'all the booklands which I have in Kent' to his eldest son, Edward: Simon Keynes and Michael Lapidge, *Alfred the Great: Asser's Life of King Alfred and Other Contemporary Sources* (Harmondsworth: Penguin, 1983), p. 175. Robin Fleming, 'Monastic lands and England's defence in the Viking Age', *English Historical Review*, 100 (1985), 247–65, at pp. 250–1 and 261–5; David Dumville, *Wessex and England from Alfred to Edgar: Six Essays on Political, Cultural, and Ecclesiastical Revival* (Woodbridge: Boydell Press, 1992), pp. 29–54.

[233] *Historia Monasterii de Abingdon*, I, 44 (ed. Stevenson, I, 50), trans. Alan Thacker, 'Æthelwold and Abingdon', in Barbara Yorke (ed.), *Bishop Æthelwold: His Career and Influence* (Woodbridge: Boydell Press, 1988), pp. 43–64, at p. 45.

[234] *EpEcg*, ch. 12 (p. 415). See plate VI; one of only three known manuscripts of this text, this is an early twelfth-century copy of the letter written at Durham cathedral priory and accompanying a text of Bede's commentary on Proverbs: London, British Library, Harley MS 4688, fo. 93v.

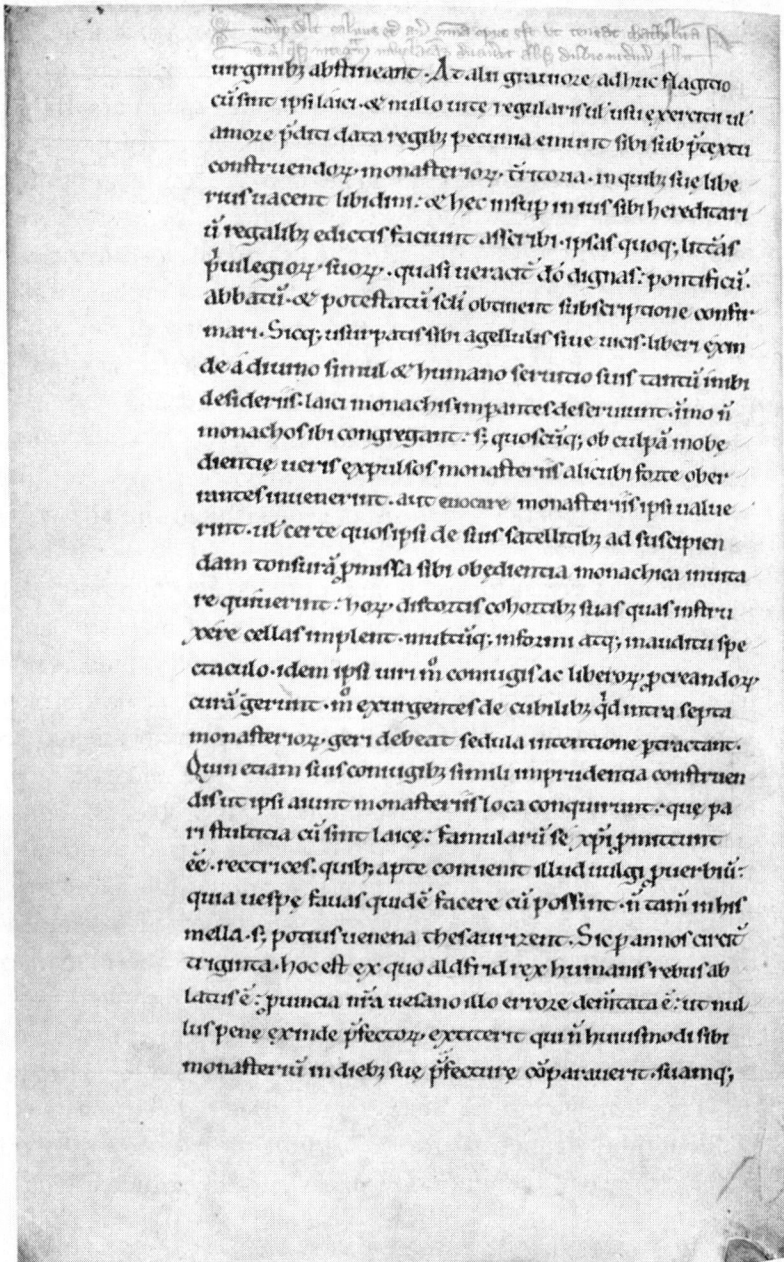

PLATE VI: Bede, Letter to Ecgberht, bishop of York, AD 734: London, British Library, Harley MS 4688, fo. 93v.

king, and who, although as laymen they could have learnt something of the monastic life not by experience but by hearsay, are yet absolutely without the character and profession which should teach it'.[235] Secondly, Bede lamented that lands which could have been used for the support and training of future warriors for the kingdom were being wasted so that there was 'a complete lack of places where the sons of nobles or of veteran thegns [could] receive an estate'; this he feared would lead to 'the dwindling of the supply of secular troops', and hence to 'a lack of men to defend our territories from barbarian invasion'.[236] Allowance must indeed be made for the rhetorical hyperbole of this letter, and Patrick Sims-Williams has rightly drawn attention to the extent to which Bede's letter conforms to a particular genre of monastic hortatory literature, dating back at least to Cassian.[237] Yet instances such as that of the three Northumbrian minsters at Coxwold, Stonegrave and *Donæmuthe*, seized from the hands of Abbot Forthred and given into lay ownership, corroborate the thrust of Bede's lament, and his was by no means an isolated voice.[238]

In a letter written to Archbishop Cuthbert of Canterbury dated AD 747, Boniface criticized the fraudulent acquisition of monastic lands by thegns purporting to be abbots in similar manner to Bede. Boniface referred to the habits of laymen of all ranks who 'relying upon secular force may wrest a minster from the power of a bishop, abbot or an abbess and begin to rule there in place of the abbot, have monks under him and hold property bought by the blood of Christ'.[239] As a solution to this problem Bede had suggested to Ecgberht that these 'innumerable places, allowed the name of minsters but having nothing at all of a monastic way of life' should be taken over for the support of the new bishoprics, which he had recommended should be created to provide adequate pastoral care for the unmanageably large diocese of York.[240]

The council of *Clofesho* of 747 tackled the problem somewhat differently. It recommended that bishops should, for the sake of the health of those who dwell in them, 'go into minsters, if it is indeed right so to name them, which in these times cannot in any way be brought back to Christianity because of the violence of tyrannical greed, that is those which are held by secular

---

[235] *EpEcg*, § 11 (p. 415).   [236] *Ibid.*, § 11. Abels, *Lordship*, pp. 28–30.
[237] Sims-Williams, *Religion and Literature*, pp. 126–9.
[238] *EHD* no. 184; M. S. Parker, 'An Anglo-Saxon monastery in the lower Don valley', *Northern History* 21 (1985), 19–32, at pp. 24–5.
[239] Boniface, *Ep.* 78 (ed. Tangl, p. 169).   [240] *EpEcg*, § 10 (p. 413).

men not by the ordinance of divine law but by presumptuous human invention'.[241] Those present at this council appear to have recognised that such establishments were not capable of total reform or eradication but were, for the foreseeable future at least, an intrinsic part of the English ecclesiastical landscape. Instead of making any alternative suggestions as to the use to which such minsters might be put, the synod urged only that bishops admonish abbots and abbesses to proper behaviour and, where minsters were run by laymen, that they should ensure all such establishments at least had access to the ministry of a priest to provide the sacraments for their inmates.[242]

Yet this edict, in allowing bishops some control over the internal management of minsters, overturned the directive of the council of Hertford in 672–3, which had expressly forbidden bishops to meddle: 'no bishop shall in any way interfere with the minsters dedicated to God nor take away forcibly any part of their property'.[243] Perhaps minsters had been suffering particularly from avaricious bishops in the period before the Hertford council, but any benefit religious houses may have gained from this edict was short-lived, for during the course of the eighth century their independence from episcopal control was steadily eroded. Clergy present at these later councils may have believed that the quality of religious observance in their day was sufficiently inferior to that found in the minsters of Theodore's time to justify the overturning of the minster's customary autonomy. Alternatively, perhaps a forceful group of abbots had contrived in 672 to maintain an

<hr/>

[241] Council of Clofesho, AD 747, ch. 5 (H&S III, 364). The canons of this council were copied into an eighth-century manuscript (British Library, Cotton MS Otho A. i), together with an abridged text of Gregory's *Regula pastoralis*, Boniface's letter to Archbishop Cuthbert, and the text of a charter issued by King Æthelbald at Gumley in Leicestershire in 747 granting privileges to minsters and churches (S 92). As Simon Keynes has shown, this collection constituted a working handbook for the reform of the eighth-century church, probably compiled by or for a Mercian bishop: 'The reconstruction of a burnt Cottonian manuscript: the case of Cotton MS Otho A. i', *British Library Journal* 22 (1996), 113–60, at pp. 135–40. See also *idem*, *The Councils of Clofesho* ([Leicester]: University of Leicester, Department of Adult Education, 1994), p. 27.

[242] Council of *Clofesho*, AD 747, chs. 4–5 (H&S III, 364); see also Hanna Vollrath, *Die Synoden Englands bis 1066* (Paderborn: Schöningh, 1985), pp. 148–9. This council did attempt to approach the problem of undue association between the laity and those devoted to the religious life from a different angle, by directing that clerics, monks and nuns might no longer dwell in the houses of seculars but should return to the minsters where they had first adopted the religious habit: ch. 29 (H&S III, 374); Catherine Cubitt, *Anglo-Saxon Church Councils c.650–c.850* (London and New York: Leicester University Press, 1995), pp. 100–1. Compare the council of Hertford, chs. 4–5 (*HE* IV. 5), which insisted that neither monks nor clerics were to wander from place to place, nor stay among the laity.

[243] Council of Hertford, ch. 3 (*HE* IV. 5, pp. 350–1).

independence from episcopal control which they had felt they were in danger of losing, but the bishops held the stronger hand in 747 and thereafter. The changed emphasis of the canons promulgated after Hertford may bear witness to the increased influence of bishops over abbots in the drafting of ecclesiastical legislation.[244]

Certainly monastic independence from episcopal interference was not restored after 747; indeed the later councils did much to increase the power of the bishops still further, especially over the appointment of abbots, justifying these restrictions on monastic autonomy by references to the external threats to the minsters' survival. Lay domination of minsters had apparently remained a problem, for the legatine synods of 786 attempted to eradicate lay abbots by urging that bishops oversee the appointment of the heads of religious houses.[245] Æthelheard's synod of 803 offered a yet more forceful statement against lay overlordship: 'the communities of all minsters . . . shall never from this time forward presume by any rash daring to elect for themselves laymen and seculars as lords over the inheritance of the Lord'.[246] In 816, the council of Chelsea, presided over by Archbishop Wulfred, made similar injunctions against the presence of seculars within religious communities.[247] This council also attempted to prevent the alienation of monastic properties into secular control by forbidding the leasing of ecclesiastical estates for longer than one lifetime, and stipulated that minsters once dedicated to God should remain minsters in perpetuity.[248]

Whatever the benefit to minsters of such edicts (should they have proved enforceable), these were obtained only at the cost of still further erosion of their independence. The bishops, being deemed responsible for ensuring

---

[244] This is, of course, to presume not only that all the attending clergy played a part in the composition of the canons, but that the abbots were present on every occasion; not every set of canons records whether they were. Bede's account of the Hertford synod (*HE* IV. 5) named all the bishops attending and says only that they met 'with many teachers of the church'. Stephen reported that bishop Wilfrid attended the council of Austerfield in 704 with his abbots, priests and deacons: *VSW* ch. 53. The canons from *Clofesho* in 747 record the presence, in addition to a long list of bishops, only 'of many priests of the Lord and also of those of the lesser dignities of the ecclesiastical order' (H&S III, 362). Abbots were, however, named among the witnesses to the canons agreed at the legatine synod of 786 (ed. Dümmler, p. 29) and at *Clofesho* in 803 and Chelsea in 816 (H&S III, 546–7, 586), although as Cubitt has noted abbots and the lower clergy were not reported in the protocols of conciliar canons before 816: *Anglo-Saxon Church Councils*, p. 42. An interesting chapter of Archbishop Theodore's Penitential (II.ii.3, ed. Finsterwalder, p. 313) stated 'a bishop should not compel an abbot to go to a synod unless there is some sound reason'. See further Cubitt, *Anglo-Saxon Church Councils*, pp. 42–4.

[245] Legatine synods, ch. 5 (ed. Dümmler, p. 22). See Vollrath, *Die Synoden*, p. 168.

[246] Council of *Clofesho*, AD 803 (H&S III, 545); Cubitt, *Anglo-Saxon Church Councils*, pp. 69 and 75.

[247] Council of Chelsea, AD 816, ch. 8 (H&S III, 582).

[248] *Ibid.*, chs. 7 and 8 (p. 582); discussed Cubitt, *Anglo-Saxon Church Councils*, pp. 194–5.

that houses were prevented from decaying either through penury or the rapacity of seculars, were provided with legitimate justification for taking control of any houses which they considered to be sufficiently ailing to be in need of support. Furthermore, the bishops were here given virtually sole charge of the appointment of abbots and abbesses.[249] Nicholas Brooks has demonstrated that this council may be seen as one step in a prolonged episcopal campaign to control the minsters in their dioceses together with their lands, a process that is visible from surviving documents relating to disputes in the eighth and ninth centuries in the Worcester diocese and also in the dispute between Canterbury and the Mercian kings over the Kentish minsters in the early ninth century.[250]

Against this background of encroachment from both the secular world and the ecclesiastical establishment, it is hardly surprising that, at least from the late seventh century onwards, many minsters had attempted to free themselves from all outside control by obtaining privileges from the papacy, which placed them under the direct control of the apostolic see and exempt them from the authority of the diocesan bishop.[251] Benedict Biscop gained a privilege from Pope Agatho (AD 678–91) for his minster at Wearmouth, granting it safety from all outside interference and perpetual freedom.[252] This was later confirmed by Pope Sergius (AD 687–701) and extended to include Jarrow as well.[253] Wilfrid also acquired liberty from secular and episcopal control over his houses at Ripon and Hexham from Pope Agatho, although the terms of his privilege were not respected by the Northumbrian kings.[254] Minsters in southern England tried equally to free themselves from outside interference; although many of the texts of such privileges which now survive are forgeries,[255] there are others which may have some claim to authenticity, such as that of Pope Hadrian in favour of St Augustine's Canterbury, or from Constantine for Bermondsey and Woking.[256] In 786 the canons of the legatine synods directed that the terms of

[249] Council of Chelsea, AD 816, ch. 4 (pp. 580–1).
[250] Brooks, *The Early History*, pp. 175–80; Cubitt, *Anglo-Saxon Church Councils*, pp. 194–202.
[251] Hans Hubert Anton, *Studien zu den Klosterprivilegien der Päpste im frühen Mittelalter: unter besonderer Berücksichtigung der Privilegierung von St. Maurice d'Agaune* (Berlin and New York: de Gruyter, 1975), pp. 51–92.
[252] *HA* ch. 6 (p. 369). Anton, *Studien*, pp. 62–7.   [253] *HA* ch. 15 (p. 380).
[254] *VSW* chs. 45, 47, 51 (pp. 92–3, 96–7, 106–7). Anton, *Studien*, pp. 63–4.
[255] For example S 69, for Sts Peter and Paul, Canterbury; BCS 56 in favour of Chertsey; and BCS 129 for Evesham (neither of the last two is listed in Sawyer's *Handlist*); Levison, *England and the Continent*, p. 26, n. 2; Anton, *Studien*, pp. 60–73.
[256] Canterbury: BCS 38, Levison, *England and the Continent*, pp. 25–6, 187–90, Kelly, *Charters of St Augustine's*, p. xv; Bermondsey and Woking: BCS 133, Levison, *England and the Continent*, p. 26, n. 2, Stenton, *Preparatory*, pp. 185–7.

ancient privileges conferred on churches by the holy Roman see should be respected by everyone, but such documents could equally be used by kings to deny episcopal interference in their proprietary rights over minsters in royal hands.[257] Offa contrived to obtain a privilege from Pope Hadrian I between 772 and 795, granting that all the minsters the king had erected or justly acquired and had established and consecrated in the name of St Peter were to remain under the control of the king, his queen Cynethryth and their heirs for ever.[258] Similarly, Pope Leo II not only gave Coenwulf of Mercia in 817 protection for his minster at Winchcombe where he intended to be buried, freeing it from all secular burdens, but also granted him and his heirs the freedom to dispose of their other minsters in England as they desired.[259] In this light, the actions of Archbishops Æthelheard and Wulfred in trying to legitimise episcopal control and reduce the rights of the laity over minsters are the more understandable.

The making of minsters

After Bede, the voice of those persons most affected by these pressures, the religious themselves, was not heard again until the tenth century, when those who wished to effect a reorganisation of the monastic life in England sought explanation for the state of decay pertaining around 960 by attributing much of the blame to the greed of secular men.[260] Bishop Æthelwold may indeed have lamented justifiably that 'the observance of this holy rule was impaired in former times through the robbery of evil men, and through the consent of kings who had little fear of God'.[261] The extent to which the spiritual quality of the minsters' religious observance and their economic status truly declined in the century before the reform can be questioned, but the reformers' attitude is in part vindicated by the fact that the prosperity of religious houses was so dependent on the support of the nobility. Herein lay both the success of Christianity in England – its capacity to inspire the interest, and more importantly the landed and monetary resources of the Anglo-Saxon aristocracy – and also the seeds of English monasticism's future ills. No quantity of charters purporting, with threats of divine sanction, to

---

[257] Legatine synod, ch. 8 (Dümmler, p. 22).
[258] Levison, *England and the Continent*, pp. 29–31; Sims-Williams, *Religion and Literature*, p. 161.
[259] Levison, *England and the Continent*, pp. 255–7. See also Cubitt, *Anglo-Saxon Church Councils*, pp. 196–202.
[260] Compare *Regularis concordia*, proem, ch. 10, quoted above, p. 17.
[261] Æthelwold, 'Old English account' (*C&S*, I, 152–3).

remove the church's lands from secular control, or of papal privileges preserving minsters from episcopal influences, could protect a religious house if its patrons chose to find other uses for its estates.

Contemporary sources, mostly concerned with larger, richer houses, and comments made by the later reformers, present a similar impression of the prosperity of early Anglo-Saxon minsters, suggesting that these institutions provided equal opportunities for material gain for avaricious laymen. Yet it has been seen that a few of the houses for which information is available did in fact have some difficulty in maintaining the religious life through the inadequacy of their endowments; the same may well have been true of many other minsters about which the sources are silent. We cannot know just how many minsters were founded in the late seventh and early eighth centuries, although we may be confident that this was the time at which interest in expressing religious zeal in this fashion was at its height. The surviving sources may have served to distort our understanding of the prevalence and wealth of early Anglo-Saxon religious communities in that they relate largely (if not exclusively) to those institutions sufficiently well-endowed for some account of their landholdings to have been preserved. Other establishments may briefly have been created by devout enthusiasts, but proved ultimately ephemeral when their lands were restored to secular purposes within a generation or so of their creation. Small and relatively ill-endowed establishments are those least likely to have found their way into the surviving record.[262]

The predominantly ecclesiastical nature of so many of the sources for early Anglo-Saxon history may further serve to accentuate unduly the proportion of lay wealth devoted to religious matters. Although, from the period before the mid-eighth century, the only surviving written records of land tenure relate to ecclesiastical estates, kings also patently gave lands to their followers in much the same way as they had done before the advent of Christianity, namely, in return for service. Benedict Biscop on his conversion to the religious life renounced not only his wife and family but also the possession of land suitable to his rank as a thegn of King Oswiu.[263] Bede's objection to the creation of pseudo-minsters was that they deprived kings of land with which to reward their followers, so leading young men to abandon their homeland in search of wealth elsewhere.[264] That gifts of money and of precious objects such as weapons, jewellery, clothing or books were regularly

[262] Compare the similar remarks I have made about the survival of sources relating to women's religious houses: *Veiled Women*, I, ch. 1.
[263] *HA* ch. 1 (p. 364).   [264] *EpEcg*, § 11 (p. 415).

exchanged and bequeathed between lay people, for example as rewards, as marks of friendship, or to commemorate betrothals, may serve to remind us that the church represented only one of a number of outlets on which the nobility expended their wealth.[265]

King Alfred apparently consigned half of his annual income to religious purposes, yet these included the giving of alms to the poor, providing for the school which he had established at court, and his own monastic foundations at Athelney and Shaftesbury; only one eighth of his revenue was to be spent on 'neighbouring minsters throughout the Saxon land and Mercia'.[266] The other half of his income was reserved for secular beneficiaries, whom he clearly, from the evidence of his will, considered at least as important as religious ones.[267] Many of the precious artefacts which survive from Anglo-Saxon England are presumed to have served a religious function, but there is also abundant evidence, not only from surviving archaeological remains, but also from the written sources for the trade in and the exchange of objects made from precious metals and adorned with jewels, to indicate that only a proportion of the aristocracy's material wealth was lavished on the church.[268] Arrangements made in the surviving wills of the Anglo-Saxon laity for the disposal of their estates and their moveable property demonstrate equally that there is no evidence that the conversion to Christianity caused the Anglo-Saxons to place the church before their loyalty to their kin.[269]

By collecting the evidence relating to the lands and wealth of early Anglo-Saxon religious houses, the separate elements of which are already

---

[265] Thomas Charles-Edwards, 'The distinction between land and moveable wealth in Anglo-Saxon England', in P. H. Sawyer (ed.), *English Medieval Settlement* (London: Edward Arnold, 1979), pp. 97–104, at pp. 97–100. The way in which the Germanic custom of gift exchange was accommodated into a Christian context in Carolingian Francia has been considered by Rosamond McKitterick, *The Carolingians and the Written Word* (Cambridge: Cambridge University Press, 1989), pp. 77–9. For the exchange of books as gifts see *ibid.*, pp. 155–7.

[266] Asser, Life of King Alfred, ch. 102 (ed. Stevenson, pp. 88–9).

[267] Compare *ibid.*, chs. 100–1 (pp. 86–8), with Alfred's will, trans. Keynes and Lapidge, *Alfred the Great*, pp. 174–8. James Campbell suggested that Asser derived his passage about Alfred's arrangement of his income from Einhard's description of the division of Charlemagne's revenues: 'Asser's *Life of Alfred*', in C. Holdsworth and T. P. Wiseman (eds.), *The Inheritance of Historiography, 350–900* (Exeter: University of Exeter, 1986), pp. 115–35, at pp. 116–17. This has been challenged by J. R. Maddicott, 'Trade, industry and the wealth of King Alfred', *Past and Present* 123 (1989), 3–51, at p. 5.

[268] D. Wilson, *Anglo-Saxon Art from the Seventh Century to the Norman Conquest* (London: Thames and Hudson, 1984); Maddicott, 'Trade'; Wormald, 'Bede, "Beowulf" and the conversion'.

[269] See for example S 1482, the will of the reeve Abba; this makes detailed provisions for the distribution of his property after his death among various religious houses in Kent, but his intention was that these institutions would only receive the bulk of his endowment in the event of his dying without heirs, and of his wife's choosing to enter a minster or go on a pilgrimage; otherwise his own family were to be the main beneficiaries.

well-known, we have seen that in material terms there is little to distinguish Bede's 'false' minsters from the majority of other religious houses, even if the way of life followed in both types of institution in fact differed markedly from that of Bede's Jarrow. Indeed it may be fruitless to attempt to distinguish those minsters apparently established for disreputable motives from those houses founded for authentically religious purposes, to satisfy the vocation of an individual, to ensure the spiritual health of a family or dynasty, or to provide for the pastoral care of a neighbourhood. As the owners of landed property, all minsters look remarkably similar, the perceptible differences lying only in the extent of their endowments. The process of creating each sort of institution was the same, they held land on terms which ultimately proved equally precarious, and the sorts of buildings erected within monastic enclosures would seem to be indistinguishable (and not only from other religious establishments but from secular dwellings also). This serves to reinforce the conclusion I have drawn previously from the evidence of the language used to describe religious houses and their inmates, namely that early Anglo-Saxon society recognised a wide diversity of types of institution as nominally distinct from secular establishments.[270] In part, it has been shown, this was because they held land on different terms from their lay counterparts, but it is not clear whether the possession of a charter booking estates for the service of God was sufficient to turn a nobleman's estate into a minster.

We need to turn to consider whether those who lived within minsters were readily distinguishable from seculars in the society around them. To do so, we shall look at the motives driving the pious to leave the world, and the factors that forced others into the cloister against their will. Investigation of the ceremonies marking the entry of seculars to the religious life may reveal not only how the intention to renounce the old life was expressed, but also whether this marked a change in a postulant's social status. Here we will want further to consider the arrangements made to receive children into the cloister. In exploring the ways in which monastic congregations functioned in our period we shall once more find ourselves questioning the accuracy of Bishop Æthelwold's assertion that all houses observed 'one holy rule'; perhaps we should be looking rather to find the same diversity that characterised the making of minsters.

[270] Sarah Foot, 'Anglo-Saxon minsters: a review of terminology', in Blair and Sharpe (eds.), *Pastoral Care before the Parish*, pp. 212–25.

CHAPTER 4

The minster community

When Abbot Ceolfrith left Northumbria to go to Rome in 716, he left a substantial community behind him at Wearmouth and Jarrow. According to his anonymous biographer the two minsters contained between them 'a company of soldiers of Christ of more than six hundred'; Bede similarly numbered the brothers left behind by Ceolfrith at 'almost six hundred'.[1] Although the two communities were clearly supported by a considerable endowment, it is difficult to know whether to take these assessments of the number of their occupants literally.[2] Certainly, no other minster at this period is known to have housed a congregation of such magnitude. The Wearmouth–Jarrow example raises one of the foremost difficulties in assessing the nature of minster communities: which individuals living on a church's estates should be counted as part of the monastic fraternity? Did the six hundred from whom Ceolfrith parted include all the peasantry dwelling on his minsters' one hundred and fifty hides?[3] The Anonymous's description of the inmates as *milites Christi* might suggest not, but Bede can

---

[1] *VSCeol.* ch. 33 (p. 400): 'reliquit autem in monasteriis cohortem militum Christi numero plus quam sexcentorum'. *HA* ch. 17 (p. 382): 'relictis in monasteriis suis fratribus numero ferme sexcentorum'.

[2] Bede's most recent biographer has accepted this figure of six hundred without question: George Hardin Brown, *Bede the Venerable* (Boston, MA: Twayne, 1987), p. 12. Richard Morris has also quoted this figure as an accurate representation of the minster's size: *Churches in the Landscape* (London: J. M. Dent and Sons, 1989), p. 95.

[3] The size of the minsters' endowment was given by Ceolfrith's biographer, *VSCeol.* ch. 33, and has been considered by Alan Thacker, 'Monks, preaching and pastoral care', in John Blair and Richard Sharpe (eds.), *Pastoral Care before the Parish* (Leicester, London and New York: Leicester University Press, 1992), pp. 137–170, at p. 141.

be seen elsewhere to have used *fratres* fairly loosely, possibly with such a broad meaning.[4]

Much information about the nature of minster communities, the reasons which inspired individuals to adopt the religious life and the manner in which their communal existence was organised may be found in early Anglo-Saxon saints' lives. Such works must necessarily be treated with some caution, especially where hagiographers sought to illustrate their subjects' conformity to accepted models of sanctity. However, these texts can illustrate the prevalence of such *topoi* within the early Anglo-Saxon church, while at the same time revealing something about the types of individuals who dwelt in minsters in the pre-Viking period. Since the information to be derived from saints' lives relates predominantly to those of noble and royal rank, less can be determined about the role within minsters of those of humbler birth, whose presence must have been essential for the continuing economic function of at least the larger institutions. Differences between cathedrals and large minsters and the smallest houses may be significant: did the former rely for their continuing communal existence on the labours of others within their enclosures and on their wider estates, whereas the brothers (or sisters) within the smallest cells were much more nearly self-sufficient? This raises a further question as to the relationship between the sexes in double houses, congregations of men and women living together under the authority of an abbess.[5] Before we can analyse the composition of monastic households we need to think about how and why men, women and children chose the cloistered life.

Monastic vocations

Adults and children came to the cloister by various routes, some driven by zealous fervour, others by necessity and a few forced against their will.[6]

---

[4] I have discussed this further in my 'Language and method: the *Dictionary of Old English* and the historian', in M. J. Toswell (ed.), *The Dictionary of Old English: Retrospects and Prospects*, Old English Newsletter, Subsidia 26 (1998), 73–87, at pp. 76–7.

[5] Many have wondered what purpose men served in double houses; see John Godfrey, 'The place of the double monastery in the Anglo-Saxon minster system', in Gerald Bonner (ed.), *Famulus Christi* (London: SPCK, 1976), pp. 344–50; Stephanie Hollis, *Anglo-Saxon Women and the Church: Sharing a Common Fate* (Woodbridge: Boydell Press, 1992), pp. 94–6; Jane Tibbetts Schulenburg, 'Strict active enclosure and its effects on the female monastic experience (500–1100)', in John A. Nichols and Lillian Thomas Shank (eds.), *Medieval Religious Women*, I: *Distant Echoes* (Kalamazoo, MI: Cistercian Publications, 1984), pp. 51–86; and my *Veiled Women*, I, 50–1.

[6] For a brief summary see James Campbell, 'Elements in the background of the life of St Cuthbert and his early life', in Gerald Bonner *et al.* (eds.), *St. Cuthbert, his Cult and his Community to AD 1200* (Woodbridge: Boydell Press, 1989), pp. 3–19, at p. 14.

Saints' lives naturally tended to concentrate on the devotional zeal of their subjects and to lay the greatest emphasis on piety among the range of factors that steered individuals towards a life of religion, but their witness is not necessarily to be trusted on such matters. Pragmatic considerations, either personal ones (illness or disability, divorce or widowhood) or those occasioned by local political circumstances are likely to have been equally important in contributing to an individual's choice of the monastic habit. The entry of children to the cloister raises different issues from those surrounding adult monastic profession and must be considered separately; particular choices also faced devout women who wished to leave their earthly lives, which I have discussed elsewhere.[7]

Children

Early medieval hagiographers frequently stressed the precociously young age at which their subject's notable piety became manifest, for to choose religion in childhood was a recognised mark of holiness and an indication of future sanctity. The anonymous Lindisfarne biographer of Cuthbert depicted the young saint as an ordinary boy, full of agility and high spirits, playing games and performing handstands until 'like Samuel and David' he was marked out by the prophetic words of a smaller child who watched him at play, and by visitations from angels.[8] Although the first intimations of his holiness thus came when he was only eight, Cuthbert was an adult before he first sought entry to a minster.[9] The child Wynfrith, later the missionary Boniface, supposedly conceived a longing to enter the service of God when only four or five years old and achieved his desire despite his father's objections. Bearing in mind Boniface's extreme youth, it is in fact more probable that the saint was dedicated by his father as an oblate; his hagiographer Willibald seems here to have conflated that gift with a common hagiographical *topos* of a disputed conversion.[10]

---

[7] *Veiled Women*, I, 39–44 and 111–26.

[8] Anon., *VSCuth*. I, 3–5 (pp. 64–9). Bede was distinctly less forgiving of the games and wantonness (*lascivia*) of childhood: *VSCuth*. ch. 1 (pp. 154–5 and 158–9); see Janet Nelson, 'Parents, children and the church in the early Middle Ages', in Diana Wood (ed.), *The Church and Childhood*, Studies in Church History 31 (Oxford: Blackwell for the Ecclesiastical History Society, 1994), 81–114, at pp. 84 and 89.

[9] According to his anonymous hagiographer, Cuthbert took the tonsure at Ripon: (*VSCuth*. II. 2, pp. 76–7); but Bede's account, in which he made his vows at Melrose, moving to Ripon with Abbot Eata on its foundation (*VSCuth*. chs. 6–7, pp. 172–6), is the more plausible. See Bertram Colgrave, *Two Lives of Saint Cuthbert* (Cambridge: Cambridge University Press, 1940), p. 317.

[10] *VSB* ch. 1 (pp. 460–2). The episode is discussed further below and by Mayke De Jong, *In Samuel's Image: Child Oblation in the Early Medieval West* (Leiden: Brill, 1996), pp. 47–8.

Children were often found in early English minsters, some perhaps born within their walls,[11] but many consecrated to God by their parents or other relations as a devotional act. Oblation, which properly means the giving of a child in permanent (irrevocable) gift to a monastic community, could provide vicariously for the donors' own spiritual welfare or indeed for the future religious health of the oblate's entire family; it might be chosen in order to fit a child for a future ecclesiastical career, or simply to dispose of the unmarried and unmarriageable (and thereby divorce them from any future entitlement to familial inheritance).[12] To equate oblation with the abandonment of children, as John Boswell has done in grouping exposure, fostering, adoption and oblation within a single category, is unconvincing.[13] Children offered to the religious life were not supposed to return to the world, but they were not thereby totally cut off from their birth families.[14] The practice of oblation, modelled in the view of most early medieval commentators on the dedication of the infant Samuel to the priesthood soon after his birth, was common in the early Christian East and West and is described in several early monastic rules.[15] Yet in reading the early English narrative sources it may be wiser to treat the status of children within minsters with some caution than to assume that a substantial proportion were oblates.[16] Early monastic rules handled differently the problem of the permanence of a donated child's residence within the cloister, but by the beginning of the seventh century both ecclesiastical and secular law in Western Europe stipulated that children given in infancy were not to leave the cloister in maturity.[17]

---

[11] See further below, pp. 145–6.

[12] This area has attracted considerable recent scholarly interest; the most significant recent study of child oblation is Mayke de Jong, *In Samuel's Image*, but see also Patricia A. Quinn, *Better than the Sons of Kings: Boys and Monks in the Early Middle Ages*, Studies in History and Culture 2 (New York: P. Lang, 1989). Children were of course found in contemporary Gallic, Spanish and Irish monasteries, too: Gisela Muschiol, *Famula Dei: zur Liturgie in merowingischen Frauenklöstern*, Beiträge zur Geschichte des alten Mönchtums und des Benediktinertums 42 (Münster: Aschendorff, 1994), pp. 300–12; Lisa Bitel, *Isle of the Saints: Monastic Settlement and Christian Community in Early Ireland* (Ithaca, NY: Cornell University Press, 1990; paperback edition Cork: Cork University Press, 1993), pp. 106–8. For discussion of oblation in the Visigothic realms see De Jong, *In Samuel's Image*, pp. 40–6.

[13] John Boswell, *The Kindness of Strangers: The Abandonment of Children in Western Europe from Late Antiquity to the Renaissance* (London: Allen Lane, 1989), ch. 5, and his '*Expositio* and *oblatio*: the abandonment of children and the ancient and medieval family', *American History Review* 89 (1984), 10–33.

[14] Nelson, 'Parents, children and the church', p. 107.

[15] I Samuel 2:11, 18; for discussion of references to oblation in early monastic rules see De Jong, *In Samuel's Image*, pp. 16–46.

[16] For a less cautious view see Mathew S. Kuefler, '"A wryed existence": attitudes toward children in Anglo-Saxon England', *Journal of Social History* 24 (1991), 823–34, at pp. 824–5.

[17] Boswell, *The Kindness*, pp. 230–4; De Jong, *In Samuel's Image*, pp. 46–7. Boniface struggled with this problem in eighth-century Thuringia and wrote to Pope Gregory II in 726 for advice about whether, 'if a father or mother have placed a son or daughter in the cloister under the discipline of the

One of the most famous child oblates of the early Anglo-Saxon period was the Venerable Bede. By his own account, having been born within the territory of the minster of Jarrow, Bede was, 'when seven years of age, by the care of my kinsmen, put into the charge of the most reverend abbot Benedict and then of Ceolfrith, to be educated'.[18] His relations may not originally have intended that he spend the rest of his life in religion if this act was, as Colgrave suggested, equivalent to putting the boy in the care of foster-parents, rather than a permanent dedication to religion.[19] Among early medieval authorities, Alcuin was alone in asserting that Bede's parents had offered him as an oblate: 'with loving concern his parents had made him enter at the age of seven the cloistered precincts of the minster of Jarrow'.[20] Yet Bede does seem to have become a full member of the community at a young age; he is usually presumed to have gone with his master Ceolfrith to Jarrow when the new minster of St Paul was founded there,[21] and is often identified with the *puerulus* who survived the plague at Jarrow and assumed responsibility for the antiphonal chanting of the office with his abbot.[22] There were other children educated at Wearmouth and Jarrow in Bede's time, for example the future abbot Hwaetberht had been brought up 'from his earliest childhood' in the same minster so, had it not been for the plague, Bede would have had companions in his childhood.[23]

rule, it is lawful for the child, after reaching the years of discretion, to leave the cloister and enter into marriage'. Gregory was unambiguous in his response: 'this we absolutely forbid, since it is an impious thing that the restraints of desire should be relaxed for children given to God': *Ep.* 26, p. 46; trans. Emerton, p. 54; De Jong, *In Samuel's Image*, pp. 46–7.

[18] *HE* V. 24 (pp. 566–7): 'Qui natus in territorio eiusdem monasterii, cum essem annorum VII, cura propinquorum datus sum educandus reuerentissimo abbati Benedicto, ac deinde Ceolfrido.' Bonner has rightly stressed that, although Bede showed in later life nothing but enthusiasm for the cloistered life, it was not seemingly one that he chose of his own volition: 'The Christian life in the thought of the Venerable Bede', *Durham University Journal* 63 (1970), 39–55, at p. 41.

[19] Bertram Colgrave and R. A. B. Mynors (eds), *Bede's Ecclesiastical History of the English People* (Oxford: Clarendon Press, 1969), p. xx; see also Peter Hunter Blair, *The World of Bede* (London: Secker and Warburg, 1970), p. 241. Bede's own reference to these people and the relationship they bore to him was somewhat vague, yet it is not necessary to argue with Brown (*Bede the Venerable*, p. 110, n. 31), that Bede sought deliberately to suppress information about his family. See also Sister M. Thomas Aquinas Carroll, *The Venerable Bede: His Spiritual Teachings* (Washington, DC: Catholic University of America Press, 1946), pp. 2–3, n. 5.

[20] Alcuin, *Versus*, lines 1294–5 (pp. 102–3).

[21] *VCeol.* ch. 11 (p. 391); De Jong, *In Samuel's Image*, pp. 48–9. For a contrary view see Judith McClure and Roger Collins, *Bede, the Ecclesiastical History of the English People* (Oxford and New York: Oxford University Press, 1994), p. xiii. Ian Wood has reasserted the case for the *puerulus* being Bede: Wood, *The Most Holy Abbot Ceolfrid*, p. 34, n. 207.

[22] *VSCeol.* ch. 14, p. 393; see Charles Plummer, *Venerabilis Bedae opera historica*, 2 vols. (Oxford: Clarendon Press, 1896), xii. But the *puerulus* might equally have been another boy, such as Hwaetberht, or the anonymous author of the Life of Ceolfrith himself: Dorothy Whitelock, 'Bede and his teachers and friends', in Gerald Bonner (ed.), *Famulus Christi* (London: SPCK, 1976), pp. 19–39, at pp. 21–2.

[23] *HA* ch. 18 (p. 383).

There are several examples from the seventh and eighth centuries of parents who decided for different reasons to dedicate their young children to the religious life. Oswiu (king of the Northumbrian kingdom of Bernicia 642–70) gave his daughter Ælfflæd to be consecrated to God in perpetual virginity when she was scarcely a year old in order to fulfil a vow, consigning her to the care of Hild at Hartlepool.[24] Willibald's mother and father dedicated their son to God at the age of five, having sworn an oath when he was seriously ill in infancy that if he were cured they would give him to God.[25] The parents of Æthelwulf, author of the poem *De abbatibus*, may also have dedicated their son in childhood; he reported that he had first entered the cell whose abbots he was celebrating as a boy (*puer*) and had attached himself to the priest Wulfsig for six years until the latter became abbot.[26] According to her hagiographer, Rudolf, St Leoba's mother, Æbba, had a vision before her daughter was born which persuaded her to consecrate her child to God as soon as she was old enough.[27]

Not all parents, however, recognised the spiritual benefits to be derived from the permanent dedication of their children to religion. Two incidents from unrelated saints' lives serve to counteract the impression generally given in such literature by demonstrating that the adoption, or imposition, of the religious life was not always welcomed with reverence, or even accepted with resignation. On one occasion, described in some detail in Stephen's Life of St Wilfrid, Bishop Wilfrid had to send his reeve to retrieve a child, Eodwald, whose mother had hidden him among the British instead of giving him up to the saint as she had previously promised. When mortally ill in infancy, Eodwald had been brought back to life by Wilfrid; the saint had baptized the child and restored him to his mother on the understanding that Eodwald would be returned to Wilfrid for the service of God once he reached seven years of age.[28] Wynfrith's father, as we have already seen, was said to have been equally reluctant to allow his five-year-old son to enter a minster. The child had been inspired to this vocation by the example of some visiting priests; a heaven-sent illness warning of the importance of

---

[24] *HE* III. 24 (pp. 290–3). In the ninth century King Alfred established a minster for women over which he placed his daughter Æthelgifu as abbess. The minster seems to have taken some responsibility for the maintenance of the cult of the West Saxon royal family, see my *Veiled Women*, II: *Female Religious Communities in England* (Aldershot: Ashgate, 2000), pp. 165–71.

[25] *Hodoeporicon of Willibald*, chs. 1–2, ed. Oswald Holder-Egger, *MGH*, *SS* XV.I (Hanover: Hann, 1887), 80–117 (pp. 88–9).

[26] *De abbatibus* ch. 18 (pp. 44–5); discussed by De Jong, *In Samuel's Image*, pp. 53–5.

[27] *VSL* ch. 6 (p. 124). Rudolf did not indicate how old Leoba was when she was placed in the minster at Wimborne, but implied that she was still a child.

[28] *VSW* ch. 18 (pp. 38–41).

concentrating on matters spiritual helped the budding saint's father into a more accepting mood.[29]

From these examples it is not possible to make any definitive statement about the age at which children were normally consigned to the religious life in seventh- and eighth-century England; nor does the conflicting advice of early monastic rules shed much light on this question. The Rule of St Benedict, rather unhelpfully, made provision 'if the boy himself is too young' for his parents to draw up on his behalf the written document, *petitio*, in which the new entrant's promises were recorded, but it is not clear when Benedict would have considered a youth old enough to speak for himself.[30] The Rule of the Master, although legislating for young children in the cloister to be treated leniently in various respects, did not contemplate either the possibility that children might make permanent vows, or that others could make them on their behalf; his rule envisages choices made by largely self-determining adolescents.[31] Basil, bishop of Caesarea (d. 379), had suggested that, although children were allowed within monasteries, they should not be required to make a personal commitment to the religious life until they were old enough to choose for themselves at sixteen or seventeen years.[32] Basil's authority was cited in the penitential canons attributed to Archbishop Theodore of Canterbury, in which, although boys were permitted to take full vows at fifteen, girls were made to wait until they reached sixteen or seventeen.[33] In his Rule for Virgins, Caesarius of Arles recommended that girls should not be accepted before they were six or seven, although he allowed for the possibility that younger children might have to be admitted, whereas Aurelian of Arles preferred to set the minimum age at ten or even twelve.[34]

---

[29] *VSB* ch. 1 (pp. 460–2); De Jong, *In Samuel's Image*, pp. 47–8.   [30] *RSB* ch. 59 (pp. 270–1).

[31] *RM* ch. 91 (p. 404); De Jong, *In Samuel's Image*, pp. 31–2. For a wider discussion of adolescents in monasteries see Fiona Harris Stoertz, 'Adolescence and authority in medieval monasticism', in Martin Gosman *et al.* (eds.), *The Growth of Authority in the Medieval West* (Groningen: E. Forsten, 1999), pp. 119–40; the attitude to the possible maturity of adolescents reflected in the Rule of the Master is discussed at p. 129, n. 36.

[32] Basil, *Epistolae*, no. 199, §8, ed. Roy J. Deferrari, *Saint Basil: The Letters*, 4 vols. (London and Cambridge, MA: William Heinemann and Harvard University Press, 1962), II, 108–9.

[33] Theodore, Penitential, II, xii, ch. 37 (p. 330); analysed fully by De Jong, *In Samuel's Image*, p. 52. For the various influences, including that of Basil, on the Canons of Theodore see Hollis, *Anglo-Saxon Women*, pp. 51–5.

[34] Caesarius, *Regula ad uirgines*, ch. 7 (p. 186); Aurelian, *Regula ad monachos*, ch. 17, col. 390. The Rule of Columbanus did not mention oblation; those Gallic writers who produced composite rules such as Donatus (d. 658), for a nunnery in Besançon, and Waldebert of Luxeuil's Rule for the nuns of Faremoutiers, followed Caesarius' recommendations on age: Boswell, *The Kindness*, p. 232, n. 15; De Jong, *In Samuel's Image*, pp. 35–7.

Whatever the rules advised, in practice it is clear from the hagiographical literature that very small children were frequently found inside English minsters, not all of whom had necessarily been formally dedicated as oblates. Some of the nobility may have seen their local minster as a convenient source of child-care, possibly even for very young children. Bede described the death at Barking of a boy called Æsica who was only three years old and 'because of his extreme youth was being looked after and learning his lessons in the dwelling of the maidens dedicated to God'. At the moment of his death he cried out for one of the sisters, Eadgyth (perhaps the one who particularly looked after him); in reporting that she too died the same day, Bede was careful to describe her as a virgin, so she cannot have been his mother.[35] Such houses may thus have found themselves in effect providing the sort of nursery facilities against which Charlemagne felt the need to legislate at the Synod of Frankfurt in 794.[36] The lack of references to wet nurses in medieval monasteries might imply, as Boswell suggested, that early medieval practice was generally to donate babies to religion after their weaning.[37] According to Alcuin, Willibrord's father took him as an infant when he was weaned and gave him to the brothers at Ripon,[38] and Alcuin's own biographer similarly reported that the saint had been 'brought to the mystical bosom of the church when he was weaned from his mother's carnal breasts'.[39] Yet there may in fact have been some tiny infants inside minsters if they were born there (and these need not necessarily have been born exclusively to visitors or to those only newly recruited). Infant boys were also, as

[35] *HE* IV. 8 (pp. 358–9). Since an early ninth-century capitulary of Charlemagne's sought to prohibit the entrusting of boys to female religious communities, one might imagine that there were small boys found in Frankish nunneries also: 804 Capitulary, ch. 7 (ed. Boretius, *MGH, Capitularia* I, 42, no. 119): 'Omnino prohibemus, ut nullus masculum filium aut nepotem uel parentem suum in monasterio puellarum ad nutriendum commendare praesumat, nec quisquam illum suscipere audeat.' Quoted by Boswell, *The Kindness*, p. 244, n. 50.
[36] Synod of Frankfurt, ch. 16, ed. *MGH, Concilia*, II, 168; compare also Louis the Pious' monastic capitularly of 817, ch. 75 (ed. Boretius, *MGH, Capitularia* I, 348, no. 170), which forbids the reception of people into monasteries for the gifts they might bring with them rather than the probity of their lives.
[37] Boswell, *The Kindness*, p. 234, n. 26. One passage in Benedict's Rule describing the steps of humility, the highest monastic virtue, echoed Psalm 130: 1–2 in saying 'Surely I have behaved and quieted myself as a child that is weaned from its mother; my soul is as a weaned child' (*RSB* ch. 7, p. 192–3). This could be an allusion to the pure humility of the child oblate, taken into the monastery at the moment of their weaning: Patricia Quinn, *Better than the Sons of Kings*, pp. 140–1.
[38] Alcuin, *Vita S. Willibrordi*, ch. 3 (pp. 117–18). Talbot thought it implausible that Alcuin intended to imply that Willibrord was given as an infant, preferring to translate the phrase 'statim ablactatum infantulum' as 'when he reached the age of reason': *The Anglo-Saxon Missionaries in Germany* (London: Sheed & Ward, 1954), p. 5, n. 1.
[39] *Vita Alcuini*, ch. 1, p. 185; De Jong, *In Samuel's Image*, p. 50.

the example from Barking makes clear, able to gain access to parts of female enclosures from which adult males would normally have been excluded.[40] Fornication by religious women and the adultery committed by laymen with professed virgins were not infrequent *topoi* in admonitory letters addressed to the English, and the fate of the children born of such unions caused equal concern; Boniface consigned the souls of murdered babies adulterously born to religious women to eternal damnation.[41]

That entry to the cloister in early medieval England was meant to be permanent is clear from the prescriptive literature. The penitential canons attributed to Theodore tried to tackle the problem of adolescents given in childhood who wanted to return to the world and marry,[42] but did also recognise that families might think better on reflection of vows made in a child's infancy. Theodore ruled that although a vow ought to be kept, one child might be given to God at a monastery instead of another, even if the other had originally been vowed.[43] For all the disapproval expressed in early monastic rules of the practice, there were even so children living within early English minsters who were not necessarily destined for the cloister.[44] Wilfrid was fourteen when he first entered the minster of Lindisfarne, where he learnt the Psalter and several other books; although Stephen said that he sought to live 'the full religious life' there, he did not take the tonsure until he visited Gaul in his early twenties.[45] Nor did the bishop envisage monastic careers for all his own pupils; secular nobles gave their sons to Wilfrid to be educated 'so that, if they chose, they might devote themselves to the service of God; or that, if they preferred, he might give them into the king's charge as warriors when they were grown up'.[46]

Adult postulants

While children were thus commonly given to a life of religion in the early Anglo-Saxon period, many monastics chose the religious life for themselves

[40] Nelson, 'Parents, children and the church', p. 88.

[41] In a letter of 746/7 to Æthelbald, king of Mercia, in which Boniface had also expressed his disapproval of the prostitution and adultery of religious women: *Epistola* 73 (pp. 151–2). Anxiety about sexual relations with professed virgins was reflected in the canons of the legatine council of 786, chs. 15–6, and such behaviour was specifically prohibited in a letter from Pope John VIII to Burgred, king of Mercia, datable 873/4, ed. Caspar, *MGH, Epp. Karol. Aevi* V, 293, trans. *EHD* no. 220.

[42] Theodore, Penitential, II, vi, 11 (p. 321).

[43] *Ibid.*, II, xiv, 5. The next provision stipulated that the same might be done with cattle.

[44] Caesarius, *Regula ad uirgines*, ch. 7 (p. 186), tried to prevent the acceptance of noble or peasant girls simply for rearing and education.

[45] *VSW* chs. 2 and 6 (pp. 6–7 and 12–15). [46] *Ibid.*, ch. 21 (pp. 44–5).

later in life, coming to an understanding of the emptiness of worldly pursuits only after experiencing these directly.[47] Guthlac and Eosterwine had both been soldiers before they renounced the world and laid down their arms to become soldiers of Christ.[48] Benedict Biscop had been one of King Oswiu's thegns (and so abandoned an earthly career in the hope of heavenly reward) but chose to leave his family on Christ's behalf, rejecting the bond of earthly marriage in favour of a life dedicated to chastity, through which he might raise spiritual not earthly children.[49] Among the obituary notices included in the set of earlier northern annals incorporated into Simeon of Durham's *Historia regum* are records for a certain Alric 'once *dux* now *clericus*' and for Edwin, 'formerly ealdorman of the Northumbrians, then indeed by the grace of the Saviour of the world an abbot strong in the service of God, ended his last day like a veteran soldier in the sight of the brothers'.[50] Cuthbert had apparently more lowly origins, having spent some of his time tending sheep before a divine vision inspired him to abandon the secular habit and enter the minster at Melrose; his possession of a horse on which to ride alone to the abbey suggests, however, that he had some independent means.[51]

Many people of both sexes came to the minsters in widowhood, or as a means of escaping from uncongenial marriages. The prologue to Aldhelm's prose *De virginitate*, dedicated to Abbess Hildelith and the sisters of Barking, suggests that both courses of action were common.[52] In recognition of the diverse backgrounds of the women at Barking, Aldhelm defined virginity somewhat differently from earlier patristic writers. Instead of the more usual three states of virginity, marriage and widowhood, he allowed

---

[47] The Anglo-Saxon evidence suggests that John van Engen may have overstated his case when he argued that '[d]own to the year 1100 and beyond, most contemplatives joined monasteries as child oblates, their religious vocation determined for them by parents': 'Professing religion: from liturgy to law', *Viator* 29 (1998), 323–43, at p. 324.

[48] *VSG* chs. 18–19 (pp. 80–2); *HA* ch. 8 (p. 371).

[49] *HA* ch. 1 (pp. 364–5); compare Bede's homily for the feast of Benedict Biscop, *Homelia*, I, 13 (p. 92), quoted Plummer, *Bedae opera*, II, 356, and Michael Lapidge and Michael Herren (eds.), *Aldhelm: The Prose Works* (Ipswich: D. S. Brewer, 1979), p. 54, and p. 192, n. 14.

[50] *Historia regum, s.a.* 796, 801 (ed. Arnold, pp. 57 and 65); compare also the obit for Osbald, *s.a.* 799 (ed. Arnold, p. 62) on whom see Alcuin, *Ep.* 109 (p. 156). These entries were discussed by Campbell, 'Elements', p. 14.

[51] Anon., *VSCuth*. I. 5 (pp. 68–9); Bede, *VSCuth*. ch. 4 and ch. 6 (pp. 164–5 and 172–3).

[52] A fuller discussion of the choices facing widows and their status in law may be found in my *Veiled Women, I: The Disappearance of Nuns from Anglo-Saxon England* (Aldershot, 2000), chs. 2 and 5. Legal protection for widows was provided in the following early law-codes: Æthelberht, chs. 75–6 and 78 (ed. Liebermann, *Die Gesetze*, I, 7–8); Hlothhere and Eadric, ch. 6 (*ibid.*, p. 10); Ine, ch. 38 (*ibid.*, p. 94). See T. J. Rivers, 'Widows' rights in Anglo-Saxon law', *American Journal of Legal History* 19 (1975), 208–15, at pp. 210–12.

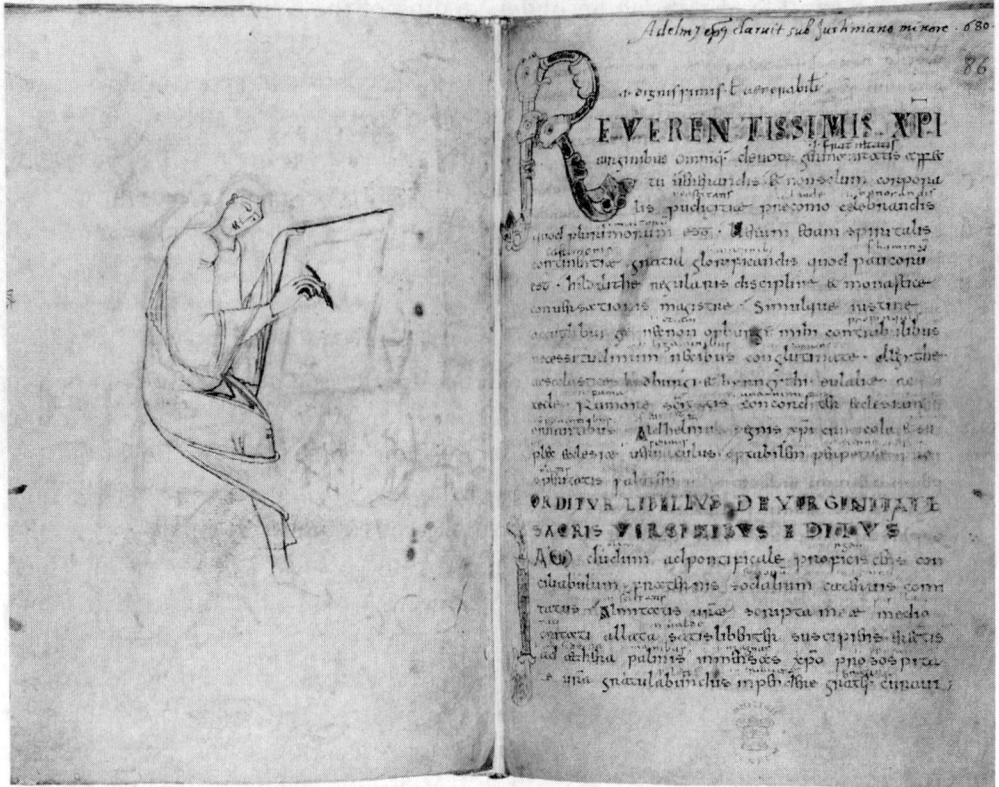

PLATE VII: Aldhelm, *De uirginitate*, London, British Library, Royal MS 7 D. xxiv, fos. 85v–86.

three conditions of virginity, chastity and marriage.[53] Chastity he defined as the condition of a person who, 'having been assigned to marital contracts, has scorned the commerce of matrimony for the sake of the heavenly kingdom'.[54] Thus Aldhelm was able to praise both those in the Barking community who had abandoned their marriages in favour of the religious life and those who were true virgins.[55] The Anglo-Saxon Chronicle reported that Cuthburg, the sister of King Ine of Wessex and the wife of King Aldfrith of the Northumbrians, separated from her husband during his lifetime; it is possible that she should be identified with the Cuthburg whose name

---

[53] Lapidge and Herren, *Aldhelm*, pp. 52–6.   [54] Aldhelm, prose *De uirginitate*, xix (p. 248).

[55] Lapidge and Herren, *Aldhelm*, pp. 55–6. The continuing popularity of Aldhelm's *De uirginitate* is illustrated by plate VII, a manuscript of the text dating from the first half of the tenth century: London, British Library, Royal MS 7 D. xxiv, fos. 85v–86.

is included among the dedicatees of Aldhelm's treatise.[56] Theodore's Penitential also allowed couples to separate in order for one or both of them to adopt the religious life and permitted an adulterous woman whose husband no longer wished to live with her to elect to enter a minster.[57] For such a purpose the wife might retain a fourth part of her property, although she would lose all of it if she chose another course;[58] Aldhelm considered neither eventuality in his *De virginitate*.

Narrative sources make references to various people who left their spouses to join minsters, not without considerable difficulty in some cases.[59] Æthelthryth had first been married to the ealdorman Tondberht, who died shortly after their marriage. She was then made the wife of Ecgfrith of Northumbria, but it was twelve years (during which time she is reputed to have retained her virginity) before she was able to achieve her long-held ambition and enter the minster of Coldingham.[60] King Sæbbi of the East Saxons also spent many years persuading his wife to allow him to leave the world to enter a minster, but only obtained her consent when after thirty years on the throne of Essex he became seriously ill.[61] The devout man, Dryhthelm, who entered the minster of Melrose after having a vision of hell following a severe illness, had previously lived 'a religious life together with his family', according to Bede ('religiosam cum domu sua gerens uitam'), but it is not known what became of his wife once he left her, other than that she received a third of Dryhthelm's property.[62] Dryhthelm may have been one of those persons described so scathingly in Bede's letter to Bishop Ecgberht, who had acquired a charter reserving his estate for ecclesiastical use but continued to dwell on it with his wife and family. That Dryhthelm went immediately on waking to the oratory of the village (*ad uillulae oratorium*) need not contradict such a supposition; the religious arrangements

---

[56] ASC *s.a.* 718; Aldhelm, *De virginitate*, prol. (p. 229). See also Pauline Stafford, *Queens, Concubines and Dowagers* (London: Batsford, 1983), p. 179, and my *Veiled Women*, I, pp. 40–1.

[57] Theodore, Penitential, II. xii. 8, 13.   [58] *Ibid.*, II. xii. 11.

[59] Julie Ann Smith has explored the question of divorce more widely: *Ordering Women's Lives: Penitentials and Nunnery Rules in the Early Medieval West* (Aldershot: Ashgate, 2001), pp. 52–4.

[60] *HE* IV. 19 (pp. 390–3). The implication of this passage is that Tondberht died before Æthelthryth's first marriage could be consummated.

[61] *HE* IV. 11 (pp. 364–5). Sæbbi was not the only king to resign his throne in favour of the cloister. Sigeberht of the East Angles entrusted his kingdom to a kinsman in order to enter his own foundation at Burgh Castle; even when dragged out of the cloister to fight Penda he refused to bear arms again and was killed on the battlefield: III. 18 (pp. 268–9).

[62] *HE* V. 12 (pp. 488–9). In the Old English Bede (V. 13), Dryhthelm was said to have lived 'piously' with his whole household, rather than in the religious life, at home: 'lufde he aefestlice his lif mid his heorde': Thomas Miller (ed.), *The Old English Version of Bede's Ecclesiastical History of the English People*, 2 vols., EETS orig. ser. 95–6 and 110–11 (London, New York, Toronto: Oxford University Press for the Early English Text Society, 1890), II, 422–3.

in such family minsters may have been so informal as not to set aside any particular place for prayer. It is clear that Dryhthelm's vision had convinced him that life with his family, however devoutly conducted, was insufficient to secure salvation, a realisation which inspired him to leave home, take the tonsure at Melrose and thereafter live in a solitary retreat provided for him by the abbot. The Kentish reeve, Abba, made different provisions in his will for his wife after his death according to whether she remarried (in which case she would receive only her own property), went on a pilgrimage, or entered the cloister. If she took the latter course, Abba made generous arrangements to ensure she was adequately provided with a suitable dowry.[63]

The motives which inspired women other than the widowed or divorced to enter minsters are less explicitly described in the sources, but some general inferences may be drawn when all the evidence for women in the religious life is assembled.[64] Bede reported that Hild, later abbess of Whitby, had 'spent the first thirty-three years of her life very nobly in the secular habit', and then been inspired by the example of her sister, Hereswith, a sister at Chelles, to enter the religious life in Francia herself. She did not, however, achieve this ambition, being recalled by Bishop Aidan to Northumbria, where she was given one hide of land on the north side of the river Wear on which to live a monastic life with a small group of companions.[65] Dagmar Schneider has shown that 'without exception women followed their mother's family when they entered a monastic community', rather than entering houses connected with their paternal relations; for example, Eorcengota did not enter Folkestone, founded by her father's sister Eanswith, but went instead to Brie where her mother's sister, Æthelburh, and half-sister, Saethryth, were abbesses.[66] It does seem to have been common when a mature woman of noble birth entered a minster for at least some of her daughters to have done likewise; a number of incidents in the sources relate to mothers and daughters within the same house.[67] For example

---

[63] S 1482 (AD 833x839); trans. Harmer, *SEHD*, p. 41, no. 2.

[64] For a detailed study of the role of women in Anglo-Saxon minsters see Dagmar Schneider, 'Anglo-Saxon women in the religious life: a study of the status and position of women in an early mediaeval society' (unpublished PhD dissertation, University of Cambridge, 1985), and now my *Veiled Women*, I, ch. 2, and for widows specifically, ch. 5, where particular attention is paid to the evidence for women who elected to take the veil but remain living within their own homes.

[65] *HE* IV.23 (pp. 406–7).

[66] Schneider, 'Anglo-Saxon women', p. 249; for Eorcengota see *HE* III. 8 (pp. 238–9).

[67] In this context, compare also Julia Smith's remarks about women's religious devotion in Francia: 'Carolingian images of female sanctity do not operate around an antithesis between family and religious calling; they present their subjects in a predominantly familial context . . . It is also

Bede related a miracle performed by John of Beverley in curing a certain Cwenburh, a sister at Watton, where her mother Hereburg was abbess.[68] A record of a dispute over the succession of a minster in Gloucestershire in the mid-eighth century shows how such family connections might extend over two generations. A certain Dunne and her daughter Bugge had been given land at Withington on which to found a minster; when Dunne was dying she left the house to her grand-daughter Hrothwaru, then still a child, since her own daughter was married, but entrusted the care of it to Bugge until Hrothwaru was old enough to preside over the minster herself. The cause of the dispute lay in Bugge's refusal to part with the possession of the minster on Hrothwaru's maturity, but the case was settled in the latter's favour.[69]

Ambitious members of the nobility of both sexes may by the late seventh century have been attracted to the religious life because of the potential promise offered by monasticism as a career, even though such motives are at odds with the purest expressions of the monastic ideal. Several noble abbesses held considerable political power and influence in the seventh and eighth centuries, not only through the richness of their lands and property but also because their houses were used as meeting places by visiting kings and for councils and synods.[70] The status of an abbess might therefore offer a woman a more secure means of achieving political power than she could hope to attain by marriage, or alternatively provide her with a means of maintaining influence in the world when widowed or otherwise separated from her husband.[71] For men the cloister might frequently be a useful route to episcopal advancement; most if not all bishops appointed from the time of Theodore onwards were trained in English minsters, and it is possible to trace links between certain individual minsters and particular episcopal sees.[72]

---

particularly common to find that, even after taking the veil, women's lives remained shaped by their family cares and attachments': 'The problem of female sanctity in Carolingian Europe, *c.* 750–920', *Past and Present* 146 (1995), 3–37, at p. 25.

[68] *HE* V. 3 (pp. 460–3). There is no indication, contrary to Kuefler's suggestion ('"A wryed existence"', pp. 824–5), that Cwenburh was a child, for Bede described her merely as a *virgo*.

[69] S 1429 (AD 736x737). This serves to demonstrate how important the minster as inheritable property was to women as well as to men; see Schneider, 'Anglo-Saxon women', pp. 243–70.

[70] See below.

[71] However, Schneider has shown ('Anglo-Saxon women', p. 274) that this was not always true; Queen Iurminburg played a significant role in contemporary Northumbrian politics while married to Ecgfrith, but once she entered the minster at Carlisle she appears to have lost her political influence.

[72] Nicholas Brooks and Catherine Cubitt have both commented on the monastic origins of seventh-century archbishops of Canterbury, who were trained in a variety of Mercian minsters rather than at the metropolitan see: Nicholas Brooks, *The Early History of the Church of Canterbury: Christ Church 597–1066* (Leicester: Leicester University Press, 1984), pp. 76–83, 114 and 120; Catherine Cubitt,

Quite apart from whatever active pastoral activities such institutions performed on behalf of their lay neighbours, the local minster must have acted as a focus for the expression of lay piety and not infrequently have inspired individuals to adopt the religious life themselves. This was supposedly the source of the vocation of the child Wynfrith, later the missionary Boniface, who heard about monasticism from visiting clerics who came to the town where he was living.[73] Equally, some of those who attempted to live in solitary devotion were frustrated in their efforts, acting instead as a magnet to similar-minded souls in the vicinity; Willibrord's father, Wilgils, retired alone to an oratory on the Humber estuary, but soon found himself surrounded by crowds seeking instruction, some of whom wanted to join him.[74]

Entry to the religious life

A person's status within society was permanently changed by their entry to the religious life, the transformation being marked with appropriate ceremony and ritual.[75] The visible alteration to a postulant's appearance, made through the adoption of the outward symbols of monastic status, notably a distinctive form of dress and a particular haircut (or for women, head-covering), was an important aspect of that transition from the secular world to the religious. These ceremonies, together with the formalised rejection of personal property, conveyed the magnitude and meaning of the entrant's transition to the new life in starkly physical manner, a process facilitated, as Roberta Gilchrist has shown, through the structuring of the new self in relation to monastic time, ordered space, religious ceremony and a new material culture.[76] Rituals followed in early Anglo-Saxon minsters to mark an individual's renunciation of his former secular life and his acceptance into a community of the servants of God may have been of variable formality, with diverse ceremonies practised in different houses; some indication

---

'Wilfrid's "usurping bishops": episcopal elections in Anglo-Saxon England *c.* 600–*c.* 800', *Northern History* 25 (1989), 18–38, at pp. 27–30. Hild's house at Whitby was obviously exceptional in having nurtured five future bishops: *HE* IV. 23 (pp. 408–9). See further below.

[73] *VSB* ch. 1 (p. 460).   [74] Alcuin, *Vita S. Willibrordi*, ch. 1 (p. 116).

[75] Giles Constable, 'The ceremonies and symbolism of entering the religious life and taking the monastic habit, from the fourth to the twelfth century', *Settimane* 33 (1987), 771–834, at pp. 808–15. We have already observed that medieval commentators commonly equated the act of religious profession with a second baptism; see above, p. 40.

[76] Roberta Gilchrist, *Gender and Material Culture: The Archaeology of Religious Women* (London and New York: Routledge, 1994), p. 18. Compare the discussion of the ordering of monastic space above in chapter 2.

of the nature of contemporary rituals may be found in the prescriptive literature but – as ever – this is not necessarily the clearest guide to local custom.

Benedict's Rule provides the most precise advice on the reception of new members to a monastic community, going to considerable lengths, indeed, to put obstacles in the way of an adult newcomer to ensure that only the fully committed were made professed members of the congregation.[77] His provisions owed much to the arrangements for the probation and profession of new monks specified by Cassian and in the Rule of the Master, but Benedict's ideas about probation were more developed than those of his sources and his ceremony of profession went further than they did in drawing together all the elements that make a monk into a single ceremony performed at one time.[78] The Rule of Columbanus (which as we have already seen is likely to have been a significant component part of the mixed rules created in individual English minsters, as it was in Gaul) made no reference to ceremonies of initiation, although it did refer to a monk's vow, *uotum*.[79] One might reasonably assume that all applicants of sufficient age made public statements about their commitment to follow a new path; whether this always included the making of a formal vow or promise is less clear.

Any adult who came knocking at the abbey's door seeking admission was, according to Benedict, to be ignored for the first four or five days and only allowed to enter the confines of the monastery if he were able to contain his impatience at being so disregarded. After a brief period in the guesthouse, he might be admitted to the *cella nouiciorum* where he was to remain for a year,[80] during which time the whole of the Rule was to be read to him three times in order that he understand fully the law under which he was choosing to serve.[81] Only those who had successfully navigated this

---

[77] Richard Yeo has made a detailed study of the history of Benedictine monastic profession: *The Structure and Content of Monastic Profession: A Juridical Study, with Particular Regard to the Practice of the English Benedictine Congregation since the French Revolution*, Studia Anselmiana, 83 (Rome: Pontificio Ateneo S. Anselmo, 1982).

[78] *Ibid.*, pp. 126–9.

[79] Columbanus, *Regula monachorum*, ch 6 (ed. Walker, pp. 128–9); the vow is referred to specifically in relation to the commitment to chastity and the necessity for a monk to remain virgin in mind as well as in body. For the influence of Columbanus's Rule, and more specifically the mixed systems adopted in his circle in the generation after his death see above, ch. 2.

[80] Both Cassian and the Rule of the Master placed potential recruits in the guest-house during their probation; the *cella nouiciorum* was a Benedictine innovation: Yeo, *The Structure and Content*, p. 128.

[81] *RSB* ch. 58, 1–5, 9–16 (pp. 266–9). The Rule of the Master demanded that the entire rule be read to a novice just once during his novitiate: *RM* chs. 87, 3 (pp. 356–7), 89, 8 (pp. 372–3), 90, 5 (pp. 378–9). Yeo, *The Structure and Content*, pp. 126–7. Rules for women also insisted on a period of probation and

period of training and preparation were permitted to come before the whole community in the *oratorium* and promise, in the presence of God and his saints, stability, fidelity to monastic life, and obedience; that promise was recorded in writing in a *petitio* deposited by the novice on the altar before he prostrated himself in front of each member of the community in turn and requested their prayers.[82] Through the *promissio* and *petitio* the aspiring monk made a binding commitment to remain in the religious life for ever; he was to be numbered among the community from that hour, according to Benedict, having already passed his year of probation before that day.[83] Only then did the newcomer rid himself of all his personal possessions (either giving them to the poor beforehand, or handing them in formal donation to the monastery) and as the final act in the admission ceremony he parted with his secular clothing and donned the clothes of the monastery.[84]

In stark contrast with this lengthy process, during which the adult postulant was frequently given the option to abandon the monastery and return to the world, Benedict's treatment of children seems, as Mayke de Jong has observed, almost indecently hasty. None of the same obstacles prevented a child's admission: his parents were directed to draw up the *petitio* on his behalf, to wrap his hand with his offering in the cloth of the altar and thereby commit him irrevocably to a life of religion.[85] At five years of age, Wynfrith was, according to his biographer, old enough to make his own petition to the abbot of Exeter, yet the offering of Willibald, also aged five,

---

testing before an aspirant woman could become a full member of the congregation. In the Rule of Caesarius of Arles, women could only assume the veil and habit after a year's novitiate: Caesarius, *Regula ad uirgines*, ch. 4 (pp. 182–3); compare the Rule of Donatus, ch. 6, ed. Adalbert de Vogüé, 'La règle de Donat pour l'abbesse Gauthstrude', *Benedictina* 25 (1978), 219–313, at pp. 249–50.

[82] *RSB* ch. 58, 17–23 (pp. 268–9). Yeo, *The Structure and Content*, pp. 130–3.

[83] *RSB* ch. 58, 23 (pp. 268–9); Yeo, *The Structure and Content*, p. 134. Cuthbert Butler discussed the significance of the Benedictine vows in his *Benedictine Monachism* (London: Longmans, Green & Co., 1919), pp. 122–45.

[84] *RSB* ch. 58, 24–8 (pp. 268–71). The clothing is not described here, but ch. 55 (pp. 260–3) provides a detailed account of the nature and quantity of the clothes supplied to each monk. Compare Caesarius, *Regula ad uirgines*, chs. 4–5 (pp. 182–5), which discuss the necessity for postulants to remain in secular garb until their vocations have been tested.

[85] *RSB* ch. 59 (pp. 270–3); De Jong, *In Samuel's Image*, pp. 26–30; Quinn, *Better than the Sons of Kings*, pp. 136–8. On the issue of the irrevocability of the parents' vow on their child's behalf see van Engen, 'Professing religion', p. 327, where the highly influential statement made at the Fourth Council of Toledo of 633 (ch. 49) is quoted: 'Monachum aut paterna deuotio aut propria professio facit; quidquid horum fuerit, alligatum tenebit': 'Either paternal devotion or personal profession makes a monk; which ever it was he will be bound': José Vives *et al.* (ed.), *Concilios visigóticos e hispano-romanos*, no. 21 (Barcelona: Consejo Superior de Investigaciones Cientificas, Instituto Enrique Flóres, 1963), p. 24. Nelson has explored the elaboration of the liturgy of oblation in the Carolingian period: 'Parents and children', pp. 107–8.

was made by a 'venerable man' called Theodred, who had been entrusted by the child's parents with making all the arrangements and dispositions on his behalf.[86]

Although the exact nature and timing of a postulant layman's reclothing in the distinctive clothing of religion varied in early medieval Europe, the assumption of the habit came increasingly to symbolise the making of a vow, to be an outward and visible sign of a person's *conversatio*. Benedict's influence is likely to have been significant here, for in linking the ceremony of reclothing more closely with the making of final vows than had earlier monastic rules, Benedict's Rule made the habit the symbol of monastic profession in a way that other monastic legislators had not.[87] For religious women, the veil – and to a lesser extent – the habit similarly came to symbolise a woman's new, holy status. When legislating to try to prevent laymen from fornicating with virgins, the canons of the 786 legatine synod asserted 'we do not hesitate to call a virgin who has devoted herself to God and put on the garment of the holy Mary, a bride of Christ'.[88] Various English texts make it clear that the act of assuming religious garb marked the moment of transition from lay to religious status. The dialogues of Ecgberht offered guidance as to the best way to handle crimes committed by a *clericus uel monachus* 'while he was still in the lay habit' ('pro causis aliquibus iam pridem sub laico habitu perpetratis').[89] At the 747 council of *Clofesho*, bishops or the heads of minsters were directed to enquire thoroughly into the way of life and moral standing of those who wanted to join religious communities while they were still in the lay habit and before they were tonsured.[90] Whether such enquiry was undertaken during a period of novitiate and before the postulant's clothing and tonsuring (as Benedict's Rule prescribed) or whether it might happen before the individual had entered the cloister at all is unclear. From this insistence on the representative function played by monastic dress, it is thus unsurprising that so much attention was paid in church councils both to the manner in which the new clothing was put

---

[86] *VSB* ch. 1; *Hodoeporicon of Willibald*, ch. 2. The donation of the young Willibald was discussed by De Jong, *In Samuel's Image*, p. 54.
[87] Constable, 'The ceremonies', pp. 808–10; Yeo, *The Structure and Content*, pp. 134–6.
[88] Legatine synod of 786, ch. 16 (p. 25): 'Virginem namque, quae se Deo uouerit et ad instar sanctae Mariae uestem induerit, sponsam Christi uocitare non dubitamus.'
[89] Dialogues of Ecgberht, *Interrogatio* XIV (H&S III, 409).
[90] Council of *Clofesho*, AD 747, ch. 24 (H&S III, 370). Trying to prevent clerics, monks and nuns from living among the laity, the same council directed that all should return 'to the minsters where they first took the habit of holy profession', ch. 29 (H&S III, 374): 'repetant monasteria ubi primitus habitum sanctae professionis sumpserant'.

on, and to the importance of religious of both sexes wearing appropriate dress at all times.[91]

Archbishop Theodore's penitential canons provide the earliest evidence from the medieval West of a sacrament for the ordaining of a new monk.

> In the ordination of a monk, indeed, the abbot ought to perform the mass and complete three prayers over his head; and for seven days he shall veil his head with his cowl, and on the seventh day the abbot shall remove the veil as in baptism the priest is accustomed to remove the veil of infants; thus the abbot should [do] for the monk, since according to the judgement of the fathers, it is a second baptism in which all sins are dismissed as in baptism.[92]

The ceremony of covering the monk's head with the *melota* from the time of his promise until the eighth day did not originate with Benedict, as is explained in a ninth-century Carolingian commentary on the Rule of St Benedict. There the custom is described as equivalent to baptism in which sacrament it was performed according to the tradition of the holy catholic fathers.[93] Presumably the allusion was here to the practice in which the newly baptised wore their white garments, *chrisom*, for the whole of the week following their baptism, an act that symbolised the transformation brought about within the soul by the cleansing sacrament of baptism.[94]

In addition to his reclothing, a man's assumption of the monastic profession involved the shaving of part of his head and the cutting of the rest of his hair according to a specified pattern, the object being once again to mark him out physically from the rest of the population.[95] The tonsure

---

[91] See further below, this chapter, pp. 161–2 and notes 121–3.

[92] Theodore, Penitential, II, iii, 3 (ed. Finsterwalder, p. 315; trans. McNeill and Gamer, p. 201); discussed by Constable, 'The ceremonies', pp. 782 and 791–2.

[93] *Pauli Warnefridi, diaconi casinensis, In sanctam regulam commentarium*, ch. 58 (Abbey of Monte Cassino, 1880), p. 443: '. . . ut caput eius promissione ueletur, et in die octauo deueltur, quia uice baptismi est Melota'; *ibid.*, p. 446: 'Ideo uero dicit monachum caput co-opertum usque ad octauum diem habere, quia secundum sanctorum patrum catholicorum dicta, uice baptismi est hoc.' The authorship of this commentary (which is more plausibly associated with a ninth-century brother at Corbie, Hildemar, than with Paul the Deacon), is discussed by Richard Yeo, *The Structure and Content*, pp. 139–43.

[94] For this practice see my '"With water in the Spirit": the administration of baptism in early Anglo-Saxon England', in John Blair and Richard Sharpe (eds.), *Pastoral Care before the Parish* (Leicester, London and New York: Leicester University Press, 1992), pp. 171–92, at p. 178. We have remarked before on the equation of monastic profession and baptism. For discussion of the use of this parallel in the Carolingian commentary on the RSB see Sister Mary Alfred Schroll, *Benedictine Monasticism as Reflected in the Warnefrid-Hildemar Commentaries on the Rule* (New York: AMS Press, 1941), pp. 69–70, quoting the passage from the commentary attributed to Paul the Deacon just cited.

[95] Edward James, 'Bede and the tonsure question', *Peritia* 3 (1984), 85–98. The Rule of the Master concentrated more on the tonsure than on the question of reclothing a new monk: RM 90, 77–81 (pp. 392–3), but Benedict's Rule made no reference to the tonsure in describing how new monks were to be admitted to the cloister. It is not clear whether tonsuring was part of Benedict's profession rite or not: Yeo, *The Structure and Content*, pp. 135–6.

represented an outward symbol of his voluntary servitude to God; it was
the sign of his inward spiritual commitment, a visual demonstration of
his renunciation of the world and the negation of his personal sexuality,[96]
as well as his choice of a life aspiring to grace. The tonsure was sufficiently
recognised as the mark of ecclesiastical status that Dryhthelm and the Saxon
boy from the community at Selsey were both in their otherworldly visions
readily able to see which men were clerics by reason of their tonsures.[97]
It was, however, further a mark of humility; hair forcibly removed from
slaves and criminals was a mark of shame, but the tonsure constituted a
self-imposed humiliation. Since there were conflicting views about the style
in which the hair should be shaved, a man's tonsure could come to represent a symbol of orthodoxy. In England, at least, the adoption of a particular
– Roman or Petrine – form of the tonsure became an outward expression
of membership of a single, unified church.[98] Abbot Ceolfrith argued in his
letter to Nechtan, king of the Picts, that it was right that those who had
taken either monastic vows or holy orders should be bound by stricter bonds
of continence and wear on their heads, by way of tonsure, the likeness of
a crown of thorns (in memory of Christ's Passion), so that He might carry
away the thorns of their sins. 'Thus they can show upon their crowns that
they are ready to endure all kinds of ridicule and disgrace gladly for His
sake; thus they can signify that they too are always waiting for the crown
of eternal life . . . and to gain it, despite both worldly adversity and prosperity.'[99] What was at issue here (since the letter was written to help the Picts

---

[96] Gilchrist, *Gender and Material Culture*, pp. 18–19. Robert Bartlett has drawn attention to the relationship between clerical hair-shaving and – in the western church – clerics' beardlessness, suggesting
that the symbolic significance of hair removal was here sexual renunciation (in contrast with the
hirsute Greek clergy, who were married): 'Symbolic meanings of hair in the Middle Ages', *TRHS*,
6th ser. 4 (1994), 43–60, at p. 57. For the association of the Christian tonsure with the full or
partial shaving of the beard in early Ireland see William Sayers, 'Early Irish attitudes towards
hair and beards, baldness and tonsure', *Zeitschrift für celtische Philologie* 44 (1991), 154–89, at p. 181.
Giles Constable has offered a more general discussion of the significance of beards and hair in
his 'Introduction' to Burchard of Bellevaux, *Apologia de barbis*, ed. R. B. C. Huygens, in *Apologiae
duae*, Corpus Christianorum, continuatio mediaevalis, 62 (Turnhout: Brepols, 1985), pp. 47–130,
with specific reference to the hair and beards of men in religion at pp. 114–30.
[97] Bede described Dryhthelm's vision, *HE* V. 12 (pp. 488–97), and that of the child at Selsey, *HE* IV.
14 (pp. 376–81). On entering Melrose, Dryhthelm was himself 'crowned with the monastic tonsure'
(pp. 496–7), which marked the end of his secular life.
[98] James, 'Bede and the tonsure question', pp. 92–5, 97.
[99] *HE* V. 21 (pp. 548–9). Although Bede attributed the letter to his abbot, Ceolfrith, he prefaced his
quotation of the lengthy text by stating that the letter sent had been written 'in hunc modum'.
The similarities between the text Bede supplied and his own writings, together with the stress on
Petrine and Roman obedience and the use of biblical quotation, might suggest that Bede had contributed to this text: Plummer, *Bedae opera*, II, 232; Colgrave and Mynors, *Bede's Ecclesiastical History*,
p. 534n.; Wallace-Hadrill, *Commentary*, p. 196; Judith McClure, 'Bede and the Life of Ceolfrid', *Peritia*   157

in their recent decision to renounce their former error and turn to follow the customs of the Roman church) was less the symbolic significance of the sign of the tonsure as that it should be fashioned in the correct manner. While acknowledging that a difference in the style of the tonsure was not hurtful to those whose faith in God was secure, the letter made much of the need to imitate the apostle Peter in choosing the manner of cutting the hair, and the inappropriateness of adopting the Celtic form.[100]

Since the question of the 'correct' manner of performing the tonsure so divided the Roman and Celtic churches in the seventh century, various contemporary texts contain lengthy excursions on the merits of the different recognised methods and their symbolism.[101] Three different forms of tonsure were known in England. In the eastern the whole head was shaved. Theodore of Tarsus having adopted this mode of tonsure (said by Bede to be modelled on that of the apostle Paul), had to wait for four months after his election to the see of Canterbury for his hair to grow before it could be cut in the Roman fashion.[102] In the Roman style, also described as the Petrine tonsure, the top of the scalp was shaved and a band of hair left to form a crown around the head, representing Christ's crown of thorns.[103] The precise nature of the Celtic tonsure is not entirely clear. It seems to have involved the shaving of the head from ear to ear, leaving a portion of hair at some point on the head. Some have argued that hair of variable length was allowed to hang down behind, but it is also possible that the back of

---

3 (1984), 71–84, at p. 83. On the other hand, it would hardly be surprising to find similarities of style between this letter and Bede's own writings, and D. P. Kirby has questioned Bede's authorship: *Bede's Historia ecclesiastica gentis Anglorum: Its Contemporary Setting*, Jarrow Lecture 1992 (Jarrow: St Paul's Church, 1993), pp. 7–8.

[100] *HE* V. 21 (pp. 548–9). The Celtic tonsure was often linked with Simon Magus and may, perhaps, have been similar to the hairstyle adopted by the druids: see Colgrave and Mynors, *Bede's Ecclesiastical History*, p. 139, n. 3. William Sayers has discussed the Irish evidence for the form of druidical tonsure – which may have left a tuft of hair at the front of the head – but he warned of the difficulty of interpreting some of the evidence because of the apparent assumption or transformation of the druidical tonsure into the Christian, Celtic monastic tonsure: 'Early Irish attitudes', p. 179. See also Natalie Venclová, 'The Venerable Bede, druidic tonsure and archaeology', *Antiquity* 76 (2002), 458–71, at pp. 467–8.

[101] James, 'Bede and the tonsure question', pp. 94–8.

[102] *HE* IV. 1 (pp. 330–1); this form was discussed by Bertram Colgrave, *The Life of Bishop Wilfrid by Eddius Stephanus* (Cambridge: Cambridge University Press, 1927; paperback edition, 1985), p. 154. The authority for St Paul's shaving of his head is *Acts* 18:18.

[103] Aldhelm explained this clearly in his letter to Geraint, king of Domnonia, in which he regretted the hostile rumour that clerics in Domnonia were preferring a false tonsure: 'We, bearing witness to our tonsure of truth . . . , assert that the Apostle Peter chose this mode for various reasons: in the first place, that he might wear the form and likeness of Christ upon his head, since (Christ) was cruelly crowned with sharp points of thorns by the cursed race of Jews before he suffered the gibbet of the cross for our redemption': *Ep.* IV (ed. Ehwald, *Aldhelmi opera*, pp. 482–3, trans. Lapidge and Herren, *Aldhelm*, p. 157).

the head was entirely bald and a fringe of hair was left across the front of the skull, creating – as Bede complained to Abbot Adamnan – a crown that had an ending (because it did not form an unbroken ring but was cut short or terminated at the nape of the neck).[104] This style was, apparently, similar to that of the druids; while critics associated it with Simon Magus, the Irish preferred to attribute its form to St John.[105]

As one might imagine from the emphasis the prescriptive literature placed on the rituals surrounding the adoption of the religious life, many of the references in narrative sources to the manner in which their subjects left the secular world did so terms that emphasised the visible marks of changed status. For example, at the age of eighteen Ceolfrith was said to have preferred to lay aside the secular habit and become a monk (*monachus*);[106] and when King Sæbbi finally obtained his wife's agreement to dissolve their marriage, with the blessing of Waldhere, bishop of London, he 'received the religious habit which he had long desired'.[107] Those whom King Osred forced into minsters were tonsured first, as much to reinforce their humiliation as to demonstrate their new status.[108] Ceolwulf, who had been king of Northumbria since 729, was also tonsured when deprived of his kingdom in 731, but since he was restored to power later the same year it would seem that a tonsure unwillingly accepted was not necessarily sufficient to confine an individual to the cloister permanently.[109] Since, as we have already seen, a shaven head was widely seen as a mark of clerical status, its improper use had to be prevented, lest the whole monastic profession were brought into disrepute. Fear of this led Bede to castigate the false abbots described in his letter to Bishop Ecgberht of York, charging these men with having persuaded their followers to promise them obedience and so receive the tonsure, turning them 'at their pleasure' into religious.[110] Those entering minsters were

---

[104] *HE* V. 21 (pp. 550–1): 'quid contrario tuae fidei habitu terminatam in capite coronae imaginem portas?'; discussed by Sayers, 'Early Irish attitudes', pp. 182–3, and Venclová, 'The Venerable Bede', pp. 467–8.

[105] Sayers, 'Early Irish attitudes', p. 181.

[106] *VSCeol.* ch. 2 (p. 388): '[Ceolfridus] deposito habitu saeculari monachus fieri maluit, intrauitque monasterium'. Compare Bede's decription of Hild's entry to religion after thirty-three years in the world, *HE* IV. 23 (pp. 406–7): 'quae cum relicto habitu saeculari illi [Christo] soli seruire decreuisset'.

[107] *HE* IV. 11 (pp. 366–7): 'et per eius benedictionem habitum religionis, quam diu desiderabat, accepit'. Compare *VSG*, ch. 20 (pp. 84–5): 'monasterium Hrypadun usque peruenit, in quo . . . accepto clericali habitu, praeterita piacula expiare certabat'.

[108] Æthelwulf, *De abbatibus*, ch. 2, lines 50–1 (pp. 6–7).

[109] James, 'Bede and the tonsure question', p. 92. Compare also the examples James has given (pp. 89–91) of the forcible tonsuring of kings in other Christian barbarian kingdoms in pre-Carolingian Europe.

[110] *EpEcg*, §§ 12–13 (pp. 415–16).

not, necessarily, always tonsured immediately. Wilfrid remained untonsured while he lived in the community at Lindisfarne and it was only after he had spent three years in Gaul that he received 'from the holy Archbishop Dalfinus the form of the tonsure of the Apostle Peter in the shape of the crown of thorns which encircled the head of Christ'.[111] The twenty-two brothers whom Ceolfrith took from Wearmouth to establish a second community at Jarrow comprised ten tonsured men, but twelve still awaiting the grace of tonsure ('decem quidem attonsis, XII uiro tonsurae adhuc gratiam expectantibus').[112] Perhaps the second group were still novices.

Women also assumed a distinctive dress and head-covering on their entry to the religious life. Their adoption of the veil in the ceremony of consecration was intended to symbolise their chastity, marking them out visually from other women.[113] Theodore decreed that religious women should (like churches) be consecrated with a mass. Further he noted a distinction between Greek and Roman custom in the blessing of virgins and widows; while the Greeks permitted virgins and widows to be consecrated together, the Romans performed these as separate ceremonies. Roman custom also restricted the consecration of virgins with a holy veil to bishops, whereas the Greeks allowed priests to do so.[114] Whether Theodore's prescriptions were closely observed in early Anglo-Saxon England it is difficult to determine; the paucity of surviving liturgical books from England before the tenth century makes it hard to establish what ritual forms were followed in minsters before the tenth-century monastic revolution.[115]

---

[111] *VSW* ch. 6 (pp. 14–5): 'Nam seruus Dei Wilfrithus desiderio concupiscens tonsurae Petri apostolic formulam in modum coronae spineae caput Christi cingentis, a sancto Dalfino archiepiscopo libenter suscepit.' Compare Anon., *VSCuth.* II, 2 (pp. 76–7): 'tonsurae Petri formam in modum corone spineae capud Christi cingentis'.

[112] *VSCeol.* ch. 11 (p. 391).

[113] Constable, 'The ceremonies and symbolism', p. 798. Several of Boniface's letters described women in the religious life as veiled. At the same time as he wrote to King Æthelbald of Mercia in 747 complaining about various aspects of the king's behaviour, including his lack of respect for women in the religious life, the missionary sent a letter to Archbishop Ecgberht of York, in which he protested about unheard of evils, such as the 'seduction of veiled and consecrated women', *Ep.* 75 (p. 158), with the clear implication that it was their veiling that marked them out from secular women (and which should, thus, have protected them from male lusts).

[114] Theodore, Penitential, II, iii, 6–8 (p. 316). Various attempts were made in the Frankish church to prevent priests from usurping the episcopal role in the consecration of virgins: René Metz, *La consécration des vierges dans l'Eglise romaine: étude d'histoire de la liturgie* (Paris, Presses universitaires de France, 1954), p. 102. Equally, some women (and men) made a private decision to enter into a life of religion, without involving any third party: that, too, the Frankish Church legislated to prevent: Council of Verneuil, ch. 6 (ed. Boretius, *MGH, Capitularia*, I, 34). I have discussed the rituals surrounding the entry of women to religion in greater detail in *Veiled Women*, I, ch. 5.

[115] For a bibliographical survey of English pontificals (collections of episcopal *ordines*, the rituals and prayers performed by a bishop at ceremonies at which he officiated) see J. Brückmann, 'Latin

Early Frankish liturgical forms linked the consecration of religious women, their veiling and subsequent blessing together, the terms *consecratio, uelatio* and *benedictio* being used equivalently in sacramentaries to denote ceremonies for reception into religion.[116] That Charlemagne had to legislate in 789 to prevent abbesses from conferring the veil upon virgins, contrary to the custom of the holy church of God, suggests that this abuse, too, had become commonplace, but this legislation must be seen in the context of a wider attempt in the late eighth and early ninth century to bring Frankish houses of female religious more directly under episcopal control.[117]

Austerity in dress was regarded by hagiographers as one of the marks of female sanctity; Abbess Æthelthryth of Ely was reputed never to wear linen but only wool,[118] and Abbot Ceolfrith was said to have shown a disregard for dress rarely found among those in authority.[119] Even though such references might be dismissed as standard hagiographical *topoi*, it does appear from the frequency of the comments found in ecclesiastical texts that many individuals of noble birth were reluctant to give up their fine clothes on entering the cloister, so that those who chose plainer garb were genuinely somewhat unusual. One of the complaints made by Adomnan about the sisters at Coldingham was that they showed no respect for their profession but occupied their time in weaving elaborate garments with which to adorn themselves as if they were brides, so imperilling their virginity.[120] Aldhelm's prose *De virginitate* included a long diatribe against the vanity of those living under the discipline of a minster and of those clergy controlled by bishops, who glamorised their dress, preferring fine linen shirts, scarlet or blue tunics, their sleeves and necks embroidered with silk, with finely trimmed shoes and crimped curls in their hair, or women who spurned dark-grey veils for bright and coloured head-dresses.[121] The letters of Boniface and Alcuin railed repeatedly against vain dress and useless adornment,[122] and

manuscript pontificals and benedictionals in England and Wales', *Traditio* 29 (1973), 391–458. The most extensive survey of the liturgical forms for the consecration of religious women is Metz, *La consécration des vierges dans l'église romaine.*

[116] René Metz, 'La consécration des vierges dans l'église franque du vi^e au ixe siècle', *Revue des sciences religieuses* 31 (1957), 105–21, at p. 114.

[117] *Admonitio generalis*, ch. 76 (ed. Boretius, *MGH, Capitularia*, I, p. 60, no. 22); Metz, 'La consécration', pp. 115–16; on the wider issue of the Carolingian reform of female religion see Suzanne F. Wemple, *Women in Francish Society: Marriage and the Cloister 500–900* (Philadelphia, PA: University of Pennsylvania Press, 1981), pp. 165–74, and my *Veiled Women*, I, 66–71, and the literature cited there.

[118] *HE* IV. 19 (pp. 392–3).   [119] *HA* ch. 16 (p. 381).   [120] *HE* IV. 25 (pp. 424–7). See further chapter 6.

[121] Aldhelm, *De virginitate*, ch. 58 (ed. Ehwald, pp. 317–18); see *Veiled Women*, I, 56–7.

[122] Compare Boniface's letter to Cuthbert, AD 747 (*Ep.* 78, p. 170) and Alcuin, *Epp.* 20 and 40 (pp. 57 and 86).

eighth-century English councils also attempted to ensure that monks, nuns, and clerics abandon their elaborate and brightly coloured clothes and adopt more appropriate garb, distinct from that of the laity. None of these texts specified the precise form such apparel should take.[123] It would appear from the canons of the 747 council at *Clofesho* that it was the responsibility of the head of a minster to supply his congregation with clothes 'suitable to the habit of their profession'. Men were recommended to assume the 'customary garb of their predecessors, whether clerics or monks', and religious women, 'veiled by the priest' (*a sacerdote uelatae*) to wear always 'the clothes of purity' (*pudicitiae uestimenta*).[124]

In Benedict's Rule, as we have already seen, new postulants made solemn vows as part of their formal ritual of entry to the religious life; early English narrative sources reinforce the notion that the declarations made on admission to minsters were thought to constitute a binding commitment. Bede described Heiu, the founder of Hartlepool, as the first woman in Northumbria to take the vows and habit of religion;[125] similarly he reported that when Benedict Biscop went to the island of Lérins, 'he gave himself there to the company of monks, received the tonsure, and marked with the vow of a monk, observed the regular discipline with due care'.[126] Abbess Eangyth, writing to ask Boniface whether she should go on a pilgrimage, stated that those who opposed the practice supported their view by arguing that the councils prescribed that everyone should remain where they were placed and wherever they had taken vows.[127]

Part of the taking of vows was the acceptance of – and subjection to – the new code of discipline that ordered the communal life in religion. Cuthbert's anonymous biographer, echoing Athanasius' Life of St Anthony, reported that when the saint left his secular life he 'arranged to bind himself by the more rigid rule of life in a minster' and 'took upon himself the

---

[123] For example, the council of *Clofesho*, AD 747, ch. 19 (H&S, III, 369), which ordered that monks and nuns ought not to wear elaborate or secular garb in case they be confused with lay-people; and the legatine councils of 786, ch. 4 (ed. Dümmler, p. 22). All these prescriptions echo Caesarius' various injunctions about the necessity for religious women to avoid clothes that might attract inappropriate attention (ch. 22, pp. 198–9), his prohibition on their wearing of lay garb (ch. 46, pp. 232–3) or purple-dyed or elaborately woven clothes (ch. 60, pp. 244–5).

[124] Council of *Clofesho*, AD 747, ch. 28 (H&S, III, 374).

[125] *HE* IV. 23 (pp. 406–7): 'religiosa Christi famula Heiu, quae prima feminarum fertur in prouincia Nordanhymbrorum propositum uestemque sanctimonialis habitus'.

[126] *HA* ch. 2 (p. 365): 'ibidem se monachorum coetui tradidit, tonsuram accepit, et disciplinam regularem monachi uoto insignitus debita cum sollicitudine seruauit'.

[127] Boniface, *Ep.* 14 (p. 25): 'ut unusquisque in eo loco ubi constitutus fuerit et ubi uotum suum uouerit, ibi maneat et ibi Deo reddat uota sua'.

yoke of service to Christ'.[128] Earthly warfare paralleled the divine combat of the monastic life: Eosterwine had been one of King Ecgfrith's thegns but laid down his arms and girded himself for spiritual warfare.[129] Equally, Eanmund left his fruitless military career to strive for heavenly armour.[130] All the saints' lives stressed that their subjects left the world voluntarily. Even though Æthelwulf implied that Eanmund was one of those whom the tyrant King Osred had forced to 'serve their parent above and to live in monastic enclosures', he presented Eanmund in the poem as one who had made a personal choice to dedicate himself to the service of God.

The monastic congregation receiving a postulant also had a role to play on his or her admission. Some texts suggest that the entire community had to consent before a potential new member could be received; when Wynfrith and Willibald were taken as children to the minsters at Exeter and Bishops Waltham, respectively, to be given to the religious life, the abbots of each house consulted with the rest of the brethren before agreeing to receive the children.[131] The rest of the congregation was not, however, permitted to agree to accept a new entrant in their abbot's absence; on his arrival at Melrose, Cuthbert was welcomed by the prior, Boisil, but it was only when Abbot Eata returned that Cuthbert was given permission to receive the tonsure and join the fellowship of the brethren.[132] The abbot would solemnly consecrate a postulant man to his new status; prospective religious women were usually consecrated by a visiting bishop. Æthelthryth received her veil and habit from Bishop Wilfrid, Heiu was consecrated by Bishop Aidan, while Cuthbert travelled to Carlisle to ordain some priests but also in order to confer the dress of the holy life on Queen Iurminburg and to bless her.[133]

On entering a minster, a postulant was supposed to renounce all personal property, handing everything over to the congregation as a whole, so that all lands and goods were held by the *familia* in common, after the example of the first Christian community in Jerusalem.[134] Dícuill and his brethren

---

[128] Anon., *VSCuth.* II, 1; II, 2 (pp. 74–7): 'seruitutis Christi iugum . . . susceperat'. Compare Bede, *VSCuth.* ch. 1 (pp. 154–5): 'ab ineunte adolescentia iugo monachicae institutionis collum subdidit'.

[129] *HA* ch. 8 (p. 371).   [130] Æthelwulf, *De abbatibus*, chs. 3, 4 (pp. 6–9).

[131] *VSB* ch. 1 (p. 462); *Hodoeporicon of Willibald*, ch. 2 (p. 89).

[132] Bede, *VSCuth.* ch. 6 (pp. 172–5). Nicholas Brooks has suggested that the different ranks accorded to Boisil and Eata here may suggest that although the former had responsibility for the day-to-day running of the abbey of Melrose, he was ultimately subject to the authority of Eata at Lindisfarne.

[133] *HE* IV. 19 (pp. 392–3); IV. 23 (pp. 406–7); Bede, *VSCuth.* ch. 28 (pp. 248–9).

[134] Bede, *Retractatio in Actus apostolorum*, IV. 32 (ed. M. W. Laistner, CCSL 121, pp. 126–7). For Bede's views on the virtue of poverty see Carroll, *The Venerable Bede*, pp. 236–41; Bonner, 'The Christian life', p. 45; and Glenn Olsen, 'Bede as historian: the evidence from his observations on the life   163

at Bosham were said to live in humility and poverty. Hild's community at Whitby was supposed to have been modelled on the example of the primitive church so that 'no one was rich, no one was in need, for they had all things in common and none had any private property', and the same example influenced the way of life at Lindisfarne.[135] Various people brought some property as a dowry with them into the cloister; Witmaer, consigning himself to Wearmouth, gave ten hides at *Daltun*, which he had formerly received from Aldfrith, to the minster.[136] Had Abba's widow (whom we have already mentioned) chosen to assume the religious life, she would have been able to rely on a substantial dowry to ease her admission. In his will, the Kentish reeve arranged that at his funeral, 'ten oxen, ten cows, one hundred ewes, and one hundred swine are to be given to Folkestone, and to the community severally, five hundred pence, in order that my wife may have the privilege of entering there, either at my funeral, or at a later day, whichever she may prefer'.[137] Presumably parents who consigned their children to minsters sent them with some sort of dowry of land, money or precious gifts; the only instances quoted in the sources, however, relate to children of royal blood. For example, Oswiu's dedication of Ælfflæd was accompanied by a donation of 120 hides to the church, and Alfred's foundation of Shaftesbury for Æthelgifu was endowed with 'estates of land and every kind of wealth'.[138]

Other postulants chose not to bring money into a minster but distributed alms to the poor before quitting the world, as Dryhthelm did before he entered Melrose; King Sæbbi took a large sum of money with him into the minster to be distributed to the poor from there.[139] Many religious men and women, however, particularly those of noble origin, seem to have retained

---

of the first Christian community at Jerusalem', *JEH* 33 (1982), 519–30, at pp. 522–3. Compare also the discussion of the apostolic community in chapter 2 above.

[135] Bosham: *HE* IV. 13 (pp. 372–3); Whitby: IV. 23 (pp. 408–9); Lindisfarne: IV. 27 (pp. 434–5); compare Acts, 2: 44–5 and 4: 32–4.

[136] *HA* ch. 15 (p. 380).

[137] S 1482 (AD 833x839); trans. Harmer, *SEHD*, p. 41, no. 2. The text continues: 'if however the community or their head will not grant her admittance into the minster, or if she herself does not desire it but prefers some other course, then one thousand pence are to be given at my funeral for my resting-place, and to the community severally, five hundred pence on behalf of my soul'. For discussion of this will see Thomas Charles-Edwards, 'Anglo-Saxon kinship revisited', in John Hines (ed.), *The Anglo-Saxons from the Migration Period to the Eighth Century: An Ethnographic Perspective* (Woodbridge: Boydell Press, 1997), pp. 171–210, at pp. 197–8, and for a more general discussion of widows, Julia Crick, 'Men, women and widows: widowhood in pre-Conquest England', in Sandra Cavallo and Lyndan Warner (eds.), *Widowhood in Medieval and Early Modern Europe* (Harlow: Longman, 1999), pp. 24–36.

[138] *HE* III. 24 (pp. 292–3); Asser, Life of King Alfred, ch. 98 (ed. Stevenson, p. 85).

[139] *HE* V. 12 (pp. 488–9), IV. 11 (pp. 366–7).

their own property after they entered the cloister. The members of the Cold-ingham community may have used their own money in order to support the luxurious life-style of which they were accused, and journeys and pilgrim-ages or gifts to other religious could all have been paid for by the more afflu-ent members of a congregation.[140] In fact it is likely that many members of even the stricter communities retained some possessions of their own; Bede, for example, on his death-bed shared out among the priests of Jarrow the pepper, napkins and incense that he owned.[141] Wilfrid was, however, clearly unusual not only in having accumulated so much personal wealth in the form of gold, silver and precious stones, but also in dividing it so carefully between his own followers and his two minsters in order that the commu-nities might be able to buy the friendship of kings and bishops.[142] One of the members of the community at Wenlock still owned a part share in a slave-girl (*ancilla*) with his brother who had remained in the world.[143] Some of the questions in Ecgberht's Dialogues addressed the resolution of disputes over the personal property of men and women who had left the world, and over the joint possession of one minster by two individuals, which implies that this may not have been an uncommon problem.[144] In ideal, if not in practice, personal possessions were supposed to be handed over to the head of the minster.[145] Ælfflæd, abbess of Whitby, had a chest in which she stored a girdle of St Cuthbert's, which is more likely to have been in her care on the

---

[140] *HE* IV. 25. Schneider, 'Anglo-Saxon Women', pp. 56–7.

[141] Cuthbert, *Epistola de obitu Bedae* (ed. Colgrave and Mynors, *Bede's Ecclesiastical History*, pp. 584–5).

[142] *VSW* ch. 63 (pp. 136–7). This passage has been much analysed; see for example D. H. Farmer, 'Saint Wilfrid', in D. P. Kirby (ed.), *Saint Wilfrid at Hexham* (Newcastle upon Tyne: Oriel Press, 1974), pp. 35–60, at pp. 56–7; and Patrick Wormald, ''Bede, "Beowulf" and the conversion of the Anglo-Saxon aristocracy', in R. T. Farrell (ed.), *Bede and Anglo-Saxon England*, BAR, British series, 46 (Oxford: BAR, 1978), pp. 32–95, at p. 55. David Pelteret has compared Wilfrid in his last days with the dying Beowulf, who rejoiced in the richness of his dragon hoard. In the division of Wilfrid's wealth, Pelteret has seen 'the Christian bishop and the Germanic lord conjoined within him': Wilfrid the politician gave cash to his abbots while the Germanic lord shared a third part among his *comitatus*; 'Saint Wilfrid: tribal bishop, civic bishop or Germanic lord?' in Joyce Hill and Mary Swan (eds.), *The Community, the Family and the Saint* (Turnhout: Brepols, 1998), pp. 159–80, at pp. 179–80.

[143] Boniface, *Ep.* 10 (p. 13). Patrick Sims-Williams drew attention to this passage, noting that in this respect at least Mildburg's minster at Wenlock was laxer than Hild's at Whitby, where all private property was forbidden: *Religion and Literature in Western England, 600–800* (Cambridge: Cambridge University Press, 1990), pp. 117–18.

[144] Ecgberht, *Dialogi, responsio* 10 (H&S III, 407–8). Mayr-Harting has argued that Ecgberht's response incorporates some elements of the *RSB*'s provisions for electing abbots, in suggesting that the community should chose one of the two to be head over the minster (with the bishop's agreement) and that the co-heir should only be allowed to succeed on the first's death if the bishop thought him suitable: *The Venerable Bede, the Rule of St Benedict and Social Class*, Jarrow Lecture 1976 (Jarrow: St Paul's Church, 1977), p. 12.

[145] Consider, for example, Caesarius, *Regula ad uirgines*, ch. 21 (p. 194): 'Those who had something in the world shall, when they enter the monastery, humbly offer it to the mother to be of use for the common needs.' Compare also *ibid.*, ch. 9 (forbidding anyone from having a chest which might be

whole community's behalf for its safe-keeping than owned by her alone.[146] Abbots and abbesses were responsible for clothing and providing all the necessities for their *familiae*, who had not the individual means from which to provide them.[147] It also fell to the minster's head to give alms to the poor and needy.[148]

The assumption of the monastic profession marked a change in status that was intended to be permanent. Theodore tried to legislate for the problem of those who attempted to abandon the religious life, decreeing in his Penitential that if anyone resumed the secular habit having once left the world, he should do penance for ten years (although after the first three of these his bishop might treat him more leniently should he seem truly penitent).[149] No former religious of either sex was to be welcomed back to any ecclesiastical position of status: it was better that such people should not come to prominence in the church.[150] Generalising about the individual factors that might have driven the once-committed out of the cloister back into the world is manifestly impossible. Austerity of life-style, social isolation or changed family circumstances are likely all to have challenged certain of the noble-born within minsters, but for this group the lack of personal freedom and independence may, perhaps, have been especially restricting. Joining a minster involved not just all the outward signs of the ontological change in status, but the obedient acceptance of a new and often repressive discipline.

Monastic discipline

Whatever the rule, or rules, they chose to follow,[151] every early English religious community appointed an *abbas* or *abbatissa* to take responsibility for the general organisation of the house and maintenance of its discipline. He or she might frequently be assisted by others, *praepositi*, *priores*, *decani* or *decanae*, who could take charge of the minster in the superior's absence. Cuthbert was made *praepositus* first at Melrose after the death of Boisil and was then transferred in the same rank to the minster at Lindisfarne in the

---

locked: pp. 186–8), 52 (a general statement about the desirability of personal poverty: p. 238) and ch. 59 (specifically forbidding the abbess from keeping her own possessions: p. 242).

[146] Bede, *VSCuth*. ch. 23 (pp. 232–3). Dagmar Schneider interpreted this differently, seeing this and other similar references as proof that abbesses retained personal possessions: 'Anglo-Saxon women', pp. 56–7.

[147] Hildelith, abbess of Barking, was said to have been 'most energetic in . . . the provision of all things necessary for the common use': *HE* IV. 10 (pp. 362–3). Compare the council of *Clofesho*, AD 747, chs. 4, 28 (H&S III, 364, 374).

[148] Alcuin, *Ep*. 105 (p. 152).   [149] Theodore, Penitential, I. viii. 12–14 (p. 301).

[150] *Ibid*., I. ix. 2–3 (p. 302).   [151] Above, ch. 2.

abbacy of Eata.[152] A sister called Frigyth was in charge of Whitby's daughter-house at Hackness; Bede gave her no specific rank, merely reporting that she presided over the minster in place of the abbess.[153] Overall control of a double house was usually taken by a woman, although there are instances in the eighth century of men ruling houses which had formerly been governed by women.[154] The head of a minster remained in that office until death or retirement – or until advanced to higher preferment elsewhere – but the lesser offices may sometimes have rotated between members of the community. This, at least, seems to be implied in one passage in Rudolf's Life of Leoba which describes a certain unpopular member of the Wimborne congregation, who because of her zeal for discipline and strict obedience (in which she surpassed the others) was often appointed prioress and frequently made a *decana*.[155] All aspects of the government of the minster did not, however, devolve exclusively upon its heads and their deputies, for some decisions were clearly taken by the whole community together. Before he died, Cuthbert advised the members of his community to keep peace among themselves and 'when necessity compels you to take counsel about your affairs, see to it most earnestly that you are unanimous in your counsels'.[156] After the departure of Ceolfrith for Rome, the brethren of the houses at Wearmouth and Jarrow agreed to meet together in council in order to discuss what they should do.[157]

Although according to Benedict's Rule the office of abbot or abbess should have been elective, it was often in effect hereditary, especially in English royal or proprietary minsters.[158] Seaxburh succeeded her sister Æthelburh at Ely; possession of Minster-in-Thanet passed to Mildred, the daughter of its first abbess Eormenburh; Abbess Hereburh at Watton planned to make her daughter Cwenburh, a member of the community, abbess in her place; while at Whitby, Ælfflæd and her mother Eanflaed ruled together.[159] Chad

[152] *HE* IV. 27 (pp. 432–5); Anon., *VSCuth.*, II, 8, III, 1 (pp. 90–1 and 94–5). Clare Stancliffe, 'Cuthbert and the polarity between pastor and solitary', in Gerald Bonner, David Rollason and Clare Stancliffe (eds.), *St Cuthbert, his Cult and his Community* (Woodbridge: Boydell Press, 1989), pp. 21–44, at p. 33.

[153] *HE* IV. 23 (pp. 412–13).

[154] For example, the three houses of Stonegrave, Coxwold and *Donaemuthe* referred to in the letter of Pope Paul I to Bishop Ecgberht of York and King Eadberht of Northumbria (H&S III, 394–5); see Schneider, 'Anglo-Saxon women', pp. 23–6, and my *Veiled Women*, I, 49–56.

[155] *VSL* ch. 4 (pp. 123–4). This woman imposed such strict discipline on the community, that when she died the sisters stamped on her grave to vent their pent-up frustration and resentment. The episode is discussed by Stephanie Hollis, *Anglo-Saxon Women*, p. 275

[156] Bede, *VSCuth.* ch. 39 (pp. 282–3).   [157] *HA* ch. 18 (pp. 382–3).

[158] *RSB* ch. 64, 1–6 (pp. 280–1). Mayr-Harting, *The Venerable Bede*, p. 12.

[159] *HE* IV. 19 (pp. 392–3); Rollason, *The Mildrith Legend*, pp. 11–13; *HE* V. 3 (pp. 460–1); *HE* IV. 26 (pp. 428–31). I have explored the close links between early English minsters for women and the

succeeded his brother Cedd at Lastingham, and various brothers succeeded one another at Æthelwulf's minster.[160] Benedict Biscop was, however, determined that his brother should not succeed him as abbot of Wearmouth, decreeing that 'no abbot was ever to be sought for the same minster by reason of hereditary succession, but for his manner of life and diligence in teaching'.[161] Whenever a new head had to be chosen, this was normally done by consultation between the minster's inhabitants,[162] but the 816 council of Chelsea directed that bishops and synods should choose abbots and abbesses for minsters, giving the *familia* only a nominal consultative role.[163] In allowing bishops to take the lead here, Wulfred's synod was reversing traditional roles and significantly extending episcopal powers over the internal running of minsters, however much the legislation purported simply to be following the example of early canon law.[164]

Individual members of minster communities owed obedience to their superiors – at *Clofesho* in 747, for example, monks and nuns were reminded of the need to be 'humbly subject to their superior'[165] – but they had a further obligation of mutual obedience to the community at large.[166] Willibald explained the value of this virtue for the maintenance of the communal life in his Life of Boniface:

He cannot prefer himself to others who has refused to be subject to others, because he will not be able rightly to apply to inferiors the service of obedience which he does not duly render to those that are set over him by the direction of heaven.[167]

royal families responsible for their foundation, *Veiled Women*, I, pp. 44–5. In addition to the literature cited there, see Catherine Cubitt, 'Universal and local saints in Anglo-Saxon England', in Alan Thacker and Richard Sharpe (eds.), *Local Saints and Local Churches in the Early Medieval West* (Oxford: Oxford University Press, 2002), pp. 423–53, at p. 438, and for comparative Carolingian examples of women who maintained their dynastic ties from within the cloister, Julia Smith, 'The problem of female sanctity', pp. 25–8.

[160] *HE* III. 23 (pp. 288–9); Æthelwulf, *De abbatibus*, chs. 13–15 (pp. 32–41).
[161] *HA* ch. 11 (pp. 374–5); *VSCeol.*, ch. 16 (p. 393). Discussed by Sims-Williams, *Religion and Literature*, p. 125.
[162] As, for example, happened after Ceolfrith went to Rome: *VSCeol.* ch. 28 (p. 398).
[163] Council of Chelsea, AD 816, ch. 4 (H&S III, 580–1).
[164] Brooks, *The Early History*, pp. 175–6. See also Catherine Cubitt, *Anglo-Saxon Church Councils c. 650–c. 850* (London and New York: Leicester University Press, 1995), pp. 196–9.
[165] Council of *Clofesho*, AD 747, ch. 19 (H&S III, 368): 'ut monachi seu nunnones sui majori regulariter constituto humiliter subjecti sint . . .' Obedience was the subject of the first chapter of Columbanus' Rule for monks, which opens with the injunction, 'At the first word of a senior, all on hearing should rise to obey, since their obedience is shown to God;' *Regula monachorum*, ch. 1 (ed. Walker, pp. 122–3). Compare Caesarius, *Regula ad uirgines*, ch. 18 (p. 192): 'all shall obey the mother after God; all should defer to the prioress'. *Ibid.*, ch. 35, also enjoined obedience to the abbess, the prioress, choir mistress and novice mistress (p. 216).
[166] Benedict's Rule placed considerable emphasis on the collective obligation to obedience: *RSB*, ch. 71 (pp. 292–3).
[167] *VSB* ch. 2 (p. 466).

Not, however, that the young Boniface was guilty of such pride: 'such obedience as befits a monk was given by the saint to all the members of the community, particularly the abbot'.[168] Disobedience may, however, have caused some problems, particularly when young members of the aristocracy were forced to live in what must have been to many of them rather uncongenial surroundings.[169] When Bede reminded his readers in his commentary on *Acts* that perfect flight from the world involved not glorying in the nobility of one's birth, he may, Mayr-Harting has plausibly suggested, have been thinking particularly of the noble brethren at Wearmouth who had once rejected Ceolfrith as their prior.[170] The list of sins which reproached the brother from Wenlock in his vision of heaven included 'stubbornness and disobedience, whereby you have failed to obey your spiritual superiors'.[171] Bede lamented in his letter to Archbishop Ecgberht of York that false abbots were able to collect in their spurious religious communities not just hapless laymen but 'whomever they may perhaps find wandering anywhere, expelled from true minsters for the fault of disobedience (*ob culpam inobaedientiae*)'.[172]

Apart from these scattered allusions to internal dissent, the sources reveal little about the difficulties of maintaining discipline within minsters. Rudolf commented on the unpopularity of the harsh *decana* at Wimborne, but in a way as much to demonstrate the inappropriateness of her behaviour as to show the indiscipline of the sisters.[173] At one time, as we have already seen, Ceolfrith had a reputation as an unpopular disciplinarian: he was driven out of Wearmouth soon after he was first appointed prior, because of the 'jealousies and most violent attacks of certain nobles who could not endure his regular discipline'.[174] In his attempts to impose a stricter rule at Lindisfarne, Cuthbert experience similar problems; often during debates in the assembly of the brothers about the rule he was 'assailed by the bitter insults of his opponents'.[175] Bede claimed the authority of his personal

---

[168] *Ibid.*
[169] Patrick Wormald has emphasised the aristocratic environment of early English Christianity: 'Bede, "Beowulf" and the conversion of the Anglo-Saxon aristocracy', pp. 55–8. See also Ian Wood, 'Ripon, Frankia and the Franks casket in the early Middle Ages', *Northern History* 26 (1990), 5–8.
[170] Bede, *Expositio actuum apostolorum*, 4. 32; *HA*, ch. 8 (p. 390); Mayr-Harting, *The Venerable Bede*, p. 11.
[171] Boniface, *Ep.* 10 (p. 10). This was not in fact one of this brother's besetting sins, for among the virtues which later spoke up in his defence was obedience.
[172] Bede, *EpEcg*, ch. 12 (p. 415).   [173] *VSL*, ch. 2 (pp. 123–4).
[174] *VSCeol.* ch. 8 (pp. 390–1). Ian Wood, *The Most Holy Abbot Ceolfrid*, Jarrow Lecture 1995 (Jarrow: [St Paul's Church], 1996), pp. 10–11.
[175] Bede, *VSCuth.* ch. 16 (pp. 210–11).

169

knowledge when he catalogued the derelictions of a certain brother who lived an ignoble life in a Bernician minster, refusing to follow the precepts of the rule or to observe the divine offices, but instead remaining drunk in his workshop (for he was a skilled smith). In the end he died – unrepentant and unshriven – thus proving Bede's point that those who failed to follow their elders' example and observe the Christian life would inevitably be damned.[176] Disputes over the performance of the rule may in fact have been more common than the sources suggest, at least in those houses where independent-minded members of the nobility met with zealous protagonists of a strictly regulated way of life. It is, however, also probable that the rules implemented in the vast majority of minsters were less stringent than those imposed in places such as Lindisfarne or Wearmouth and Jarrow.

Where we are markedly better informed is over the problem presented by wandering clergy. Recurrent references in the literature to the importance of enforcing the concept of monastic *stabilitas* suggest that this was a perennial difficulty for the early leaders of the English church.[177] When Boniface wanted to move to the minster at Nursling in order to receive a more advanced education, his biographer reported that he first sought the consent of the abbot and the rest of the community at Exeter; equally, Guthlac left Repton to adopt the solitary life with the willing consent of his elders in the minster.[178] Yet Aldhelm wrote to the abbots of Wilfrid's monastic affinity urging them to place the claims of lordship above those of monastic stability, reminding them of their obligation to follow their leader into exile. If, Aldhelm wrote, worldly men (deprived of divine teaching) were to desert a lord whom they had followed willingly in prosperity as soon as he fell on hard times, they would be derided by all: 'What then, will be said of you, if you cast into solitary exile the bishop who nourished and raised you?'[179] While other writers did not articulate the tension

---

[176] *HE* V. 14 (pp. 502–5). Catherine Cubitt has discussed this and other exemplary 'bad' deaths in Bede's History: 'Monastic memory and identity in early Anglo-Saxon England', in William O. Frazer and Andrew Tyrell (eds.), *Social Identity in Early Medieval Britain* (London and New York: Leicester University Press, 2000), pp. 252–76, pp. 268–9.

[177] Compare the council of Hertford, chs. 4–5, quoted by Bede, *HE* IV. 5 (pp. 350–1); council of *Clofesho*, AD 747, ch. 29 (H&S III, 374–5); legatine council, AD 786, ch. 6 (ed. Dümmler, p. 22). See also Boniface, *Ep.* 14 (p. 25), quoted above.

[178] *VSB* ch. 2 (p. 466); *VSG* ch. 24 (pp. 86–7).

[179] Aldhelm, *Ep.* 12 (ed. Ehwald, p. 502; trans. Lapidge and Herren, pp. 169–70). This passage was quoted by R. P. Abels, *Lordship and Military Obligation in Anglo-Saxon England* (Berkeley and Los Angeles, CA: University of California Press, 1988), p. 17. For discussion of the letter, its survival (only as an excerpt in William of Malmesbury's *Gesta pontificum Anglorum*), and the light it sheds on the complex politics of Wilfrid's career see Lapidge and Herren, *Aldhelm*, pp. 150–1.

between monastic and Germanic social codes so clearly, many religious of both sexes manifestly paid little attention to the church's injunctions that sought to restrict their mobility.[180] Boniface's comments about the undesirability of women going on pilgrimage suggest that it was not unknown for religious women to travel outside their minsters on whatever pretext; his view was that such actions were bringing all religious women into disrepute.[181] If Rudolf is to be believed, the sisters at Wimborne were very tightly enclosed and kept apart from all representatives of the male sex. This view may reflect more of Rudolf's abhorrence of mixed communities, with which in ninth-century Germany he was quite unfamiliar, than the arrangements at Wimborne.[182] Among early monastic rules, the rule for virgins by Caesarius of Arles makes the most explicit statements about the necessity to protect virgins dedicated to God from contact with the exterior world; Caesarius' obsession was with keeping the doors secured (so that unauthorised men might not pass inside, nor the women without).[183] Irish monastic legislation also favoured the creation of physical boundaries separating sacred space and protecting religious women in particular.[184] On the other hand, the maintenance of regular pastoral ministry to the laity was incompatible with complete enclosure, and the personal histories of various individuals demonstrate that some monastic populations could at times be quite fluid.[185]

---

[180] This was not a problem exclusive to Anglo-Saxon England. The difficulty of coping with wandering religious and with those who attempted to establish unauthorised monasteries had been addressed as early as 451 at the council of Chalcedon (ch. 4, ed. Mansi, *Concilia*, VI, col. 1226) where it was stipulated that monks should not take part in secular matters, nor leave their own monasteries unless permitted to do so for necessary purposes by the bishop of the city. Benedict identified *gyrovagi* as the fourth sort of monks, those who spend all their lives drifting from place to place, staying in different monasteries, always on the move and never settled; to his mind they were worse than sarabaites (tonsured men living in small groups without being subject to any law or rule): *RSB*, ch. 1, 10 (pp. 170–1); see Fry, *The Rule*, p. 319, for discussion of the problem of wandering, homeless monks in early sixth-century Italy and Benedict's indebtedness to the Rule of the Master (and thus to Cassian) here.

[181] Boniface, *Ep.* 78 (p. 169), addressed to Cuthbert, archbishop of Canterbury.

[182] *VSL* ch. 2 (p. 123). It is important to remember that Rudolf's account, written on the continent after the monastic reforms of Louis the Pious, may not reflect earlier English circumstances accurately; see Hollis, *Anglo-Saxon Women*, pp. 271–5; Julia Smith has shown how little use Rudolf made of the evidence of those who had known Leoba and how much he was dependent on male hagiographical models, submerging her within a traditional male texture: 'The problem of female sanctity', pp. 16–17.

[183] Caesarius, *Regula ad uirgines*, ch. 36 (pp. 218–20). This chapter permits the 'provisor' to come in as needed, and priests or other clergy at appropriate times; if the roof needed mending, or windows and doors replacing, the provisor was to accompany carefully chosen workmen and ensure that the women's cloister was not violated. Several chapters forbid the sisters to step outside the door either of the monastery, or the basilica: chs. 2, 50, 59, 73 (pp. 180, 236, 242 and 272).

[184] Bitel, *Isle of the Saints*, pp. 58–66.   [185] Discussed further below, ch. 7.

The minster community

Contemporary texts reflect the centrality of the corporate and familial in the construction of monastic ideals in early Anglo-Saxon England, as we have already seen.[186] Terms such as *familia*[187] and *congregatio*[188] are found frequently, and the descriptions of religious as *fratres* or *sorores* and of an abbess as 'mother of the handmaidens of Christ' all reinforce the collective identity of minster communities.[189] Establishing the precise composition of any one monastic congregation, or determining with any certainty how many of those who dwelt within the enclosure or on a minster's estates were deemed to belong to the *familia* (strictly the 'household', not the kindred group),[190] can be problematical, particularly in light of the concentration of most sources on the activities of those of noble birth.

This is obviously of importance for consideration of the question of the size of monastic communities. At the beginning of this chapter we questioned the accuracy of the statement that 600 brothers (or soldiers of Christ) occupied the minsters at Wearmouth and Jarrow on Ceolfrith's departure for Rome in 716.[191] When Ceolfrith had first arrived at Jarrow his anonymous biographer said that he brought only twenty-two brothers with him, all of whom seem to have died in the plague in 686, leaving only the abbot and one small boy.[192] A house begun on such a small scale and suffering such a set-back so early in its history would surely have found it hard to increase in size so rapidly in the thirty years before Ceolfrith's departure. On a more practical level, the dimensions of the surviving portions of the early Anglo-Saxon church at Jarrow render it unlikely that a congregation of anything approaching even half this number of professed religious could have worshipped regularly inside the building.[193] Other texts indicate that

---

[186] Discussed in more detail above, ch. 2.

[187] *VSW* ch. 23 (pp. 46–7); this is the term commonly used to describe religious communities in charters, for example S 86 (AD 733?) and S 31 (*c.* AD 767).

[188] Alcuin, *Ep.* 20 (p. 57); in the same letter Alcuin also used the word *comitatus*.

[189] Bede, *VSCuth.* ch. 10 (pp. 188–9), described Æbbe as 'sanctimonialis femina et mater ancillarum Christi'. See further my 'Language and method', p. 76.

[190] *Dictionary of Medieval Latin from British Sources* (Oxford: Oxford University Press, 1975–), fasc. IV, *s.v. familia.* David Herlihy, *Medieval Households* (Cambridge, MA, and London: Harvard University Press, 1985), pp. 2–3 and 57.

[191] *HA* ch. 17 (p. 382); *VSCeol.* ch. 33 (p. 400).

[192] *VSCeol.* chs. 11 and 14 (pp. 391 and 393). Bede numbered the first community at seventeen: *HA*, ch. 7 (370). The confusion might have arisen, Ian Wood suggested, from confusion in transcribing XXII as XVII: *The Most Holy Abbot Ceolfrid*, p. 2 and n.

[193] For a description of the church at Jarrow, its layout and dimensions see H. M. Taylor and Joan Taylor, *Anglo-Saxon Architecture*, 3 vols. (Cambridge: Cambridge University Press, 1965–78), I, 338–49; Rosemary Cramp, 'Jarrow church', *AJ* 133 (1976), 220–8; *eadem*, 'Monkwearmouth and Jarrow in

the term *frater* could be used with reference to those working for a minster and was not restricted to those who had taken monastic vows.[194] It seems much more likely that the number given here relates to those who lived on the minster's estates (or possibly to the heads of each household living on the church's lands). The author of the life of Ceolfrith may simply have chosen this figure as a nominal indication of the relative size of the whole Wearmouth and Jarrow community, including the peasants as well as those in monastic habits. Alternatively, it is possible this figure appealed to Ceolfrith's biographer because in the first book of Samuel, the armies of first Saul and then King David were said to number almost 600 men.[195]

Few other texts provide any evidence as to the size of the congregations they describe. There were supposedly fifty sisters at Wimborne during the abbacy of Tetta when Leoba lived there, but one might question the reliability of Rudolf's testimony here.[196] When a certain Lulla (*ancilla Christi*) sold some land to Glastonbury Abbey in 744, six members of the minster's community were named in the record of the transaction: Cunbert (for Tunberht) *abbas*, Bosa, Urta, Walcstod, and Tidbert, *sacerdotes*, and Cuthwine, *praepositus*.[197] While it is probable that the community was larger than this, including some professed men who were not priests as well as novices and

their cultural context' in Catherine E. Karkov (ed.), *The Archaeology of Anglo-Saxon England: Basic Readings* (New York and London: Garland Publishing, 1999), pp. 137–53, at pp. 147–8.

[194] Thomas Charles-Edwards offers a useful Irish parallel, noting that a lay-tenant of a monastery in Ireland could be called a *manach* or monk: 'The pastoral role of the church in the early Irish laws', in John Blair and Richard Sharpe (eds.), *Pastoral Care before the Parish*, pp. 63–77, at p. 67; and cf. Kathleen Hughes, *The Church in Early Irish Society* (London: Methuen, 1966), pp. 136–7. Also Thacker, 'Monks, preaching and pastoral care', p. 141.

[195] For Saul's army see I *Samuel* 13:15, 14:2; 23:13. David's companions were numbered at 600 in I *Samuel* 23: 13; 27: 1; 30: 9, and II *Samuel* 15: 18.

[196] *VSL* ch. 5. Dagmar Schneider ('Anglo-Saxon Women', p. 48) was more inclined than I to take this number literally, comparing it with the figure of fifty-four sisters (including two abbesses) listed in the community of Romsey early in the eleventh century in the *Liber vitae* of Hyde Abbey: *Liber vitae: Register and Martyrology of New Minster and Hyde Abbey, Winchester*, ed. W. de G. Birch (Hampshire Record Society, 1892), pp. 62–3; cf. Simon Keynes, *The Liber vitae of the New Minster and Hyde Abbey Winchester* (Copenhagen: Rosenkilde and Bagger, 1996), p. 96; discussed by me in *Veiled Women*, II, 154. It is worth noting that post-reform houses are likely to have been considerably larger than those of the early period; a congregation of fifty would have been remarkable in the eighth century.

[197] S 1410 (AD 744). Although the text of this charter has been much manipulated, and the form of these personal names considerably corrupted, there seems no good reason to doubt its authenticity. See J. Armitage Robinson, 'The Saxon abbots of Glastonbury', in his *Somerset Historical Essays* (London: Oxford University Press for the British Academy, 1921), pp. 26–53, at p. 36; Lesley Abrams, *Anglo-Saxon Glastonbury: Church and Endowment* (Woodbridge: Boydell Press, 1996), pp. 53–4; Sarah Foot, 'Glastonbury's early abbots', in Lesley Abrams and James P. Carley (eds.), *The Archaeology and History of Glastonbury Abbey* (Woodbridge: Boydell Press, 1991), pp. 163–89, at pp. 177–8 (on Abbot Tunberht).

perhaps others being educated there, it is equally possible that the community was not substantially larger than these six named. The cathedral church at Worcester had a rather larger congregation of ordained clergy in the late eighth (or early ninth) century when Bishop Denebert leased some land in Gloucestershire, with the consent of his venerable *familia*, to a priest called Balthun; that grant was witnessed by nine priests, four deacons, two *clerici* and three other men whose names are given without appellation.[198] At Christ Church, Canterbury, in 805 a community of seventeen witnessed a charter in the cathedral's favour: two *praepositi*, ten priests, an archdeacon, two deacons, and two others given no title.[199] Again, if only some of the clergy were available when the grant was made, it is possible that the community was larger than this; others might have been working outside the minster. Most minster communities in early Anglo-Saxon England were probably relatively small, perhaps numbering between five and twenty individuals. It is important to remember that the shape and size of communities could and did fluctuate for various reasons (political, economic or personal) and that no house is likely to have supported a community of a constant size throughout the pre-Viking Age period.[200]

A further problem (which I have addressed more fully elsewhere) relates to the gender-distribution within minster communities. Those pre-Viking-Age congregations that are known to have included women among their number are plotted on figure 10. What proportion of these were all-female establishments and which housed men as well as women is uncertain, for as already explained contemporaries made no linguistic distinction between male, female and mixed communities: all were minsters (*monasteria*). The institution of the double house, that is the mixed-sex congregation ruled by an abbess, was a peculiarly English and Frankish one and, furthermore, a relatively short-lived phenomenon. A number of double houses are described by Bede and others can be identified as having been active in the seventh and eighth centuries with varying degrees of confidence from a range of different sources; stating with certainty that any minster housed women

---

[198] S 1262 (AD 798x822); J. Armitage Robinson, *St Oswald and the Church of Worcester*, British Academy supplemental papers 5 (London: Oxford University Press for the British Academy, 1919), p. 9. Compare S 1261 (AD ?814), attested by twelve members of the *familia*, and S 1272–3; see further Robinson, *St Oswald*, p. 10.

[199] S 1259 (AD 805). See Brooks, *The Early History*, p. 155.

[200] To give just one example, Bede revealed that the nature of the community at South Shields had changed since Cuthbert's time: 'there is a minster not far from the mouth of the Tyne, on the south side, filled with a noble company of men but now, changed like all else by time, of virgins who serve Christ', *VSCuth*. ch. 3 (pp. 160–3). See further *Veiled Women*, I, 51–3.

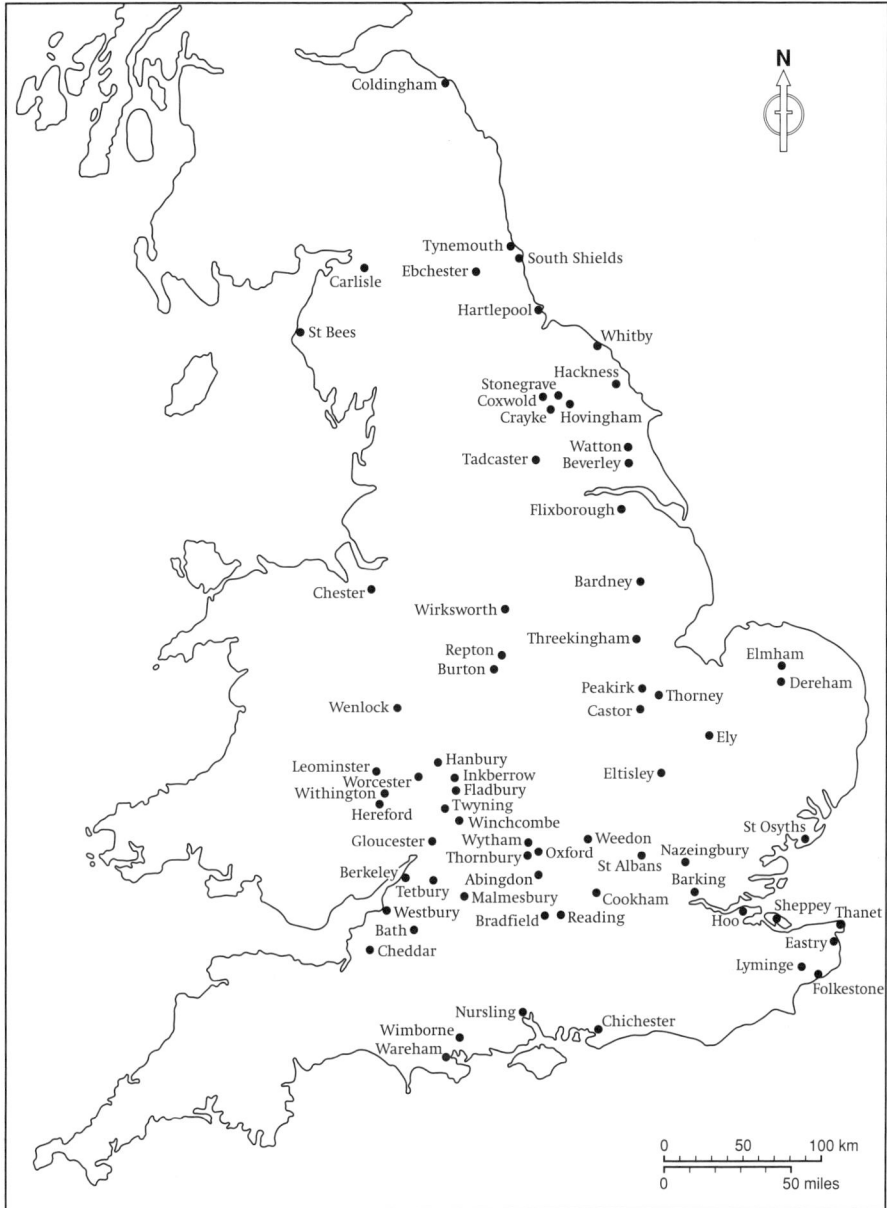

FIGURE 10: Map of minsters housing women to *c.* 850.

exclusively before the early tenth century is impossible.[201] Yet at some point long before the monastic revolution of Edgar's reign imposed full sex-segregation on all monastic houses, the double house ceased to exert the same appeal over the Anglo-Saxon royal and aristocratic patrons of new minsters: no double house is identifiable with certainty after 796.[202] One might offer various reasons both for the popularity of the notion of the double house and for its subsequent decline. An obvious attraction to aspiring female religious (and probably their less spiritually driven relatives) was the potential protection male companions could provide as well as the practical physical advantages of their stronger arms.[203] That some of the men could be ordained to the ranks of the clergy was of further benefit.

No minster could function effectively without the services of at least one priest: the whole congregation (and their guests and tenants) needed regular access to the sacraments. If established near a cathedral, a minster congregation could turn to the episcopal community for a priest to celebrate the eucharist, but for many minsters this would have proved impracticable. The presence of a priest was thought sufficiently important for the legislators at *Clofesho* in 747 to relax their otherwise uncompromising stance on the question of 'lay minsters' and urge bishops to go inside those irregular houses established by secular men, lest the health of those within be further compromised for the lack of a priest.[204] Early monastic rules expressed some ambivalence about the place of priests within monastic communities and it is difficult to determine in some instances even whether early Anglo-Saxon abbots were ordained, let alone to establish how many of any given community were in clerical orders.[205] Once we look away from cathedral congregations such as Worcester and Christ Church, Canterbury, which obviously contained larger numbers of priests and men in the lesser clerical orders than would a small family minster, the sources are not particularly helpful. Many of the men described in saints' lives were ordained, but these were,

---

[201] For a general discussion of double houses see *Veiled Women*, I, 49–56. Lists of double houses have been compiled by Dagmar Schneider, 'Anglo-Saxon women in the religious life: a study of the status and position of women in an early mediaeval society' (unpublished PhD thesis, University of Cambridge, 1985), pp. 19–20 and Roberta Gilchrist, *Gender and Material Culture: The Archaeology of Religious Women* (London and New York: Routledge, 1994), pp. 28–9.

[202] *Veiled Women*, I, 62–3 and 78–9; P. Wormald, 'St Hilda, saint and scholar (614–80)', in Jane Mellanby (ed.), *The St Hilda's College Centenary Symposium: A Celebration of the Education of Women* (Oxford: St Hilda's College, 1993), pp. 93–103, at p. 95.

[203] *Veiled Women*, I, 50–1.   [204] Council of *Clofesho*, AD 747, ch. 5 (H&S III, 364).

[205] For Benedict's reservations see above, ch. 2, n. 144; Giles Constable, 'Monasteries, rural churches and the *cura animarum* in the early Middle Ages', *Settimane* 28 (1982), 349–89, at p. 359. Patrick Sims-Williams has also considered this problem in the context of the early English church: *Religion and Literature*, p. 170.

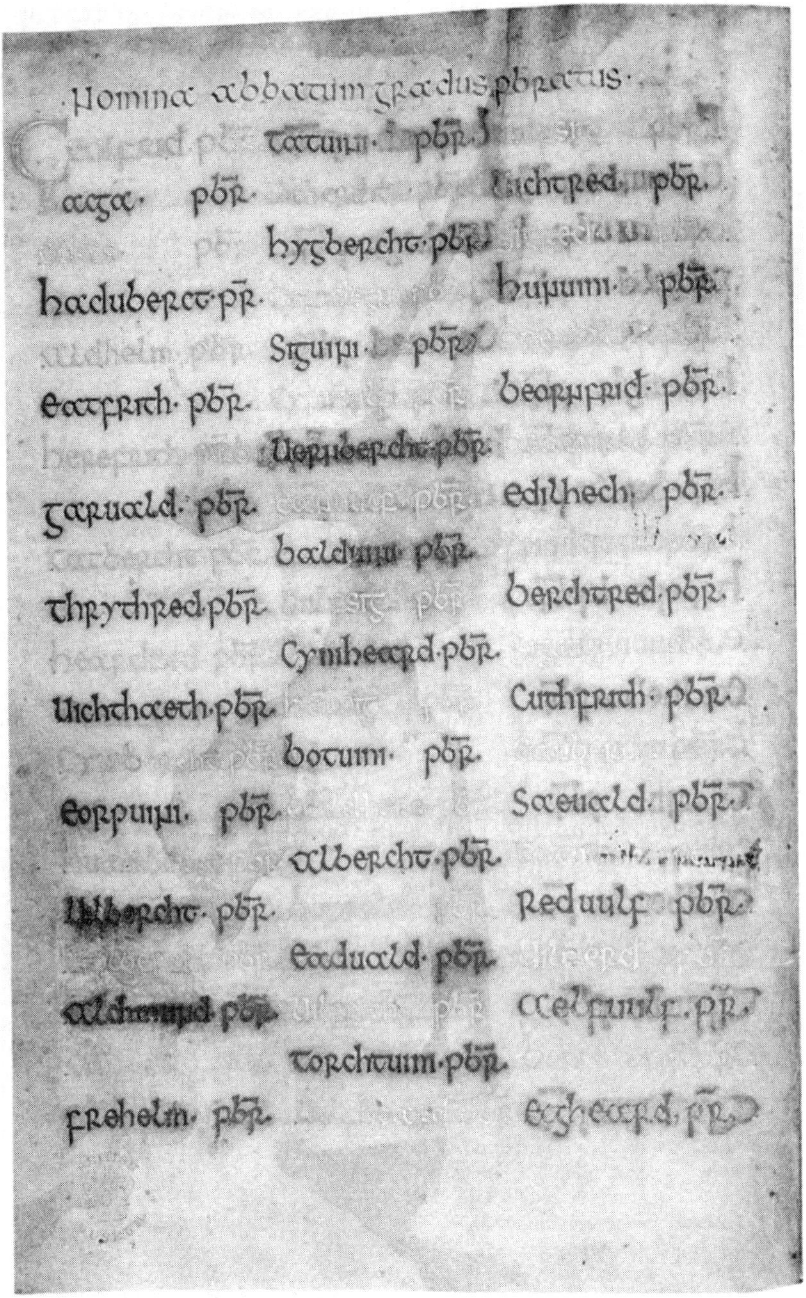

PLATE VIII: Durham *Liber vitae*, London, British Library, Cotton MS Domitian A. vii, fo. 18b (list of abbots beginning with Ceolfrith).

by definition, exceptional figures, unrepresentative of the majority of those living in religious houses. In the Lindisfarne *Liber vitae* the names of abbots were recorded under three headings – abbots of the grade of priest, abbots who were deacons, and plain abbots – the first and third lists being of more or less equivalent length.[206] According to Bede's account of the organisation of Columba's community on Iona, the abbots of that community were always priests.[207] Certain minsters with high standards of scholarship and learning may have trained a higher proportion of their inmates for the priesthood and diaconate than did the mass of smaller, less exceptional establishments. At Whitby, Hild 'compelled those under her direction to devote so much time to the study of the holy Scriptures and so much time to the performance of good works, that there might be no difficulty in finding many there who were fitted for holy orders'; in fact five men from this minster later became bishops.[208] Early ninth-century abbots of St Augustine's, Canterbury who described themselves as 'priest-abbot' had formerly been trained in the episcopal community at Christ Church;[209] other Kentish minsters in the same period also acquired heads who styled themselves *presbyter abbas* or *praepositus*, and Nicholas Brooks has shown that at Lyminge, at least, this was not a new development.[210] Headda, abbot of the Worcestershire minster of Dowdeswell in the late eighth century, but formerly a member of the episcopal *familia* at Worcester, described himself as 'priest and abbot' (*presbiter et abbas*) and tried to ensure that his inheritance should pass into the hands of the cathedral community if no one could be found in holy orders among his heirs to maintain the monastic rule there, in an attempt to ensure that the

---

[206] See plate VIII: a page from the Durham *Liber Vitae*; A. H. Thompson (ed.), *Liber Vitae ecclesiae Dunelmensis. A Collotype Facsimile of the Original Manuscript with Introductory Essays and Notes*, Surtees Society 136 (Durham: published for the Society by Andrews & Co., 1923); *Liber Vitae ecclesiae Dunelmensis nec non obituaria duo ejusdem ecclesiae*, ed. J. Stevenson, Surtees Society 8 (London: J. B. Nichols and Son, 1841). For recent discussion of the *Liber vitae* see Jan Gerchow, *Die Gedenküberlieferung der Angelsachsen: mit einem Katalog der libri vitae und Necrologien* (Berlin: de Gruyter, 1988), pp. 109–54.

[207] *HE* III. 4 (pp. 222–5); for discussion of the implications of Bede's statement that these priest-abbots held sway over the whole *prouincia* including the bishops see Wallace-Hadrill, *Commentary*, pp. 93–4 and 230; Richard Sharpe, 'Some problems concerning the organisation of the church in early medieval Ireland', *Peritia* 3 (1984), 230–70

[208] *HE* IV. 23 (pp. 408–9). Peter Hunter Blair, 'Whitby as a centre of learning in the seventh century', in Michael Lapidge and Helmut Gneuss (eds.), *Learning and Literature in Anglo-Saxon England* (Cambridge: Cambridge University Press, 1985), pp. 3–32, at pp. 3 and 25–9.

[209] Brooks, *The Early History*, pp. 163–4. For the most recent discussion of the abbots of St Augustine's see Susan Kelly (ed.), *Charters of St Augustine's Abbey, Canterbury and Minster-in-Thanet* (Oxford: Oxford University Press for the British Academy, 1995), pp. 205–13. See also Sims-Williams, *Religion and Literature*, pp. 156, 170–1 and 357; Simon Keynes, *The Councils of Clofesho* (Leicester: University of Leicester, Department of Adult Education, 1994), p. 46 and n. 202.

[210] Brooks, *The Early History*, pp. 187–8. Berhtwald, *presbyter abbas*, was abbot of Lyminge in 689 (S 12), Dun in 723 (S 23).

lands did not pass into lay control.[211] Patrick Sims-Williams speculated as to whether Headda thought that his minster had a duty to take the sacraments to its lay neighbours, or if alternatively he was influenced by the provisions of the 747 council of *Clofesho* relating to the need to ensure priestly ministry for minster congregations which were quoted above.[212] Despite the disquiet of early monastic rules about the presence of priests within monastic houses, it seems that in England as elsewhere in Europe, it became increasingly common for men living in religion to take clerical orders, and for priest-monks to have obligations towards the spiritual care of their lay neighbours as well as their fellow religious brethren.[213]

If early Anglo-Saxon monastic congregations really were fairly small, one might wonder how their – often substantial – estates were managed. At Glastonbury a congregation of six (or even twice that number) could scarcely have hoped themselves to cultivate more than a tiny proportion of the numerous estates held by the minster in 744.[214] Land was generally given to minsters together with the peasants and slaves already living on it, as we have seen; these will have continued to cultivate the lands under the supervision of the minster's representative (rather than their former, lay lord), but parts of an estate may have been looked after by those more directly connected with the minster. Some of Whitby's estates were managed on the minster's behalf by a reeve responsible to the abbess,[215] others were cultivated by individuals who apparently belonged to the wider community, and might even be described as *fratres*, even though they seemingly had no intention of becoming professed religious.[216]

Both Lives of St Cuthbert report an occasion on which the saint, while feasting with Abbess Ælfflæd, had a vision of the death of a shepherd called

---

[211] S 1413 (? AD 781x800).

[212] Sims-Williams, *Religion and Literature*, p. 156. Another Worcestershire charter, also discussed by Sims-Williams (*ibid.*, p. 157), made similar provision: Bishop Milred gave Sodbury to a certain Eanbald provided that there was a man in his family willing to take holy orders and qualified to do so; Eanbald passed the estate onto to a certain Eastmund (possibly a priest) who repeated the same condition in his own will: S 1446.

[213] Constable, 'Monasteries', pp. 360–1. Mayr-Harting has also commented on the intensification of monastic clericalisation in the eighth century, attributing it to a variety of reasons, including the growth of daily mass in monasteries as well as the need for missionary work: *The Venerable Bede*, p. 17.

[214] For Glastonbury's early endowment see Heather Edwards, *The Charters of the Early West Saxon Kingdom*, BAR, Brit. ser. 198 (Oxford: BAR, 1988), 10–78, and Abrams, *Anglo-Saxon Glastonbury*, ch. 3.

[215] See, for example, the account given by Bede of the origins of Cædmon, who worked with the cattle on one of Whitby's estates: *HE* IV. 24.

[216] Rosemary Cramp, 'Northumbria and Ireland', in Paul E. Szarmach with the assistance of Virginia Darrow Oggins (eds.), *Sources of Anglo-Saxon Culture* (Kalamazoo, MI: Medieval Institute Publications, Western Michigan University, 1986), pp. 185–201, at p. 193.

Hadwald who worked for Whitby. The anonymous brother of Lindisfarne described Hadwald as 'seruus Dei ex familia tua [Ælfflaeda]' and as one of the *fratres* from the shepherds' huts;[217] Bede referred to him firstly merely as a holy man (*quidam sanctus*) from Ælfflaed's minster, but later more explicitly as *frater* and *quidam de pastoribus*.[218] Although the term *frater* is somewhat ambiguous, particularly when used by Bede, who employed the word *monachus* seldom, it is more probable that Hadwald was not one of the professed brethren at Whitby, but a member of the community in its broadest sense: he was the minster's tenant.[219]

Not all of those who adopted the religious life were noble, even though the sources tend to concentrate on the activities of those who were. A celebrated exception was the British-named herdsman, Cædmon, who supposedly (if any truth lies behind this famous account) lived in the secular habit until he was well advanced in years tending the cattle on one of Whitby's estates before his remarkable gift of song came to his reeve's attention. According to Bede's narrative, when the abbess heard of his talent she ordered him to take monastic vows and had him instructed in the whole course of sacred history; thereafter he was said to have become a notably devout member of the Whitby community, submitting himself wholeheartedly to the discipline of the rule.[220] The minster of a certain Abbess Cynethryth contained a *paupercula sanctimonialis*, notable for having a withered arm which was cured by contact with the water in which Wilfrid's dead body had been washed. This impoverished sister seems to have been a poor woman in the world, whose lowly status was not forgotten after her entry to the religious life.[221] In other cases, non-noble origins may only be guessed at. Bede's account of the unworthy smith in the Bernician minster contrasted the nobility of the community to which he belonged with the ignobility of his life-style, but Bede did not comment specifically on the man's origins. Whether the exceptional craftsmanship for which he was renowned is any clue as to his social origins is unclear, for he might have acquired his skill within the cloister.[222]

---

[217] Anon., *VSCuth*. IV, 10 (pp. 126–7).   [218] Bede, *VSCuth*., ch. 34 (pp. 262–5).

[219] Rosemary Cramp suggested ('Northumbria and Ireland', pp. 193–4) that Hadwald could have been either a monk or a 'lay associate' of the minster. See also Thacker, 'Monks, preaching and pastoral care', pp. 141–2.

[220] *HE* IV. 24 (pp. 416–19).

[221] *VSW* ch. 66 (pp. 144–5); this suggestion was made by Schneider, 'Anglo-Saxon women', p. 51.

[222] *HE* V. 14 (pp. 502–5). That craftsmen were commonly found within monastic houses is suggested by the inclusion of a chapter devoted to artisans (*artifices*) in the Rule of St Benedict (ch. 57, pp. 264–7). Benedict warned craftsmen of the need for humility lest they take undue pride in their skilfulness and urged the community as a whole not to sell manufactured goods fraudulently or at exalted prices.

Allusions to those who served senior members of monastic communities need not relate to people of low birth but may rather reflect the custom of using younger members of a congregation to care for the elderly and frail within the minster. Two of the sisters at Barking had people ministering to their needs, one as she was nearing death from the plague, the other over a longer period since 'her whole body had for years been so disabled that she could not move a single limb'; in both cases their attendants are likely to have been younger, stronger noble members of the community rather than servants.[223] A paralysed brother in Æthelwulf's minster also had a boy (*puer*) to wait upon his needs and the young Wilfrid looked after a disabled nobleman called Cudda at Lindisfarne.[224] When he knew his death was approaching, Cædmon was reputed to have asked his attendant (*ministrum suum*) to prepare a place for him in the building for the infirm or those close to death, to the bemusement of the other brothers who did not share the former shepherd's divine foreknowledge.[225] There may have been some servants at Melrose, for when Cuthbert arrived there, still in secular clothes, he handed in horse and spear to a 'servant' (*minister*) before entering the church to pray, but it also possible that the servant was Cuthbert's companion.[226] There were, however, certainly both male and female servants (*minister* and *ministra*) in Æthelhild's double minster, who ran errands for the abbess in the different parts of the enclosure.[227]

There can be no doubt that some of those who worked the estates of minsters and cathedral churches in the early Anglo-Saxon period were slaves, or that some slaves lived within monastic enclosures, although there is little evidence relating to slavery in England before the tenth century.[228] The penitential attributed to Theodore includes various comments about the status of slaves and their rights, and appears to imply that English religious were in the habit of keeping slaves, as were Roman monks, by specifying that 'a bishop or an abbot may keep a criminal as a slave if he [the criminal] has not the means of redeeming himself'.[229] The laws of King Wihtred of Kent legislated for the clearing of accusations against bishops' servants, the

---

[223] *HE* IV. 8, 9 (pp. 358–63).   [224] Æthelwulf, *De abbatibus*, ch. 8 (pp. 20–1); *VSW*, ch. 2 (pp. 6–7).

[225] *HE* IV. 24 (pp. 418–21).   [226] Bede, *VSCuth*. ch. 6 (pp. 172–3).   [227] *HE* III. 11 (pp. 248–9).

[228] There are also various terminological problems, since the Latin *servus* and Old English *esne* can be used in relation to free servants rather than slaves, and so are less explicit than *mancipium* and *þeow*, which seem to have had more restricted meanings: David A. E. Pelteret, *Slavery in Early Mediaeval England: From the Reign of Alfred until the Twelfth Century* (Woodbridge: Boydell Press, 1995), pp. 41–9.

[229] Penitential of Theodore, II. xiii (p. 331); II. viii. 4: 'Grecorum monachi seruos non habent; Romanorum habent' (p. 323); II. ii. 5 (p. 313).

181

servants of ecclesiastics, and the unfree servants of a (?monastic) community.[230] The 816 council of Chelsea made provision on the death of a bishop
for the freeing of every Englishman of his who had been enslaved during his
lifetime.[231] It is clear from Domesday Book that many religious houses in
the eleventh century owned sizeable numbers of slaves; for example, 40 per
cent of all the slaves mentioned in the survey of Worcestershire were owned
by only four abbeys, Evesham, Pershore, Westminster and Worcester.[232] No
conclusions can be drawn, however, about the number of slaves owned by
earlier English minsters. Only one text refers to the ownership of a slave by
an individual member of a religious house; the visionary brother from Wenlock requested on his death-bed that the slave-girl whom he owned jointly
with his brother, who had remained in the world, be set free.[233]

Ecgberht's Dialogues prohibited the ordination of anyone of servile origin,[234] and also directed that anyone who wished to submit to the service
of the holy profession should be asked whether he were 'guilty of a servile
condition', as well as whether he had committed any serious offences or
owned the property of another, all of which would render him ineligible for
admission to a minster.[235] The only other text to comment on the selection
of suitable applicants for entry to the religious life was the 747 council of
Clofesho. Its canons directed merely that the heads of minsters (and also bishops) should attempt to ensure that those who wanted to enter the service
of the holy profession be suitably morally qualified, without commenting

[230] Wihtred, laws, chs. 22, 24, 23 (ed. Liebermann, *Die Gesetze*, I, 14). Liebermann understood ch. 23 to relate to bond-servants in religious communities, but the chapter makes alternative provisions for instances where the slave's lord was not a communicant (which one would presume the head of a minster to be). Compare F. L. Attenborough, *The Laws of the Earliest English Kings* (Cambridge: Cambridge University Press, 1922), pp. 181–2.
[231] Council of Chelsea, AD 816, ch. 10 (H&S III, 583).
[232] David A. E. Pelteret, 'Slavery in Anglo-Saxon England', in Jon Douglas Woods and David A. E. Pelteret (eds.), *The Anglo-Saxons: Synthesis and Achievement* (Waterloo, Ontario: Wilfrid Laurier University Press, 1985), pp. 116–33, at p. 131.
[233] Boniface, *Ep.* 10 (p. 13).
[234] Ecgberht, *Dialogi, Responsio* 15 (H&S III, 410). The late-tenth-century will of Æthelgifu contains the first reference to an unfree priest in Anglo-Saxon England; the list of those freed by the will included a priest, Edwin, who was to be able to keep the church during his lifetime provided he kept it in good repair, and who could have a slave himself: ed. Dorothy Whitelock, *The Will of Æthelgifu: A Tenth-Century Anglo-Saxon Manuscript* (Oxford: Oxford University Press for the Roxburghe Club, 1968), p. 9. One clause of the so-called First Synod of St Patrick, a collection of ecclesiastical canons compiled in Ireland possibly in the mid-sixth or the seventh century, which refers to a priest 'under the yoke of servitude', was taken by Kathleen Hughes to refer to a servile cleric: *The Church*, p. 47. However D. A. Binchy has pointed out that the word *servitus* can refer to various kinds of unfreedom such as captivity or hostageship, and argued that it would be safer to assume that there were no servile priests in the early Irish church: 'St Patrick's "First synod"', *Studia Hibernica* 8 (1968), 49–59, at pp. 53–4.
[235] Ecgberht, *Dialogi, Responsio* 14 (H&S III, 409–10).

on their other attributes, but the council also insisted that even the most unsuitable, once tonsured, should only actually be expelled in exceptional circumstances on the decree of a synod.[236] It is not clear whether, if slaves were ineligible to join religious communities, men and women could be freed in order to enter the cloister. Wallace-Hadrill suggested that some of the 250 male and female slaves at Selsey whom Wilfrid freed and baptised joined the bishop's community there and that 'from them [Wilfrid] could have formed the nucleus of the local clergy'.[237] That there are no specific references in the narrative sources to slaves becoming professed members of religious communities does not prove that it was impossible for men of servile birth to take the monastic habit in early Anglo-Saxon England; in the canon law of the early church such an action was possible, provided that the permission of the slave's owner was first obtained.[238]

Another group of people who may frequently have been found inside early English minsters, but who are seldom mentioned in the sources, are the mentally and physically disabled. In the fourth century Jerome had complained to one of his correspondents about the frequency with which children who were physically deformed or otherwise unmarriageable were put into monasteries.[239] Although there is little direct evidence for the prevalence of similar practices in early medieval England, one wonders to what extent minsters were treated as general repositories for the otherwise unemployable: not just surplus daughters, who could be much more cheaply wedded to Christ than to man, but also the maimed and the imbecile may quietly have been consigned to the privacy as well as the protection of the cloister. Such individuals were not the natural subjects of saints' lives (unless they happened to be cured by a miracle) and they were (according to Ecgberht) denied elevation to the priesthood;[240] so it is unlikely that the available contemporary sources would comment on their presence within religious communities. But the appeal of such a sheltered environment to the parents of those disabled children who did not die in infancy, or to

---

[236] Council of *Clofesho*, AD 747, ch. 24 (p. 370).
[237] *HE* IV. 13 (pp. 374–7); Wallace-Hadrill, *Commentary*, p. 153. See also Henry Mayr-Harting, 'St Wilfrid in Sussex', in M. J. Kitch (ed.), *Studies in Sussex Church History* (London: Leopard's Head Press in association with the Centre for Continuing Education, University of Sussex, 1981), pp. 1–17.
[238] Council of Chalcedon, AD 451, ch. 4 (ed. Mansi, *Concilia*, VI, col. 1226).
[239] Jerome, *Ep.* 130, 6 to Demetriades (ed. Hilberg, III, 182): 'Solent miseri parentes et non plenae fidei christiani deformes et aliquot membro debiles filias, qui dignos generos non inveniunt, uirginitati tradere . . . certe, qui religiosiores sibi uidentur paruo sumptu et qui uix ad alimenta sufficiat uirginibus dato omnem censum in utrosque sexu saecularibus liberis largiuntur.' Quoted by Quinn, *Better than the Sons of Kings*, p. 31.
[240] Ecgberht, *Dialogi, Responsio* 15 (H&S III, 410).

those who were injured later in life, seems obvious. Since religious houses played a prominent part in the care of the sick and many of them included men described as doctors, it seems likely that minsters also took responsibility for some of those unsuited to life in the world.[241] Wilfrid first entered the minster at Lindisfarne in order to accompany one of the king's former thegns, Cudda, who chose the religious life after having acquired a paralytic infirmity; one of the noble sisters at Barking had for many years been so disabled that she could not move a single limb.[242] However, the boy who had been dumb from birth, although willing to stay in a hut within the enclosure of Bishop John's oratory near Hexham while receiving the saint's healing and instruction, once able to speak and cured also of his skin disease, rejected John's offer of a permanent place in his *familia* (whether as a servant or to be educated for the religious life it is not clear), preferring to return home.[243]

As well as people from a wide variety of social backgrounds, minsters housed people of all ages. The presence of children within religious houses has already been mentioned, including, at Barking, one as young as three, the boy Æsica; the same minster also housed several elderly sisters, such as the paralysed woman already mentioned and a certain Torhtgyth.[244] Various members of the all-male cell described by Æthelwulf were reputed to have reached considerable ages, including the minster's founder, Eanmund, and the priest Ultán.[245] Since the cloister was often a refuge in widowhood, most minsters probably sheltered several men and women in their last years.[246]

Conclusion

All sorts of motives led people to leave the world for a life of religion in the early Anglo-Saxon period. It is hard to take the remarks about the piety of infants found so commonly in saints' lives too seriously, but there is no doubt that a considerable number of children were educated in the cloister and themselves came voluntarily to stay there in later life. However one might want to question Bede's seven-year-old reaction to life at Jarrow, his

---

[241] For the role of minsters in the care of the sick see below, chapter 7.

[242] *VSW* ch. 2 (pp. 6–7), discussed by William Trent Foley, *Images of Sanctity in Eddius Stephanus' 'Life of Bishop Wilfrid', an Early English Saint's Life* (Lewiston, NY, Queenston, ON, and Lampeter: Edwin Mellen Press, 1992), p. 55; *HE* IV. 9 (pp. 360–1).

[243] *HE* V. 2 (pp. 456–9).   [244] *HE* IV. 8, IV. 9 (pp. 358–9; 360–1).

[245] Æthelwulf, *De abbatibus*, chs. 8, 12 (pp. 20–1, 32–3).

[246] For the church's encouragement of chastity and the cloister for the widowed of both sexes, see *Veiled Women*, I, 120–6.

adult vocation cannot be denied. It does also seem that many people made (or their relations made on their behalf) a deliberate choice to enter a particular minster, one within their native kingdom, and where they had family connections. Women followed the example of their maternal relations, but men were attracted to houses with local or family associations, too.

What has also clearly emerged from this analysis of the composition of minster communities is that there is very little specific information on the basis of which any broad generalisations may be made; indeed the very paucity of detailed evidence, dating as it does from a wide chronological period and relating to houses geographically far removed, serves only to reinforce the ambiguity of the comments found in contemporary materials. Without surviving autobiographical accounts, it is especially difficult to probe questions as personal as the nature of individual vocation. On the basis of the sorts of evidence that do survive we can never wholly comprehend what an early English monastic community was really like; not only is there insufficient material to search for patterns across the country, it is patently unwise to attempt to extrapolate from one region to another. Early Anglo-Saxon monastic congregations were in essence local communities, assuming their peculiar characters from a number of individual factors, both personal and regional, which were unlikely to be replicated elsewhere in England.

In composition, minster communities do not appear far removed from their secular counterparts: they housed people of all ages, from different social classes, who – whether bound by kinship or economic ties – lived together on one estate or group of estates. Once more it is difficult to distinguish the proprietary minster from the noble household. Although a minster's character was indubitably profoundly affected by the geographical location in which it lay and also by the family or families responsible for its foundation and later endowment, a postulant's decision to enter a particular minster was often inspired by other factors unrelated to the locality. A minster's role within its local community and within the wider church, the nature of the activities pursued within its walls, and above all the spiritual qualities of the abbot and leading brethren, were of equal importance to new entrants; these may provide a key to our better understanding of early Anglo-Saxon monasticism.

CHAPTER 5

Daily life within minsters

Eosterwine was renowned at Wearmouth for his readiness to share in the daily round of the minster and his complete identification with the other brothers, in which he refused to take advantage either of his noble birth or of his kinship with Benedict Biscop. He was willing humbly to take his share 'in winnowing and threshing, milking the cows and ewes, in the bake-house, the garden, the kitchen', rejoicing to participate 'gladly and obediently in all the tasks of the minster'.[1] Even after Eosterwine became abbot, the one-time royal thegn would often help the brothers in their work when he came upon them as he went about the minster's business: 'he was happy to put his hand to the plough, hammer iron into shape, wield the winnowing iron, or assist in performing any other task'.[2] Few other texts offer so detailed an insight into the life of an essentially self-sufficient Anglo-Saxon minster in the seventh century as that given by Bede in his *Historia abbatum*; only the anonymous Life of Ceolfrith and Æthelwulf's poem *De abbatibus* provide equivalent pictures of the daily round in individual minsters.[3] It is hard to escape the view that Bede's lengthy treatment of Eosterwine's virtues was intended at least in part to accentuate the contrast between this holy man and other nobly-born religious of the day who were markedly less likely to engage in such menial tasks. More usually, hagiographers accentuated those incidents in their subjects' lives and the particular aspects of their behaviour

---

[1] *HA* ch. 8 (pp. 371–2).   [2] *Ibid.* (p. 372).

[3] The Life of Ceolfrith includes a number of descriptions of aspects of the daily life at Wearmouth and Jarrow which complement the descriptions in Bede's *Historia abbatum*. Æthelwulf's *De abbatibus* concerns events in an unnamed cell of Lindisfarne, possibly Crayke.

which distinguished saints spiritually from their less exalted companions. Since they hoped to teach by example, encouraging their listeners and readers to emulate the heights of saintly conduct, hagiographers often ignored as irrelevant the more mundane details of their heroes' daily lives with which their monastic audience was familiar from its own experience.

Prescriptive literature is similarly unhelpful here. It is easier to find statements in the canons of early English church councils and in the admonitory letters of leading churchmen about inappropriate aspects of the behaviour of religious or the ways in which the organisation of minsters was deemed deficient than it is to locate clear and specific pronouncements about how such men and women ought to live that extend beyond the most general platitudes. This is not to argue that there was not a clear understanding among contemporary church-leaders as to how the monastic life should properly be led, or that this ideal was not one to which all current and aspirant religious were expected to subscribe. At the reforming council held at *Clofesho* in 747, bishops were charged with making vigilant inspection in their dioceses to ensure that *monasteria* lived up to their name. Minsters, the council determined, should be honest dwellings for the silent, the quiet and those who labour for God, not shelters for the arts of the theatre (*ludicrae artes*), that is for poets, harpists, musicians and buffoons. They should be houses for those who pray, read and praise God, and permission should not be given to laymen to wander at will in unsuitable places within them, that is in the rooms in the interior of the minster, lest they see or hear any indecency in the cloister and thus have occasion to reproach the inmates. The dwellings of nuns (*sanctimoniales*) were not to be dens of filthy chatter, feasting, drunkenness, or nests of luxury but should be habitations of those who live continently and soberly in reading and psalmody; sisters should spend their time in reading books and singing psalms rather than weaving and lacing vainglorious clothes in bright colours.[4]

Prayer lay at the heart of the monastic life. The same council decreed that 'henceforth churchmen and monastics should in their canonical hours entreat the divine clemency not only for themselves, but for kings, ealdormen and for the safety of all Christian people'.[5] It was in order that prayers might be offered daily for the redemption of the souls of kings Oswiu and Oswine that the minster at Gilling in North Yorkshire was established at

---

[4] Council of *Clofesho*, AD 747, ch. 20 (H&S III, 369). As Catherine Cubitt has observed, this account of banned occupations in devout minsters reads like a description of Bede's Coldingham: *Anglo-Saxon Church Councils c. 650–c. 850* (London and New York: Leicester University Press, 1995), p. 121.

[5] Council of *Clofesho*, AD 747, ch. 30 (p. 375); discussed by Cubitt, *Anglo-Saxon Church Councils*, pp. 111–13.

the request of Queen Eanflæd.[6] Many texts stressed the intercessory role of minsters, sometimes explicitly linking that function to the church's exemption from earthly financial burdens. In the first chapter of his law-code, the Kentish king, Wihtred (690–725), freed the church from taxation while in the second he ordered that the king should be prayed for and honoured by churchmen of their own free will.[7] At the synod of Gumley in 749, Æthelbald (king of Mercia 716–57) confirmed that all churches and minsters were to be released from public burdens, taxation and the requirement to provide hospitality to the king and his followers, so that they might be free to serve God in peaceful contemplation (*in contemplatione pacifica*), throughout Æthelbald's realm for ever.[8] More difficult to interpret is the markedly more elaborate statement made in a charter attributed to King Ine of Wessex (688–726) which ordered that minsters should serve God alone and practise monastic discipline according to the rule ('et monasticam cenobii disciplinam . . . regulariter exerceant'), so that 'they be worthy to pour out prayers for the condition and prosperity of our kingdom and for the forgiveness of sins committed before the face of the divine majesty, attending the offices of prayer in churches and striving to intercede for our fragility'. The authenticity of this text is questionable and it is far from clear that this passage was written in the eighth century.[9]

Our search for the nature of the daily round in early English minsters must take us beyond the prescriptions and admonitions of the conciliar literature and between the lines of hagiographical narratives of spiritual and

---

[6] *HE* III. 14 and 24 (pp. 256–7, 292–3).

[7] Laws of Wihtred, 695, chs. 1–2 (ed. Liebermann, *Die Gesetze*, I, 12); Richard P. Abels, *Lordship and Military Obligation in Anglo-Saxon England* (Berkeley and Los Angeles, CA: University of California Press, 1988), pp. 50–1.

[8] S 92; discussed by Nicholas Brooks, 'The development of military obligations in eighth- and ninth-century England', in Peter Clemoes and Kathleen Hughes (eds.), *England before the Conquest* (Cambridge: Cambridge University Press, 1971), pp. 69–84, at pp. 76–7; Abels, *Lordship*, pp. 52–3; Cubitt, *Anglo-Saxon Church Councils*, pp. 112–13.

[9] S 245 (AD 704), a charter freeing all the minsters in Ine's kingdom from secular obligations and fiscal tribute; the passage is translated and quoted in full by Cubitt, *Anglo-Saxon Church Councils*, p. 112. Opinions differ as to the authenticity of this charter, but even if it were derived from a genuine text, a number of difficulties would remain; see Brooks, 'The development', p. 75, n. 1; Patrick Sims-Williams, *Religion and Literature in Western England, 600–800* (Cambridge: Cambridge University Press, 1990), p. 225. The same statement about minsters' prayerful obligations is found otherwise only in S 246 (a spurious charter of Ine's in favour of Glastonbury, closely modelled on S 245), and in two spurious charters for Chertsey abbey, one supposedly granted by King Edgar in 967 (S 752) and the other in Edward the Confessor's name and dated 1062 (S 1035). In many ways the references to the regular discipline and to prayer for the king's realm might seem better suited to the conditions of the tenth-century monastic revolution than to the early eighth century. However, that religious had a duty to pray for kings and specifically for the forgiveness of royal sins is not anachronistic; compare the discussion in chapter 3 above of the granting of lands and privileges to minsters in return for intercession for the donor.

ascetic prowess. Even by piecing together a variety of sources of different date and relating to diverse geographical areas, we may succeed in assembling only a partial picture of the shape of a monastic day. It might, however, be unwise to strive too hard to bring this divergent material together to create a standardised image of monastic daily life in the early English church. Since uniformity characterised neither the foundation nor the regulation of separate minsters,[10] diversity in the working out of monasticism in practice is probably to be anticipated, even if some texts may seem to witness to deceptively consistent practices. Without attempting to identify the characteristics of a 'typical' day in the life of an early Anglo-Saxon religious man or woman, we will explore here the practices and activities that characterised a life dedicated to God, emphasising those elements of this life-style that were distinctively religious and noting those aspects of monastic behaviour that conformed more closely to that of secular households.

Prayer and worship

In the last chapter we saw the preoccupation of legislators for the early English church with the outward appearance of men and women devoted to religion; habits, veils and tonsures were to be symbols of a life professed, and testify not just to the rejection of earthly vanities, but to the bearer's active decision to dedicate that life to the worship of God. Devotion – corporate and individual – lay at the core of the monastic day and it was its performance that centrally distinguished the religious from the secular way of life. Further, since participation in the liturgy involved the whole community, a minster's sense of its shared identity was expressed through its liturgical life.[11] For minsters (and, indeed, for cathedral churches), the timetable of the monastic office governed the ordering of the day, sending religious from their beds during the night and structuring the division of daylight hours. Precisely which model individual minsters chose to follow was, as we shall see, their own affair and it may not be sensible to look for a standardised liturgical *cursus* even shared by churches within one early Anglo-Saxon kingdom, let alone over the whole country.[12] Yet it is here that we must start, for nothing else so encapsulates what it meant to leave the world for the seclusion of the cloister.

---

[10] Above, chapters 2 and 3.

[11] Catherine Cubitt, 'Unity and diversity in the Anglo-Saxon liturgy', in R. N. Swanson (ed.), *Unity and Diversity in the Church*, Studies in Church History 32 (Oxford: Blackwell, 1996), 45–57, at p. 52.

[12] See Cubitt, 'Unity and diversity', p. 46.

When Eanmund, founder of the minster described in Æthelwulf's poem, *De abbatibus*, sent to Ireland to seek Ecgberht's guidance about where to locate his new church, the bishop advised him to clear the top of a hill of thorn and other vegetation, so as to reveal a smooth top where a fair church for God might be built, in which 'faithful hearts may both by day and night fulfil for Christ the vows made from pure breasts'.[13] The church of York in the time of Bishop Bosa (formerly a member of the community at Whitby), was also, according to Alcuin, constantly engaged in praising God:[14]

This father of the church endowed its fabric and made its clergy live a life apart from the common people, decreeing that they should serve the one God at every hour: that the mystical lyre should sound in unbroken strain, that human voices, forever singing heavenly praises to the Lord, should beat upon the heights of Heaven: regulating every hour with alternate duties: now a reading, now a holy prayer.

When one reads the narrative descriptions of early English monastic practice it is, however, striking how much less emphasis is laid there on the place of daily office within the coenobitic life in comparison with the close focus cast on individual examples of private prayer and devotion. Saints' lives were, of course, narratives about the exceptional, those who were marked out during their lives on earth as destined for future sanctity. The devotional behaviour of a Cuthbert or a Guthlac attracted attention precisely because it was far removed from that of their less exalted companions in the cloister.[15] Perhaps hagiographers assumed that their audiences were sufficiently familiar with the monastic office to render explanations of its form and purpose unnecessary. Alternatively, the English may have perceived the height of spiritual devotion to have lain in private contemplation, for which the conventual life with its round of common offices was only a preparation. It was a hagiographical convention to portray a saintly individual as continuously engaged in praise of God and ceaselessly chanting psalms. Cuthbert was accustomed to sing psalms even before he entered the religious life; Wilfrid could not be prevented from chanting psalms perpetually when in prison.[16] While Bede was dying, he spent all of his time when he was not teaching his pupils reciting the Psalter, singing antiphons and repeating prayers, even though

---

[13] Æthelwulf, *De abbatibus*, lines 137–9 (ed. Campbell, pp. 12–13).

[14] Alcuin, *Versus*, lines 857–64 (ed. and trans. Godman, pp. 70–3).

[15] James Campbell, 'Elements in the background to the Life of St Cuthbert and his early cult', in Gerald Bonner *et al.* (eds.), *St Cuthbert, his Cult and his Community to AD 1200* (Woodbridge: Boydell, 1989), pp. 3–19, at pp. 13–16.

[16] Bede, *VSCuth.* ch. 5 (pp. 170–1); *VSW* chs. 36 and 38 (pp. 72–7).

he was too weak to attend the office with his brethren.[17] Yet, although Bede had previously urged his brethren not to lose opportunities to retreat to the minster's oratory where God might be thanked for gifts or petitioned for grace in private, the less spiritually athletic who constituted the majority of most congregations were more likely to have restricted their devotion to the set hours of the office.[18]

The daily office

The office dictated the rhythm of the monastic day. Sleeping, eating, reading, working and leisure each had their allotted times within a framework determined by the sequence of corporate worship and by the liturgical calendar of the church year.

The months revolve with their successive feast-days and cycles of years shall pass with the feasts in fixed order: on this day each year may antiphons strike the ear with their pleasing harmonies and the singing of psalms reverberate from twinned choirs . . . Brothers, let us praise God in harmonious voice, and let the throngs of sisters (*turba sororum*) also burst forth in continual psalmody. On those feast days let us all chant hymns and psalms and appropriate responds beneath the roof of the church, intoning the melodies with the continuous accompaniment of the psaltery; and let us strive to tune the lyre with ten strings . . . Let each one of us adorn the new church with his singing and let each *lector* – whether male or female – read the lessons from Holy Scripture.

This metrical *titulus* written by Aldhelm of Malmesbury in celebration of a West Saxon church dedicated to the Virgin Mary and built by a certain Bugga offers valuable insights into the performance of the liturgy in a double minster.[19] In this establishment, music was as important as was the word in the celebration of the office: the psalms were accompanied by psaltery (a ten-stringed, triangular-shaped instrument, strung over a hollow box),[20] hymns, antiphons and responses were sung and the worship was led by 'the trained

---

[17] Cuthbert, *Epistola de obitu Bedae* (ed. Colgrave & Mynors, pp. 580–3).

[18] Bede, *Homelia*, I. 23 (ed. Hurst, p. 165); A. G. P. van der Walt has drawn attention to the link between this passage and *RSB*, ch. 52, 4 (pp. 254–5): 'Reflections of the Benedictine Rule in Bede's homiliary', *JEH*, 37 (1986), 367–76, at p. 372.

[19] Aldhelm, *Carmen ecclesiasticum* III, lines 44–58 (ed. Ehwald, *Aldhelmi opera*, pp. 16–17, trans. Michael Lapidge and James L. Rosier, *Aldhelm: The Poetic Works* (Cambridge: D. S. Brewer, 1985) pp. 48–9). The location of this minster is not known; it was apparently founded during the reign of King Ine of Wessex (688–726) and before Aldhelm's death in 709; see Barbara Yorke, *Nunneries and the Anglo-Saxon Royal Houses* (London and New York: Continuum, 2003), pp. 20 and 27.

[20] Lapidge and Rosier, *Aldhelm: The Poetic Works*, pp. 236–7, n. 26.

voice of the precentor, resounding repeatedly and shaking the summit of heaven with its sonorous chant' (lines 48–9). Women as well as men read the lessons from Scripture.[21] Celebration in other churches may have been less elaborate than this (and Aldhelm's description clearly referred to the worship on a special occasion: either the dedication of the church or a feast of the Virgin);[22] yet this was the essential shape of the early medieval Divine Office in England.

We know little about the details of the form of the office in England in this period, because of the lack of surviving office books.[23] Although only three manuscript collectars survive from Anglo-Saxon England (and just one of those – the Durham Collectar – pre-dates the tenth-century Benedictine revolution), Alicia Corrêa has argued convincingly that no Anglo-Saxon minster could have performed the daily offices without possessing such a standard book of collects and chapters. Among the factors militating against the preservation of such manuscripts may have been their pragmatic function, derivative nature and workaday appearance: these were not deluxe altar books like sacramentaries, but working manuals.[24] Similarly, no Anglo-Saxon service-books survive from the early period that contain the entire corpus of psalm texts arranged for use in formal worship, even though the principal component of the daily office was the recitation of psalms in set order.[25] In considering the nature and content of the monastic office we might expect early English practice to owe much to Rome, but southern Italian, Gallican and Irish prayers were also influential.[26]

A bell or other signal summoned the devout from their various activities to prayer. At Hackness, a sister called Begu woke from her rest in the sisters'

---

[21] For discussion of the shape of the canonical office and the role of the *lector* in its performance see Karl Young, *The Drama of the Medieval Church*, 2 vols. (Oxford: Clarendon Press, 1933), I, 46–75.

[22] 'With her own birth the Virgin Mary consecrated this very day, on which the dedication of Bugga's church gleams brightly – the day on which the month of August perpetually renews . . .': Aldhelm, *Carmen ecclesiasticum*, III, lines 59–62 (ed. Ehwald, p. 17); Lapidge and Rosier, *Aldhelm*, p. 237, n. 28; Mary Clayton, 'Feasts of the Virgin in the liturgy of the Anglo-Saxon church', *Anglo-Saxon England* 13 (1984), 209–33, at pp. 213–21, and also *eadem, The Cult of the Virgin Mary in Anglo-Saxon England* (Cambridge: Cambridge University Press, 1990), pp. 38–47.

[23] Compare Helmut Gneuss, 'Liturgical Books in Anglo-Saxon England and their Old English terminology', in Michael Lapidge and Helmut Gneuss (eds.), *Learning and Literature in Anglo-Saxon England* (Cambridge: Cambridge University Press, 1985), pp. 91–141, at pp. 110–21.

[24] Alicia Corrêa, 'Daily office books: collectars and breviaries', in Richard W. Pfaff (ed.), *The Liturgical Books of Anglo-Saxon England* (Kalamazoo, MI: The Medieval Institute, Western Michigan University, 1995), pp. 45–66, at pp. 46–7.

[25] Phillip Pulsiano, 'Psalters', *ibid.*, pp. 61–85, at pp. 61–2.

[26] See Henry Mayr-Harting, *The Coming of Christianity to Anglo-Saxon England* (3rd edn, London: Batsford, 1991), pp. 168–90; Cubitt, 'Unity and diversity', pp. 49–52; Donald Bullough, 'Roman books and the Carolingian *renovatio*', in his *Carolingian Renewal: Sources and Heritage* (Manchester and New York: Manchester University Press, 1991), pp. 1–38, at pp. 4–6.

dormitory when she heard 'the well-known sound of the bell (*notum campanae sonum*) with which sisters were used to be roused to their prayers or called together when one of them had been summoned from the world'.[27] They gathered together in their church several times each day in order to chant psalms, sing hymns and antiphons, listen to Scripture and recite prayers. On a couple of occasions in his homilies, Bede alluded to the daily recitation of the Lord's Prayer in the monastic office, reminding his hearers how 'we daily ask the Father in genuflexion, "Thy kingdom come",' and commending the Lord's injunction to cure daily-committed sins by the daily exercise of prayer, particularly in the words He taught: 'Forgive us the wrong we have done as we have forgiven those who have wronged us.'[28]

Even more than his historical and hagiographical works, Bede's homilies and biblical commentaries supply some of our most valuable information about the place of the liturgy within the religious life; Bede's own particular devotion to the monastic office was remembered by later generations.[29] He was confident that angels were often present beside the devout, particularly 'when we give ourselves to divine services, that is when we enter a church and open our ears to sacred reading, or give our attention to psalm-singing, or apply ourselves to prayer, or celebrate the solemnity of the mass . . . Hence we must strive meticulously my brothers, when we come into the church to pay the due service of divine praise or to perform the solemnity of the mass, to be always mindful of the angelic presence, and to fulfil our heavenly duty with fear and fitting veneration.'[30] Quoting *Acts*, Bede urged his fellow brothers meticulously to imitate the apostolic work through prayer: 'we who have the heavenly promises, [and] are commanded painstakingly to offer supplication to receive them should all come together to pray, and should persist in prayer, and should entreat the Lord with single-minded devotion'.[31] Prayer was not an activity to be undertaken only within the confines of the office or other set liturgical forms. 'We cannot', he wrote in his homily for the greater litanies, 'otherwise fulfil the command of the apostle to "pray

---

[27] *HE* IV. 23 (pp. 412–13).

[28] Bede, *Homelia*, II. 12, lines 31–2 (ed. Hurst, p. 261); *Homelia*, II. 14, lines 228–33 (ed. Hurst, p. 278). Van der Walt has remarked on the closeness of these comments (particularly the second quoted) to *RSB*, ch. 13, 13–14 (pp. 208–9): 'Reflections of the Benedictine Rule', p. 374.

[29] Alcuin, *Ep.* 284 (p. 443); quoted by Gerald Bonner, 'The Christian life in the thought of the Venerable Bede', *Durham University Journal*, 63, n.s. 32 (1970), 39–55, at p. 42.

[30] Bede, *Homelia*, II. 10 (ed. Hurst, p. 249), which alluded to Rule of St Benedict, ch. 19, discussed by Bonner, 'The Christian life', p. 42. See also Bede's reference to the presence of angels at the Eucharist: *In Lucam* vi, ed. D. Hurst, *Bedae venerabilis opera*, II: *Opera exegetica* 3, CCSL, 120 (Turnhout: Brepols, 1960), p. 411.

[31] Bede, *Homelia*, II. 15 (ed. Hurst, p. 285), quoting Acts, 1: 14.

without ceasing" unless by the gift of God we so direct all our actions, words, thoughts and even silences so that each may become tempered by regard for him and all may become profitable for our salvation.'[32] Bede had argued similarly in his commentary on Mark's Gospel, where he linked prayer with fasting, not just abstaining from food 'but from all the allurements of the flesh and self-restraint from every kind of vicious passion. Likewise, prayer in general consists not only in the word with which we invoke the mercy of God but in everything we do in devout faith to serve our Creator.'[33] Not only must prayer be made continually, it must be made correctly. It is all right for 'the citizens of the heavenly fatherland, while they are pilgrims on this earth', to ask God for peace, prosperity and abundant crops provided that they do so in the right spirit; but 'there are some who look for temporal rest and prosperity from their Creator, not that they may obey their Creator with more devoted souls, but that they may be free for more abundant eating and drinking'. This is not the correct way to petition the Almighty and those that do so in such a way are not worthy to have their prayers answered; 'let us strive, dearly beloved, both to ask well and to obtain what we ask'.[34]

Hagiographers used references to the monastic office and its timetable to set particular incidents in their subjects' lives in context, confirming – were such confirmation necessary – our presumption that their subjects' lives did indeed revolve around their liturgical obligations. Stories were often introduced into larger narratives by reference to some fixed point in the liturgy, the notable event having occurred 'after the psalmody of the third hour',[35] or 'when the accustomed time of nightly prayer arrived'.[36] Before the tenth century (when the *Regularis concordia* supplied the first detailed account of a monastic *cursus* to be followed in England)[37] it is not easy either to establish a certain timetable for the monastic offices or to be certain of

---

[32] *Homelia*, II. 14 (p. 279); quoted by Benedicta Ward, *The Venerable Bede* (London: Geoffrey Chapman, 1990; 1998 edition), p. 64.

[33] Bede, *Mark*, 9:29, p. 550; Ward, *The Venerable Bede*, p. 62.

[34] Bede, *Homelia*, II. 14 (ed. Hurst, p. 275; trans. Martin and Hurst, p. 128).

[35] *HA* ch. 18 (p. 382): 'completa horae tertiae psalmodia'.

[36] Bede, *VSCuth*. ch. 39 (pp. 284–5): 'ubi consuetum nocturnae orationis tempus aderat'.

[37] *Regularis concordia*, chs. 14–26 (ed. Hallinger, pp. 77–87). Even after this time, it is not clear which houses other than those known to have been reformed or newly founded as Benedictine establishments actually conformed to all the details of this timetable, nor what alternative customaries may have been in use: M. Bradford Bedingfield, *The Dramatic Liturgy of Anglo-Saxon England* (Woodbridge: Boydell Press, 2002), pp. 11–18. For discussion of the votive observances imposed as part of the tenth-century monastic revolution see Sally Elizabeth Roper, *Medieval English Benedictine Liturgy: Studies in the Formation, Structure and Content of the Monastic Votive Office, c. 950–1540* (New York and London: Garland Publishing, 1993), pp. 23–41.

what each office consisted beyond the broad outline already sketched. Many early medieval monastic rules explained at some length how to observe the synaxis, the office of psalms and prayers, in the canonical manner,[38] but considerable variations may be seen between the recommendations of individual rules, for example in the number of offices to be celebrated in each day.[39] Diversity may, as Cubitt has persuasively argued, have been the keynote of the early Anglo-Saxon liturgy.[40]

'Seven times a day I have given praise to thee,' sang the Psalmist, and St Benedict quoted this passage approvingly in his Rule for monks.[41] Yet Benedict used the same psalm to argue for the addition of a night office ('At midnight I arose to give you praise': Psalm 118:62) creating for his monks an eight-fold office: 'Therefore, we should praise our Creator for his just judgements at these times: Lauds, Prime, Terce, Sext, None, Vespers and Compline; and let us arise at night to give him praise.'[42] Western monastic patterns of daily worship developed from the forms first established in the eastern church, but tended to be both more elaborate in content and more frequent during each day. Cassian noted this tendency to diversity in his monastic *Institutes*: 'We have found different rules appointed in different places, and the systems and regulations that we have seen are almost as many in number

---

[38] Columbanus, *Regula monachorum*, ch. 7 (ed. Walker, p. 128): 'De synaxi uero, id est de cursu psalmorum et orationum modo canonico quaedam sunt distinguenda, quia uarie a diversis memoriae de eo traditum est.'

[39] Cuthbert Butler offered a detailed account of the shape of the Benedictine *horarium* in his *Benedictine Monachism: Studies in Benedictine Life and Rule* (London and New York: Longmans, Green, 1919).

[40] Cubitt, 'Unity and diversity', p. 52.

[41] Psalm 118: 164; *RSB*, ch. 16, 1 (pp. 210–11). For the relationship between Benedict's daily office (and that of the Rule of the Master) and the early Roman monastic office, see Paul F. Bradshaw, *Daily Prayer in the Early Church: A Study of the Origin and Early Development of the Divine Office*, Alcuin Club collections no. 63 (London: SPCK: 1981), pp. 134–42. The centrality of the office in Benedict's thinking about the nature of monasticism was discussed by Adalbert de Vogüé, 'Problems of the monastic conventual mass', *Downside Review* 87 (1969), 327–38, at pp. 329–30 and 334–6.

[42] *RSB*, ch. 16, 5 (pp. 210–11). 'Ergo his temporibus referamus laudes creatori nostro super iudicia iustitiae suae, id est matutinis, prima, tertia, sexta, nona, uespera, completorio; et nocte surgamus ad confitendum ei.' Compare *RM*, ch. 34 (pp. 186–91). The translation of the terms describing these offices is somewhat complicated by the vocabulary used by modern Benedictines, who call the night office (*nocturna oratio*) matins, and the office at daybreak (*matutinae*) lauds. Indeed, the history of the nightly and early morning offices, nocturns and matins, and of prime is a highly complex and much disputed question; for a general survey of the problem see Robert F. Taft, *The Liturgy of the Hours in East and West: The Origins of the Divine Office and its Meaning for Today* (Collegeville, MN: Liturgical Press, 1986), pp. 191–209. It seems better when discussing the early Anglo-Saxon period to avoid modern terminology as far as possible; but where I have resorted to these terms for brevity, I have used 'nocturns' to describe the night office, and 'matins' in relation to the early morning service. The place of these offices in early Benedictine practice was discussed by J. B. L. Tolhurst, *The Monastic Breviary of Hyde Abbey*, Henry Bradshaw Society, 6 vols. (London: printed for the Society by Harrison and Sons, 1932–42), VI. 7–14; and Bradshaw, *Daily Prayer*, pp. 143–8. See also Thomas Symons, *Regularis concordia* (London: Thomas Nelson and Sons, 1953), pp. xxxi, xlii–xliii.

195

as the monasteries and cells that we have visited.[43] In southern Gaul in the sixth century, Caesarius of Arles described a monastic *cursus* (which he said in his rule for nuns was based on that of the monastery at Lérins) that seems to have been seven-fold, with prayer at midnight, in the early morning, at the third, sixth and ninth hours and with two dusk offices: *lucernarium* and *duodecima*.[44] Caesarius' arrangements were amplified and clarified by his successor Aurelian (bishop of Arles 546–53); in his rule the number of daily offices was increased to nine and the brethren were prevented from returning to sleep after rising for morning prayer, being instructed instead to say prime immediately after the completion of matins and then spend time in reading until the third hour.[45] The sixth-century rule of the Irishman Columbanus, written for his Gallic and Italian monasteries, reflects a relatively simple cycle of daily worship. He explained 'the manner of canonical prayers, in which all gather together at appointed hours in common prayer', allowing in the course of each day for a six-fold office, services being held at midnight, in the early morning, at the third, sixth, and ninth hours, and at nightfall.[46] Columbanus' recommendation that only three psalms be said at each of the day-time offices was made with the potential disruption to work in mind; at nightfall and at midnight, he allowed for twelve psalms and in the early morning, twenty-four.[47] English practice may, as we have already seen, have drawn on each of these traditions, depending on the particular rule or rules with which each minster was familiar as well as the previous experience – in England or elsewhere – of the community's early members.[48] A customary, such as that Benedict Biscop may have written for Wearmouth and Jarrow, would naturally have dealt in some detail with the organisation of the liturgy, but no such texts survive.[49]

---

[43] Cassian, *Institutes*, 2.2 (ed. and Fr. trans. Guy, SC 109. 58–9). Bradshaw, *Daily Prayer*, pp. 124–7.

[44] Caesarius of Arles, *Regula ad uirgines*, ch. 66 (pp. 254–5). Taft, *The Liturgy*, p. 105. On the inclusion of two evening offices see Bradshaw, *Daily Prayer*, pp. 127–8.

[45] Aurelian, *Regula ad monachos*, ch. 28 (PL 68, cols. 385–98); quoted by Bradshaw, *Daily Prayer*, p. 127.

[46] Columbanus, *Regula monachorum*, ch. 10 (ed. Walker, pp. 130–1). This pattern would seem to have been followed by monastic groups in the city of Rome as early as the fourth century; Taft, *The Liturgy*, pp. 131–2. Columbanus recommended that each monk should, at the conclusion of the office, return to his own cell to pray: *Regula monachorum*, ch. 7 (ed. Walker, pp. 130–1).

[47] *Ibid.*, pp. 130–1.

[48] For the diversity of rules known and observed in England see above, ch. 2. Many leading churchmen (and indeed some women) had close contacts with the Frankish church in the seventh century: James Campbell, 'The first century of Christianity in England', in his *Essays in Anglo-Saxon History* (London: Hambledon Press, 1986), pp. 49–67; Ian N. Wood, 'Ripon, Francia and the Franks casket in the early Middle Ages', *Northern History* 26 (1990), 1–19, at pp. 8–17.

[49] Klaus Zelzer, 'Zur Frage der Observanz des Benedict Biscop', in Elizabeth A. Livingstone (ed.), *Studia patristica 20: Papers Presented to the Tenth International Conference on Patristic Studies held in Oxford 1987* (Leuven: Peeters Press, 1989), pp. 323–9; discussed further above, pp. 54–6.

There are two references to a seven-fold recitation of the office in England, both dating from the late 740s. The reforming council of *Clofesho* in 747 stipulated that 'the seven canonical hours of prayer by day and night be diligently observed, by singing proper psalms and canticles; and that the uniformity of the monastic psalmody be everywhere followed, and nothing be read or sung which is not allowed by common use; but only what is derived from the authority of holy Scriptures and what the custom of the Roman Church permits'.[50] Writing to Boniface between 747 and 749, King Ælfwald of East Anglia promised that 'your name will be remembered perpetually in the seven-fold synaxis in our minsters'.[51] The bishop of the East Angles, Heardwulf, was present at *Clofesho*; so Ælfwald's remarks might be linked to that council's recommendations. Bearing in mind the impossibility of reconstructing precisely how the office was celebrated in any one house, it is probably unwise to attempt to read too much into these isolated references. It would obviously be easier to determine the effect of this legislation (should it ever have been enforced) on the liturgical practices of early English minsters, had any monastic prayer-books survived from this period, and were more known about the content of the Roman service-books of which the English appear to have had copies.[52] The same *Clofesho* council stipulated that priests were to celebrate the mass 'in the manner of singing according to the written copy which we have from the Roman Church', and to observe saints' days according to the Roman martyrology.[53] In 801, Archbishop Eanbald II of York wrote to Alcuin asking him about the order and arrangement of the missal, which surprised the latter who replied 'Surely you have plenty of missals following the Roman rite? You also have enough of the larger missals of the old rite. What need is there for new when the old are adequate? I would have you introduce the Roman order among your

---

[50] Council of *Clofesho*, AD 747, ch. 15 (H&S III, 367). The insistence of this canon on uniformity of practice may seem surprising in comparison with the much less specific remarks made (ch. 4, p. 364) on systems of monastic regulation, but all the liturgical provisions of this council lay great stress on consistency. Compare for example ch. 11 (p. 366), which instructed that priests should perform all their priestly ministry, in baptising, teaching and judging, in the same way and fashion. See Cubitt, *Anglo-Saxon Church Councils*, pp. 147–52.

[51] Boniface, *Ep*. 81 (ed. Tangl, p. 181): 'memoria nominis uestri in septenis monasteriorum nostrorum sinaxis perpetua lege censeri debet'.

[52] For one approach to this problem see Christopher Hohler, 'The type of sacramentary used by St Boniface', in Cuno Raabe *et al*. (eds.), *Sankt Bonifatius: Gedenkgabe zum Zwölfhundertsten Todestag* (Fulda: Parzeller, 1954), pp. 89–93.

[53] Council of *Clofesho*, AD 747, ch. 13 (H&S III, 367); compare also the statement in chapter 18 (p. 368) about the celebration of Ember Days according to the exemplar which we have describing the rite of the Roman church (*ibid*., p. 368). These Roman models have been discussed by Cubitt, *Anglo-Saxon Church Councils*, pp. 144–7.

clergy that you might set the precedent and church offices be carried out in a reverent and praiseworthy manner.'[54]

However diverse the modalities of liturgical performance within separate minsters, a degree of consistency linked the religious practices of all those houses to whose activities the narrative sources bear witness. Every minster congregation engaged in some form of corporate devotional activity at more than one point in the day, and these offices were everywhere based on a mixture of psalmody, hymnody, reading from Scripture, and intercession.[55]

On occasions when a service is described in sufficient detail, it may be possible to determine reasonably accurately at what point in the day it took place; whether the event in question was a part of the minster's regular liturgical *cursus*, or rather celebrated to mark a special occasion or set of unusual circumstances, is not always so clear. The vigil kept by the brothers of the church of Hexham every year on the eve of King Oswald's death was patently a special celebration. On that day they went to Heavenfield, where they recited psalms all night before celebrating mass for his soul the following morning.[56] Equally, the imminence of Bishop Wilfrid's death led his followers at Oundle to adopt special measures: in his last days, the whole community sang psalms for him 'day and night without ceasing'; once he had died, his body was transported to Ripon and there prepared for burial with further psalmody.[57] When the deacon from Jarrow, Cuthbert, described the death of his master Bede, he related how those who were sitting with the dying man had to leave him at the third hour on the morning of the day before his death to go in procession with relics 'as was the custom of the day'. This also was not a regular event, but one of the Rogation Day processions specified in the Gallican liturgy for the days before Ascension.[58] On other occasions no obvious inspiration is apparent; some of these episodes may relate to normal offices, even where this is not clarified.

Perhaps, considering the preoccupations of hagiographers, we should not be surprised that saints' lives tend to reveal much more about the

---

[54] Alcuin, *Ep.* 226 (ed. Dümmler, p. 370; trans. Allott, *Alcuin*, pp. 27–8); Donald Bullough, *Alcuin: Achievement and Reputation* (Leiden and Boston: Brill, 2004), p. 204. For discussion of the fragmentary surviving early examples of English mass-books, see also Richard W. Pfaff, 'Massbooks', in Richard W. Pfaff (ed.), *The Liturgical Books of Anglo-Saxon England* (Kalamazoo, MI: The Medieval Institute, Western Michigan University, 1995), pp. 7–34, especially pp. 9–10.

[55] This is to ignore for the time being establishments created under false pretences, where no serious effort was made to pursue a devotional life.

[56] *HE* III. 2 (pp. 216–17).   [57] *VSW* chs. 65–6 (pp. 140–3).

[58] Cuthbert, *Epistola de obitu Bedae* (ed. Colgrave and Mynors, pp. 584–5); for discussion of Rogation Day processions see Colgrave and Mynors, *Bede's Ecclesiastical History*, p. 76, n. 1. Bede died on Wednesday 25 May, which in 735 was Ascension Eve.

night-time offices than about the normal daytime routine of the minsters they describe. Several lives contain lengthy accounts of the extraordinary nocturnal devotions practised by their subjects, which incidentally reveal not only the approximate timing of the ordinary nightly offices, but also the fact that the less ascetic religious were accustomed to return to bed in the intervals between them. Some saints, like Cuthbert, or the smith in Æthelwulf's minster, Cwicwine, seem to have made a habit of staying up all night to pray and sing psalms while the rest of their brethren were asleep.[59] The day-time devotions of such individuals, being much less extraordinary, were less worthy of comment and are accordingly more seldom described.

Most religious began and ended each day with some corporate worship, these two services being considered the most important offices of the day. When plague had killed all who could 'read or preach or say the antiphons and responses' at Jarrow, apart from Ceolfrith and one small boy, it was at the morning and evening offices that psalm-singing with antiphons was retained, the services during the rest of the day being curtailed.[60] The office described as *matutinae*, or *psalmodia matutinalis*, took place at daybreak or soon thereafter. When Cuthbert was staying on one occasion at Coldingham, 'while the others were resting at night', he spent the hours in vigil in the sea, returning in the morning at daybreak 'just at the hour of common worship' to sing the 'canonical hymns with the brothers at the appointed hour'.[61] Aldhelm's *Carmen rhythmicum* relates the poet's experiences one night when staying at a minster in Devon: 'When the fourth cockcrow – as if it were the fourth vigil of the night – had roused the slumbering masses with its clarion calls, then standing in two responding ranks we were celebrating matins and the psalmody of the divine office.'[62] The evening office, *uesperae*,

---

[59] Anon, *VSCuth*. II. 3 (pp. 78–83); Æthelwulf, *De abbatibus*, ch. 10 (ed. Campbell, pp. 24–5). The *Regula magistri* in describing the dual night office (celebrated in winter at midnight and completed before cockcrow, so that the brothers could return to bed before matins if they so wished) recommended that it would be more profitable not to return to bed then (or in the summer between matins and prime), but rather to read or meditate: RM 33, 44 (pp. 184–5). See Bradshaw, *The Daily Office*, p. 140 and for discussion of Benedict's adjustments to the timing of the night hours (probably made to ensure that monks did get enough sleep to be able to function effectively during the day), *ibid.*, pp. 143–4.

[60] *VSCeol.* ch. 14 (p. 393). Éamonn Ó Carragáin, *The City of Rome and the World of Bede*, [Jarrow : St Paul's Church, 1995], pp. 24–5.

[61] Bede, *VSCuth*. ch. 10 (pp. 188–91); anon, *VSCuth*. II. 3 (pp. 78–80). Compare also Æthelwulf, *De abbatibus*, chs. 10 and 18 (ed. Campbell, pp. 24–5 and 44–5), which show clearly that this office was held simultaneously with the coming of the light of day, at cockcrow.

[62] Aldhelm, *Carmen rhythmicum*, lines 123–30 (ed. Ehwald, *Aldhelmi opera*, p. 527; trans. Lapidge and Rosier, *Aldhelm*, p. 178): 'Cum quarta gallicinia/Quasi quarta vigilia/Suscitarent sonantibus/ Somniculosos cantibus/Tum binis stantes classibus/Celebramus concentibus/Matutinam melodiam/ Ac synaxis psalmodiam.'

was at sunset; according to Æthelwulf, 'when dark night comes and the stars are about to replace the daylight, men hasten from outside to the summons of ringing'.[63] Stephen's Life of Wilfrid made one reference to the celebration of a dusk-office (*completorium*) at Ripon; whether this was being sung instead of or in addition to an office corresponding to vespers is unclear.[64] Bearing in mind Stephen's assertion that Wilfrid had instituted the Rule of St Benedict for his minsters at Ripon and Hexham, it may be significant that the only other reference I have found to the celebration of the Benedictine office of compline in an English minster in this period relates to Wimborne and comes from another text which reflects aspects of the Benedictine Rule, Rudolf's Life of Leoba.[65]

Between the evening and early morning offices many houses held a further service during the night, usually described as *nocturna oratio* or *nocturna psalmodia*; its precise timing is hard to determine and may have varied from house to house.[66] All the accounts state quite explicitly that such an office took place in the dark, and that most members of the community had to be woken perhaps by a bell or some other signal, in order to attend.[67] Normally, the community would return to bed after this, rising again for the dawn office, but the particularly devout might remain in the church in prayer between the night-time office and daybreak.[68] Colgrave interpreted an isolated reference in Bede's Life of Cuthbert as relating to the Benedictine office of 'lauds', but it may be unwise to attempt to match any individual offices too closely with the precepts of any one rule, and in fact the phrase in question could be translated in more general terms.[69]

---

[63] Æthelwulf, *De abbatibus*, ch. 20, lines 613–14 (ed. Campbell, pp. 48–9).

[64] *VSW* ch. 68 (pp. 148–9): 'coena finita, in crepusculo vespertino abbates cum omni familia ad completorium orationis exierunt'.

[65] *VSL* ch. 5 (p. 124): 'Alio quoque tempore contigit, ut soror cui oratorii cura commissa erat, cum post completorium cubitum itura fores aecclesiae obseraret, claues uniuersas ipsa nocte nesciens perderet.' Compare *RSB*, ch. 16, 5 (pp. 210–11), quoted above, n. 42.

[66] The community at Coldingham held no such service, for Adomnan was occupied in vigils and singing psalms alone on the night when he received his warning about the fate of the minster: *HE* IV. 25 (pp. 424–5). See pp. 216 and 244 for discussion of the inmates' behaviour during that night.

[67] Bede, *VSCuth.* ch. 45 (pp. 300–1): 'ubi consuetum in monasterio nocturnae orationis signum insonuit . . .'

[68] For example, Bede attributed this habit to a brother who had as a small boy at Æthelhild's minster been cured by a miracle at the tomb of St Oswald, and to the abbess of Ely, Æthelthryth: *HE* III. 12, IV. 19 (pp. 250–1, 392–3).

[69] This passage relates to the moment (on Wednesday 20 March 687) at which Cuthbert died, when by Bede's account the communities on Farne and at Lindisfarne happened to be singing the same psalm. Those at Lindisfarne were said to be gathered in the church 'celebrating the solemnities of nightly psalmody' (Bede, *VSCuth.* ch. 40, pp. 286–7: 'collectus omnis fratrum coetus nocturnae psalmodie solennia celebrabat'). On Farne, the brothers were 'according to the order of night-time praise' singing Psalm 59 (*ibid.*: 'sub ordine nocturnae laudis dicebant psalmum quinquagesimum

Narrative sources have rather less to say about when and how offices were celebrated during daylight hours, although there clearly was a recognised sequence of services, which varied at different times of year and at the particular festivals in the calendar of the liturgical year. Aldhelm referred in his poem for the dedication of Bugga's church to the 'rotation' of the months with successive feast-days, and the passing of years with feasts in fixed order.[70] When Benedict Biscop was dying and too weak to get up to pray or to recite the psalms 'in their appointed order', he had some of the brethren come to him 'at the individual hours for prayer day and night', and chant the accustomed psalms in two choirs.[71] Commenting on the prosperity of his minster, Æthelwulf remarked on the flourishing numbers in the community: 'faith brings many to the stars and causes great troops to gather, and the faithful commend themselves to God at the customary hours'.[72] Alcuin wrote to the brothers at York, asking them to keep him continually in their hearts and on their lips in their 'hours of common prayer' as well as in their private intercessions.[73]

Only for two houses can the time of one daytime office be determined. Both lives of St Cuthbert indicate that the short-lived community at Ripon before the time of Wilfrid was accustomed to hold an office at the third hour. As guest-master, Cuthbert received an angelic visitor, whom he had difficulty persuading to stay and eat at the minster, but at length compelled him and 'as soon as the prayers of the third hour were finished and the time for food had come, placed a table before him and offered him food'.[74]

---

nonum'). Colgrave translated this phrase as 'according to the order of lauds', and pointed out in a note (p. 357) that Psalm 59 'forms part of the office for mattins or lauds on Wednesday in both the Roman and Benedictine breviaries'. But this only confuses the issue, particularly since the place of lauds in the western monastic liturgy is so controversial (Taft, *The Liturgy*, pp. 191–209). Since Bede described the psalmody in each house quite explicitly as nocturnal, and linked its singing to the signalling of Cuthbert's death by torches which were visible to the watchman on the mainland, it is clear that Bede was referring to the celebration by both communities simultaneously of a night-time not a dawn office. Benedicta Ward has discussed Cuthbert's last days and death: 'The spirituality of St Cuthbert', in Gerald Bonner *et al.* (eds.), *St Cuthbert, his Cult and his Community to AD 1200* (Woodbridge: Boydell, 1989), pp. 65–76, at pp. 74–6.

[70] Aldhelm, *Carmen ecclesiasticum*, III, lines 44–5 (ed. Ehwald, p. 16): 'Menstrua uoluuntur alternis tempora festis/Et uicibus certis annorum lustra rotabunt.' Compare Æthelwulf, *De abbatibus*, ch. 15, line 495 (ed. Campbell, pp. 40–1): 'dum ueneranda dei sanctorum festa redirent'.

[71] *HA* ch. 12 (p. 376): 'per singulas diurnae siue nocturnae orationis horas aliquos ad se fratrum uocare, quibus psalmos consuetos duobus in choris resonantibus'. Compare *VSCeol.* ch. 28 (p. 398): 'psalmos non paucos per congruas canonice orationis horas augendos . . .'

[72] Æthelwulf, *De abbatibus*, ch. 20 (ed. Campbell, pp. 48–9).

[73] Alcuin, *Ep.* 42 (pp. 85–6): 'Vos . . . seu in communibus sanctae orationis horis uel in secretis deprecationum uestrarum intercessionibus Alchuinum, filium uestrum, per Dei deprecor caritatem, iugiter in corde habete in ore.'

[74] Bede, *VSCuth.* ch. 7 (pp. 176–7); anon, *VSCuth.* II. 2 (pp. 78–9): 'facto iam signo diei hore tertiae et oratione consummata, mensam statim adposuit praeparato cibo desuper quem habebat'.

An office was also held at the third hour at Wearmouth. In his Lives of the Abbots Bede explained how, after Abbot Ceolfrith had finally departed from them, the sorrowing brothers returned to the church tearfully to commend their anxieties to God; this was not, seemingly a regular office but once, a short time later, the brethren had recited the psalms for the third hour (*completa horae tertiae psalmodia*), they were in a state to start organising their next move.[75]

Defining the content of the monastic office in early Anglo-Saxon England is as difficult as is the task of establishing the number and times of the hours.[76] Bede referred in a homily for Advent to the daily singing of the Magnificat 'with the psalmody of evening praise', in order that devotion for the memory of Christ's incarnation and recognition of the example of his virgin mother might increase and be strengthened.[77] We have already seen that he also referred to the daily recitation of the Lord's Prayer, which St Benedict had recommended should be said at matins and at vespers each day 'in order that the thorns of scandal that are wont to arise' can be cleansed from the community when the brothers petition God to forgive them their trespasses as they forgive those who have trespassed against them.[78] In another echo of Benedict's Rule, Bede emphasised the more frequent singing of the Alleluia in the period between Easter and Pentecost, contrasting this time of joy with the fasting of Lent and the necessity then to pray kneeling.[79] Otherwise, the sources refer more vaguely to prayer, reading, and the singing of hymns and litanies, but above all to psalmody, indicating that the saying or chanting of psalms was as central to the early Anglo-Saxon monastic liturgy as it was to the other medieval systems of monastic organisation for which we have more information.

As the vehicle through which the unlettered learnt to read, the Psalter was the first religious text with which a young postulant would become familiar and its words would structure all of their prayerful life.[80] Recitation of the Psalter, according to Cassian, made the Psalmist's thoughts one's own;[81] even one with poor Latin might devoutly apply the Psalmist's intentions to his

---

[75] *HA* ch. 18 (p. 382).

[76] Alicia Corrêa discussed the manuscript evidence for the content of the office before the Benedictine revolution in 'Daily office books', pp. 46–7 and 52.

[77] Bede, *Homelia*, I. 4 (ed. Hurst, p. 30).   [78] *RSB*, ch. 13, 12–13 (pp. 208–9).

[79] Bede, *Homelia*, II. 16, lines 159–61 and 293–5 (ed. Hurst, pp. 294 and 298); van der Walt, 'Reflections of the Benedictine Rule', p. 375; Bradshaw, *Daily Prayer*, p. 136.

[80] *VSG* ch. 22 (pp. 84–5). *Hodoeporicon of Willibald*, ch. 2 (ed. Holder-Egger, p. 89).

[81] Cassian, *Conlationes*, X. 11, ed. and trans. E. Pichery, *Conférences*, 3 vols, SC 42, 54, 64 (Paris: du Cerf, 1955–9), II, 92–3; quoted by Sims-Williams, *Religion*, p. 119.

own heart and thus make his own petitions to God.[82] Considerable care was devoted in some English institutions to the proper chanting of psalms. Benedict Biscop invited the Roman *archicantator*, John, to Wearmouth to teach the method of chanting to the brothers,[83] and Bishop Acca brought to Hexham a famous singer called Maban (who had been taught how to chant in Kent) to teach the skill to Acca and his people.[84] James the Deacon, who assisted Paulinus in his mission to Northumbria, and Putta, one-time bishop of Rochester, were both renowned for their musical abilities and spent their latter years travelling round teaching church music to others.[85] Wilfrid counted among his own achievements that he had instructed the Northumbrian people 'in accordance with the rite of the primitive church to make use of a double choir singing in harmony with reciprocal responsions and antiphons', for he had taken from Kent two notable singers, Ædde and Æona.[86] Other texts also refer to the singing of psalms in double choir: this was practised as we have seen at Bugga's church, in the minster visited by Aldhelm in Devon, and at Æthelwulf's house.[87] The latter community had at least one member described as a *lector*, who was very learned in books, and had presumably been specially trained to 'pour forth song'.[88] Bede referred to singers and readers belonging to Bishop Eata's community at Lindisfarne, but these may have been men in minor orders, since he mentioned them in conjunction with the priests, deacons and other ecclesiastical grades that constituted the episcopal congregation there.[89]

---

[82] Council of *Clofesho*, AD 747, ch. 20 (H&S III, 372); quoted by Bullough, *Alcuin*, p. 181.

[83] *VSCeol.* ch. 10 (p. 391), *HA* ch. 6 (p. 369); compare *HE* IV. 18 (pp. 388–9); discussed by Ó Carragáin, *The City of Rome*, pp. 18–9. When he went to Jarrow, Ceolfrith instituted the same canonical method of chanting and reading which was observed at Wearmouth: *VSCeol.* ch. 11 (p. 392). Ian Wood has discussed Ceolfrith's devotion to correct liturgical performance and the innovations he made, particularly in commemorative observance: *The Most Holy Abbot Ceolfrid*, Jarrow Lecture 1995 [Jarrow: St Paul's Church, 1996], pp. 16–18. See also Simon Coates, 'Ceolfrid: history, hagiography and memory in seventh- and eighth-century Wearmouth-Jarrow', *Journal of Medieval History* 25 (1999), 69–86, at pp. 74–6.

[84] *HE* V. 20 (pp. 530).

[85] *HE* II. 20 and IV. 12 (pp. 306–7, 368–9). Wallace-Hadrill, *Commentary*, p. 86; Peter Hunter Blair, *The World of Bede* (London: Secker and Warburg, 1970), pp. 96–8.

[86] *VSW* chs. 47, 14 (pp. 98–9, 30–1). It is no longer thought that Ædde should be identified with the author of Wilfrid's Life; see D. P. Kirby, 'Bede, Eddius Stephanus and the "Life of Wilfrid"', *English Historical Review* 98 (1983), 101–14, at pp. 102–4.

[87] Bugga's church: Aldhelm, *Carmen ecclesiasticum*, III, lines 42–53 (ed. Ehwald, pp. 16–17); the Devon minster: Aldhelm, *Carmen rhythmicum*, lines 127–30 (*ibid.*, p. 527); Æthelwulf, *De abbatibus*, ch. 15, lines 496–8, and ch. 20, lines 615–17 (ed. Campbell, pp. 40–1 and 48–9).

[88] *De abbatibus*, ch. 15, lines 499–500 (pp. 40–1). The office of *lector* might be given both to a teacher in a church and to a member of one of the minor orders. Aldhelm also appeared to suggest that there was a trained hymn-singer (*ymnista*) at Bugga's church: *Carmen ecclesiasticum*, III, line 48 (ed. Ehwald, p. 16).

[89] Bede, *VSCuth.* ch. 16 (pp. 208–9).

In some double houses, men and women worshipped separately; according to Rudolf of Fulda, the women at Wimborne had their own church, which no men were allowed to enter apart from priests invited to celebrate mass,[90] and the men at Barking also had a separate oratory.[91] When Cuthbert stayed at Coldingham, the brothers celebrated the canonical hours on their own, but it is not known whether they had a church or oratory separate from that used by the women.[92] It is possible that in other houses both sexes worshipped together regularly, but the only references to this relate to special occasions.[93] In his poem on the dedication of Bugga's church, Aldhelm mentioned male and female *lectors* reading from Holy Scripture on feast days;[94] Bede reported that at the translation of Æthelthryth's body at Ely the whole congregation stood around the sepulchre singing, the brothers on one side and the women on the other.[95]

Attendance at the office was generally expected of all members of a congregation other than the seriously ill. Bede told of a recalcitrant brother who refused to 'go to the church with the brothers to sing psalms and pray and listen to the word of life', and implied that he encountered his unpleasant end as a direct consequence of this: 'He who is not willing to enter the church gate humbly of his own accord, is bound to be carried against his will to the gates of hell, a damned soul.'[96] However, there were circumstances in which certain individuals might be excused from this obligation. In his Life of Cuthbert, Bede mentioned a member of the Lindisfarne community who was charged with looking out from a watch-tower for the signal to say that Cuthbert had died, which sign eventually came while the rest of the

---

[90] *VSL* chs. 2, 5 (pp. 123–4). Stephanie Hollis has argued that Rudolf's didactic intent makes his account of the strict segregation of the women from the men at Wimborne representative only of ninth-century Carolingian views about claustration: *Anglo-Saxon Women and the Church: Sharing a Common Fate* (Woodbridge: Boydell Press, 1992), p. 272; see also Yitzhak Hen, 'Milites Christi utriusque sexus: gender and politics of conversion in the circle of Boniface', *Revue bénédictine* 109 (1999), 17–31, at pp. 23–5; Barbara Yorke, *Nunneries and the Anglo-Saxon Royal Houses* (London and New York: Continuum, 2003), pp. 19–20.

[91] *HE* IV. 7 (pp. 356–7); Hollis, *Anglo-Saxon Women*, pp. 245–6.

[92] Anon., *VSCuth.* II. 3 (pp. 80–1); Bede, *VSCuth.* ch. 10 (pp. 190–1). Hollis, *Anglo-Saxon Women*, pp. 101–2.

[93] Dagmar Schneider has argued that the sexes would have been segregated in these churches on ordinary days, but this cannot be presumed on the basis of the scant evidence: 'Anglo-Saxon women in the religious life: a study of the status and position of women in an early mediaeval society' (unpublished PhD thesis, University of Cambridge, 1985), pp. 30–1.

[94] Aldhelm, *Carmen ecclesiasticum*, III, line 58 (ed. Ehwald, p. 17): 'Et lector lectrixue uolumina sacra reuoluant.' Theodore's Penitential stated that women – that is the female servants of God – were permitted to read lections and perform the ministries relating to the confession of the holy altar other than those which were the special function of priests and deacons: II. vii. 1–2 (ed. Finsterwalder, *Die Canones*, p. 322).

[95] *HE* IV. 19 (pp. 394–5).   [96] *HE* V. 14 (pp. 502–3).

brothers were singing the night-time office.[97] The liturgical obligations of those who were engaged in activities outside the confines of their parent house, whether in ministering to their lay neighbours or attending to estate-business, are unclear. Cuthbert certainly tried to say the offices wherever he was, but he may well be a far from representative example.[98] Perhaps those working in distant parts of the estate stopped whatever they were doing to say the office in the fields; they may even have continued to work while singing psalms and praying.[99]

The mass

Minster communities approached the question of the celebration of the mass and reception of communion in different ways. Although the earliest Egyptian monks did not celebrate the Eucharist every day, the Rule of the Master recommended that the whole community for which he legislated should receive communion (from the reserved sacrament) in both kinds every day at a service held between part of the office and the daily meal. Mass itself was probably said rarely in the oratory of the Master's monastery.[100] St Benedict's intentions are less clear; he may, like the Master, have envisaged that the monks would receive communion daily but it is far from apparent that a conventual mass was celebrated in his monastery on Sundays and major feasts.[101] In England, Bede was keen to encourage the more frequent participation in the Eucharist of both professed religious and lay people, reminding Bishop Ecgberht of York, 'how salutary for every Christian is the daily partaking of the body and blood of our Lord'.[102] That there are several references to the celebration of mass daily and on special occasions and feasts in the *Historia ecclesiastica, Historia abbatum* and in Bede's Life of Cuthbert is thus not surprising. How many of Bede's contemporaries heeded his advice

---

[97] Bede, *VSCuth*. ch. 40 (pp. 286–7); see above, n. 68.   [98] Ward, 'The spirituality'.

[99] George Ovitt, 'Manual labour and early medieval monasticism', *Viator*, 17 (1986), 1–18. That monks should pray wherever they happened to find themselves was recommended by St Augustine, *De opere monachorum*, ch. 17 (ed. Migne, *PL*, 40, col. 565). Benedict and the Master both legislated for the circumstances in which monks found themselves working too far away from their monastery to be able to return to the choir in time for the office: *RM*, ch. 55, 9–14 (pp. 260–3); *RSB*, ch. 50 (pp. 252–5). See A. de Vogüé, 'Travail et alimentation dans les règles de saint Benoît et du Maître', *Revue bénédictine* 74 (1964), 242–51. The *Regularis concordia* directed that when monks were travelling they should always busy themselves with psalms and not with idle talk: proem 11 (ed. Hallinger, p. 76).

[100] *RM* chs. 21, 1–3 and 22, 1–6 (pp. 102–3; 106–7); de Vogüé, 'Problems', pp. 327–8.

[101] *RSB* chs. 38, 2; 38, 10; 63, 4 (pp. 236–7 and 278–9); de Vogüé, 'Problems', pp. 327–30; Fry, *The Rule*, pp. 410–12.

[102] Bede, *EpEcg*, § 15 (p. 419).

is hard to tell. Boniface would seem to have been unusual in electing to celebrate the holy sacrifice daily (at least his so-doing occasioned comment), but Alcuin also recommended the daily celebration of mass to Æthelburh, abbess of Fladbury.[103] The council held at *Clofesho* in 747 directed that monastics and ecclesiastics should keep themselves always ready to receive the sacrament but made no clear statement about daily celebration.[104] It seems unlikely that most religious took communion every day; Theodore's Penitential listed the frequency with which the Greeks and Romans, laymen as well as clerics, were accustomed to communicate, implying that the English generally received the Eucharist less frequently.[105] Priests were instructed at the same *Clofesho* council to spend their time in reading, celebrating masses and psalmody, and directed to discharge their duties at the altar and in divine service with care, but the canons failed to indicate how often such duties would be expected of them.[106] Clearly, masses were to be said on Sundays, for then abbots and priests were supposed to remain in their minsters and say mass, laying aside all travelling and secular business.[107] If ordained members of many minster congregations spent a good deal of time away from their parent house, ministering to the surrounding population, they may sometimes have celebrated mass on their behalf, perhaps in the open air where the largest possible number of people could be gathered together.[108]

One of the abbots of Æthelwulf's cell, Wulfsig, said a private mass every day: 'When in the middle of the day the brothers began already to seek food, he withdrew sparingly from every meal, and pressed the floor of the chapel with bended knees, and in very suitable attire offered on the altar with sacred songs that which releases the world from malignant death.'[109] That this is described in such detail and Wulfsig's motive explained – he did not wish any day to pass without a fine offering with which to adorn it – implies that Æthelwulf considered this to be a sufficiently unusual practice to be worthy of remark. Stephen referred to a priest, appointed abbot of Oundle by Wilfrid, who elected to say a private mass for the bishop every day;[110] according to Bede, a priest said a mass every Saturday at the altar of Pope Gregory at St Augustine's, Canterbury, for the souls of all the archbishops

---

[103] Liudger, *Vita S. Gregorii*, ch. 3 (ed. Holder-Egger, *MGH, SS*, XV, 70); Alcuin, *Ep.* 102 (p. 149): 'Et uelim te cotidiana consuetudine usum habere offerendi Deo munus ad altare.'
[104] Council of *Clofesho*, AD 747, ch. 22 (H&S III, 370).
[105] Penitential of Theodore, I. xii. 1–2 (ed. Finsterwalder, p. 305).
[106] *Ibid.*, ch. 8 (p. 365).   [107] Council of *Clofesho*, AD 747, ch. 14 (H&S III, 367).
[108] The role of minster communities in pastoral ministry is discussed further below, ch. 7.
[109] Æthelwulf, *De abbatibus*, ch. 18, lines 562–6 (ed. Campbell, pp. 44–5).
[110] *VSW* ch. 65 (pp. 410–11): 'omni die pro eo missam singularem celebrare'.

buried there.[111] Otherwise the mass would appear to have been a corporate spiritual activity, even where it was celebrated only to mark particular events, on feast-days, or on Sundays. For example, Bede accounted for a reference to the celebration of the mass at Lindisfarne by explaining that the day in question was a Sunday, which suggests that a daily conventual mass was not held there.[112] However, a sick boy at Selsey was visited by Sts Peter and Paul at the second hour of the day, just before mass was to be celebrated in the minster, implying that in this minster communion was celebrated every day. Since the day in question was the second of three appointed as fast-days by the Selsey brothers (who hoped that their abstinence would lead God to deliver them from the plague) it is most unlikely to have been a Sunday.[113] On his journey to Rome, Ceolfrith celebrated mass every day for himself and his companions, even when he was so ill he could no longer stand, but whether a daily conventual mass was also the norm within the Jarrow community is unclear.[114] Masses were also said for the souls of the dead; the priest Tunna, abbot of the minster in a town called *Tunnacaestir*, celebrated mass daily at the third hour for the soul of his brother whom he wrongly believed to have died.[115] Obviously houses which were founded to maintain the cult of an individual or family,[116] or which received endowments making specific liturgical provisions (such as the saying of psalms and masses on behalf of the benefactor on certain days)[117] may have perforce celebrated masses more often than others, and may also have therefore contained a higher proportion of priests in order to fulfil such obligations. Whether such masses were attended by members of the community other than the presiding clergy is not always clarified in the sources, but, when one considers the role of liturgical commemoration in reinforcing a community's sense of common identity, it seems likely that these were not often said as private masses.[118]

[111] *HE* II. 3 (pp. 144–5).   [112] Bede, *VSCuth.* ch. 44 (pp. 296–7).   [113] *HE* IV. 14 (pp. 376–9).

[114] *VSCeol.* ch. 33 (p. 401). The Life of Ceolfrith and Bede's *Historia abbatum* both describe the singing of masses in the two Wearmouth churches early on the morning of the day when Abbot Ceolfrith was to leave the minster, but this might have been a special celebration to mark Ceolfrith's departure; *ibid.*, ch. 25 (p. 396); *HA* ch. 17 (pp. 381–2). There can certainly be no doubt as to the extraordinary nature of the community's subsequent actions: Ceolfrith's procession to the oratory of St Lawrence, his use of incense, and kissing of all the brothers, all of which were accompanied by the singing of antiphons, psalms and litanies; Ó Carragáin, *The City of Rome*, pp. 12–14.

[115] *HE* IV. 22 (pp. 402–5).

[116] Such as Gilling (*HE* III. 14 and 24, pp. 256–7 and 292–3) or Minster in Thanet: David Rollason, *The Mildrith Legend: A Study in Early Medieval Hagiography in England* (Leicester: Leicester University Press, 1982), pp. 49–51, 56; see above, p. 84.

[117] For example, S 1188 (AD 805 × 810).

[118] Cubitt, 'Unity and diversity', p. 46; *eadem*, 'Monastic memory and identity in early Anglo-Saxon England', in William O. Frazer and Andrew Tyrell (eds.), *Social Identity in Early Medieval Britain*   207

Contemplation

Many religious whose deeds were recorded in saints' lives consigned a part of each day to private devotional exercises often far exceeding whatever portion of the daily routine was normally assigned to individual contemplation. Since exceptional piety was one of the recognised marks of sanctity, we might treat the devotional excesses of these saints with some caution, but there seems no reason to doubt that certain individuals did spend more time in private prayer and contemplation than did many of their companions in the cloister. Wilfrid was said to have occupied his time continually in prayers, fastings, reading and vigils;[119] Cuthbert was supposedly able to endure 'such fastings and watchings that his strength silenced unbelief. He very often spent the whole night in prayer, sometimes even enduring a second and a third night, and refreshed himself only on the fourth day.'[120] While the band of brothers was at rest, one of the abbots of Æthelwulf's minster, Wulfsig, also kept vigil at night singing hymns and psalms. He was said to sing the entire psalter through each night and again every day, a practice also attributed to Abbot Ceolfrith of Wearmouth and Jarrow.[121]

Those whose position within the church required them to spend a lot of time ministering to the laity or engaged in other ecclesiastical business had more difficulty finding time for their own devotions. Both Chad, bishop of Lichfield, and John of Beverley, bishop of Hexham, built themselves oratories a little distance from their cathedrals, to which they retired whenever they were able with a few companions in order to read and pray.[122] Eadberht, bishop of Lindisfarne, had a similar retreat, a place remote from the minster and surrounded by the sea on all sides at flood-tide, where he would retire alone especially during Lent and Advent.[123] Cuthbert's career above all others epitomises the struggle between the irreconcilable demands of a cleric's ecclesiastical obligations and his anchoritic ambitions. In his retreat

---

(London and New York: Leicester University Press, 2000), pp. 252–76, at pp. 270–1. Prayer for the dead is considered also in chapter 7 below.

[119] *VSW* ch. 3 (pp. 8–9).

[120] Anon., *VSCuth.* II. 1 (pp. 74–5); the anonymous was here quoting verbatim from Athanasius' Life of St Anthony.

[121] Æthelwulf, *De abbatibus*, ch. 18 (ed. Campbell, p. 45); *VSCeol.* ch. 33 (p. 401). On his journey to Rome, the anonymous asserted that Ceolfrith had chanted the psalter right through three times every day until four days before his death (*ibid.*), although Bede said he did so only twice daily: *HA* ch. 22 (p. 386). Wood, *The Most Holy Abbot*, p. 16; Coates, 'Ceolfrid', p. 75.

[122] *HE* IV. 3 and V. 2 (pp. 336–9; 456–7).   [123] Bede, *VSCuth.* ch. 42 (pp. 292–3).

on Farne Cuthbert could achieve his contemplative desire 'to be silent and hear no human speech', but even there he could not remain wholly cut off from the world.[124] It may not be fanciful to seek to associate some of the known pocket Gospel books and personal prayer-books that have survived from the Anglo-Saxon period with monastics whose work took them outside the cloister.

Although somewhat beyond our period, the prayer-book of Ælfwine would be a particularly good example of a volume compiled for just such an over-burdened monk; Ælfwine was dean of the New Minster at Winchester in the early eleventh century. His prayer-book contained a calendar and computus with an Easter Table, two texts of St John's Gospel and three offices (for the Trinity, Holy Cross and the Virgin) as well as a litany, a number of private prayers and various sets of prognostications showing its owner's particular preoccupation with the days most appropriate for blood-letting.[125] The group of late eighth- and early ninth-century Southumbrian prayer-books (British Library MSS Harley 7653, Harley 2965 and Royal 2 A. xx, and Cambridge University Library, MS Ll. 1. 10, the Book of Cerne) contain both private devotional material and also some liturgical texts that may have had a more public use. One of these, the Book of Cerne, may have been associated with Aedeluald, bishop of Lichfield 818–30,[126] but the others cannot be linked with any individual men (or women) even though they contain prayers associated with particular men.[127] The Royal prayer-book gives prominent place to a prayer of confession of an Abbot Hygbald (included also in the Book of Cerne); Kathleen Hughes identified him with the seventh-century 'abbot of the province of Lindsey', who visited Ireland, according to Bede, and was buried at *Cecesigi* (later Hibaldstowe) near the river Ancholme.[128] Prayers of an anchorite Alchfrith are copied into the Book of Cerne; he is known also from a letter written to Hygelac, *lector* and *presbyter* described in Æthelwulf's

---

[124] Bede, *VSCuth*. ch. 1 (pp. 154–5); see Clare Stancliffe, 'Cuthbert and the polarity between pastor and solitary', in Gerald Bonner *et al.* (eds.), *St Cuthbert, his Cult and his Community to AD 1200* (Woodbridge: Boydell, 1989), pp. 21–44.

[125] Beate Günzel (ed.), *Ælfwine's Prayerbook (London, British Library, Cotton Titus D. xxvi + xxvii)*, Henry Bradshaw Society 108 (London: Boydell Press for the Henry Bradshaw Society, 1993). I am grateful to Simon Keynes for drawing this edition to my attention.

[126] Michelle Brown, *The Book of Cerne: Prayers, Patronage and Power in Ninth-Century England* (London: British Library, 1996), pp. 151–60 and 181–4.

[127] *Ibid.*, p. 181.

[128] Bede, *HE* IV. 3 (pp. 344–5); *Die Heiligen Englands*, II. 7 (ed. Liebermann, pp. 11–12). Kathleen Hughes, 'Some aspects of Irish influence on early English private prayer', *Studia Celtica* 5 (1970), 48–61, at pp. 56–7.

De abbatibus and probably resident there *c.* 780.[129] The attractions of this sort of devotional material to monastics whose pastoral or administrative tasks regularly required them to be away from the minster (and hence from the choir office) are obvious, but (despite the rules' proscriptions against personal possessions) aristocratic religious of both sexes may have commissioned personal prayer-books for use inside the cloister, and perhaps sought to have had them lavishly decorated.[130]

The popularity of the solitary life among early Anglo-Saxon religious may in part reflect the external pressures on the lives of those within minsters, which prevented the pious from devoting as much time as they would have liked to uninterrupted contemplation. A period of training within the cloister was, however, deemed a necessary preparation for the eremitic life. Ultán, the brother of Fursa, passed on to the life of a hermit 'after a long time of probation in the minster',[131] while Guthlac spent two years at Repton before he requested permission to adopt the life of the desert.[132] Cuthbert had been many years at Lindisfarne before 'he entered into the remote solitudes which he had long desired, sought and prayed for . . . he rejoiced because, after a long and blameless active life, he was now held worthy to rise to the repose of divine contemplation'.[133] Withdrawal from the world did not however guarantee permanent solitude; Guthlac was continually visited at Crowland by other ecclesiastics and laymen,[134] and Wilgils, having entered his cell on the Humber estuary in order to lead the austere life of a solitary, became so celebrated that people flocked to him in large numbers.[135] Others, as well as Cuthbert, were brought back from the hermitage into the world to assume positions of ecclesiastical responsibility. Caelin, *praepositus* at Ripon, had previously been a solitary, and held office in Wilfrid's minster for a long time before the bishop gave him permission to return to his former way of life.[136] While these examples all refer to the contemplative aspirations of notably devout and holy men whose spiritual attainments attracted hagiographical interest, a general picture does emerge of the minster as a frequently unquiet place within which the more modestly devout may similarly have struggled to find peace for private contemplation.

---

[129] Wilhelm Levison, *England and the Continent in the Eighth Century* (Oxford: Clarendon Press, 1946), pp. 295–302 (appendix ix); Hughes, 'Early English private prayer', p. 59.

[130] Michael Lapidge, 'Latin learning in ninth-century England', in his *Anglo-Latin Literature, 600–899* (London: Hambledon, 1996), pp. 409–39, at p. 413.

[131] *HE* III. 19 (pp. 276–7).   [132] *VSG* ch. 24 (pp. 86–7).   [133] Bede, *VSCuth.* ch. 17 (pp. 214–15).

[134] *VSG* chs. 35–49 *passim*.   [135] *Vita S. Willibrordi*, ch. 1 (ed. Levison, p. 116).

[136] Anon., *VSCuth.* IV. 1 (pp. 110–13); Stancliffe, 'Cuthbert', pp. 34–6. *VSW* ch. 64 (pp. 138–9).

Manual labour

Prayer and work were intimately connected in early monasticism; indeed to many commentators work was itself a form of prayer, an ascetic task undertaken (like fasting or keeping vigil) to subdue the flesh, as well as a valuable defence against idleness.[137] 'Monks supplement their prayer with labour so that sleep does not creep upon them,' wrote Cassian in his monastic *Institutes*.[138] To Cassian, the ideal spiritual life offered so delicate a balance of the virtues of body and soul that one might struggle to be certain whether it were in order to perfect spiritual meditation that monks practised incessant manual labour, or if it were as a result of the assiduousness of their labour that monks advanced so in the spirit and acquired such a light of knowledge.[139] In his *De opere monachorum*, written in *c*. 400, St Augustine sought to mediate between two groups of monks following different biblical injunctions as to the value of work. While one group followed St Paul's instruction ('if any man will not work, neither let him eat') the other group were guided by Matthew: 'Behold the birds of the air, for they neither sow, nor do they reap nor gather into barns: and your heavenly Father feedeth them. Are you not of much more value than they?'[140] Augustine's view was that only those who laboured and produced a surplus would be able to practise charity,[141] and that idle monks would be better to fill their time by praying while working: 'Those working with their hands can easily sing the psalms and thereby ease their labour at the divine call.'[142] In the sixth-century Italian *Regula magistri*, physical labour was commended to all monks, both in order to provide them with occupation to prevent absent-mindedness and to add virtue to the making of goods to give to the poor; but physical labour was broadly defined to include reading (or the study of Latin for those who could not yet read)[143] and each brother was urged to work at whatever he was most skilled. 'Field-work . . . should be considered the province of those brothers who are not skilled in the arts and have neither the ability nor the desire to learn them. The skilled craftsmen, on

[137] Claude J. Peifer, 'The relevance of the monastic tradition to the problem of work and leisure', *American Benedictine Review* 28 (1977), 373–96, at p. 379.

[138] Cassian, *Institutes* II. 14 (ed. Guy, *SC* 109, pp. 82–3).

[139] *Ibid.*, pp. 84–5, and compare X. 21, pp. 418–19; Ovitt, 'Manual labour', p. 12.

[140] *2 Thessalonians* 3:10; *Matthew* 6:26.

[141] George Ovitt, Jr., 'The cultural context of western technology: early Christian attitudes towards manual labour', in Allen J. Frantzen and Douglas Moffat, *The Work of Work: Servitude, Slavery, and Labor in Medieval England* (Glasgow: Cruithne Press, 1994), pp. 71–94, at p. 82, n. 54.

[142] Augustine, *De opere monachorum*, ed. Migne, *PL* 40, col. 565; Ovitt, 'Manual labour', pp. 10–11; Peifer, 'The relevance of the monastic tradition', p. 383.

[143] RM ch. 50, 5–7, 9–13 (pp. 222–5).

the other hand, are to stay in their respective crafts every day, having their daily quota of work assigned and checked.' Only if there were urgent need for fieldwork, should craftsmen leave their tools behind and help the other brothers.[144]

It was Benedict of Nursia who most successfully reconciled the monks' personal spiritual needs and the economic demands of a collective community. In a chapter 'de opera manuum cotidiana', Benedict argued that 'idleness is the enemy of the soul. Therefore the brothers should have specified periods for manual labour as well as for prayerful reading.'[145] Such work might well include agricultural labour: 'they must not become distressed if local conditions or their poverty should force them to do the harvesting themselves. When they live by the labour of their hands, as our fathers and the apostles did, then they are really monks.'[146] Labour involved a degree of bodily humiliation but was not intended to be punitively demanding: 'All things are to be done with moderation on account of the fainthearted.'[147] Columbanus took a rather different line here, seeing work primarily as a means of chastening the flesh.[148] In Benedict's vision, prayer and labour were inextricably bound: he placed his chapter on work in the part of the Rule where he explained the shape and timing of the monastic day. Even the amount of food and drink assigned to each monk was dependent on the work he had performed.[149] Thus, as Ovitt has shown, Benedict's monastery became 'a workshop of the soul' designed to be self-sufficient and independent of

---

[144] RM ch. 50, 72–4 (pp. 236–9). Ovitt, 'Manual labour', p. 14; idem, 'The cultural context', pp. 85–6.

[145] RSB ch. 48, 1 (pp. 248–9); Ovitt, 'Manual labour', p. 15.

[146] RSB ch. 48, 7–8 (pp. 248–51); contrast RM 86, 1–3 (pp. 350–1), which directed that all the lands of the monastery should be rented out so that the tenant had the burden of the fieldwork and the monks did not become preoccupied with worldly affairs.

[147] RSB ch. 48, 9 (pp. 250–1). Janet Nelson, 'The church and a revaluation of work in the ninth century?' in R. N. Swanson (ed.), The Use and Abuse of Time in Christian History, Studies in Church History 37 (Woodbridge: Boydell Press for the Ecclesiastical History Society, 2002), 35–43, at p. 36.

[148] Columbanus, Regula monachorum, ch. 9 (ed. Walker, p. 138; cf. Columbanus' Instructio IV, 1, ed. Walker, pp. 78–81).

[149] RSB chs. 39, 6 and 40, 5 (pp. 238–9, 240–1); compare also ch. 41, 2–4 (pp. 240–1), which adjusts the timing of the main meal of the day if the monks have work to perform in the fields. By contrast, the Master increased the provision of food only on special occasions or when guests were present (ch. 26, 11–13, pp. 138–9) and was particularly uncompromising about limiting the quantity of water available even to the thirsty (ch. 27, 23–6, pp. 144–5). Adalbert de Vogüé has drawn attention to the extent to which Benedict, in concentrating on the physical well-being of his monks, here diverged from the Master, who was more preoccupied by the need to sustain a principle of monastic deprivation, even to the extent of getting others to cultivate the fields on the monks' behalf so that they might concentrate exclusively on things spiritual and eternal: 'Travail et alimentation', pp. 242–5.

its neighbours while integrating the spiritual impulses of eremiticism and the economic requirements of coenobitism.[150]

Bede's account of the passion of his abbot Eosterwine for physical tasks quoted at the head of this chapter fits well within a Benedictine conception of the spiritual value of manual labour. As Ian Wood has argued, Bede may here have been trying to depict Eosterwine as an ideal brother, reflecting his wider concern to make Wearmouth and Jarrow appear as 'regular' in their monastic observance as possible.[151] Cuthbert also considered manual labour to be an important element of the spiritual life, singling it out as an admirable activity in which brothers were subject to the commands of their abbot.[152] When Oswine, who had been head of the household of Æthelthryth, wife of Ecgfrith of Northumbria, decided to leave the world and join a monastery, he arrived at Lastingham dressed in plain garments and carrying an axe and an adze in his hands. According to Bede, this demonstrated that Owine had not chosen the minster in search of a life of ease (like some people) but in order to work hard: *non enim ad otium, ut quidam, sed ad laborem*.[153] Such sentiments were not necessarily shared by all those who came to the cloister from noble backgrounds. Not always the best of witnesses to early English monastic life, Rudolf of Fulda may for once have reflected the state of affairs in many minsters fairly accurately when he described the activities of Leoba at Wimborne:

When she was not praying, she worked with her hands at whatever was commanded her, for she had learned that he who will not work should not eat. However, she spent more time in reading and listening to Sacred Scripture than she gave to manual labour.[154]

Leoba's own correspondence bears witness to her interest in scholarly pursuits: in a letter to Boniface she reported that an Abbess Eadburga had taught her to write Latin verse.[155] Equally, there are references to the

---

[150] Ovitt, 'Manual labour', pp. 16–17. For Benedict's views on self-sufficiency see his statement in *RSB*, ch. 66, 6 (pp. 288–9), quoted above in chapter 2, that a monastery should be so constructed that all necessities were contained within it.

[151] *HA* ch. 8 (pp. 371–2), quoted above, p. 186. Wood, *The Most Holy Abbot Ceolfrid*, p. 10.

[152] Bede, *VSCuth.*, ch. 22 (pp. 228–31): 'est coenobitarum uita miranda, qui abbatis per omnia subiciuntur imperiis. Ad eius arbitrium cuncta uigilandi, orandi, ieiunandi, atque operandi tempora moderantur.'

[153] *HE* IV. 3 (pp. 338–9).   [154] *VSL* ch. 7 (p. 125).

[155] Boniface, *Ep.* 29 (pp. 52–3). Eadburga has conventionally been identified with the abbess of Thanet who died *c.* 751, but she may in fact have been at Wimborne, which would explain her correspondence with Boniface more readily: Barbara Yorke, 'The Bonifacian mission and female religious in Wessex', *Early Medieval Europe* 7 (1998), 145–72, at pp. 170–2.

production of manuscripts at Eadburga's minster in the letters the abbess exchanged with the missionary bishop.[156] This potential conflict between the life of the mind and the drudgery of physical labour brings us once more to the tension between the monastic desire for separation from the world and the need to support a community in essentials. As was discussed in chapter 3, the size of a minster's endowment (and the nature and agricultural quality of that land) directly affected the size of community that could sustain itself independently; yet the larger a minster's estates, the less likely it was that the brothers themselves could farm them with their own hands. Much of the agricultural labour on an abbey's wider landed holdings must have been performed by those who had lived on the land before it came into the church's hands, tenants who merely exchanged a secular landlord for an ecclesiastical one.[157]

Hagiographical narratives about religious who laboured with their own hands may perhaps better be imagined as allusions to the performance of lighter tasks such as weeding or fruit-picking, than references to the physically demanding agricultural labour like ploughing which fell to their slaves and servants. Cuthbert was said to have ensured that he was not so abstinent in food that 'he should become unfitted for necessary labour', and to have worked with his hands even while watching at night, but the nature of the labours in which he engaged is unclear until the time he went to live on Farne.[158] At Gilling, Ceolfrith was diligent in every way in reading, labouring and in the discipline of the rule, and at Nursling Boniface 'applied himself assiduously, as the Rule of St Benedict prescribes, to the daily manual labour and the regular performance of his duties', but neither man's hagiographer tried to define the sorts of work in which he engaged.[159]

Solitaries may genuinely have laboured arduously with their hands at more specifically described tasks; they were dependent on their own endeavours to maintain their separate existence, erecting their own shelters, finding water or growing food. Yet none of the solitary religious whom the early Anglo-Saxon sources describe lived in total isolation: each was assisted and brought gifts of food by visitors and some had more regular help from a companion of some kind. When Cuthbert first lived on Farne the brethren

---

[156] Boniface, *Epp.* 30 and 35 (pp. 54 and 60); see further below.

[157] As, for example, was seemingly the shepherd from Whitby called Hadwald: Anon., *VSCuth.* IV, 10 (pp. 126–7); above, p. 180.

[158] Bede, *VSCuth.* chs. 6 and 16 (pp. 174–5 and 210–11).

[159] *VSCeol.* ch. 3 (pp. 388–9). *VSB* ch. 2 (ed. Rau, p. 468): 'ut labore manuum cottidiano et disciplinali officiorum administratione incessanter secundum praefinitam beati patris Benedicti rectae constitutionis formam insisteret'.

at Lindisfarne gave him bread, 'but afterwards in accordance with the example of the fathers, he considered it more fitting to live by the labour of his own hands'.[160] The anonymous Lindisfarne author described how Cuthbert made a space to dwell in from the rock of the island, excavated a well, and dug and ploughed the land so that he might gain food by the work of his hands.[161] Ultán was joined in his solitude by his brother Fursa, who 'for a whole year lived with him in austerity and prayer labouring daily with his hands'.[162] Surprisingly, Felix did not describe Guthlac's physical labours beyond saying that he built himself a hut on top of the barrow where he chose to live. Felix did not mention any agricultural activities, nor explain whence Guthlac obtained the pieces of barley bread which he occasionally ate; he concentrated rather on the saint's prayers, vigils and fasts. Guthlac's servant, Beccel, assisted him in some matters and may have taken responsibility for obtaining food; alternatively they may both have depended upon gifts made by the saint's numerous visitors.

Not all the manual labour performed by religious was agricultural. The brothers from the community at South Shields were responsible for finding wood suitable for the use of the minster, for which they had to travel down the river on rafts, while the brethren at Ely were sent by their abbess to Cambridge in search of stone from which to make a coffin for the translated body of Æthelthryth.[163] Ceolfrith was given the office of baker at Ripon, but this did not prevent him from learning and practising the ceremonies of the priesthood 'in the midst of sieving the flour, lighting and cleansing the oven and baking in it the loaves'.[164] Some houses tried to find labours specifically suited to their occupants' talents; Bede tells of a brother at Lastingham, Oswine, who since he was less capable of the study of the Scriptures applied himself more earnestly to manual labour, and when the other brothers were reading inside he was working outside 'at whatever seemed necessary'.[165]

Women in minsters seem to have spent much time in weaving, making materials for various purposes such as altar coverings or ecclesiastical vestments as well as garments for themselves.[166] Many such objects were given by religious women as presents; for example, Cuthbert had been sent a linen

---

[160] Bede, *VSCuth.* ch. 19 (pp. 220–1). [161] Anon., *VSCuth.* III. 1–5 (pp. 96–101).
[162] *HE* III. 19 (pp. 276–7). [163] Bede, *VSCuth.* ch. 3 (pp. 162–3); *HE* IV. 19 (pp. 394–5).
[164] *VSCeol.* ch. 4 (p. 389). [165] *HE* IV. 3 (pp. 338–9).
[166] Loom-weights have been found from the excavations at Whitby; Rosemary Cramp, 'Northumbria and Ireland', in Paul E. Szarmach with the assistance of Virginia Darrow Oggins (eds.), *Sources of Anglo-Saxon Culture* (Kalamazoo, MI: Medieval Institute Publications, Western Michigan University, 1986), pp. 185–201, at p. 194. But see also *ibid.*, p. 201 n. 28, where Cramp suggested that weaving may in some places have been a male activity, women engaging rather in spinning and sewing.

cloth by Abbess Verca, which he refused to wear while alive but directed should be used to wrap his body after death.[167] Abbess Bugga sent Boniface an altar cloth and other unspecified *vestimenta* as presents.[168] While weaving may have been considered an appropriate occupation for female religious,[169] it might also lead to one of the most often-mentioned abuses they were said to have perpetrated, namely the manufacture of brightly coloured, elaborate garb for their own use. Thus, according to Adomnan, were the women at Coldingham engaged: 'Even the virgins who are dedicated to God put aside all respect for their profession and, whenever they have leisure, spend their time weaving elaborate garments with which to adorn themselves as if they were brides.'[170]

Copying manuscripts was also probably considered to be a form of work in early Anglo-Saxon minsters.[171] Both Augustine and Cassian had specifically allowed the copying of manuscripts to be classified as manual labour, although the rules of Benedict, Caesarius and Columbanus made no reference to the activity at all.[172] Yet in houses with active scriptoria responsible for creating significant numbers of texts (particularly decorated texts), such work must have occupied a substantial proportion of the time of those capable of its execution.[173] The creation of a collection of necessary books for a newly established monastic house was as much a part of the process of

---

[167] Bede, *VSCuth.* ch. 37 (pp. 272–3).   [168] Boniface, *Epp.* 15 and 27 (pp. 28 and 48).

[169] It is, however, also possible that some female houses provided homes for lay women who were skilled in spinning and weaving; Rosemary Cramp, 'Northumbria and Ireland', p. 195; Schneider, 'Anglo-Saxon women', pp. 72–3.

[170] *HE* IV. 25 (pp. 424–7). We have already seen that the *Clofesho* council of 747 (ch. 20, H&S III, 369, quoted above) tried to dissuade women from weaving unsuitable clothes for their own adornment. This canon did not, however, forbid women in minsters to weave at all, as was suggested by Dagmar Schneider, 'Anglo-Saxon women', p. 72.

[171] See plate IX, a Gospel book from Durham, Cathedral Library, A. II. 10, fo 2v, showing the beginning of St Mark's Gospel. This is the earliest Anglo-Saxon illuminated manuscript, demonstrating a sophisticated capacity to synthesise Celtic and English ornamental styles. Where it was made is not known, but it is probably Northumbrian and – since later held at Durham – might have been written at Lindisfarne. David Wilson, *Anglo-Saxon Art from the Seventh Century to the Norman Conquest* (London: Thames and Hudson, 1984), pp. 32–3.

[172] Cassian, *De institutis*, 10, 8–14 (pp. 400–9); see Owen Chadwick, *John Cassian: A Study in Primitive Monasticism* (Cambridge: Cambridge University Press, 1950), p. 62, and Ovitt, 'The cultural context', p. 81. Rosamond McKitterick has discussed the silence of other monastic rules on the subject: 'Women and literacy in the early Middle Ages', in her *Books, Scribes and Learning in the Frankish Kingdoms 6th–9th Centuries* (Aldershot: Variorum, 1994), no. XIII, p. 8.

[173] For a general discussion of manuscript production in monastic and cathedral scriptoria see Michael Lapidge, 'Scriptorium', in Michael Lapidge *et al.* (eds.), *The Blackwell Encyclopaedia of Anglo-Saxon England* (Oxford: Blackwell, 1999), p. 411. For discussion of the impact of a single scriptorium see Michelle Brown, 'The Lindisfarne scriptorium from the late seventh to the early ninth century', in Gerald Bonner *et al.* (eds.) *St Cuthbert, his Cult and his Community to AD 1200* (Woodbridge: Boydell, 1989), pp. 151–63, and Rosemary Cramp, 'The artistic influence of Lindisfarne within Northumbria', *ibid.*, pp. 213–28.

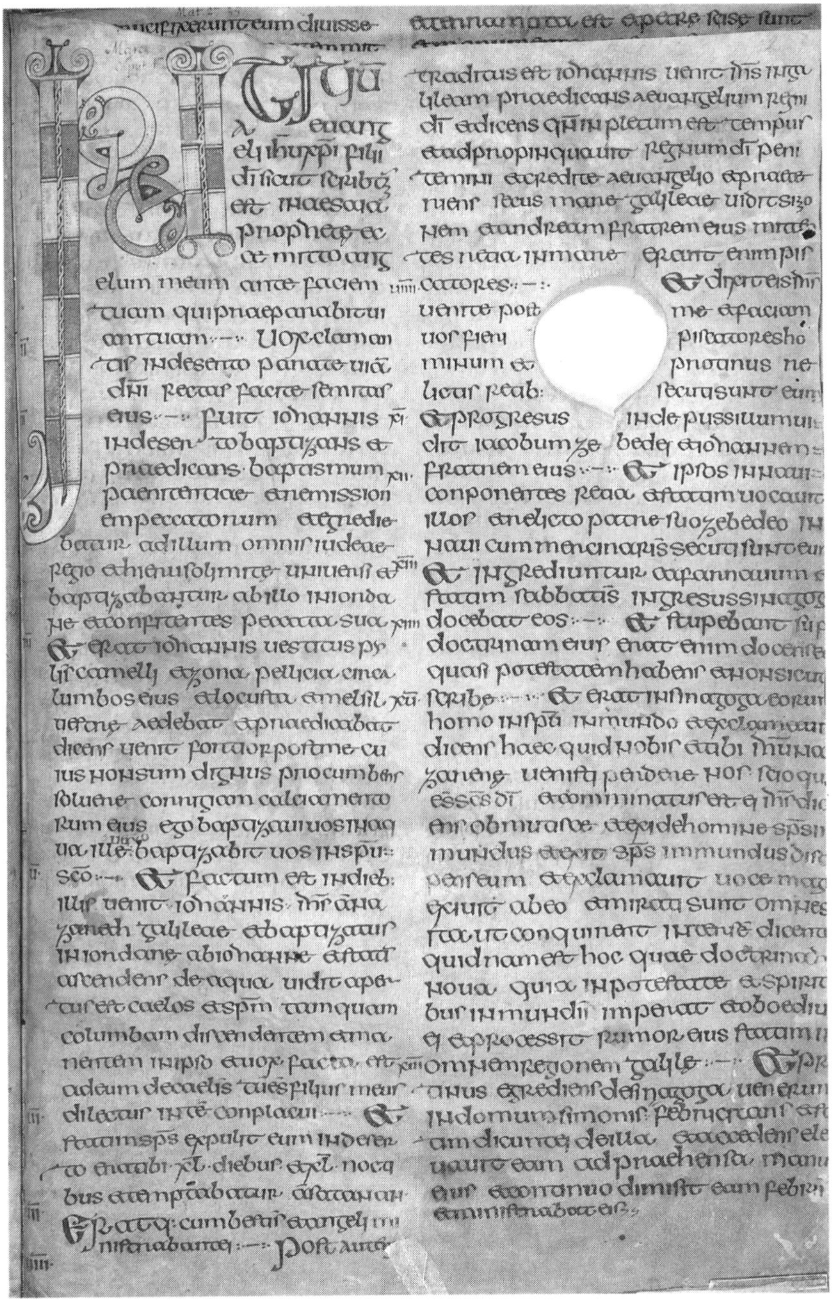

PLATE IX: Durham Gospel Book, Durham, Cathedral Library, MS A. II. 10, fo. 2v.

making it self-sufficient as was the productive organisation of its agricultural lands; it was in these early stages that a minster's particular 'house-
style' might first emerge, as the first members of the new scriptorium were
trained to write a similar hand.[174] That women as well as men played a part
in copying manuscripts seems highly probable.[175] Boniface wrote to Abbess
Eadburga to ask her to have a copy of the Epistles of St Peter written in gold
for him, sending the materials she would need for the task with a priest
Eoban.[176] Among the finds from the excavated double house at Whitby are
twelve styli and two vellum prickers,[177] although only one surviving text is
generally agreed to have been produced at Whitby: the anonymous Life of
Pope Gregory the Great (which now survives only in a ninth-century continental copy in the monastic library of St Gall, Switzerland).[178] The priest
Ultán in Æthelwulf's minster 'could ornament books with fair marking, and
by this art he accordingly made the shape of letters beautiful one by one
so that no modern scribe could equal him'.[179] Ceolfrith had the brothers
at Wearmouth and Jarrow transcribe manuscripts, including three Bibles,
one for each church and a third to take to Rome,[180] while Wilfrid had
a copy of the Gospels made for the church at Ripon, written in gold on
purple parchment and illuminated, together with a gold book-cover inlaid
with gems.[181] Binding these volumes was an additional labour-intensive and

---

[174] McKitterick, 'Women and literacy', p. 6.

[175] For discussion of the failure of any monastic rules for women specifically to mention the task of
manuscript copying among the activities suitable for women, see Rosamond McKitterick, 'Nuns'
scriptoria in England and Francia in the eighth century', in her *Books, Scribes and Learning in
the Frankish Kingdoms 6th–9th Centuries*, no. VII, pp. 30–1. McKitterick there contrasted the failure
of Caesarius' Rule for nuns to mention the copying of books with the description in the *Vita
Caesarii* of the mother Caesaria, under whose rule the nuns' community 'so flourished that amidst
psalmody and fasting, vigils and readings, the virgins of Christ lettered most beautifully the divine
books, having the mother herself as teacher' (*Vita Caesarii*, I, ch. 58, ed. B. Krusch, *MGH*, *SSRM* III,
p. 481).

[176] Boniface, *Ep.* 35 (p. 60). Compare also *Ep.* 30 (p. 54) in which Boniface thanked Eadburga for 'the
gift of sacred books' sent to him as an exile in Germany; these may also have been copied within
her minster.

[177] Cramp, 'Northumbria and Ireland', p. 194.

[178] Bertram Colgrave, *The Earliest Life of Gregory the Great* (Cambridge: Cambridge University Press,
1985), pp. 63–9; Rosemary Cramp, 'A reconsideration of the monastic site of Whitby', in R. Michael
Spearman and John Higgitt (eds.), *The Age of Migrating Ideas: Early Medieval Art in Northern Britain
and Ireland* (Edinburgh: National Museums of Scotland; Stroud: Alan Sutton, 1993), pp. 64–73, at
p. 64.

[179] Æthelwulf, *De abbatibus*, ch. 8, lines 211–13 (ed. Campbell, pp. 18–19).

[180] *VSCeol.* ch. 20 (p. 395). The third of these massive pandects, known as the *Codex Amiatinus*, survives
in the Biblioteca Laurenziana in Florence (MS Amiatino 1); see R. L. S. Bruce-Mitford, *The Art of
the Codex Amiatinus*, Jarrow: Lecture 1967 (Jarrow: [St Paul's Church, 1968]); Paul Meyvaert, 'Bede,
Cassiodorus and the Codex Amiatinus', *Speculum* 71 (1996), 827–83.

[181] *VSW* ch. 17 (pp. 36–7). For the use of purple dye, which was extremely expensive, see Christopher De Hamel, *A History of Illuminated Manuscripts* (Oxford: Phaidon, 1986), p. 46, and Rosamond

time-consuming task, that required a range of different skills (sewing quires together, manufacturing boards to which the sewn quires could be attached and – for display books at least, decorating the exterior of the cover). These tasks were not necessarily performed by the same men and women who had copied or illustrated the texts.[182]

Several early Anglo-Saxon minsters engaged in the manufacture of other valuable objects as well as books, such as liturgical vessels and ornaments made from precious metals and adorned with jewels, glass objects and complex figural and decorative sculpture, all of which would have required the labour of skilled craftsmen. The carved and inscribed rectangular whalebone box known as the Franks casket (plate XI) seems, on stylistic grounds, to have been made in Northumbria in the early or mid-eighth century and must have originated in a highly educated environment, for the decoration is extremely sophisticated and text (in both Latin and Old English) and image work closely together. Fusing Roman, Christian and Germanic traditions, it is difficult to imagine that this was created in any but a monastic environment, although where it was made is unknown; a case has recently been made for Wilfrid's Ripon, which could help also to explain how the casket found its way to Francia.[183] While Lindisfarne made use of the talents of a certain Billfrith the anchorite, who may have lived near the minster, to make a cover of gold, silver and jewels for the Lindisfarne Gospels, other monastic congregations had their own smiths.[184] A thin silver plaque dating from *c.* 700 discovered at Hexham (plate XII) may have formed part of a book cover,

---

McKitterick, *The Carolingians and the Written Word* (Cambridge: Cambridge University Press, 1989), pp. 142–4.

[182] There is a general discussion of Anglo-Saxon book-binding in Michael Gullick, 'Bookbindings', in Lapidge *et al.* (eds.), *The Blackwell Encyclopaedia of Anglo-Saxon England*, pp. 70–1. See also Graham Pollard, 'Some Anglo-Saxon book-bindings', *The Book Collector* 24 (1975), 130–59, and for a technical analysis of the binding process, J. A. Szirmai, *The Archaeology of Medieval Bookbinding* (Aldershot: Ashgate, 1999), pp. 99–139, where Anglo-Saxon bindings are discussed with Carolingian ones. See also plate X, showing the binding of the Stonyhurst Gospel of St John. This volume was discovered in the tomb of St Cuthbert in Durham in 1104, and may have been placed there when the saint's relics were translated at Lindisfarne in 698; it is the earliest surviving western book-binding.

[183] Plate XI. The front (shown on this plate) depicts two scenes: the left taken from the Germanic legend of Weland the Smith, and the right showing the Adoration of the Magi, labelled 'maegi' in runes. See Leslie Webster and Janet Backhouse, *The Making of England: Anglo-Saxon Art and Culture AD 600–900* (London: British Museum Press, 1991), pp. 101–3, no. 70; Leslie Webster, 'The iconographic programme of the Frank's casket', in Jane Hawkes and Susan Mills (eds.), *Northumbria's Golden Age* (Stroud: Sutton, 1999), pp. 227–46; and for the suggestion that the casket was made at Ripon see Ian N. Wood, 'Ripon, Francia and the Franks casket in the early Middle Ages', *Northern History* 26 (1990), 1–19.

[184] T. D. Kendrick *et al., Codex Lindisfarnensis (The Lindisfarne Gospels) published by permission of the Trustees of the British Museum*, 2 vols. (Oltun and Lausanne: Urs Graf, 1956–60), II, 5; Cramp, 'Northumbria and Ireland', p. 193.

PLATE X: Binding of the Stonyhurst Gospel of St John, on loan to the British Library from Stonyhurst College.

PLATE XI: Franks casket: London, British Museum. Front face; *left*: scene from legend of Weland the smith; *right*: Adoration of the Magi.

or been placed on a reliquary; it depicts a haloed cleric wearing the robes of a bishop and holding a book marked with a cross (presumably a Bible or book of Gospels.[185] The ninth-century gold plaque found at Brandon in Suffolk depicting St John the Evangelist with an eagle's head (plate XIII) may also have been a book-cover, or might alternatively have been attached to a standing cross; the plaque has holes at each of its four corners for fixing. The evangelist is shown holding a quill and book and the inscription around him reads SCS EVANGELISTA IOHANNIS ('St John the Evangelist').[186] At Æthelwulf's minster there was a smith called Cwicwine who made metal vessels for the brothers' table, and who was clearly a full member of the community and active in fasts and devotions.[187] Archaeological evidence from Crayke (plausibly shown by Lapidge to have been the site of Æthelwulf's

---

[185] Hexham plaque, plate XII. This is an impressed silver plaque, 9.9 cm high, 7.4 cm wide. See Richard N. Bailey, 'The Anglo-Saxon metalwork from Hexham', in D. P. Kirby (ed.), *St Wilfred at Hexham* (Hexham: Oriel Press, 1974), pp. 141–67; Webster and Backhouse, *The Making of England*, p. 138, no. 104.

[186] Brandon plaque, plate XIII. A gold plaque, 34 × 34 mm. See Webster and Backhouse, *The Making of England*, p. 82, no. 66 (a).

[187] Æthelwulf, *De abbatibus*, ch. 10 (ed. Campbell, pp. 25–6).

PLATE XII: Hexham plaque: London, British Museum.

PLATE XIII: Brandon plaque: London, British Museum.

minster) points to an unusually high quality of iron-working at this site. Since, as Lapidge observed, few iron-smelting sites have been identified from pre-Conquest England, the association of the remains of iron-working and the textual evidence is significant.[188] Cwicwine may have been responsible for making some of the precious objects which Æthelwulf said adorned the church – bronze bowls, the gold chalice and silver paten, the various silver plaques with images stamped on them or the gilded book-covers.[189] By contrast, Bede tells of a *monasterium nobile* in Bernicia, where there was a particularly recalcitrant and drunken brother (the same who refused to attend services and ended up in Hell) who was only tolerated by the others because he was an exceptionally skilful smith.[190] It seems from the excavated materials that bronze and silver were worked at Whitby together with jet and glass, and from Jarrow there was evidence for working in metal and glass in the workshops along the river-front.[191]

---

[188] Michael Lapidge, 'Aediluulf and the School of York', in *Lateinische Kultur im VIII. Jahrhundert: Traube Gedenkschrift*, ed. A. Lehner and W. Berschin (St Ottilien: Eos Verlag, 1990), pp. 161–78, at pp. 176–7.
[189] *De abbatibus*, ch. 20 (pp. 49–50).
[190] *HE* V. 14 (pp. 502–3).   [191] Cramp, 'Northumbria and Ireland', pp. 194, 198.

Benedict Biscop had to bring masons and glaziers from Francia in order to build his church at Wearmouth,[192] and masons were subsequently found among the communities of other Northumbrian minsters, for example at Hexham.[193] Stone was used by Benedict Biscop and by Wilfrid, Jane Hawkes has argued, as a means of asserting the existence and the status of these new ecclesiastical centres; Hawkes has stressed the impact multi-storeyed buildings such as Wilfrid's church at Hexham would have had in a landscape in which all other structures were low and made of wood, thatch and wattle-and-daub.[194] The use of carved ornament to adorn these early churches added to their impact (and of course represented a substantial investment of time and labour in addition to the materials employed). As well as the architectural stone sculpture that decorated the minster churches of Northumbria in the late seventh century and Mercia in the eighth, sculptors working in monastic environments created other forms of monument. Stone grave-markers, some with inscriptions identifying the dead and asking for prayer for their souls, have been found in monastic sites from Northumbria, particularly Whitby and Hartlepool.[195] More visible to the wider population were the elaborately decorated free-standing crosses erected first in Northumbria but later found elsewhere in England. Although the origins of this tradition are not entirely clear, it seems that their development followed the introduction of architectural sculpture and that the first examples (probably dating from the early eighth century) were produced under the patronage of monastic houses such as Wearmouth–Jarrow and Hexham and were built by masons with experience of decorating churches.[196] From the complexity of the iconography of these monuments, and the advanced

---

[192] VSCeol. ch. 7 (p. 390); HA, ch. 5 (p. 368). Hunter Blair, The World of Bede, pp. 165–6; idem, Northumbria in the Days of Bede (London: Book Club Associates, 1976), pp. 122–6; Rosemary Cramp, 'Monkwearmouth and Jarrow in their continental context', in Catherine E. Karkov (ed.), The Archaeology of Anglo-Saxon England: Basic Readings (New York and London: Garland Publishing, 1999), pp. 137–53, at p. 140.

[193] VSW ch. 23 (pp. 46–7); Rosemary Cramp, Early Northumbrian Sculpture, Jarrow Lecture 1965 (Jarrow: Saxby, 1965), p. 2. For discussion of the significant stone sculpture subsequently produced at Hexham see Rosemary Cramp, 'Early Northumbrian sculpture at Hexham', in D. P. Kirby (ed.), Saint Wilfrid at Hexham (Newcastle upon Tyne: Oriel Press, 1974), pp. 115–40; and Jane Hawkes, 'Statements in stone: Anglo-Saxon sculpture, Whitby and the Christianization of the North', in Karkov (ed.), The Archaeology of Anglo-Saxon England, pp. 403–21, at pp. 404–10.

[194] Hawkes, 'Statements in stone', p. 404.

[195] Richard N. Bailey, 'Grave-markers', in Lapidge et al. (eds.), The Blackwell Encyclopaedia of Anglo-Saxon England, p. 220; Cramp, 'A reconsideration', p. 65.

[196] Richard N. Bailey, 'Crosses, stone', in Lapidge et al. (eds.), The Blackwell Encyclopaedia of Anglo-Saxon England, p. 129; Richard N. Bailey, England's Earliest Sculptors (Toronto: Pontifical Institute of Mediaeval Studies, 1996), pp. 42–52; Hawkes, 'Statements in stone', pp. 405 and 410; Ian Wood, 'Anglo-Saxon Otley: an archiepiscopal estate and its crosses in a Northumbrian context', Northern History 23 (1987), 20–38, at pp. 26–30.

literate skills required of those who both wrote and designed the layout of the inscriptions, it is generally accepted that the earliest sculpture produced in England was made in a monastic context.[197] We should thus add sculpture and its design to the range of manual activities in which men devoted to religion may have engaged. Stylistic similarities between for example the Ruthwell and Bewcastle crosses and the minster at Jarrow suggest that some skilled craftsmen may have worked outside monastic ateliers;[198] whether these were professed brothers who obtained permission to work for substantial periods of time away from home, or rather laymen who had learnt the skill in a monastic workshop without taking vows, is unclear.

While not all minsters will have engaged in such skilled production, every community had need of more mundane artefacts for daily living: pottery for eating and cooking, clothes, belts, shoes, knives, metal and wooden tools, and so on. If not produced within a minster's own workshops, such items would have to be acquired from elsewhere, paid for either in cash or by the exchange of goods or agricultural produce.[199] The presence of craft workshops within monastic enclosures is well-attested from known monastic sites that have been excavated, such as Jarrow, Wearmouth, Whitby and Barking, and evidence for similar sorts of production has also been found at other sites which may at some time in their history have supported monastic congregations, such as Brandon and Flixborough.[200] Just as there is no archaeological evidence for the use of a uniform plan governing the layout of early Anglo-Saxon minsters, nor does it appear that each community engaged in the same craft activities. Rosemary Cramp has drawn attention to the fact that there is no sign of the textile manufacture and working attested at Whitby among the craft workshops found at Jarrow; she has wondered 'whether male and female monasteries maintained

---

[197] Bailey, 'Sculpture', p. 412.

[198] *Ibid.*; Jane Hawkes, 'Anglo-Saxon sculpture: questions of context', in Jane Hawkes and Susan Mills (eds.), *Northumbria's Golden Age* (Stroud: Sutton, 1999), pp. 204–15, at pp. 211–13.

[199] We have already noted the injunction made at *Clofesho* in 747 that the heads of minsters were to be responsible for providing suitable food and clothing for the inhabitants of their houses, and the recommendation in the same chapter that abbots and abbesses should ensure that they did not admit a larger congregation than they could maintain and support in necessities: ch. 28 (H&S III, 374).

[200] Cramp, 'Monkwearmouth and Jarrow', pp. 150–1; Cramp, 'A reconsideration of the monastic site at Whitby'; Kenneth MacGowan, 'Barking Abbey', *Current Archaeology* 149 (1996), 172–8; R. D. Carr, *et al.*, 'The Middle Saxon Settlement at Staunch Meadow, Brandon', *Antiquity* 62 (1988), 371–7; C. P. Loveluck, 'A high-status Anglo-Saxon settlement at Flixborough, Lincolnshire', *Antiquity* 72 (1998), 146–61.

specialised workshops and operated an exchange system'.[201] The question the evidence least equips us to answer is who within a community engaged in craft production. Designing high-quality metalwork for the service of the altar, determining an iconographic sequence to decorate a standing cross or drafting an inscription for a sacred object, standing monument or tombstone were all activities of the intellectually learned (and the last, a task only performable by the literate). However, it does not necessarily follow that the execution of patterns designed by professed religious was not undertaken by lay workmen (or of course women) skilled in a particular craft. Although we have just observed that some religious were technically expert in specific crafts, they may have been remarked upon in the narrative sources precisely because these skills were not normally found among choir brothers.

Education and learning

A good deal of the monastic day in many houses was devoted to intellectual pursuits, ranging from the learning of sufficient literate skills for the proper performance of the liturgy, through the private reading of Scripture and exegesis, to more advanced theological study and the composition of original literary works. Determining the proportion of time spent by religious each day in such activities is difficult: there were presumably considerable variations between both the accepted practices of different establishments and the habits of individuals within any one minster. As with skilled craft activities, much will have depended on the aptitude of the individual for the task.

Early monastic rules considered reading to be appropriate activity for monks and nuns; Caesarius of Arles recommended it to the sisters for whom he wrote, and Benedict of Nursia's Rule set aside variable portions of the day for sacred reading according to the season, directing that each brother be given a book to read through at the beginning of Lent every year.[202] The writings of Anglo-Saxon ecclesiastics show that they too laid considerable stress on reading. Bede expressed much anxiety at the generally low

---

[201] Cramp, 'Monkwearmouth and Jarrow', p. 150.

[202] Caesarius of Arles, *Regula ad uirgines*, ch. 19 (pp. 192–5); *RSB*, ch. 48, 14–16 (pp. 250–1). See McKitterick, *The Carolingians and the Written Word*, pp. 166–8. Benedict's provisions also made allowance for those who were incapable of such study, advising that they be given some work to perform to keep them from idleness. Compare Bede's account of the brother of Lastingham, Owine, who was less capable of the study of Scripture and so applied himself more earnestly to manual labour, *HE* IV. 3 (pp. 338–9), quoted above.

levels of clerical education in his day, and urged Bishop Ecgberht of York to meditate on Scripture, especially on Paul's letters to Timothy and Titus, and Pope Gregory's *Cura pastoralis*.[203] However, he also recommended that no one who was sufficiently learned to teach the word of God should scorn the simplicity of another brother.[204] Reading was singled out as one of the activities appropriate to those in the religious life at the council held at *Clofesho* in 747, which lamented how few of those living in minsters laboured for sacred knowledge.[205] The letters of Boniface and Alcuin contain similar comments on the value of reading Scripture and its relevance to the lives and situations of their correspondents. Alcuin urged the abbot of Wearmouth–Jarrow to ensure that boys learnt to read the scriptures so that they might teach them when grown-up.[206] To the brothers of Hexham he said, 'it is necessary to read the Holy Scriptures for from them each may understand what to follow and what to avoid. Let the light of learning dwell among you and give light through you to other churches, that all may praise you and your reward in heaven may be everlasting.'[207] Among the sins that confronted the brother from Wenlock in his vision were sloth and negligence in studying divine reading.[208]

New converts to the religious life and any children being brought up within the minster needed to be educated and trained for their future service, whether in the choir or in the world.[209] Indeed, the establishment of schools to train native clergy for the religious life was one of the first tasks of missionaries to the English; Augustine rapidly created a school in Canterbury, which by the 630s was able to send masters to Sigeberht, king of East Anglia, who wanted to found a school for his kingdom, having been impressed by the institutions he had seen in Gaul.[210] Oswald of Northumbria also gave land to Irish religious in order to establish schools in which English children as well as adults were instructed by Irish teachers.[211] In a double

---

[203] Bede, *EpEcg*, § 3 (p. 406); compare his remarks about clerical literacy, ch. 5 (pp. 408–9).

[204] Bede, *Super parabolam Salomonis*, II. 20 (ed. Migne, *PL* 91, 997): 'Nemo cum scripturarum se scientia institutum, et ad dicendum uerbum Dei uiderit idoneum, despiciat simplicitatem fratris qui etsi minus doctus ad praedicandum, non tamen minus promptus est ad discendum uel ad implendum bona quae didicit.' Quoted by Pierre Riché, *Education and Culture in the Barbarian West: Sixth through Eighth Centuries*, translated from the third French edition by John J. Contreni (Columbia: University of South Carolina Press, 1976), pp. 394–5.

[205] Council of *Clofesho*, AD 747, chs. 7 and 20 (H&S III, 364–5).   [206] Alcuin, *Ep*. 19 (p. 55).

[207] Alcuin, *Ep*. 31 (p. 73). Compare Alcuin, *Ep*. 21 (p. 59), and Boniface, *Ep*. 30 (p. 54). See Hunter Blair, *Northumbria in the Days of Bede*, pp. 153–4.

[208] Boniface, *Ep*. 10 (p. 10); Sims-Williams, *Religion and Literature*, p. 177.

[209] For the education of the children of the Anglo-Saxon nobility in the cloister see Riché, *Education and Culture*, pp. 322–3, and compare *VSW* ch. 21 (pp. 44–5), quoted above, p. 146.

[210] *HE* III. 18 (pp. 268–9).   [211] *HE* III. 3 (pp. 220–1).

house like Barking, the children lived and were educated in the women's part of the minster; here one of the sisters, Torhtgyth, was responsible for teaching them.[212] Alcuin advised the community at Hexham diligently to teach the boys and young men the knowledge of Christian books, so that they might be worthy to succeed their teachers and pray for them.[213] At *Clofesho* in 747, the heads of minsters were told to confine boys in schools and train them in sacred knowledge so that they might become useful to the church of God, and reminded that they were not to exact so much worldly labour from the boys as to deprive them of such an education.[214]

Felix described the nature of the basic monastic education at Repton in his Life of Guthlac. First the saint was taught his letters, then he advanced to study of the Psalter, and for the next two years he was initiated in canticles, psalms, hymns, prayers and ecclesiastical customs.[215] Wilfrid also began his studies with the Psalter, which he was said already to have learnt by heart, together with several other books, even before he was tonsured.[216] Once a student had mastered sufficient Latin, he would go on to read the wisdom books of the Old Testament and then start to explore the more demanding poetic texts of the school curriculum in Late Antiquity together with examples of Christian Latin poetry.[217] From here, having by this stage covered the 'arts' elements of the classical curriculum (the *trivium*: grammar, rhetoric and dialectic), the advanced student might have proceeded to the more scientific elements of the *quadrivium* (arithmetic, geometry, astronomy and music), although there are few surviving pre-Conquest manuscripts that cover these subjects.[218] The extent to which any brother may have advanced beyond the basic study of Latin will have depended in part on the teaching available to him in his own minster, but also on his own abilities; many must have learnt little more than the rudiments, while others may have remained barely literate, able to participate in the liturgy by learning the Latin required through its constant repetition rather than by genuine understanding.[219]

---

[212] *HE* IV. 8–9 (pp. 358–61).   [213] Alcuin, *Ep.* 31 (p. 73).

[214] Council of *Clofesho*, AD 747, ch. 7 (H&S III, 365).   [215] *VSG* chs. 22–3 (pp. 84–7).

[216] *VSW* ch. 2 (pp. 6–7). At Lindisfarne, Wilfrid learnt Jerome's version of the Psalter, but during the year in which he waited at Canterbury before accompanying Benedict Biscop to Rome, he committed the Roman Psalter to memory: *ibid.*, ch. 3 (pp. 8–9).

[217] Riché, *Education and Culture*, pp. 419–49.

[218] Michael Lapidge, 'Schools', in Lapidge *et al.* (eds.), *The Blackwell Encyclopaedia*, p. 409.

[219] Benedict Biscop brought back a number of pictures from Rome with which to decorate the walls of the church of St Peter at Wearmouth, in order to inspire and teach all those who entered the building, even those who could not read: *HA* ch. 6 (pp. 369–70).

Unambiguous evidence for the existence of schools in seventh-century minsters is sparse; there are references to schools at Barking, Malmesbury, Melrose, Repton, Ripon, Wearmouth–Jarrow and Whitby, as well as in cathedral minsters such as Canterbury, Hexham, Lindisfarne and York.[220] Alcuin provided a particularly detailed account of the nature of the curriculum he had experience as a young man at York in the time of Archbishop Ælberht (776/7–8; died 780): 'He watered parched hearts with diverse streams of learning and the varied dew of knowledge: skilfully training some in the arts and rules of grammar and pouring upon others a flood of rhetorical eloquence.'[221] To some he taught dialectic, others music; astronomy, computus and the study of Scripture were also part of this advanced curriculum.[222] In the metrical epitaph Alcuin wrote for his teacher after his death, he recalled particularly his teaching of the *artes liberales*.[223] That this somewhat idealised picture of Ælberht's teaching of the *trivium* and the *quadrivium* at York may reflect with some accuracy the nature of the education Alcuin received there is, Donald Bullough argued, suggested by the fact that this provided a pattern for Alcuin's later educational writings.[224] We know also of the extensive library inherited by Alcuin from his teacher, which included a substantial collection of Latin poets, and sheds further light on the texts available for teaching at York.[225] Only a few minsters were able to support more advanced learning; indeed Pierre Riché has argued that with the exception of grammar, which was essential for learning the Latin necessary to read the Bible, the liberal arts were largely ignored by the majority of Anglo-Saxon religious houses.[226] More academically-inclined members of monastic communities often sought, and obtained, permission to leave their own minster to study elsewhere.

As a young man, Boniface progressed quickly through the basic training offered at Exeter and was allowed to leave there because of its lack of suitable teachers in order to go to Nursling, where he became proficient in grammar, rhetoric, the writing of verses and the literal and spiritual exposition

---

[220] Lapidge, 'Schools', p. 408; Michael Lapidge, 'The school of Theodore and Hadrian', *Anglo-Saxon England* 15 (1986), 45–72; reprinted in his *Anglo-Latin Literature 600–899* (London: Hambledon, 1996), pp. 141–68; Sims-Williams has traced the intellectual links between Whitby and Worcester: *Religion and Literature*, pp. 184–90.

[221] Alcuin, *Versus*, lines 1432–3 (ed. and trans. Godman, pp. 112–13).

[222] *Ibid.*, lines 1436–49 (pp. 112–5).

[223] Alcuin, *Carmen* II (ed. Dümmler, *MGH Poetae*, p. 206); Bullough, *Alcuin*, p. 253; Lapidge, 'Aediluulf', p. 162.

[224] Bullough, *Alcuin*, pp. 253–5.   [225] Lapidge, 'Aediluulf', pp. 163–4.

[226] Riché, *Education and Culture*, pp. 384–91.

of the Bible.[227] Aldhelm also went on from the house where he was first educated, possibly Malmesbury, to study with Hadrian at Canterbury, learning under his tutelage Roman law, metrics, computus and astronomy.[228] He might have been one of those mentioned by Bede who learned Greek in the Canterbury school, but this cannot be proved.[229] Later, Aldhelm himself attracted pupils, and we know from a letter he wrote to a certain Heahfrith that such persons came to study with him only after completing their elementary education.[230] Lull may be an example of just such a pupil; although he studied at Malmesbury and probably adopted a life of religion there, he (and Burchard, later bishop of Würzburg, and Denehard) studied also with Cuniburg, abbess of Inkberrow, presumably spending their early years in her care before proceeding to more advanced study at a later age.[231] Certainly Aldhelm's correspondents required considerable Latin knowledge if they were to cope with his style, with its abstruse vocabulary and complex periods; his praise for the learning of the women of Barking to whom he dedicated his treatise on virginity cannot be dismissed as mere rhetoric.[232] Others studied outside England; according to Bede, in the 630s many English people went to Gaul to practise the monastic life,[233] and in the eighth century English scholars were still attracted to the Frankish court.[234] Ireland

---

[227] *VSB* ch. 2 (pp. 464–6). Writing to Bishop Daniel of Winchester from Germany, Boniface later remembered the quality of the library of Abbot Winberht of Nursling, asking Daniel particularly for a book of Winberht's which contained the six books of the Prophets in one volume, copied in clear letters, without abbreviations: Boniface, *Ep.* 63 (p. 131).

[228] Aldhelm, *Ep.* 1 (ed. Ehwald, pp. 475–8, trans. Lapidge and Herren, *Aldhelm*, pp. 152–3). See also Lapidge, 'The school of Theodore and Hadrian', and *idem*, 'The career of Archbishop Theodore', in Michael Lapidge (ed.), *Archbishop Theodore: Commemorative Studies on his Life and Influence* (Cambridge: Cambridge University Press, 1995), pp. 1–29, at pp. 17–18. Sims-Williams, *Religion and Literature*, p. 184. For discussion of the nature of the Roman law studied by Aldhelm see J. M. Wallace-Hadrill, 'Rome and the early English church: some questions of transmission', in his *Early Medieval History* (Oxford: Blackwell, 1975), pp. 115–37, at pp. 127–8.

[229] *HE* IV. 2 (pp. 332–5): 'ita ut etiam metricae artis, astronomiae et arithmeticae ecclesiasticae disciplinam inter sacrorum apicum uolumina suis auditoribus contraderent. Indicio est quod usque hodie supersunt de eorum discipulis, qui Latinam Graecamque linguam aeque ut propriam in qua nati sunt norunt.' For Aldhelm's education see Lapidge and Herren, *Aldhelm*, pp. 8–9.

[230] Aldhelm, *Ep.* 5 (ed. Ehwald, p. 490).

[231] Lull mentioned his study at Malmesbury in Boniface, *Ep.* 135 (p. 274); the three men wrote from Germany to Abbess Cuniburg asking her to pray for their work in the mission field: *Ep.* 49 (pp. 78–80). Discussed by Rosamond McKitterick, *Anglo-Saxon Missionaries in Germany: Personal Connections and Local Influences*, Vaughan Paper 36 (1991), reprinted in her *Frankish Kings and Culture in the Early Middle Ages* (Aldershot: Variorum, 1995), no I, p. 21.

[232] Aldhelm, *De virginitate*, chs. 1–4 (ed. Ehwald, pp. 228–32). For a discussion of Aldhelm's use of Latin see Michael Winterbottom, 'Aldhelm's prose style and its origins', *Anglo-Saxon England* 6 (1977), 39–76.

[233] *HE* III. 8 (pp. 236–9).

[234] Alcuin himself attracted pupils; in a letter to Offa, king of Mercia, he requested that one such pupil whom he was sending back to England be looked after and encouraged to teach others

was also frequently visited by Anglo-Saxon religious, either seeking divine instruction or hoping to live a more ascetic life.[235] Aldhelm deplored the fact that so many English scholars were accustomed in his day to flock to Ireland, as if there were no one at home to teach them the Latin and Greek necessary to unravel the mysteries of Scripture.[236]

Additional information about the sort of literature read in a wider variety of minsters may be found in the letters exchanged between England and the continent in the eighth century, which included requests for individual books the writers were unable to obtain in their own country.[237] Boniface in particular demanded various books with which to 'lighten his exile in Germany'.[238] In part his needs were clearly liturgical; he asked for a copy of the epistles of St Peter written in gold in order that 'a reverence for and love of the Holy Scriptures might be impressed upon the minds of the heathens' to whom he preached.[239] Boniface may, however, have wanted for his own reading the works of Bede, which he requested from Abbot Hwaetberht of Wearmouth.[240] The missionary also continued to correspond with his pupils, such as Leoba, who wrote asking him to correct her unpolished style and to help her with her composition of verses, a sample of which she had added to the end of her letter.[241] Cuthswith, abbess of Inkberrow in Worcestershire, apparently owned a fifth-century Italian copy of Jerome's Commentary on *Ecclesiastes*, which may have been brought back from Rome for her minster by Bishop Oftfor of Worcester.[242]

---

properly: Alcuin, *Ep.* 64 (p. 107). On Alcuin's role as a teacher in the late 780s see Bullough, *Alcuin*, pp. 371–2 and 436–7.

[235] *HE* III. 27 (pp. 312–13). Among the individuals mentioned by Bede who studied in Ireland are Ecgberht (III. 4, pp. 224–5), Trumhere (III. 24, pp. 292–3) and Chad (IV. 3, pp. 344–5). Pierre Riché (*Education and Culture*, p. 376) stressed the importance of Irish influences on those Englishmen who left their country to evangelise Gaul and Germany, such as Egbert, Wiehtberht and Willibrord.

[236] Aldhelm, *Ep.* 5 (ed. Ehwald, *Aldhelmi Opera*, p. 492).

[237] The acquisition of books by the English from Rome and elsewhere in the early Anglo-Saxon period was examined by Wallace-Hadrill, 'Rome', pp. 123–33.

[238] Boniface, *Ep.* 30 (p. 54). Levison, *England and the Continent*, pp. 139–48; McKitterick, *Anglo-Saxon Missionaries in Germany*, pp. 18, 21–3.

[239] Boniface, *Ep.* 35 (p. 60). Compare *Ep.* 34 to Abbot Duddo (pp. 58–9) in which Boniface requested not only, as an aid in sacred learning, part of a treatise on St Paul which he lacked, but also 'whatever you may find in your church library which you think would be useful to me and which I may not know, or may not have in written form'.

[240] *Ep.* 76 (p. 159); compare *Ep.* 75 (p. 158) in which Boniface asked Archbishop Ecgberht of York for some of the treatises of Bede, in return for a copy of some of the letters of Pope Gregory which he had obtained from the papal archives.

[241] Boniface, *Ep.* 29 (pp. 52–3).

[242] The manuscript is Würzburg, Universitätsbibliothek, MS. M. p. th. q. 2; its probable connection with Cuthswith was traced by Patrick Sims-Williams, 'Cuthswith, seventh-century abbess of Inkberrow, near Worcester, and the Würzburg manuscript of Jerome on Ecclesiastes', *Anglo-Saxon England* 5 (1976), 1–21. Also his *Religion and Literature*, pp. 190–3 and 237–40.

231

In addition to the few institutions famed for the excellence of their learning, other establishments were also able to sustain some more advanced study; even if some of these have yet to be identified, it is not necessary to conclude with Riché that 'whenever Bede described a minster without stating exactly what kinds of studies the brothers there pursued, we can conclude that they were content with the daily office and the simple reading of the Bible'.[243] Nor should the significance of Bible-reading (one assumes with the assistance of an appropriate commentary) be down-played; this was, as Patrick Sims-Williams has argued, the fundamental literary activity of Anglo-Saxon religious, frequently pursued at a demandingly intellectual level.[244] Yet it is apparent that the vast majority of those minsters at which any sort of academic endeavour was regularly attempted lacked both the material and intellectual resources to engage in the range of studies offered at a school like Canterbury's. The complaints made by Bede in his letter to Ecgberht about the deplorable standards of latinity among the Northumbrian clergy may reflect conditions in the mass of lesser-known minsters more accurately than do the letters of Boniface.[245] Bede certainly took the problem seriously enough to transate various important texts from Latin into English; on his death-bed he was engaged in making a translation of St John's Gospel and a selection from Isidore's *De natura rerum*, lest after he was gone his pupils might learn what was not true and lose the labour they had already expended.[246]

Food and drink

A minster was, as we have already remarked, a particular kind of social institution in which the tensions between the ascetic ideals of the monastic rules and the aristocratic values common to most religious were only partially resolved. In matters of the detail of liturgical performance or the allocation of uncongenial yet necessary manual tasks, frictions between personalities within one community could be reconciled in private, without reference to outsiders. While we may have noted considerable variation in the expression of specific aspects of monasticism and perhaps some blurring

---

[243] Riché, *Education and Culture*, p. 394.

[244] Sims-Williams, *Religion and Literature*, pp. 177–210. Compare also the remarks of Boniface and Alcuin about the benefits of reading, quoted above.

[245] Bede, *EpEcg*, §5 (pp. 408–9). Those centres at which few brothers were literate are of course precisely those least likely to have left any written records for posterity.

[246] Cuthbert, *Epistola de obitu Bedae* (ed. Colgrave and Mynors, pp. 582–3).

over the articulation of its ideals, we have predominantly been exploring aspects of a closed society. Yet once we turn from the activities particular to the monastic way of life and explore those aspects of daily living common to all early medieval households, it becomes increasingly difficult to hold the cloister's boundary against incursion from the outside world. In their habits of eating and drinking, and also in their play, early Anglo-Saxon religious were literally, not merely metaphorically, closer to their secular counterparts.

Food (and still more alcohol) were no less value-laden issues within early medieval monasticism than were dress and hairstyles. Fasting in moderation, when coupled with prayer, was a useful way for Christians to strengthen the spirit by weakening the desires of the flesh; the Gospels illustrate Christ's teaching and practice of fasting,[247] and the Christian church specified particular days and longer periods of abstinence which various early monastic rules amplified.[248] Excessive consumption led not only to indigestion (*RSB*, ch. 39, 7) but more importantly to the sin of gluttony, defined by Alcuin in his book on the virtues and vices as 'intemperate pleasure in food and drink' (*intemperans cibi uel potus uoluptas*) 'through which the first parents of the human race lost the happiness of paradise'. Gluttony might be exemplified by eating earlier than the established canonical hour, asking for specially elaborate or delicious foods to be prepared, or eating or drinking to excess. Its consequences included not just scurrilous enjoyment, frivolity and boastful talk, but uncleanness of body, unsteadiness of mind and lust (*libido*).[249] Aldhelm named Gluttony (*ingluuies uentris*) first among the vices in the allegorical battle between virtue and vice which forms the final section of his *Carmen de uirginitate*; gluttony – excess of food, drunkenness and intoxication of the soul – led inevitably in his view to debauchery. The remedy for gluttony was fasting and abstinence: in Aldhelm's account, 'the virtues continually wage harsh wars against Gluttony which overcomes iron-clad hearts; Integrity, however, opposes it with strength of fasting, so that the fortress of the spirit may not be overwhelmed by feasting'.[250] Alcuin's advice was similar: 'from fullness of the stomach is built up lust of the body, which is best overcome through fasting and abstinence and the constant

[247] *Matthew* 6: 16–18; *Mark* 2: 20; *Luke* 4: 2.
[248] Caesarius of Arles addressed fasts in his *Regula ad uirgines*, chs. 67 and 71 (pp. 258–9, 268–9).
[249] Alcuin, *Liber de uirtutibus et uitiis*, ch. 28 (*PL* 101, 633A–B); quoted and translated by Hugh Magennis, *Anglo-Saxon Appetites: Food and Drink and their Consumption in Old English and Related Literature* (Dublin: Four Courts Press, 1999), pp. 93–4.
[250] Aldhelm, *Carmen de uirginitate*, lines 2485–9 and 2537–40 (ed. Ehwald, pp. 454 and 456).

practice of any sort of work'.[251] Both writers were following established patristic conventions here, particularly Gregory the Great's *Moralia* on the book of Job and the fifth of Cassian's *Collationes*, which deals with the eight principal vices, starting with gluttony (which he too associated with carnal desire).[252]

Since gluttony had such significance in early medieval Christian teaching, we might expect to find that food and drink were carefully regulated in early monastic rules and fasting strongly recommended. Benedict's provisions were, predictably, moderate and tempered by a consciousness of the weaknesses of his fellows; indeed he clearly felt some uneasiness in legislating to restrict the food of others, recognising that the gift of abstinence was not granted to all.[253] In the matter of food Benedict allowed for the provision of two separate dishes at any meal (to help tempt the palate of the faddy eater) and, as well as a daily ample distribution of bread, recommended that the abbot arrange for larger quantities on days when the labour had been particularly onerous. He was anxious to avoid overindulgence, 'since in all matters frugality is the rule'.[254] A half bottle of wine per day for each he thought sufficient, provided more could be supplied in great heat, 'but those to whom God gives the strength to abstain must know that they will earn their own reward'.[255] By contrast, Columbanus' Rule was rather stricter: 'Let the monks' food be poor and taken in the evening, so as to avoid repletion, and their drink such as to avoid intoxication, so that it may both maintain life and not harm.' Instead of providing for enhanced supplies if the labour was arduous, Columbanus recommended that toil should be moderated, for the journey towards spiritual progress required a careful balance of temperance and supply: 'therefore we must fast daily, just as we must feed daily, and while we must eat daily, we must gratify the body more poorly and sparingly'.[256]

---

[251] Alcuin, *Liber de uirtutibus et uitiis*, ch. 28; Magennis, *Anglo-Saxon Appetites*, p. 94.

[252] Lapidge and Rosier, *Aldhelm*, pp. 99–100; Magennis, *Anglo-Saxon Appetites*, pp. 95–8. St Jerome took a particularly hard-line attitude to drink and was not willing even to countenance the consumption of wine in moderation, recommending rather that one should flee from it as a poison: *Ep.* 22 (ed. Hilberg, *CSEL* 54, 154); see Hugh Magennis, *Images of Community in Old English Poetry* (Cambridge: Cambridge University Press, 1996), p. 57, n. 107.

[253] *RSB* ch. 40, 1–2 (pp. 238–9).   [254] *RSB* ch. 39, 10 (pp. 238–9).

[255] *RSB* ch. 40, 4 (pp. 240–1). For a general discussion of these provisions, with particular attention to Benedict's concern for the proper nourishment of those who had to labour, see de Vogüé, 'Travail et alimentation'.

[256] Columbanus, *Regula monachorum*, ch. 3 (ed. and trans. Walker, pp. 122–5). Lisa Bitel has explored the politics of food in early Irish monasticism: *Isle of the Saints: Monastic Settlement and Christian Community in Early Ireland* (Ithaca, NY, and London: Cornell University Press, 1990; paperback edition Cork: Cork University Press, 1993), pp. 207–21.

Against this background, we should not be surprised that English hagiographers took great interest in the austerities practised by the saints they described. While the fasts and privations of saints attracted attention as clear signs of their remarkable holiness, normal monastic habits of eating and drinking excited little comment. Although the Anglo-Saxons do not generally seem to have practised the excessive privations common to Irish ascetics, there were some saints with reputations for austerity in eating and drinking. Æthelthryth of Ely reputedly rarely ate more than once a day,[257] while Eorpwine, abbot of Æthelwulf's minster, also ate very sparingly, nourishing himself only on dry food, and maintaining his fast throughout the day.[258] Several saints' lives remarked specifically that their subjects did not carry such practices to extremes: Wulfsig, another of Æthelwulf's abbots, ate when his body needed nourishment, providing it with precisely the right amount, and Cuthbert ensured that he did not fast to the extent that he could not work.[259] There are no references in the sources to whole communities engaging in canonical fasts, and we can only guess whether Wednesdays, Fridays, Advent and Lent were observed as fasts in early Anglo-Saxon minsters. Bede did relate one episode in the Life of Cuthbert when the saint refused to eat at the third hour one day because it was a fast-day, explaining that it was a Friday, the day 'on which most of the faithful are accustomed to protract their fast until the ninth hour out of reverence for the passion of the Lord'.[260] Fasts and extra devotions were sometimes practised by an entire minster as a penitential exercise: the Selsey congregation observed a three-day fast when several of its members were suffering from the plague.[261] Tetta made the Wimborne community fast and pray for three days for the soul of the harsh *decana*, and the brothers at Wearmouth and Jarrow fasted and added extra psalms to the canonical prayers after Ceolfrith's departure, so that amid prayer and fasting they might inquire of the Lord whom to appoint as their new abbot.[262]

Meal-times were presumably arranged at each community's convenience. The Wearmouth brethren delayed the start of their fast until they had eaten the midday meal on the Thursday on which Ceolfrith left, refreshing themselves again only at the ninth hour on Saturday.[263] A meal was also normally eaten at midday in Æthelwulf's minster. However, at Melrose in Cuthbert's

[257] *HE* IV. 19 (pp. 392–3).
[258] Æthelwulf, *De abbatibus*, ch. 13 (ed. Campbell, pp. 32–5). Compare the account of the fastings practised by Cwicwine the smith in the same minster, ch. 10 (pp. 24–5).
[259] *Ibid.*, ch. 18 (pp. 46–7); Bede, *VSCuth.* ch. 6 (pp. 174–5), quoted above.
[260] Bede, *VSCuth.* ch. 5 (pp. 168–9).   [261] *HE* IV. 14 (pp. 376–7, 380–1).
[262] *VSL* ch. 4 (p. 124); *VSCeol.* ch. 28 (p. 398).   [263] *Ibid.*

day the time for eating was the third hour,[264] and the meal would also seem to have been eaten at approximately this hour at Selsey. The sick boy in that minster had his vision of the apostles at the second hour of the day; when he had related what he had seen to the priest, the latter ordered the immediate celebration of mass and the preparation of food.[265] Midday cannot have been the normal meal-time at Verca's minster either, for Bede reported that this was the hour of rest in that house.[266]

Feasting and its necessary accompaniment, drinking, were as much a part of the monastic life as they were central to contemporary aristocratic culture.[267] James Campbell has portrayed the late seventh- and early eighth-century Anglo-Saxon minster as a 'special kind of nobleman's club', and rightly stressed how much 'conviviality mattered even in the best-conducted monasteries'.[268] This was one of the main spheres in which churchmen retained direct contact with their secular neighbours and – inevitably – where behaviour more fitting to a warrior's hall (mead, merriment and music) penetrated the silences of the cloister. After the dedication of Wilfrid's new church at Ripon, the community, together with the kings Ecgfrith and Ælfwine, abbots, reeves, sub-kings and other dignitaries, held a great feast lasting for three days and three nights.[269] Cuthbert feasted with Ælfflæd, abbess of Whitby, at a place in his diocese called Ovington, where he had gone to dedicate a church.[270] He also once, when staying at Verca's minster at South Shields and thirsty on rising from a midday rest, turned water drawn from the well into wine, which at least two brothers in the minster tasted with pleasure and amazement.[271] But when the same saint was invited from his hermitage on Farne to spend Christmas Day with the rest of the community of Lindisfarne, he three times interrupted their feasting, rejoicing and story-telling to urge upon them the merits of fasting and vigils.[272] The reforms of the tenth century did not put an end to monastic

---

[264] Anon., *VSCuth.* II. 2 (pp. 78–9).   [265] *HE* IV. 14 (pp. 380–1).

[266] Bede, *VSCuth.* ch. 35 (pp. 264–5). For a general discussion of the monastic diet see Ann Hagen, *A Handbook of Anglo-Saxon Food: Processing and Consumption* (Pinner: Anglo-Saxon Books, 1992), pp. 94–9.

[267] Hugh Magennis has observed that some Old English poetry, particularly *Beowulf*, gives a diluted image of Anglo-Saxon culture in which drinking is liberal but not riotous or immoderate and thus not inconsistent with the tastes and predilections of a Christian audience: *Images of Community*, p. 52. There is a general account of Anglo-Saxon feasting in Hagen, *A Handbook of Anglo-Saxon Food*, pp. 76–88.

[268] Campbell, 'Elements in the background', p. 12. David Knowles commented on the 'heroic scale' of the quantity of drink seemingly consumed in pre-Conquest religious houses: *The Monastic Order in England: A History of its Development from the Times of St Dunstan to the Fourth Lateran Council, 940–1216* (2nd edn, Cambridge: Cambridge University Press, 1963), p. 717.

[269] *VSW* ch. 17 (pp. 36–7).   [270] Anon., *VSCuth.* IV. 10 (pp. 126–7); Bede, *VSCuth.* ch. 34 (pp. 262–3).

[271] Bede, *VSCuth.* ch. 35 (pp. 264–7).   [272] *Ibid.*, ch. 27 (pp. 246–7).

feasting; indeed the *Regularis concordia* advised abbots to be zealous in providing hospitality for guests in their guest-houses.[273] Wulfstan of Winchester recounted an incident in his Life of St Æthelwold when King Eadred visited the monastery at Abingdon with his retinue, which included a number of Northumbrian thegns, and the abbot, Æthelwold, invited the king and his party to dine in the guest-house (*hospicium*). Servants poured mead all day to satisfy the drinkers' needs but miraculously the container never ran dry and the Northumbrians got extremely drunk as, Wulfstan observed wryly, they tended to do.[274] Wulfstan also described at some length the bibulous feasting that followed the dedication of the new cathedral church at Winchester in 980 in his metrical *Narratio* on the life St Swithun, completed in 996.[275] As Christopher Hohler observed, 'among the few apparently indisputable contributions of England to the Latin liturgy is the formula, to be read over the cask by the priest, to improve the quality of beer in which mice or weasels have got drowned'.[276]

Bishops' public roles may have laid still greater social obligations upon their congregations than upon those of some minsters and we should note that two of the most outspoken statements against over-enthusiasm for feasting and fraternising with lay people made in our period were addressed to bishops not abbots.[277] It would, however, be a mistake to minimise monastic participation in the same activities, or indeed to imagine that the churchmen who sought to condemn, or at least to restrict such behaviour, represented majority opinion within the early English church.[278] The brothers at Repton who were said to have ostracised Guthlac for his refusal to drink any sort of intoxicating drink may have been rather more typical of contemporary Anglo-Saxon attitudes.[279]

---

[273] *Regularis concordia*, ch. 63 (ed. Hallinger, p. 139).

[274] Wulfstan of Winchester, *Vita Æthelwoldi*, ch. 12 (ed. and trans. Lapidge and Winterbottom, pp. 22–5). Hugh Magennis has drawn attention to the fact that although Ælfric of Eynsham normally preached the advantages of moderation in drink, he repeated this story in his own version of Æthelwold's life, apparently without censure: *Images of Community*, pp. 55–6.

[275] *Narratio metrica de sancti Swithuno*, dedicatory letter, lines 85–100, in Michael Lapidge (ed.), *The Cult of St Swithun*, Winchester Studies 4, ii (Oxford: Clarendon Press for the Winchester Excavations Committee, 2003), pp. 378–9.

[276] C. E. Hohler, 'Some service books of the later Saxon church', in David Parsons (ed.), *Tenth-Century Studies* (London and Chichester: Phillimore, 1975), pp. 60–83, at p. 71, and see also pp. 222–3, n. 43,

[277] Bede's letter to Bishop Ecgberht of York and Alcuin's letter to a bishop 'Speratus'; see below.

[278] Richard Fletcher, *The Conversion of Europe: From Paganism to Christianity 371–1386 AD* (London: Harper-Collins, 1997), p. 192; Magennis, *Anglo-Saxon Appetites*, p. 108.

[279] *VSG* chs. 20–1 (pp. 84–5). Campbell, 'Elements in the background', p. 12. See also Martha Bayless, 'Humour and the comic in Anglo-Saxon England', in Paul Hardwick (ed.), *English Medieval Comedy* (Turnhout: Brepols, forthcoming).

Conviviality could, however, be taken to extremes and there were concerns in various quarters about the excesses of English religious and clergy, particularly in their consumption of alcohol. Bede complained about the behaviour of episcopal communities in his letter to Ecgberht, bishop of York:

It is rumoured abroad about certain bishops that they serve Christ in such a fashion that they have with them no men of any religion or continence, but rather those who are given to laughter, jests, tales, feasting and drunkenness, and the other attractions of a lax life, and who daily feed the stomach with feasts more than the soul on the heavenly sacrifice.[280]

The vice of drunkenness particularly disturbed Boniface, who writing to Archbishop Cuthbert lamented 'it is said that the vice of drunkenness is far too common in your *parochiae*, and that some bishops not only do not prohibit it, but themselves drink to the point of intoxication'. He thought this habit peculiar to the heathen and the English: 'neither the Franks, nor the Gauls, nor the Lombards, nor the Romans, nor the Greeks practise it', he claimed.[281] Writing to a bishop of Lindisfarne, Alcuin recommended him to surround himself with 'such men as are always learning and who rejoice more in learning than in being drunk'.[282] His most famous and outspoken statement on the subject came in a letter to 'Speratus', long identified with Bishop Higbald of Lindisfarne but shown by Bullough in fact to have been addressed to Unuuona (bishop of Leicester 781×785–801×803). Alcuin urged the bishop to pay more attention to his performance in church than to the pomp of his banquets:

What kind of praise is it that your table is loaded so high that it can hardly be lifted and yet Christ is starving at the door? . . . It is better that the poor should eat at your table than entertainers and persons of extravagant behaviour. Avoid those who engage in heavy driving, as blessed Jerome says, 'like the pit of Hell' . . . Splendour in dress and the continual pursuit of drunkenness are insanity . . . May you be the example of all sobriety and self-control.[283]

---

[280] Bede, *EpEcg*, ch. 4 (p. 407).

[281] Boniface, *Ep.* 78 (pp. 170–1). The force of this last remark is somewhat weakened by the charge of drunkenness Boniface had laid on the Frankish episcopate in an earlier letter to Pope Zacharias: *Ep.* 50 (p. 83).

[282] Alcuin, *Ep.* 285 (p. 444). Compare *Epp.* 20, 21, 230, 290 (pp. 58, 58–9, 374, 448). See Donald Bullough, *Friends, Neighbours and Fellow-Drinkers: Aspects of Community and Conflict in the Early Medieval West* (Cambridge: Department of Anglo-Saxon, Norse and Celtic, 1991), pp. 9–10.

[283] Alcuin, *Ep.* 124 (p. 183); translated by Donald Bullough, 'What has Ingeld to do with Lindisfarne?', *Anglo-Saxon England* 22 (1993), 93–125, at p. 124.

An indication of the extent of the problem in the early English church is provided by the first chapter of the penitential canons attributed to Archbishop Theodore, which was concerned with 'excess and drunkenness'. Bishops and ordained clergy could be removed from office for persistent drunkenness.[284] A brother who drank to the point of vomiting was to do penance for thirty days, but if he drank to excess because he had previously been abstinent for some time or because he had been celebrating a saint's day or one of the greater festivals such as Christmas or Easter (and if he had drunk no more than his seniors had recommended him), then he was to be let off the penance.[285] At *Clofesho* in 747, monks and clerics were advised to avoid the vice of drunkenness as a deadly poison, and also recommended to ensure that they did not allow others to drink intemperately, but rather to have wholesome and sober entertainments lest they bring disrepute on the habit that symbolised their religious status.[286] Yet, in other contexts, both Alcuin and Boniface could be more relaxed about the dangers of alcoholic drink. While visiting York, Alcuin wrote to Joseph, an Irish pupil of his on the continent, complaining that his hosts were running out of wine and the bitter beer was playing havoc with his stomach, but he hoped that Uinter, *medicus*, was soon going to send him two cartloads of best clear wine from Francia.[287] Boniface sent two small casks of wine to Ecgberht of York, 'so that you may have a merry day with the brethren'.[288] Whatever the difficulties its provision might cause, it is clear that alcohol was drunk in Anglo-Saxon minsters throughout our period even if certain notably holy men and women chose to be abstinent.[289] Some houses may have been able to make their own wine: there were a number of vineyards in southern England in 1066 and at least one minster, Glastonbury, is known to have owned one in the tenth century.[290]

Leisure

Conviviality was as significant an element of feasting as were the food and drink consumed, and the associated entertainment and merriment caused a similar degree of difficulty for adherents of strict monastic principles.

[284] Theodore, *Penitential*, I. i. 1 (ed. Finsterwalder, p. 288). Bullough, *Friends, Neighbours and Fellow-Drinkers*, p. 10, n. 18; Campbell, 'Elements in the background', p. 12.

[285] Theodore, *Penitential*, I. i. 2; I. i. 4 (p. 289).   [286] Council of *Clofesho*, AD 747, ch. 21 (H&S III, 369).

[287] Alcuin, *Ep.* 8 (p. 33).   [288] Boniface, *Ep.* 91 (p. 208).

[289] Cuthbert was said to have abstained from all intoxicants: Bede, *VSCuth.* ch. 6 (pp. 174–5). See further Magennis, *Images of Community*, pp. 57–9.

[290] S 626 (AD 956).

Separating entertainment from consumption is patently somewhat artificial, but the decision to do so here reflects a wider argument about the fusion of Germanic and Christian ideals within early Anglo-Saxon monasticism which understands the minster to have been an essentially aristocratic institution.[291] For those who worried about the incursion of secular values within the cloister, one of the most substantial problems about the reception of lay guests was that visitors expected to be entertained while they ate and drank. Alcuin's advice is the most celebrated, written to his episcopal friend 'Speratus':

Let God's words be read at the episcopal dinner-table. It is right that a reader should be heard, not a harpist, patristic discourse, not pagan song. What has *Hinield* [Ingeld] to do with Christ? The house is narrow and has no room for both. The Heavenly King does not wish to have communion with pagan and forgotten kings listed name by name: for the eternal King reigns in Heaven, while the forgotten pagan king wails in Hell. The voices of readers should be heard in your dwellings, not the laughing rabble in the courtyards.[292]

It was the recitation, to the harpist's accompaniment, of tales of pagan heroes, the singing of poems like *Beowulf* or *Widsith* in which Ingeld appears, to which Alcuin was objecting, on the grounds that these were entertaining, not edifying tales. He paints a picture of just that sort of *convivium* from which the young Cædmon had been wont to crawl away despondently when the circulating harp was nearing him, for he then believed that he could not sing.[293] Cædmon was not, then, participating in a monastic feast for it is quite clear from Bede's narrative that the herdsman was still at that time living a secular life and feasting in the company of his rustic companions, albeit as a tenant of Whitby and responsible for some of the abbey's cattle.[294] That such feasts and entertainments did occur also within minsters – as well as bishops' communities – seems more than probable.

Adomnan's vision of the iniquities perpetrated at Coldingham gives a picture of a house devoted to feasting, drinking and gossip.[295] We noted at

---

[291] Compare Patrick Wormald, 'Bede, "Beowulf" and the conversion of the Anglo-Saxon aristocracy', in R. T. Farrell (ed.), *Bede and Anglo-Saxon England*, BAR, British series, 46 (Oxford: BAR, 1978), 32–95; Fletcher, *The Conversion of Europe*, pp. 160–92. As Bullough pointed out, the word *convivium* is not known in either insular or continental monastic rules: 'What has Ingeld to do with Lindisfarne?', p. 108.

[292] Alcuin, *Ep.* 124 (p. 183); transl. Bullough, 'What has Ingeld to do with Lindisfarne?', p. 124.

[293] Bede, *HE* IV. 23 (pp. 414–17).

[294] Bullough drew attention to Cædmon's secular status: 'What has Ingeld to do with Lindisfarne?', p. 106.

[295] *HE* IV. 25 (pp. 424–6). See further below.

the beginning of this chapter the recommendation made at *Clofesho* in 747 that minsters should not be filled with poets, cithara players, musicians and buffoons, and that solemn religious festivals be properly observed and not consigned to games, horse-racing and feasting.[296] The specificity of this advice suggests it was couched in response to perceived problems within the eighth-century church, a presumption that other sources would tend to support. Cuthbert, abbot of Wearmouth and Jarrow, wrote to Lull in Germany in 764 asking if he were able to send a harpist for, Cuthbert said, 'I have a cithara but no one skilled to play it'. He begged Lull not to scorn his request, or to laugh at him for asking.[297] Bede's letter to Ecgberht had also warned against the habits of bishops who surrounded themselves with men given to laughter, jests and tales.[298] In other letters Alcuin made references to the inappropriateness of 'shows and devilish feignings' (*spectacula et diabolica figmenta*) and to the advisability of avoiding players and entertainers.[299] Ingeld had, indeed, little to do with Christ, but the songs of the harpist were far from silent in monastic halls, and may not have confined their tunes to the songs of David or to the biblical narratives preferred by Cædmon.[300]

Idleness was abhorred by monastic legislators as the enemy of the soul.[301] Its avoidance was best achieved by ensuring that every hour of the day was set to useful and prayerful tasks, such as reading, not idle chatter.[302] Yet it is hard to imagine other than in the strictest of English minsters that there were not some parts of the day as well as meal-times when religious had no designated tasks and when they did not seek some sort of relaxation or amusement. A humorous corrective to the strictures of the prescriptive literature is offered in the colloquies of the Benedictine schoolmaster, Ælfric Bata, written *c.* 1000 (and so falling outside our period). These shed an entirely different light on English monastic culture around the first millennium, showing for example how monks learned in the schoolroom and something of their activities elsewhere.[303] But while the contrast with the formality, discipline and strict asceticism of more conventional texts is marked (especially in the attitudes shown here to food and drink, in the references to brothers' personal possessions, and the prevalence of the

[296] Council of *Clofesho*, AD 747, chs. 20 and 16 (H&S III, 369, 368).
[297] Boniface, *Ep.* 116 (p. 251). Fletcher, *The Conversion of Europe*, p. 186.
[298] *EpEcg*, §4 (p. 407).   [299] Alcuin, *Epp.* 175 and 281 (pp. 290 and 439).
[300] Bede, *HE* IV. 23 (pp. 418–19); Fletcher, *The Conversion of Europe*, p. 186; Campbell, 'Elements in the background', p. 12.
[301] *RSB* ch. 48, 1 (pp. 248–9); see above, p. 212.   [302] *RSB*, ch. 48, 18.
[303] Scott Gwara (ed.), *Anglo-Saxon Conversations: The Colloquies of Aelfric Bata*, trans. with an introduction by David W. Porter (Woodbridge: Boydell Press, 1997).

humour and its frequently scatological nature), it is important to remember that these texts were designed as much for entertainment as for instruction, and that they were perhaps meant to shock.[304]

In earlier Anglo-Saxon minsters we might perhaps take gossip, chatter and some harmless joking for granted but we might also wonder whether they played games. No Anglo-Saxon text can parallel the account Gregory of Tours gave of the activities of the abbess of Poitiers (who had been summoned before her bishop to answer a variety of charges of wrong-doing): 'As to the *tabulae* she used to play during the lifetime of the Lady Radegund, she saw nothing wrong in it, and it was not expressly forbidden in the Rule, or in the canons.'[305] *Tabula* or *alea* (a board-game similar to backgammon, involving both skill and chance) was certainly known in Anglo-Saxon England, although finds of the boards are rare. Up to a further six distinct board-games may have been played in England; gaming-pieces have been found in high-status and more modest graves widely distributed across the country.[306] One of the most intriguing finds is that of a board-game incised onto the base of an Anglo-Saxon cross shaft (dated to between the seventh and tenth centuries); unfortunately it is not possible to establish whether the design was initially an integral part of the cross-base or whether – as might seem more plausible – it was added at a later date and in a secular context, when the base had become detached from the shaft of the cross.[307] A page in an twelfth-century Irish Gospel Book (Oxford, Corpus Christi College, MS 122, fo. 5v) shows a squared board with pieces set out for a game; above the picture is the title 'Alea evangelii (the game or playing board of the Gospel) which Dubinsi bishop of Bangor brought away from the king of the English, that is from the house of Adelstan king of the English.'[308] The church's attitude to board-games was predictably negative, although the best evidence comes from beyond

---

[304] Porter, 'Introduction', *ibid.*, pp. 1–15.

[305] Gregory of Tours, *Decem libri historiarum*, X. 16 (ed. B. Krusch and W. Levison, *MGH, SSRM* I. 1, p. 428).

[306] Susan M. Youngs, 'The gaming-pieces', in Rupert Bruce-Mitford, *The Sutton Hoo Ship-Burial*, III, part 2, ed. Angela Care Evans (London: British Museum Publications for the Trustees of the British Museum, 1983), pp. 853–74; the finds are mapped and listed at pp. 872–3. See also Martha Bayless, '*Alea tæfl* and related games: vocabulary and context', in Katherine O'Brien O'Keefe and Andy Orchard (eds.), *Latin Learning and English Lore: Studies in Anglo-Saxon Literature for Michael Lapidge*, 2 vols. (Toronto: University of Toronto Press, 2005), II, 9–27.

[307] M. A. Hall, 'A possible merels board incised on the pre-Conquest cross-base at Addingham, St Michael's church, Cumbria', *Transactions of the Cumberland and Westmorland Antiquarian and Archaeological Society*, 3rd ser., 1 (2001), 45–51.

[308] J. Armitage Robinson, *The Times of St Dunstan* (Oxford: Clarendon Press, 1923), pp. 70–1; the page of OCCC 122 is illustrated as a frontispiece to that volume. See also Claude Sterckk, 'Les jeux de damier celtiques', *Etudes celtiques* 13 (1973), 733–49, at pp. 743–5.

our period. In the so-called 'Canons of Edgar', an early-eleventh-century text attributed to Wulfstan, clergy were reminded 'a priest should be neither a hunter nor a hawker nor a player of games, but should occupy himself with his books as his office requires'.[309] One of the Vercelli homilies also warned against 'worthless speech, gaming and gatherings' (*idele spæca & tæflunga gebeorscipas*).[310] With the Poitiers example in mind we might be naïve to imagine that earlier generations of Anglo-Saxon religious were not aware of the possibilities for amusement offered by board-games.

As for the other aristocratic pursuits mentioned disapprovingly at the council of *Clofesho* in 747 and in Wulfstan's later strictures, we are on firmer ground in supposing these to have been pursued in some early minsters. There is plentiful evidence that religious owned horses and it may be imagined that young noble brothers not infrequently enjoyed riding, and racing, them.[311] Bede related a tale told by a cleric Herebald from John of Beverley's *familia*, who had been seriously injured one day when, against the bishop's orders, he had joined his companions in racing their horses along a flat piece of ground.[312] Boniface reported to Archbishop Cuthbert that his synod had legislated to prevent the Frankish servants of God from hunting, going about in woods with dogs, and keeping hawks and falcons,[313] and although these are not specifically mentioned in English church councils, there is every reason to think that English religious indulged in the same sports. King Æthelberht of Kent wrote to Boniface in Germany asking if he could procure him a pair of tame falcons capable of bringing down cranes; while we cannot infer from this that Boniface himself lived in a community that trained hunting birds, it is interesting that the Kentish king assumed he moved in circles in which he could easily procure such birds.[314] The missionary had, moreover, on a previous occasion sent a hawk and two falcons (with two shields and lances) to King Æthelbald of Mercia.[315] Alcuin accused the boys at Wearmouth and Jarrow of digging out the earths of foxes and hare-coursing,[316] and when advising Archbishop Eanbald of York to choose himself suitable companions, directed that these 'should not gallop over

---

[309] 'Canons of Edgar', §65 (*C&S* I, 334–5).
[310] Homily for Monday in Rogationtide, in Donald Scragg (ed.), *The Vercelli Homilies and Related Texts*, EETS 300 (London: Oxford University Press for the Early English Text Society, 1992), pp. 315–26, line 88. I owe this reference to Martha Bayless.
[311] For discussion of the ownership of horses by Frankish religious and clerics see F. Irsigler, 'On the aristocratic character of early Frankish society', in Timothy Reuter (ed. and trans.), *The Medieval Nobility: Studies on the Ruling Classes of France and Germany from the Sixth to the Twelfth Century* (Amsterdam and Oxford: North-Holland Publishing Co., 1979), pp. 103–36, at pp. 121–2.
[312] *HE* V. 6 (pp. 464–7).   [313] Boniface, *Ep.* 78 (p. 169).   [314] Boniface, *Ep.* 105 (p. 231).
[315] *Ep.* 69 (p. 142); McKitterick, *Anglo-Saxon Missionaries in Germany*, p. 19.   [316] Alcuin, *Ep.* 19 (p. 55).   243

fields after the fox, but ride with you singing psalms in harmony'.[317] That all these aristocratic pursuits were apparently followed by the members of minster communities indicates once again how difficult it can be to distinguish many aspects of the religious life from that of their secular noble counterparts.[318]

If we turn from group activities to consider more private forms of amusement, we find ourselves on rather less certain ground. Although the history of sexuality has in recent years attracted growing attention, this remains an opaque area of early medieval social activity and, despite the energetic efforts of some scholars to make this more accessible, it is extremely difficult to reconstruct patterns of sexual behaviour in this period, still less to say much that is meaningful about contemporary attitudes.[319] Ecclesiastical views may to some degree be observed through administrative and prescriptive texts, but since these deal with what should not be done they may best be seen as 'deviance-defining sources'; they reveal nothing of the responses of those at whom such prescriptions were directed.[320] That the cloister should have been sexless is, of course, self-evident. A central element of the renunciation of the self involved in the adoption of the religious life was the abjuring of sexual congress and embracing of chastity. Yet here, as elsewhere, ideal may have fallen some way behind reality.

As well as the chatter and vainglorious weaving to which Adomnan objected at Coldingham were 'other delights' he was too coy to mention; his visionary companion noted that the cells and beds of the men and women were not being put to proper use. Either the inmates were sunk in slothful slumber, or they were awake for the purposes of sin. Our imaginations are left to reflect on the likely consequences for virgins who wove 'elaborate garments with which to adorn themselves as if they were brides, so imperilling their virginity, or else to make friends with strange men'.[321] Other than this instance, few specific charges of immorality were levelled at individual religious men or women in the contemporary sources (there

---

[317] *Ibid.*, no. 114 (p. 168). In the tenth century the *Regularis concordia* directed that monks were not, when travelling, to celebrate the regular hours on horseback, but were to dismount and kneel to do so: proem, 11 (ed. Hallinger, p. 76).

[318] Wormald, 'Bede, "Beowulf"', pp. 54–6.

[319] Particularly significant have been Michel Foucault, *The History of Sexuality*, I, trans. Robert Hurley (New York: Vintage, 1980); John Boswell, *Christianity, Social Tolerance and Homosexuality: Gay People in Western Europe from the Beginning of the Christian Era to the Fourteenth Century* (Chicago: University of Chicago Press, 1980).

[320] Allen J. Frantzen, *Before the Closet: Same-Sex Love from Beowulf to Angels in America* (Chicago and London: University of Chicago Press, 1998), pp. 138–9.

[321] Bede, *HE* IV. 25 (pp. 424–7). Hollis, *Anglo-Saxon Women*, pp. 100–2.

is no Anglo-Saxon equivalent of the nun of Watton), but the tone of some of the more sweeping condemnations suggests that these were not entirely abstract criticisms. Bede castigated those who established minsters on their own estates, buying land on which they might freely devote themselves to lust and filling their congregations with the former members of minsters or any of their own followers willing to join them; 'with the unseemly companies of these persons they fill the minsters which they have built and – a very ugly and unheard-of spectacle – the very same men now are occupied with wives and the procreation of children, now rising from their beds perform with assiduous attention what should be done within the precincts of minsters'.[322] Boniface charged King Æthelbald and his followers with the violation of holy women and virgins and also lamented the moral laxity of Englishwomen who travelled abroad on pilgrimage.[323] Lull sent a fierce letter to an Abbess Switha in Germany threatening her with excommunication for having allowed two sisters in her community to travel into a distant region; while the sisters had clearly thereby imperilled their virginity it is not entirely clear that they had in fact done anything worse than travel in the company of some laymen.[324] At the legatine councils in 786, marriage with *ancillae Dei* was condemned as unrighteous.[325] Although here the crime was imputed to the men who contracted such marriages, the next chapter roundly condemned religious women who had illegitimate offspring and so polluted the virgin's habit, the garment of the Holy Mary, spouse of Christ.[326]

Having struggled to say much beyond the bland and platitudinous about attitudes to or the elicit practice of heterosexual relations within the early medieval cloister (or between cloistered women and lay men in the outside world), we might expect the question of homoeroticism to be yet further from our reach. According to David Porter, however, this is a misconception: 'for one growing up in the monastery, to be sexual must have meant to be homosexual, to state a patent truth, and not all manifestations of sexuality can have gone unshared'.[327] This seems to me to be far from patent truth, for it requires us to make unwarranted assumptions not just about

---

[322] Bede, *EpEcg* ch. 12 (ed. Plummer, p. 416; trans. Whitelock, *EHD*, no. 170).

[323] Boniface, *Epp.* 73, 78 (pp. 148, 169).

[324] Boniface, *Ep.* 128 (pp. 265–6); Christine Fell explored the meaning of this letter, from which the precise nature of the sisters' offence remains uncertain: 'Some implications of the Boniface correspondence', in Helen Damico and Alexandra Hennessey Olsen (eds.), *New Readings on Women in Old English Literature* (Bloomington: Indiana University Press, 1990), pp. 29–43, at pp. 36–7.

[325] Legatine synods, ch. 15 (ed. Dümmler, p. 25).   [326] *Ibid.*, ch. 16, p. 25.

[327] Porter, 'Introduction', in Gwara (ed.), *Anglo-Saxon Conversations*, p. 14, n. 29.

individual sexual desire but about its physical expression on behalf of a social group who have left no first-hand evidence of their erotic vocabulary or behaviour. Not only can we not speculate about the stimuli that might have aroused a pubescent brother, we cannot automatically assume that an enclosed, same-sex environment created homosexuals out of all oblates. Admittedly, there are several references to sexual activity between cloistered boys and between boys and adult religious in early medieval penitentials and a few also to lesbian activities (although general awareness of the possibilities of non-penetrative sex was no better in the early Middle Ages than in later periods).[328] The potential that certain situations might offer for older brothers to prey on young oblates concerned a number of monastic legislators from Pachomius onwards and led them to offer guidance to limit the opportunities for men (even the novice-master) to be alone with boys.[329] If we can assume that penitentials were used as practical handbooks by priests trying to enforce ecclesiastical discipline then these texts do suggest that homosexual activity was something with which they had to deal, but most of the references found within them are to homosexual activity outside the cloister. Although Theodore's Penitential contains no reference to homosexual acts by religious men or clerics, the Penitential attributed to Bede imposed a heavier penance on a religious who performed such acts than on a layman, and Egbert's Penitential made a number of references to clerical fornication one of which imposed the same penalty for intercourse with a professed woman as for fornicating *cum masculo* (with an additional penalty for one who perpetrated such abuse habitually).[330] Yet there is an enormous gulf between the proposition that some religious, unable to handle the non-fulfilment of persistent desire, chose to satisfy bodily urges with willing homosexual partners and the suggestion that all religious were gay. And it requires a still greater imaginative leap to accept that the atmosphere of the Anglo-Saxon cloister was 'homoerotically charged'.[331]

---

[328] Frantzen, *Before the Closet*, pp. 150–2; Nina Rulon-Miller, 'Sexual humor and fettered desire in Riddle 12', in Jonathan Wilcox (ed.), *Humor in Anglo-Saxon Literature* (Cambridge: D. S. Brewer, 2000), pp. 99–126, at p. 118.

[329] Frantzen, *Before the Closet*, pp. 159–61. See for example *Regularis concordia*, ch. 12 (ed. Hallinger, pp. 76–7), which directs that a monk should not on any excuse presume to take with him a young boy alone for any purpose.

[330] Bede's 'Penitential', 3. 19–20 (H&S III, 328); Egbert, Penitential, 5. 4 (H&S III. 421). For further examples see Frantzen, *Before the Closet*, pp. 153–63. A general introduction to penitentials and their use in the early medieval period is given by Allen J. Frantzen, *The Literature of Penance in Anglo-Saxon England* (New Brunswick, NJ: Rutgers University Press, 1983).

[331] Rulon-Miller, 'Sexual humor', p. 101.

Conclusion

No attempt has been made in this chapter to establish the shape or form of a 'typical' monastic day in the early Anglo-Saxon period, although, as one might have anticipated, we have seen that different monastic households organised their waking and sleeping hours in broadly similar fashion throughout our period. Hagiographers tended to use the same aspects of the monastic day with which to illustrate their subjects' performance of those ascetic and devotional feats considered to be typical of the holy, for they could more graphically depict the uniqueness of saintly behaviour if they located their subjects within an environment immediately familiar to their audience. How better to demonstrate the length and ardour of fasts and vigils than to place them within the context of the ordinary monastic liturgy, or beside the patterns of eating and sleeping adopted by more ordinary mortals? As we have seen, it is in matters relating to the liturgy, especially to the performance of the night-office, that we have most information and where we may most easily draw parallels between the practices current in different houses. In other spheres, particularly the educational, it has proved rather easier to detail exemplary behaviour within certain celebrated institutions (the specialist colleges and centres of excellence of their day) than it has been to define how the members of more ordinary minsters filled their days. The comparative paucity of references to the sorts of manual labour done by those without special skills or crafts implies that its performance was also of lesser interest to the hagiographer than were feats of learning or ascetic prowess, although its performance did, interestingly, excite much more comment as a *topos* when performed by solitaries.

While a group of the most excellent monastic houses sharing similar ideals and practices may now seem to stand out more clearly against a background of widespread mediocrity, this must to a large degree merely reflect the imbalance in the sources, which rarely touch on the activities of less exceptional houses other than when these fell short of the goals for which professed religious were deemed to strive. A house unable to supply an alumnus worthy of sanctity would not readily attract the attention of historians or hagiographers; but life in a minster that had housed saints would be depicted by these authors in such a way as to demonstrate how it paralleled the life-styles and habits of previous generations of the holy. Once we move beyond those establishments which outwardly conformed so well to monastic standards and attempt to define more closely the nature of other sorts of minster, the inexactitude of the allusions in the written sources,

247

coupled with the apparent ambiguity of the archaeological evidence, makes it extremely difficult to differentiate between religious and secular households.[332] Those religious who conformed most closely to the ideals promoted by writers such as Bede, Boniface, and Alcuin, and who regularly engaged in contemplative prayer, communal worship and the study of Latin writings would more easily have been distinguished from laymen of their class than would those who had taken the habit but not entirely abandoned their secular aristocratic pastimes. This may help to explain why it has always proved so hard to identify with any confidence the false minsters castigated by Bede in his letter to Ecgberht, but also why many commentators have concluded that life within an Anglo-Saxon minster was, for all classes of society, little removed from life within any noble household.[333] In the second part of this volume, we shall move outside the cloister walls and look at the roles played by minsters and their members within secular Anglo-Saxon society. First we shall consider the ways in which groups of minsters may have sought to link themselves together into associations of varying degrees of formality.

[332] Compare Edward James, 'Archaeology and the Merovingian monastery', in H. B. Clarke and Mary Brennan (eds.), *Columbanus and Merovingian Monasticism*, BAR, Internat. ser., 113 (Oxford: BAR, 1981), 33–55, at pp. 34–6.

[333] Schneider, 'Anglo-Saxon women', p. 73; Patrick Wormald, 'Bede, "Beowulf"', pp. 53–8; Campbell, 'Elements in the background'.

PART II

Without the walls

CHAPTER 6

Dependencies, affinities, clusters

No minster was an island, entire of itself. Every minster – to continue Donne's analogy – was a piece of the continent of Christendom, a part of the main. Early Anglo-Saxon monasticism cannot only be explored from within cloister walls: the minster provided the immediate (and private) context within which individuals could test their own spiritual ambitions, but each minster was also a component element of an institutional church. It was liable to be seen and treated as a useful resource by its diocesan bishop and provincial archbishop, to whose authority the community was, at least in some measure, subject. More immediately, the minster acted as a focus for the population dwelling in its locality. Many lay people of both sexes proved keen to share, if only vicariously, in the undoubted spiritual and material benefits of monastic living; their needs as well as the demands of the ecclesiastical authorities had a significant impact on the expression of monasticism in the first Christian centuries in England. Thus every minster's death (in the sense of the dissolution of any minster community and the return of its lands to secular status) diminished secular society as much as it damaged the church.

Aspirations to isolation and the monastic quest for economic self-sufficiency were, we have already observed, frequently compromised by the realities of temporal existence. Here, in the second half of this volume we will be exploring the permeation of that boundary between religious and secular cultures in early Anglo-Saxon England. Before we turn to look directly at the interactions of minster communities with their lay neighbours, I want first to investigate a rather different aspect of minsters' external affairs, namely the question of whether formal links connected discrete monastic institutions. Heads of some minsters clearly considered themselves to be part of wider religious federations or loosely organised monastic associations, although we may struggle to find the most appropriate language in which to describe such connections. Bishop Wilfrid's group of minsters has frequently been termed a monastic 'empire'; Stenton wrote about *Medeshamstede* and its 'colonies'; small congregations founded out of larger, more celebrated institutions are often called cells or daughter houses, for example Hackness, founded from Whitby, or Bradford-on-Avon, established by the sisters of Shaftesbury in the tenth century.[1] Can we say anything about the prevalence of such institutional groups, about how they were organised, and particularly about the leadership or centralised direction of such collectivities? Is the monastic federation (or affinity) an identifiable and regular feature of the early English religious landscape, or did special circumstances govern the creation of those we can identify? One might explore whether there were any discernible models for the creation of affinities of this kind. Further, we should ask whether specific characteristics distinguished the dependencies (or colonies) of a monastic confederation from contemporary minsters not formally linked to other institutions.

It is important to be clear what this discussion will not be talking about, namely the continuing contacts many (perhaps most) minsters maintained with their lay founders and benefactors. In the process of their foundation monastic communities usually acquired formal ties with and future responsibilities towards the donor or donors whose munificence supplied their original endowment, their families and heirs. Sometimes a donor would join the community he or she had created, either at the time of its first establishment or later in life. In either case the physical bond with the founder's kin would be strengthened, finding expression in the congregation's continuing prayerful commemoration of the family and the souls of its dead and – the minster must have hoped – in a reciprocal sense of continuing obligation on the part of the living kin.[2] Some of those links we have already explored; the incursions of the world into the cloister that their

---

[1] Simon Keynes, *The Councils of Clofesho* ([Leicester]: University of Leicester, Department of Adult Education, 1994), p. 35; Frank M. Stenton, '*Medeshamstede* and its colonies', in J. G. Edwards *et al.* (eds.), *Historical Essays in honour of James Tait* (Manchester: privately printed, 1933), pp. 313–26; reprinted in Doris M. Stenton (ed.), *Preparatory to Anglo-Saxon England* (Oxford: Clarendon Press, 1970), pp. 179–92; *HE* IV. 23 (pp. 412–15); *Charters of Shaftesbury*, ed. S. E. Kelly (1996), no. 29 (S 899).

[2] Catherine Cubitt, ''Monastic memory and identity in early Anglo-Saxon England', in William O. Frazer and Andrew Tyrrell (eds.), *Social Identity in Early Medieval Britain* (London and New York: Leicester University Press, 2000), pp. 252–76.

maintenance necessarily occasioned will be the subject of the next chapter. Here we will be concerned with the associations and networks of friendship that minsters made with one another.

Monastic friendships

Single houses were frequently associated with one another from their first foundation, as were the pair of houses at Chertsey and Barking set up by Eorcenwald, bishop of London, one for men and the other for women, or Bede's own abbey of Monkwearmouth and Jarrow, established by Benedict Biscop as two separate houses bound together by the spirit of peace and harmony and united by continuous friendship, goodwill and brotherly love.[3] As we have already seen, the same monastic ideals and thus, one assumes, significant similarities in the practice of daily life characterised such twinned minsters. Their focus was, however, predominantly introspective; these were sibling-houses within a small family lying in one locality, not the seeds from which a larger federation might grow. Some minsters are categorised by historians as 'cells' or 'daughter houses' of larger, more prominent establishments,[4] terms which had precise and readily comprehensible meanings in the high Middle Ages, when Benedictines, Cistercians and others ordered groups of houses in families whose hierarchies may be depicted in the form of family trees. In the early Anglo-Saxon church, matters were seldom so transparent, yet we might, continuing the familial imagery, expect to find close similarities between a dependent foundation and its parent abbey, particularly in its internal organisation, liturgical forms and probably also in its estate management. Even where direct connections did not inspire minsters' foundation, commemorative obligations (to living donors or to dead saints) linked other houses, possibly even to the extent of the sharing of common liturgical forms.[5]

At a less formal level, friendly and prayerful greetings passed regularly between monastic houses around the country, between abbots and their

---

[3] *HE* IV. 6 (pp. 354–5); *HA* ch. 7 (p. 370).

[4] The house described in Æthelwulf's poem *De abbatibus* has for instance often been called a 'daughter house' of Lindisfarne. Lindisfarne was termed the 'mother house' of Æthelwulf's minster by D. Ó Cróinín, 'Rath Melsigi, Willibrord, and the earliest Echternach manuscripts', *Peritia* 3 (1984), 17–49, at pp. 36–7. For the identification of this cell with Crayke see Michael Lapidge, 'Aediluulf and the School of York', in A. Lehner and W. Berschin (eds.), *Lateinische Kultur im VIII. Jahrhundert: Traube Gedenkschrift* (St Ottilien: EOS Verlag, 1990), pp. 161–78, at pp. 174–8.

[5] Catherine Cubitt, 'Universal and local saints in Anglo-Saxon England', in Alan Thacker and Richard Sharpe (eds.), *Local Saints and Local Churches in the Early Medieval West* (Oxford: Oxford University Press, 2002), pp. 423–53, at pp. 432–8.

diocesan and sometimes metropolitan bishops; similar expressions of good will went to religious houses elsewhere in Britain, in Ireland and on the continent, particularly to those in the German mission-fields.[6] Some such communication between houses was sustained through the exchange of amicable greetings by letter or in the person of visitors; other houses created formal confraternity agreements of mutual prayer.[7] Alcuin wrote to Æthelbald, abbot of Wearmouth and Jarrow, to renew a previous connection reminding the abbot that 'the holy fathers who preceded you once ordered my humble name to be written on your roll of blessing out of gratitude to me, unworthy though I am of your friendship, so that, wherever God's will took me, I might be one of you'.[8] The heads of three unnamed minsters made an agreement about mutual intercession with Coengils (probably abbot of Glastonbury),[9] an abbot Ingeld and priest Wietberht in the mid-eighth century, in a letter preserved with the Boniface correspondence.[10] Ælfwold, king of East Anglia, promised Boniface himself that after his departure for the German mission-field his name would be remembered in prayer in the East Anglian minsters and that the names of the dead would be communicated on both sides (by Boniface and by the East Anglian religious) so that they also could be commemorated.[11]

Intellectual connections between minsters singly and in groups can further be explored through the transmission of texts (including, of course, texts relating to the organisation of the religious life),[12] or the diffusion of artistic styles in manuscript-illumination, metalwork or sculpture.[13] Education offered another route both for the spread of ideas about monastic practice and the maintenance of personal connections between members of widely dispersed institutions. Whitby was famed in Hild's day for having trained a number of future bishops. Bosa and Wilfrid (II) both became

---

[6] Barbara Yorke, 'The Bonifacian mission and female religious in Wessex', *Early Medieval Europe* 7 (1998), 145–72; Rosamond McKitterick, *Anglo-Saxon Missionaries in Germany: Personal Connections and Local Influences* ([Leicester]: Department of Adult Education, University of Leicester, 1991); reprinted in her *The Frankish Kings and Culture in the Early Middle Ages* (Aldershot: Variorum, 1995), no. I.

[7] J. Hirst, 'On guildship in Anglo-Saxon monasteries', *AJ* 49 (1892), 107–19.

[8] Alcuin, *Ep.* 67 (ed. Dümmler, p. 110; trans. Allott, *Alcuin*, p. 33, no. 24).

[9] Sarah Foot, 'Glastonbury's early abbots', in Lesley Abrams and James P. Carley (eds.), *The Archaeology and History of Glastonbury Abbey* (Woodbridge: Boydell Press, 1991), pp. 163–89, at pp. 170–1.

[10] Boniface, *Ep.* 55 (pp. 97–8). [11] Boniface, *Ep.* 81 (p. 181).

[12] Hild, for example, established a rule of life in her new minster at Whitby on the model of that she had previously followed at Hartlepool: *HE* IV. 23 (pp. 408–9). The regulation of the monastic life and the sharing of rules between houses was explored at length in chapter 2.

[13] Rosemary Cramp, 'The artistic influence of Lindisfarne within Northumbria', in Gerald Bonner *et al.* (eds.), *St Cuthbert, his Cult and his Community* (Woodbridge: Boydell Press, 1989), pp. 213–28; Jane Hawkes, 'Anglo-Saxon sculpture: questions of context', in Jane Hawkes and Susan Mills (eds.), *Northumbria's Golden Age* (Stroud: Sutton, 1999), pp. 204–15.

bishops of York; John was bishop of Hexham and a certain Ætla took the see of Dorchester.[14] Tatfrith, a brother at Whitby, was chosen bishop of the Hwicce although he died before being consecrated; Oftfor, bishop of the Hwicce (*c.* 691–9?) had studied both with Hild and at Theodore's school in Canterbury.[15] That school trained a number of future luminaries, both in the English church and the German mission-fields.[16] One house frequently supplied a new abbot or abbess for another and there are several instances of Anglo-Saxon religious who moved from minster to minster for various reasons. Cuthbert was expelled from Ripon by Alhfrith and went from there to Melrose before he joined the community at Lindisfarne; it was, however, Boniface's own decision to leave his first minster, probably Exeter, to go to Nursling.[17] We might reasonably expect both to have shared their earlier experiences of monastic life with their new companions.

In investigating the existence of confederations or affinities of monastic houses it is not, however, sufficient to demonstrate the making or sustaining of contact between separate houses. Many of the examples just discussed might best be understood as separate instances of *amicitia* or *confraternitas*, but some of those we have already mentioned seem to have been discrete institutions linked by more formal arrangements. If we were to demonstrate that such associations did connect independent minsters, we would need to show that these went further than friendly words and mutual prayer and we might want to consider whether they continued at least in memory if not in practice over a substantial period, beyond the lifetime of the individuals responsible for making the initial connection. Further, we need to explore whether there was a single type of 'monastic association' or whether we can identify more than one model on which groups of connected houses were organised. At first sight, a cell dependent on a parent abbey would seem to

---

[14] *HE* IV. 23 (pp. 408–9 and n. 2). Peter Hunter Blair, 'Whitby as a centre of learning in the seventh century', in Michael Lapidge and Helmut Gneuss (eds.), *Learning and Literature in Anglo-Saxon England* (Cambridge: Cambridge University Press, 1985), pp. 3–32, at p. 25.

[15] *HE* IV. 23 (pp. 408–9); Patrick Sims-Williams, *Religion and Literature in the West of England, 600–800* (Cambridge: Cambridge University Press, 1990), pp. 102–3. It is possible that a further direct link between Whitby practices and a Mercian minster might be shown if Oftfor had encouraged Ælfflæd to found the minster at Fladbury in Worcestershire. Ælfflæd was a Northumbrian princess, daughter of Oswiu and Eanflæd and sister of Osthryth, who married the Mercian king, Æthelred; she spent her early years in the minster at Whitby and her putative connection with Fladbury depends on the interpretation of the place-name Fladbury (*Fledanburg*) as 'Flæde's burg or minster'. If Ælfflæd did come south to Mercia with her sister, she returned later to Northumbria, for we know that she helped her mother to govern the abbey of Whitby after Hild's death: *HE* IV. 26 (pp. 428–31); Sims-Williams, *Religion and Literature*, pp. 92–3, 102.

[16] Michael Lapidge, 'The school of Theodore and Hadrian', *Anglo-Saxon England* 15 (1986), 45–72.

[17] Anon., *VSCuth.* II. 2, 3–4; III. 1 (pp. 76–83, 94–5); *VSB* ch. 2 (ed. Rau, p. 466).

belong to a rather different sort of relationship from an affinity of several institutions spread over a wide geographical area.

One of the difficulties facing us in this task is that while historians have often been ready to postulate the existence of monastic 'federations' there are no agreed criteria by which to determine where mere *amicitia* became formal association. As well as the example of the Wilfridian houses and the celebrated instance of the colonies of the minster at *Medesham-stede*, there are other minsters in different parts of England which various modern commentators have depicted as constituent members of more or less tightly organised connections. Yet no one has yet analysed the formal arrangements governing the making and running of such associations. The lack of clarity over the working of confederations can lead to confusion as is amply demonstrated in Patricia Coulstock's book on Wimborne minster.

The abbess of Wimborne might have been responsible not only for the religious at Wimborne but for the supervision of a group of nunneries within the diocese of Sherborne or even the kingdom of Wessex. The evidence has yet to be discovered, even the identification of the nunneries, but it is not without significance that the Wessex monk Boniface sent to Wimborne for Lioba, not only to govern Taufbishofsheim, but to be responsible for the administration of the central German nunneries within his mission.[18]

Coulstock has cited a number of examples from the seventh and eighth centuries of what she has taken to be houses founded by the members of one royal or noble family and grouped under the overall control of one minster, under the abbacy of a bishop or a member of the founding family. Her list includes Frome and Bradford-on-Avon, which she has argued were the responsibility of Aldhelm, bishop of Sherborne and abbot of Malmesbury; the 'six' Mercian minsters under Wilfrid's charge; the Northumbrian abbot Forthred's three houses; and the Midland houses for religious women including Weedon, Hanbury and Threekingham, which were supposedly under the control of the Mercian princess Werburg.[19] The evidence that might support the existence of these mother houses with dependencies is not of equal status, and each would need careful consideration on its own merits. Such a list does, however, raise broader questions similar to those articulated above. Clarification of the sorts of organisational relationships that can be shown to have existed between houses would

---

[18] Patricia Coulstock, *The Collegiate Church of Wimborne Minster* (Woodbridge: Boydell Press, 1993), p. 87.
[19] *Ibid.*

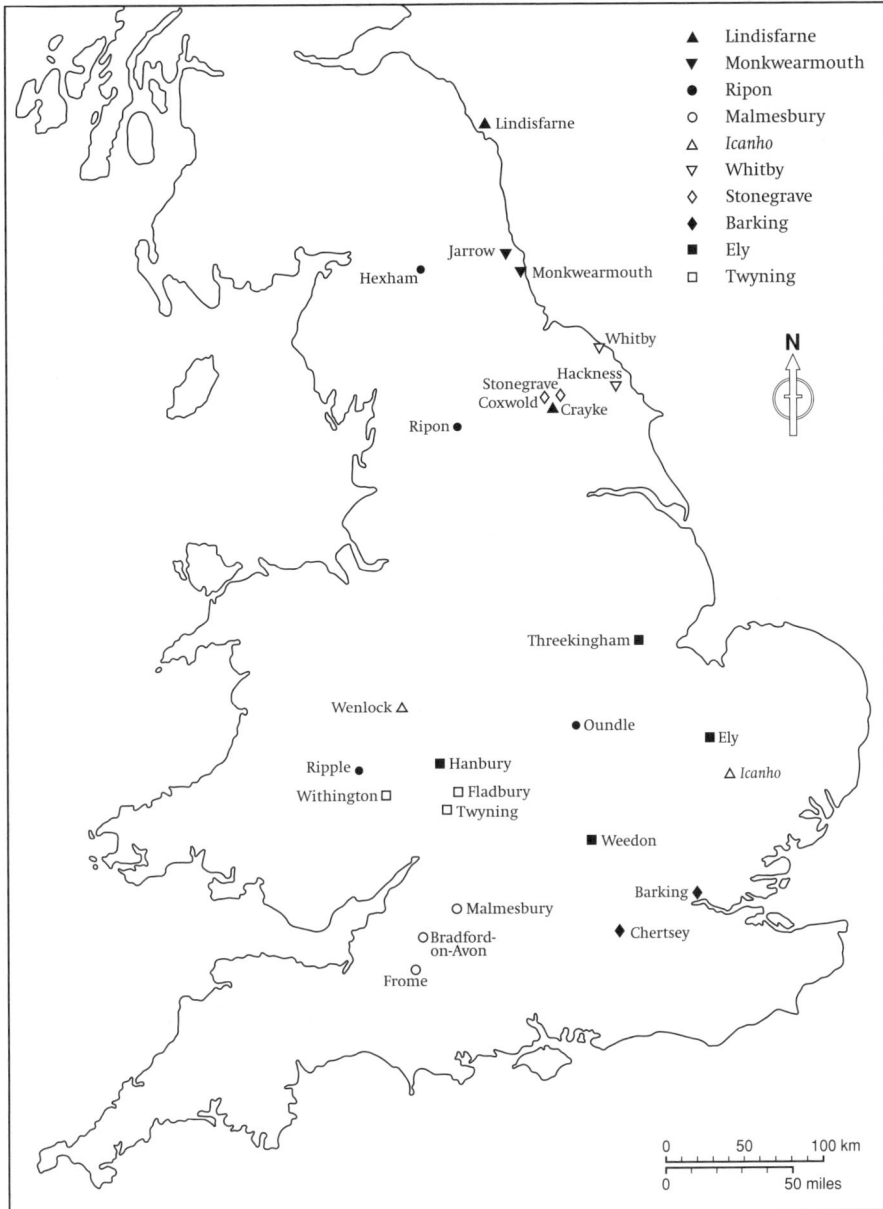

FIGURE 11: Map of monastic affinities (excluding *Medeshamstede* and its colonies).

provide a better framework against which statements such as Coulstock's could be measured.

The Wilfridian affinity

When Bishop Wilfrid was displaced from the see of York in 678 on its division into three new bishoprics, his biographer, Stephen, blamed Ecgfrith's queen, Iurminburg, for having instigated Wilfrid's deposition by setting her husband's mind against the saint and inciting him to condemn Wilfrid unjustly to Archbishop Theodore. Stephen attributed the queen's enmity to her jealousy of Wilfrid's temporal glories: 'his riches, the number of his minsters (*coenobiorum multitudinem*), the greatness of his buildings, and his countless army of followers arrayed in royal vestments and arms'.[20] At the heart of Wilfrid's personal dominion lay his own religious houses; it was thus peculiarly humiliating that all three of the bishops newly-appointed came from houses independent of the Wilfridian axis. Stephen reported, 'In the absence of our bishop, Theodore consecrated, by himself over parts of Wilfrid's own diocese, irregularly and contrary to all precedent, three bishops who had been found elsewhere and were not subjects of Wilfrid's *parochia*.'[21] The nature of Wilfrid's *parochia*, a monastic empire, extending north and south of the Humber, raises almost as many problems as it helps to solve, but because his confederation of minsters is one of the best attested and most frequently cited instances of the association of independent houses, it offers an appropriate place at which to begin.

Wilfrid was, however, far from typical of the Anglo-Saxon bishops of his day: in the manner in which he treated his monastic foundations he may have stood as far apart from his contemporaries as he demonstrably did in other spheres of action. It is notable that Bede's account of Wilfrid's life, while referring to separate houses he established, did not hint at any closer connection between those establishments than the fact that they shared a common founder.[22] Even defining the extent of Wilfrid's monastic connection is not simple. At its core lay the two minsters at Ripon and

---

[20] *VSW* ch. 24 (pp. 48–9).

[21] *Ibid.*: 'Nam tres episcopos aliunde inventos et non de subiectis illius parrochiae in absentia pontificis nostri in sua propria loca episcopatus sui nouiter inordinate solus ordinauit.' Wilfrid's involvement in Northumbrian politics has been much discussed: see D. P. Kirby, 'Northumbria in the time of Wilfrid', in D. P. Kirby (ed.), *Saint Wilfrid at Hexham* (Newcastle upon Tyne: Oriel Press, 1974), pp. 1–34, at pp. 23–9; D. H. Farmer, 'Saint Wilfrid', in Kirby (ed.), *St Wilfrid at Hexham*, pp. 35–59, at pp. 47–50; Walter Goffart, *The Narrators of Barbarian History (AD 550–800): Jordanes, Gregory of Tours, Bede, and Paul the Deacon* (Princeton, NJ: Princeton University Press, 1988), pp. 288–9.

[22] *HE* V. 19 (pp. 520–9).

Hexham – *duo optima coenobia*[23] – founded by the saint early in his career and always treated by him as the most precious of his possessions.[24] In his disputes with the kings of Northumbria this was the issue over which Wilfrid was least willing to capitulate: concessions might be made in other areas but never over his control of these minsters.[25] From the arrangements he made towards the end of his life it would seem that Wilfrid always considered himself Ripon's abbot, for he appointed the priest Tatberht as head (*praepositus*) over the minster to rule with him during his own lifetime and alone only after the bishop's death.[26] Control of the headship of his minster at Hexham was more problematical after 678, when it became a bishop's seat and passed from Wilfrid's own control. The saint still considered it his to bequeath, however, for he left it after his death to the priest Acca, himself later bishop of Hexham.[27] Even when absent, Wilfrid retained a degree of direct control over both the internal organisation of these two minsters and their economic status. One of the ways in which Wilfrid sought to protect his monastic empire was in the acquisition of privileges for his houses (something to which we shall return shortly); here Ripon and Hexham were again treated as a distinct pair in being protected together by one privilege.[28]

Stephen named just one other Wilfridian minster, the Mercian house at Oundle (Northamptonshire) dedicated to St Andrew, where the saint spent his last hours.[29] Wilfrid's connection with the Mercian church seems to have begun when he assumed some episcopal responsibilities in the kingdom at the request of King Wulfhere and founded various minsters, perhaps

---

[23] *VSW* ch. 60 (pp. 132–3).

[24] Wilfrid was first given the minster at Ripon with thirty hides of land by King Alhfrith, perhaps *c.* 660: *VSW* ch. 8 (pp. 16–17). The church of Ripon Wilfrid had built during the 670s, before his expulsion by King Ecgfrith and Archbishop Theodore, and he was given an estate at Hexham by Queen Æthelthryth during the same period: *ibid.*, chs. 17 and 22 (pp. 36–7 and 44–7).

[25] Michael Roper, 'Wilfrid's landholdings in Northumbria', in Kirby (ed.), *Saint Wilfrid at Hexham*, pp. 61–79, at p. 63; Catherine Cubitt, 'Wilfrid's usurping bishops: episcopal elections in Anglo-Saxon England, *c.* 600–*c.* 800', *Northern History* 25 (1989), 18–38, at pp. 37–8.

[26] *VSW*, ch. 63 (pp. 136–9); Wilfrid was appointed abbot of Ripon when he was given possession of the minster by Alhfrith, and before his ordination to the priesthood: chs. 8–9 (pp. 16–19). Bede also described Wilfrid's acquisition of Ripon (*HE* V.19, pp. 520–3), explaining that the site of the minster had originally been offered by Alhfrith to some Irish monks but that they had abandoned it rather than agree to follow Roman rites.

[27] *VSW* ch. 65.

[28] *VSW* ch. 51 (pp. 104–7); see Patrick Wormald, 'Bede and Benedict Biscop', in Gerald Bonner (ed.), *Famulus Christi* (London: SPCK, 1976), pp. 141–69, at pp. 147–8; Ian N. Wood, 'Ripon, Francia and the Franks casket in the early Middle Ages', *Northern History* 26 (1990), 1–19, at p. 18.

[29] *VSW* chs. 65 and 67 (pp. 140–1 and 144–5); *HE* V. 19 (pp. 516–17 and 528–9). According to Bede, Oundle's abbot was called Cuthbald (pp. 528–9). Cuthbald has been identified as Seaxwulf's successor at *Medeshamstede*; on this basis the twelfth-century Peterborough historian Hugh Candidus claimed that Oundle was one of *Medeshamstede*'s colonies: see further below, p. 275.

including Oundle.[30] In 680, while in exile from Northumbria, he took refuge with Berhtwald, nephew of the Mercian king Æthelred, who seems to have had charge of a Mercian dependency in northern Wessex. Berhtwald gave Wilfrid an estate from his own lands, on which Wilfrid founded a little minster (*monasteriolum*) which – Stephen reported – his *monachi* possess 'to this day'.[31] Although Wilfrid himself was not able to stay there long, being driven out to Wessex and on into Sussex, his brothers remained behind in the unnamed minster, not following their abbot into exile.[32] Ripple in Worcestershire may have been another Wilfridian minster. A charter dated 680 and surviving in the early eleventh-century Worcester cartulary records the grant of *Rippel* by Oshere, king of the Hwicce, to Frithowald, *monacho Uuinfridi episcopi*, made on condition that Frithowald maintain the monastic life at Ripple. There had previously been a bishop Wynfrith at Lichfield, but he had been removed from office some years earlier by Archbishop Theodore and was living in the minster at Barrow; it seems more than likely, as Sims-Williams has proposed, that in copying the charter Wilfrid's and Wynfrith's names have been confused.[33] According to Stephen, Wilfrid's name had been confused in his own lifetime with that of Bishop Wynfrith, by the error of a single syllable.[34] If so, Frithowald might be seen as one of Wilfrid's brethren and his minster at Ripple conceivably identified with the *Rippel* included in the list of royal estates owned by Wilfrid and read out in the dedication of the church at Ripon.[35] Beyond these examples, it is impossible either to identify or even number the others of Wilfrid's houses although there would seem to have been quite a number in Mercia by the end of his life.[36] He may well have had others in the north also, but this, too, remains uncertain.[37]

---

[30] *VSW* ch. 14 (p. 30); Farmer, 'Saint Wilfrid', p. 52; Keynes, *The Councils of Clofesho*, p. 34, n. 145; Nick Higham, 'Bishop Wilfrid in southern England: a review of his political objectives', *Studien zur Sachsenforschung* 13 (1999), 207–17, at pp. 211–12.

[31] *VSW* ch. 40 (pp. 80–1).

[32] Sims-Williams, *Religion*, pp. 104–5; perhaps, Sims-Williams suggested, it was this that led Aldhelm to write to Wilfrid's brethren urging them to follow their abbot into exile: see further below.

[33] *HE* IV. 3 and 6 (pp. 346–7 and 354–5); Sims-Williams, *Religion*, p. 105.   [34] *VSW* ch. 25 (pp. 50–1).

[35] *VSW* ch. 17 (pp. 36–7); this suggestion was made by Sims-Williams: *Religion*, p. 105. Since Wilfrid dedicated the church at Ripon before he was expelled from Northumbria in 678 by Ecgfrith, the identification of the *Rippel* granted by Oshere in 680 with the *Rippel* in Stephen's list would depend on that being not a report of the precise list of place-names articulated by Wilfrid on the day of the church's dedication, but a summary list of places the bishop had owned, compiled after the event.

[36] Keynes, *The Councils of Clofesho*, p. 34. Patricia Coulstock has suggested that Wilfrid founded six minsters in Mercia during his second exile from Northumbria (692–703): *The Collegiate Church*, p. 87. Wilfrid regained his minster at Ripon in 703, but his episcopal office only in 706.

[37] Both Stephen and Bede explained that King Alhfrith had given Wilfrid an estate of ten hides at a place called Stamford (*Aetstanforda*) before making him the grant of Ripon, but neither suggested that this place was a minster: *VSW* ch. 8 (pp. 16–17); *HE* V. 19 (pp. 520–1).

What can be said about Wilfrid's monastic connection is that it included houses in both Northumbria and Mercia; indeed its geographical extent may have been one of its most distinctive features. Stephen described how, when King Ecgfrith was at the height of his power and his earthly realm was extending both north and south, at the same time Wilfrid's 'ecclesiastical kingdom' (*regnum ecclesiarum*) was increasing both to the south among the Saxons (viz. the people of Mercia) and to the north among the British, the Picts and the Scots.[38] Such was Wilfrid's success in advancing the church's interests and so impressive was the example of pious devotion he presented to others that 'almost all the abbots and abbesses of the minsters dedicated their substance to him by vow, either keeping it themselves in his name, or intending him to be their heir after their death'.[39] Affinity with the bishop was patently considered advantageous by religious in institutions other than those he himself had founded, at least at this stage in Wilfrid's career. That Wilfrid retained a degree of influence, even authority over his Mercian houses after his restoration in Northumbria in 706 is indicated by his continuing involvement in their affairs. On the occasion of what turned out to be Wilfrid's final meeting with his *familia* at Ripon two of 'his' Mercian abbots (*duo abbates nostri*) were also present, sent by Ceolred, king of Mercia. These men, Tibba and Eabba, persuaded the bishop to agree to travel to meet with the Mercian king 'for the sake of the position of our minsters' in Ceolred's kingdom;[40] Wilfrid thus went with them from Northumbria 'to the southern lands where he found all his abbots rejoicing at his coming'.[41]

Wilfrid's Life gives the strong impression that, although geographically dispersed, the saint's community was spiritually and emotionally close and that the bond they felt was to their bishop (and perhaps hence to other houses in his affinity, although this is less clear). Stephen consistently described the bishop's own followers in such a manner as to imply that they were seen, at least within Wilfrid's own circle, as a coherent, identifiable body of religious, distinct from the congregations of other Mercian or Northumbrian religious houses. To outsiders Wilfrid's brethren also appeared as a discrete group. Writing to the abbots of his minsters (perhaps in 678), Aldhelm lamented the bishop's fate in being exiled to a 'transmarine country', reminding the abbots how tenderly Wilfrid had nourished and educated them and of their consequent obligation to support him in his difficulties.[42] The personal clerical retinue that travelled with the bishop and was exiled with him (among whose company his biographer was apparently himself numbered from about 703 onwards)[43] is to be distinguished from Wilfrid's other brothers, the inhabitants of the minsters he had founded and supported. His immediate companions the bishop also remembered before his death; although he gave them neither lands nor estates he had a portion of his treasure divided between them for their future material support.[44]

Beyond the personal ties linking the members of these communities with Bishop Wilfrid, material prosperity seems both to have marked out the Wilfridian houses and to have bound them to their patron. The account given by Stephen of the dispositions made by Wilfrid in the last year and a half of his life show clearly that the bishop was at least as preoccupied with ensuring that his minsters were adequately provided for financially as that they were all governed suitably. When in old age the bishop was taken ill while travelling to Hexham, his *familia* was apparently filled with dismay; they prayed urgently that the Lord 'would grant him an extension of life, at any rate so that he could speak to them, and dispose of his minsters and divide his possessions and not leave us as it were orphans, without any abbots'. As reports of his illness spread, all his abbots from their minsters and his anchorites came hastening by day and night to reach him while he was still alive, and so it happened that 'He arranged the lives of all of us in various places according to his desire, under the superiors chosen by himself, and shared his substance . . . between God and men according to his judgement.'[45] Most attention was given in the Life to the precise provisions made for Wilfrid's particular minsters of Ripon and Hexham, the nomination of abbots to succeed the saint and the allocation of a quarter of Wilfrid's accumulated treasure so that these two abbeys 'may be able to purchase the friendship of kings and bishops'.[46] Yet his other minsters were not forgotten; on his final visit to Mercia Wilfrid reiterated his testamentary arrangements in detail to certain of his abbots 'and for each of them in due proportion he either increased the livelihood of their brethren by gifts of land, or rejoiced their hearts with money, as though, endowed with the

---

[42] Aldhelm, *Ep.* 12, to the abbots of Wilfrid (ed. Ehwald, pp. 500–2; trans. Lapidge and Herren, *Aldhelm*, pp. 168–70). Lapidge and Herren have discussed this excerpt from a longer letter preserved only by William of Malmesbury and its probable date, *ibid.*, pp. 150–1. It was also discussed above, p. 71, n. 162.

[43] *VSW* ch. 49 (pp. 100–1): 'we and those who participated with us . . .' ('nos . . . et eos, qui nobiscum participarent . . .).

[44] *VSW* ch. 63 (pp. 136–7).   [45] *VSW* ch. 62 (pp. 134–5).   [46] *VSW* ch. 63 (pp. 136–7).

spirit of prophecy, he were sharing his inheritance among his heirs before his death'.[47]

Bishop Wilfrid can thus be seen to have retained an interest in an indeterminate number of houses lying both north and south of the Humber to the end of his career. He was not himself the direct head of most of these institutions (some were governed by abbots, others by abbesses) yet he retained a nominal headship over all his minsters to the extent that their leaders turned to him for spiritual succour and guidance over the management of their worldly affairs. Indeed Stephen's account of the Mercian minsters indicates that by making their earthly substance over to Wilfrid they were consigning more than nominal authority to him.[48] Similarly, the bishop clearly expected to exert some influence over the way of life observed within his houses, although whether all his minsters followed the same rule of life is unclear. Wilfrid himself was credited by his hagiographer with having introduced the Rule of St Benedict into England,[49] which implies at the very least that the bishop might have taken a specific interest in the manner of the communal life observed within his own institutions. In a period in which no single rule was prescribed for general observance among the English churches it would have been unusual to find a body of geographically dispersed minsters adhering to a single rule rather than each devising their own customs according to local taste and convenience, but there were precedents outside England for such an affinity or confederation namely among the Columbanian monasteries of Francia, whose model was certainly known to Wilfrid by direct experience.[50]

Beyond Wilfrid's death his houses apparently continued at least for a time to see themselves as part of a wider connection, albeit one now linked by their commemoration of Wilfrid's memory as a saint.[51] Our difficulty lies in determining how distinctive these bonds were. In the broad context of the territorial expansion of Wilfrid's sphere of episcopal authority Stephen referred to the saint's *regnum ecclesiarum*, a term which was almost certainly chosen to parallel Ecgfrith's earthly realm whose bounds Wilfrid's spiritual one followed.[52] Although Stephen need have intended to denote

---

[47] *VSW* ch. 65 (pp. 140–1).

[48] *VSW* ch. 21 (pp. 44–5); Eric John, 'The social and political problems of the early English church', in Joan Thirsk (ed.) *Land, Church, and People: Essays presented to Professor H. P. R. Finberg* (Reading: British Agricultural History Society, 1970), pp. 39–63, at p. 60.

[49] *VSW* chs. 46–7 (pp. 93–9); above, pp. 50–4.

[50] Northumbrian power south of the Humber would seem to have been at a peak between 675 and 679, to judge by the account in Stephen's Life of Wilfrid. See further below.

[51] *VSW* chs. 65–8 (pp. 140–9).   [52] *VSW* ch. 21 (pp. 42–3).

nothing more than an expanding diocese, the most interesting feature about Wilfrid's 'empire' (and that which caused the greatest offence to his enemies) was that it transcended contemporary political boundaries, comprising as it did houses on both sides of the Humber. It was in order to break up this politically dangerous supra-regional alliance that Ecgfrith strove so hard to deprive Wilfrid of land and power. It can hardly have been coincidental, as Eric John has noted, that the moment at which this happened – in 678 – Northumbrian–Mercian relations were at breaking point, and the dissolution of Wilfrid's connection, supported as it was by Ecgfrith's Mercian rival, was an important object of Northumbrian royal policy.[53] Similarly, the Northumbrian *Ouestræfelda* synod of 703, against whose decisions Wilfrid made his last appeal to Rome, tried to force Wilfrid to surrender by force to Archbishop Berhtwald 'whatever he had gained in Mercia under King Æthelred', so that the archbishop might 'give it to whom he wished', in other words presumably appoint new abbots and abbesses in place of Wilfrid's nominees.[54] Wilfrid's appeals to Rome may have been driven primarily by his desire to maintain the integrity of his monastic connection, rather than to argue against the division of his diocese.[55]

Identifying this distinct group of minsters associated with Bishop Wilfrid is much more straightforward than is the task of defining the affinity's precise nature, a matter not helped by the vagueness of the language with which Stephen described it. When he spoke of Wilfrid's *regnum ecclesiarum*, Stephen was seemingly referring to the entire realm of the bishop's influence, not merely to 'his' monastic houses. He may, however, have used the term *parochia* to serve on one occasion as a collective noun. Recording the names for the new bishops among whom Wilfrid's former dominion was divided – Bosa from Whitby, Eata from Lindisfarne and Eadhæd who had been Oswiu's priest – Stephen observed that all three of them came from outside Wilfrid's *parochia*.[56] Colgrave, as editor of Wilfrid's Life, took *parochia* to mean diocese; these were men from beyond Wilfrid's episcopal realm.[57] Eric John suggested, however, that we should understand *parochia* in the Irish sense of a monastic connection, an idea for which Catherine Cubitt has recently offered some support.[58] It is worth looking a little further at the possible models for connections of this sort, bearing in mind that the

---

[53] John, 'Social and political problems', p. 51.
[54] *VSW* ch. 47 (pp. 96–7); John, 'Social and political problems', p. 51.
[55] Eric John, *Reassessing Anglo-Saxon England* (Manchester: Manchester University Press, 1996), p. 35.
[56] *VSW* ch. 24 (pp. 48–9).   [57] Colgrave, *The Life of Wilfrid*, p. 168.
[58] John, 'Social and political problems', p. 50, n. 3, p. 60, n. 3; Cubitt, 'Wilfrid's "usurping bishops"', p. 23 and n. 20. For a contrary view see Hanna Vollrath, *Die Synoden Englands bis 1066* (Paderborn:

time Wilfrid spent away from Britain may have proved rather more influential here than were his early experiences in this country.[59]

Irish and Frankish models

One of the characteristics of Irish church organisation used to be thought to be the grouping of monastic churches into non-territorial units of jurisdiction, confederations or *paruchiae*, under the headship of their founder and his heirs. The classic examples of such federations were the *paruchia Patricii* dependent on Armagh (the instance from which the term itself was borrowed) and the foundations made by St Columba on both sides of the Irish Sea and united under his headship in Iona.[60] This latter arrangement appears analogous to one of secular overlordship, particularly in this case Uí Néill overlordship.[61] Richard Sharpe's work has now challenged many aspects of the conventional model of the Irish monastic church. He has argued that the family of Iona is appropriately to be termed a monastic confederation, since it embraced the great monasteries of Iona, Durrow and Derry, which were together headed by a priest-abbot under arrangements that survived in some form from the sixth until the twelfth century.[62] The monasteries within the federation were subject to Iona and its abbot, who had the power to appoint heads (*praepositi*) to rule the dependent houses.[63] There is, however, no reason to suppose that Iona's was the standard pattern of ecclesiastical organisation in the seventh century. Indeed, Bede implied as much in his description of the rulership of Iona by a priest-abbot, stating explicitly that such an arrangement was not usual, but rather *ordo inusitatus*.[64]

Schöningh, 1985), p. 79, n. 157. For discussion of Irish *paruchiae* now see also Thomas Charles-Edwards, *Early Christian Ireland* (Cambridge: Cambridge University Press, 2000), pp. 245 and 250–59.

[59] Higham, 'Bishop Wilfrid', p. 210.

[60] Richard Sharpe, 'Some problems concerning the organisation of the church in early medieval Ireland', *Peritia*, 3 (1984), 230–70, at pp. 239–47, and *idem*, 'Armagh and Rome in the seventh century', in Próinséas Ní Chatháin and Michael Richter (eds.), *Irland und Europa: die Kirche im Frühmittelalter* (Stuttgart: Klett-Cotta, 1984), pp. 58–72, at pp. 61–2; Charles-Edwards, *Early Christian Ireland*, p. 251. See also Colmán Etchingham, *Church Organisation in Ireland AD 650–1000* (Maynooth: Laigin Publications, 1999), especially in this context pp. 126–30.

[61] Máire Herbert, *Iona, Kells, and Derry: The History and Hagiography of the Monastic Familia of Columba* (Oxford: Clarendon Press, 1988), p. 34. See also Kathleen Hughes, *The Church in Early Irish Society* (London: Methuen, 1966), pp. 65–78.

[62] Sharpe, 'Some problems', pp. 244–5.   [63] Charles-Edwards, *Early Christian Ireland*, p. 256.

[64] *HE* III. 4 (pp. 224–5); see Plummer, *Baedae opera*, II. 133–4; Wallace-Hadrill, *Commentary*, pp. 93–4; addenda, p. 230. Donald Bullough took the exceptionality remarked by Bede to have related to Iona's assumption of *principatus* (authority) over all the minsters established by Columba's disciples in Britain and Ireland: 'Missions to the English and Picts and their heritage (to *c.* 800)', in Heinz Löwe (ed.), *Die Iren und Europa im früheren Mittelalter* (Stuttgart: Klett-Cotta, 1982), pp. 80–98, at p. 90 and n. 33.

The Ionan model needs to be distinguished from the *paruchiae* which can be seen to have grown up from the seventh century onwards, which, Sharpe has argued, were not monastic in the sense of families of contemplatives, but were rather collegiate or communal families concerned with the control of temporal possessions, membership of a *paruchia* meaning the owing of some kind of *census* or rent to the abbot of the controlling church.[65] This argument about Irish ecclesiastical structures is important for our purposes, for Sharpe has stressed the territorial focus of native church organisation, each territory having a mother church (equivalent to an English minster) as well as a number of lesser local churches, possibly served by one priest, or one priest taking charge of three or four such places, but the four-tier organizational superstructure differing from the English pattern.[66] Thomas Charles-Edwards has also commented on the sorts of economic factors that might have stimulated the growth of Irish *paruchiae*, notably 'the wish to defend oneself from the tentacles of a powerful ecclesiastical neighbour, by seeking the patronage of [a] more distant church', an arrangement that might have involved no change in the economic position of the newly subject church 'beyond some, possibly token, tribute', but could have led in some cases to 'a genuine accumulation of economic resources'.[67] While some federations, he has suggested, may have been only defensive alliances designed to preserve economic independence, lordship over distant churches and their lands might have conferred considerable political power.[68] On this reading, Irish *paruchiae* are to be understood as economic federations concerned with the control of temporal possessions; this superstructure of non-territorial association is thus apparently different from the sorts of arrangement found in England.

Although Eric John's suggestion, that Wilfrid's monastic connection was derived from an Irish model, was based on an understanding of the nature of the Irish monastic *paruchia* that Sharpe and Charles-Edwards have now shown to be invalid, John's point would still stand. Wilfrid's minsters were not members of one monastic family governed by *praepositi* all following a single rule of life and answerable to a single abbot at a parent house. Yet Wilfrid's monastic empire might best be categorised as a non-territorial

[65] Sharpe, 'Some problems', pp. 246–7 and 257–8; *idem*, 'Churches and communities in early medieval Ireland', in John Blair and Richard Sharpe (eds.), *Pastoral Care Before the Parish* (Leicester, London and New York: Leicester University Press, 1992), pp. 81–109, at pp. 107–9.
[66] Sharpe, 'Churches and communities', pp. 108–9.
[67] Thomas Charles-Edwards, 'The church and settlement', in Ní Chatháin and Richter (eds.), *Irland und Europa*, pp. 167–75, at p. 168.
[68] *Ibid.*, p. 169.

connection of houses bound under the nominal authority of one bishop in an economically dependent federation not dissimilar to the Irish model.[69] An Irish example was not, however, necessarily the one that Wilfrid would most obviously have chosen to adopt. As a young man he had been trained in the monastic way of life by Irish religious at Lindisfarne, but much the most significant influences on his ideas about ecclesiastical organisation are likely to have been those customs he encountered in Rome and above all in Gaul. The grouping of houses in Gaul associated with Columbanus perhaps represented the closest contemporary model for Wilfrid's creation of a monastic empire.

Wilfrid might be expected to have learned much about contemporary Frankish ideas of monastic organisation during the three years he spent with Archbishop Annemundus of Lyons, between 655 and 658, and in the two years after 664, when he spent time with his patron Agilbert, himself a member of the Columbanian connection.[70] As we have already seen (in chapter 2), this was a confederation of houses, all of which had some direct connection with the Irish monk Columbanus, originally from the monastery of Bangor, who founded a number of monasteries including Luxeuil in Burgundy and Bobbio in northern Italy.[71] Many of the houses with Columbanian connections followed a mixed rule, combining the saint's own directions for monastic living with the Rule of St Benedict, albeit sometimes modified by an abbey's own head to suit the community's particular needs.[72] The close bond felt between these houses and particularly their first founder, Columbanus, appears closely to be paralleled in the manner in which Wilfrid's minsters were connected. But there are also important differences. In many ways, as Ian Wood has stressed, it was the second generation of Columbanus' followers who were the most significant in spreading the Columbanian

---

[69] It is worth here considering the possibility that Wilfrid, who showed himself keen to extend his authority among the Picts in the period 670–8, might there have sought to replace Iona's authority with his own and – in rivalling that network – in some ways have tried to imitate it.

[70] *VSW* chs. 6, 12 and 28 (pp. 12–15, 24–7, 54–7); Wormald, 'Bede and Benedict Biscop', pp. 145–6; Henry Mayr-Harting, *The Venerable Bede, the Rule of St Benedict and Social Class*, Jarrow Lecture, 1976 (Jarrow, 1977), p. 6. Also Higham, 'Bishop Wilfrid', p. 210.

[71] Pierre Riché, 'Columbanus, his followers and the Merovingian Church', in H. B. Clarke and Mary Brennan (eds), *Columbanus and Merovingian Monasticism*, BAR, International series 113 (Oxford: BAR, 1981), 59–72; Ian Wood, *The Merovingian Kingdoms 450–751* (London and New York: Longman, 1994), pp. 184–9.

[72] Friedrich Prinz, *Frühes Mönchtum im Frankenreich: Kultur und Gesellschaft in Gallien, den Rheinlanden und Bayern am Beispiel der monastischen Entwicklen (4. bis 8. Jahrhundert)* (Munich and Vienna: R. Oldenbourg, 1965), pp. 286–7 and 149–51; Jane Barbara Stevenson, 'The monastic rules of Columbanus', in *Columbanus: Studies on the Latin Writings*, ed. Michael Lapidge (Woodbridge: Boydell Press, 1997), pp. 203–16.

tradition, and the influence of the saint's rule was often more important in spreading his spiritual ideas than was direct contact with his main foundation at Luxeuil.[73] Wilfrid may have modelled his monastic connection on patterns he had observed in Francia, but his affinity was distinguished from the Columbanian connection by the closeness of the personal bond between the bishop and his followers. The Wilfridian connection consisted of independent establishments, none dependent on any other but all linked by their devotion to the bishop and, after his death, to his cult. His was not, however, the only such confederation in England. Wilfrid's affinity and its legacy may have proved an inspiration to other abbots, particularly in Mercia, where *Medeshamstede* would seem, in Simon Keynes's words, 'to have been the centre of a veritable monastic empire, as other houses in various parts of the "Mercian" world were colonised from it, or turned to it for development and guidance'.[74]

Medeshamstede and its colonies

According to Peterborough tradition, the abbey of *Medeshamstede* was founded by the *princeps* Peada, son of Penda (king of the Mercians c. 632–55), and his brother Wulfhere (king of the Mercians 657–75), with the assistance of Seaxwulf, a prominent local nobleman – *uir potentissimus*. Seaxwulf donated the land on which the minster was founded and became its first abbot.[75] A twelfth-century Peterborough monk, Hugh Candidus, wrote a history of his abbey, drawing on a variety of early memoranda and other sources, on the basis of which he established that *Medeshamstede* had once been the centre of a network of connected minsters.[76] It was either in Seaxwulf's time or, according to Hugh Candidus during the abbacy of his successor, Cuthbald, that 'it came to pass that from that very minster were founded many others with brothers and abbots from the same congregation as at *Ancarig*, which is now called Thorney, at Brixworth, Breedon (*Bredun*), Bermondsey, *ad Repingas* (either Repton in Derbyshire or Rippingdale, Lincs),

[73] Wood, *The Merovingian Kingdoms*, p. 189.
[74] Keynes, *The Councils of Clofesho*, pp. 35 and 43; Stenton, '*Medeshamstede* and its colonies'.
[75] Anglo-Saxon Chronicle *s.a.* 656 and 675E; S 68, 72 and 68A; *The Chronicle of Hugh Candidus*, ed. W. T. Mellows (London: Oxford University Press for the Friends of Peterborough Cathedral, 1949), pp. 7–14. Keynes, *The Councils of Clofesho*, pp. 33–5.
[76] Stenton, '*Medeshamstede* and its colonies', p. 185. For discussion of the early Peterborough memoranda and the evidence they may provide for Peterborough's pre-tenth-century archive, see William Stubbs, 'On the foundation and early fasti of Peterborough', *AJ* 18 (1861), 193–211, and Keynes, *The Councils of Clofesho*, pp. 34–7.

FIGURE 12: *Medeshamstede* and its colonies.

PLATE XIV: Sarcophagus panel from Breedon-on-the-Hill, Leicestershire.

Woking (*ad Wochingas*) and many other places'.[77] Stenton expressed some scepticism about parts of this list (doubting, in particular, whether the adjacent minster at Thorney were ever a colony of its neighbour), but *Medeshamstede* does seem to have played a central role in a federation of largely, but not exclusively, Mercian minsters.[78] This connection, like Wilfrid's, might be compared with Irish patterns of monastic organisation, particularly the notion of a *paruchia* or group of daughter houses controlled by the abbot of a mother house, in which a monk from the daughter house might be promoted to the abbacy of the mother house, as for example Applecross and Bangor, or Antrim and Bangor.[79]

Breedon-on-the-Hill in Leicestershire was seemingly a colony of *Medeshamstede* from the time of its first creation.[80] Situated at the site of a prehistoric hillfort, the later medieval church at Breedon dominates the local landscape as must have its Anglo-Saxon precursor; all the surviving fabric of the present-day church is post-Conquest but there are some important pre-Conquest carved friezes and relief-panels built into the walls of the medieval

---

[77] *The Chronicle of Hugh Candidus*, p. 15; trans. C. Mellows and W. T. Mellows, *The Peterborough Chronicle of Hugh Candidus* (2nd edn, Peterborough: Museum Society, 1966), p. 8.

[78] Stenton, '*Medeshamstede* and its colonies', p. 35; Dorothy Whitelock, 'The pre-Viking Age church in East Anglia', *Anglo-Saxon England* 1 (1972), 1–22, at p. 13; Keynes, *The Councils of Clofesho*, p. 35.

[79] Charles-Edwards, *Early Christian Ireland*, p. 245 and n. 22.

[80] Stenton, '*Medeshamstede* and its colonies', pp. 182–4, Keynes, *The Councils of Clofesho*, pp. 37–9.

PLATE XV: Arched panel from Breedon-on-the-Hill, Leicestershire.

church.[81] Although the foundation charter for this house now survives only in the form of a record entered into the twelfth-century register of Peterborough Abbey, it seems to be based on a seventh-century text. This record purports to provide for a grant of twenty hides from the *princeps* Frithuric to St Peter's *familia* dwelling at *Medeshamstede*, made in order that the community 'should found a minster and *monachorum oratorium* serving God at [Breedon] and should also appoint a priest of commendable life and good reputation to minister the grace of baptism and teaching of Gospel doctrine to the people assigned to him'. The *Medeshamstede* community chose a priest named Hædda from their number, and appointed him abbot at Breedon on condition that he would acknowledge himself to be one of their fraternity.[82] A further grant recorded in the same Peterborough memorandum reveals that when Frithuric knew Hædda to be diligent in preaching to the people committed to him, he added a further grant of land at *Hrepingas*, bringing the total endowment of Breedon to fifty-one hides.[83] After this Abbot Hædda bought fifteen hides of land at *Cadenan ac* from Æthelred, king of the Mercians (675–704), for the sum of 500 *solidi*.[84]

If the wording of these memoranda can be accepted as preserving something of the original seventh-century documents, it does seem to suggest that the abbot of Breedon had a specific responsibility for the pastoral care of the lay people entrusted to him. Indeed, this house has attracted particular attention from historians interested in the example it provides of a congregation apparently assembled specifically to provide for the spiritual needs of the laity. It need not be, as Richard Morris has argued, that the priest was merely attached to the community to serve the local laity, the roles of pastor and abbot were clearly intended to be combined.[85] Even if we presume that the people entrusted to the priest-abbot's care were merely

---

[81] See plate XIV, a panel from a sarcophagus, depicting three figures, two with scrolls and one carrying a book, and plate XV, an arched panel which probably depicts the Virgin Mary. For a recent discussion of the figural and other carving from Breedon see Richard Jewell, 'Classicism of Southumbrian sculpture', in Michelle P. Brown and Carol A. Farr (eds.), *Mercia: An Anglo-Saxon Kingdom in Europe* (London and New York: Leicester University Press, 2001), pp. 247–62.

[82] S 1803 (BCS 841); Stenton, '*Medeshamstede* and its colonies', p. 182; Ann Dornier, 'The Anglo-Saxon monastery at Breedon-on-the-Hill, Leicestershire', in Ann Dornier (ed.), *Mercian Studies* (Leicester: Leicester University Press, 1977), pp. 155–68, at p. 157.

[83] S 1805 (BCS 842). The identification of *Hrepingas* is disputed. Stenton doubted that this was Rippingdale in Lincolnshire, on the grounds that this was too far from Breedon, but suggested no alternative ('*Medeshamstede* and its colonies', p. 185, n. 3); Alexander Rumble has suggested that it is more likely to have been Repton in Derbyshire: '*Hrepingas* reconsidered', in Dornier (ed.), *Mercian Studies*, pp. 169–72.

[84] S 1804 (BCS 843). *Cadenan ac*, Cadda's oak, is sometimes identified with Cadney in Lincolnshire.

[85] Richard Morris, *Churches in the Landscape* (London: Dent, 1989), p. 132; see also Alan Thacker, 'Monks, preaching and pastoral care in early Anglo-Saxon England', in John Blair and Richard Sharpe (eds.),

those lay people who lived and worked on the minster's estates, the size of the minster's endowment would preclude all this activity being undertaken by the abbot alone, and some of it must surely have devolved upon other members of the community.[86] We know of at least one other priest at Breedon, Tatwine, described by Bede as 'a man renowned for his devotion and wisdom and excellently instructed in the Scriptures', who was archbishop of Canterbury from 731 to 734, a role in which some previous pastoral experience would obviously have been useful.[87] Breedon's pastoral cares may have extended beyond its immediate neighbours and tenants to encompass the royal Mercian court at Tamworth; this at least is one interpretation one might place on the evidence of a charter issued in 848 by Berhtwulf, king of the Mercians, and Humberht, *princeps* of the 'Tonseti', which gave privileges to Abbot Eanmund and the community at Breedon. The grant freed the abbey from the obligation to supply food to passing royal officials, but required them still to offer shelter and sustenance to messengers from overseas, from Wessex or Northumbria, who were passing on their way to the royal court, suggesting that the abbey had some part to play in supporting aspects of the running of royal administration, and thus conceivably some spiritual functions at court.[88]

As important to Breedon's foundation as its pastoral role was its close and enduring association with the 'parent house' at *Medeshamstede*. This relationship is complicated by the ambiguities in the evidence relating to the career of Breedon's first abbot, Hædda, who had been a priest at *Medeshamstede* before assuming the task of running the new Leicestershire minster. In another composite document preserved in the Peterborough cartulary (the so-called *Liber niger*) Hædda, 'abbot of *Medeshamstede*', is said to have been present *c.* 690 when an Ecgbald, abbot of the minster at Hoo in Kent, came to *Medeshamstede* in order to obtain confirmation from the Mercian king Æthelred for some earlier grants.[89] As Simon Keynes has suggested, the level of circumstantial detail in this composite document is testimony to its probably authentic roots, in which case we need to take seriously its suggestion that Hædda was an abbot of *Medeshamstede* even

---

Pastoral Care before the Parish (Leicester, London and New York: Leicester University Press, 1992), pp. 137–70, at pp. 140 and 146, n. 55.

[86] Morris, *Churches*, p. 132.

[87] *HE* V. 23 (pp. 558–9). This is to assume that Bede's *Briudun* is correctly to be identified with Breedon-on-the-Hill in Leicestershire and not with Bredon in Worcestershire.

[88] S 197; Keynes, *The Councils of Clofesho*, pp. 39–40.

[89] S 233 (BCS 89); Stenton, '*Medeshamstede* and its colonies', pp. 189–91; Keynes, *The Councils of Clofesho*, pp. 41–2.

though he is not credited with that role in the twelfth-century versions of Peterborough's history.[90] If Hædda did assume the abbacy of his first minster at some time in the 680s, Keynes argued that he must have succeeded Abbot Seaxwulf when the latter became bishop of the Mercians and Middle Angles, soon after the synod of Hertford of 672.[91] Alternatively, we might accept the twelfth-century Peterborough tradition represented by the abbey's version of the Anglo-Saxon Chronicle and by Hugh Candidus and interpose Cuthbald between Seaxwulf and Hædda.[92]

A privilege issued by Pope Constantine (708–15) in favour of Hædda, abbot and priest of two minsters at Bermondsey and Woking in the *prouincia* of the West Saxons, and preserved in Peterborough's archive adds one further layer of confusion. The privilege placed the two minsters under the pope's protection, decreeing that the local bishop (of Winchester) should ordain a priest or deacon for the community of his own choosing, should consecrate whomsoever the congregation chose as their abbot without imposing any stranger upon them and should otherwise interfere in their affairs only if they committed faults contrary to the sacred canons.[93] It seems probable that this Hædda is the same priest whom we have just been discussing; what is less obvious is whether this document supports our presumption that Hædda was abbot of *Medeshamstede* (and thereby abbot of two of that minster's dependencies in Surrey), or whether it rather suggests that the minsters of Bermondsey and Woking were colonies of Breedon-on-the-Hill.[94] Hædda is usually identified with the bishop of Lichfield appointed in 691 on the division of the Mercian diocese, who became bishop of Leicester also after Wilfrid's removal. It might have been, as Keynes suggested, that it was in an episcopal capacity that Hædda sought papal advice about the rights of the bishop of Winchester in his Surrey minsters, but that the precise relationship between the different institutions was not fully understood in Rome.[95]

These various documents offer some support for Hugh Candidus' assertion that *Medeshamstede* lay at the centre of a nexus of minsters in the Midlands and beyond. Lists of the minsters belonging to this confederation are found

---

[90] *Ibid.*   [91] *HE* IV. 6 (pp. 354–5); Keynes, *The Councils of Clofesho*, p. 41.

[92] Anglo-Saxon Chronicle s.a. 656E; *The Chronicle of Hugh Candidus*, p. 15.

[93] BCS 133; Stenton, '*Medeshamstede* and its colonies', pp. 185–7; Keynes, *The Councils of Clofesho*, p. 42. See also John Blair, *Early Medieval Surrey: Landholding, Church and Settlement before 1300* (Stroud: Alan Sutton and Surrey Archaeological Society, 1991), pp. 95–7 (Woking) and 102–3 (Bermondsey).

[94] Whitelock suggested that Hædda had founded these two minsters: 'The pre-Viking Age church', p. 13.

[95] Keynes, *The Councils of Clofesho*, p. 43.

also in spurious charters for *Medeshamstede* in the names of Wulfhere and
Æthelred, kings of the Mercians, and an Old English version of the Æthelred
document which was inserted into the Peterborough version of the Anglo-
Saxon Chronicle.[96] The close connection between the parent house and Breedon is clear; there may have been a link with the Kentish house at Hoo
(although it might have been in error that a copy of the Mercian king's confirmation for Hoo made its way into the Peterborough archive). Bermondsey and Woking in Surrey were also apparently associated with the abbey,
whether directly or as offspring of the daughter-house at Breedon is less
clear. Hugh Candidus's statement that *ad Repingas* was a colony was based,
one assumes, on the preservation in the Peterborough archive of a note
of Frithuric's grant of the land there to Hædda;[97] if this were the original grant of land on which Repton minster were founded, as Ann Dornier
has suggested, that minster too would be included among *Medeshamstede's*
colonies.[98] Thorney's link with Peterborough is rather less clear, although if
there were an early minster there, such a link is not impossible.[99] Oundle,
however, belonged not to the *Medeshamstede* affinity but to Wilfrid's monastic
empire.[100] The confusion seems to arise here from the fact that Bede named
the abbot of the minster where Wilfrid died as Cuthbald, a name later
attributed to one of *Medeshamstede's* abbots.[101] Hugh Candidus was alone in
associating the minster at Brixworth with *Medeshamstede*, including it in the
list of places founded from that abbey and peopled by religious whom it had
trained.[102] A link with Bardney in Lincolnshire is suggested by its inclusion
in the lists of places incorporated into the charters in the names of Wulfhere
and Æthelred, although is not otherwise supported in narrative or documentary sources.[103] Since nothing is known about the foundation of Bardney,
Stenton suggested that it might have been established as a colony from
Medeshamstede and all record of that direct connection subsequently lost
with the abbey's other muniments.[104] While this is plausible, it is no longer

---

[96] S 68 and 72; the Old English version of S 72 (BCS 49) is given in Anglo-Saxon Chronicle *s.a.* 675.

[97] S 1805; discussed above.   [98] Dornier, 'The Anglo-Saxon monastery', p. 158.

[99] Stenton, '*Medeshamstede*', p. 185; Keynes, *The Councils*, pp. 44–5.

[100] *Contra* Hugh Candidus: *The Chronicle of Hugh Candidus*, p. 22.

[101] *HE* V. 19 (pp. 528–9); *VSW* chs. 65 and 67 (pp. 140–1 and 144–5); Whitelock, 'The pre-Viking Age church', p. 13, n. 7. For discussion of different identifications of this minster see Keynes, *The Councils*, p. 44, n. 187.

[102] *The Chronicle of Hugh Candidus*, p. 15. Whitelock argued ('The pre-Viking Age church', p. 13) that Abbot Cuthbald of *Medeshamstede* had founded Brixworth, but Hugh's text does not admit of such a reading. Keynes has observed that the re-use of Roman fabric in the surviving Anglo-Saxon church at Brixworth points rather to a connection with Leicester than Peterborough: *The Councils*, p. 45.

[103] Keynes, *The Councils*, p. 43, n. 183.   [104] Stenton, '*Medeshamstede* and its colonies', pp. 180–1.   275

possible to explain the inclusion of the place-names Shifnal, the Lizard and Wattlesborough in Shropshire among the lands of *Medeshamstede* listed in the Old English version of S 68.[105]

The similarity between this group of houses and the Wilfridian affinity has already been observed; both were spread over a wide geographical area and it may not be insignificant that abbots of *Medeshamstede* (and Breedon) were – like Wilfrid – elected to episcopal office. Yet there is a significant difference between the two sorts of connection: while Wilfrid's houses were independent foundations bound by affection for their bishop, *Medeshamstede* created colonies, separate minsters dependent not on a man but on a founding institution. Quite how the parent house ran its dependencies is no longer clear. We might surmise that they would all have followed a similar rule of life but we can say nothing about what that rule, or set of customs, might have been like. If Peterborough tradition correctly associated the minster's foundation with Peada, Christian son of the pagan Mercian king Penda, then there would have been scope for the priests who accompanied the newly converted young king back from Northumbria to the kingdom of the Middle Angles to exert some influence, particularly the Irishman Diuma who later became bishop of the Middle Angles and Mercians.[106]

Clusters and dependencies

Two further eastern minsters appear to have had interests in western Mercia. The minster at *Icanho* was founded in 654 by Botulf and rapidly acquired a reputation outside the bounds of East Anglia.[107] When, *c.* 669, the Northumbrian Ceolfrith travelled from his minster at Ripon to Kent to study the practices of the monastic life, he went on to East Anglia 'to see the monastic practices of Abbot Botulf, whom report had proclaimed on all sides to be a man of unparalleled life and learning and full of the grace of the Holy Spirit'.[108] At

---

[105] *Ibid.*; Sims-Williams (*Religion*, p. 99) points out that the abbey's claim to these estates might be related to the Seaxwulf's tenure of the Mercian bishopric.

[106] *HE* III. 21 (pp. 278–81).

[107] The foundation of *Icanho* was recorded in the Anglo-Saxon Chronicle in the same year as the obit of King Anna of East Anglia, AD 654AB; 653C. The site used to be identified as Boston, but this is in Lincolnshire not East Anglia; other possible suggestions are Iken in Suffolk and Hadstock in Essex: Whitelock, 'The pre-Viking Age church', p. 10, n. 3.

[108] *VSCeol.* ch. 4 (p. 389); Whitelock, 'The pre-Viking Age church', p. 10. The late eleventh-century life of St Botulf states that the saint had studied on the continent before founding *Icanho*; it is hard to know how much reliance to place on this text, but Whitelock was right to argue that we could be confident that Botulf would not have promoted Celtic monastic practices, since it was dissatisfaction with those that had led Ceolfrith to leave his first minster at Gilling and go to Ripon: *ibid.*, p. 11.

some time this community appears to have been given a minster at Wenlock in Shropshire, together with all its possessions. They may have run Wenlock as a daughter house of *Icanho*, with its own independent abbess, or it is conceivable that the brothers of *Icanho* saw the Shropshire minster as one element within in a wider monastic federation similar to that organised from *Medeshamstede*.[109] Evidence for these arrangements is found in a record of transactions relating to Wenlock incorporated in the eleventh-century Life of St Mildburg which Finberg described as 'St Mildburg's Testament'. According the foundation charter datable to 674×690 incorporated within this text, Æthelheah, abbot of the minster of *Icheanog*, 'with the consent of the whole *familia* of Abbot Botulf of blessed memory' gave to Mildburg, the consecrated virgin, Wenlock and other estates totalling 144 hides, 'on condition that the aforesaid *locus* [Wenlock] shall by the grace of God remain unalterably under the tutelage of the worshipful abbot Botulf, not under compulsion but of its own accord, since it is with the money of that same church that the land is being purchased from the king named Merwald'. The grant was made in exchange for sixty hides at *Homtun* which Mildburg gave to 'the two parties to whom authority over the *locus* belonged', namely Abbot Æthelheah and an abbess *Liobsynda*.[110] It would seem that Botulf had bought the minster at Wenlock from Merewalh, king of the Magonsæte, and ran the abbey as a daughter house of *Icanho* under the authority of the Frankish abbess, *Liobsynda*. When Merewalh's daughter, Mildburg, acquired possession of it she continued to acknowledge the spiritual authority of Botulf's community.[111] Wenlock was a church of some significance in Mercia, probably associated with royal administration and continuing to function, albeit with some changes to the composition of the one-time mixed congregation, into the tenth century and beyond.[112] How long its connection with *Icanho* remained is not clear, nor is it possible to say whether that minster had other Mercian interests. On a smaller scale, this arrangement appears more closely to resemble the *Medeshamstede* pattern of parent house with dependent colonies than it does the Wilfridian model.

A legend current in the twelfth century that Anna, king of the East Angles, had founded a wooden church on the border between the Mercians and the

[109] Sims-Williams, *Religion*, p. 99.
[110] S 1798; edited and translated by H. P. R. Finberg, *Early Charters of the West Midlands* (Leicester: Leicester University Press, 1972), pp. 201–6; Whitelock, 'The pre-Viking Age church', p. 12.
[111] Sims-Williams, *Religion*, pp. 98–9.
[112] Alan Thacker, 'Kings, saints and monasteries in pre-Viking Mercia', *Midland History* 10 (1985), 1–25, at pp. 4–5. See also *Veiled Women*, II, *s.n.* Wenlock.

277

Welsh dedicated to his daughter, St Æthelthryth of Ely, seems implausible.[113] But it is not impossible that Ely could, like *Icanho*, have had some connection with the west Midlands. Bishop Wilfrid might have fostered such an association: he was close to Æthelthryth and maintained his connection with Ely beyond her death, since he was reported by Bede as one of the witnesses to the finding of her incorrupt body.[114] Alternatively St Werburg, daughter of King Wulfhere of Mercia and his Kentish wife, Eormenhild, could have promoted Æthelthryth's cult in Mercia. Werburg adopted a religious life at Ely but was said later to have lived on her father's estates, having been given some unspecified authority over the minsters of Mercia. She died at Threekingham in Lincolnshire and was buried at Hanbury in Staffordshire. These, together with Weedon in Northamptonshire, another church claiming connection with Werburg, may have been part of another monastic affinity and might have sustained some contact with Ely.[115] That abbey's later traditions claimed that Werburg returned to become abbess of Ely on her mother's death.[116]

The Northumbrian minster of Whitby provides another example of a church with dependent colonies. Abbess Hild constructed a minster at Hackness, thirteen miles away from the main abbey. From Bede's account of the sisters' life it is clear that this was a fully conventual establishment with a dormitory and its own church; although a deputy (Frigyth) presided over Hackness in Hild's stead, the sisters considered Hild to be 'mother of them all'.[117] In the time of Hild's successor Ælfflæd, Whitby had another dependency at *Osingadun* where St Cuthbert had a vision when dedicating a church there; Abbess Ælfflæd had to send back to her main minster (*ad maius suum monasterium*) to find out whose death it was that Cuthbert had seen.[118] It is tempting to wonder, as Eric Cambridge has done, about the physical relationship between Whitby and the dwelling in which postulants lived before they became full members of the community. Bede placed this 'at the remotest part of the minster' (*in extremis monasterii locis*) which must

---

[113] Osbert of Clare is the authority for this tale, reporting it in a letter to the monks of Ely, who were clearly ignorant of the connection: *The Letters of Osbert of Clare, Prior of Westminster*, ed. E. W. Williamson (London: Oxford University Press, 1929), *Ep.* 33 (pp. 116–19). The church may have been at Hyssington in Montgomeryshire, or in Shropshire: *Liber Eliensis*, ed. E. O. Blake, Camden third series, XCII (London: Royal Historical Society, 1962), pp. 281–3; Whitelock, 'The pre-Viking Age church', p. 12, n. 3; Sims-Williams, *Religion*, pp. 99–100.

[114] *HE* IV. 19 (pp. 390–5); Whitelock, 'The pre-Viking Age church', p. 13, n. 7.

[115] Thacker, 'Kings, saints and monasteries', p. 4.

[116] *Liber Eliensis*, ed. Blake, p. 52 (and cf. pp. 32, 35 and 42 for discussion of Werburg's activities); Whitelock, 'The pre-Viking Age church', p. 13, n. 7.

[117] *HE* IV. 23 (pp. 412–13).   [118] Anon., *VSCuth*. IV. 10 (pp. 126–9); Bede, *VSCuth*. ch. 34 (pp. 260–5).

certainly imply a location on the very edge of Whitby's site. Since this build-ing was too far from the main house for these handmaidens of Christ to reach Hild's death-bed (one of their number being treated to a vision of the abbess's soul ascending to heaven instead), it might in fact have lain beyond the perimeter of the Whitby site itself and could even have been another dependency.[119]

Drawing on the material evidence for early Northumbrian ecclesiasti-cal buildings and particularly for Anglian sculpture (long recognised to be closely connected with monasticism), Eric Cambridge has noted that monas-tic sites in County Durham appear to have been organised into a distinctive pattern of zones and clusters. In addition to the Whitby cluster, he has noted one associated with Wearmouth and Jarrow, including Seaham and Dalton, a relationship between Escomb and Auckland and a possible major church at Billingham with a dependency four miles away at Greatham.[120] Docu-mentary sources offer further instances in which a particular person, often an abbot or abbess of royal birth, is linked with more than one monastic house. One Northumbrian abbot Forthred went to Rome in 757 or 758 to complain to Pope Paul I that three minsters at Stonegrave, Coxwold and *Donaemuthe*, which had been granted to him by a certain abbess, had been seized by the king, Eadberht, and given to his brother.[121] Æthelburh, a mem-ber of the Hwiccian royal family and an eighth-century abbess of Twyning in Worcestershire, acquired a minster at Withington in Gloucestershire (for-merly subject to a dispute over its inheritance)[122] from Bishop Milred in 774 on condition that both it and Twyning reverted to the church of Worces-ter after her death.[123] Another minster at Fladbury came into Æthelburg's hands when she leased that from the diocese on similar terms; all three houses ended up in Worcester's possession, thus ensuring the preserva-tion of these documents in that abbey's archive.[124] According to William of Malmesbury, Aldhelm founded two additional minsters at Frome and Bradford-on-Avon while he was abbot of Malmesbury, conferring lands and privileges on both, including the right for each to elect its own abbot after

---

[119] *HE* IV. 23 (pp. 414–15); Eric Cambridge, 'The early church in County Durham: a reassessment', *Journal of the British Archaeological Association*, 137 (1984), 65–85, at p. 74.

[120] Cambridge, 'The early church', pp. 75–6.

[121] Pope Paul wrote to Eadberht and to his brother, Ecgberht archbishop of York, to complain about the king's behaviour; his letter is printed in BCS no. 184 and H&S III, 394–6, and translated in *EHD* no. 184. For discussion of the possible identity of *Donaemuthe* see M. S. Parker, 'An Anglo-Saxon monastery in the lower Don valley', *Northern History* 21 (1985), 19–32.

[122] S 1429; *EHD*, no. 68; Sims-Williams, *Religion*, pp. 130–2.   [123] S 1255; *EHD*, no. 75.

[124] S 62; Sims-Williams, *Religion*, pp. 37 and 132–3.

his death.[125] Although the two had been destroyed by his own time, William did note that at Bradford-on-Avon the *ecclesiola*, dedicated to St Laurence, was still standing, as indeed it is today (see plate V).[126] These small groups of minsters resemble less the federations or affinities we discussed earlier but rather point towards the idea of a monastic cluster or plurality of separate houses ephemerally connected with a single person who was head of each.

Conclusion

Apart from the two celebrated examples – the Wilfridian affinity and the *Medeshamstede* federation with dependent colonies – and the rather less certain East Anglian/Mercian pairings with *Icanho* and Ely, it can, as we have just seen, be difficult to distinguish other associations or groups of minsters from instances of houses connected by association with a single abbot or abbess or by broader ties of confraternity. We are, however, now in a better position to suggest a typology for categorising monastic associations. Perhaps the most formalised arrangement was that of the type run from *Medeshamstede*: a federation of separate houses, spread across a wide geographical area, founded from that head-minster and run as subject colonies. Some at least of these had their own independent abbot (Hædda was appointed from the *Medeshamstede* congregation to establish and run the new colony at Breedon); one abbot may at different times have been in charge of more than one colonial minster, although the sources are not always pellucid here. It is possible that a similar arrangement was organised from *Icanho*, and other examples may also have existed. The closest parallel for such a monastic federation is that organised from Iona. Bishop Wilfrid's connection was rather different and might better be termed an affinity. All the congregations of Wilfrid's minsters saw themselves as connected by their association with their bishop; they found themselves scattered widely both north and south of the Humber and each had its own abbot. Presumably Wilfrid's approval was sought for

---

[125] William of Malmesbury, *De gestis pontificum Anglorum*, ed. N. E. S. A. Hamilton, Rolls Series 52 (London, 1870), pp. 346–7. The charter in Aldhelm's name surviving in Malmesbury's archive that supposedly confirms freedoms of Frome and Bradford has no claim to authenticity: S 1251a (BCS 114); see Heather Edwards, *The Charters of the Early West Saxon Kingdom*, BAR, Brit. ser., 198 (Oxford: BAR, 1988), pp. 115–16.

[126] The church of St Laurence at Bradford is probably not that originally built by Aldhelm but rather a tenth- or early-eleventh-century rebuilding of that earlier church. Most striking is the height of the building (which is slightly greater than the length of the nave and almost twice the width); see H. M. Taylor and Joan Taylor, *Anglo-Saxon Architecture*, 3 vols. (Cambridge: Cambridge University Press, 1965–78), III, 86–9. See plate V.

each new abbatial appointment, if he did not, as he did in nominating Tatberht to take over at Ripon, issue direct instructions. Wilfrid's monastic arrangements bear some similarity to the affinity of Columbanian houses in Francia, and also with the federation of Ionan monasteries, which were also united in their devotion to the cult of Columba (and so, like Wilfrid's, bound by a particularly personal tie). As described in the sources, Wilfrid's affinity does not readily find any parallel within the English church, but it is of course possible that personal allegiances were also significant at *Medeshamstede*, although they are less obvious in the evidence we happen to have. Both the federation with colonies and the affinity are distinguished from any other sort of monastic association in that they encompassed separate institutions dispersed over a wide geographical area extending beyond a single kingdom.

A third model I have called a cluster, following Eric Cambridge's suggestion: instances in which several minsters, lying within a reasonably confined area, if not all in the same immediate locality, were associated either by being among the possessions of a single abbot or abbess or as proximate colonies of a main, parent minster. Where such arrangements were closely tied to one person, even if they were not forcibly and prematurely terminated as was Forthred's possession of his Yorkshire houses, they may often have been relatively short-lived, the cluster being rearranged on the disposal of their owner's inheritance. Local clusters, such as those seen in County Durham, which had an institutional focus might be expected to have endured longer. One additional type of monastic connection was arguably found more commonly and spread more diversely than any of these: the single dependency, the institution or community founded as an offspring of a parent house, such as the retreat houses, or *mansiones*, associated with episcopal minsters at Lindisfarne, Hexham and Lichfield and described by Bede.[127] Among many other examples, one might cite, for example, the establishment created on land inside the city of Canterbury by Selethryth, abbess of Lyminge in Kent early in the ninth century, to serve as a refuge in case of external attack, to which the sisters did ultimately repair. Similarly, in the early eleventh century, the cloistered women of Shaftesbury established a second dwelling at Bradford-on-Avon, again in case they needed a safer place to care for their precious relics during the Viking wars.[128] The dependency

---

[127] Lindisfarne (Cuthbert's retreat on Farne): *HE* IV. 28 (pp. 434–7); Hexham: *HE* V. 2 (pp. 456–9); Lichfield: *HE* IV. 3 (pp. 336–9); Cambridge, 'The early church', p. 76.
[128] S 160 (AD 804); discussed in *Veiled Women*, II, *s.n.* Lyminge. S 899 (AD 1001); see *Veiled Women*, II, *s.n.* Bradford and Shaftesbury.

of Lindisfarne described in Æthelwulf's poem *De abbatibus* was presumably of a similar type. None of these instances led either to the creation of a cluster, or of a wider affinity or federation.

This typology takes territorial extent to be the defining feature of a feder-ation, and an intimate personal bond (similar to that of secular lordship) to characterise an affinity. On such terms, arrangements of those two types can more readily be distinguished from the relationships that existed between individual abbeys and separate houses immediately dependent upon them, whether those dependencies represented a minster's sole venture into exter-nal expansion or were part of a regional plurality of such related houses.

CHAPTER 7

Minsters in the world

An Englishman called Wilgils had lived a devout Christian life with his family before he determined to give up his worldly career and devote himself to the monastic life. Soon after:

as his zeal for the spiritual life increased, he entered with even more intense fervour on the austere life of a solitary, dwelling in the headlands that are bounded by the North Sea and the river Humber. In a little chapel there, dedicated to St Andrew . . . he served God for many years in fasting, prayer, and watching, with the result that he became celebrated for his miracles and his name was in everyone's mouth. People flocked to him in great numbers, and when they did so he never failed to instruct them with sound advice and the Word of God. He was held in such high esteem by the king and the nobles of that nation that they made over to him in perpetual gift a number of small landed properties that lie near those headlands for the purpose of building there a church to God. In this church the reverend father gathered together a rather small but devout company of those who wished to serve God.[1]

Alcuin's account of the dilemmas that confronted St Willibrord's father encapsulates the paradox that faced any aspiring religious in the early English church. However much he might envisage that the adoption of the

---

[1] Alcuin, *Vita S. Willibrordi*, ch. 1 (ed. Levison, p. 116). Such a narrative is, of course, reflective of a stock monastic *topos*, found in saints' lives from the Life of St Anthony onwards; see Eric Cambridge and David Rollason, 'Debate: the pastoral organization of the Anglo-Saxon church: a review of the "minster hypothesis"', *Early Medieval Europe* 4 (1995), 87–104, at p. 93, and my 'The role of the minster in earlier Anglo-Saxon society', in Benjamin Thompson (ed.), *Monasteries and Society in Medieval Britain: Proceedings of the 1994 Harlaxton Symposium* (Stamford: Paul Watkins, 1999), pp. 35–58, at pp. 35–7.

monastic life would separate him from contact with the world and enable him to concentrate exclusively on contemplation and devotion, the reality that confronted him in the cloister was very different. The gathering of a community at Spurn Head does not represent an instance in which any formalised arrangement had been made for the provision of pastoral care to the laity in the area (rather it reflected an *ad hoc* arrangement, arising from the saint's peculiar spiritual charisma),[2] yet Alcuin's narrative points to an important context in which we should be investigating relationships between religious and laymen. In practice, no institutions of which record has survived maintained total isolation from their surroundings.[3] All religious communities in the early Anglo-Saxon church interacted regularly with their lay neighbours in a range of contexts and at varying degrees of formality. As we saw in chapter 3, a minster's physical character and its geographical location could have a significant impact on the nature and the extent of its dealings with secular society. Yet, even in remote places, few religious found themselves wholly immune from external incursion into their private, prayerful lives. For some religious men and women, particularly those to whom the community had assigned specific tasks or offices whose performance required them to work outside the confines of the cloister, those contacts will have been regular and the presence and activities of such office-holders within a predominantly lay environment will have excited little comment. Others from the same congregations may have encountered lay people less regularly, but no less closely, on occasions of social or religious festivities when one group entertained the other. One might think here of the feasts we discussed in chapter 5, of high religious festivals when the laity were asked to share in the celebration of the religious feast and subsequently in celebratory eating and drinking; equally pertinent would be those occasions when the king entertained his leading men on one of his own estates, inviting bishops and abbots and their retinues as well as the secular nobility to feast and make merry.

All the sources reveal that close contacts – spiritual, economic and social – existed between minster communities and local lay populations from the

---

[2] Catherine Cubitt has suggested that the accumulation of visitors around Guthlac's fenland cell should be seen in the same context: 'Pastoral care and conciliar canons: the provisions of the 747 council of *Clofesho*', in John Blair and Richard Sharpe (eds.), *Pastoral Care before the Parish* (Leicester, London and New York: Leicester University Press, 1992), pp. 193–211, at p. 201.

[3] Some solitaries or small groups of brethren may of course have contrived to achieve such total withdrawal from not only the laity in their vicinity but all their ecclesiastical neighbours, too, so that no record of their deeds ever reached outsiders or survived for posterity. Such congregations cannot, however, have been widespread.

beginning of the Anglo-Saxon Christian period. This chapter explores the
ways in which the expression of monasticism in England came to be so
intimately fused with secular aristocratic society and shows how a better
informed understanding of the benefits the laity sought from the church
can shed new light on the distinctiveness of the English monastic experience
before the first Viking Age. We have already considered how the situation
of monastic congregations in the physical landscape can help to explain
the social prominence of the institution and hence the economic as well as
spiritual advantages the laity might have expected to obtain from minsters
in their neighbourhood.[4] Here we shall look first at the various aspects of
pastoral ministry that minsters may have supplied, ranging from the provision of sacraments, through teaching and preaching to charitable services
such as care of the sick and alms-giving. Then we shall turn to investigate
the spheres in which the laity may have initiated contact with communities
of religious, exploring the role of minsters as sites of pilgrimage or places
of refuge. This will shed some light on the role minsters may have played
in the fostering of lay piety as well as on the other, less obviously religious
benefits lay people may have expected their local minster to supply.

The cure of souls

Historians have argued over the appropriateness of drawing distinctions in
the early medieval church between houses that took an active pastoral role
and those institutions devoted exclusively to contemplation.[5] Pastoral care,
the cure of souls, could encompass a variety of services provided by ecclesiastics for lay people ranging from charitable work (alms-giving, care for
the sick, the poor and the needy), through preaching and teaching to the
imposition of penance and the administration of the sacraments of baptism,
the Eucharist and extreme unction.[6] While there is manifestly some overlap between charitable work and the ministry of the word and sacraments,
it cannot automatically be presumed that a community able and willing
to provide the former was also engaged in the latter. In part, a minster's
attitude to and involvement in such activities may have depended on the
purpose for which it was first founded. As Eric Cambridge has explained,

---

[4] Above, chapter 3.
[5] For a thorough analysis of the important issues see U. Berlière, 'L'exercice du ministère paroissial par les moines dans le haut Moyen-Age', *Revue bénédictine* 39 (1927), 227–50.
[6] Giles Constable, 'Monasteries, rural churches and the *cura animarum* in the early Middle Ages', *Settimane* 28 (1982), 349–89, at p. 353; Cubitt, 'Pastoral care and conciliar canons', p. 192.

'however blurred it became in practice, there is an important functional difference in principle between a church whose *raison d'être* is to provide for the pastoral needs of a lay population . . . and one whose prime purpose is to accommodate the liturgical requirements of a community which has come into being as a result of a desire to live according to a monastic rule'.[7]

Anglo-Saxon clergy appear not to have seen any incongruity in the participation by brothers in activities outside the cloister, as we saw when we explored the ideals that may have governed the early expression of monasticism in England.[8] Because of the way in which the creation of the first minsters in England was so closely connected with the conversion of the Anglo-Saxons to Christianity, many of the earliest religious houses assumed an active role in their locality from the outset, in which concern they had perforce to persist after the population was nominally converted. It would, however, be wrong to see these as exclusively 'active' establishments; all their inmates, including those in clerical orders, appear to have led lives which mixed contemplation with external ministry. This is true not only of those houses which became episcopal sees such as Canterbury and Lindisfarne, but also of others like Bradwell-on-Sea and Tilbury, or Melrose.[9] Active ministry and contemplative devotion thus became inextricably linked in early Anglo-Saxon monasticism; it was only in the tenth century that formal efforts were made to differentiate between religious establishments according to the functions performed by their inmates.[10] Bede envisaged that all those who adopted the religious life would mix devotion with action; he laid considerable stress in his writings on the responsibilities of teachers and preachers towards the laity and on the performance of good works by religious and clerics, whether these took the form of alms-giving and succouring the needy, or were expressed, as by Bede himself, through the work of scholarship and teaching. As he said in his sermon for the feast of John the Evangelist, 'few indeed ascend to the contemplative life and they do

---

[7] Eric Cambridge, 'The early church in County Durham: a reassessment', *Journal of the British Archaeological Association* 137 (1984), 65–85, at p. 66.

[8] Above, chapter 2.

[9] The way of life practised in the two earliest Canterbury houses and at Lindisfarne was discussed above, chapter 2. For Bradwell and Tilbury see *HE* III. 22 (pp. 282–4) John Blair, 'Debate: Ecclesiastical organization and pastoral care in Anglo-Saxon England', *Early Medieval Europe* 4 (1995), 193–212, at p. 205; his anonymous biographer described the pastoral activities undertaken by Cuthbert while a brother at Melrose: Anon., *VSCuth*. II. 5–8 (pp. 84–93).

[10] I discussed this previously in my 'Parochial ministry in early Anglo-Saxon England: the role of monastic communities', in W. J. Sheils and Diana Wood (eds.), *The Ministry: Clerical and Lay*, Studies in Church History 26 (Oxford: Basil Blackwell for the Ecclesiastical History Society, 1989), pp. 43–54.

the more exaltedly who come after the perfection of pious action'.[11] One of the aspects of Hild's congregation at Whitby that Bede particularly admired was that those under the abbess's direction devoted a great deal of time not merely to study but also to the performance of good works.[12]

It may be inappropriate to attempt to differentiate between early Anglo-Saxon religious houses according to the function they were designed to pursue.[13] When we explored the daily lives of religious within the cloister in an earlier chapter, the only notable distinctions we observed between individual congregations lay in the extent to which they engaged in certain activities which might be seen as characteristic of the monastic life, whether liturgical, intellectual, or manual. Might it not therefore be reasonable to expect to observe a similar correspondence between the behaviour of religious from different establishments outside their separate communities? To argue that action and contemplation were inextricably connected in early Anglo-Saxon conceptions of the nature of the religious life is not, however, to argue that the provision of spiritual care for the laity was organised on any systematic basis. Eric John even went so far as to argue that 'it scarcely seems that there was any trace of a true parochial organisation in England before the tenth century'.[14]

Historiographical debate over the organisation of pastoral ministry in the early English church became particularly heated during the 1990s when a series of articles was written about the validity of what came to be called the 'minster hypothesis'. In this debate, arguments about the manner in which early Anglo-Saxon ecclesiastics provided for the spiritual care of a newly-Christianised lay population became part of a wider discussion about the institutional development of the English church. At its crudest the minster hypothesis (largely articulated in two collections of papers that addressed

---

[11] Bede, *Homelia*, I. 9 (ed. Hurst, p. 64, lines 149–51): 'ad contemplatiuam uero perpauci et hoc sublimiores quique post perfectionem piae actionis ascendunt'. See Mary Thomas Aquinas Carroll, *The Venerable Bede: His Spiritual Teachings, a Dissertation* (Washington, DC: Catholic University of America Press, 1946), pp. 246–9; A. G. P. van der Walt, 'Reflections of the Benedictine Rule in Bede's homiliary', *JEH* 37 (1986), 367–76, at p. 371; Alan Thacker, 'Monks, preaching and pastoral care in early Anglo-Saxon England', in John Blair and Richard Sharpe (eds.), *Pastoral Care before the Parish* (Leicester, London and New York: Leicester University Press, 1992), pp. 137–70, at pp. 141–2. Bede may have meant something rather special by 'contemplation' here, not the prayerful life to which all were called but something closer to mystical contemplation.

[12] *HE* IV. 23 (pp. 408–9). Marilyn Dunn, *The Emergence of Monasticism: From the Desert Fathers to the Early Middle Ages* (Oxford: Blackwell, 2000), pp. 196–7.

[13] Others have also made this point, for example, Nicholas Brooks, *The Early History of the Church of Canterbury: Christ Church 597–1066* (Leicester: Leicester University Press, 1984), p. 187.

[14] Eric John, "The social and political problems of the early English church', in Joan Thirsk (ed.), *Land, Church, and People: Essays presented to Professor H. P. R. Finberg* (Reading: British Agricultural History Society, 1970), pp. 39–63, at p. 56, n. 2.

the origins of the parochial system)[15] asserted that most pre-Viking Age English churches (minsters) were staffed by communities of clergy who took pastoral responsibility for defined territorial areas, a coherent network of *parochiae* gradually being created through acts of royal and episcopal policy.[16] From the tenth century onwards, those areas of pastoral responsibility were fragmented as the parish system began to develop, although minsters retained some traces of their earlier position and original territory. Persuasive as this argument is, it depends to a great extent on a number of assumptions about the nature of early Anglo-Saxon ecclesiastical structures made on the basis of much later evidence for parochial boundaries.[17] The essential 'minster model' was challenged in articles by David Rollason and by Rollason writing with Eric Cambridge, and then defended by John Blair, perhaps the single scholar most closely associated with the pastoral model. A short review of the whole debate was also written by David Palliser.[18]

The relevance of this debate to our current preoccupations is obvious. If it were indeed the case that all early Anglo-Saxon minsters had spiritual, pastoral obligations towards their lay neighbours, those responsibilities would fundamentally have shaped the evolution of their relationships with the

---

[15] John Blair (ed.), *Minsters and Parish Churches: The Local Church in Transition 950–1200* (Oxford: Oxford University Committee for Archaeology, 1988); Blair and Sharpe (eds.), *Pastoral Care before the Parish*.

[16] John Blair, 'Introduction: from minster to parish church', in Blair (ed.), *Minsters and Parish Churches*, pp. 1–19, at p. 1.

[17] Thus, for example, Patrick Hase matched the evidence for mother churches and their *parochiae* in the area around Southampton Water in the eleventh and twelfth centuries with the foundation of minsters at *villae regales* in the seventh century, even though no early sources refer explicitly to a network of *parochiae* controlled by minsters: 'The mother churches of Hampshire', in Blair (ed.), *Minsters and Parish Churches*, pp. 45–66, at pp. 45–8. Compare also John Blair's argument that the silence of the sources on this point may be because 'the most familiar areas of life are often the most liable to be taken for granted'; 'Minster churches in the landscape', in Della Hooke (ed.), *Anglo-Saxon Settlements* (Oxford: Basil Blackwell, 1988), pp. 35–58, at p. 36. Also useful here are Michael Franklin, 'The identification of minsters in the Midlands', in R. Allen Brown (ed.), *Anglo-Norman Studies VII* (Woodbridge: Boydell Press, 1985), pp. 69–88, and Steven Bassett, 'The administrative landscape of the diocese of Worcester in the tenth century', in Nicholas Brooks and Catherine Cubitt (eds.), *St Oswald of Worcester* (London and New York: Leicester University Press, 1996), pp. 147–73.

[18] David Rollason, 'Monasteries and society in early medieval Northumbria', in Thompson (ed.), *Monasteries and Society*, pp. 59–74; Cambridge and Rollason, 'Debate'; Blair, 'Debate'; David Palliser, 'Review article: the 'minster hypothesis': a case study', *Early Medieval Europe* 5 (1996), 207–14. Patrick Sims-Williams has taken a different perspective and argued that no deliberate policy served to shape a planned matrix of minsters in the west Midlands, and that the later medieval church-pattern there emerged in more haphazard fashion: *Religion and Literature*, pp. 168–72. Nicholas Brooks has also criticised the retrospective reading of later ecclesiastical boundaries onto the Anglo-Saxon landscape: 'Alfredian government: the West Saxon inheritance', in Timothy Reuter (ed.), *Alfred the Great* (Aldershot: Ashgate, 2003), pp. 153–74, at pp. 163–73.

lay society in the midst of which they were obliged to reside. Self-evidently, such duties would have conflicted with the monastic aspiration to isolation, depriving at least those members on whom the charge of providing spiritual services fell of their own opportunities for solitude and contemplation. If, however, pastoral care were provided by only some of the religious houses in pre-Viking Age England, we would need to determine how to distinguish such institutions from those without a pastoral charge. Further it would be necessary to explore how separate were the ways in which the two categories of monastic house interacted with the lay population (and, indeed, with the ecclesiastical hierarchy of the church).

Previously I have argued for the significance of contemporary linguistic use in both Latin and Old English for the insight it offers into the nature of communal religious establishments in England before the mid-ninth century.[19] In that period, the single Latin term *monasterium* (and its Old English equivalent, *mynster*) were not used monolithically to denote a religious community of a particular type; rather they were deployed in a broad sense to encompass a wide diversity of houses. Not all congregations were uniform, as John Blair has emphasised: the single term *monasterium* embraced diversity. It was not a precise descriptor of an institutional type or organisational character, for it signified only the communality of the inmates' existence.[20] A minster was simply a 'community church' and all early English religious lived in communities (apart from hermits and they, as already shown, had to train for the solitary life in a communal context and probably never wholly severed their ties with that group).[21] One important distinction was sustained linguistically and in the prescriptive literature relating to the roles of priests, other clergy and monks between congregations subject to the authority of an abbot and those responsible to a bishop. Episcopal seats were located more sparsely in the English kingdoms than elsewhere in contemporary Europe and, perhaps in part as a result of their relative scarcity, were seen as special places with particular functions.[22] Apart from differentiating it from a cathedral church and community it is difficult to define a minster more tightly: minsters reflected a broad church.

---

[19] Particularly in my 'Anglo-Saxon minsters: a review of terminology', in Blair and Sharpe (eds.), *Pastoral Care before the Parish*, pp. 212–25 and 'Language and method: the *Dictionary of Old English* and the historian', in M. J. Toswell (ed.), *The Dictionary of Old English: Retrospects and Prospects*, Old English Newsletter, Subsidia 26 (1998), 73–87.

[20] Blair, 'Debate', p. 194.   [21] *Ibid.*, p. 210.

[22] James Campbell, 'The church in Anglo-Saxon towns', in his *Essays in Anglo-Saxon History* (London: Hambledon, 1986), pp. 139–54, at pp. 139–40; Foot, 'Anglo-Saxon minsters', p. 219; Cambridge and Rollason, 'Debate', pp. 89–90.

This argument merely reiterates points made earlier in this volume and gets us little further in resolving this problem. Blair is right to argue that 'the semantic debate leads nowhere. Religious communities were diverse in size and character, but distinguishing between them on the basis of contemporary terminology is a lost cause.'[23] An alternative perspective on this problem was offered in an essay by Catherine Cubitt that sought to move the argument away from the discussion of institutions to look at the personnel involved in the provision of pastoral services. She focused on the single most important text from the period to tackle the *cura animarum*, the canons of the council that met at *Clofesho* in 747.[24] At this council an ambitious and complex programme was advanced offering systematic guidance for the improvement of the spiritual health of the English nation. Cubitt's detailed analysis of the canons draws attention to the focus of the legislators on the importance of episcopal authority, their desire to reform the internal organisation (and religious observance) of minsters by emphasising the contemplative and intellectual activities of their inmates, and their concern for the provision by ordained clergy of effective spiritual care for the laity. As she stresses,

> The canons are concerned not with institutions but with office. Pastoral duties are not portrayed as devolving upon organizations and communities, but upon individuals by virtue of their ordination. The cure of souls was seen in a spiritual rather than an institutional or geographical dimension. Priests may indeed have lived in communities, but *monasteria* are not viewed as the organizing structure for pastoral care. Where the canons do display an interest in regulations concerning where clergy and monks should live, it is to prevent them from living in lay households.[25]

This analysis draws attention to one of the main limitations of the 'minster model', its predominantly topographical emphasis and its failure to focus – as the contemporary sources did – on the people who administered pastoral care not the places where they lived. Important as it is to reposition the emphasis on the responsibilities of ordained clergy and to show that in their clerical roles priests and deacons were answerable directly to bishops (not to the abbots of their conventual houses), this does not remove the question of how pastoral care was delivered from the scope of an investigation of the role of the minsters in Anglo-Saxon lay society. For all the sources show that communal living was the norm for religious of every grade and status. Priests and deacons manifestly lived in minsters as well as

[23] Blair, 'Debate', p. 196.   [24] Cubitt, 'Pastoral care and conciliar canons'.   [25] *Ibid.*, p. 206.

in episcopal churches. We need to consider how their presence (and their manifest obligation to engage in external activities) affected the lives of the houses in which they dwelt.

Preaching and teaching

At the centre of all pastoral ministry lay the spiritual instruction of the laity, ranging from the most rudimentary explanations of the faith given to those who were yet to be converted, through basic catechetical teaching, to the more profound exposition of particular passages of Scripture for the benefit of mature believers. Its proper performance was of paramount importance to Bede, who, as Alan Thacker has demonstrated, saw the *doctores* and *praedicatores* of his own day as the spiritual leaders of the entire nation, the successors of the prophets and apostles.[26] In eighth-century terms 'preaching' may have been used as a shorthand for what we might prefer to call ministry, referring not just to the act of talking to the people about the faith, but the whole duty of bishops and priests to the people under their care.[27] Bede attributed much of the blame for the ills he perceived in the church of his own day to the lack of sufficient teachers of adequate learning; in his letter to Bishop Ecgberht of York he recommended that more suitable teachers should be appointed who might teach the people the truth of the faith and the difference between good and evil,[28] so that the laity might learn by what works to please God and from what sins to abstain, with what sincerity to believe, and with what devotion to pray.[29] In some of his writings, Bede extended his definition of 'pastor' to include not just bishops, priests and deacons, 'but also the heads of minsters and all the faithful who have the care of even small households'.[30] This wider understanding of pastoral responsibility included all Christians, even women.[31]

[26] Alan Thacker, 'Bede's ideal of reform', in Patrick Wormald *et al.* (eds.), *Ideal and Reality in Frankish and Anglo-Saxon Society* (Oxford: Basil Blackwell, 1985), pp. 130–53, at p. 130. Bede's own views on the subject were heavily indebted to those of Gregory the Great, whose writings are filled with allusions to teaching, presenting it as the particular province of those trained in the ascetic life, proficient in both active and contemplative virtues; *ibid.*, pp. 133–5. For discussion of the significance of Gregory's *Dialogues* to the formation of ideas about ministry in seventh-century Northumbria (and the radical suggestion that this text is in fact a Northumbrian composition), see Dunn, *The Emergence*, pp. 130–6, 189 and 199–200.

[27] Compare council of *Clofesho*, AD 747, ch. 9 (H&S III, 365), discussed further below, n. 55, where baptism is included under preaching and alongside teaching.

[28] *EpEcg*, § 7 (p. 410).   [29] *Ibid.*, ch. 15, p. 418.

[30] Bede, *Homelia*, I, 7 (ed. Hurst, p. 49); quoted by Cubitt, 'Pastoral care', p. 202.

[31] *In Ezram et Neemiam*, I (ed. Hurst, CCSL, 119A, p. 257), quoted in Thacker, 'Bede's ideal', p. 131. Compare also the use made of women in the mission to Germany: Barbara Yorke, 'The Bonifacian mission and female religious in Wessex', *Early Medieval Europe* 7 (1998), 145–72.

Nor was Bede alone in laying such stress on preaching and ministry in general; other English ecclesiastics also emphasised the importance of teaching the laity. Although Boniface was mostly concerned in his hortatory letters to the English with urging the eradication of the specific evils which he believed were present among both laymen and religious, he did comment on the role of teachers. These, he argued, were set over the church of God in order to give an example of good living to the people and through their diligent preaching to bring 'every man's sins before his eyes and show him what penalty awaits the hard of heart and what glory the obedient'.[32] Alcuin attributed to a lack of teachers many of the woes suffered by the English church in the late eighth century. Writing to the people of Kent in 797 after the rebellion of Eadberht Præn, he urged them to get themselves teachers and masters of the Scriptures so that there might be no want of the Word of God among them, for 'those who serve God in the church of Christ must take care to . . . maintain and preach the catholic faith which our teachers founded among them. For ignorance of the Scriptures is ignorance of God.'[33] He wrote in similar vein to Bishop Æthelberht of Hexham and his community: 'without teachers such a place as yours can hardly be saved, if at all. It is good to give alms to feed the poor with physical food, but satisfying the hungry soul with spiritual teaching is better.'[34] It is notable however, as Bullough observed, that in none of his letters to monastic communities among the English did Alcuin argue that their members should be involved in pastoral work with lay people.[35] His emphasis was on the priestly (and conceivably diaconal) responsibility for teaching.[36]

Many of the instances the sources narrate of occasions when priests and other religious left their own houses to go out to preach to the laity relate to the initial work of conversion. As soon as St Augustine's companions had acquired a place in which to settle at Canterbury, they preached the Word of life to as many as they could; once the king had been converted 'they received greater liberty to preach everywhere and to build or restore churches'.[37] Cedd and the priest sent with him to preach the Word to the East Saxons traversed the whole kingdom of Essex in order to build up a church for the Lord.[38] Oswald asked the Irish for a bishop by whose 'teaching and ministry' the race over whom he ruled might be brought to the faith; thereafter many men, mostly apparently professed religious, came

---

[32] Boniface, *Ep.* 78 (ed. Tangl, p. 166).   [33] Alcuin, *Ep.* 129 (ed. Dümmler, pp. 191–2).
[34] *Ibid.*, 31 (ed. Dümmler, pp. 72–3).
[35] Donald Bullough, *Alcuin: Achievement and Reputation* (Leiden and Boston: Brill, 2004), p. 311.
[36] *Ibid.*, pp. 304–13.   [37] *HE* I. 26 (pp. 76–7).   [38] *Ibid.*, III. 22 (pp. 282–3).

from Ireland to Northumbria to preach, the priests among them baptised the new believers, churches were built in various places and 'people flocked together with joy to hear the Word'.[39] Peripatetic clergy were, however, still to be found beyond the conversion period; indeed so frequently do narrative sources describe clergy travelling away from their own minsters to visit the laity such activities seem to have been, at least for a significant minority, part of the normal monastic round.

Boniface, who as a child was brought up near Exeter, was said first to have come into contact with the religious life 'when priests or clerics, travelling abroad, as is the custom in those parts to preach to the people, came to the town and the house where his father dwelt'.[40] Similar customs pertained in Northumbria; according to Bede, at the time when Cuthbert was at Melrose:

it was the custom among the English people, when a cleric or a priest came to a village, for all to gather at his command to hear the Word, gladly listening to what was said and still more gladly carrying out in their lives whatever they heard and could understand.[41]

Preaching was one of the principal functions of priests preoccupying the legislators at church councils. At *Clofesho* in 747, bishops were instructed not to ordain any monk or cleric to the priesthood without first examining his way of life, behaviour and knowledge of the faith, 'for how can he reasonably preach to others the soundness of faith, or provide knowledge of the word . . . who has not first with diligent effort studied these matters, so that, according to the Apostle, he may be able to "exhort with sound doctrine"'.[42] Successive church councils legislated against the unconditional ordination of priests, and there is every reason to presume that bishops tried both to maintain some control over all the parochial workers in their own dioceses and to ensure that such men were fit for their duties and continued to perform them diligently.[43] Except in the immediate vicinity of cathedral churches, priests living in minsters may have found it hard to evade their

---

[39] *Ibid.*, III. 3 (pp. 218–21).   [40] Willibald, *Vita S. Bonifatii*, ch. 1 (ed. Rau, p. 462).
[41] *HE* IV. 27 (pp. 432–3).
[42] Council of *Clofesho*, ch. 6 (H&S III, 364; quoting Titus 1: 9). Compare *ibid.*, ch. 9, which refers to the duties of priests in teaching and visiting, and ch. 11, which directs that each priestly function, whether baptising, teaching or judging should be performed in one uniform fashion (pp. 365–6).
[43] Compare council of Chelsea, AD 816, ch. 5 (H&S III, 581) and Ecgberht, *Dialogi*, ch. 9 (*ibid.*, p. 407) which ordered that priests should not be ordained *absolute*, that is without a charge. Foot 'Parochial ministry', pp. 50–2.

obligation to share their knowledge of the faith and its doctrines with a lay audience beyond the minster's walls.

Bede's accounts of Cuthbert's ministry to the local population suggest that the saint travelled purposefully to preach to specific groups of people. For example, Cuthbert and the boy attending him were apparently making a long journey towards a particular village on the occasion when an eagle fed them. Although they stopped at a village on the way to have the divinely provided food cooked for them – and Cuthbert took the opportunity to preach to their hosts – once they had eaten the two 'resumed their journey and set out to reach those whom they intended to teach'.[44] His preaching took Cuthbert far from home; he made a habit of teaching in 'those villages which were far away on steep and rugged mountains, which others dreaded to visit and whose poverty and ignorance kept others away' and such journeys might keep him away from Melrose for up to a month at a time.[45] It is not clear to what extent Cuthbert was alone in travelling such distances, nor whether others organised their teaching in a similarly systematic manner.

It is equally hard to determine from contemporary evidence the size, nature or distribution of the populations to which early Anglo-Saxon minster communities felt obliged to preach, if indeed such territories were as well-defined as some have argued.[46] None of the early sources in fact state explicitly that particular minsters were to take charge of specified areas; the word *parochia* is most usually used in sources from the early period with reference to a bishop's diocese, although as we saw in the previous chapter it could be used to describe a monastic 'empire'.[47] The *parochiae* of the first bishops seem to have been essentially coterminous with the boundaries of the kingdoms in which their sees were placed, although some of these enormous dioceses were subsequently divided, for example that of the West Saxons and those in the Northumbrian kingdoms. Bishops were generally described more often in relation to the people for whom they took responsibility rather by reference to the territory they served, which points again to an emphasis on people (in this case those whose souls had need of care) not space.[48] The relationship between non-cathedral churches and the

---

[44] Bede, *VSCuth.* ch. 12 (pp. 196–7). Compare Bede's account of Cuthbert's ministry: *HE* IV. 27 (pp. 432–5).

[45] *HE* IV. 27 (pp. 432–4).   [46] See for example Blair, 'Introduction'.

[47] See above, pp. 264–7. Asser did refer to the *parochia* of the church of Exeter, apparently in the sense used by Celtic Latin authors, to designate the jurisdiction of a church or minster, rather than with reference to an area administered by a bishop: Life of Alfred, ch. 81 (ed. Stevenson, p. 68); see Keynes and Lapidge, *Alfred the Great*, pp. 50–1, and 264–5, n. 193.

[48] For example, the proceedings of the 747 council of *Clofesho* begin by listing all the bishops who were present according to the peoples for whom they were responsible: council of *Clofesho*, prologue (H&S

laity is far less well-defined in any of the early sources. Partly this reflects the fact that almost nothing is known about the lay population to whom such communities ministered; they are usually described by such anonymous collective terms as *gentes*, *prouinciales*, or, most often, *populi*.[49] Even where a lay person comes into closer focus as a key player in a particular incident or as the recipient of a saint's miraculous powers, he or she is seldom depicted in much detail, for the hagiographer's focus was not on the recipient of grace (or divine displeasure) but on the saint whose holy powers the episode served to prove.

The close correspondence visible between minsters and *villae regales* has led some to presume that such ecclesiastical communities would take charge of the cure of souls over an area coterminous with that administered from the vill, which was likely to comprise several villages.[50] Certainly Aidan may be seen to have organised his ministry around royal estates; Bede reported that he had a church and a cell on a royal estate not far from Bamburgh 'where he often used to go and stay, travelling about in the neighbourhood to preach. He did the same on the other royal estates.'[51] Lay people may have felt some loyalty towards the particular church in their neighbourhood. In the time of the Irish at Lindisfarne the local people used apparently to flock on Sundays to the church and the minster there in order to hear the Word of God.[52] The council held at *Clofesho* in 747 recommended that on Sundays and at the major feasts the laity should be invited to churches to hear the Word of God and the preaching of sermons.[53] Presumably those who attended such services went regularly to one local minster not to a variety of different churches, but their opportunities for so doing must have varied considerably in different parts of the country.

In his letter to Bishop Ecgberht of York, Bede had commented on the many portions of the wide Northumbrian diocese which were deprived of access to a priest or indeed of any spiritual teaching. He advised the bishop to appoint some assistants to help him 'by ordaining priests and instituting teachers who may devote themselves to preaching the word of God in the various

III, 362). Bede frequently described bishops in similar fashion, for example reporting that Diuma was consecrated bishop of the Middle Angles and Mercians by Bishop Finan: *HE* III. 21. But compare *ibid.*, V. 23, where Bede listed all the bishops reigning in 731 by reference to the *prouinciae* they served. Campbell, 'The church', pp. 139–40.

[49] *HE* III. 21 (p. 278); IV. 13 (p. 372); Willibald, *Vita S. Bonifatii*, ch. 1 (ed. Rau, p. 464).

[50] G. W. O. Addleshaw, *The Pastoral Organisation of the Modern Dioceses of Durham and Newcastle in the Time of Bede*, Jarrow Lecture 1963 (Jarrow [St Paul's Church, 1964]), pp. 11–2; Sawyer, 'The royal *tun*', pp. 277–8.

[51] *HE* III. 17 (pp. 262–3).   [52] *Ibid.*, III. 26 (pp. 310–11).   [53] Council of *Clofesho*, ch. 14 (H&S III, 367).

villages . . . wherever opportunity arises'.[54] In the light of the statements made in later church councils about the appointing of priests to specific places which imply that priests were appointed by bishops to a particular cure, one might surmise that Bede here imagined that Ecgberht would assign specific areas to the care of individual teachers.[55] At *Clofesho* in 747, bishops were recommended to visit all the portions of their dioceses every year in order to call together in convenient places the people of every condition and sex, 'especially those who rarely hear the word of God', to teach them plainly.[56] The insufficiency of clerical provision in rural areas was obviously a continuing problem. In which case, it is difficult to imagine that the sort of teaching provided by bishops or any others on such occasions was more than the most rudimentary instruction in the basics of Christian belief and behaviour; while the hold of Christianity on the population remained apparently so tenuous, more advanced exegetical or theological preaching could have had no meaning for the majority of the laity.

Not all teaching and preaching was necessarily welcomed enthusiastically by the laity; it may not invariably have been through ecclesiastical neglect that certain areas remained predominantly pagan in their beliefs. Dícuill and his companions at Bosham could not get any of the native South Saxons to follow their way of life or listen to their preaching.[57] The first Irishman invited by Oswald also made no impression on the Northumbrian people, whom he apparently thought were 'intractable, obstinate and barbarous'; Aidan, who was sent to replace him, was said to have had greater success because he offered the people 'the milk of simpler teaching until they were capable of receiving more advanced instruction'.[58] English resistance to missionary methods was, however, less violently stated than were the objections of some of the pagans among whom Anglo-Saxon and Irish missionaries tried to preach in the eighth century.[59]

---

[54] *EpEcg*, § 5 (p. 408).

[55] The council of *Clofesho*, AD 747, ch. 9 (H&S III, 365) directed that priests should take care to perform their duty of evangelical and apostolic preaching in baptising, teaching, and visiting 'in the places and districts of the laity assigned to them by the bishops of the province'. It was also stipulated at the legatine synods of 786 that priests and deacons were to remain in that *titulus* to which they had been consecrated, so that no one should presume to accept a priest or deacon from the title of another without good reason: Legatine synods, ch. 6 (ed. Dümmler, p. 22).

[56] Council of *Clofesho*, ch. 3 (H&S III, 363–4). Compare legatine synod, AD 786, ch. 3 (ed. Dümmler, p. 21), which directed that on their annual visitations bishops should set up meeting points at convenient places so that all can meet to hear the Word of God. The bishops were advised to preach diligently to their flock, giving warning like watchful shepherds and condemning sin.

[57] *HE* IV. 13 (pp. 372–3).   [58] *Ibid.*, III. 5 (pp. 228–9).

[59] Compare, for example, the sad fate of the two Hewalds, *HE* V. 10 (pp. 482–3), and for a wide discussion of northern European missions see Richard Fletcher, *The Conversion of Europe: From Paganism to Christianity 371–1386 AD* (London: HarperCollins, 1997), ch. 7.

Baptism

Baptism, the initiation ceremony by which new believers were admitted to the fellowship of the church, was perhaps the most important of all the Christian sacraments, and certainly had particular significance in the missionary phase of the evolution of the early English church. In his commentary on Luke's Gospel, Bede argued that 'no-one unless he is baptized, unless he is united to the body of Christ, shall enter the church'.[60] Everlasting damnation awaited those who died unbaptised. The anonymous author of the Whitby Life of Gregory the Great believed that those blessed people who, having been slain at the battle of Hatfield Chase, returned later in splendour to view their earthly bodies had undoubtedly been baptised.[61] Boniface was equally sure that the adulterously conceived offspring of English religious women who were murdered by their mothers at birth would be crowding hell, but it is unclear whether it was their illegitimacy or their lack of baptism (or both) which would have condemned them to such a fate.[62] Confirmation was administered as a separate rite in the early Anglo-Saxon period and was an episcopal prerogative.[63]

Most of the references in the narrative sources to the administration of baptism during our period relate to the conversion of different English peoples to Christianity. For example, the anonymous author of the Whitby Life of Gregory recorded how Paulinus converted King Edwin to the faith, and then instructed him and the other new converts as catechumens before baptising the king as his spiritual father.[64] Since many of the sources implied that baptism was an immediate consequence of the acceptance of Christianity, this passage is particularly interesting for it implies that there could be an interval between conversion and baptism. In describing the conversion of Æthelberht of Kent, for instance, Bede made no reference to any formal period of catechism but stated merely: 'at last the king, as well as others,

---

[60] Bede, *In Lucam*, III (ed. Hurst, CCSL 120, 5–425); see my '"By water in the Spirit": the administration of baptism in Anglo-Saxon England', in Blair and Sharpe (eds.), *Pastoral Care before the Parish*, pp. 171–92, at p. 172.

[61] *LBG* ch. 19 (pp. 104–5). Compare also Gregory, *Moralia*, II. 21 (*PL* LXXV, 877; quoted by Colgrave, *The Earliest Life of Gregory the Great*, pp. 150–2, n. 76), which argued for the damnation of unbaptised babies.

[62] Boniface, *Ep.* 73 (ed. Tangl, p. 151). Boniface's belief in the importance of apostolic ministry, and in the central role played by instruction, together with the administration of baptism, in the furtherance of the evangelical faith, is clear from the glosses to the epistle of James in the Codex Fuldensis (Fulda, Landesbibliothek, Codex Bonifatianus 1, fos. 435v–441v) which are thought to have been written in Boniface's own hand: Malcolm Parkes, 'The handwriting of St Boniface: a reassessment of the problems', *Beiträge zur Geschichte der deutschen Sprache und Literatur*, 98 (1976), 161–79, at pp. 171–9.

[63] Discussed fully in my '"By water in the Spirit"', p. 179.   [64] *LBG* ch. 15 (ed. Colgrave, pp. 96–9).   297

believed and was baptized, being attracted by the pure life of the saints and by their most precious promises, whose truth [the missionaries] confirmed by performing many miracles'.[65] Several narratives describe bishops, accompanied by groups of priests, travelling around the countryside taking teaching and baptism to the people; others show priests working alone, or in small groups.[66]

Our other information about the regular provision of the sacrament of baptism by the members of religious communities between the conversion and the First Viking Age derives largely from the prescriptive literature of penitentials and church councils, which repeatedly stressed the importance of its proper performance.[67] The council of *Clofesho* of 747 emphasised the apostolic nature of the priestly functions of baptism, preaching and visiting, seeking to ensure that all priests would perform their duties in these spheres in like fashion, according to the manner of the Roman Church.[68] The canons also directed that priests should learn the words of the baptismal office in order to be able to explain their spiritual significance.[69] At the council held at Chelsea in 816, while priests were told not to seek greater duties than those laid on them by their bishops, baptism was specifically excluded from this injunction; instead priests everywhere were charged to ensure that they never refused to perform the ministry of baptism, those that did refuse it through negligence being directed to cease from their ministry until corrected by their bishop.[70] Secular legislators showed similar concern about the availability of baptism. King Wihtred of Kent directed in his law-code that any priest who neglected the baptism of a sick man should abstain from all ministry until he had been reconciled to his bishop.[71] The prominence accorded to baptism in these texts shows that it was considered as essential a part of pastoral ministry as was preaching and that its overall organisation fell once more to bishops, but the legislators had little to say about where baptism was performed.

---

[65] *HE* I. 26 (pp. 76–7); Henry Mayr-Harting, *The Coming of Christianity to Anglo-Saxon England* (London: Batsford, 1972; 3rd edn, 1991), pp. 61–8. Compare, however, *HE* IV. 13 (pp. 374–5), where Wilfrid instructed the people of Selsey in the faith of Christ before he washed them in the waters of baptism: '"By water in the Spirit"', pp. 175–7.

[66] Cubitt, 'Pastoral care', p. 200.   [67] Foot, '"By water in the Spirit"', pp. 183–6.

[68] Council of *Clofesho*, AD 747, chs. 9, 11, 13 (H&S III, 365–7).

[69] *Ibid.*, ch. 10, p. 366. Compare also the injunction of the 786 legatine synod, ch. 2 (ed. Dümmler, p. 21) that baptism should be administered according to the canonical statutes.

[70] Council of Chelsea, AD 816, ch. 11 (H&S III, 584). See my 'Parochial ministry', p. 52.

[71] Laws of King Wihtred, ch. 6 (ed. Liebermann, *Die Gesetze*, I, 12); compare Laws of King Ine, chs. 2–2.1 (*ibid.*, p. 90).

In contrast to Gaul and Italy during the same period, where baptismal churches were widely distributed not only in cities but also in rural areas, there were seemingly few special baptismal churches in early Anglo-Saxon England. Cathedrals obviously had fonts or separate baptisteries and acted as a focal point for the administration of the sacrament for the diocese; some other baptisteries have been identified from archaeological excavation.[72] For the majority of the rural population who lived too far from such places, however, alternative arrangements will have been necessary and it is hard to resist the assumption that this obligation fell on the congregations of minster churches. According to Theodore, the administration of baptism was not an exclusively priestly function, for his Penitential permitted deacons to baptise, in the same way that preaching was deemed the responsibility of instituted teachers not just priests.[73] Theodore did decree that 'if anyone who is not ordained performs baptism through temerity, he is cut off from the Church and shall never be ordained'.[74] Should we assume that away from the vicinity of cathedral churches, baptism was provided by clerics – and possibly others, not in clerical orders – who lived in minster communities?

Later evidence relating to the collection of the chrism – the holy oil for baptism and extreme unction, collected from the bishop in return for a payment of chrism-money each Maundy Thursday – points to a system for the organised provision of baptism within a diocese. For Kent the *Domesday Monachorum* provides a list of those churches entitled to collect the chrism, including Dover, Folkestone, Lyminge and St Augustine's, Canterbury, of the pre-viking minsters.[75] As Nicholas Brooks suggested, 'their annual payment of chrism-money to the archbishop is best understood as a jealously maintained relic of an age when the Kentish "monasteries" were true baptismal churches, taking a dominant role in the pastoral work of the diocese'.[76] Similar evidence for the supply of the chrism in other dioceses does not survive, but it is hard to suggest any alternative to the minsters as the main providers of the sacrament of baptism in Kent and elsewhere in the seventh and eighth centuries. That obligation need not have fallen on all members of a minster's congregation, but unless we are to treat the legislative

---

[72] For examples see '"By water in the Spirit"', pp. 180–2.

[73] Theodore, Penitential, II. ii. 16 (ed. Finsterwalder, p. 315); Compare Thacker, 'Bede's ideal of reform', pp. 131–3; Cubitt, 'Pastoral care', p. 201.

[74] Theodore, Penitential, I. ix. 11 (ed. Finsterwalder, p. 303).

[75] David C. Douglas, *The Domesday Monachorum of Christ Church, Canterbury* (London: Royal Historical Society, 1944), pp. 77–8; '"By water in the Spirit"', pp. 181–2.

[76] Brooks, *The Early History*, p. 189. See also Frank Barlow, *The English Church 1066–1154* (London: Longman, 1979), pp. 179–80.

pronouncements about the importance of baptism as mere rhetoric, we may have to envisage some disruption to the tranquillity of the cloister occasioned by the arrival of adults demanding the cleansing ritual of baptism either for themselves or for their children.[77]

Arrangements had also to be made for those who did not choose to present themselves at churches for baptism. According to his biographers, Cuthbert spent much of his time in preaching and also baptising the people in the mountains in the name of the Trinity on his many lengthy journeys away from his own minster.[78] From Bede's account of Cuthbert's ministry it would seem that much of his teaching was directed towards those who had nominally received the faith, and so presumably already been baptised, even if they retained a rather fragile grasp of Christian precepts.[79] If this is an accurate representation it must be assumed that at least some of those whom Cuthbert baptised were the children of Christian parents. An incident related in Stephen's life of Bishop Wilfrid in which a woman offered her dead baby to the saint for baptism in the hope that he would thereby be restored to life might point to the mother's faith in the efficacy of the baptismal sacrament, although it could of course represent only her confidence in Wilfrid's thaumaturgic powers.[80] Even if the proportion of children baptised did gradually increase, a sizeable proportion of the English population was probably still being newly converted in adulthood. Theodore's Penitential certainly appears to address the eventuality that in practice many adults may never have received baptism; he ordered (separately from those instructions relating to unbaptised children) the deposition of any priest who refused, because of the exertion of the journey, to travel to a sick person in order to baptise them with the result that the individual died without receiving that sacrament.[81] If we accept that some clerics left their minsters to go out and preach to the people, we should probably expect them, like Cuthbert and Wilfrid, to have been prepared to administer baptism to those who had need of it.

When after the end of the evangelising phase of England's Christianisation infant baptism began to replace the initiation of mature believers will have depended both on the success of missionary endeavours and on the

---

[77] I argued in '"By water with the Spirit"' (pp. 190–2) that the church's success in persuading the laity of the benefits of baptism can be seen from the increasing evidence for parental demands for its provision. It is likely that, as in sixth-century Gaul, baptism was commonly performed at the liturgical seasons of Easter and Whitsun.

[78] Anon., *VSCuth*. II. 5–6 (pp. 86–7).   [79] Bede, *VSCuth*. ch. 9 (pp. 184–5).

[80] *VSW* ch. 18 (pp. 38–9).   [81] Theodore, Penitential, I. ix. 7 (ed. Finsterwalder, p. 302).

local availability of sufficient clergy to perform the rite for new parents.[82] In his commentary on Mark, Bede stated that parents were accustomed to speak the *fides* and *confessio* for their infants at the font in order to deliver them from the devil, which implies that by his day infant baptism was usual.[83] The compilers of the canons of the legatine councils of 786 also assumed that infant baptism was the norm, directing that those who acted as sponsors for children (*paruuli*) at the font and spoke for them renouncing Satan and all his works, should know the Creed and be able to teach this and the Lord's Prayer to their godchildren when they were older.[84] Yet, we gain a rather different impression from the various pieces of ecclesiastical legislation dealing with the problems caused by the death of unbaptised children and infants. Theodore clearly considered infant baptism to be the ideal, although he recognised that it was frequently never performed at all. If the parents were responsible for failing to have a child who died in infancy baptised, he imposed a penance of one year, but should the child have been as old as three at its death and still unbaptised, a period of three years was prescribed.[85] Ine's laws imposed similarly harsh penalties for parents who failed to have their children baptised; if a child had still to be baptised after thirty days, thirty shillings' compensation was to be paid, but should it die without baptism 'he is to compensate for it with all that he possesses'.[86] Priests were apparently as often responsible for omitting to perform baptisms; Theodore directed that 'if an infant that is weak and is a pagan has been recommended to a presbyter for baptism and dies unbaptised, the presbyter shall be deposed'.[87]

While organisation of the provision of baptism was an episcopal task, and those who administered the sacrament were clearly answerable to the bishop for their competence and diligence in its performance, it is impossible to imagine that all the ministers of baptism belonged to episcopal households. The practical difficulties of a widely dispersed population demanded a different solution, one that the clergy who dwelt in minsters were best placed

[82] Foot, '"By water in the Spirit"', pp. 187–9.
[83] Bede, *In Marci evangelium expositio*, II. vii. 29, lines 1419–23 (ed. Hurst, CCSL 120, p. 525); quoted by Joseph H. Lynch, *Godparents and Kinship in Early Medieval Europe* (Princeton, NJ: Princeton University Press, 1986), p. 243.
[84] Legatine synod, AD 786, ch. 2 (ed. Dümmler, p. 21).
[85] Penitential of Theodore, I. xiv. 29 (p. 310). To this last injunction, the compiler of the penitential added the statement that Theodore had given this decision at a certain time because it happened to be referred to him, which implies that, however much infant baptism was the ideal, it was often not performed.
[86] Laws of Ine, chs. 2, 2.1 (ed. Liebermann, *Die Gesetze*, I, 90); Allen J. Frantzen, *The Literature of Penance in Anglo-Saxon England* (New Brunswick, NJ: Rutgers University Press, 1983), p. 79.
[87] Theodore, Penitential, I. xiv. 28 (ed. Finsterwalder, p. 310).

to supply. Not all such men will have welcomed the task, but the attitude of both secular and ecclesiastical hierarchies to those who failed in this critical duty of pastoral care was clear.

The mass

Clerical commentators were keen to encourage lay participation in the sacrament of the Eucharist. Writing to Ecgberht, bishop of York in 734, Bede urged, 'how salutary for every class of Christian is the daily partaking of the body and blood of our Lord, according to what you know is wisely done by the Church of Christ throughout Italy, Gaul, Africa, Greece and the whole East'. In the circumstances of the early eighth century this was probably somewhat over-ambitious an aspiration. Bede himself recognised that although there were 'innumerable people of chaste conduct, boys and girls, young men and maidens, old men and women, who could without a doubt participate in the celestial mysteries every Sunday, or also on the nativities of the holy apostles or martyrs', the practice of regular communion among such people was virtually unknown because of the 'carelessness of teachers'.[88] Bearing in mind the low opinion of the married state expressed elsewhere in his writings, it is unlikely that Bede's recommendations about lay participation in the mass were intended to encompass the majority of the married laity who had not vowed to remain chaste.[89] Contemporary penitential literature certainly displayed a strict attitude towards the taking of sacraments by the sexually active; if these lay people had paid any attention to such proscriptions, the occasions on which they would have been permitted to communicate would have been very limited.[90]

Those responsible for drafting the canons of the council held at *Clofesho* in 747 also appear not to have endorsed the regular participation in the Eucharist for all the laity. They recommended only that young boys be encouraged to communicate more frequently while, by virtue of their youth, they remained uncorrupted. As for older men only the unmarried and 'the married who refrain from sin' were exhorted to regular communion. The

---

[88] *EpEcg*, § 15 (p. 419).

[89] For Bede's attitude to the married state see his commentary on I Peter, 3 (*PL* XCIII, 55); Thacker, 'Monks, preaching and pastoral care', pp. 155–6.

[90] Theodore's Penitential contains various canons restricting the access of married people to communion, see for example I. xii. 3; I. xiv. 1; and II. xii. 1–4 (ed. Finsterwalder, pp. 305, 306 and 326).

same council did direct in addition that the people should attend churches on Sundays in order to be present at the sacraments of the masses as well as to hear sermons preached; whether those who attended in this fashion actually received communion is unclear.[91] Earlier, Archbishop Theodore had also envisaged that members of the laity would be present in churches, for he stipulated that a layman ought not to recite a lection in a church or say the Alleluia, but only say the psalms and responses without the Alleluia.[92] Again it is not apparent whether this remark implies that lay people were present at other services than the mass, nor does this clarify the problem of the lay receipt of communion. Nevertheless, the paucity of references in saints' lives to daily, or even weekly, communication by the members of religious communities renders it improbable that many of the laity received the sacrament in churches at all frequently.[93]

Travelling priests may have taken the sacrament to the laity in their villages. Theodore's Penitential made provision for the celebration of masses outside church buildings in fields, stipulating that the elements should not be allowed to touch the ground but always be held by the priest or a deacon.[94] Yet the directives made at the church councils about episcopal visitations and about the duties of priests outside their minsters do not refer to the saying of masses. While the council of *Clofesho* of 747 laid considerable stress on the duties of priests at the altar, and the proper celebration of the sacraments, in discussing priests' duties towards the laity the canons referred only to teaching, preaching and baptising, never to the saying of masses outside the minster.[95] The Dialogues of Ecgberht devoted a good deal of attention to the behaviour of priests outside minsters, for several of the questions dealt with the activities of foreign priests or of English clergy away from their own dioceses. His answers were worded in rather vague terms, however, and refer for the most part simply to the act of 'ministering' (*ministrare*).[96] Ecgberht does seem to have understood external ministry to include the administration of sacraments. When asked, for example, whether priests

---

[91] Council of *Clofesho*, chs. 23 and 14 (H&S III, 370 and 367).
[92] Theodore, Penitential, II. i. 10 (ed. Finsterwalder, p. 313).
[93] The statement in Theodore's Penitential that 'the Greeks, clergy and laymen communicate every Lord's day, and those who do not communicate for three Lord's days are to be excommunicated' (I. xii. 1; p. 305) may have been made to draw direct comparison with the less regular habits of the English. We investigated the place of the Eucharist in minsters in chapter 5, pp. 205–7.
[94] Theodore, Penitential II. ii. 2 (p. 313).
[95] The sacramental obligations of priests were addressed by the council held at *Clofesho* in 747, chs. 8, 10, 13, 14, 16 (H&S III, 365–8). Canon 9 dealt with the duties of priests entrusted by bishops with care for 'places and regions of the laity' (p. 365); Cubitt, 'Pastoral care', p. 196.
[96] Ecgberht, *Dialogi, Responsiones* 5, 6, 9 (H&S III, 405–7).

were permitted to minister anywhere without the consent of the bishop in whose diocese they were staying, he replied:

Foreign priests, or those ordained without charge, going around the country without letters of commendation, are not allowed to minister or give the sacraments without the consent of the bishop of that place.[97]

Saints' lives offer a similar picture, concentrating more on their subjects' activities of preaching or baptising than on their celebration of communion. Both the prose Lives of Cuthbert described his work among the laity in the districts around Melrose and Lindisfarne, but neither referred to his celebration of masses other than those said within his own minster or cell, or that which he performed on one occasion for the dedication of a church on one of Whitby's estates.[98] Administering communion to the laity is not among the activities described by Stephen in his Life of St Wilfrid. It is difficult to escape the conclusion that in the early Anglo-Saxon period lay people seldom received communion, either at a church in their locality or on occasions when visiting religious came to their villages.

Confession and penance

Public penitential rituals presided over by a bishop of the type practised in the early church may have been used in Anglo-Saxon England; if they were, they existed beside rituals of private penance. These provided church-men with a valuable missionary tool, in giving them an opportunity to explain the essentials of the faith to individuals rather than to groups; it also allowed them to exercise some degree of control over the religious behaviour of members of the laity with whom they established a relationship as con-fessor.[99] In this role they were guided by penitential handbooks such as that compiled by the *discipulus Umbrensium*, who recorded Theodore's judgements about penance as he learnt them from a certain priest Eoda.[100] According to Theodore, reconciliation was not in his time 'publicly established in this province for the reason that there is no public penance either',[101] but the Dialogues of Ecgberht barred anyone who had previously committed crimes requiring public penance from ordination to the priesthood. The same text also decreed that any existing priests who, after ordination, were guilty of

---

[97] *Ibid., Responsio* 9 (p. 407).   [98] Anon., *VSCuth*. IV.10 (pp. 126–7); Bede, *VSCuth*. ch. 34 (pp. 262–5).
[99] Frantzen, *The Literature of Penance*, pp. 4–7.
[100] Theodore, Penitential, preface (ed. Finsterwalder, p. 287).
[101] Theodore, Penitential, I. xiii. 4 (p. 306); compare Frantzen, *The Literature of Penance*, p. 66.

the worship of idols or other pagan practices, of murder, fornication, theft or perjury should be deposed, and might not be readmitted to communion as laymen until they had done public penance.[102] It is possible that this passage derives from a canon of the early church, although no liturgical records of public penance earlier than the prayers for the reconciliation of penitents on Maundy Thursday found in the tenth-century Ecgberht Pontifical survive.[103] Whether the ritual was actually performed in the early Anglo-Saxon period is not clear.

One of the roles of seventh- and eighth-century pastoral workers appears to have been the hearing of individual confessions and the imposition of private penance. Bede reported that when Cuthbert went out to the villages, the people gathered round him, did not hide their secrets from him, 'but they all made open confession of what they had done, because they thought that these things could certainly never be hidden from him, and they cleansed themselves from the sins they had confessed by "fruits worthy of repentance" as he commanded'.[104] At the council of *Clofesho* in 747, bishops were instructed to ensure that they ordained no one to the priesthood until they had investigated his knowledge of the faith in order that he might, among other things, properly be able to fulfil the function of enjoining penance to others.[105] If the laity had taken communion as often as some churchmen thought they should (and as frequently as the council recommended), those laypeople would have had to confess their sins regularly as part of their preparation for the sacrament. Having already cast considerable doubt on the frequency of lay communion, we would be unwise to try to deduce much about penitential practices from these edicts.[106] Nevertheless, the inclusion in the canons of the *Clofesho* council of a long chapter about general Christian behaviour, commending particularly alms-giving, fasting, and psalmody, does seem to indicate that at the very least penances were being imposed, even if all penitents did not necessarily adhere rigorously to their terms. No one was to 'relax fasting imposed for sins', nor attempt to pay for the vicarious performance of his own penance by others who fasted or sang psalms on his behalf.[107]

Secular law supports the presumption that penances were performed in this period. The laws of Wihtred directed that men living in illicit

[102] Ecgberht, *Dialogi, Responsio* 15 (H&S III, 410).
[103] John T. McNeill and Helena M. Gamer, *Medieval Handbooks of Penance* (New York: Columbia University Press, 1938), p. 240, n. 8. H. M. J. Banting, *Two Anglo-Saxon Pontificals (the Egbert and Sidney Sussex Pontificals)*, Henry Bradshaw Society, 104 (Woodbridge: Boydell Press, 1989), pp. 130–2, 145.
[104] Bede, *VSCuth.* ch. 9 (pp. 186–7).   [105] Council of *Clofesho*, AD 747, ch. 6 (H&S III, 364).
[106] Frantzen, *The Literature of Penance*, p. 81.   [107] Council of *Clofesho*, AD 747, ch. 27 (H&S III, 373).

cohabitation were to turn to a right life with repentance of sins or to be excluded from the fellowship of the church.[108] Similarly, there may be a reference to penitential books (or to the canons of church councils) in the injunction in the same code that if 'any *gesith*-born man chooses to enter into an illicit union in spite of the command of the king and the bishop and the decree of the books, he is to pay to his lord 100 shillings according to the ancient law'.[109] Alfred's law-code contained further references to ecclesiastical confession, decreeing that 'If any man has recourse to the church on account of any crime which has not been discovered and there confesses himself in God's name, it is to be half-remitted.'[110]

The hearing of confession, the appointment of penance, and granting of absolution were all functions restricted by the early medieval Church to priests and bishops, and the exclusive rights of such men in this sphere were reinforced by Theodore in his Penitential: 'A deacon may not give penance to a layman but a bishop or a presbyter ought to give it.'[111] All were required to confess capital sins, but members of religious communities were expected also to confess their venial sins for which the head of their minster would impose penance. Some women (presumably abbesses) may have attempted to prescribe penances to the sisters in their convents, for to the instruction 'it is the function of bishops and priests to prescribe penance', some manuscripts add: 'No woman may adjudge penance for anyone since in the canons no one may do this except the priest alone.'[112] It was a liberty (*libertas*, i.e. a privilege, not an obligation) for *monasteria* to adjudge penance to laymen for, Theodore repeated, 'this is properly a function of the clergy'.[113] Whether monastic tenants were expected also to follow monastic penitential discipline is not clear, but that they would have had to confess daily seems unlikely.

One of the other-worldly visions included by Bede in his *Historia ecclesiastica* sheds an interesting sidelight on the place of penance in the life of a layman. The visionary was an unnamed Mercian of military rank, who failed to take adequate care of his own soul and ignored the salutary advice given apparently not by a priest or bishop but by his king, Cenred, who 'warned him constantly to make confession, mend his ways, and give up

---

[108] Wihtred, Laws, ch. 3 (ed. Liebermann, *Die Gesetze*, I, 12).

[109] *Ibid.*, ch. 5, p. 12; Frantzen, *The Literature of Penance*, p. 79.

[110] Laws of Alfred, ch. 5. 4 (ed. Liebermann, *Die Gesetze*, I, 52). Compare also *ibid.*, ch. 14, which, although relating to the payment of secular compensation, does in the language it employs seem also to allude to a penitential practice: 'If anyone is born dumb or deaf so he cannot deny sins or confess them, the father is to pay compensation for his misdeeds.'

[111] Theodore, Penitential, II. ii. 15 (ed. Finsterwalder, p. 315).

[112] *Ibid.*, II. vii. 2 (p. 322).   [113] *Ibid.*, II. vi. 16 (p. 321).

his sins, before sudden death robbed him of all opportunity of repentance and amendment'. When he fell ill, it was again the king who urged him to repent before he died, but he refused on the grounds that he did not want to be accused of doing, for fear of death, something which he would not do when he was in good health. However, he then had a vision that he was visited by angels from heaven and devils from hell; these showed him written record of his good deeds and his many crimes, and agreed between them that he was bound for everlasting damnation, and he died shortly thereafter.[114] Bede drew the moral very clearly: 'Now he suffers everlasting and fruitless punishment in torment because he failed to submit for a brief spell to the penance which would have brought him the fruit of pardon.'[115] The legatine synods of 786 expressed this doctrine with equal force, decreeing 'If any man die without repentance and confession (which God forbid) prayers must not be made for him.'[116]

Frantzen's assertion that 'penance is not the practice of a small segment of society living near a minster, but a prescription for social observance intended for all devout Christians', seems to be supported by the evidence for the practice of confession from the early period.[117] Here, as in the performance of other strictly clerical roles, we may imagine that the labour devolved to some only of a minster's inmates. When we turn to more general charitable tasks, we may find that these were more widely distributed among professed religious, not just those who had been ordained.

Care of the sick

Miracles of healing occupied a prominent place in the stock repertoire of early medieval hagiography, since all saints' lives included accounts of such incidents as a means of demonstrating their subjects' divine powers. These narratives often provide insights into lay attitudes towards holy men and sacred places, which although rarely central to the narrator's preoccupations, can tell us much about the expectations placed upon churches by the laity. The church showed considerable willingness in this period to adapt its

---

[114] *HE* V. 13 (pp. 498–502).

[115] *HE* V. 13 (pp. 500–3). That the vehicle of the salutary advice in the story happened to be a layman, would, if accurate, provide some indication of the pervasiveness of Christian ideals and teaching among a certain sector of Mercian society. In fact King Cenred was probably unusually interested in religious matters, for after only five years as king he followed his predecessor and uncle, King Æthelred, into the cloister, going to Rome where he was tonsured by Pope Constantine: Colgrave and Mynors, pp. 498–9, n. 2.

[116] Legatine synods, ch. 20 (ed. Dümmler, p. 27).   [117] Frantzen, *The Literature of Penance*, p. 67.   307

rituals to accommodate the needs of the sick, maimed and possessed, and their relatives and carers, notably by encouraging such unfortunates to come to seek cures at saints' shrines.[118] By linking sickness with divine displeasure and portraying illness and disfigurement as the outward manifestations of God's punishment, churchmen appropriated to themselves a central role in the management of illness as a route to ultimate salvation. We should not be too ready to dismiss hagiographical evidence for the involvement of minsters and their inmates in the care of the sick. Whether they welcomed the task or not, many – perhaps most – minster communities found that the care of the sick occupied a significant place in their lives, the responsibilities it entailed falling on women as well as on men.[119]

Medicine seems to have been studied in at least some religious communities; others certainly possessed books about medicine, although it is unclear what these contained. Cyneheard, bishop of Winchester, wrote to Bishop Lull of Mainz in *c.* 760 asking for some medical treatises, because although he already had some, the medical recipes prescribed by scholars from overseas were unknown to him and difficult to prepare.[120] Archbishop Theodore took considerable interest in medicine: among the collection of canons known as his Penitential is a recipe for dysentery: the gall of hare to be mixed with pepper for the relief of pain.[121] John of Beverley learnt about blood-letting from Theodore. On one occasion, John was asked to visit Cwenburh, a sister at Watton who, being seriously ill, had recently been bled in the arm, which had since become swollen and agonisingly painful. John declared that those treating her had acted 'foolishly and ignorantly to bleed her on the fourth day of the moon; I remember how Archbishop Theodore of blessed memory used to say that it was very dangerous to bleed a patient when the moon is waxing and the ocean tide flowing'.[122]

[118] Janet L. Nelson, 'Parents, children and the church in the early Middle Ages', in Diana Wood (ed.), *The Church and Childhood*, Studies in Church History 31 (Oxford: Blackwell for the Ecclesiastical History Society, 1994), 81–114, at p. 91.
[119] For consideration of the care of the sick Christian by clerics in sixth-century Gaul, compare Henry J. G. Beck, *The Pastoral Care of Souls in South-East France during the Sixth Century*, Analecta Gregoriana 51 (Rome: Apud Aedes Universitatis Gregorianae, 1950), pp. 239–43; see also *ibid.*, pp. 243–54, for discussion of the role of unction in this ministry.
[120] Boniface, *Ep.* 114 (ed. Tangl, pp. 246–7); quoted by Pierre Riché, *Education and Culture in the Barbarian West, Sixth through Eighth Centuries*; translated from the 3rd French edn by John J. Contreni (Columbia: University of South Carolina Press, 1976), p. 386.
[121] Theodore, Penitential, II. xi. 5 (p. 325). A ninth-century manuscript from St Gall (St Gallen, Stiftsbibliothek MS 44) also contains a collection of medical recipes, some of which are attributed to Theodore and others to Hadrian; see Michael Lapidge, 'The school of Theodore and Hadrian', *Anglo-Saxon England* 15 (1986), 45–72, at p. 50.
[122] *HE* V. 3 (pp. 460–1).

John was in fact renowned for his medical skills, but all the cures which Bede attributed to his actions were portrayed as miraculous. He recounted an incident when, after having dedicated a church, John was persuaded to visit the nearby home of a *gesith* called Puch whose wife had been seriously ill for some time. Giving her some of the water consecrated for the church's dedication, the bishop told her to drink it, and bathe the worst affected area with the water, after which her health was rapidly restored to the point that she could minister to her husband and his exalted guest at their meal.[123] Although it was John who taught the dumb youth who visited his shrine to talk, the bishop handed him over to a physician (*medicus*) to have his scabby head healed;[124] similarly John used prayer and vigil to initiate the cure of Herebald, who had been injured in a riding accident, but the bishop called a *medicus* to set and bind up the young man's fractured skull.[125]

Several other religious houses had doctors, that is inmates described in literary texts as *medici*. If we were to rely on the evidence presented in the saints' lives, few of these doctors had any success in effecting cures, yet they were obviously, from the examples just narrated, able to draw on some practical expertise in handling injury and presumably using plants and herbs to make healing and soothing potions. The doctors at Dacre argued among themselves as to the most appropriate course of action to cure a tumour on a brother's eye, some applying potions and ointments and others recommending surgery; in the end the youth was cured by some hairs from St Cuthbert's head.[126] Æthelthryth, abbess of Ely, was attended on her deathbed by a doctor, Cynefrith, who drained the tumour under her jaw, but she still died soon thereafter. Hagiographers generally related such stories to prove the medics' ineptitude in comparison with the divine power of healing. When Æthelthryth's body was elevated later, the same doctor from Ely was present and testified that his gaping wound had been reduced to an almost invisible scar.[127] The boy who fell from the roof at Hexham during the building of Wilfrid's church there, and smashed his limbs on a stone pavement, was attended by *medici* who bound up his broken limbs with bandages, but Stephen's account makes it quite clear that it was the power of the community's prayers, and specifically the prayers of Wilfrid, that really cured the child.[128] Again, Lindisfarne had some doctors who were even considered sufficiently skilled for a paralytic boy to be brought to that house

---

[123] *HE* V. 4 (pp. 462–3). [124] *Ibid* V. 2 (pp. 458–9). [125] *Ibid.*, V. 6 (pp. 466–9).
[126] *Ibid.*, IV. 32 (pp. 448–9). [127] *Ibid.*, IV. 19 (pp. 394–5). [128] *VSW* ch. 3 (pp. 46–7).

from another minster to be cured, but their efforts were completely unsuccessful, and only once they had given up altogether were St Cuthbert's shoes able to heal him.[129]

The care of the sick was clearly considered part of a minster's normal obligations towards its neighbours; Cuthbert healed a number of lay people while on his missionary journeys, including on one occasion a woman who had been ill with a pain in her head and down one side for nearly a year which the doctors had been unable to cure by poulticing, but which the saint relieved by anointing her with the consecrated chrism.[130] Minsters also had a responsibility towards any visiting strangers who fell ill. When a guest visiting Æthelhild's minster was taken ill during the night, the abbess was summoned from the female part of the minster and went with a priest to the guest-house to try to calm the possessed man; according to Bede there was already a crowd of people trying to hold him down, but there is no evidence that a doctor had been summoned.[131] One of the clergy of Bishop Willibrord became ill while staying at Lindisfarne, and lay sick in the guest-house for some days until he thought to ask to be taken to Cuthbert's shrine where he was healed.[132]

The coincidence of the availability of medical services at the shrines of many saints encouraged the sick to seek out such places; should the powers of earthly healing prove ineffective, there was always the possibility of a miraculous cure. Felix told the story of a young East Anglian man, Hwætred, who had for four years so suffered from madness that his body became emaciated and weak; his parents decided to take him to the holy places of the saints so that he could be washed in holy water by priests and bishops, but none of them were successful, and every remedy having failed, his parents began to wish for his death. When, however, they heard of the fame of the hermit Guthlac, they carried Hwætred to his shrine, and the boy was miraculously healed.[133] Similarly, Bede told how the wife of a certain *gesith* in the neighbourhood of Barking visited the cemetery of the holy virgins there and prayed before the relics of the saints for her sight to be restored.[134] However, Bede also explained in his Life of Cuthbert why the girdle which the saint had given to Ælfflæd, abbess of Whitby, disappeared after effecting two cures:

---

[129] Anon., *VSCuth.* IV. 17 (pp. 136–9).   [130] *Ibid.*, IV. 4 (pp. 116–17).
[131] *HE* III. 11 (pp. 248–9).   [132] Bede, *VSCuth.* ch. 44 (pp. 296–7).
[133] *VSG* ch. 41 (pp. 126–31).   [134] *HE* IV. 10 (pp. 364–5).

For if that girdle had always been there, sick people would have wished to flock to it; and when perhaps one of them did not deserve to be healed of his infirmity, he would disparage its power because it did not heal him, when really he was not worthy of being healed.[135]

Not everyone sought healing at minsters; some preferred to carry their sick to holy sites not necessarily associated with religious communities. When the infant Willibald was taken ill his parents took him not to their nearest church but to a standing cross, for according to his hagiographer, Huneberc, 'On the estates of the nobles and good men of the Saxon race it is a custom to have a cross, which is dedicated to our Lord and held in great reverence, erected on some prominent spot for the convenience of those who wish to pray daily before it.'[136]

It is not clear whether all the members of religious communities would have had some obligations towards the care of the sick and it is quite possible that the burden fell more heavily on those who were not ordained and thus had no other obligations to the cure of souls. Unction of the sick and dying was, however, another clerical function. Among the virtues which spoke in defence of the brother from Wenlock during his visionary other-worldly journey was 'the service of the weak which he has shown by kindness to the sick', which might suggest that such duties were not restricted to a specific group within a minster.[137] Theodore's Penitential allowed that the reception of infirm persons into a minster was within the authority and liberty of the minster;[138] many of those attracted to religion later in life may have been influenced at least in part by the relative security of the monastic environment and the prospect of comfortable care in their last sickness. Some of the elderly members of the Barking community were clearly infirm and disabled and required the particular care of other members of the congregation, and the women there also had charge of sickly children in the minster.[139] The Northumbrian nobleman Cudda entered the minster at Lindisfarne when he acquired a paralytic infirmity which prevented him from continuing in his military career; Wilfrid accompanied him into the cloister, charged with ministering to his needs, but this task must have fallen on others after Wilfrid left for Gaul.[140]

---

[135] Bede, *VSCuth.* ch. 23 (pp. 232–3).
[136] *Hodoeporicon of Willibald*, ch. 1 (ed. Holder-Egger, *MGH*, *SS*, XV.1, 88).
[137] Boniface, *Ep.* 10 (ed. Tangl, p. 10). Compare Theodore, Penitential, II. viii. 6 (ed. Finsterwalder, p. 323), which commented on the importance of visiting the sick, as the Lord had commanded.
[138] *Ibid.*, II. vi. 14 (p. 321).   [139] *HE* IV. 8–9 (pp. 358–63).   [140] *VSW* ch. 2 (pp. 6–7).

Burial

The association of minsters with cemeteries, whether or not these burial grounds pre-dated the founding of the Anglo-Saxon religious community on the site, further reinforced essential links between the churches and the lay population throughout all stages of the latter's lives. Tombs of the saints attracted not only pilgrims and relic-collectors but also those who hoped to gain from the *virtus* associated with their shrines and wanted to be buried *ad sanctos*. During the early Middle Ages, the western European church developed and refined rituals to mark the rite of passage by which the dying passed into the other world. Rituals for the anointing of the sick were formalised in the liturgy, death-bed confession and absolution encouraged as a further means of purifying and healing the parting soul, which was strengthened after death by the celebration of votive masses and the ritualisation of the commemoration of the dead by the community of the living. As Fred Paxton has argued, the joining of heaven and earth at the graves of the saints marked not the end but the start of the process of socialising death.[141]

The transition in England from the use of pagan burial grounds, lying predominantly on the boundaries of territories and settlements, to burial within Christian graveyards, attached to minster churches, depended on a number of local factors and no single pattern can be postulated for the entire country.[142] There was no single model to which all churches conformed; patterns of burial in the countryside would have differed from those of urban settlements, particularly before the early ninth century, while the Roman prohibition on intra-mural burial was still respected.[143] Whether a particular minster took responsibility for the burial of its lay neighbours

---

[141] Frederick S. Paxton, *Christianizing Death: The Creation of a Ritual Process in Early Medieval Europe* (Ithaca, NY, and London: Cornell University Press, 1990), p. 18. See also Megan McLaughlin, *Consorting with the Saints: Prayer for the Dead in Early Medieval France* (Ithaca, NY, and London: Cornell University Press, 1994).

[142] Richard Morris has shown how further understanding of this question is dependent on more intensive archaeological fieldwork: *The Church in British Archaeology* (London: Council for British Archaeology, 1983), pp. 49–62. For a more recent analysis of burial on boundaries see Andrew Reynolds, 'Burials, boundaries and charters in Anglo-Saxon England: a reassessment', in Sam Lucy and Andrew Reynolds (eds.), *Burial in Early Medieval England and Wales* (London: Society for Medieval Archaeology, 2002), pp. 171–94.

[143] I discussed this issue in detail in my thesis: 'Anglo-Saxon minsters AD 597–*ca* 900: the religious life in England before the Benedictine reform' (unpublished PhD thesis, University of Cambridge, 1990), pp. 275–8. It was the eighth-century archbishop of Canterbury, Cuthbert, who was credited with moving the burial-place for the archbishops inside the walls of the city, at much the same time as the ban on intra-mural burial was lifted in Rome.

could, therefore, depend on the house's geographical position and status in relation to lay society.[144]

There were early Anglo-Saxon minsters established at the sites of pre-existing graveyards, some of which, such as Wells, may have housed the bodies of Christians of the late or sub-Roman periods,[145] but others may have been associated with pagan cemeteries.[146] Theodore's Penitential directed that an altar might not be sanctified in a church in which the bodies of dead unbelievers (*cadavera infidelium*) were buried; should, however, the church seem suitable for consecration, the bodies were to be removed, and the timber cleaned and then re-erected.[147] It is not clear whether Theodore envisaged that the timbers would be reassembled on a different site. His next canon directed that if such a church were already consecrated, masses could be celebrated there even if religious men were buried within it, but that if there were a pagan buried there, it would be better to cleanse the church and throw (the pagan?) out.[148]

The English seem equally to have interpreted the canonical prohibition on burial within churches fairly liberally, as is apparent from the remarks in Theodore's Penitential quoted above, although it would appear that burial within the confines of a church was restricted to those of royal birth and notable ecclesiastics. The eighth- and ninth-century English church councils did not comment on burial or repeat the prohibitions of the earlier Frankish canons, but an eleventh-century text, the so-called *Canons of Edgar* (in fact a collection of ecclesiastical legislation compiled by Wulfstan of York) specified that 'no man be buried inside the church unless one knows that in his life he pleased God so well that on that account one may consider that he is entitled to that burial-place'.[149] Nevertheless, it was seemingly common for the bodies of the dead to be laid in *porticus* or side-chapels, rather than in the main body of the church itself. At Wearmouth,

---

[144] Anglo-Saxon liturgical rites for consecrating cemeteries are found only in manuscripts from the tenth century and later, but as Helen Gittos has shown, the custom was probably well-established before this period, and perhaps emerged in the late seventh century: 'Creating the sacred: Anglo-Saxon rites for consecrating cemeteries', in Lucy and Reynolds (eds.), *Burial in Early Medieval England and Wales*, pp. 195–208, at p. 201.

[145] Richard Morris, *Churches in the Landscape* (London: Dent, 1989), pp. 29–39.

[146] For a general survey see E. O' Brien, *Post-Roman Britain to Anglo-Saxon England: Burial Practices Reviewed*, BAR Brit. ser., 289 (Oxford: John and Erica Hedges, 1999).

[147] Theodore, Penitential, II. i. 4 (ed. Finsterwalder, p. 312).

[148] *Ibid.*, II. i. 5, p. 312: 'Si autem consecratum prius fuit missas in eo celebrare licet si relegiosi ibi sepulti sunt. Si uero paganus sit mundare et iactare foras melius est.' For discussion of these canons see Donald Bullough, 'Burial, community and belief in the early medieval West', in Wormald *et al.* (eds.), *Ideal and Reality*, pp. 177–201, at p. 189.

[149] 'Canons of Edgar', ch. 29 (*C&S* I, 324).

for example, the bones of Abbot Eosterwine were buried in the *porticus* at the entrance to the church and those of Sigfrith south of the sanctuary; Abbot Hwætberht had them both placed in one casket and reburied with the body of Benedict Biscop, which had been laid in the *porticus* of the blessed Peter, to the east of the altar.[150] Presumably only the abbots were buried in the *porticus* of the church; the other brothers may have been buried in the cemeteries which archaeological excavation has shown lay to the south of the churches at both Wearmouth and Jarrow,[151] although the place or manner of their deposition is not mentioned by Bede or the anonymous biographer of Ceolfrith. In fact, most of the references in the sources as to where or how a person was buried relate to kings or prominent ecclesiastics.

Some English religious houses were also founded specifically to serve as burial-places, such as the minster of Sts Peter and Paul at Canterbury, placed outside the walls of the city to be the burial place for the kings of Kent and their archbishops.[152] Œthelwald of Deira granted land to Cedd for a minster at Lastingham, where he might eventually be buried, 'for he firmly believed that the daily prayers of those who served God there would greatly help him'.[153] Minsters founded for other reasons might also find themselves responsible for the maintenance of cults of the dead, particularly the royal dead. The body of King Edwin was moved from its original burial place at Hatfield Chase to Whitby, where it was reburied with the other kings on the south side of the altar dedicated to St Peter and east of St Gregory's altar.[154] A minster at Derby promoted the cult of the murdered Mercian prince Ealhmund, and Repton was associated with the cult of Wigstan.[155] There are certain sites which are recorded as the burial places of kings, but which are not otherwise known to have housed religious communities at the time of the individual's deposition; one such is Wareham, where the body of Brihtric, king of the West Saxons, was said by the compilers of the

---

[150] *HA* ch. 20 (p. 385). The burial place of Benedict was described by the anonymous author of the Life of Ceolfrith: ch. 18 (p. 394).

[151] Rosemary Cramp, 'Monastic sites', in David Wilson (ed.), *The Archaeology of Anglo-Saxon England* (Cambridge: Cambridge University Press, 1976), pp. 201–52, at pp. 231–3 and 236. The cemetery at Wearmouth appears to have been divided into two, the eastern portion being reserved for members of the minster community, whereas the western one acted as the burial ground for the local lay population: *ibid.*, p. 231.

[152] *HE* I. 22 (pp. 114–15).   [153] *HE* III. 23 (pp. 286–7).   [154] *LBG* ch. 19. (pp. 104–5).

[155] *Die Heiligen Englands*, II, 11 (ed. Liebermann, pp. 11–12); William of Malmesbury, *Gesta regum Anglorum*, ch. 212 (ed. Mynors *et al.*, I, 392–3); David Rollason, *The Search for St Wigstan, Prince-Martyr of the Kingdom of Mercia*, Vaughan Occasional Papers (Leicester: Department of Adult Education, University of Leicester, 1981).

Anglo-Saxon Chronicle to have been buried.[156] Presuming that the annal which records this fact was based on an early-ninth-century one, and does not merely indicate where Brihtric's body was to be found at the end of the ninth century when the Chronicle was compiled, it could perhaps be argued that there was a graveyard at Wareham in 802, and hence a church with a community to serve it.[157]

Although references may be found in the narrative sources to cemeteries for the members of religious communities, for example the separate sites for men and women found at Barking, or the sisters' graveyard at Wimborne, it is much harder to determine where the bodies of the laity other than kings were placed.[158] The problem here is the remarkable paucity of written evidence relating to lay burial in England before the tenth century.[159] Donald Bullough has pointed out that although Cuthbert is seen both in the anonymous Lindisfarne Life and in Bede's prose version as regularly engaged in the cure of souls, 'none of his pastoral acts or miracles is linked with any burial place or tomb except, finally, his own'.[160] Cuthbert's pastoral responsibilities did, however, clearly include ministry to the dying. When the king's reeve Hildmer thought that his wife, who was afflicted with demons, was close to death, he went to Lindisfarne to summon Cuthbert or another priest to her bedside in order that, although she was mad in life, 'she would have peace in the grave'.[161] The fact that she was actually cured of her madness and had no need of the last rites should not divert us from the purposes for which Cuthbert was originally summoned; in Bede's version of the story Hildmer asked for a priest to be sent to bring his wife the sacrament of communion, and also that Cuthbert would permit her to be buried *in locis sanctis*.[162] Whether this last request was made because there was no other Christian burial ground in the area, or because Hildmer thought the cemetery at Lindisfarne a particularly holy place for his wife's remains we cannot know.[163] If the monastic burial ground was available normally only for the community's own dead, this raises a related question of who was counted among those privileged to such a burial. One of the defining features of an

---

[156] The Anglo-Saxon Chronicle recorded *s.a.* 784 ADE, 783 C (*recte* 786), that Brihtric, who died in 802, was buried at Wareham.

[157] See further *Veiled Women*, II, 201.   [158] *HE* IV. 7, 10 (pp. 356–9, 362–5); *VSL* ch. 4 (p. 123).

[159] Morris, *The Church*, p. 50. For a general review of the problem of locating unfurnished burials in early Christian England see Helen Geake, 'Persistent problems in the study of conversion-period burials in England', in Lucy and Reynolds (eds.), *Burial in Early Medieval England and Wales*, pp. 144–55, at pp. 152–4.

[160] Bullough, 'Burial', p. 185.   [161] Anon., *VSCuth.* II. 8 (pp. 90–3).

[162] Bede, *VSCuth.* ch. 15 (pp. 204–5); see Bullough, 'Burial', p. 192.   [163] Morris, *The Church*, p. 50.   315

Irish *manach,* or monastic tenant, was that he should have the right to burial in the monastic cemetery.[164] It is difficult to be certain whether the same privilege was afforded to their English counterparts, but it may not be an unreasonable assumption that it was.

Carolingian liturgical reforms of the eighth and ninth centuries enhanced the role of the clergy in the rituals of death performed outside the cloister, encouraging clergy to visit dying lay people and get them to confess their sins and receive absolution and be purified with unction.[165] Although these reforms spread only gradually to England, the frequency with which saints' lives from an earlier period recorded miracles of healing performed on the dying or terminally ill suggests that holy men were often summoned to visit them, and that their help was valued in this transitional phase between life and death. The Dialogues of Ecgberht addressed the question of whether a priest or deacon should be able to be witness of the last words of a dying man concerning his estates, which further suggests that ecclesiastics were present on such occasions.[166] Theodore's Penitential laid great stress on the importance of priests giving penance to the dying: 'if any presbyter denies penance to the dying he is answerable for their souls . . . For true conversion is possible in the last hour since the Lord sees not only the time but the heart.'[167]

Lay concern for the fate of the soul after death is apparent from charters recording grants lay people made to the places where they hoped to be buried.[168] Whether they could reasonably hope to be buried in immediate physical proximity to the saints is uncertain, for it is possible that the actual ground in which their bodies were placed was separated from that reserved for the members of the community.[169] In 804 a certain Æthelric, son of Æthelmund, made known at a synod at *Aclea* the names of the lands he intended to give to the place (that is presumably to the minster)

---

[164] O'Brien, *Post-Roman Britain,* p. 53; Charles-Edwards, *Early Christian Ireland,* pp. 117–19.

[165] Paxton, *Christianizing Death,* chs. 4–5. For consideration of this question in Gaul in an earlier period compare Beck, *The Pastoral Care,* pp. 254–7.

[166] Ecgberht, *Dialogi, Responsio* 2 (H&S III, 404).

[167] Theodore, Penitential, I. viii. 5 (ed. Finsterwalder, p. 300).

[168] For a general discussion of the symbolism of such gifts see Patrick Geary, *Living with the Dead in the Middle Ages* (Ithaca, NY, and London: Cornell University Press, 1994), ch 4. David Postles has argued that the economic aspects of this form of gift exchange (whereby land or other possessions were given to a monastic house by lay people in exchange for a promise of future burial) were less important than the symbolic and spiritual aspects of the transaction: 'Monastic burials of non-patronal lay benefactors', *JEH* 47 (1996), 620–37.

[169] This was certainly the case at Wearmouth.

called Deerhurst 'if it befall me that my body shall be buried there'.[170] The will of the Kentish reeve Abba detailed a substantial grant to be made to his burial place, the minster of Folkestone, on the day of his funeral on behalf of his soul.[171] It is first in the late ninth century that reference is found to the collection of a burial tax (the 'soul-scot') at the graveside and the obligation to pay such a tax was imposed in law only in the eleventh century.[172]

The responsibilities of minster communities certainly included the celebration of masses, singing of psalms, and saying of prayers for the souls of the dead buried on their ground. This was patently true of those houses founded primarily to promote specific cults, such as Minster-in-Thanet or Gilling, and of those which acquired notable relics later in their history, such as Shaftesbury. This women's community was founded originally for Alfred's daughter Æthelgifu (and hence from the outset arguably associated with the cult of the West Saxon royal family); from 979 it was the resting-place of King Edward the Martyr and served as the focus for his cult.[173] Minsters were also expected to pray for the souls of those of lesser status whom they had buried. Theodore's Penitential made a number of provisions relating to the celebration of masses for dead laymen (and children) as well as for brothers who died,[174] quoting the authority of Augustine in saying that 'masses are to be performed for all Christians, since it either profits them or consoles those who offer or those who seek to have it done'. He decreed, however, that masses might not be said for those who had killed themselves: 'we may only pray and dispense alms'.[175] Bede also commended the practice of praying for the dead, as well as the giving of alms and saying of masses on their behalf, all of which activities could bring souls more swiftly to the eternal rest awaiting the blessed.[176] On his other-worldly journey,

---

[170] S 1187. Patrick Sims-Williams, *Religion and Literature in Western England, 600–800* (Cambridge: Cambridge University Press, 1990), pp. 59–64.

[171] S 1482.

[172] Blair, 'Introduction', p. 8; the first references in charters are in texts from the 870s: S 1275 and 1279; the obligation was imposed in law in V Æthelred, 12.1, and VIII Æthelred, 13 (ed. Liebermann, *Die Gesetze*, I, 240–1, 265); see Gittos, 'Creating the sacred', p. 201.

[173] Anglo-Saxon Chronicle, *s.a.* 980 D; *Veiled Women*, II, *s.n.* Shaftesbury.

[174] Theodore, Penitential, II. v. 1–10 (ed. Finsterwalder, pp. 318–19); compare *ibid.*, II. xiv. 2 (p. 322, which referred to the beneficial effects of fasting for the dead.

[175] *Ibid.*, II. v. 9 (p. 194); II. x. 3 (p. 324).

[176] Bede, *Homelia*, I. 2 (ed. Hurst, p. 13): 'uel certe prius amicorum fidelium precibus eleemosynis ieiuniis fletibus et hostiae salutaris oblationibus absoluti a poenis et ipsi ad beatorum peruenient requiem'. Compare Bede, *In Marcum*, I. iii. 30 (ed. Hurst, CCSL 120, 477). See Carroll, *The Venerable Bede*, pp. 178–80.

Dryhthelm was taken to purgatory, where he saw those souls who had delayed making confession for their sins until they were on the point of death; as the angel explained, 'because they did repent and confess, even though on their death-bed, they will all come to the kingdom of heaven on judgement day; and the prayers of those who are still alive, their alms and fastings and especially the celebration of masses, help many of them to get free even before the day of judgement'.[177]

To live in a minster meant in a very real sense to live with the dead. While the living and the dying might be kept at a distance (or only brought into the daily lives of religious men and women in tightly controlled circumstances and within defined spaces), the dead were never absent and represented a constant presence in their collective memory.

Alms

A number of texts from the early Anglo-Saxon period recommended the performance of good works, and specifically of alms-giving, by the members of religious communities, presumably following Christ's injunction: 'If thou wilt be perfect, go sell what thou hast and give to the poor and thou shalt have treasure in heaven.'[178] Bede considered that all Christians had an obligation to charitable action, including the giving of alms and care for the needy; he commented favourably on Abbess Hild's enjoining of the performance of good works upon all the members of her community at Whitby, but did not specify what these were. From Hild's insistence on the individual poverty of members of her congregation, we might assume that they included alms-giving.[179] Several of Alcuin's letters commended the practice of alms-giving to individual religious women; writing to Abbess Æthelthryth in 796, he urged her, 'while you have control of your property, use it for alms . . . God will welcome the gifts that go before us more than those that follow'.[180] In a letter to Æthelburh, Alcuin extolled the virtues of works of mercy, love and chastity, and warned especially against avarice, recommending generosity in alms.[181]

---

[177] *HE* V. 12 (pp. 494–5).
[178] Matt. 19: 21. Part of this chapter was quoted in Columbanus, *Regula monachorum*, ch. 4 (ed. Walker, p. 126).
[179] Bede, *Homelia*, I. 9 (ed. Hurst, p. 64); *HE* IV. 23 (pp. 408–9).
[180] Alcuin, *Ep.* 105 (ed. Dümmler, p. 152).
[181] Alcuin, *Ep.* 36 (p. 78). Compare also *Epp.* 79, 102 and 300 (pp. 121, 149, and 459).

References in the literary sources to the charitable activities of minster communities relate for the most part to the actions of individuals, particularly of abbots, rather than to corporate giving. Since individual religious were, ideally, not supposed to have personal property, one might hesitate over the source of such pecuniary gifts. St Wilfrid represents an obvious exception, poverty not being a virtue to which he subscribed. Stephen reported admiringly his 'giving of alms in the Lord's name to the poor, the orphan and the widow, and those afflicted by any kind of infirmity' and his death-bed instruction that ordered that a quarter of his not inconsiderable wealth be divided among the poor of his people for the redemption of his soul.[182] The abbot of the minster at Oundle where Wilfrid died may have found it rather more painful to persist in his determination to make a grant of his whole share of the tithes he received to the poor among his flock on the anniversary of the saint's death. This gift was made in addition to the alms which the abbot was accustomed every day to give to God and the needy for himself and for the soul of the bishop.[183] Abbot Ceolfrith of Wearmouth and Jarrow was also renowned for his generosity and support of the poor: 'Consequently when he was about to depart, and was setting out [for Rome], the unanimous lamentation of the poor and homeless bore witness that they were deprived, as it were, of a father and sustainer.'[184] Some people marked their entry into the religious life by the giving of alms, an action specifically recommended by the Rule of St Benedict.[185] A slightly different impression to that given by this widespread concentration on personal charity is presented by Bede's statement that the Irish congregation at Lindisfarne was remarkable for making a point of corporately giving away all its material wealth beyond that which it needed for its survival: the brethren 'had no money but only cattle; if they received money from the rich they promptly gave it to the poor'.[186]

Wills of various lay men and women included bequests of alms to be given to the poor on the anniversaries of their deaths by the religious communities who were their beneficiaries. The Kentish ealdorman Oswulf and his wife Beornthryth, for example, in leaving an estate at Stanstead to Christ

---

[182] *VSW* ch. 8 (pp. 18–19) and ch. 63 (p. 136): 'unam [partem] pauperibus populi mei pro redemptione animae mea dividite'. It is not entirely clear whom Wilfrid meant by *populi mei*; perhaps they were the poor living on the estates of his various minsters.

[183] *Ibid.* ch. 65 (pp. 140–3).

[184] *VSCeol.* ch. 34 (p. 401); see Wood, *The Most Holy Abbot Ceolfrid*, Jarrow Lecture 1995 (Jarrow: [St Paul's Church], 1996), p. 18.

[185] *RSB* ch. 58, 24 (pp. 268–9); see above, p. 164.   [186] *HE* III. 26 (pp. 310–11).

Church, Canterbury, willed that their anniversary might be celebrated every year with religious offices and the distribution of alms; in confirming this bequest Archbishop Wulfred clarified its terms:

and from the common provisions of the community at the minster itself one hundred and twenty *gesufl* loaves are to be given as charity for the good of their souls as is done at the anniversaries of lords. And . . . [these] provisions are to be given to the provost (*reogolweard*), and he is to distribute them as may be most advantageous to the brethren and most efficacious for the souls of Oswulf and Beornthryth.[187]

In like fashion King Alfred (who had by Asser's account during his lifetime assigned an eighth of his annual income to be 'judiciously expended on the poor of every race who came to him'),[188] left fifty pounds in his will to be distributed to the poor and the destitute: 'for my sake, for my father and the friends for whom he used to intercede and I intercede'.[189]

The poor might reasonably have grounds for anticipating that they would benefit from a minster's own largesse or from lay bequests made with charitable intent if they congregated around the enclosures of monastic houses. Æthelwulf indeed demonstrated that such expectations could be gratified, for he described the practice of one of his abbots, Sigwine, who gave gifts to the wretched poor who lay at the gates of the minster.[190] Similarly, the dumb boy who was cured by John of Beverley had originally come to the bishop's oratory in search of alms.[191]

Minsters' charitable activities may have inspired laymen to follow their example. A lengthy chapter of the canons of the council of *Clofesho* in 747 dealt with the profitability of daily alms-giving by all Christians, including the laity, pointing out specifically that alms could not be used to commute other penitential activities such as fasting: 'for it is good to be assiduous in psalmody and often to bow the knee with a sincere intention, and daily to give alms; yet abstinence is not to be remitted; fasting once imposed by the rule of the Church, without which no sins are forgiven, is not to be remitted on account of these'.[192] Whether some laymen really were trying to commute their penances in this way remains uncertain; nor can we be sure

---

[187] S 1188; trans. *SEHD*, pp. 39–40, no. 1.

[188] Asser, Life of Alfred, ch. 102 (ed. Stevenson, p. 88; trans. Keynes and Lapidge, *Alfred*, p. 107).

[189] S 1507; trans. Keynes and Lapidge, *Alfred*, p. 107.

[190] Æthelwulf, *De abbatibus*, ch. 15 (ed. Campbell, pp. 38–9); see Campbell, 'The church in Anglo-Saxon towns', p. 142. Cubitt has noted that the contact made by the congregation described in this poem with the laity seems to have been restricted to alms-giving and care for the poor: 'Pastoral care', p. 207.

[191] *HE* V. 2 (pp. 456–7).   [192] Council of *Clofesho*, AD 747, ch. 26 (H&S III, 372).

how much reliance to place on the assertion in the Dialogues of Ecgberht that the custom had grown up among the English of observing a twelve-day fast before Christmas marked by the *clerici* in minsters and also laymen with their wives and families, with tears, abstinence and the giving of alms.[193] This leads us to think further about the laity as active participants in the life of the church, not just the recipients of its services.

The laity and the minster

In our exploration of the place of the minster within early Anglo-Saxon lay society, we have thus far, as in all preceding chapters, considered our questions largely from the perspective of the cloister. Although we have looked a little at the attractions presented by minsters to devout (or indigent) lay people, our focus has been predominantly on the ecclesiastical provision of care and spiritual services for the laity's benefit. The lay population was not, however, a passive force in this relationship, and I want to turn now to explore the ways in which lay men and women of different social status actively sought out minsters, and the sorts of advantages (spiritual or material) they might have hoped to acquire by initiating such contact.

Pilgrims and visitors

Holy men attracted pious visitors anxious to learn from and have a share in their special relationship with God throughout the Christian period.[194] Some, as we saw at the start of this chapter, came to visit a charismatic man because of his reputation for particular asceticism or notably effective and spiritually rewarding instruction. Others were drawn to the dead as much as to the living, inspired to travel to seek spiritual relief from contact with the tomb and relics of a saint housed within the church, possibly travelling some distance to visit a shrine of known thaumaturgic power.

There were, as Diana Webb has observed, 'pilgrims in what is now England not only before there were Englishmen, but before there were Christians'. The practice of travelling to a sacred place in search of a cure or of intellectual enlightenment was familiar to the Romans and practised in Roman

---

[193] Ecgberht, *Dialogi, Responsio* 16.4 (H&S, III, 412–13).

[194] The classic study of this relationship is Peter Brown, 'The rise and function of the holy man in Late Antiquity', in his *Society and the Holy in Late Antiquity* (London: Faber, 1982), pp. 103–52; see also his *The Cult of the Saints: Its Rise and Function in Latin Christianity* (London: SCM Press, 1981).

Britain; Germanic pagans also venerated particular places, both temple-sites and natural features such as woods, springs or groves of trees.[195] In the early Christian Latin West the objects of veneration were early Christian martyrs, conventionally buried (in accordance with Roman legal practice) outside city walls, although not necessarily thus buried in obscurity, for the sites of such tombs could be marked with elaborate basilicas.[196] Britain had her own early martyr, St Alban, supposedly martyred during the Diocletian persecution and buried near the Roman city of *Verulamium*; according to Bede, who narrated the saint's story in some detail, 'here when peaceful Christian times returned, a church of wonderful workmanship was built a worthy memorial of his martyrdom. To this day sick people are healed in this place and the working of frequent miracles continues to bring it renown.'[197] Augustine of Canterbury showed some interest in another potential Romano-British martyr, Sixtus, writing to Pope Gregory to express some hesitation about this man's sanctity on the grounds that no miracles were performed at his shrine and no narrative of his passion had survived; Gregory sent the relics of Pope Sixtus II to replace this dubious local saint.[198] The conversion of the Anglo-Saxons was, however, remarkable for being achieved without the shedding of Christian blood and it was to the shrines of the holy men and women renowned in life and death for their sanctity to which Anglo-Saxon pilgrims flocked.[199] In the early Middle Ages the notion of pilgrimage could encompass journeys made for various overlapping purposes: penitential, ascetic or missionary.[200] These might range from *peregrinatio*, the act of deliberately dissociating oneself from home and kin to travel as a stranger for the Lord's sake; missionary journeys, undertaken to bring the Christian faith to a still pagan people; travel to another country to study with a remarkable holy man (as for example those who visited particular teachers in Ireland) or at a particular religious house (consider the women who went to Brie, Chelles and Les Andelys to learn about monasticism before there were minsters for women in England); as well as travel to a

---

[195] Diana Webb, *Pilgrimage in Medieval England* (London and New York: Hambledon and London, 2000), p. 1; David Wilson, *Anglo-Saxon Paganism* (London: Routledge, 1992), pp. 5–43.

[196] Geary, *Living with the Dead*, p. 166.   [197] *HE* I. 7 (pp. 34–5); Webb, *Pilgrimage*, p. 2.

[198] Brooks, *The Early History*, p. 20; for discussion of the authenticity of this portion of the *Libellus responsionum*, the so-called *Obsecratio Augustini*, which was not included in the version to which Bede had had access see Paul Meyvaert, 'Bede's text of the Libellus responsionum', in Peter Clemoes and Kathleen Hughes (eds.), *England before the Conquest* (Cambridge: Cambridge University Press, 1971), pp. 15–33, at p. 24.

[199] Frankish ecclesiastical reformers tried to reorder the shrines of the saints, asserting episcopal control over the distribution of relics and thus imposing central control over the veneration of the sacred: Geary, *Living with the Dead*, chs. 8 and 9.

[200] Webb, *Pilgrimage*, p. 6.

notable shrine, or city filled with shrines, such as the home of the apostles, Rome.[201]

Pilgrims who came to the monastic churches of early Anglo-Saxon England either hoped to gain spiritual benefits from the simple act of visiting the shrine, or more specifically sought to petition the saint to intercede in heaven on the pilgrim's behalf, perhaps to effect a cure of some physical or mental infirmity.[202] The horse-litter on which the ailing bishop Eorcenwald of London had been carried was preserved by his followers up to Bede's day, when it continued to cure many people afflicted with plague and other complaints; not only could the sick be healed if brought into close proximity to the litter, or placed on it, but even splinters of the wood had curative powers.[203] Although initially a little reluctant to receive the bones of the Northumbrian king, Oswald, the brothers of Bardney became energetic defenders of his reputation once they saw the healing powers of his bones for themselves; even the soil over which they had poured the water with which they had washed the saint's bones before re-housing them in the abbey church proved to have 'the power and saving grace of driving devils from the bodies of people possessed'.[204] Most minsters went to some lengths to maintain the shrines of any notable persons buried within them; the Penitential of Theodore recommended, for instance, that a candle should always be left burning beside the shrines of saints, although it did allow that the poverty of a church might prevent this.[205] Possession of a notable shrine would not only increase the prestige of the community responsible for its upkeep, but might have implications for the secular status of the site.[206] Early in

---

[201] Thomas M. Charles-Edwards, 'The social background to Irish *peregrinatio*', *Celtica* 11 (1976), 43–59. For an important re-evaluation of the notion of *peregrinatio* that shows how travel for the purpose of evangelisation should be distinguished from the idea of spiritual exile, see now James T. Palmer, 'Locating sanctity: community and place in the hagiography of the eighth-century Anglo-Saxon missions to the continent' (unpublished PhD thesis, University of Sheffield, 2004), ch. 1. Travel to Ireland: *HE* III. 27 (pp. 312–3); women travelling to Francia; *ibid.* III. 8 (pp. 236–9), for which see *Veiled Women*, I, 36–7. All these instances and pilgrimage to Rome are explored by Webb, *Pilgrimage*, pp. 4–6. For kings who made the last kind of pilgrimage see Clare Stancliffe, 'Kings who opted out', in Wormald *et al.* (eds.), *Ideal and Reality*, pp. 154–76.

[202] Brown, *The Cult of the Saints*; David Rollason, 'The shrines of saints in later Anglo-Saxon England: distribution and significance', in L. A. S. Butler and R. K. Morris (eds.), *The Anglo-Saxon Church* (London: Council for British Archaeology, 1986), pp. 32–43.

[203] *HE* IV. 6 (pp. 354–5). Compare *ibid.*, III. 13 (pp. 254–5), where Bede recorded the curative power of splinters of the stake onto which the martyred King Oswald's head had been fixed, a piece of which the missionary Willibrord had carried with him on his mission to the Frisians; Peter Clemoes, *The Cult of St Oswald on the Continent*, Jarrow Lecture 1983 (Jarrow: St Paul's Church, 1984), pp. 4–5. In contrast to the other examples given here, it was the object itself that was worthy of veneration, not the place with which it was associated.

[204] *HE* III. 11 (pp. 246–7).   [205] Theodore, Penitential, II. i. 8 (ed. Finsterwalder, p. 312).

[206] Compare the important role played by St-Riquier as a place of pilgrimage because of its large collection of relics; around the monastery there with its three churches a town of considerable   323

the tenth century the relics of various Northumbrian saints were translated from their original resting-places to sites in southern England which
hoped to benefit from the *uirtutes* of these notable figures. The relics of St
Oswald were translated from Bardney to Gloucester in 909 by the Mercian
rulers Æthelflæd and Æthelred; the translations of Ealhmund from Derby to
Shrewsbury and of Werburg from Hanbury to Chester were also associated
with Æthelflæd's creation of new burhs, and were clearly designed to serve
a political purpose.[207] Visiting pilgrims represented an important source of
income to many minsters which, in order to foster the interest and hence the
offerings of the faithful, promoted the cults of their local saints deliberately
in a number of ways: by the composition of *uitae*, or by liturgical means,
celebrating masses on the anniversaries of saints' deaths, and through the
entering of these dates into Kalendars.[208]

Others as well as pilgrims would also look to minsters for lodging, and
religious communities served an important role in their localities in ful-
filling these needs. Among the recommendations that St Cuthbert made to
his brethren before he died was the injunction not to 'despise those of the
household of faith who come to you for the sake of hospitality, but see that
you receive such, keep them, and send them away with friendly kindness'.[209]
In writing a general letter of introduction to kings, princes, bishops, abbots,
priests and his 'spiritual sons' on behalf of Wynfrith (later the missionary,
Boniface), Bishop Daniel extolled the merits of hospitality to travellers as recommended by Scripture: 'in receiving the servants of God you also receive
Him whose majesty they serve and who promises: "He that receiveth you
receiveth me."'[210] Even where this activity is not explicitly described in the
surviving sources, all religious establishments must perforce have made provision for the reception of visitors. Relatives of professed religious within a

---

size grew up: Centula–St-Riquier. The accounts of Angilbert, who restored the monastery in the
late eighth century, demonstrate the relationship between the abbey community and the urban
population who participated ceremonially in various feast-day celebrations in which the relics were
prominently borne in procession: Rosamond McKitterick, 'Town and monastery in the Carolingian
period', in Derek Baker (ed.), *The Church in Town and Countryside* (Oxford: Basil Blackwell, 1979),
pp. 93–102, pp. 99–101.

[207] Mercian Register, *s.a.* 909; William of Malmesbury, *Gesta pontificum Anglorum*, IV. 155 (ed. Hamilton, p. 293). For the Chester saints see Alan Thacker, 'Chester and Gloucester: early ecclesiastical
organisation in two Mercian burhs', *Northern History* 18 (1982), 199–211; Rollason, 'The shrines
of saints', pp. 38–40. Compare also the acquisition of relics by Glastonbury during the tenth
century, described by William of Malmesbury, *Gesta pontificum*, ch. 91 (ed. Hamilton, p. 92); *De
antiquitate Glastonie ecclesiae*, ch. 55 (ed. Scott, p. 116). Also *Resting Places*, II. 37 (ed. Liebermann,
p. 17).

[208] See, for example, the account of the spread of the cult of St Oswald to Selsey given by Bede: *HE*
IV. 14 (pp. 378–80).

[209] Bede, *VSCuth.* ch. 39 (pp. 282–3).   [210] Boniface, *Ep.* 9 (ed. Tangl, p. 16), quoting Matt. 10: 40.

community might have expected to be entertained periodically, as – perhaps rather more regularly – would those who had made substantial benefactions to a particular institution. Bishops might also expect hospitality from minsters when travelling round their dioceses. Alcuin wrote to two of his pupils in 801 lamenting the harm done to religious houses by the excessive size of episcopal retinues.[211]

Various houses indeed made particular provisions for the care of those who came to stay within their walls. At Ripon, Cuthbert was elected guest-master by the rest of the community, taking charge of a separate dwelling (*diuersorium*) set aside for visitors, which consisted of at least two rooms, and was some distance away from the other monastic buildings.[212] Visitors were not necessarily expected to conform to the habits of the monastic community, for Cuthbert was able to offer his angelic guest a meal at the third hour of the day, even though the fact that the day's baking had not yet been completed demonstrates that this was not the hour at which the brothers were accustomed to dine.[213] The Irish congregation at Lindisfarne, however, made no special arrangements for visitors; according to Bede, the brethren there 'had no need to provide dwellings for the reception of worldly and powerful men, since these only came to the church to pray and to hear the word of God'. Neither were such guests given special food: 'if they happened to take a meal there, they were content with the simple daily fare of the brothers and asked for nothing more'.[214] On the other hand, after Cuthbert's time, there was a place described by Bede as a *hospicium* at Lindisfarne in which the member of Bishop Willibrord's clergy referred to above had been staying as a guest when he fell ill.[215] There was also at this time an individual responsible for ministering to visitors, for a long time one Baduthegn; among his duties was the washing of the blankets used in the guest-house.[216]

Female houses also regularly received visitors of both sexes; for example, Hild received a number of religious men at Hartlepool,[217] Abbess Æbbe invited Cuthbert to Coldingham,[218] and Æthelhild's minster, as has already

---

[211] Alcuin, *Ep.* 233 (p. 378).

[212] When Cuthbert sought a table to set out a meal for the visitor, he had to fetch it from another room from that in which he received the angel; this additional room was described by Bede (*VSCuth.* ch. 7, pp. 176–7) as a store-house, *conclauus*, but by the anonymous as a *cubiculum*: Anon., *VSCuth.* II. 2 (pp. 76–9). Cuthbert had, further, to walk to another part of the minster in order to fetch his guest some bread: *ibid.*

[213] *Ibid.*: 'Ille etiam homo Dei reuertens ad monasterium querens panem, et non inuento eo, adhuc enim coquebant panes in fornace, reuersus uero ad hospitem.'

[214] *HE* III. 26 (pp. 310–11).   [215] Bede, *VSCuth.* ch. 44 (pp. 296–9).   [216] *HE* IV. 31 (pp. 444–7).

[217] *HE* IV. 23 (pp. 408–9).   [218] Bede, *VSCuth.* ch. 10 (pp. 188–9).

been seen, had a dwelling for guests set apart from the monastic build-ings.[219] Wimborne would have been exceptionally strict in refusing to allow lay people access to the female part of the community, but it is quite pos-sible that there was a guest-house in the men's part of the enclosure about which Rudolf (our main, if late, source for the early minster at Wimborne) was silent.[220] Members of royal families were frequent monastic visitors; Hild attracted kings and princes seeking her counsel when at Whitby,[221] Queen Iurminburh waited at her sister's minster at Carlisle during her hus-band Ecgfrith's war with the Picts,[222] and Æthelbald used to visit Guthlac's cell at Crowland.[223]

Minsters and the law

Asylum-seekers constituted a discrete group of those who came to a minster's doors, people driven to seek sanctuary in the church through the pressing need for shelter from the force of the law.[224] In the early medieval West, such refuge was sought as often with a person as at a place, for a bishop or other venerable figure could intercede with the authorities on the fugitive's behalf; the seeking of sanctuary at a tomb or altar with relics appears to have been a secondary development from the idea that charismatic individuals could offer succour in need.[225] Cuthbert apparently foresaw the consequences of this in his own case all too clearly, arguing (in the words put into his mouth on his death-bed) 'I think it expedient for you that I rest here [on the island of Farne] because of the influx of fugitives and criminals of every sort, who will perhaps flee to my body, since, unworthy as I am, my reputation as a servant of Christ has gone forth among the multitude.'[226]

Early Anglo-Saxon law-codes provide evidence that churches were recog-nised to afford sanctuary to those who sought shelter within them. Ine's code directed that anyone liable to the death penalty who reached a church would retain his life and that a due flogging would also be remitted if the

---

[219] HE III. 11 (pp. 248–9).   [220] VSL ch. 3 (ed. Waitz, p. 123).   [221] HE IV. 23 (pp. 408–9).
[222] Bede, VSCuth. ch. 27 (pp. 242–3).   [223] VSG chs. 40, 49, 52 (pp. 124–5, 148–51, 164–5).
[224] Charles H. Riggs, Jnr, *Criminal Asylum in Anglo-Saxon Law* (Gainesville, FL: University of Florida Press, 1963).
[225] Gervase Rosser, 'Sanctuary and social negotiation in medieval England', in John Blair and Brian Golding (eds.), *The Cloister and the World* (Oxford: Clarendon Press, 1996), pp. 57–79, at pp. 61–2. Such arrangements were available early in Gaul; see Council of Orléans I, ch. 1.
[226] Bede, VSCuth. ch. 37 (pp. 278–9); quoted and discussed by Thacker, 'Monks, preaching', p. 168; Rosser, 'Sanctuary', p. 61.

guilty person reached a church.[227] Similarly Alfred decreed: 'If anyone for any guilt flees to any one of the monastic houses to which the king's food rent belongs, or to some other privileged community which is worthy of honour, he is to have a respite of three days to protect himself unless he wishes to be reconciled.'[228] However, the same code also recognised that providing sanctuary could prove very inconvenient for a minster and recommended: 'If the community have more need of their church he is to be kept in another building and it is to have no more doors than the church; the head of that church is to take care to give him food during that period.'[229]

Churches could also provide the setting for solemn judicial acts. The laws of the seventh-century Kentish kings, Hlothhere and Eadric, make provision for the swearing of oaths at altars,[230] as does the code of King Wihtred.[231] The latter code made arrangements for the performing of manumissions too, which were also to be given at the altar.[232] A written record of the act of freeing a slave was often made in a set of Gospels or some other book belonging to the church where the manumission was made (or a neighbouring one if, as could also occur, the act took place at a public meeting or at a crossroads);[233] all the surviving records of manumissions date from beyond the period of this study, the earliest being in a Gospel book from St Augustine's, Canterbury, possibly that on which King Æthelstan had made his coronation oath, since the individual Ealdhelm is stated to have been freed by Æthelstan immediately after he had been made king.[234] Ordeals might also be conducted in minsters, but again our best information comes from beyond our period. King Æthelstan's second law-code gave priests a central role in preparing the accused with three days of prayer and fasting before the trial, as well as giving them responsibilities in the organisation and adjudication of the trial itself.[235] The tenth-century legal tract *Ordal*

[227] Ine, laws, chs. 5, 5.1 (ed. Liebermann, *Die Gesetze*, I, 90); Riggs, *Criminal Asylum*, pp. 9–10 and 21–2.
[228] Alfred, laws, ch. 2 (ed. Liebermann, p. 48); Riggs, *Criminal Asylum*, pp. 33–5.
[229] Alfred, laws, ch. 5.1–2 (p. 52); compare ch. 42.2 (p. 76).
[230] Hlothhere and Eadric, laws, c. 16.2 (*ibid.*, p. 11).   [231] Wihtred, laws, chs. 18–21 (*ibid.*, pp. 13–14).
[232] *Ibid.*, ch. 8.   [233] Dorothy Whitelock in *EHD*, p. 383.
[234] London, British Library, MS Royal I. B. vii; the text is printed and translated in Harmer, *SEHD*, no. 19, and was also translated by Whitelock in *EHD*, no. 140. See J. A. Robinson, *The Times of St Dunstan* (Oxford: Clarendon Press, 1923), pp. 66–7; Simon Keynes, 'King Æthelstan's books', in Michael Lapidge and Helmut Gneuss (eds.), *Learning and Literature in Anglo-Saxon England* (Cambridge: Cambridge University Press, 1985), pp. 143–201, at pp. 185–9.
[235] II Æthelstan, ch. 23 (ed. Liebermann, *Die Gesetze*, I, 162). For the guarding of the historic right to hold ordeals by St Peter's minster at Northampton in the twelfth century see Blair, 'Minster churches in the landscape', p. 48, n. 44. For the early development of the ordeal see Robert Bartlett, *Trial by Fire and Water: The Medieval Judicial Ordeal* (Oxford: Clarendon Press, 1986), pp. 4–12.

gives details of the nature of the ceremony which compare closely with contemporary liturgical *ordines* relating to ordeals.[236]

Minsters might moreover fulfil important political functions within their own kingdoms, acting as meeting places for the king's councils and for ecclesiastical synods. We have already observed the close connections that persisted between religious houses and local ruling royal families, such as Whitby, where Oswiu's daughter Ælfflæd was brought up; the minster served as the burial-place of the Bernician and Deiran royal families and was the site of the synod which met there in 664 to discuss the Roman and Celtic methods of religious observance.[237] While the texts of some charters state that they were drawn up in places where there are known to have been minsters, it is seldom apparent whether the transfer of ownership which the document records took place within the minster itself. For example, the earliest surviving original, recording a grant of land in Thanet to Abbot Brihtwold of Reculver in AD 679, was merely said to have been 'done' (*actum*) in the *ciuitas* of Reculver.[238] There is a charter of King Cuthred to Glastonbury of dubious authenticity (it purports to confirm all the grants made to the house by previous kings) which does claim to have been promulgated within the minster of Glastonbury: 'Prouulgatum est in predicto cenobio sub presencia Cudredi regis quod propriae manus munificentia altario sacro commendauit.'[239] Similarly, another spurious charter, allowing Aldhelm to retain the abbacy of his minsters at Frome and Bradford-on-Avon at the request of the brothers in these houses, claimed to have been drawn up in the minster which is situated beside the river called Wimborne.[240] It might be unwise to conclude too much from such statements, which could easily have been added to forged instruments in the interests of verisimilitude. There are, however, instances where we see members of religious communities being sucked into participation in royal government, even to the extent

---

[236] *Ordal* (datable to either *c.* 936 × 958 or *c.* 1000; ed. Liebermann, *Die Gesetze*, I, 383–7, and see Liebermann's comments, *Die Gesetze*, II, 601–4); Paul R. Hyams, 'Trial by ordeal: the key to proof in the early common law', in Morris S. Arnold (ed.), *On the Laws and Customs of England: Essays in honor of Samuel E. Thorne* (Chapel Hill, NC: University of North Carolina Press, 1981), pp. 90–126, at pp. 106–11.

[237] *HE* III. 25 (pp. 294–309); *VS*, ch. 10 (pp. 20–3). Peter Hunter Blair, 'Whitby as a centre of learning in the seventh century', in Lapidge and Gneuss (eds.), *Learning and Literature*, pp. 3–32. Catherine Cubitt has produced a list of the sites at which pre-Viking Age Anglo-Saxon church councils were held: *Anglo-Saxon Church Councils c. 650–c. 850* (London and New York: Leicester University Press, 1995), appendix 2.

[238] S 8.   [239] S. 257 (AD 745). I owe this reference to Lesley Abrams.

[240] S 1251a (BCS 114) (AD 705). Lapidge and Herren, *Aldhelm*, p. 204, n. 2, dismiss this as 'patently spurious', and Heather Edwards (*The Charters of the Early West Saxon Kingdom*, BAR, Brit. ser., 198 (Oxford: BAR, 1988), pp. 115–16), considered that only the witness list had any claim to authenticity.

that the demands of kings could have interfered with normal monastic life. The anonymous hagiographer of Ceolfrith reported that Benedict Biscop had been forced to appoint Eosterwine as an additional abbot of Wearmouth because he himself was wont so often to be summoned from the minster to the king 'on account of his innate wisdom and the ripeness of his counsels' that he could no longer take full responsibility for the house's governance.[241]

Lay obligations towards minsters

Although land booked to churches in perpetuity by means of charters was freed from all but the three essential secular burdens, minsters were dependent in part on the material support of their lay neighbours in order to function effectively, particularly in carrying out their pastoral obligations. Most of the evidence for the nature of the payments collected by Anglo-Saxon minsters dates from the later tenth and eleventh centuries and relates to the period after the monastic reform of Edgar's reign, when it became necessary to distinguish between the rights of types of religious community performing distinct functions. For example, King Edgar's second law-code stipulated that all payment of tithe was to be paid to the 'old minster to which the parish belongs', but, 'if there is any thegn who has on his bookland a church with which there is a graveyard, he is to pay the third part of his own tithes into his church'.[242] Anyone who had on his land a church without a graveyard was, after paying tithe to the old minster, free to pay to his own priest whatever he liked from the remaining nine parts.[243]

Theodore's Penitential is the earliest extant English text to mention the payment of tithes (that is a tribute amounting to a tenth portion of all types of an individual's revenue),[244] but this does not suggest that their payment had newly been introduced into England during his archiepiscopacy: 'Let the tribute of the church be according to the custom of the province; that is so that the poor suffer no violence in paying tithes or anything.'[245] Tithes came later to be payable specifically for the support of the clergy, yet Theodore apparently envisaged wider uses to which they could be put, directing: 'It is not legitimate to give tithes except to the poor or to pilgrims or for laymen

---

[241] Anon., *VSCeol.* ch. 12 (p. 392).

[242] II Edgar, 1–2 (ed. Liebermann, *Die Gesetze*, I. 196; trans. Whitelock in *EHD*, p. 431, no. 40).

[243] II Edgar, 2.1, *ibid.*

[244] For the early history of tithing see Giles Constable, *Monastic Tithes from their Origins to the Twelfth Century* (Cambridge: Cambridge University Press, 1964), pp. 9–56.

[245] Theodore, Penitential, II. xiv. 10 (ed. Finsterwalder, p. 333; trans. Constable, *Monastic Tithes*, p. 25, n. 1).

[to give] theirs [except] to the church.'[246] Only priests were exempt from their payment.[247] At the 786 legatine synods, the payment of tithes was urged upon all: 'We recommend with solemn entreaty that everyone should strive to give the tenth part of all that they possess, for that peculiarly belongs to the Lord our God; and from the nine parts let them live and give alms.'[248] It was only in the tenth century that secular legislation enforced the payment of tithes; King Edgar introduced elaborate and severe penalties for non-payment, and Æthelred likewise insisted that those who failed to pay God's dues should be brought to justice.[249]

Other dues were also payable to the local minster from the produce of the land. The payment of first fruits or church-scot was due on St Martin's Day (11 November);[250] Ine of Wessex was the first to insist on this due, imposing penalties for non-payment: 'Church-scot is to be given by Martinmas; if anyone does not discharge it he is to be liable to 60 shillings and to render the church-scot twelve-fold.'[251] Plough-alms, a penny payable for each plough or plough-land, was according to the tenth-century legislation to be paid within fifteen days of Easter;[252] its payment also is likely to be a much older custom.

The act of giving money, precious objects or land to the place of one's burial we have already seen as one of the ways in which the laity became involved in the Christianisation of the rituals of death and dying.[253] From King Æthelstan's reign, however, the payment of soul-scot was legally enforced, and from Æthelred's time these dues were payable to the minster in whose *parochia* the dead person had lived, even if his body was buried in another church.[254] Some later Anglo-Saxon wills made specific provision for

---

[246] *Ibid.*, II. xiv. 11 (ed. Finserwalder, p. 333, trans. Constable, *Monastic Tithes* p. 25, n. 1).

[247] *Ibid.*, II. ii. 8, p. 314.   [248] Legatine synod, AD 786, ch. 17 (ed. Dümmler, p. 25, no. 3).

[249] II Edgar, ch. 3.1 (ed. Liebermann, *Die Gesetze*, I, 196–8); VIII Æthelred, chs. 14–15, *ibid.*, p. 265. See Frank M. Stenton, *Anglo-Saxon England* (3rd edn, Oxford: Clarendon Press, 1971), pp. 154–6; Frank Barlow, *The English Church 1000–1066: A History of the Later Anglo-Saxon Church* (1963, 2nd edn, London: Longman, 1979), p. 145.

[250] Stenton, *Anglo-Saxon England*, pp. 153–4; Barlow, *The English Church*, pp. 160–2.

[251] Ine, laws, ch. 4 (ed. Liebermann, *Die Gesetze* I, 90; trans. Whitelock in *EHD*, p. 399, no. 32). Compare *ibid.*, ch. 61 (ed. Liebermann, p. 116, trans. Whitelock, p. 406): 'church-scot is to be paid from the *haulm* and the hearth where one resides at midwinter'.

[252] I Æthelstan, 4 (*C&S*, I, 44–6, at p. 46, no. 11). Compare I Edmund, 2 (ed. Liebermann, *Die Gesetze*, I, 184); V Æthelred, 11.1 (*ibid.*, p. 240).

[253] Above. Stenton suggested that this might have been a relict of pagan customs, since the gifts made in such circumstances can resemble the grave-furniture which accompanied heathen burials: *Anglo-Saxon England*, pp. 152–3. See also Dorothy Whitelock, *Anglo-Saxon Wills* (Cambridge: Cambridge University Press, 1930), notes pp. 110–1: *saulsceatte*; see also Gittos, 'Creating the sacred', p. 201.

[254] I Æthelstan, ch. 4 (*C&S*, I, 46, no. 11). V Æthelred, ch. 12.1 (ed. Liebermann, *Die Gesetze*, I, 240). Compare also II Edgar, ch. 5.2 (*ibid.*, p. 198); VI Æthelred, ch. 20 (*ibid.*, p. 252); VIII Æthelred, ch. 13 (*ibid.*, p. 265).

the payment of this obligation: a certain Æthelwold whose will is datable to after AD 987 bequeathed twenty mancuses of gold for his soul to the New Minster at Winchester and a cup for his soul-scot.[255] The tenth-century testatrix Wynflaed, however, used the term soul-scot in a more general sense to mean any charitable payment for the good of her soul, not specifically her burial-price.[256]

Responsibility for ensuring that all such dues were paid rested either on the landowner or on his representative. Early in King Alfred's reign, Bishop Ealhferth and the community at Winchester leased to an ealdorman Cuthred and his wife Wulfthryth land at Easton near Winchester for three lives; this was to be freed from all but the three common burdens and 'the payment of eight-fold church dues, and priests' dues, and burial fees'.[257] King Æthelstan's first law-code enjoined reeves to pay their tithes and to see that those under them did likewise, and to ensure 'that church-scot, soul-scot and plough alms go to their lawful recipients'.[258] In similar vein King Eadred, in granting five hides at Alwalton to Ælfsige Hunlafing, freed it from every burden except the repair of fortifications, the building of bridges and military service, and advised 'a prudent landowner [will also make himself responsible for] church dues, burial fees and tithes'.[259] The maintenance of ecclesiastical establishments within Anglo-Saxon society was a burden that fell increasingly on all the faithful, not merely on those who had the means and the pious ambition to make over part of their material possessions to the church's use.

Conclusion

The issue of the provision of spiritual care for the laity has dominated this exploration of the interactions between lay and monastic society in the early Anglo-Saxon period, as it has the recent historiography. The pastoral functions of an active religious community were summarised by Bede in the oft-quoted passage relating to the Irish congregation at Lindisfarne:

If by chance a priest came to a village, the villagers crowded together, eager to hear from him the word of life; for the priests and the clerics visited the villages for no other reason than to preach, to baptize and to visit the sick, in brief to care for their souls.[260]

---

[255] S 1505; Whitelock, *Anglo-Saxon Wills*, no. 12.   [256] S 1539; Whitelock, *Anglo-Saxon Wills*, no. 3.
[257] S 1275 (AD 871 × 877).   [258] I Æthelstan, ch. 4 (*C&S*, I, 44–6, no. 11).
[259] S 566 (AD 955); trans. Robertson, *Anglo-Saxon Charters*, no. 30.   [260] *HE* III. 26 (pp. 310–11).

In chapter 5 I argued that, although adherence to the strictest principles of monastic observance varied considerably between minsters, the one activity common to all ostensibly-professed religious, and that which distinguished their life-style from that of their secular counterparts, was their commitment to give a portion of every day to prayer and devotion. Is it possible to go so far as to argue, as some have done, that engagement in external ministry on behalf of the laity along the lines drawn by Bede was another distinguishing characteristic of the institution?

The answer to this question depends in part, as we have already seen, on how one defines pastoral ministry. Some would describe such work in purely sacramental terms as, for example, has Giles Constable, who has described the *cura animarum* as the 'pastoral activities of administrating the sacraments, especially baptism and the eucharist, imposing penance and preaching', distinguishing these functions from charitable works such as alms-giving and caring for the sick and indigent.[261] In practice, however, there was clearly a good deal of overlap between sacramental and charitable work and if we are investigating this question from an institutional perspective, an over-rigid distinction seems inappropriate to the circumstances of the early English church. We have already seen, however, that trying to answer this question institutionally is doomed to failure. Since no distinctions were drawn by contemporaries between religious houses founded to pursue a purely devotional life and those established to provide for local pastoral needs, nor (with the exception of cathedral congregations) did the early sources differentiate between types of congregation according to the religious status (or, indeed gender) of their inhabitants, we have to address the issue from a different perspective.

Looking at the work of priests and those ordained to the lesser ranks of the clergy has proved much more rewarding, for here it does seem that ecclesiastical legislators differentiated between their obligations and responsibilities and those of *monachi*. The burdens of pastoral care, preaching and teaching, and the administration of the sacraments, fell to the former, and cannot realistically have been performed only within cloister walls, where the latter were mostly encouraged to stay. That these pastorally active priests and clerks lived in communities (and that those communities also contained men devoted to a life of religion who were not ordained) cannot be doubted. There were members of minster communities, most if not all of whom were probably ordained clergy, who left the sheltered confines of their cloisters

[261] Constable, 'Monasteries', p. 353.

to offer spiritual succour to lay people unable or unwilling to seek it at the church's gates. The obligation to offer the sacraments to those who did come to the minster in search of them will also have fallen to the ordained among each congregation; minsters that were without the services of any clerical members caused some anxiety to ecclesiastical legislators and will have struggled to meet the needs of their lay neighbours except in the charitable sphere. All ordained clergy were responsible in this pastoral work to their diocesan bishop and – unless we are to envisage a chaotic free-for-all in which priests raced to get to an untaught village before anyone else – it is not unreasonable to imagine that the bishops had some system for assigning workers to specific areas. In some regions, the organisation of that pastoral provision was perhaps better, and more systematically, arranged in defined territorial areas than it was in others. Occasionally new foundations were made specifically to minister to a particular pastoral need, as for example the creation of the minster at Breedon-on-the-Hill as a colony of *Medeshamstede*.[262] Caritative work of caring for the sick and giving alms to the poor were tasks that seem to have fallen more widely upon an entire minster's congregation; considering the spiritual benefits thought to accrue from such action, it is hard to imagine that these were tasks in which many religious houses refused to participate. Although the nature of the sources is such that no house is described as engaged in every form of ministry – the provision of sacraments and basic religious teaching, the care of the sick, the giving of alms, or the reception of visitors – it is difficult to accept that there could have been many minsters that performed no pastoral roles at all within their localities.[263] If we abandon the notion that action and contemplation were binary opposites and mutually exclusive activities, it is easier to see how one minster congregation might have led a corporate life that fused active (pastoral) and enclosed (contemplative) pastimes. Anglo-Saxon minster communities led mixed lives, encompassing a diverse range of religious ideals worked out through a variety of practices suited to their own circumstances. We have seen previously that no one model fits all houses.

A religious house might foster the religious sentiments of its neighbours in a number of ways through its external ministry, and at the same time provide (by means of a visible presence in the locality) models of devout

---

[262] Morris, *Churches in the Landscape*, p. 132. See further above, pp. 270–4.

[263] Compare Palliser, 'Review article', p. 214: 'No doubt some minsters with pastoral functions were new creations by tenth-century kings on Carolingian lines, but it is going much too far to deny *any* role for minsters as centres of pastoral care before the Scandinavian invasions.'

behaviour for the laity. But not all of the pastoral activities of either the non-ordained brethren or the priests were performed away from their own house. Minsters fulfilled an equally important function in their own areas by providing a focus for the expression of lay devotion. The importance of their intercessory function of praying and saying masses regularly for the souls of their king and his people in general, or petitioning for particular individuals, we explored in a previous chapter. Lay penitents were told at the council of *Clofesho* in 747 to pray first for themselves, but then to bring as many servants of God as they could to make their common prayers to God for them.[264] Prayer was not a duty restricted to those who came directly into contact with the laity in the world; it seems more than likely that those professed religious of both sexes who led a more enclosed life took a major role in the performance of such intercessory prayer.[265]

Bede obviously considered that all religious should set an example not only of good living, but also of Christian devotion to the rest of the laity; the individuals whom Bede most extolled in his writings, such as Cuthbert or Aidan, were exemplary figures to whose pastoral ascetic and spiritual ideals all should aspire.[266] One of the gravest concerns which he voiced in his letter to Bishop Ecgberht was that pseudo-minsters were being filled with laymen who although they 'as laymen could have learnt something of the religious life not by experience but by hearsay, are yet absolutely without the character or profession which should teach it'.[267] Similar concerns exercised the compilers of the canons of the *Clofesho* council of 747, who ordered bishops, abbots and abbesses to ensure that their *familiae* turned their minds ceaselessly to reading, and that their congregations' actions 'be made known by the voices of many for the gaining of souls'.[268] Priests should fulfil all their duties, the same council urged, so that by their example and advice others might be inspired to enter the service of God.[269] A minster's buildings could equally act as a magnet attracting all classes of the laity to its gates not just at major festivals but more regularly in search of baptism, masses, or burial, or as pilgrims hoping to benefit from the *uirtus* accruing to a famous collection of relics. As we have seen, the church deliberately fostered the religious behaviour of laypeople

---

[264] Council of *Clofesho*, AD 747, ch. 27 (H&S III, 373).   [265] Compare *ibid.*, ch. 10, p. 366.
[266] Thacker, 'Bede's ideal', pp. 140–6.   [267] *EpEcg*, § 13 (p. 416).
[268] Council of *Clofesho*, AD 747, ch. 7 (H&S III, 364–5).   [269] *Ibid.*, ch. 8, p. 365.

in a number of ways, but the laity was also an active player in these interactions.

A minster was more than a place of worship. It could be a meeting-place for the poor and destitute, for pilgrims and for relic-collectors, as well as for kings and their associates. Traders might gather at its gates to buy the minster's surplus produce and sell in exchange such items as the church could not itself manufacture. Minsters were also – perhaps from the perspective of their neighbours, above all – landowners and thus preoccupied at a local level with the management of their, often substantial, estates, and the disposition of their agricultural produce. We looked previously at the church's accumulation of wealth, but the point is worth restating: minsters were not only numerous in the English landscape by the end of the eighth century, they were also extremely wealthy. Ecclesiastical landlords were in material terms at least the equals of their secular noble counterparts in most regions, and in some areas substantially richer.[270] Closely related to local royal and noble families, few men or women seem to have seen their entry into a life of religion as separating them entirely from lay society; benefactors, relatives and friends of professed religious were those most likely to have been invited to enjoy minsters' hospitality at feasts and on the occasions of major church festivals. It was, however, as an inspiration to devotion and in the celebration of sacraments that minsters came into the closest contact with their lay neighbours, and it was through such 'ministry' that the church arguably had the greatest impact on the lives of all laypeople, not just those who could claim the friendship of religious within cloisters. This was by no means a static process; there were wide fluctuations in the level of monastic pastoral activity between individual areas and at different periods, as well as in the extent to which the laity were brought into contact with the ideals of organised Christianity. In collecting together all the evidence for the exercise of various types of pastoral ministry, I may inevitably have over-simplified the process by which the church cared for the spiritual health of the lay population and so presented an unduly homogeneous picture, albeit one that differs radically from that offered either by Bede or by the monastic reformers of Edgar's reign. We have already seen that Bede's ideas about the essential unity of the early English church were not only of major importance in determining the way in which he portrayed its customs but

---

[270] Consider, for example, the size of the endowment of the cathedral church of Canterbury: Brooks, *The Early Church*, pp. 105–7.

335

also underlay Æthelwold's propaganda. Turning in conclusion to consider how our reassessment of the nature of early Anglo-Saxon monasticism necessarily requires us to view the ecclesiastical reforms of the tenth century in a new light, there is one other major facet of the justification for reform still to be addressed. Was there really a decline in the number and quality of English religious institutions in the latter part of the ninth century, to the virtual extinction of monasticism?[271]

[271] Compare Æthelwold's remarks on the subject quoted in chapter 1.

Coda

CHAPTER 8

Horizons

Anxiety about the spiritual health of the English people pervades much of the literature relating to the ninth-century church. When he was making preliminary enquiry about the possibility of going on pilgrimage to Rome which would mean travelling through the lands of the Frankish empire, Æthelwulf, king of the West Saxons from 839 until 858, wrote a letter to the Emperor Louis the Pious, some of which was preserved in the collection of contemporary annals then being kept at the Frankish court and known to us as the Annals of St-Bertin. The portion copied describes an out-of-body vision experienced by 'a certain pious priest of the land of the English'. The priest's visionary guide showed him boys writing in lines of blood the various sins of the Christian people committed because of their refusal to obey the orders and precepts of holy Scripture, and he received an unambiguous warning:

If Christian people do not quickly do penance for their various vices and crimes and do not observe the Lord's Day in a stricter and worthier way, then a great and crushing disaster will swiftly come upon them: for three days and nights a very dense fog will spread over their land, and then all of a sudden pagan men will lay waste with fire and sword most of the people and land of the Christians along with all they possess. But if instead they are willing to do true penance immediately and carefully atone for their sins according to the Lord's command with fasting, prayer and alms-giving, then they may still escape those punishments and disasters through the intercession of the saints.[1]

---

[1] *Annals of St-Bertin*, s.a. 839 (trans. Janet Nelson, *The Annals of St-Bertin*, p. 43). For the composition in the 830s of the annals (which were a continuation of the court-based Royal Frankish Annals)

Wessex was, of course, in the late 830s already no stranger to the sudden raids of small fleets of foreign ships along its exposed coastlines, yet in the light of the subsequent escalation of Danish raiding and the disruption that warfare brought to the maintenance of regular religious life, these remarks seem remarkably prescient. Commentators writing at the end of the century were convinced that religion had sunk to an unprecedented low among the English. Fulk, archbishop of Rheims, believed that 'the beneficial and religious observation and ever-cherished transmission of them was either not fully observed among your peoples, or else has largely fallen into disuse'.[2] Pope Formosus worried that the 'abominable rites of the pagans have sprouted again in your parts' and that the bishops were suffering 'the Christian faith to be violated, the flock of God to wander . . . for lack of pastors'.[3] The rot had spread beyond the episcopal church, if we are to believe Asser's assertion that men would not join the newly founded minster at Athelney because 'for many years past the desire for the monastic life had been totally lacking in that entire race [of the English]'.[4] Such comments may give time-depth to the disparaging remarks tenth-century Benedictines made about the state of English monasticism which were quoted in the introduction, but they were of course no less rhetorical. Perhaps what these late-ninth-century laments most indicate is not a fear that minsters had ceased to exist in England during the Viking Age, but that the ecclesiastical reforms promoted by the Carolingians had finally had sufficient impact that it was difficult for anyone familiar with that discourse to describe the communal religious life of English houses as 'monastic'.

Æthelwulf's youngest son, Alfred, ascended to the West Saxon throne at the height of the Danish wars in 871, when the so-called Great Army was in the midst of a concerted attack on his kingdom, having already played some role in the removal of native royal lines from Northumbria, Mercia

---

see Janet L. Nelson, 'The annals of St Bertin', in Margaret Gibson and Janet L. Nelson (eds.), *Charles the Bald: Court and Kingdom* (2nd rev. edn, Aldershot: Variorum, 1990), pp. 23–40. Æthelwulf did not in the end make his planned trip to Rome until 855. For English–Frankish relations during this period, see Pauline Stafford, 'Charles the Bald, Judith and England', *ibid.*, pp. 139–53, and M. J. Enright, 'Charles the Bald and Æthelwulf of Wessex: the alliance of 856 and strategies of royal succession', *Journal of Medieval History* 5 (1979), 291–302; and Janet L. Nelson, 'Alfred's Carolingian contemporaries', in Timothy Reuter (ed.), *Alfred the Great: Papers from the Eleventh-Centenary Conferences* (Aldershot: Ashgate Publishing, 2003), pp. 293–310, at pp. 293–8.

[2] Fulk, letter to Alfred, AD 885×886 (*C&S* I, 9, no. 4; trans. Keynes and Lapidge, *Alfred the Great*, p. 184).

[3] Formosus, letter to the bishops of England, AD 891×896 (*C&S* I, 36, no. 8; *EHD*, no. 227).

[4] Asser, Life of Alfred, ch. 92 (ed. Stevenson, p. 80; trans. Keynes and Lapidge, *Alfred the Great*, p. 103).

and East Anglia.[5] His success in defeating the Danes in battle and not just preserving but strengthening the West Saxon realm is justly famed. From the perspective of the relative peace of the 880s, Alfred embarked on a whole sale programme of reform, designed to reinforce his kingdom's defences on both military and spiritual fronts. Looking back at an earlier era, the king's recollections were characterised by nostalgic idealism. He recalled wistfully the happy times there were formerly throughout England, the profusion of men of learning and 'how, before everything was ransacked and burnt – the churches throughout England stood filled with treasures and books'. Urging his bishops to institute the educational reforms he planned, the king warned them to 'remember what punishments befell us in this world when we ourselves did not cherish learning nor transmit it to other men. We were Christians in name alone, and very few of us possessed Christian virtues.'[6]

Quite how much permanent damage was done to the ecclesiastical structures of Anglo-Saxon England by the political and military disruption of the ninth century is not easy to gauge and has been much disputed.[7] Conventional wisdom that 'the England of the great days of Wilfred and Benet Biscop, or Aldhelm, the Venerable Bede and Boniface had all but passed away under the pressure of Viking raids', as monastic life in England was 'almost destroyed' no longer finds many adherents.[8] Yet, as John Blair has argued,

---

[5] The Danes capitalised on a civil war among the Northumbrians in 867 which led to the death of both rival kings and a forced peace-making between the Northumbrian people and the viking army; in the winter of 869, the army fought against the East Anglian king, Edmund, who was killed (either in or after the battle), and conquered all his land; in 874 the Danes drove the Mercian king Burgred across the sea, installing a puppet king, Ceolwulf, in his stead. Numerous historians offer narratives of the ninth-century viking wars drawing on the contemporary accounts of the Anglo-Saxon Chronicle and Asser's Life of King Alfred; particularly accessible versions are Simon Keynes and Michael Lapidge in their introduction to *Alfred the Great* (Harmondsworth: Penguin, 1983) and Simon Keynes, 'The vikings in England *c.* 790–1016', in P. H. Sawyer (ed.), *The Oxford Illustrated History of the Vikings* (Oxford: Oxford University Press, 1997), pp. 48–82.

[6] Alfred, prose preface to the *Cura pastoralis* (ed. Henry Sweet, *King Alfred's West Saxon Version of Gregory's Pastoral Care*, 2 vols., EETS, o.s. 45 and 50 (London: N. Trübner, 1871–2), I, 4–5; trans. Keynes and Lapidge, *Alfred the Great*, p. 125).

[7] This is not the place at which to attempt to survey the effects of Danish raiding and settlement on individual minsters. For surveys of the wider question see my 'Violence against Christians? The vikings and the church in ninth-century England', *Medieval History* 1.3 (1991), 3–16 and 'Remembering, forgetting and inventing: attitudes to the past in England after the First Viking Age', *TRHS*, 6th series 9 (1999), 185–200, at pp. 189–92; Guy Halsall, 'Playing by whose rules? A further look at viking atrocity in the ninth century', *Medieval History* 2.2 (1992), 2–12. A Frankish perspective is given by Simon Coupland, 'The rod of God's wrath or the people of God's wrath? The Carolingians' theology of the viking invasions', *JEH* 42 (1991), 535–54.

[8] Thomas Symons, *Regularis concordia* (London: Thomas Nelson and Sons, 1953), p. ix; Nigel Ramsay and Margaret Sparks, *The Image of Saint Dunstan* (Canterbury: Dunstan Millennium Committee, 1988), p. 13.

'Although the old view that the minsters perished for good in the Viking raids is clearly wrong, the late ninth century was for many of them a time of loss, disruption and change.' Other factors certainly contributed to the fate of the minsters in this period, some of which I explored previously when I looked specifically at the reduction in the number of religious houses for women in England after 800. There I set the effects of viking raiding in the context of changing aristocratic patterns of patronage and the influence of Carolingian ecclesiastical reforms, and concluded that the Danish wars were just one, albeit important, factor in a series of overlapping contexts, masked for us to some extent by the paucity of ninth-century evidence.[9] From whatever perspective one chooses to approach this problem, a remarkably consistent picture does emerge of the ninth century as a low-point in monastic fortunes.

Much ecclesiastical property passed into lay hands during and after the second half of the ninth century and it is hard to escape the conclusion that the Danish wars contributed substantially to the dispersal of monastic estates. Northumbria, East Anglia and eastern Mercia suffered disproportionately, together with the exposed coastal minsters of Kent, but this was not a happy time for West Saxon minsters either, and it was not only houses for women that passed from ecclesiastical control.[10] Considering the wider political and military circumstances it is not surprising that few new grants were made to the church in this era, still less that the only new minsters were those the king himself created, both founded to satisfy particular personal needs. Athelney Alfred created in thanksgiving for his victory at Edington; Shaftesbury he founded for his daughter, who was to pray there for the spiritual health of her family then and in the hereafter.[11] Land that was needed so badly for the defence of the realm was a commodity not lightly to be spared for the support of non-fighting mouths. Nor, as I have remarked before, did contemporary experience suggest that an undefended minster would offer a suitable place of safety for nobles of either sex or any age.[12] In fact the palpable reduction in noble enthusiasm for the endowment

---

[9] Veiled Women, I, ch. 3, and particularly pp. 83–4.

[10] David N. Dumville, Wessex and England from Alfred to Edgar (Woodbridge: Boydell Press, 1992), ch. 2, particularly pp. 53–4. This essay offers a critical reading of Robin Fleming, 'Monastic lands and England's defence in the Viking Age', English Historical Review 100 (1985), 247–65, while accepting her essential view that the viking invasions led to the redistribution of much church land.

[11] Asser, Life of Alfred, chs. 92 and 98 (ed. Stevenson, pp. 79–80 and 85).

[12] Compare my remarks about the declining appeal of double houses in time of war, made in Veiled Women, I, 74.

of minsters housing women preceded the onset of the Viking Age.[13] Shifts in patterns of aristocratic patronage are visible before the start of the viking wars and affect all monastic endowments, not just those for women. They may have been related as much to the formalisation of arrangements for the provision of military service from booked land (which made the permanent alienation of land by means of charter rather less attractive than it might previously have appeared) as to either external pressures or any diminution in spiritual fervour.[14]

Episcopal sees faced substantial disruption in the period, including the two archiepiscopal sees, both of which experienced brief interregna. Three English bishoprics disappear entirely from the record in this period (both of those in East Anglia and the see of Hexham); two more were transferred to new locations (Leicester to Dorchester and Lindisfarne temporarily to Chester-le-Street, before eventually being re-established in Durham). The Midland dioceses of Lindsey and Lichfield suffered periods of vacancy or restricted jurisdiction. Only the sees of Hereford, Rochester, Winchester and Worcester functioned apparently unaffected through the period, at least if we are to rely on the evidence of the surviving episcopal lists.[15] Although bishops-elect continued to make professions of obedience to the metropolitan archbishop of Canterbury up to 870, no church council met in the southern province after the meeting held at Kingston in 838.[16]

In intellectual terms, standards were low. Much of the discussion of the level of Latin learning in England at this time has revolved around the frequently quoted statement made by Alfred in his preface to his translation of Gregory's *Cura pastoralis* that when he ascended to the throne there were few men on the southern side of the Humber who could translate a letter from Latin into English. One might dismiss this as rhetorical hyperbole, but study of manuscript-production in England after *c.* 800 and particularly of the deplorable level of Latinity demonstrated by those who tried

---

[13] Patrick Wormald, 'St Hilda, saint and scholar (614–80)', in Jane Mellanby (ed.), *The St Hilda's College Centenary Symposium: A Celebration of the Education of Women* (Oxford: St Hilda's College, 1993), pp. 93–103, at p. 95.

[14] Richard P. Abels, *Lordship and Military Obligation in Anglo-Saxon England* (Berkeley and Los Angeles, CA: University of California Press, 1988), pp. 43–57; Eric John, *Reassessing Anglo-Saxon England* (Manchester: Manchester University Press, 1996), pp. 51–3; *Veiled Women*, I, 65.

[15] For full details see Mary Anne O'Donovan, 'An interim revision of episcopal dates for the province of Canterbury, 850–950: part 1', *Anglo-Saxon England* 1 (1972), 23–44, and *eadem*, 'An interim revision: part 2', *Anglo-Saxon England* 2 (1972), pp. 91–113.

[16] Nicholas Brooks, *The Early History of the Church of Canterbury: Christ Church 597–1066* (Leicester: Leicester University Press, 1984), pp. 164–7; Catherine Cubitt, *Anglo-Saxon Church Councils c. 650–850* (London and New York: Leicester University Press, 1995), pp. 235–40.

to write in the language, notably charter-scribes, confirms the king's view. Expertise in practising and – more importantly – in teaching this skill was pretty much absent from southern England in Alfred's reign.[17] In comparison with the remembered and the historical past, late-ninth-century commentators had some cause to lament the circumstances in which they found themselves.

Memory did not fail Alfred's generation. Minsters had once been happier places and (some) kings of the English godly.[18] Caveats added to a number of ninth-century charters that grants should be made as long as the Christian faith or as long as baptism should endure among the English were heartfelt, and not unwarranted, expressions of insecurity.[19] Seeking causes for the misfortunes they experienced, contemporaries distributed blame widely. Alcuin struggled to make any sense of the pagan attack on Lindisfarne in 793 and wrote to the Northumbrian king to enquire whether 'this unaccustomed and unheard-of evil was merited by some unheard-of evil practice' among the people, and to Bishop Higbald and his congregation to insist that they correct any sins in their own behaviour.[20] Asser worried that the minsters remaining in Wessex in his day did not maintain the rule of life in any consistent way and wondered whether it was 'the people's enormous abundance of riches of every kind' that meant that 'this kind of monastic life came all the more into disrespect'.[21] A catalogue of evils accounted for the ruin Fulk saw in England's ecclesiastical order: the frequent invasion and onslaught of vikings; decrepitude; the carelessness of the bishops; or the ignorance of those subject to them.[22] While pagan incursions brought

---

[17] Alfred, prose preface (ed. Sweet, p. 5; trans. Keynes and Lapidge, *Alfred the Great*, p. 125). Jennifer Morrish argued that Alfred was exaggerating for effect: 'King Alfred's letter as a source on learning in England in the ninth century', in Paul Szarmach (ed.), *Studies in Earlier Old English Prose* (Albany, NY: State University of New York Press, 1986), pp. 87–107. Helmut Gneuss looked at the king's words in the context of contemporary book production: 'King Alfred and the history of Anglo-Saxon libraries', in Phyllis Rugg Brown *et al.* (eds.), *Modes of Interpretation in Old English Literature* (Toronto, Buffalo, and London: University of Toronto Press, 1986), pp. 29–49. Nicholas Brooks explored the evidence of the charters: 'England in the ninth century: the crucible of defeat', *TRHS* 5th ser. 29 (1979), 1–20, especially pp. 14–16; and *The Early History*, pp. 164–74. Most convincing is Michael Lapidge's assessment 'Latin learning in ninth-century England', in his *Anglo-Latin Literature 600–899* (London and Rio Grande: Hambledon, 1996), pp. 409–39.

[18] As remarked by Pope John VIII in a letter to Æthelred, archbishop of Canterbury datable to Sept. 877×Aug. 878 (*C&S* I, 5, no. 3; *EHD*, no. 222).

[19] Brooks, 'England in the ninth century', p. 13; also my '"By water in the Spirit": the administration of baptism in Anglo-Saxon England', in John Blair and Richard Sharpe (eds.), *Pastoral Care before the Parish* (Leicester, London and New York: Leicester University Press, 1992), pp. 171–92, at p. 191.

[20] Alcuin, *Epp.* 16 and 20 (ed Dümmler, pp. 43 and 57).

[21] Asser, Life of Alfred, ch. 93 (ed. Stevenson, p. 81).

[22] Fulk, archbishop of Rheims, letter to King Alfred (trans. Keynes and Lapidge, *Alfred the Great*, pp. 182–3).

immediate misery to congregations directly attacked or forced to flee in face of imminent danger, these were not alone responsible for the poor state into which organised religion was felt to be sliding, nor in many respects were the Danes seen as more than the tools by which the Almighty vented his anger on a sinful people.[23] At least in Wessex, the solution to Danish attacks lay in military reform (better-organised defences, restriction of the Danes' mobility on land, sea and river, and the invention of an orderly system for army-service), but the solution to the 'viking problem' was the eradication of sin and the setting of the people back on the track towards righteousness through education.[24] To that end, a confidence in a prior golden age when 'the religious orders in England were eager both in teaching and in learning as well as in all the holy services which it was their duty to perform for God' was a useful hortatory tool.[25]

This language of regret finds echoes among past and also future generations, so bringing our argument full circle, back to the point at which this study began: the historical location of tenth-century Benedictine justifications for the reform of the English monasteries. In his account of the events preceding the reform, Bishop Æthelwold described the conversion of the English and showed how 'this apostolic mode of life, through the admonition of [Augustine] was for a long time progressing and prospering well in the minsters of the English nation'.[26] To Æthelwold and his contemporaries there was a time when English monasticism had been properly organised (that is according to the 'right rule of life'), but at some later point, things deteriorated spiritually and materially. Our difficulty is to establish when that decline might have occurred. If nostalgia had its attractions for each generation, each necessarily looked back to a different era. At the turn of the eighth century, Alcuin had written to Æthelbald, abbot of Wearmouth and Jarrow, regretting that 'almost everywhere in our country the monastic life is being given up and the secular way of life spreading', and had complained to the bishop of Winchester that there were fewer priests and teachers able to explain to the people how to live rightly than in former

---

[23] Coupland, 'The rod of God's wrath'.

[24] In areas where Danes had already begun to settle – predominantly the north and the east – a solution was not so readily to be found. The failure of the tenth-century Benedictine revolution to have any impact north of the Humber is testament to the magnitude of the problems there. For discussion of the effects of Scandinavian settlement on the English church see Lesley Abrams, 'Conversion and assimilation', in Dawn M. Hadley and Julian D. Richards (eds.), *Cultures in Contact: Scandinavian Settlement in England in the Ninth and Tenth Centuries* (Turnhout: Brepols, 2000), pp. 135–53, and Julia Barrow, 'Survival and mutation: ecclesiastical institutions in the Danelaw in the ninth and tenth centuries', *ibid.*, pp. 155–76.

[25] Alfred, prose preface (ed. Sweet, p. 4).   [26] Æthelwold, 'An account' (*C&S* I, 150, no. 33).   345

times.[27] Alcuin regretted the passing of the time of his youth, especially the era of his teacher Archbishop Ælberht of York (767–80). For Bede, the high point of English Christianity had certainly been the period of Theodore's archiepiscopate in Canterbury.

Never before had there been such happy times since the English first came to Britain . . . the desires of all men were set on the joys of the heavenly kingdom of which they had only lately heard, while all who wished for instruction in sacred studies had teachers ready at hand.[28]

Alarmed at what he saw as a decline from those standards in his own day, Bede wrote to Ecgberht, bishop of York, urging him to obtain the co-operation of King Ceolwulf to bring about 'the restoration of the ecclesiastical condition of our race better than it has been hitherto'.[29]

We have already seen how the tenth-century reformers made particular use of the writings of Bede to support an argument that the improvements they planned for the ordering of English monasticism would do no more than to restore the church to its former condition. Our close study of the ways in which early English minsters used monastic rules and the relationship between ideal and practice in the practical ordering of individual religious houses has shown us how unrealistic the reforming rhetoric was.[30] Theirs was not a reform (a restoration of a past state) but rather a revolution in monastic organisation.[31] The monastic 'irregularities' that so perturbed Dunstan, Æthelwold and their contemporaries did not result from misfortunes suffered by the English church during the viking wars, or reflect a decline in the spiritual fervour of the Anglo-Saxon laity or even the avarice of rapacious strangers. There was nothing 'regular' about English monasticism before c. 900. For all the peremptory demands of canon lawyers that minsters should open their doors to inspection by episcopal authority and the consequent efforts of the bishops to rein in the worst excesses of behaviour and impose some minimal standards, particularly on those houses run by the nobility on estates booked to them in perpetuity, a minster was organised on lines devised by its own abbot or abbess. That one term minster conceals

---

[27] Alcuin, *Epp.* 67 and 189 (ed. Dümmler, pp. 111 and 316–17).
[28] HE IV. 2 (pp. 21–2). Compare here Alfred's wish to have been born earlier, in his regret that 'At the time when he was of the right age and had the leisure and capacity for learning, he did not have the teachers.' Asser, Life of Alfred, ch. 25 (ed. Stevenson, pp. 21–2).
[29] *EpEcg*, ch. 9 (p. 412).   [30] Chapter 2.
[31] Further it occasioned, as observed in chapter 1, a geographical revolution: no reformed houses for religious of either gender were founded north of the Humber; see figure 1 and p. 14, n. 33.

and celebrates a multiplicity of expressions of the ideal of communal living in the name of religion.[32]

Herein lay the phenomenal success of the monastic church of the early Anglo-Saxon era and also the necessary conditions for its later replacement. Earlier I suggested that the language of the family might offer a valuable metaphor for understanding the nature of seventh- and eighth-century English monasticism.[33] Recognising that the family is itself a functional institution, not just a social classification, we have seen how comparison between Germanic family structures and the interactions between separate family groups can help us to understand the internal organisation and external roles of minster communities. Minsters occupied a liminal space between the society of the secular aristocracy from which most of their professed members were drawn and the ecclesiastical society of the Christian church. Inevitably they were part of particular noble and royal networks and bound by reciprocal bonds of hospitality and obligation. In their roles as landowners and patrons, they were the equals of secular lords when it came to the managing of their own, often substantial, landed endowments and the men who were their tenants.[34] But minsters were also part of the wider family of the church and could thus divorce themselves from kin (and king) to appeal to a higher authority, that of bishop, archbishop or even pope.

Monasticism established itself as a powerful force within the nascent English church during an early phase of the Christianisation of the Anglo-Saxon people. In the context of this developing church, religious men and women sought to carve out functions for themselves that were adapted to the particular social situations in which they lived. As they sought to define and create a distinctive 'religious' identity, these first minster communities had to grapple with the very issue which has lain at the heart of this study: their continuing connection with noble society (and thus to some extent its ideals) served only to impede their aspirations to separation. Recognition of the closeness of the enduring links that bound minsters and the aristocracy is vital to our understanding of the nature of early English minsters and their role and place within contemporary society. If the models that shaped the choices made by the first aspiring religious were largely those of familial, noble communality, not isolation in separate solitude, we should scarcely be surprised that the first minsters resembled much more

[32] Illustrated most forcibly in our discussion of daily life within minsters in chapter 5.
[33] In chapter 2.
[34] Monastic landholdings were examined in chapter 3 and the nature of monastic communities in chapter 4.

347

'a special kind of nobleman's club' than they did Benedict's Monte Cassino.[35] The success and widespread appeal of monasticism in these early Christian centuries owes much to the capacity of its early leaders to recognise these factors as integral to the monastic experience they sought to establish and to capitalise on methods of integrating features they particularly admired into a higher spiritual ideal. In part this may account for the tendency of the prescriptive literature to dwell particularly on extreme models of ascetic perfection. Patrick Wormald showed this most effectively when he argued that 'Christianity in Anglo-Saxon England was successfully assimilated by a warrior nobility which had no intention of abandoning its culture, or seriously changing its way of life, but which was willing to throw its traditions, customs, tastes and loyalties into the articulation of the new faith.'[36] The early Anglo-Saxon minster offered members of the aristocracy an opportunity to join an institution with defined spiritual and social roles without having to compromise too many of the noble and heroic ideals that characterised the world in which their new home would continue to play an integral part.[37]

Seventh- and eighth-century ecclesiastics were not complacent about monastic standards in their own day and made efforts in various ways to remove the abuses that particularly concerned them and to improve general standards of clerical and monastic education and literacy. What they never sought to do was to make all minsters the same. Regularity of observance, especially adherence to a single set of organising precepts, was not an ideal to which they aspired. This is where the tenth-century monastic revival was so revolutionary, in that its exponents insisted on the imposition of one rule so that all monks and cloistered women would 'carry out the self-same monastic customs openly and with one uniform observance'. Diversity of practice was anathema to Æthelwold who strove to avoid the possibility that 'differing ways of observing the customs of one Rule and one country should bring the holy monastic life into disrepute'.[38] Having demonstrated the pluralism of early English monasticism and the intimacy of its involvement with lay society, this study forces us to view the pre-Viking Age church

[35] James Campbell, 'Elements in the background to the Life of St Cuthbert and his early cult', in Gerald Bonner et al. (eds.), St Cuthbert, his Cult and his Community to AD 1200 (Woodbridge: Boydell, 1989), pp. 3–19, at p. 12.

[36] Patrick Wormald, 'Bede, "Beowulf" and the conversion of the Anglo-Saxon aristocracy', in R. T. Farrell (ed.), Bede and Anglo-Saxon England, BAR, British series, 46 (Oxford: BAR, 1978), 32–95, at p. 57.

[37] Compare my 'The role of the minster in earlier Anglo-Saxon society', in Benjamin Thompson (ed.), Monasteries and Society in Medieval England (Stamford: Paul Watkins, 1998), pp. 35–58, at pp. 57–8.

[38] Regularis concordia, prologue, 6 and 4 (ed. Hallinger, pp. 73 and 71).

from a different perspective, neither coloured by the normalising tendencies of Bede's narrative or the admonitory literature, nor distorted through the lens of the historically-suspect rhetoric of King Edgar's reforming bishops. Contemporary continental influence was to have a profound significance in shaping the minds of those who adapted the model of Benedictine monastic observance and imposed it upon the conventual communities of tenth-century England.[39] But more significant in the achievement of their goals was perhaps the consolidation under Edgar of a politically-unified English realm. 'What man is there dwelling in England', asked Æthelwold, 'who does not know how Edgar advanced and protected God's kingdom, that is God's church, with benefits both spiritual and worldly, with all his strength?'[40] Only in the new political circumstances of the 960s was it to prove possible to begin to realise Bede's ambition of a homogeneous church united in uniform religious practice.

[39] Donald Bullough, 'The continental background of the reform', in David Parsons (ed.), *Tenth-Century Studies* (Chichester: Phillimore, 1975), pp. 20–36; Patrick Wormald, 'Æthelwold and his continental counterparts: contact, comparison, contrast', in, Barbara Yorke (ed.), *Bishop Æthelwold: His Career and Influence* (Woodbridge: Boydell Press, 1988), pp. 13–42.

[40] Æthelwold, 'An account' (*C&S* I, 147).

Bibliography

Primary sources

Abbo, *Passio sancti Eadmundi*, ed. Michael Winterbottom, *Three Lives of English Saints* (Toronto: Pontifical Institute of Mediaeval Studies for the Centre for Medieval Studies, 1972)

Adomnán's Life of Columba, ed. and trans. Alan Orr Anderson and Marjorie Ogilvie Anderson (London: Nelson, 1961; revised edition, Oxford: Clarendon Press, 1991)

Ælfric's Lives of Saints: Being a Set of Sermons on Saints' Days formerly Observed by the English Church, ed. from manuscript Julius E. VII in the Cottonian collection, with various readings from other manuscripts, ed. Walter W. Skeat, EETS 76, 82, 94, 114 (London: 1881–1900; reprinted in 2 vols. Oxford: Oxford University Press for the Early English Text Society, 1966)

Ælfwine's Prayerbook (London, British Library, Cotton Titus D. xxvi and xxvii), ed. Beate Günzel, Henry Bradshaw Society vol. 108 (London: Boydell Press for the Henry Bradshaw Society, 1993)

Æthelwold, 'An account of King Edgar's establishment of monasteries', ed. and trans. Dorothy Whitelock *et al.*, *Councils and Synods*, I, 142–54, no. 33

Æthelwulf, *De abbatibus*, ed. and trans. Alistair Campbell (Oxford: Clarendon Press, 1967)

Alcuin, *Epistolae*, ed. Ernst Dümmler, *MGH*, *Epistolae Karolini Aevi*, II (Berlin: Weidmannos, 1895)

Alcuin, 'Versus de patribus regibus et sanctis Euboricensis ecclesiae', ed. Peter Godman, *Alcuin: The Bishops, Kings and Saints of York* (Oxford: Clarendon Press, 1982)

Alcuin, *Vita sancti Willibrordi*, ed. Wilhelm Levison, *MGH, SSRM*, VII, 81–141 (Hanover and Leipzig: Hahn, 1920)

Aldhelm, *Opera*, ed. Rudolf Ehwald, *Aldhelmi opera*, *MGH, AA*, XV (Berlin: Weidmannos, 1919)

Aldhelm, *Prosa de virginitate*, revised edn with Latin and Anglo-Saxon glosses by Scott Gwara, CCSL, 124–124A (Turnhout: Brepols, 2001)

King Alfred's West Saxon Version of Gregory's Pastoral Care, ed. Henry Sweet, 2 vols., EETS, o.s. 45 and 50 (London: N. Trübner, 1871–2)

Anglo-Saxon Charters, ed. A. J. Robertson, Cambridge Studies in English Legal History (Cambridge: Cambridge University Press, 1939)

The Anglo-Saxon Chronicle: A Collaborative Edition, ed. D. N. Dumville and Simon Keynes, III: *MS A: A Semi-Diplomatic Edition with Introduction and Indices*, ed. Janet M. Bately (Cambridge: Brewer, 1986)

Anglo-Saxon Wills, ed. Dorothy Whitelock, Cambridge Studies in English Legal History (Cambridge: Cambridge University Press, 1930)

The Annals of St-Bertin, translated and annotated by Janet L. Nelson (Manchester: Manchester University Press, 1991)

Asser, Life of King Alfred, ed. W. H. Stevenson, *Life of King Alfred: Together with the Annals of Saint Neots erroneously ascribed to Asser* (Oxford: Clarendon Press, 1904, reprinted with an introductory essay by Dorothy Whitelock, 1959)

Augustine, *De opera monachorum*, ed. Migne, *PL*, 40, cols. 548–82

'B', *Vita sancti Dunstani*, ed. William Stubbs, *Memorials of St Dunstan*, Rolls Series 63 (London, 1874), pp. 3–52

Basil, *Epistolae*, ed. Roy J. Deferrari, *Saint Basil: The Letters*, 4 vols. (London and Cambridge, MA: William Heinemann and Harvard University Press, 1962)

Bede, *Epistola ad Ecgberhtum episcopum*, ed. Charles Plummer, *Venerabilis Bedae, opera historica*, 2 vols. (Oxford: Clarendon Press, 1896), I, 405–23

Bede, *Historia abbatum*, ed. Charles Plummer, *Venerabilis Bedae, opera historica*, 2 vols. (Oxford: Clarendon Press, 1896), I, 364–87

Bede, *Historia ecclesiastica*, ed. and trans. Bertram Colgrave and R. A. B. Mynors, *Bede's Ecclesiastical History of the English People* (Oxford: Clarendon Press, 1969)

The Old English Version of Bede's Ecclesiastical History of the English People, ed. Thomas Miller, EETS, o.s. 95–6 (Oxford: EETS, 1890; reprinted 1959)

Bede, *Homelia*, ed. David Hurst, *Bedae venerabilis opera*, III: *Opera homiletica*, CCSL 122 (Turnhout: Brepols, 1955)

Bede, *In Ezram et Neemiam*, ed. David Hurst, *Bedae venerabilis opera*, II: *Opera exegetica*, 2A, CCSL 119A (Turnhout: Brepols, 1949), 235–392

Bede, *In Lucae evangelium expositio*, ed. David Hurst, *Bedae venerabilis opera*, II: *Opera exegetica*, 3: *In Lucae evangelium expositio. In Marci evangelium expositio*, CCSL 120 (Turnhout: Brepols, 1960), 5–425

Bede, *In Marci evangelium expositio*, ed. David Hurst, *Bedae venerabilis opera*, II: *Opera exegetica*, 3: *In Lucae evangelium expositio. In Marci evangelium expositio*, CCSL 120 (Turnhout: Brepols, 1960), 431–648

Bede, *Retractatio in Actus apostolorum*, ed. M. L. W. Laistner, *Bedae venerabilis opera*, II: *Opera exegetica*, 4, CCSL 121 (Turnhout: Brepols, 1983), 101–63

Bede, *Vita sancti Cuthberti*, ed. and trans. Bertram Colgrave, *Two Lives of Saint Cuthbert: A Life by an Anonymous Monk of Lindisfarne and Bede's Prose Life* (Cambridge: Cambridge University Press, 1940), pp. 142–307

Boniface, *Epistolae*, ed. Michael Tangl, *Die Briefe des Heiligen Bonifatius und Lullus*, MGH, *Epistolae selectae*, I (Berlin, 1916)

Byrhtferth, *Vita S. Oswaldi*, ed. James Raine, *The Historians of the Church of York and its Archbishops*, Rolls Series 71, 3 vols. (London, 1879–94), I, 399–475

Caesarius, *Regula ad uirgines*, ed. A. de Vogüé and J. Courreau, *Césaire d'Arles, Oeuvres monastiques*, I: *Oeuvres pour les moniales*, SC 345 (Paris: Editions du Cerf, 1988); translated by Mary Caritas McCarthy, *The Rule for Virgins of Saint Caesarius of Arles: A Translation with a Critical Introduction* (Washington, DC: Catholic University of America Press, 1960)

Cassian, *Conlationes*, ed. and trans. E. Pichery, *Conférences*, 3 vols., SC 42, 54, 64 (Paris: Editions du Cerf, 1955–9)

Cassian, *De institutis coenobiorum et de octo principalium vitiorum remediis libri xii*, ed. Jean-Claude Guy, *Institutions cenobitiques*, SC 109 (Paris: Editions du Cerf, 1965)

Charters of Abingdon Abbey, ed. S. E. Kelly, Anglo-Saxon Charters VII–VIII (Oxford: Oxford University Press for the British Academy, 2000–1)

Charters of St Augustine's Abbey, Canterbury and Minster-in-Thanet, ed. S. E. Kelly, Anglo-Saxon Charters IV (Oxford: Oxford University Press for the British Academy, 1995)

Charters of Selsey, ed. S. E. Kelly, Anglo-Saxon Charters VI (Oxford: Oxford University Press for the British Academy, 1998)

Charters of Shaftesbury Abbey, ed. S. E. Kelly, Anglo-Saxon Charters V (Oxford: Oxford University Press for the British Academy, 1996)

Chrodegang of Metz, *Regula canonicorum*, ed. Wilhelm Schmitz, *S. Chrodegangi Metensis Episcopi (742–766) Regula canonicorum aus dem Leidener Codex Vossianus Latinus 94* (Hanover, 1889)

The Chronicle of Hugh Candidus, a Monk of Peterborough, ed. W. T. Mellows (London: Oxford University Press for the Friends of Peterborough Cathedral, 1949)

Chronicon abbatiae Rameseiensis, ed. W. D. Macray, Rolls Series 83 (London, 1886)

Chronicon monasterii de Abingdon, ed. Joseph Stevenson, 2 vols., Rolls Series 1 (London, 1858)

Columbanus, *Regula monachorum*, ed. and trans. G. S. M. Walker, *Sancti Columbani Opera* (Dublin: Dublin Institute for Advanced Studies, 1970)

Concilios visigóticos e hispano-romanos, ed. José Vives, Tomás Marín Martínez and Gonzalo Martínez Díez (Barcelona: Consejo Superior de Investigaciones Cientificos, Instituto Enrique Flórez, 1963)

Councils and Synods, I: *AD 871–1204, with Other Documents Relating to the English Church*, ed. Dorothy Whitelock, Martin Brett and C. N. L. Brooke (Oxford: Clarendon, 1981)

Cuthbert, *Epistola de obitu Bedae*, ed. and trans. Bertram Colgrave and R. A. B. Mynors, *Bede's Ecclesiastical History of the English People* (Oxford: Clarendon Press, 1969), pp. 580–7

Eigil, *Vita S. Sturmi*, ed. G. H. Pertz, *MGH SS*, II (Hanover: Hahn, 1829), 366–77

Felix, *Vita S. Guthlaci*, ed. and trans. Bertram Colgrave, *Felix's Life of Saint Guthlac* (Cambridge: Cambridge University Press, 1956; paperback edition, 1985)

Die Gesetze der Angelsachsen, ed. Felix Liebermann, 3 vols. (Halle: Niemeyer, 1903–16)

Gregory the Great, *Epistolae*, ed. Dag Norberg, *S. Gregorii Magni registrum epistularum*, 2 vols., CCSL 140–140A (Turnholt: Brepols, 1982)

Die Heiligen Englands, ed. Felix Liebermann (Hanover: Hahn, 1889)

Historia de Sancto Cuthberto: A History of Saint Cuthbert and a Record of his Patrimony, ed. Ted Johnson South (Cambridge: D. S. Brewer, 2002)

Hughe Candidus, *Chronicle*, ed. W. T. Mellows, *The Chronicle of Hugh Candidus* (London: Oxford University Press for the Friends of Peterborough Cathedral, 1949), and trans. C. Mellows and W. T. Mellows, *The Peterborough Chronicle of Hugh Candidus* (2nd edn, Peterborough: Museum Society, 1966)

Jerome, *Epistolae*, ed. Isidorus Hilberg, *Sancti Eusebii Hieronymi epistulae*, Corpus scriptorum ecclesiasticorum Latinorum, vols. 54–6, S. Eusebii Hieronymi Opera, sect. 1, partes 1–3 (Vienna: F. Tempsky; Leipzig: G. Freytag, 1910–18)

John of Worcester, ed. R. R. Darlington and P. McGurk, trans. J. Bray and P. McGurk, *The Chronicle of John of Worcester*, II: *The Annals from 450 to 1066* (Oxford: Clarendon Press, 1995)

Liber beatae Gregorii papae, ed. Bertram Colgrave, *The Earliest Life of Gregory the Great* (Cambridge: Cambridge University Press, 1968)

Liber Eliensis, ed. E. O. Blake, Camden third series, XCII (London: Royal Historical Society, 1962)

Liber vitae: Register and Martyrology of New Minster and Hyde Abbey, Winchester, ed. Walter de G. Birch, Hampshire Record Society (London: Simpkin & Co., 1892)

Liudger, *Vita S. Gregorii*, ed. Oswald Holder-Egger, *MGH, Scriptores*, XV.1 (Hanover: Hahn, 1887), 63–79

353

Pauli Warnefridi, diaconi casinensis, in sanctam Regulam commentarium archi-coenobii casinensis monachi nunc primum ediderunt ([Monte Cassino]: Abbey of Monte Cassino, 1880)

Regularis concordia, ed. Kassius Hallinger, *Consuetudinum saeculi X/XI/XII monumenta non-Cluniacensia*, Corpus consuetudinum monasticarum, 7 (Siegburg: F. Schmitt, 1984), 69–147

Regularis concordia anglicae nationis monachorum sanctimonialiumque: The Monastic Agreement of the Monks and Nuns of the English Nation, ed. and trans. Thomas Symons (London and New York: Nelson, 1953)

Rudolf, *Vita Leobae abbatissae Biscofesheimensis*, ed. G. Waitz, MGH, SS, XV.I (Hanover: Hahn, 1887), 118–31

Rule of the Master, ed. Adalbert de Vogüé, *La Règle du Maître*, SC, 105–7 (Paris: Editions du Cerf, 1964–5)

Rule of St Benedict, ed. Timothy Fry, *The Rule of St Benedict in Latin and English with Notes* (Collegeville, MN: Liturgical Press, 1981)

Rule of St Benedict, ed. Adalbert de Vogüé and Jean Neufville, *La Règle de Saint Benoît*, SC 181–6, 6 vols. (Paris: Editions du Cerf, 1971–2)

Sanctorum conciliorum et decretorum collectio nova, ed. G. D. Mansi, 6 vols. (Lucca: Ex Typographia Josephi Salani et Vincentii Junctinii, 1748–52)

Simeon of Durham, *Historia Dunelmensis ecclesiae*, ed. Thomas Arnold, *Symeonis monachi opera omnia*, Rolls Series 75, 2 vols. (London, 1882–5), I, 3–160

Simeon of Durham, *Historia regum*, ed. Thomas Arnold, *Symeonis monachi opera omnia*, Rolls Series 75, 2 vols. (London, 1882–5), II, 2–283

Stephen, *Vita sancti Wilfridi*, ed. and trans. Bertram Colgrave, *The Life of Bishop Wilfrid by Eddius Stephanus* (Cambridge: Cambridge University Press, 1927)

Theodore, Penitential, ed. Paul Willem Finsterwalder, *Die Canones Theodori Cantuariensis und ihre Uberlieferungsformen* (Weimar: H. Böhlaus, 1929)

Vita Ædwardi Regis, ed. and trans. Frank Barlow, *The Life of King Edward, who Rests at Westminster: Attributed to a Monk of St. Bertin* (London: Nelson, 1962)

Vita sancti Alcuini, ed. Wilhelm Arndt, *MGH, Scriptores*, XV. 1 (Hanover: Hahn, 1887), 182–97

Vita sancti Ceolfridi, ed. Charles Plummer, *Venerabilis Bedae, opera historica*, 2 vols. (Oxford: Clarendon Press, 1896), I, 388–404

Vita sancti Cuthberti, ed. and trans. B. Colgrave, *Two Lives of Saint Cuthbert: A Life by an Anonymous Monk of Lindisfarne and Bede's Prose Life* (Cambridge: Cambridge University Press, 1940), pp. 60–139

Vita Filiberti abbatis Gemeticensis et Heriensis, ed. Wilhelm Levison, *MGH, SSRM*, V (Hanover and Leipzig: Hahn, 1910), 589–90

William of Malmesbury, *De antiquitate Glastonie ecclesie*, ed. and trans. John Scott, *The Early History of Glastonbury: An Edition, Translation and Study of William of Malmesbury's De antiquitate Glastonie ecclesie* (Woodbridge: Boydell Press, 1981)

William of Malmesbury, *Gesta regum Anglorum*, ed. and trans. R. A. B. Mynors, completed by R. M. Thomson and Michael Winterbottom, 2 vols. (Oxford: Clarendon Press, 1998–9)

William of Malmesbury, *De gestis pontificum Anglorum*, ed. N. E. S. A. Hamilton, Rolls Series 52 (London, 1870)

William of Malmesbury, *Vita sancti Dunstani*, ed. W. Stubbs, *Memorials of St Dunstan*, Rolls Series 63 (London, 1874)

Willibald, *Hodoeporicon*, ed. Oswald Holder-Egger, *MGH, Scriptores*, XV. 1 (Hanover: Hahn, 1887), 80–117

Willibald, *Vita sancti Bonifatii*, ed. Reinhold Rau, *Briefe des Bonifatius: Willibalds Leben des Bonifatius. Nebst einigen zeitgenössischen Dokumenten* (Darmstadt: Wissenschaftliche Buchgesellschaft, 1968)

Wulfstan, *Institutes of Polity*, ed. Karl Jost, *Die 'Institutes of Polity, Civil and Ecclesiastical': Ein Werk Erzbischof Wulfstans von York*, Schweizer anglistische Arbeiten 47 (Bern: Francke, 1959)

Wulfstan of Winchester, *Vita sancti Æthelwoldi*, ed. Michael Lapidge and Michael Winterbottom, *Wulfstan of Winchester, the Life of St Æthelwold* (Oxford: Clarendon Press, 1991)

Secondary sources

Abels, Richard P., *Lordship and Military Obligation in Anglo-Saxon England* (Berkeley and Los Angeles, CA: University of California Press, 1988)

Abrams, Lesley, *Anglo-Saxon Glastonbury: Church and Endowment* (Woodbridge: Boydell Press, 1996)

Abrams, Lesley, 'Conversion and assimilation', in Dawn M. Hadley and Julian D. Richards (eds.), *Cultures in Contact: Scandinavian Settlement in England in the Ninth and Tenth Centuries* (Turnhout: Brepols, 2000), pp. 135–53

Addleshaw, G. W. O., *The Pastoral Organisation of the Modern Dioceses of Durham and Newcastle in the Time of Bede*, Jarrow Lecture 1963 (Jarrow [St Paul's Church, 1964])

Allison, Thomas, *English Religious Life in the Eighth Century as illustrated by Contemporary Letters* (London: SPCK and New York: Macmillan, 1929)

Allott, Stephen, *Alcuin of York: His Life and Letters* (York: William Sessions Ltd, 1974)

Angenendt, Arnold, 'The conversion of the Anglo-Saxons considered against the background of early medieval mission', *Settimane* 32 (1986), 747–92

Anton, Hans Hubert, *Studien zu den Klosterprivilegien der Päpste im frühen Mittelalter: unter besonderer Berücksichtigung der Privilegierung von St. Maurice d'Agaune* (Berlin and New York: de Gruyter, 1975)

Attenborough, F. L., *The Laws of the Earliest English Kings* (Cambridge: Cambridge University Press, 1922)

Bailey, Richard N., 'The Anglo-Saxon metalwork from Hexham', in D. P. Kirby (ed.), *St Wilfred at Hexham* (Hexham: Oriel Press, 1974), pp. 141–67

Bailey, Richard N., 'St Wilfrid, Ripon and Hexham', in Catherine Karkov and Robert Farrell (eds.), *Studies in Insular Art and Archaeology* (Oxford, OH: American Early Medieval Studies and the Miami University School of Fine Arts, 1991), pp. 3–25

Bailey, Richard N., *England's Earliest Sculptors*, Publications of the Dictionary of Old English, 5 (Toronto: Pontifical Institute of Mediaeval Studies, 1996)

Banham, Debby, *Food and Drink in Anglo-Saxon England* (Stroud: Tempus, 2004)

Banton, N., 'Monastic reform and the unification of tenth-century England', in Stuart Mews (ed.), *Religion and National Identity*, Studies in Church History 18 (Oxford: Basil Blackwell for the Ecclesiastical History Society, 1982), pp. 71–85

Barlow, Frank, *The English Church 1000–1066: A History of the Later Anglo-Saxon Church* (1963, 2nd edn, London: Longman, 1979)

Barlow, Frank, *The English church 1066–1154* (London: Longman, 1979)

Barnard, L. W., 'Bede and Eusebius as church historians', in Gerald Bonner (ed.), *Famulus Christi* (London: SPCK, 1976), pp. 106–24

Barrow, Julia, 'Survival and mutation: ecclesiastical institutions in the Danelaw in the ninth and tenth centuries', in Dawn M. Hadley and Julian D. Richards (eds.), *Cultures in Contact: Scandinavian Settlement in England in the Ninth and Tenth Centuries* (Turnhout: Brepols, 2000), pp. 155–76

Bartlett, Robert, *Trial by Fire and Water: The Medieval Judicial Ordeal* (Oxford: Clarendon Press, 1986)

Bartlett, Robert, 'Symbolic meanings of hair in the Middle Ages', *TRHS*, 6th ser. 4 (1994), 43–60

Bascombe, Kenneth, 'Two charters of King Suebred of Essex', in Kenneth Neale (ed.), *An Essex Tribute: Essays presented to Fredrick G. Emmison* (London: Leopard's Head, 1987), pp. 85–96

Bassett, Steven, 'The administrative landscape of the diocese of Worcester in the tenth century', in Nicholas Brooks and Catherine Cubitt (eds.), *St Oswald of Worcester* (London and New York: Leicester University Press, 1996), pp. 147–73

Bayless, Martha, '*Alea*, *tæfl*, and related games: vocabulary and context', in Katherine O'Brien O'Keeffe and Andy Orchard (eds.), *Latin Learning and English Lore: Studies in Anglo-Saxon Literature for Michael Lapidge*, 2 vols. (Toronto: University of Toronto Press, 2005), II, 9–27

Beck, Henry J. G., *The Pastoral Care of Souls in South-East France during the Sixth Century*, Analecta Gregoriana, 51 (Rome: Apud Aedes Universitatis Gregorianae, 1950)

Bedingfield, M. Bradford, *The Dramatic Liturgy of Anglo-Saxon England* (Woodbridge: Boydell Press, 2002)

Bell, R. D. and Maurice Beresford (eds.), *Wharram Percy: The Church of St Martin*, J. G. Hurst and P. H. Rahtz (gen. eds.), *Wharram: A Study of Settlement on the Yorkshire Wolds*, III (London: Society for Medieval Archaeology, 1987)

Berlière, U., 'L'exercice du ministère paroissial par les moines dans le haut Moyen-Age', *Revue bénédictine* 39 (1927), 227–50

Biddle, Martin, 'Archaeology and the beginnings of English society', in Peter Clemoes and Kathleen Hughes (eds.), *England before the Conquest* (Cambridge: Cambridge University Press, 1971), pp. 391–408

Biddle, Martin, 'The archaeology of the church: a widening horizon', in Peter Addyman and Richard Morris (eds.), *The Archaeological Study of Churches*, Council for British Archaeology, Research Report 13 (London: Council for British Archaeology, 1976), pp. 65–71

Biddle, Martin (ed.), *Winchester in the Early Middle Ages: An Edition and Discussion of the Winton Domesday*, Winchester Studies 1 (Oxford: Clarendon Press, 1976)

Biddle, Martin, 'Archaeology, architecture, and the cult of saints in Anglo-Saxon England', in L. A. S. Butler and R. K. Morris (eds.), *The Anglo-Saxon Church* (London: Council for British Archaeology, 1986), pp. 1–31

Binchy, D. A., 'St Patrick's "first synod"', *Studia Hibernica* 8 (1968), 49–59

Birch, W de Gray (ed.), *Liber vitae: Register and Martyrology of New Minster and Hyde abbey*, Hampshire Record Society Publications, 5 (London: Simpkin & Co., 1892)

Bitel, Lisa, *Isle of the Saints: Monastic Settlement and Christian Community in Early Ireland* (Ithaca, NY, and London: Cornell University Press, 1990; paperback edition Cork: Cork University Press, 1993)

Blair, John, 'Wimborne Minster', *Arch J* 140 (1983), 37–8

Blair, John, 'Secular minster churches in Domesday Book', in P. H. Sawyer (ed.), *Domesday Book: A Reassessment* (London and Baltimore: Edward Arnold, 1985), pp. 104–42

Blair, John, 'Introduction: from minster to parish church', in John Blair (ed.), *Minsters and Parish Churches: The Local Church in Transition 950–1200*, Oxford University Committee for Archaeology, Monograph 17 (Oxford: Oxford University Committee for Archaeology, 1988), pp. 1–19

Blair, John, 'Minster churches in the landscape', in Della Hooke (ed.), *Anglo-Saxon Settlements* (Oxford: Basil Blackwell, 1988), pp. 35–58

Blair, John (ed.), *Minsters and Parish Churches: The Local Church in Transition 950–1200*, Oxford University Committee for Archaeology, Monograph 17 (Oxford: Oxford University Committee for Archaeology, 1988)

Blair, John, 'The early churches at Lindisfarne', *Archaeologia Aeliana* 5th series, 19 (1991), 47–53

Blair, John, *Early Medieval Surrey: Landholding, Church and Settlement before 1300* (Stroud: Alan Sutton and Surrey Archaeological Society, 1991)

Blair, John, 'Anglo-Saxon minsters: a topographical review', in John Blair and Richard Sharpe (eds.), *Pastoral Care before the Parish* (Leicester, London and New York: Leicester University Press, 1992), pp. 226–66

Blair, John, 'Debate: ecclesiastical organization and pastoral care in Anglo-Saxon England', *Early Medieval Europe* 4 (1995), 193–212

Blair, John, 'The minsters of the Thames', in John Blair and Brian Golding (eds.), *The Cloister and the World: Essays in Medieval History in honour of Barbara Harvey* (Oxford: Oxford University Press, 1996), pp. 5–28

Blair, John, 'A saint for every minster? Local cults in Anglo-Saxon England', in Alan Thacker and Richard Sharpe (eds.), *Local Saints and Local Churches in the Early Medieval West* (Oxford: Oxford University Press, 2002), pp. 455–94

Blair, John, and Richard Sharpe (eds.), *Pastoral Care before the Parish* (Leicester, London and New York: Leicester University Press, 1992)

Böhmer, Heinrich, 'Das Eigenkirchentum in england', in Heinrich Böhmer *et al.* (eds.), *Texte und Forschungen zur englischen Kulturgeschichte: Festgabe für Felix Liebermann zum 20. Juli 1921* (Halle: M. Niemeyer, 1921), pp. 301–53

Bonner, Gerald, 'The Christian life in the thought of the Venerable Bede', *Durham University Journal* 63, n.s. 32 (1970), 39–55

Bonner, Gerald (ed.), *Famulus Christi: Essays in commemoration of the Thirteenth Centenary of the Birth of the Venerable Bede* (London: SPCK, 1976)

Bonner, Gerald, David Rollason and Clare Stancliffe (eds.), *St Cuthbert, his Cult and his Community to AD 1200* (Woodbridge: Boydell Press, 1989)

Boswell, John, *Christianity, Social Tolerance and Homosexuality: Gay People in Western Europe from the Beginning of the Christian Era to the Fourteenth Century* (Chicago: University of Chicago Press, 1980)

Boswell, John, '*Expositio* and *oblatio*: the abandonment of children and the ancient and medieval family', *American History Review* 89 (1984), 10–33

Boswell, John, *The Kindness of Strangers: The Abandonment of Children in Western Europe from Late Antiquity to the Renaissance* (London: Allen Lane, 1988)

Bradshaw, Paul F., *Daily Prayer in the Early Church: A Study of the Origin and Early Development of the Divine Office*, Alcuin Club Collections, 63 (London: SPCK, 1981)

Brooke, C. N. L., 'Rural ecclesiastical institutions in England: the search for their origins', *Settimane* 28 (1982), 685–711

Brooks, Nicholas, 'The development of military obligations in eighth- and ninth-century England', in Peter Clemoes and Kathleen Hughes (eds.), *England before the Conquest* (Cambridge: Cambridge University Press, 1971), pp. 69–84

Brooks, Nicholas, 'England in the ninth century: the crucible of defeat', *TRHS*, 5th series, 29 (1979), 1–20

Brooks, Nicholas, *The Early History of the Church of Canterbury: Christ Church 597–1066*, Studies in the Early History of Britain (Leicester: Leicester University Press, 1984)

Brooks, Nicholas, *Bede and the English*, Jarrow Lecture 1999 (Jarrow: [St Paul's Church], 2000)

Brooks, Nicholas, 'Alfredian government: the West Saxon inheritance', in Timothy Reuter (ed.), *Alfred the Great* (Aldershot: Ashgate Publishing, 2003), pp. 153–74, at pp. 163–73.

Brooks, Nicholas, and Catherine Cubitt (eds.), *St Oswald of Worcester: Life and Influence* (London and New York: Leicester University Press, 1996)

Brown, George Hardin, *Bede the Venerable* (Boston, MA: Twayne, 1987)

Brown, Michelle, 'The Lindisfarne scriptorium from the late seventh to the early ninth century' in Gerald Bonner *et al.* (eds.), *St Cuthbert, his Cult and his Community to AD 1200* (Woodbridge: Boydell Press, 1989), pp. 151–63

Brown, Michelle, *The Book of Cerne: Prayers, Patronage and Power in Ninth-Century England* (London: British Library, 1996)

Brown, Peter, 'Art and society in Late Antiquity', in Kurt Weitzmann (ed.), *Age of Spirituality: A Symposium* (New York: Metropolitan Museum of Art, 1980), pp. 17–27

Brown, Peter, *The Cult of the Saints: Its Rise and Function in Latin Christianity* (London: SCM Press, 1981)

Brown, Peter, 'The rise and function of the holy man in Late Antiquity', in his *Society and the Holy in Late Antiquity* (London: Faber, 1982), pp. 103–52

Bruce-Mitford, R. L. S., *The Art of the Codex Amiatinus*, Jarrow Lecture 1967 (Jarrow: [St Paul's Church, 1968])

Brückmann, J., 'Latin manuscript pontificals and benedictionals in England and Wales', *Traditio* 29 (1973), 391–458

Bullough, Donald, 'The educational tradition in England from Alfred to Ælfric: teaching *utriusque linguae*', *Settimane* 19 (1972), 453–94

Bullough, Donald, 'Social and economic structure and topography in the early medieval city', *Settimane* 21 (1974), 351–99

Bullough, Donald, 'The continental background of the reform', in David Parsons (ed.), *Tenth-Century Studies* (Chichester: Phillimore, 1975), pp. 20–36

359

Bullough, Donald, 'Hagiography as patriotism: Alcuin's "York poem" and the early Northumbrian "vitae sanctorum"', in Pierre Riché and Evelyne Patlagean (eds.), *Hagiographie, cultures et sociétés iv*ᵉ*–xii*ᵉ *siècles: Actes du colloque organisé a Nanterre et a Paris (2–5 mai, 1979)* (Paris: Etudes augustiniennes, 1981), pp. 339–59

Bullough, Donald, 'Missions to the English and Picts and their heritage (to *c.* 800)', in Heinz Löwe (ed.), *Die Iren und Europa im früheren Mittelalter* (Stuttgart: Klett-Cotta, 1982), pp. 80–98

Bullough, Donald, 'Burial, community and belief in the early medieval West', in Patrick Wormald *et al.* (eds.), *Ideal and Reality in Frankish and Anglo-Saxon Society* (Oxford: Basil Blackwell, 1983), pp. 177–201

Bullough, Donald, *Friends, Neighbours and Fellow-Drinkers: Aspects of Community and Conflict in the Early Medieval West* (Cambridge: Department of Anglo-Saxon, Norse and Celtic, 1991)

Bullough, Donald, 'Roman books and the Carolingian *renovatio*', in his *Carolingian Renewal: Sources and Heritage* (Manchester and New York: Manchester University Press, 1991), pp. 1–38

Bullough, Donald, 'What has Ingeld to do with Lindisfarne?', *Anglo-Saxon England* 22 (1993), 93–125

Bullough, Donald, 'The career of Columbanus', in Michael Lapidge (ed.), *Columbanus: Studies on the Latin Writings* (Woodbridge: Boydell Press, 1997), pp. 1–28

Bullough, Donald, *Alcuin: Achievement and Reputation* (Leiden and Boston: Brill, 2004)

Butler, Cuthbert, *Benedictine Monachism: Studies in Benedictine Life and Rule* (London and New York: Longmans, Green, 1919)

Butler, L. A. S., and R. K. Morris (eds.), *The Anglo-Saxon Church: Papers on History, Architecture and Archaeology in honour of Dr H. M. Taylor*, Council for British Archaeology, Research Report 60 (London: Council for British Archaeology, 1986)

Cambridge, Eric, 'The early church in County Durham: a reassessment', *Journal of the British Archaeological Association* 137 (1984), 65–85

Cambridge, Eric, and David Rollason, 'Debate: the pastoral organization of the Anglo-Saxon church: a review of the "minster hypothesis"', *Early Medieval Europe* 4 (1995), 87–104

Campbell, James, 'Bede', in T. A. Dorey (ed.), *Latin Historians* (London: Routledge and Kegan Paul, 1966), pp. 159–90; reprinted as 'Bede I', in his *Essays in Anglo-Saxon History* (London and Ronceverte: Hambledon Press, 1986), pp. 1–27

Campbell, James, 'Bede II', in his *Essays in Anglo-Saxon History* (London and Ronceverte: Hambledon Press, 1986), pp. 29–48; originally published in *idem* (trans.), *Bede: The Ecclesiastical History of the English People and other selections* (New York: Washington Square Press, 1968), pp. vii–xxxii

Campbell, James, 'The first century of Christianity in England', *Ampleforth Journal* 76 (1971), 12–29; reprinted in his *Essays in Anglo-Saxon History* (London and Ronceverte: Hambledon Press, 1986), pp. 49–67

Campbell, James, 'Bede's words for places', in P. H Sawyer (ed.), *Names, Words and Graves* (Leeds: School of History, University of Leeds, 1979), pp. 34–54; reprinted in his *Essays in Anglo-Saxon History* (London and Ronceverte: Hambledon Press, 1986), pp. 99–119

Campbell, James, 'The church in Anglo-Saxon towns', in Derek Baker (ed.), *The Church in Town and Countryside*, Studies in Church History 16 (Oxford: Basil Blackwell, 1979), 119–35; reprinted in his *Essays in Anglo-Saxon History* (London and Ronceverte: Hambledon Press, 1986), pp. 139–54

Campbell, James, 'Asser's *Life of Alfred*', in Christopher Holdsworth and T. P. Wiseman (eds.), *The Inheritance of Historiography*, Exeter Studies in History 12 (Exeter: University of Exeter, 1986), 115–35; reprinted in his *The Anglo-Saxon State* (London and New York: Hambledon and London, 2000), pp. 129–55

Campbell, James, *Essays in Anglo-Saxon History* (London and Ronceverte: Hambledon Press, 1986)

Campbell, James, 'Elements in the background to the Life of St Cuthbert and his early cult', in Gerald Bonner *et al.* (eds.), *St Cuthbert, his Cult and his Community to AD 1200* (Woodbridge: Boydell Press, 1989), pp. 3–19; reprinted in his *The Anglo-Saxon State* (London and New York: Hambledon and London, 2000), pp. 85–106

Campbell, James, 'The East Anglian sees before the Conquest', in Ian Atherton *et al.* (eds.), *Norwich Cathedral: Church, City and Diocese, 1096–1996* (London: Hambledon Press, 1996), pp. 3–21; reprinted in his *The Anglo-Saxon State* (London and New York: Hambledon and London, 2000), pp. 107–27

Carr, R. D. *et al.*, 'The middle Saxon settlement at Staunch Meadow, Brandon', *Antiquity* 62 (1988), 371–7

Carroll, Mary Thomas Aquinas, *The Venerable Bede: His Spiritual Teachings, a dissertation* (Washington, DC: Catholic University of America Press, 1946)

Carver, Martin O., 'Exploring, explaining, imagining: Anglo-Saxon archaeology 1998', in Catherine E. Karkov (ed.), *The Archaeology of Anglo-Saxon England: Basic Readings* (New York and London: Garland Publishing, 1999), pp. 25–52

Cassidy-Welch, Megan, *Monastic Spaces and their Meanings: Thirteenth-Century English Cistercian Monasteries* (Turnhout: Brepols, 2001)

Chadwick, Owen, *John Cassian: A Study in Primitive Monasticism* (Cambridge: Cambridge University Press, 1950)

Chaplais, Pierre, 'Some early Anglo-Saxon diplomas on single sheets: originals or copies?', reprinted in Felicity Ranger (ed.), *Prisca munimenta* (London: University of London Press, 1973), pp. 62–87

Chaplais, Pierre, 'The origin and authenticity of the royal Anglo-Saxon diploma', reprinted in Felicity Ranger (ed.), *Prisca munimenta* (London: University of London Press, 1973), pp. 28–42

Charles-Edwards, Thomas, 'Kinship, status and the origins of the hide', *Past and Present* 56 (1972), 3–33

Charles-Edwards, Thomas M., 'The social background to Irish *peregrinatio*', *Studia Celtica* 11 (1976), 43–59

Charles-Edwards, Thomas, 'The distinction between land and moveable wealth in Anglo-Saxon England', in Peter H. Sawyer (ed.), *English Medieval Settlement* (London: Edward Arnold, 1979), pp. 97–104

Charles-Edwards, Thomas, 'The church and settlement', in Próinséas Ní Chatháin and Michael Richter (eds.), *Irland und Europa: Die Kirche im Frühmittelalter = Ireland and Europe: The Early Church* (Stuttgart: Klett-Cotta, 1984) pp. 167–75

Charles-Edwards, Thomas, 'The pastoral role of the church in the early Irish laws', in John Blair and Richard Sharpe (eds.), *Pastoral Care before the Parish* (Leicester, London and New York: Leicester University Press, 1992), pp. 63–77

Charles-Edwards, Thomas, 'Anglo-Saxon kinship revisited', in John Hines (ed.), *The Anglo-Saxons from the Migration Period to the Eighth Century: An Ethnographic Perspective* (Woodbridge: Boydell Press, 1997), pp. 171–210

Charles-Edwards, T. M., *Early Christian Ireland* (Cambridge: Cambridge University Press, 2000)

Clarke, H. B., and Mary Brennan (eds.), *Columbanus and Merovingian Monasticism*, BAR, Internat. ser., 113 (Oxford: BAR, 1981)

Clayton, Mary, 'Feasts of the Virgin in the liturgy of the Anglo-Saxon Church', *Anglo-Saxon England* 13 (1984), 209–33

Clayton, Mary, *The Cult of the Virgin Mary in Anglo-Saxon England* (Cambridge: Cambridge University Press, 1990)

Clayton, Mary, 'Ælfric's *Judith*: manipulative or manipulated?' *Anglo-Saxon England* 23 (1994), 215–27

Clemoes, Peter, *The Cult of St Oswald on the Continent*, Jarrow Lecture 1983 (Jarrow: St Paul's Church, 1984)

Clemoes, Peter, and Kathleen Hughes (eds.), *England before the Conquest: Studies in Primary Sources presented to Dorothy Whitelock* (Cambridge: Cambridge University Press, 1971)

Coates, Simon, 'The bishop as pastor and solitary: Bede and the spiritual authority of the monk-bishop', *JEH* 47 (1996), 601–19

Coates, Simon, 'The role of bishops in the early Anglo-Saxon Church: a reassessment', *History* 81 (1996), 177–96

Coates, Simon, 'Perceptions of the Anglo-Saxon past in the tenth-century monastic reform movement', in R. N. Swanson (ed.), *The Church Retrospective* (Woodbridge: Boydell Press for the Ecclesiastical History Society, 1997), pp. 61–74

Coates, Simon, 'Ceolfrid: history, hagiography and memory in seventh- and eighth-century Wearmouth–Jarrow', *Journal of Medieval History* 25 (1999), 69–86

Colgrave, Bertram, 'The earliest saints' lives written in England', *Proceedings of the British Academy* 44 (1958), 35–60

Colgrave, Bertram (ed.), *The Earliest life of Gregory the Great* (Lawrence, KS: University of Kansas Press, 1968; paperback edition Cambridge: Cambridge University Press, 1985)

Constable, Giles, *Monastic Tithes from their Origins to the Twelfth Century*, Cambridge Studies in Medieval Life and Thought, n.s. 10 (Cambridge: Cambridge University Press, 1964)

Constable, Giles, 'Monasteries, rural churches and the *cura animarum* in the early Middle Ages', *Settimane* 28 (1982), 349–89

Constable, Giles, 'The ceremonies and symbolism of entering religious life and taking the monastic habit from the fourth to the twelfth century', *Settimane* 33 (1987), 771–834

Corrêa, Alicia, 'Daily office books: collectars and breviaries', in Richard W. Pfaff (ed.), *The Liturgical Books of Anglo-Saxon England*, Old English Newsletter, Subsidia 23 (Kalamazoo, MI: The Medieval Institute, Western Michigan University, 1995), pp. 45–66

Coulstock, Patricia, *The Collegiate Church of Wimborne Minster* (Woodbridge: Boydell Press, 1993)

Coupland, Simon, 'The rod of God's wrath or the people of God's wrath? The Carolingians' theology of the viking invasions', *JEH* 42 (1991), 535–54

Cowdrey, H. E. J., 'Bede and the "English People"', *Journal of Religious History* 11 (1981), 501–23

Cramp, Rosemary, *Early Northumbrian Sculpture*, Jarrow Lecture 1965 (Jarrow: Saxby, 1965)

Cramp, Rosemary, 'Excavations at the Saxon monastic sites of Wearmouth and Jarrow, Co. Durham: an interim report', *Medieval Archaeology*, 13 (1969), 21–66

Cramp, Rosemary, 'Early Northumbrian sculpture at Hexham', in D. P. Kirby (ed.), *Saint Wilfrid at Hexham* (Newcastle upon Tyne: Oriel Press, 1974), pp. 115–40

Cramp, Rosemary, 'Jarrow church', *Arch J* 133 (1976), 220–8

Cramp, Rosemary, 'Monastic sites', in David Wilson (ed.), *The Archaeology of Anglo-Saxon England* (Cambridge: Cambridge University Press, 1976), pp. 201–52

Cramp, Rosemary, 'Schools of Mercian sculpture', in Ann Dorrier (ed.), *Mercian Studies* (Leicester, 1977), pp. 191–231

Cramp, Rosemary, 'Anglo-Saxon settlement', in J. C. Chapman and H. C. Mytum (eds), *Settlement in North Britain 1000 BC–AD 1000*, BAR, Brit. ser., 118 (Oxford: BAR, 1983), 263–97

Cramp, Rosemary, 'Northumbria and Ireland', in Paul E. Szarmach with the assistance of Virginia Darrow Oggins (eds.), *Sources of Anglo-Saxon Culture* (Kalamazoo, MI: Medieval Institute Publications, Western Michigan University, 1986), pp. 185–201

Cramp, Rosemary, 'The artistic influence of Lindisfarne within Northumbria', in Gerald Bonner *et al.* (eds.), *St Cuthbert, his Cult and his Community* (Woodbridge: Boydell Press, 1989), pp. 213–28

Cramp, Rosemary, 'A reconsideration of the monastic site of Whitby', in R. Michael Spearman and John Higgitt (eds.), *The Age of Migrating Ideas: Early Medieval Art in Northern Britain and Ireland, proceedings of the second international conference on insular art held in the National Museums of Scotland in Edinburgh, 3–6 January 1991* (Edinburgh: National Museums of Scotland; Stroud: Alan Sutton, 1993), pp. 64–73

Cramp, Rosemary, 'Monkwearmouth and Jarrow in their continental context', in Catherine E. Karkov (ed.), *The Archaeology of Anglo-Saxon England: Basic Readings* (New York and London: Garland Publishing, 1999), pp. 137–53

Cramp, R. J., and R. Daniels, 'New finds from the Anglo-Saxon monastery at Hartlepool, Cleveland', *Antiquity* 61 (1987), 424–32

Crick, Julia, 'Men, women and widows: widowhood in pre-Conquest England', in Sandra Cavallo and Lyndan Warner (eds.), *Widowhood in Medieval and Early Modern Europe* (Harlow: Longman, 1999), pp. 24–36

Cross, J. E., 'The latinity of the Old English martyrologist', in Paul E. Szarmach (ed.), *Studies in Earlier Old English Prose: Sixteen Original Contributions* (Albany, NY: State University of New York Press, 1986), pp. 275–99

Cubitt, Catherine, 'Wilfrid's "usurping bishops": episcopal elections in Anglo-Saxon England, *c.* 600–*c.* 800', *Northern History* 25 (1989), 18–38

Cubitt, Catherine, 'Pastoral care and conciliar canons: the provisions of the 747 council of *Clofesho*', in John Blair and Richard Sharpe (eds.), *Pastoral Care before the Parish* (Leicester, London and New York: Leicester University Press, 1992), pp. 193–211

Cubitt, Catherine, *Anglo-Saxon Church Councils c. 650–c. 850*, Studies in the Early History of Britain (London and New York: Leicester University Press, 1995)

Cubitt, Catherine, 'Unity and diversity in the Anglo-Saxon liturgy', in R. N. Swanson (ed.), *Unity and Diversity in the Church*, Studies in Church History 32 (Oxford: Blackwell, 1996), 45–57

Cubitt, Catherine, 'Memory and narrative in the cult of early Anglo-Saxon saints', in Matthew Innes and Yitzak Hen (eds.), *The Uses of the Past in the Early Middle Ages* (Cambridge: Cambridge University Press, 2000), pp. 29–66

Cubitt, Catherine, 'Monastic memory and identity in early Anglo-Saxon England', in William O. Frazer and Andrew Tyrrel (eds.), *Social Identity in Early Medieval Britain*, Studies in the Early History of Britain (London and New York: Leicester University Press, 2000), pp. 252–76

Cubitt, Catherine, 'Universal and local saints in Anglo-Saxon England', in Alan Thacker and Richard Sharpe (eds.), *Local Saints and Local Churches in the Early Medieval West* (Oxford: Oxford University Press, 2002), pp. 423–53

Daniels, R., 'The Anglo-Saxon monastery at Church Close, Hartlepool, Cleveland', *Arch J* 145 (1988), 158–210

Davey, N., 'A pre-Conquest church and baptistery at Potterne', *Wiltshire Archaeological and Natural History Magazine* 59 (1964), 116–23

De Hamel, Christopher, *A History of Illuminated Manuscripts* (Oxford: Phaidon, 1986)

De Jong, Mayke, *In Samuel's Image: Child Oblation in the Early Medieval West* (Leiden: Brill, 1996)

Deanesly, Margaret, 'The *familia* at Christ Church, Canterbury, 597–832', in A. G. Little and F. M. Powicke (eds.), *Essays in Medieval History presented to Thomas Frederick Tout* (Manchester: Manchester University Press, 1925), pp. 1–13

Deanesly, Margaret, 'English and Gallic minsters', *TRHS*, 4th series, 23 (1941), 25–69

Deanesly, Margaret, *The Pre-Conquest Church in England* (London: A. and C. Black, 1961; 2nd edn, London: Adam & C. Black, 1963)

Deanesly, Margaret, *Augustine of Canterbury* (London: Nelson, 1964)

Dornier, Ann, 'The Anglo-Saxon monastery at Breedon-on-the-Hill, Leicestershire', in Ann Dornier (ed.), *Mercian Studies* (Leicester: Leicester University Press, 1977), pp. 155–68

Dornier, Ann (ed.), *Mercian Studies* (Leicester: Leicester University Press, 1977)

Douglas, David C., *The Domesday Monachorum of Christ Church, Canterbury* (London: Royal Historical Society, 1944)

Dudden, F. H., *Gregory the Great: His Place in History and Thought*, 2 vols. (London, New York [etc.]: Longmans, Green, and Co., 1905)

Dumville, David N., *Liturgy and the Ecclesiastical History of Late Anglo-Saxon England: Four Studies* (Woodbridge: Boydell Press, 1992)

Dumville, David N., *Wessex and England from Alfred to Edgar: Six Essays on Political, Cultural, and Ecclesiastical Revival* (Woodbridge: Boydell Press, 1992)

Dumville, David N., *English Caroline Script and Monastic History: Studies in Benedictinism, AD 950–1030* (Woodbridge: Boydell Press, 1993)

Dunn, Marilyn, *The Emergence of Monasticism: From the Desert Fathers to the Early Middle Ages* (Oxford: Blackwell, 2000)

Dyer, Christopher, *Lords and Peasants in a Changing Society: The Estates of the Bishopric of Worcester, 680–1540* (Cambridge: Cambridge University Press, 1980)

Edwards, Heather, *The Charters of the Early West Saxon Kingdom*, BAR, Brit. ser., 198 (Oxford: BAR, 1988)

Engen, John van, 'Professing religion: from liturgy to law', *Viator* 29 (1998), 323–43

Enright, M. J., 'Charles the Bald and Æthelwulf of Wessex: the alliance of 856 and strategies of royal succession', *Journal of Medieval History* 5 (1979), 291–302

Esposito, M., 'La vie de Sainte Vulfhilde', *Analecta Bollandiana* 32 (1913), 10–26

Etchingham, Colmán, *Church Organisation in Ireland AD 650–1000* (Maynooth: Laigin Publications, 1999)

Faith, Rosamond, *The English Peasantry and the Growth of Lordship* (London and Washington: Leicester University Press, 1997)

Farmer, D. H., 'Saint Wilfrid', in D. P. Kirby (ed.), *Saint Wilfrid at Hexham* (Newcastle upon Tyne: Oriel Press, 1974), pp. 35–60

Fell, Christine, 'Some implications of the Boniface correspondence', in Helen Damico and Alexandra Hennessey Olsen (eds.), *New Readings on Women in Old English Literature* (Bloomington: University of Indiana Press, 1990), pp. 29–43

Ferrari, Guy, *Early Roman Monasteries: Notes for the History of the Monasteries and Convents at Rome from the V through the X Century*, Studi di antichita cristiana 23 (Città del Vaticano: Pontificio Istituto di archeologia cristiana, 1957)

Finberg, H. P. R., *The Early Charters of the West Midlands* (Leicester: Leicester University Press, 1972)

Fisher, D. J. V., 'The anti-monastic reaction in the reign of Edward the Martyr', *Cambridge Historical Journal* 10 (1950–2), 254–70

Flaskamp, Franz, 'Das Geburtsjahr des Wynfrith–Bonifatius', *Zeitschrift für Kirchengeschichte* 45 (1927), 339–44

Fleming, Robin, 'Monastic lands and England's defence in the Viking Age', *English Historical Review* 100 (1985), 247–65

Fletcher, Eric, 'The influence of Merovingian Gaul on Northumbria in the seventh century', *Medieval Archaeology* 24 (1980), 69–86

Fletcher, Richard, *The Conversion of Europe: From Paganism to Christianity 371–1386 AD* (London: HarperCollins, 1997)

Flint, Valerie I. J., 'Space and discipline in early medieval Europe', in Barbara A. Hanawalt and Michal Kobialka (eds.), *Medieval Practices of Space* (Minneapolis and London: University of Minnesota Press, 2000), pp. 149–66

Foley, William Trent, *Images of Sanctity in Eddius Stephanus' 'Life of Bishop Wilfrid', an Early English Saint's Life* (Lewiston, NY, Queenston, ON, and Lampeter: Edwin Mellen Press, 1992)

Foot, Sarah, 'Parochial ministry in early Anglo-Saxon England: the role of monastic communities', in W. J. Sheils and Diana Wood (eds.), *The Ministry: Clerical and Lay,*

Studies in Church History 26 (Oxford: Basil Blackwell for the Ecclesiastical History Society, 1989), 43–54

Foot, Sarah, 'Anglo-Saxon minsters AD 597–*ca* 900: the religious life in England before the Benedictine reform' (unpublished PhD thesis, University of Cambridge, 1990)

Foot, Sarah, 'What was an Anglo-Saxon monastery?', in Judith Loades (ed.), *Monastic Studies* (Bangor: Headstart History, 1990), pp. 48–57

Foot, Sarah, 'Glastonbury's early abbots', in Lesley Abrams and James P. Carley (eds.), *The Archaeology and History of Glastonbury Abbey: Essays in honour of the Ninetieth Birthday of C. A. Ralegh Radford* (Woodbridge: Boydell Press, 1991), pp. 163–89

Foot, Sarah, 'Violence against Christians? The vikings and the church in ninth-century England', *Medieval History* 1.3 (1991), 3–16

Foot, Sarah, 'Anglo-Saxon minsters: a review of terminology', in John Blair and Richard Sharpe (eds.), *Pastoral Care before the Parish* (Leicester, London and New York: Leicester University Press, 1992), pp. 212–25

Foot, Sarah, '"By water in the Spirit": the administration of baptism in Anglo-Saxon England', in John Blair and Richard Sharpe (eds.), *Pastoral Care before the Parish* (Leicester, London and New York: Leicester University Press, 1992), pp. 171–92

Foot, Sarah, 'The making of *Angelcynn*: English identity before the Norman Conquest', *TRHS*, 6th series, 6 (1996), 25–49

Foot, Sarah, 'Language and method: the *Dictionary of Old English* and the historian', in M. J. Toswell (ed.), *The Dictionary of Old English: Retrospects and Prospects*, Old English Newsletter, Subsidia 26 (1998), 73–87

Foot, Sarah, 'The role of the minster in earlier Anglo-Saxon society', in Benjamin Thompson (ed.), *Monasteries and Society in Medieval Britain*: *Proceedings of the 1994 Harlaxton Symposium* (Stamford: Paul Watkins 1999), pp. 35–58

Foot, Sarah, 'Remembering, forgetting and inventing: attitudes to the past in England after the First Viking Age', *TRHS*, 6th series, 9 (1999), 185–200

Foot, Sarah, *Veiled Women*, I: *The Disappearance of Nuns from Anglo-Saxon England* (Aldershot: Ashgate, 2000)

Foot, Sarah, *Veiled Women*, II: *Female Religious Communities in England, 871–1066* (Aldershot: Ashgate, 2000)

Foot, Sarah, 'Reading Anglo-Saxon charters: memory, record or story?', in E. M. Tyler and Ross Balzaretti (eds.), *Narrative and History in the Early Medieval West* (Turnhout: Brepols, forthcoming 2006), pp. 39–65

Foucault, Michel, *Discipline and Punish: The Birth of the Prison*, trans. Alan Sheridan (London: Allen Lane, 1977) originally published as *Surveiller et punir: Naissance de la prison* (Paris: Editions Gallimard, 1975)

Foucault, Michel, *The History of Sexuality*, I, trans. Robert Hurley (New York: Vintage, 1980)

Franklin, Michael, 'Minsters and parishes: Northamptonshire studies' (unpublished PhD thesis, University of Cambridge, 1982)

Franklin, M., 'The identification of minsters in the Midlands', *Anglo-Norman Studies VII*, Proceedings of the Battle Conference 1984, ed. R. Allen Brown (Woodbridge: Boydell Press, 1985), pp. 69–88

Frantzen, Allen J., *The Literature of Penance in Anglo-Saxon England* (New Brunswick, NJ: Rutgers University Press, 1983)

Frantzen, Allen J., *Before the Closet: Same-Sex Love from Beowulf to Angels in America* (Chicago and London: University of Chicago Press, 1998)

Gamer, Helena M., and J. T. McNeill, *Medieval Handbooks of Penance: A Translation of the Principal libri poenitentiales and Selections from Related Documents* (New York: Columbia University Press, 1938)

Gameson, Richard (ed.), *St Augustine and the Conversion of England* (Stroud: Sutton, 1999)

Ganz, David, 'The ideology of sharing: apostolic community and ecclesiastical property in the early Middle Ages', in Wendy Davies and Paul Fouracre (eds.), *Property and Power in the Early Middle Ages* (Cambridge: Cambridge University Press, 1995), pp. 17–30

Geake, Helen, 'Persistent problems in the study of conversion-period burials in England', in Sam Lucy and Andrew Reynolds (eds.), *Burial in Early Medieval England and Wales* (London: Society for Medieval Archaeology, 2002), pp. 144–55

Geary, Patrick, *Living with the Dead in the Middle Ages* (Ithaca, NY, and London: Cornell University Press, 1994

Gelling, Margaret, 'Further thoughts on pagan place-names', in Kenneth Cameron (ed.), *Place-Name Evidence for the Anglo-Saxon Invasion and Scandinavian Settlements: Eight Studies* (Nottingham: English Place-Name Society, 1975), pp. 99–114

Gerchow, Jan, *Die Gedenküberlieferung der Angelsachsen: mit einem Katalog der Libri vitae und Necrologien* (Berlin: de Gruyter, 1988)

Gilchrist, Roberta, *Gender and Material Culture: The Archaeology of Religious Women* (London and New York: Routledge, 1994)

Gittos, Helen, 'Creating the sacred: Anglo-Saxon rites for consecrating cemeteries', in Sam Lucy and Andrew Reynolds (eds.), *Burial in Early Medieval England and Wales* (London: Society for Medieval Archaeology, 2002), pp. 195–208

Gneuss, Helmut, 'Liturgical books in Anglo-Saxon England and their Old English terminology', in Michael Lapidge and Helmut Gneuss (eds.), *Learning and Literature in Anglo-Saxon England* (Cambridge: Cambridge University Press, 1985), pp. 91–141

Gneuss, Helmut, 'King Alfred and the history of Anglo-Saxon libraries', in Phyllis Rugg Brown *et al.* (eds.), *Modes of Interpretation in Old English Literature* (Toronto, Buffalo, and London: University of Toronto Press, 1986), pp. 29–49

Godfrey, J., 'The place of the double monastery in the Anglo-Saxon minster system', in Gerald Bonner (ed.), *Famulus Christi* (London: SPCK, 1976), pp. 344–50

Godfrey, John, *The Church in Anglo-Saxon England* (Cambridge: Cambridge University Press, 1962)

Goffart, Walter, *The Narrators of Barbarian History (AD 550–800): Jordanes, Gregory of Tours, Bede, and Paul the Deacon* (Princeton, NJ: Princeton University Press, 1988)

Goffman, Erving, *Asylums: Essays on the Social Situation of Mental Patients and Other Inmates* (Chicago: Aldine Pub. Co., 1961)

Goffman, Erving, 'On the characteristics of total institutions: the inmate world', in Donald R. Cressey (ed.), *The Prison: Studies in Institutional Organization and Change* (New York: Holt, Rinehart and Winston, 1961), pp. 15–67

Goffman, Erving, 'On the characteristics of total institutions: staff–inmate relations', in Donald R. Cressey (ed.), *The Prison* (New York: Holt, Rinehart and Winston, 1961), pp. 68–106

Gransden, Antonia, 'Traditionalism and continuity during the last century of Anglo-Saxon monasticism', *Journal of Ecclesiastical History* 40 (1989), 159–207

Gwara, Scott (ed.), *Anglo-Saxon Conversations: The Colloquies of Ælfric Bata*, translated with an introduction by David W. Porter (Woodbridge: Boydell Press 1997)

Hagen, Ann, *A Handbook of Anglo-Saxon Food: Processing and Consumption* (Pinner: Anglo-Saxon Books, 1992)

Hall, M. A., 'A possible merels board incised on the pre-Conquest cross-base at Addingham, St Michael's Church, Cumbria', *Transactions of the Cumberland and Westmorland Antiquarian and Archaeological Society*, 3rd series, 1 (2001), 45–51

Hallinger, Kassius, 'Papst Gregor der Grosse und der heilige Benedikt', *Studia Anselmiana* 42 (1957), 231–319

Halsall, Guy, 'Playing by whose rules? A further look at viking atrocity in the ninth century', *Medieval History* 2.2 (1992), 2–12

Hase, Patrick, 'The development of the parish in Hampshire, particularly in the eleventh and twelfth centuries' (unpublished PhD thesis, University of Cambridge, 1975)

Hase, P. H., 'The mother churches of Hampshire', in John Blair (ed.), *Minsters and Parish Churches: The Local Church in Transition, 950–1200* (Oxford: Oxford University Committee for Archaeology, 1988), pp. 45–66

Haslam, Jeremy, *Anglo-Saxon Towns in Southern England* (Chichester: Phillimore, 1984)

Hawkes, Jane, 'Anglo-Saxon sculpture: questions of context', in Jane Hawkes and Susan Mills (eds.), *Northumbria's Golden Age* (Stroud: Sutton, 1999), pp. 204–15,

Hawkes, Jane, 'Statements in stone: Anglo-Saxon sculpture, Whitby and the Christianization of the north', in Catherine E. Karkov (ed.), *The Archaeology of Anglo-Saxon England: Basic Readings* (New York and London: Garland Publishing, 1999), pp. 403–21

Hen, Yitzhak, '*Milites Christi utriusque sexus*: gender and politics of conversion in the circle of Boniface', *Revue bénédictine* 109 (1999), 17–31

Herbert, Máire, *Iona, Kells, and Derry: The History and Hagiography of the Monastic Familia of Columba* (Oxford: Clarendon Press, 1988)

Herity, M., 'The buildings and layout of early Irish monasteries before the year 1000', *Monastic Studies* 14 (1983), 247–84

Herity, M., 'The layout of Irish early Christian monasteries', in P. Ní Chatháin and M. Richter (eds.), *Irland und Europa: Die Kirche im Frühmittelalter* (Stuttgart: Klett-Cotta, 1984), 105–16

Herlihy, David, *Medieval Households* (Cambridge, MA, and London: Harvard University Press, 1985)

Higham, Nick, 'Bishop Wilfrid in southern England: a review of his political objectives', *Studien zur Sachsenforschung* 13 (1999), 207–17

Hill, David, *An Atlas of Anglo-Saxon England 700–1066* (Oxford: Blackwell, 1981)

Hill, Rosalind, 'Christianity and geography in early Northumbria', *Studies in Church History* 3 (1966), 126–39

Hirst, J., 'On guildship in Anglo-Saxon monasteries', *Arch J* 49 (1892), 107–19

Hodges, Richard, 'San Vincenzo al Volturno and the plan of St Gall', in Richard Hodges (ed.), *San Vincenzo al Volturno, 2: The 1980–86 Excavations, part II*, Archaeological Monographs of the British School at Rome 9 (London: British School at Rome, 1995), 153–75

Hohler, Christopher, 'The type of sacramentary used by St Boniface', in Cuno Raabe *et al.* (eds.), *Sankt Bonifatius: Gedenkgabe zum Zwölfhundertsten Todestag* (Fulda: Parzeller, 1954), pp. 89–93

Hohler, C. E., 'Some service books of the later Saxon church', in David Parsons (ed.), *Tenth-Century Studies* (London and Chichester: Phillimore, 1975), pp. 60–83

Holdsworth, Christopher, 'Boniface the monk', in Timothy Reuter (ed.), *The Greatest Englishman: Essays on St Boniface and the Church at Crediton* (Exeter: Paternoster Press, 1980), pp. 49–67

Hollis, Stephanie, *Anglo-Saxon Women and the Church: Sharing a Common Fate* (Woodbridge: Boydell Press, 1992)

Hope-Taylor, Brian, *Yeavering: An Anglo-British Centre of Early Northumbria* (London: HMSO, 1977)

Horn, W., 'On the origins of the medieval cloister', *Gesta* 12 (1973), 13–52

Horn, Walter, and Ernest Born, *The Plan of Saint Gall: A Study of the Architecture and Economy of, and Life in, a Paradigmatic Carolingian Monastery*, 3 vols. (Berkeley, Los Angeles and London: University of California Press, 1979)

Hughes, Kathleen, *The Church in Early Irish Society* (London: Methuen, 1966)

Hughes, Kathleen, 'Some aspects of Irish influence on early English private prayer', *Studia Celtica* 5 (1970), 48–61

Hunter Blair, Peter, *The World of Bede* (London: Secker and Warburg, 1970)

Hunter Blair, Peter, *Northumbria in the Days of Bede* (London: Book Club Associates, 1976)

Hunter Blair, Peter, 'Whitby as a centre of learning in the seventh century', in Michael Lapidge and Helmut Gneuss (eds.), *Learning and Literature in Anglo-Saxon England* (Cambridge: Cambridge University Press, 1985), pp. 3–32

Hyams, Paul R., 'Trial by ordeal: the key to proof in the early common law', in Morris S. Arnold (ed.), *On the Laws and Customs of England: Essays in honor of Samuel E. Thorne* (Chapel Hill, NC: University of North Carolina Press, 1981), pp. 90–126

Irsigler, F., 'On the aristocratic character of early Frankish society', in Timothy Reuter (ed. and trans.), *The Medieval Nobility: Studies on the Ruling Classes of France and Germany from the Sixth to the Twelfth Century* (Amsterdam and Oxford: North-Holland Publishing Co., 1979), pp. 103–36

James, Edward, 'Merovingian cemetery studies and some implications for Anglo-Saxon England', in Philip Rahtz *et al.* (eds.), *Anglo-Saxon Cemeteries 1979: The Fourth Anglo-Saxon Symposium at Oxford*, BAR, Brit. ser., 82 (Oxford: BAR, 1980), pp. 35–55

James, Edward, 'Archaeology and the Merovingian monastery', in H. B. Clarke and Mary Brennan (eds.), *Columbanus and Merovingian Monasticism*, BAR, Internat. ser., 113 (Oxford: BAR, 1981), pp. 33–55

James, Edward, 'Bede and the tonsure question', *Peritia* 3 (1984), 85–98

James, Edward, *Britain in the First Millennium* (London: Arnold, 2001)

Jewell, Richard, 'Classicism of Southumbrian sculpture', in Michelle P. Brown and Carol A. Farr (eds.), *Mercia: An Anglo-Saxon Kingdom in Europe* (London: Leicester University Press, 2001), pp. 247–62

John, Eric, *Land Tenure in Early England: A Discussion of Some Problems* (Leicester: Leicester University Press, 1964)

John, E., '"Secularium prioratus" and the Rule of St Benedict', *Revue bénédictine* 75 (1965), 212–39

John, Eric, 'The king and the monks in the tenth-century reformation', in his *Orbis Britanniae and Other Studies* (Leicester: Leicester University Press, 1966), pp. 154–209

John, Eric, 'The social and political problems of the early English church', in Joan Thirsk (ed.), *Land, Church, and People: Essays presented to Professor H. P. R. Finberg* (Reading: British Agricultural History Society, 1970), pp. 39–63

John, Eric, *Reassessing Anglo-Saxon England* (Manchester: Manchester University Press, 1996)

Johnson, Stephen, *Burgh Castle: Excavations by Charles Green 1958–61*, East Anglian Archaeology 20 (Dereham: Norfolk Archaeological Unit, 1983)

Karkov, Catherine, 'The decoration of early wooden architecture', in Catherine Karkov and Robert Farrell (eds.), *Studies in Insular Art and Archaeology*, American Early Medieval Studies 1 (Oxford, OH: American Early Medieval Studies and the Miami University School of Fine Arts, 1991), pp. 27–48

Kendall, Calvin B., 'Imitation and the Venerable Bede's *Historia ecclesiastica*', in Margot King and Wesley Stevens (eds.), *Saints, Scholars and Heroes: Studies in Medieval Culture in honor of Charles W. Jones*, 2 vols. (Collegeville, MN: Hill Monastic Manuscript Library, Saint John's Abbey and University, 1979), I, 161–90

Kendall, Calvin B., 'The Plan of St Gall: an argument for a 320-foot church prototype', *Mediaeval Studies* 56 (1994), 179–97

Kendrick, T. D., *et al.* (eds.), *Codex Lindisfarnensis (The Lindisfarne Gospels) published by permission of the Trustees of the British Museum*, 2 vols. (Oltun and Lausanne: Urs Graf, 1956–60)

Ker, N. R., 'The provenance of the oldest manuscript of the Rule of St Benedict', *Bodleian Library Record* 2 (1941), 28–9

Keynes, Simon, 'King Æthelstan's books', in Michael Lapidge and Helmut Gneuss (eds.), *Learning and Literature in Anglo-Saxon England* (Cambridge: Cambridge University Press, 1985), pp. 143–201

Keynes, Simon, *The Councils of Clofesho*, Eleventh Annual Brixworth Lecture ([Leicester]: University of Leicester, Department of Adult Education, 1994)

Keynes, Simon, *The Liber vitae of the New Minster and Hyde Abbey, Winchester*, Early English Manuscripts in Facsimile 26 (Copenhagen: Rosenkilde and Bagger, 1996)

Keynes, Simon, 'The reconstruction of a burnt Cottonian manuscript: the case of Cotton MS Otho A.i', *British Library Journal* 22 (1996), 113–60

Keynes, Simon, 'The vikings in England *c.* 790–1016', in P. H. Sawyer (ed.), *The Oxford Illustrated History of the Vikings* (Oxford: Oxford University Press, 1997), pp. 48–82

Keynes, Simon, 'King Alfred the Great and Shaftesbury Abbey', in Laurence Keen (ed.), *Studies in the Early History of Shaftesbury Abbey* (Dorchester: Dorset County Council, 1998), pp. 17–72

Keynes, Simon, and Michael Lapidge (trans. with an introduction and notes), *Alfred the Great: Asser's Life of Alfred and Other Contemporary Sources* (Harmondsworth: Penguin, 1983)

Kirby, D. P., 'Northumbria in the time of Wilfrid', in D. P. Kirby (ed.), *Saint Wilfrid at Hexham* (Newcastle upon Tyne: Oriel Press, 1974), pp. 1–34

Kirby, D. P., *Saint Wilfrid at Hexham* (Newcastle upon Tyne: Oriel Press, 1974)

Kirby, D. P., 'Bede, Eddius Stephanus and the "Life of Wilfrid"', *English Historical Review* 98 (1983), 101–14

Kirby, D. P., *Bede's Historia ecclesiastica gentis Anglorum: Its Contemporary Setting*, Jarrow Lecture 1992 (Jarrow: St Paul's Church, 1993)

Knowles, David, *The Monastic Order in England: A History of its Development from the Times of St Dunstan to the Fourth Lateran Council, 940–1216* (1949, 2nd edn, Cambridge: Cambridge University Press, 1963)

Knowles, David, C. N. L. Brooke and Vera C. M. London (eds.), *Heads of Religious Houses, England and Wales, 940–1216* (Cambridge: Cambridge University Press, 1972)

Krüger, Karl Heinrich, *Königsgrabkirchen der Franken, Angelsachsen, und Langobarden bis zur Mitte des 8. Jahrhunderts: Ein historischer Katalog*, Munstersche Mittelalter-Schriften, 4 (Munich: Wilhelm Fink Verlag, 1971)

Kuefler, Mathew S., '"A wryed existence": attitudes toward children in Anglo-Saxon England', *Journal of Social History* 24 (1991), 823–34

Kuypers, A. B., *The Prayer Book of Aedeluald the Bishop, Commonly Called the Book of Cerne edited from the MS in the University Library, Cambridge* (Cambridge: Cambridge University Press, 1902)

Langefeld, Brigitte, '*Regula canonicorum* or *Regula monasterialis uitae*? The Rule of Chrodegang and Archbishop Wulfred's reforms at Canterbury', *Anglo-Saxon England* 25 (1996), 21–36.

Lapidge, Michael, 'The school of Theodore and Hadrian', *Anglo-Saxon England*, 15 (1986), 45–72; reprinted in his *Anglo-Latin Literature 600–899* (London and Rio Grande: Hambledon Press, 1996), pp. 141–68

Lapidge, M., 'Aediluulf and the school of York', in A. Lehner and W. Berschin (eds.), *Lateinische Kultur im VIII. Jahrhundert: Traube Gedenkschrift* (St Ottilien: EOS Verlag, 1990), pp. 161–78; reprinted in his *Anglo-Latin Literature 600–899* (London and Rio Grande: Hambledon Press, 1996), pp. 381–98

Lapidge, Michael, 'B. and the *Vita sancti Dunstani*', in Nigel Ramsay, Margaret Sparks and Tim Tatton-Brown (eds.), *St Dunstan: His Life, Times and Cult* (Woodbridge: Boydell Press, 1992), pp. 247–59

Lapidge, Michael, 'The career of Archbishop Theodore', in Michael Lapidge (ed.), *Archbishop Theodore: Commemorative Studies on his Life and Influence*, Cambridge Studies in Anglo-Saxon England 11 (Cambridge: Cambridge University Press, 1995), pp. 1–29; reprinted in his *Anglo-Latin Literature 600–899* (London and Rio Grande: Hambledon Press, 1996), pp. 93–121

Lapidge, Michael, 'Latin learning in ninth-century England', in his *Anglo-Latin Literature, 600–899* (London and Rio Grande: Hambledon, 1996), pp. 409–39

Lapidge, Michael (ed.), *Columbanus: Studies on the Latin Writings* (Woodbridge: Boydell Press, 1997)

Lapidge, Michael, and Michael Herren (eds.), *Aldhelm: The Prose Works* (Ipswich: D. S. Brewer, 1979)

Lapidge, Michael, and James L. Rosier (eds.), *Aldhelm: the Poetic Works* (Cambridge: D. S. Brewer, 1985)

Lapidge, Michael *et al.* (eds.), *The Blackwell Encyclopaedia of Anglo-Saxon England* (Oxford: Blackwell, 1999)

Lawrence, C. H., *Medieval Monasticism: Forms of Religious Life in Western Europe in the Middle Ages* (London: Longman, 1984)

Levison, Wilhelm, 'Bede as historian', in A. Hamilton Thompson (ed.), *Bede: His Life, Times and Writings* (Oxford: Clarendon Press, 1935), pp. 111–51

Levison, Wilhelm, *England and the Continent in the Eighth Century: The Ford Lectures, delivered in the University of Oxford in the Hilary Term, 1943* (Oxford: Oxford University Press, 1946)

Leyser, Conrad, 'St Benedict and Gregory the Great: another dialogue', in Salvatore Pricoco *et al.* (eds.), *Sicilia e Italia suburbicaria tra IV e VIII secolo* (Rubbettino: Soveria Mannelli, 1991), pp. 21–43

Leyser, Conrad, *Authority and Asceticism from Augustine to Gregory the Great* (Oxford: Clarendon Press, 2000)

Leyser, Henrietta, *Hermits and the New Monasticism: A Study of Religious Communities in Western Europe 1000–1150* (London: Macmillan, 1984)

Leyser, K. J., *Rule and Conflict in an Early Medieval Society: Ottonian Saxony* (London: Edward Arnold, 1979)

Loveluck, C. P., 'A high-status Anglo-Saxon settlement at Flixborough, Lincolnshire', *Antiquity* 72 (1998), 146–61

Loyn, H. R., *The English Church 940–1154* (London: Longman, 2000)

Lucy, Sam, and Andrew Reynolds (eds.), *Burial in Early Medieval England and Wales*, Society for Medieval Archaeology, Monograph series, 17 (London: Society for Medieval Archaeology, 2002)

Lynch, Joseph H., *Godparents and Kinship in Early Medieval Europe* (Princeton, NJ: Princeton University Press, 1986)

McCarthy, Mother Maria Caritas, *The Rule for Nuns of St Caesarius of Arles: A Translation with a Critical Introduction*, The Catholic University of America, Studies in Mediaeval History, n.s. 16 (Washington, DC: Catholic University of America Press, 1960)

McClure, Judith, 'Bede and the Life of Ceolfrid', *Peritia* 3 (1984), 71–84

McClure, Judith, and Roger Collins, *Bede, the Ecclesiastical History of the English People* (Oxford and New York: Oxford University Press, 1994)

MacDonald, A. D. S., 'Aspects of the monastery and monastic life in Adomnan's Life of Columba', *Peritia* 3 (1984), 271–302

MacGowan, Kenneth, 'Barking Abbey', *Current Archaeology* 149 (1996), 172–8

McKitterick, Rosamond, *The Frankish Church and the Carolingian Reforms, 789–895* (London: Royal Historical Society, 1977)

McKitterick, Rosamond, 'Town and monastery in the Carolingian period', in Derek Baker (ed.), *The Church in Town and Countryside*, Studies in Church History 16 (Oxford: Basil Blackwell, 1979), pp. 93–102

McKitterick, Rosamond, *The Carolingians and the Written Word* (Cambridge: Cambridge University Press, 1989)

McKitterick, Rosamond, 'The diffusion of insular culture in Neustria between 650 and 850: the implications of the manuscript evidence', in *La Neustrie: les pays au nord de la Loire de 650 à 850*, Francia Beihefte, 16 (Sigmaringen: Thorbecke, 1989), 395–431; reprinted in her *Books, Scribes and Learning in the Frankish Kingdoms 6th–9th Centuries* (Aldershot: Variorum, 1994), no. III

McKitterick, Rosamond, 'Nuns' scriptoria in England and Francia in the eighth century', *Francia* 19 (1989), 1–35; reprinted in her *Books, Scribes and Learning in the Frankish Kingdoms 6th–9th Centuries* (Aldershot: Variorum, 1994), no. VII

McKitterick, Rosamond, *Anglo-Saxon Missonaries in Germany: Personal Connections and Local Influences*, Eighth Brixworth Lecture, Vaughan paper no. 36 ([Leicester]: Department of Adult Education, University of Leicester, 1991); reprinted in her *The Frankish Kings and Culture in the Early Middle Ages* (Aldershot: Variorum, 1995), no. I

McKitterick, Rosamond, 'Women and literacy in the early Middle Ages', in her *Books, Scribes and Learning in the Frankish Kingdoms 6th–9th Centuries* (Aldershot: Variorum, 1994), no. XIII

McNeill, J., and Helena M. Gamer, *Medieval Handbooks of Penance: A Translation of the Principal Libri poenitentiales and Selections from Related Documents* (New York: Columbia University Press, 1938)

Maddicott, J. R., 'Trade, industry and the wealth of King Alfred', *Past and Present* 123 (1989), 3–51

Magennis, Hugh, *Images of Community in Old English Poetry* (Cambridge: Cambridge University Press, 1996)

Magennis, Hugh, *Anglo-Saxon Appetites: Food and Drink and their Consumption in Old English and Related Literature* (Dublin: Four Courts Press, 1999)

Maine, Henry Sumner, *Ancient Law: Its Connection with the Early History of Society and its Relation to Modern Ideas* (1861; with introduction and notes by Frederick Pollock, London: John Murray, 1906)

Markus, Robert, 'Gregory the Great and a papal missionary strategy', *Studies in Church History* 6 (1970), 29–38

Markus, Robert, 'Augustine and Gregory the Great', in Richard Gameson (ed.), *St Augustine and the Conversion of England* (Stroud: Sutton, 1999), pp. 41–9

Markus, Robert, 'Living within sight of the end', in Chris Humphrey and W. M. Ormrod (eds.), *Time in the Medieval World* (Woodbridge: York Medieval Press, 2001), pp. 23–34

Mayr-Harting, Henry, *The Coming of Christianity to Anglo-Saxon England* (London: Batsford, 1972; 3rd edn, 1991)

Mayr-Harting, Henry, *The Venerable Bede, the Rule of St Benedict and Social Class*, Jarrow Lecture, 1976 (Jarrow: St Paul's Church, 1977)

Mayr-Harting, Henry, 'St Wilfrid in Sussex', in M. J. Kitch (ed.), *Studies in Sussex Church History* (London: Leopard's Head Press in association with the Centre for Continuing Education, University of Sussex, 1981), pp. 1–17

Metz, René, *La consécration des vierges dans l'église romaine: Etude d'histoire de la liturgie*, Bibliothèque de l'Institut de Droit Canonique de l'Université de Strasbourg 4 (Paris, Presses Universitaires de France, 1954)

Metz, René, 'La consécration des vierges dans l'église franque du vi^e au ixe siècle', *Revue des sciences religieuses* 31 (1957), 105–21

Meyvaert, Paul, *Bede and Gregory the Great*, Jarrow Lecture 1963 (Jarrow: [St Paul's Church], 1964)

Meyvaert, Paul, 'Bede's text of the *Libellus responsionum*', in Peter Clemoes and Kathleen Hughes (eds.), *England before the Conquest* (Cambridge: Cambridge University Press, 1971), pp. 15–33

Meyvaert, Paul, 'Diversity within unity, a Gregorian theme', reprinted in his *Benedict, Gregory, Bede and Others* (London: Variorum, 1977), no. VI

Meyvaert, Paul, 'Bede, Cassiodorus and the Codex Amiatinus', *Speculum* 71 (1996), 827–83

Milis, L. J. R., *Angelic Monks and Earthly Men: Monasticism and its Meaning to Medieval Society* (Woodbridge: Boydell Press, 1992)

Miller, Molly, 'The dates of Deira', *Anglo-Saxon England* 8 (1979), 35–61

Morris, Christopher D., *Church and Monastery in the Far North: An Archaeological Evaluation*, Jarrow Lecture, 1989 [Jarrow: Saint Paul's Church, 1990]

Morris, Richard, *The Church in British Archaeology*, Council for British Archaeology, Research Report 47 (London: Council for British Archaeology, 1983)

Morris, Richard, 'Alcuin, York and the *alma sophia*', in L. A. S. Butler and R. K. Morris (eds.), *The Anglo-Saxon Church* (London: Council for British Archaeology, 1986), pp. 80–9

Morris, Richard, *Churches in the Landscape* (London: Dent, 1989)

Morrish, Jennifer, 'King Alfred's letter as a source on learning in England in the ninth century', in Paul Szarmach (ed.), *Studies in Earlier Old English Prose* (Albany, NY: State University of New York Press, 1986), pp. 87–107

Muschiol, Gisela, *Famula Dei: Zur Liturgie in merowingischen Frauenklöstern*, Beiträge zur Geschichte des alten Mönchtums und des Benediktinertums, 42 (Münster: Aschendorff, 1994)

Nees, Lawrence, 'The plan of St. Gall and the theory of the program of Carolingian art', *Gesta* 25 (1986), 1–8

Nelson, Janet L., 'The Annals of St Bertin', in Margaret Gibson and Janet L. Nelson (eds.), *Charles the Bald: Court and Kingdom* (2nd rev. edn, Aldershot: Variorum, 1990), pp. 23–40

Nelson, Janet L., 'Parents, children and the church in the early Middle Ages', in Diana Wood (ed.), *The Church and Childhood*, Studies in Church History 31 (Oxford: Blackwell for the Ecclesiastical History Society, 1994), 81–114

Nelson, Janet, 'The church and a revaluation of work in the ninth century?' in R. N. Swanson (ed.), *The Use and Abuse of Time in Christian History*, Studies in Church History 37 (Woodbridge: Boydell Press for the Ecclesiastical History Society, 2002), 35–43

Nelson, Janet L., 'Alfred's Carolingian contemporaries', in Timothy Reuter (ed.), *Alfred the Great: Papers from the Eleventh-Centenary Conferences* (Aldershot: Ashgate Publishing, 2003), pp. 293–310

Ní Chatháin, Próinséas, and Michael Richter (eds.), *Irland und Europa: Die Kirche im Frühmittelalter = Ireland and Europe: The Early Church* (Stuttgart: Klett-Cotta, 1984)

Ní Chatháin, Próinséas, and Michael Richter (eds.), *Irland und die Christenheit: Bibelstudien und Mission* (Stuttgart: Klett-Cotta, 1987)

Noble, T. F. X., 'From brigandage to justice: Charlemagne, 785–794', in Celia M. Chazelle (ed.), *Literacy, Politics and Artistic Innovation in the Early Medieval West* (Lanham, MD, and London: University Press of America, 1992), pp. 49–75

Noisette, Patrice, 'Usages et représentations de l'espace dans la Regula Benedicti: une nouvelle approche des significations historiques de la règle', *Regula Benedicti studia, Annuarium internationale* 14/15 (1985), 69–93

Ó Carragáin, Éamonn, *The City of Rome and the World of Bede*, Jarrow Lecture, 1994 [Jarrow: St Paul's Church, 1995]

Ó Cróinín, D., 'Rath Melsigi, Willibrord, and the earliest Echternach manuscripts', *Peritia* 3 (1984), 17–49

O'Donovan, Mary Anne, 'An interim revision of episcopal dates for the province of Canterbury, 850–950: part 1', *Anglo-Saxon England* 1 (1972), 23–44

O'Donovan, Mary Anne, 'An interim revision: part 2', *Anglo-Saxon England* 2 (1972), 91–113

O'Sullivan, Deirdre, 'The plan of the early Christian monastery on Lindisfarne: a fresh look at the evidence', in Gerald Bonner *et al.* (eds.), *St Cuthbert, his Cult and his Community* (Woodbridge: Boydell Press, 1989), pp. 125–42

Oexle, Otto Gerhard, 'Les moines d'occident et la vie politique et sociale dans le haut Moyen Age', *Revue bénédictine* 103 (1993), 255–72

Okasha, Elizabeth, *Handlist of Anglo-Saxon Non-Runic Inscriptions* (Cambridge: Cambridge University Press, 1971)

Olsen, Glenn, 'Bede as historian: the evidence from his observations on the life of the first Christian community at Jerusalem', *Journal of Ecclesiastical History* 33 (1982), 519–30

Ovitt, George, 'Manual labour and early medieval monasticism', *Viator* 17 (1986), 1–18

Ovitt, George Jr, 'The cultural context of western technology: early Christian attitudes towards manual labor', in Allen J. Frantzen and Douglas Moffat (eds.), *The Work of Work: Servitude, Slavery, and Labor in Medieval England* (Glasgow: Cruithne Press, 1994), pp. 71–94

Palliser, David, 'Review article: the 'minster hypothesis': a case study', *Early Medieval Europe* 5 (1996), 207–14

Palmer, James T., 'Locating sanctity: community and place in the hagiography of the eighth-century Anglo-Saxon missions to the continent' (unpublished PhD thesis, University of Sheffield, 2004)

Parker, M. S., 'An Anglo-Saxon monastery in the lower Don valley', *Northern History* 21 (1985), 19–32

Parkes, Malcolm, 'The handwriting of St Boniface: a reassessment of the problems', *Beiträge zur Geschichte der deutschen Sprache und Literatur* 98 (1976), 161–79

Parkes, Malcolm, *The Scriptorium of Wearmouth–Jarrow*, Jarrow Lecture 1982 (Jarrow: [St Paul's Church, 1983])

Parsons, David, 'England and the low countries at the time of St Willibrord', in Elisabeth de Bièvre (ed.), *Utrecht: Britain and the Continent, Archaeology, Art and Architecture* ([London?]: British Archaelogical Association, 1996)

Parsons, David, 'The Mercian church: archaeology and topography', in Michelle P. Brown and Carol A. Farr (eds.), *Mercia: An Anglo-Saxon Kingdom in Europe* (London: Leicester University Press, 2001), pp. 50–68

Paxton, Frederick S., *Christianizing Death: The Creation of a Ritual Process in Early Medieval Europe* (Ithaca, NY, and London: Cornell University Press, 1990)

Peifer, Claude J., 'The relevance of the monastic tradition to the problem of work and leisure', *American Benedictine Review* 28 (1977), 373–96

Pelteret, David, 'Slavery in Anglo-Saxon England', in Jon Douglas Woods and David A. E. Pelteret (eds.), *The Anglo-Saxons: Synthesis and Achievement* (Waterloo, ON: Wilfrid Laurier University Press, 1985), pp. 116–33

Pelteret, David, 'Saint Wilfrid: tribal bishop, civic bishop or Germanic lord?' in Joyce Hill and Mary Swan (eds.), *The Community, the Family and the Saint* (Turnhout: Brepols, 1998), pp. 159–80

Pfaff, Richard W., 'Massbooks', in Richard Pfaff (ed.), *The Liturgical Books of Anglo-Saxon England*, Old English Newsletter, Subsidia 23 (Kalamazoo, MI: The Medieval Institute, Western Michigan University, 1995), pp. 7–34

Pharr, Clyde, *The Theodosian Code and Novels and the Sirmondian Constitutions* (Princeton, NJ: Princeton University Press, 1952)

Plummer, Charles, *Venerabilis Baedae opera historica*, 2 vols. (Oxford: Clarendon Press, 1896)

Pocock, M., and H. Wheeler, 'Excavations at Escomb church, County Durham, 1968', *Journal of the British Archaeological Association*, 3rd series, 34 (1971), 11–29

Pollard, Graham, 'Some Anglo-Saxon book-bindings', *The Book Collector* 24 (1975), 130–59

Poole, Reginald Lane, 'The Alpine son-in-law of Edward the Elder', in Austin Lane Poole (ed.), *Studies in Chronology and History* (Oxford: Clarendon Press, 1934, reprinted 1969), pp. 115–22

Postles, Dave, 'Monastic burials of non-patronal lay benefactors', *Journal of Ecclesiastical History* 47 (1996), 620–37

Prinz, Friedrich, *Frühes Mönchtum im Frankenreich: Kultur und Gesellschaft in Gallien, den Rheinlanden und Bayern am Beispiel der monastischen Entwicklen (4. bis 8. Jahrhundert)* (Munich and Vienna: R. Oldenbourg, 1965)

Prinz, Friedrich., 'Columbanus, the Frankish nobility and the territories east of the Rhine', in H. B. Clarke and Mary Brennan (eds.), *Columbanus and Merovingian Monasticism*, BAR, International series, 113 (Oxford: BAR, 1981), 73–87

Pulsiano, Phillip, 'Psalters', in Richard Pfaff (ed.), *The Liturgical Books of Anglo-Saxon England*, Old English Newsletter, Subsidia 23 (Kalamazoo, MI: The Medieval Institute, Western Michigan University, 1995), pp. 61–85

Quinn, Patricia, *Better than the Sons of Kings: Boys and Monks in the Early Middle Ages* Studies in History and Culture 2 (New York: P. Lang, 1989)

Radford, C. R., 'Glastonbury Abbey before 1184: interim report on the excavations 1908–64', in *Medieval Art and Architecture at Wells and Glastonbury*, British Archaeological Association Conference Transactions for 1978 (London: British Archaelogical Association, 1981)

Rahtz, Philip, 'Artefacts of Christian death', in S. C. Humphries and H. King (eds.), *Mortality and Immortality: The Anthropology and Archaeology of Death* (London: Academic Press, 1981), pp. 117–36

Ramsay, Nigel, and Margaret Sparks (eds.), *The Image of St Dunstan* (Canterbury, 1988)

Ramsay, Nigel, Margaret Sparks and Tim Tatton-Brown (eds.), *St Dunstan: His Life, Times and Cult* (Woodbridge: Boydell Press, 1992)

379

Ranger, Felicity, *Prisca munimenta: Studies in Archival and Administrative History presented to A. E. J. Hollaender* (London: University of London Press, 1973)

Reuter, Timothy (ed.), *The Greatest Englishman: Essays on St Boniface and the Church at Crediton* (Exeter, 1980)

Reuter, Timothy (ed.), *Alfred the Great: Papers from the Eleventh-Centenary Conferences* (Aldershot: Ashgate Publishing, 2003)

Reynolds, Andrew, 'Burials, boundaries and charters in Anglo-Saxon England: a reassessment', in Sam Lucy and Andrew Reynolds (eds.), *Burial in Early Medieval England and Wales* (London: Society for Medieval Archaeology, 2002), pp. 171–94

Richards, Jeffrey, *Consul of God: The Life and Times of Gregory the Great* (London: Routledge and Kegan Paul, 1980)

Riché, Pierre, *Education and Culture in the Barbarian West, Sixth through Eighth Centuries*, trans. from the 3rd French edn. by John J. Contreni (Columbia: University of South Carolina Press, 1976)

Riché, Pierre, 'Columbanus, his followers and the Merovingian church', in H. B. Clarke and Mary Brennan (eds.), *Columbanus and Merovingian Monasticism*, BAR, International series, 113 (Oxford: BAR, 1981), 59–72

Richter, Michael, 'Practical aspects of the conversion of the Anglo-Saxons', in Próinséas Ní Cháthain and Michael Richter (eds.), *Irland und die Christenheit* (Stuttgart: Klett-Cotta, 1987), pp. 362–76

Ridyard, Susan, '*Condigna veneratio*: post-Conquest attitudes to the saints of the Anglo-Saxons', *Anglo-Norman Studies* 9 (1986), 179–206

Ridyard, Susan, *The Royal Saints of Anglo-Saxon England: A Study of West Saxon and East Anglian Cults*, Cambridge Studies in Medieval Life and Thought, 4th series, 9 (Cambridge: Cambridge University Press, 1988)

Riggs, Charles H., Jnr, *Criminal Asylum in Anglo-Saxon Law*, University of Florida Monographs, Social Sciences, 18 (Gainesville, FL: University of Florida Press, 1963)

Rivers, T. J., 'Widows' rights in Anglo-Saxon law', *American Journal of Legal History* 19 (1975), 208–15

Robinson, J. Armitage, *St Oswald and the Church of Worcester*, British Academy supplemental papers 5 (London: Oxford University Press for the British Academy, 1919)

Robinson, J. Armitage, 'The Saxon abbots of Glastonbury', in his *Somerset Historical Essays* (London: Humphrey Milford, Oxford University Press for the British Academy, 1921), pp. 26–53

Robinson, J. Armitage, *The Times of Saint Dunstan: The Ford Lectures delivered in the University of Oxford in the Michaelmas Term, 1922* (Oxford: Clarendon Press, 1923)

Robinson, J. Armitage, 'The early community at Christ Church Canterbury', *Journal of Theological Studies* 27 (1926), 225–40

Robinson, J. Armitage, 'The historical evidence as to the Saxon church at Glastonbury', *Proceedings of the Somersetshire Archaeological and Natural History Society* 73 (1928), 40–9

Rodwell, Warwick, 'Churches in the landscape: aspects of topography and planning', in Margaret Faull (ed.), *Studies in Late Anglo-Saxon Settlement* (Oxford: Oxford University Department for External Studies, 1984), 1–23

Rollason, David, *The Search for St Wigstan, Prince-Martyr of the Kingdom of Mercia*, Vaughan Occasional Papers (Leicester: Department of Adult Education, University of Leicester, 1981)

Rollason, David, 'The cults of murdered royal saints in Anglo-Saxon England', *Anglo-Saxon England* 11 (1982), 1–22

Rollason, David, *The Mildrith Legend: A Study in Early Medieval Hagiography in England*, Studies in the Early History of Britain (Leicester: Leicester University Press, 1982)

Rollason, David, 'The shrines of saints in later Anglo-Saxon England: distribution and significance', in L. A. S. Butler and R. K. Morris (eds.), *The Anglo-Saxon Church* (London: Council for British Archaeology, 1986), pp. 32–43

Rollason, David, 'Monasteries and society in early medieval Northumbria', in Benjamin Thompson (ed.), *Monasteries and Society in Medieval Britain: Proceedings of the 1994 Harlaxton Symposium* (Stamford: Paul Watkins, 1999), pp. 59–74

Roper, Michael, 'Wilfrid's landholdings in Northumbria', in D. P. Kirby (ed.), *Saint Wilfrid at Hexham* (Newcastle upon Tyne: Oriel Press, 1974), pp. 61–79

Roper, Sally Elizabeth, *Medieval English Benedictine Liturgy: Studies in the Formation, Structure and Content of the Monastic Votive Office, c. 950–1540* (New York and London: Garland Publishing, 1993)

Ross, Margaret Clunies, 'Concubinage in Anglo-Saxon England', *Past and Present* 108 (1985), 3–34

Rulon-Miller, Nina, 'Sexual humor and fettered desire in Riddle 12', in Jonathan Wilcox (ed.), *Humor in Anglo-Saxon Literature* (Cambridge: D. S. Brewer, 2000), pp. 99–126

Sanderson, Warren, 'The plan of St Gall reconsidered', *Speculum* 60 (1985), 615–32

Sawyer, Peter H., 'Fairs and markets in early medieval England', in Niels Skyum-Nielsen and Niels Lund (eds.), *Danish Medieval History: New Currents* (Copenhagen: Museum Tusculanum Press, 1981), pp. 153–68

Sawyer, Peter, 'The royal tun in pre-Conquest England', in Patrick Wormald *et al.* (eds.), *Ideal and Reality in Frankish and Anglo-Saxon Society* (Oxford: Basil Blackwell, 1983), pp. 273–99

Sayers, William, 'Early Irish attitudes towards hair and beards, baldness and tonsure', *Zeitschrift für celtische Philologie* 44 (1991), 154–89

Scharer, Anton, *Die angelsächsische Königsurkunde im 7. und 8. Jahrhundert*, Veröffentlichungen des Instituts für Österreichische Geschichtsforschung, 26 (Vienna: Böhlau, 1982)

Schiebe, Friedrich-Karl, 'Alcuin und die *Admonitio generalis*', *Deutsches Archiv* 14 (1958), 221–29

Schneider, Dagmar, 'Anglo-Saxon women in the religious life: a study of the status and position of women in an early mediaeval society' (unpublished PhD thesis, University of Cambridge, 1985)

Schroll, Sister Mary Alfred, *Benedictine Monasticism as Reflected in the Warnefrid–Hildemar Commentaries on the Rule* (New York and London: Columbia University Press and P. S. King & Son, Ltd, 1941)

Schulenburg, Jane Tibbetts, 'Strict active enclosure and its effects on the female monastic experience (500–1100)', in John A. Nichols and Lillian Thomas Shank (eds.), *Medieval Religious Women*, I: *Distant Echoes* (Kalamazoo, MI: Cistercian Publications, 1984), pp. 51–86

Scott, John, *The Early History of Glastonbury: An Edition, Translation and Study of William of Malmesbury's De antiquitate Glastonie ecclesie* (Woodbridge: Boydell Press, 1981)

Scragg, Donald (ed.), *The Vercelli Homilies and Related Texts*, EETS 300 (London: Oxford University Press for the Early English Text Society, 1992)

Sharp, Sheila, 'The West Saxon tradition of dynastic marriage with special reference to the family of Edward the Elder', in N. J. Higham and D. H. Hill (eds.), *Edward the Elder 899–924* (London and New York: Routledge, 2001), pp. 79–88.

Sharpe, Richard, 'Armagh and Rome in the seventh century', in Próinséas Ní Chatháin and Michael Richter (eds.), *Irland und Europa: Die Kirche im Frühmittelalter* (Stuttgart: Klett-Cotta, 1984), pp. 58–72

Sharpe, Richard, 'Some problems concerning the organisation of the church in early medieval Ireland', *Peritia* 3 (1984), 230–70

Sims-Williams, Patrick, 'Cuthswith, seventh-century abbess of Inkberrow, near Worcester, and the Würzburg manuscript of Jerome on Ecclesiastes', *Anglo-Saxon England* 5 (1976), 1–21

Sims-Williams, Patrick, 'St Wilfrid and two charters dated AD 676 and 680', *JEH* 39 (1988), 163–83

Sims-Williams, Patrick, *Religion and Literature in Western England, 600–800*, Cambridge Studies in Anglo-Saxon England 3 (Cambridge: Cambridge University Press, 1990)

Smith, Julia M. H., 'The problem of female sanctity in Carolingian Europe, *c.* 750–920', *Past and Present* 146 (1995), 3–37

Smith, Julie Ann, *Ordering Women's Lives: Penitentials and Nunnery Rules in the Early Medieval West* (Aldershot: Ashgate Publishing, 2001)

Smyth, A. P., *Scandinavian York and Dublin: The History and Archaeology of Two Related Viking Kingdoms*, 2 vols. (Dublin: Templekieran Press, 1975–9)

Stafford, Pauline, 'Sons and mothers: family politics in the early middle ages', in Derek Baker (ed.), *Medieval Women: dedicated and presented to Rosalind M. T. Hill*, Studies in Church History, Subsidia 1 (Oxford: Blackwell for the Ecclesiastical History Society, 1978), pp. 79–100

Stafford, Pauline, *Queens, Concubines and Dowagers* (London: Batsford, 1983)

Stafford, Pauline, 'Charles the Bald, Judith and England', in Margaret Gibson and Janet L. Nelson (eds.), *Charles the Bald: Court and Kingdom* (2nd rev. edn, Aldershot: Variorum, 1990), pp. 139–53

Stafford, Pauline, 'Queens, nunneries and reforming churchmen: gender, religious status and reform in tenth- and eleventh-century England', *Past and Present* 163 (1999), 3–35

Stancliffe, Clare E., 'Kings and conversion: some comparisons between the Roman mission to England and Patrick's to Ireland', *Frühmittelalterliche Studien* 14 (1980), 59–94

Stancliffe, Clare, 'Kings who opted out', in Patrick Wormald *et al.* (eds.), *Ideal and Reality in Frankish and Anglo-Saxon Society* (Oxford: Blackwell, 1983), pp. 154–76

Stancliffe, Clare, *St Martin and his Hagiographer: History and Miracle in Sulpicius Severus* (Oxford, 1983)

Stancliffe, Clare, 'Cuthbert and the polarity between pastor and solitary', in Gerald Bonner *et al.* (eds.), *St Cuthbert, his Cult and his Community* (Woodbridge: Boydell Press, 1989), pp. 21–44

Stancliffe, Clare, and Eric Cambridge (eds.), *Oswald: Northumbrian King to European Saint* (Stamford: Paul Watkins, 1995)

Stenton, Doris M. (ed.), *Preparatory to Anglo-Saxon England: Being the collected papers of Frank Merry Stenton* (Oxford: Clarendon Press, 1970)

Stenton, F. M., *The Early History of the Abbey of Abingdon* (Reading: University College, 1913; reprinted Stamford: Paul Watkins, 1989)

Stenton, Frank M., 'Medeshamstede and its colonies', in J. G. Edwards *et al.* (eds.), *Historical Essays in honour of James Tait* (Manchester: privately printed, 1933), pp. 313–26; reprinted in Doris M. Stenton (ed.), *Preparatory to Anglo-Saxon England: Being the collected papers of Frank Merry Stenton* (Oxford: Clarendon Press, 1970), pp. 179–92

Stenton, F. M., *Anglo-Saxon England* (Oxford: Clarendon Press, 1943; 3rd edn, 1971)

Sterckk, Claude, 'Les jeux de damier celtiques', *Etudes celtiques* 13 (1973), 733–49

Stevenson, J. (ed.), *Liber Vitae ecclesie Dunelmensis nec non obituaria duo ejusdem ecclesiae*, Surtees Society 8 (London: J. B. Nichols and Son, 1841)

Stevenson, Jane Barbara, 'The monastic rules of Columbanus', in Michael Lapidge (ed.), *Columbanus: Studies on the Latin Writings* (Woodbridge: Boydell Press, 1997), pp. 203–16

Stoertz, Fiona Harris, 'Adolescence and authority in medieval monasticism', in Martin Gosman *et al.* (eds.), *The Growth of Authority in the Medieval West* (Groningen: E. Forsten, 1999), pp. 119–40

Stubbs, William, 'On the foundation and early fasti of Peterborough', *Archaeological Journal* 18 (1861), 193–211

Stutz, Ulrich, 'The proprietary church as an element of mediaeval Germanic ecclesiastical law', in Geoffrey Barraclough (ed. and trans.), *Mediaeval Germany 911–1250: Essays by German Historians*, 2 vols. (Oxford: Blackwell, 1938), II, 35–70

Sullivan, Richard E., 'What was Carolingian monasticism?', in Alexander Callander Murray (ed.), *After Rome's Fall: Narrators and Sources of Early Medieval History* (Toronto, Buffalo and London: University of Toronto Press, 1998), pp. 251–87

Symons, Thomas, *Regularis concordia anglicae nationis monachorum sanctimonialiumque* (London and New York: Thomas Nelson and Sons, 1953)

Szirmai, J. A., *The Archaeology of Medieval Bookbinding* (Aldershot: Ashgate Publishing, 1999)

Taft, Robert F., *The Liturgy of the Hours in East and West: The Origins of the Divine Office and its Meaning for Today* (Collegeville, MN: Liturgical Press, 1986)

Talbot, C. H., *The Anglo-Saxon Missionaries in Germany* (London: Sheed & Ward, 1954; 2nd edn., 1981)

Taylor, H. M., and Joan Taylor, *Anglo-Saxon Architecture*, 3 vols. (Cambridge: Cambridge University Press, 1965–78)

Thacker, Alan, 'Chester and Gloucester: early ecclesiastical organisation in two Mercian burhs', *Northern History* 18 (1982), 199–211

Thacker, Alan, 'Bede's ideal of reform', in Patrick Wormald *et al.* (eds.), *Ideal and Reality in Frankish and Anglo-Saxon Society* (Oxford: Basil Blackwell, 1985), pp. 130–53

Thacker, Alan, 'Kings, saints and monasteries in pre-viking Mercia', *Midland History* 10 (1985), 1–25

Thacker, Alan, 'Æthelwold and Abingdon', in Barbara Yorke (ed.), *Bishop Æthelwold: His Career and Influence* (Woodbridge: Boydell Press, 1988), pp. 43–64

Thacker, Alan, 'Monks, preaching and pastoral care in early Anglo-Saxon England', in John Blair and Richard Sharpe (eds.), *Pastoral Care before the Parish* ((Leicester, London and New York: Leicester University Press, 1992), pp. 137–70

Thacker, Alan, and Richard Sharpe (eds.), *Local Saints and Local Churches in the Early Medieval West* (Oxford: Oxford University Press, 2002)

Thomas, Charles, *The Early Christian Archaeology of North Britain: The Hunter Marshall lectures delivered at the University of Glasgow in January and February 1968* (London and New York: Oxford University Press for the University of Glasgow, 1971)

Thompson, A. H. (ed.), *Liber Vitae ecclesiae Dunelmensis: A Collotype Facsimile of the Original Manuscript with Introductory Essays and Notes*, Surtees Society 136 (Durham: Andrews & Co for the Society, 1923)

Thompson, A. Hamilton (ed.), *Bede: His Life, Times, and Writings. Essays in Commemoration of the Twelfth Centenary of his Death* (Oxford: Clarendon Press, 1935)

Thompson, A. Hamilton, 'Northumbrian monasticism', in A. Hamilton Thompson (ed.), *Bede: His Life, Times, and Writings* (Oxford: Clarendon Press, 1935), pp. 60–101

Thompson, Benjamin (ed.), *Monasteries and Society in Medieval Britain: Proceedings of the 1994 Harlaxton Symposium*, Harlaxton Medieval Studies VI (Stamford: Paul Watkins, 1999)

Timson, R. A., 'English monasticism before 735', (unpublished MA dissertation, University of London, 1956)

Tolhurst, J. B. L. (ed.), *The Monastic Breviary of Hyde Abbey, Winchester: MSS Rawlinson liturg. e. 1*, and Gough liturg. 8, in the Bodleian Library, Oxford*, Henry Bradshaw Society, 6 vols. (London: Harrison and Sons for the Society, 1932–42)

Van der Walt, A. G. P., 'Reflections of the Benedictine Rule in Bede's homiliary', *JEH* 37 (1986), 367–76

Venclová, Natalie, 'The Venerable Bede, druidic tonsure and archaeology', *Antiquity* 76 (2002), 458–71

Vogüé, Adalbert de, 'Travail et alimentation dans les règles de saint Benoît et du Maître', *Revue bénédictine* 74 (1964), 242–51

Vogüé, Adalbert de, 'Problems of the monastic conventual mass', *Downside Review* 87 (1969), 327–38

Vogüé, Adalbert de, 'La règle de Donat pour l'abbesse Gauthstrude', *Benedictina* 25 (1978), 219–313

Vogüé, Adalbert de, *Les règles monastiques anciennes (400–700)*, Typologies des sources, 46 (Turnhout: Brepols, 1985)

Vollrath, Hanna, *Die Synoden Englands bis 1066* (Paderborn: Schöningh, 1985)

Wallace, Samuel E., *Total Institutions* (Chicago: Aldine Pub. Co., 1971)

Wallace-Hadrill, J. M., 'Rome and the early English church: some questions of transmission', in his *Early Medieval History* (Oxford: Blackwell, 1975), pp. 115–37

Wallace-Hadrill, J. M., *The Frankish Church* (Oxford: Clarendon Press, 1983)

Wallace-Hadrill, J. M., *Bede's Ecclesiastical History of the English People: A Historical Commentary* (Oxford: Clarendon Press, 1988)

Ward, Benedicta, 'The spirituality of St Cuthbert', in Gerald Bonner *et al.* (eds.), *St Cuthbert, his Cult and his Community to AD 1200* (Woodbridge: Boydell, 1989), pp. 65–76

Ward, Benedicta, *The Venerable Bede* (London: Geoffrey Chapman, 1990; 1998 edition)

Webb, Diana, *Pilgrimage in Medieval England* (London and New York: Hambledon and London, 2000)

Weber, Max, *General Economic History*, trans. Frank H. Knight (London: Allen and Unwin, 1927)

Webster, Leslie, 'The iconographic programme of the Franks casket' in Jane Hawkes and Susan Mills (eds.), *Northumbria's Golden Age* (Stroud: Sutton, 1999), pp. 227–46

Webster, Leslie, and Janet Backhouse (eds.), *The Making of England: Anglo-Saxon Art and Culture, AD 600–900* (London: British Museum Press, 1981)

Wemple, Suzanne F., *Women in Frankish Society: Marriage and the Cloister 500–900* (Philadelphia, PA: University of Pennsylvania Press, 1981)

West, S. E., N. Scarfe and R. Cramp, 'Iken, St Botolph, and the coming of East Anglian Christianity', *Proceedings of the Suffolk Institute of Archaeology and Natural History* 35 (1984), 279–301

Whitelock, Dorothy, *The Will of Æthelgifu: A Tenth-Century Anglo-Saxon Manuscript* (Oxford: Oxford University Press for the Roxburghe Club, 1968)

Whitelock, Dorothy, 'William of Malmesbury on the works of King Alfred', in D. A. Pearsall and R. A. Waldron (eds.), *Medieval Literature and Civilization: Studies in memory of G. N. Garmonsway* (London: Athlone Press, 1969), pp. 78–93

Whitelock, Dorothy, 'The pre-Viking Age church in East Anglia', *Anglo-Saxon England* 1 (1972), 1–22

Whitelock, Dorothy, 'Bede and his teachers and friends', in Gerald Bonner (ed.), *Famulus Christi* (London: SPCK, 1976), pp. 19–39

Whitelock, Dorothy, 'The authorship of the account of King Edgar's establishment of monasteries', reprinted in her *History, Law and Literature in 10th–11th-Century England* (London: Variorum, 1981), no. VII

Wickham-Crowley, Kelley M., 'Looking forward, looking back: excavating the field of Anglo-Saxon archaeology', in Catherine E. Karkov (ed.), *The Archaeology of Anglo-Saxon England: Basic Readings* (New York and London: Garland Publishing, 1999), pp. 1–23

Wilson, David M. (ed.), *The Archaeology of Anglo-Saxon England* (Cambridge: Cambridge University Press, 1976)

Wilson, David M., *Anglo-Saxon Art from the Seventh Century to the Norman Conquest* (London: Thames and Hudson, 1984)

Wilson, David, *Anglo-Saxon Paganism* (London: Routledge, 1992)

Winterbottom, Michael, 'Aldhelm's prose style and its origins', *Anglo-Saxon England* 6 (1977), 39–76

Wood, Ian, 'A prelude to Columbanus: the monastic achievement in the Burgundian territories', in H. B. Clarke and Mary Brennan (eds.), *Columbanus and Merovingian Monasticism*, BAR, Internat. ser., 113 (Oxford: BAR, 1981), 3–32

Wood, Ian, 'The *Vita Columbani* and Merovingian hagiography', *Peritia* 1 (1982), pp. 63–80

Wood, Ian, 'The audience of architecture in post-Roman Gaul', in L. A. S. Butler and R. K. Morris (eds.), *The Anglo-Saxon Church: Papers on History, Architecture, and Archaeology in honour of Dr H. M. Taylor*, Council for British Archaeology, Research Report 60 (London: Council for British Archaeology, 1986), pp. 74–9

Wood, Ian, 'Anglo-Saxon Otley: an archiepiscopal estate and its crosses in a Northumbrian context', *Northern History* 23 (1987), 20–38

Wood, Ian N., 'Ripon, Francia and the Franks casket in the early Middle Ages', *Northern History* 26 (1990), 1–19

Wood, Ian, *The Merovingian Kingdoms 450–751* (London and New York: Longman, 1994)

Wood, Ian, 'The mission of Augustine of Canterbury to the English', *Speculum* 69 (1994), 1–17

Wood, Ian, *The Most Holy Abbot Ceolfrid*, Jarrow Lecture 1995 (Jarrow: [St Paul's Church], 1996)

Wormald, Patrick, 'Bede and Benedict Biscop', in Gerald Bonner (ed.), *Famulus Christi* (London: SPCK, 1976), pp. 141–69

Wormald, Patrick, 'Bede, "Beowulf" and the conversion of the Anglo-Saxon aristocracy', in R. T. Farrell (ed.), *Bede and Anglo-Saxon England: Papers in honour of the 1300th Anniversary of the Birth of Bede, given at Cornell University in 1973 and 1974*, BAR, Brit. ser., 46 (Oxford: BAR, 1978), 32–95

Wormald, Patrick, *Bede and the Conversion of England: The Charter Evidence*, Jarrow Lecture 1984 (Jarrow: [St Paul's Church], 1985)

Wormald, Patrick, 'Charters, law and the settlement of disputes in Anglo-Saxon England', in Wendy Davies and Paul Fouracre (eds.), *The Settlement of Disputes in Early Medieval Europe* (Cambridge: Cambridge University Press, 1986), pp. 149–68

Wormald, P., 'In search of Offa's law-code', in I. N. Wood and N. Lund (eds.), *People and Places in Northern Europe 500–1600* (Woodbridge: Boydell Press, 1986), pp. 25–45.

Wormald, Patrick, 'Æthelwold and his continental counterparts: contact, comparison, contrast', in Barbara Yorke (ed.), *Bishop Æthelwold: His Career and Influence* (Woodbridge: Boydell Press, 1988), pp. 13–42

Wormald, Patrick, 'A handlist of Anglo-Saxon lawsuits', *Anglo-Saxon England* 17 (1989), 247–81

Wormald, Patrick, 'The Venerable Bede and the "church of the English"', in Geoffrey Rowell (ed.), *The English Religious Tradition and the Genius of Anglicanism* (Wantage: Ikon, 1992), pp. 13–32

Wormald, Patrick, 'St Hilda, saint and scholar (614–80)', in Jane Mellanby (ed.), *The St Hilda's College Centenary Symposium: A Celebration of the Education of Women* (Oxford: St Hilda's College, 1993), pp. 93–103

Wormald, Patrick, Donald Bullough and Roger Collins (eds.), *Ideal and Reality in Frankish and Anglo-Saxon Society: Studies presented to J. M. Wallace-Hadrill* (Oxford: Basil Blackwell, 1983)

Yeo, Richard, *The Structure and Content of Monastic Profession: A Juridical Study, with particular regard to the Practice of the English Benedictine Congregation since the French Revolution*, Studia Anselmiana 83 (Rome: Pontificio Ateneo S. Anselmo, 1982)

Yorke, Barbara (ed.), *Bishop Æthelwold: His Career and Influence* (Woodbridge: Boydell Press, 1988)

Yorke, Barbara, *Wessex in the Early Middle Ages* (London and New York: Leicester University Press, 1995)

Yorke, Barbara, 'The Bonifacian mission and female religious in Wessex', *Early Medieval Europe* 7 (1998), 145–72

Yorke, Barbara, *Nunneries and the Anglo-Saxon Royal Houses* (London and New York: Continuum, 2003)

Young, Karl, *The Drama of the Medieval Church*, 2 vols. (Oxford: Clarendon Press, 1933)

Youngs, Susan M., 'The gaming-pieces', in Rupert Bruce-Mitford, *The Sutton Hoo Ship-Burial*, III, part 2, ed. Angela Care Evans (London: British Museum Publications for the Trustees of the British Museum, 1983), pp. 853–74

Zelzer, Klaus, 'Zur Frage der Observanz des Benedict Biscop', in Elizabeth A. Livingstone (ed.), *Studia Patristica 20: Papers Presented to the Tenth International Conference on Patristic Studies held in Oxford 1987* (Leuven: Peeters Press, 1989), pp. 323–9

Zimmermann, W., '*Ecclesia lignea* und *ligneis tabulis fabricata*', *Bonner Jahrbücher* 158 (1958), 414–58

Index

393